MW01055742

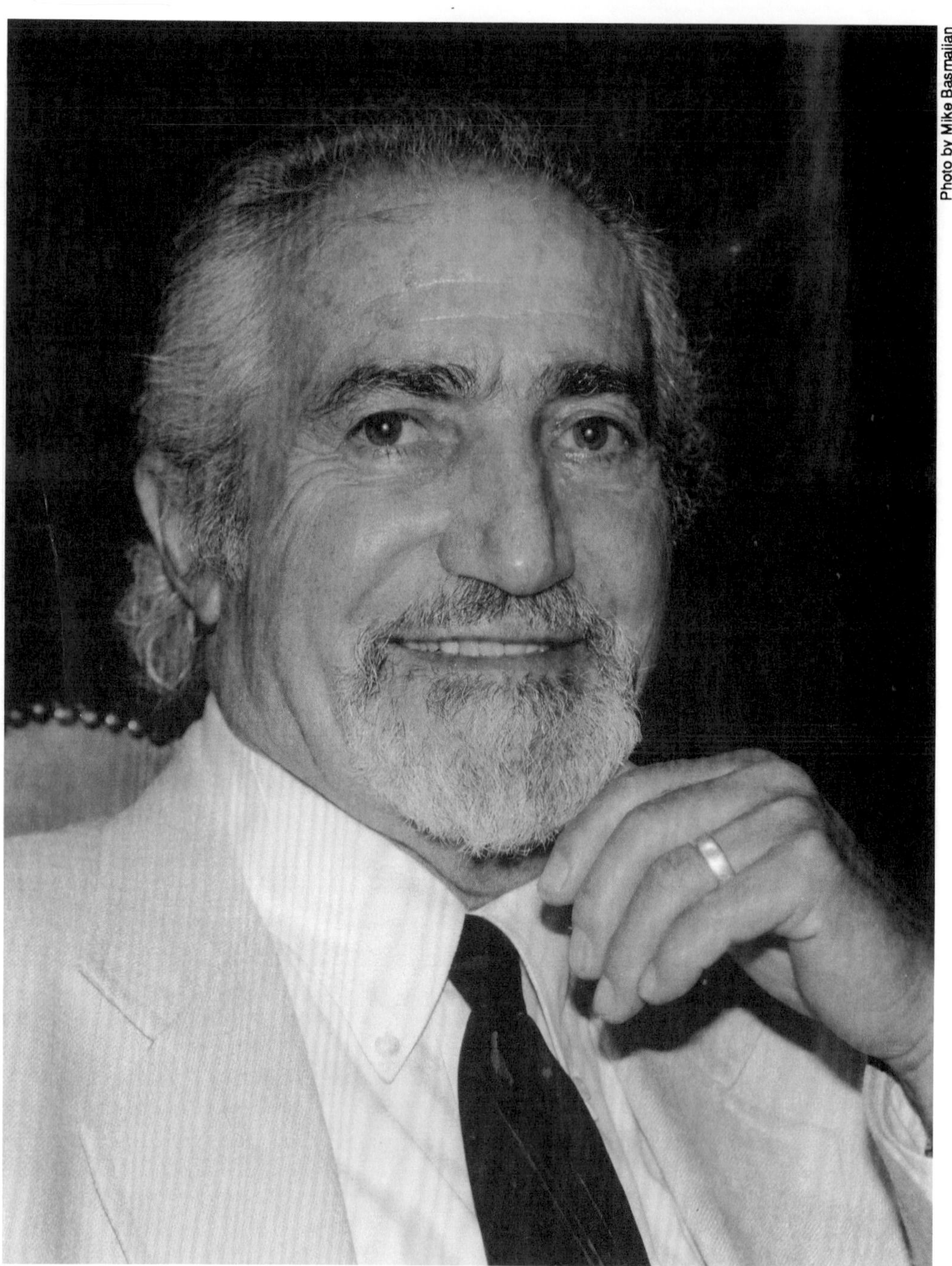

Photo by Mike Basmajian

NEW DIMENSIONS IN HEALING

HEALING AND THE FUTURE

TORKOM SARAYDARIAN

Visions for the Twenty-First Century®

New Dimensions in Healing

ISBN: 0929874-21-8 (Softcover)
ISBN: 0929874-20-X (Hardcover)

Library of Congress Catalog Number 91-75267

Printed in the United States of America

Cover design: *Fine Point Graphics*
Sedona, Arizona

Printed by: Delta Lithograph Co.
Valencia, California

Published by: **T.S.G. Publishing Foundation, Inc.**
Visions for the Twenty-First Century
P.O. Box 4273
West Hills, California 91308
United States of America

Note: The visualizations, meditations, prayers and exercises contained in this book are given to the reader as a guideline. Please consult a medical professional before proceeding. Then proceed carefully, with discretion and at your own risk.

Dedicated to my father

Yervant Toros Saraydarian

published in memory of

Jan F. Czernek

with blessings

Torkom Saraydarian

Table of Contents

Diagrams

A Few Words

My father was a pharmacist and a composer. In 1915 millions of Armenians were killed by the Turks. In our city alone, thousands of Armenians were taken out of their homes and led into the deserts to be butchered. My father and mother were in that caravan when, one night, the police came and announced that Yervant Saraydarian and his family must return to the city so that he could serve in a Turkish hospital that needed a pharmacist.

They were withdrawn from the caravan whose members were later butchered in the desert. Thus, my father and mother said their final goodbyes to their fathers, mothers, sisters, and brothers and were brought back to the city.

Cholera was everywhere. People were dying by the hundreds. The police took my father to the hospital. When they were on the first steps of the hospital, my father knelt on the steps and, raising his hands in prayer, said, "Almighty Lord, I will be working in this hospital to serve You. I will give my whole life to serve human beings with all my heart, and, Lord, please let Your hand be over me as a shield."

"What are you talking about and to whom?" asked one of the policemen.

"I am talking to the Lord so that He gives me the strength to serve."

As the years went on and the conditions became worse, many doctors and nurses passed away. Yet, my father was working almost around the clock, not only in the pharmacy but also as a doctor and surgeon, helping hundreds of soldiers brought to the hospital from the war.

He lived to be 97 years old. When people asked him the secret of his health and energy, he used to say, "A joyful heart dedicated to the service of human beings will never have time to be sick."

To the last moment of his life he was full of joy and blessings.

Before he passed away he said, "I am so happy that I did not lose a moment to help people, even if they were the enemies of my nation."

This book is written in his memory.

Torkom Saraydarian
1992

To the Reader

Dear Reader,

You do not need to believe what I have written in the following pages. Use your mind and try to see the vision behind the words.

Should you see value in these pages, do not practice what you read in a hurry. Take your time. If you do practice it, do so at your own risk.

Those of you who are interested in the healing arts must read this book at least four times to see the overall view.

After you have a full grasp of the entire topic, in its many facets, you may take specific chapters that correspond to the level of your needs and the level of your evolution and practice them, if you want, after consulting with a qualified physician.

If you want to change your course of study to another chapter and want to do another exercise, you may do so. But you must remember that if you want substantial results you must stay with an exercise for at least two months. During these two months, you must do the exercise exactly as it is given. No change or addition or subtraction must be introduced to it. If anything is introduced into the exercise, either you will not gain any result or you will create a reaction against the exercise.

Also, you must obey the time limit given in each exercise. Exaggeration and fanaticism open the gates of troubles.

These exercises must be done according to the following:

1. Your stomach must not be full.

2. You must have emptied your bowels.

3. The exercises must not be done when you are physically exhausted, emotionally in turmoil, or mentally unbalanced.

4. It is suggested that mediums, channels, lower psychics, and those who are engaged in the black arts keep themselves away from these exercises.

5. Those who use hallucinogenic drugs or alcohol must not try these exercises.

6. These exercises are dangerous also for those who have been heavily hypnotized, are lunatics, or are hospitalized in asylums.

7. Every one must use his discretion and gradually introduce himself to these exercises. They can turn into a source of golden happiness and health on many levels.

The science of healing must be based upon the healer's inner development and achievements and upon his varied experiences gathered from his experiments.

Healing is achieved by those who strive toward perfection. Those who are preparing themselves for healing must regularly do visualization exercises, many of which are given in this book. Visualization is the power through which the creative and reconstructive energies of Nature can scientifically be utilized.

Also, it is important that the healer stand inwardly detached from the sick and remain without anxieties and worries, as thoughtforms created by such turbulences block the currents of the healing energy.

For me, mental and emotional health is more important than the health of the physical body.

Again for me, the reasons why we live are more important than our physical health.

This book is written as a guide to create your future lives and build a diamond foundation for you in the coming eternities.

I can only say to you — be daring, fearless, and open minded, and Life will bless you.

Introduction

The Process of Healing

When we speak about healing, we speak about the process of attunement, just as an orchestra tunes every musical instrument with the keynote. Our physical-etheric, emotional, and mental bodies are like musical instruments. The whole individuality is an orchestra.

The healing process is the process of tuning each instrument to the fixed note.

Often in our musical rehearsals we have the "tuning fork" which gives the standard pitch on which all instruments are tuned.

But what is the *standard pitch* — the standard frequency — in man on which all his bodies must be tuned?

Medicine, psychology, and psychiatry do not give us any information about this *pitch.* The only source we have is in the Ageless Wisdom.

According to the Ageless Wisdom, there exists the standard pitch in the Core of man and it is called by various names:

— The radiation of the Divine Spark in man

— The creative AUM

— The note of the Soul, the note of the Self

— The note that resounds with the Cosmic Magnet

— The note that opens the gates for Higher Realms

— The note that makes all things new

— The note that regenerates or harmonizes, uplifts, transforms, and even shatters the form side of life when the form is no longer cooperating with it

Every human being in his Core has that keynote on which he is supposed to tune all his mental, emotional, etheric, and physical systems.

Every step in tuning our system to that keynote is the healing process.

That inner sound stands for our highest visions — the "hope of glory," the archetype of perfection. This inner note, or the key sound, not only tunes our atoms, cells, organs, and system, but it also tunes us to the keynote of the Universe which, as a Cosmic Sound, tries to harmonize and attune all parts of Creation.

For some people, the Inner Sound, the Core Sound, is the Voice of God. If any one hears this sound, he enters into an intense process of transfiguration.

For others, it is the Will of God to which every thought, emotion, action, and motive must be tuned.

For still others it is the supreme vision of beauty, harmony, joy, and bliss which must penetrate into all the vehicles and expressions of man.

Still for others it is the source of Creativity, the currents of which bring transmutation and transfiguration in man.

Still for others it is the Inner Architect, the Inner Conductor who builds the new Temple of Spirit out of the world of matter and orchestrates its relationship with the Universe.

The Ageless Wisdom says that before conception takes place the human soul releases his creative note upon which his vehicles form themselves. And when the time of departure comes, the human soul stops sounding the note and the disintegration of the bodies takes place.

The Ageless Wisdom says that "the One began to sound His note and the manifestation of the Universe began." Soon we will find that all manifestation is a condensed sound. It is on the keynote of creation that all forms of life are striving in order to reach perfection — a supreme state of health.

The healing process involves all the facets of man. There is no true health unless a person physically, emotionally, and mentally tunes to that inner keynote. Unless all the instruments of the vehicles are tuned to the keynote, the *Conductor* cannot lead the orchestra and bring into manifestation the supreme beauty — the perfection — latent in every human being.

For some people this inner keynote is the highest standard of spirituality and morality — without which there can be neither health nor happiness.

The healing process is not only related to the physical and etheric bodies but also to the emotional and mental bodies. Many people are apparently healthy in their physical body but are really sick in their emotions and thinking.

You can heal the physical body for a while, but if you forget to heal the rest of the man, the physical body does not stay healthy.

The health of a human being is the sum total of the degrees of attunement that his vehicles reach. This is why more and more we are entering an era of holistic healing.

People have thought that man is a chemical compound, while others thought that man is a pool of emotions or nothing else but a machine producing thoughts. These may be true, but a human being is also a spirit, a beauty, a condensed bliss, a source of Cosmic Creativity — he is the Space. All that exist in him, all that he is, is the sum of the Universe — he is the microcosm within the macrocosm.

The healing process also includes the process of elimination of those elements from the physical, etheric, astral, and mental nature which create discord and cannot attune with the principles that are not of our Core.

Many habits, vices, dark urges and drives coming from our past; our negative emotions; thoughts based on self-interest, exploitation, and greed — these are elements that prevent the expansion of consciousness; elements that cause separation and discord. All these elements are seeds of disease in our various vehicles for which we pay a very high price.

The keynote, the nature of our essential pitch, the pure sound of our being is ever expanding, liberating, and inclusive. To discover this note and to create harmonious cords within all our systems is the process of advanced healing of the future.

The healing process through which a person must go was defined by one of the greatest thinkers, the Christ, Who said, "Be perfect as your Father in heaven is perfect."

The process of perfection, the striving toward perfection, is the process of attunement with your Conscience, with the heartnote of the entire humanity, with the standard note of the planet, with the keynote of the solar system, and with the AUM of the Universe.

The AUM is the symbol of energy which sustains life in manifestation.

All diseases are the result of dissonance. Healing is a process carried out by every life form trying to attune its vehicles of expression to its essential purpose of life.

1

Striving Toward Perfection

The Ageless Wisdom teaches us that the major foundation of health is striving toward perfection.... There are three stages of perfection. The first is called Transfiguration. The second is called Mastery. The third one is called Resurrection.

All branches of the Ageless Wisdom — religions, traditions, legends, myths, etc. — have one major goal: to bring to the people of the world all the laws, rules, principles, ideas, and teachings which will make them healthy physically, emotionally, and mentally.

Of course health, in turn, brings happiness, prosperity, and success.

To be healthy means to be healthy in all your personality vehicles — the physical, emotional, and mental bodies. Unless these bodies are healthy, you cannot be considered a healthy person. And, these three bodies must unfold and develop simultaneously until they reach a high degree of integration in which they cooperate with maximum efficiency and without hindering each other's growth.

The entire person cannot be healthy if one body is taken care of and the others are neglected. Any disharmonious development in the three bodies creates friction between them, and eventually illness comes into being.

The Ageless Wisdom teaches us that the major foundation of health is striving toward perfection. Striving toward perfection means to make every kind of effort to make your physical body healthy, your emotional and mental bodies healthy, and to tune this triple instrument to the keynote of your Soul.

Doctors and the medical profession as a whole never tell their patients to strive for perfection. Striving toward perfection means the elimination of all those hindrances in your threefold vehicles which prevent their individual growth and their integration.

Through striving toward perfection, we make our bodies invulnerable to various kinds of attacks and keep our health and happiness.

All present sicknesses and diseases, as well as future ones, are proof that we have not achieved perfection in the three bodies. Life after life, these sicknesses repeat themselves until they are exhausted.

All that we do to heal people is superficial and temporary. The cure is not permanent; it lasts for ten days, twenty years, or a few lives.

Perfection gradually makes it impossible for the bodies to be sick. The bodies are thus able to work in their maximum capacity and are able to reject destructive agents from penetrating into them.

Integration of the vehicles and their alignment with the Soul leads to perfection.

There are three stages of perfection. The first is called **Transfiguration**. The second one is called **Mastery**. The third one is called **Resurrection**.

In the first stage, the vibrations of your threefold bodies are attuned with the Soul, and their latent light is released.

In the second stage, your threefold personality is attuned with the Spiritual Triad, and your consciousness is elevated into the Atmic Plane.

In the third stage, your vehicles are attuned with the Monad within you, and the glory of your Divinity is released to function in the next Cosmic Plane.

The Ageless Wisdom or the Teaching is the medicine, and whoever tries to actualize the Teaching in his life, or to live according to the Teaching, is making himself healthy and happy. The Teaching contains all those spiritual medicines through which you can reach health and happiness.

The Teaching expands your consciousness, and it conditions your body.

Striving means to make efforts to raise the vibration of our vehicles to the keynote of our Inner Guide. We are trying to tune our threefold vehicles to the keynote of our Inner Guide until our notes resonate with that keynote.

Slow and continuous striving purifies our vehicles and eliminates all those impediments which prevent the process of tuning in.

Striving gradually liberates the human soul from the control of the three lower vehicles.

Striving makes it possible for us to sense, and then to be aware of, the One Self. Such an awareness will eliminate all the pain and suffering of humanity.

Striving will release the light of the human soul and let it shine out.

M.M., in speaking about striving, states:

> *Sickness rises from sin — says the Scripture. We say that sickness comes from the imperfections of past and present. One should know how to approach the cure of sickness. To the regret of physicians, the process toward perfection is the true prophylactic measure. It can be understood that the process toward perfection begins with the heart, and it has not only a spatial but also a narrow material meaning. Mothers carry their children close to their hearts as a panacea for calming them, but usually one is unaware that this holding close to the heart creates a powerful reaction. Thus, also in the Subtle World we gather people close to the heart for strengthening and for cure. Of course, the heart loses a great deal of energy through such strong*

application. But, then, more than once has the heart of a mother been represented as transfixed by swords and arrows, a symbol of the acceptance into the heart of all actual pains.

Not only in developed sicknesses but at their inception is the cure through the heart especially potent. At present, this remedy is almost forgotten, but it is no less powerful than a blood transfusion, for through the reaction of the heart the finest energy is transmitted without the unpleasant low admixture of blood. When one thinks about the process of perfectment, one must not forget solicitude for the heart that gives.[1]

Thus, striving leads to perfection, and perfection casts out all seeds of illness for the present and for the future.

Thus, the first labor of the striving one consists of making his threefold personality perfect by eliminating all the habits, negative emotions, and ways of thinking which hinder the process of perfection within the bodies. This is done through meditation, which is mental striving.

Meditation gradually eliminates from your whole system those past and present elements which prevent your spiritual progress and burns them away. It also builds progressive standards in your system which automatically reject all those elements which do not fit your principles and goals.

Meditation increases the radioactivity of your soul and lets your soul purify your vehicles of unwanted elements.

The second labor of striving leads to the liberation of the human soul from the domination of the threefold vehicles. This is done by building the Antahkarana and raising the focus of consciousness beyond the mental plane.

The third labor of your striving is to create a sense of unity with the All Self. This is done by functioning on the Intuitional Plane, where the unity of all selves is seen within the One Self.

The fourth labor of striving is to make the human soul shine out its glory. This is done through real creativity and through sacrificial service.

Striving is an urge within us to actualize our real spiritual archetype through our thoughts, emotions, and actions.

When the three bodies are tuned to the keynote of the Soul, the human soul liberates himself and tries to use the threefold personality as a musical instrument on which to play his music, which means: he tries to bring into outer expression the glory hidden within him.

Great glory is hidden within our soul. All divine potentials are there waiting for manifestation. When these divine potentials increase their manifestation, they make our vehicles invincible and fiery.

---

1. Agni Yoga Society, *Heart*, para. 96.

Striving toward perfection is an ever expanding process in which your personality tunes to your Soul and to the Souls of all living creatures. This is how real personalities, real groups, real nations, and a real humanity are formed. Imagine humanity as one human being, the threefold vehicles of which are perfectly in tune with the Soul of humanity. What a glory such a humanity will manifest! And how healthy and happy will be each cell and each atom in that one humanity.

Of course, to understand the concept of one humanity requires freedom from our vanity, greed, egoism, separatism, and illusions.

Striving is a spiritual effort to get rid of such impediments, to actualize individual, group, national, and global integration and alignment with the higher centers of the Universe.

This one Universe has a center which is called the Cosmic Magnet. All true striving is an effort to tune to that Cosmic Magnet.

As we go closer to such an attunement, we eliminate all poison-producing thoughts, emotions, and actions. We eliminate all those habits that hurt our body or waste our energy. We let healing power, joy, and inspiration circulate throughout our systems, uniting, uplifting, and synthesizing us with the power of the Cosmic Magnet within us, within the solar system, and within the galaxy.

Healing energy cannot flow through us if our bodies are full of cleavages. Healing energy cannot be available to a group which is not united by real love, understanding, cooperation, and sacrificial service.

The healing energy of the Hierarchy cannot manifest through humanity when there is competition, hatred, and war. Thus, a human being, a group, a nation, and humanity deprive themselves of the fiery energy of the Higher Worlds if there is no unity in them.

Unity is power because unity creates those conditions in which the power of the Cosmic Magnet can manifest.

As long as there is hatred within a person, within a group, within a nation, within humanity, healing will be impossible and pain and suffering will be always existent within the life of humanity.

The same effect will manifest in our life as long as our thoughts, emotions, and actions are galvanized by anger, fear, revenge, jealousy, treason, vanity, separatism, and egoism. Permanent happiness and health will be impossible until we eliminate such sources of poison from our system.

The Teaching is the medicine because it advises us to strive toward perfection, toward the search for "the Kingdom of God." Each step on the path of perfection is like taking the most effective medicine.

All healing efforts are efforts of failure if they are not based on the principle of striving toward perfection. All such efforts are like building mansions on sand dunes.

Permanent healing is impossible with the present systems of healing. All present systems of healing create temporary results. A result lasts a short time or becomes a cause for another sickness, and eventually you die. But death does not terminate your sickness. Often you take your sickness to the astral plane and even to the lower mental plane. When you incarnate, you bring all the tendencies or seeds of previous sicknesses back to earth with you and continue to suffer.

There is only one way to overcome any sickness — **strive toward perfection**. As you advance on the path of perfection, you gradually develop immunity to all diseases and sicknesses and eventually develop vehicles which are charged by the fire which burns away all causes of disease.

The physical, emotional, and mental health of every individual can be guaranteed only if all humanity is healthy. Real health and happiness can be achieved only through inspiring all humanity to strive toward perfection. The real health of the cells of the body is based on the health of the entire body. The real health of every individual can be guaranteed only by the health of all humanity. This is why every effort of unification is an effort to reach an ultimate global health.

The Ageless Wisdom gives us the "medicine" for permanent health on all planes, through all our incarnations, and on all journeys in the Higher Worlds. It gives us the inspiration to strive toward perfection by developing the qualities of Beauty, Goodness, Righteousness, Joy, Freedom, gratitude, and sacrificial service. These are steps that take us to the path of everlasting health, happiness, and bliss.

All healing processes at this time are methods of suppression. This does not mean that we can live in this world without these healing processes, but we must know that they offer temporary cures and actually suppress the causes of sickness.

The causes of sickness are removed through achieving gradual perfection. When a wounded finger heals itself, it achieves its former perfection. When one perfects his vehicles with the current of his expanding and increasingly fiery energy, his nature becomes perfect, and in perfection sickness cannot exist because sickness is imperfection.

A person must realize that the health of his neighbor is as important as his own health. A person must realize that one cannot have health if he is making others unhealthy.[2]

A person must realize that in trying to make others healthy, he will be healthy. If these principles are studied, one will find the panacea of healing.

Health is equilibrium — a state of equilibrium in all the raging waves of chaos. A state of equilibrium is a state of intelligent relationship with all forces and forms existent in Nature. A state of equilibrium is a state of consciousness in which one is able to absorb shocks and not lose his direction toward perfection.

---

2. See also *The Psychology of Cooperation and Group Consciousness*, and *The Sense of Responsibility in Society.*

As we go toward higher and higher perfection, we learn how to live and move through events, cycles, inflowing and outflowing energies, and through the destructive and constructive phases of life. This is done by striving toward perfection.

Instead of teaching our children how to strive, all over the world we teach them how to commit crime and engage in violence and killing. We teach them greed and tell them to make every kind of effort to make money at the expense of others. When such seeds are planted in the consciousness of the youth all over the world, we must not wonder when epidemics spread and when pain and suffering increase.

Any effort toward cleavages, separatism, and self-interest is an effort to perpetuate the pain and suffering in the world.

Instead of encouraging the youth to achieve physical, emotional, mental, and spiritual perfection, we encourage actions that lead them toward degeneration.

All unhappy or painful conditions that we have in our present life have their roots in our past, in our present activities, and in our future plans. This chaos continues to repeat itself life after life in a vicious circle.

Temporary healings may even worsen a situation in the future if striving toward the future is not nurtured in our soul.

Every step of healing must be a step forward on the path of perfection.

Once a wounded boy said to my father, who was binding the boy's wound, "Just you wait. When I am cured, I will kill the man who hurt me."

My father said, "If you are going to kill him after you recover, I will not cure you so that I am not responsible for your crime."

"Well," said the boy, "I am paying you to help me be healed."

"The healing of your body is not the answer if you do not heal your heart," said my father.

This conversation had a tremendous effect on me. M.M. says, "What a tragedy will come to the world if people carry hate and revenge and crime in their hearts, but have healthy bodies."

Every time we disturb the harmony in the system of energies in the Universe, we suffer. We break the law of love and harmony; we break the law of synthesis and unity; then we "enjoy" our pain and suffering. Something in our heart must fundamentally change in order to discover the path of everlasting health.

It is very interesting to notice that after people become seriously sick, they express humility, goodwill, forgiveness, love, etc. This is a subtle expression of an instinct that suggests if we live a better life, we will not fall into pain and suffering.

After much suffering, many people confess their "sins" and promise to live a noble life. They do not realize that if they had lived a noble life, a life of spiritual striving toward perfection, they would not have needed to go through pain and suffering.

The principle of striving toward perfection is within our Core. If we do things against this principle, we feel ashamed just as, for example, a child is ashamed of his first experience of lying.

Some kill thousands of people and feel happy for their victory. A person kills one man and suffers until he dies. Another person feels ashamed for having harmful thoughts against someone.

I once saw my Teacher in tears. When I asked the reason, he said, "I had an opportunity to encourage someone, but I didn't." Another Teacher was sad for many hours because he unintentionally destroyed a beautiful flower bush under his feet. All such attitudes show the measure of our perfection or the measure of our degeneration.

Striving toward perfection is the only way to eliminate suffering and pain in our future incarnations or the days of our soul.

For sensitive and advanced people, a moment of disharmony is a moment of suffering because of that principle which challenges us to strive toward perfection.

One can speed his striving toward perfection if he sits down and makes a list of habits, behaviors, activities, emotions, thoughts, and motives that he does not like in himself. Such a list may help him improve himself systematically and speed his striving toward perfection.

It is possible that the current of energy created by striving toward perfection may stir and bring to the surface much trash hidden in various parts of one's nature which manifests as sicknesses and psychological and mental problems. Striving toward perfection not only will bring this trash to the surface but will also burn it off forever.

Every element within our nature that we think hinders our spiritual progress must be handled cautiously and eliminated if we wish to be healthy.

There is a very strange mechanism within us. We like to suffer. When we discover this, we say this tendency is a sickness. But if we go deeper, we will discover that those who want or like to suffer have committed hidden crimes in this life or in previous lives. They want to punish themselves. They think that by suffering they can pay for the crime they committed and thus be free from the consequences of their crime. This shows that there is a principle within us which makes us strive toward perfection and makes us uncomfortable if we hinder this process.

Health is secured by eliminating elements that work against our health. But people often prefer to have heavy smog and pollution rather than live a simple life.

When we want to be sick rather than healthy, the reasons are these:

1. We want to punish ourselves.

2. Our Inner Lord left us because of our vices.

3. We chose to go on the involutionary path which leads to disintegration, decay, separatism, pain, and suffering.

Individuals as well as groups and nations fall into such traps. Once a national consciousness wants to punish itself because of past accumulated crimes, once its Guardian Angel leaves because of its increasing vices, once a nation chooses the path of corruption, nothing can stop it from final self-destruction.

The tendency of our threefold bodies is toward involution, which means toward pain and suffering. Once we stop striving toward perfection, we fall victim to the currents of the involutionary forces.

Spiritual striving leads us to cooperate with the creative forces of Nature and inspires us to follow the path leading to perfection. It is on this path that we enjoy health. Defective bodies or vehicles prevent us from enjoying our lives in the three worlds, but healthy physical, emotional, mental bodies allow us to enjoy life on the three corresponding planes.

Even in the Subtle Worlds we have those who, like our mothers, try to encourage us to find the path of striving toward perfection if the spark of such a striving is already lit within our heart.

Health is also based on our sacrificial and heroic deeds. Such heroic deeds may wipe out accumulated piles of karma and release us from our suffering.

Every time we are defeated and have failed, we must know that before our defeat and failure we, in some way, worked against our soul's striving toward perfection. Striving toward perfection is a response of our soul to the Cosmic Magnet, to the All Self existing behind all living forms.

A consciousness that is imbued by thoughts of the One Self is a powerful healing source. When one tunes himself to the One Self, he cannot do anything against that One Self. If he does not act against that One Self, he harmonizes himself with It.

People say, "Are you crazy enough to think that you are one with the All Self existing in every form? What about your individual life? What about your possessions?" It is true that people will laugh at you, but they will never discover a better panacea to heal themselves from their suffering and pain.

In the recognition of your oneness with the One Self, you are preparing your future health, happiness, prosperity, and success. Imagine how many people have been killed, destroyed, paralyzed, and annihilated throughout thousands of years because of separatism.

The highest law of the Universe, or even in the whole Cosmos, is the Law of Unity. Every law is a branch of this major law. Any crime is, in its essence, a violation of this law, and all pain and suffering are the result of actions taken against this law.

"...The entire perfectment of the heart rests upon moral foundations."[3]

The moral foundation is the awareness of the One Self, the Law of Unity.

One must never think that he can be happy by making others unhappy; or he can be healthy by ruining the health of others; or be prosperous by manipulating others. The Law of Unity stands against such people and eventually brings them to their senses through much suffering and pain.

Healing is a living process. Actually, evolution is the law of healing because its intention is to lead us to perfection.

Evolution can be involuntary and voluntary. In the first instance, Nature makes you proceed on the path of perfection, and each of your resistances becomes a cause for pain and suffering. If you discover the cause of your pain and suffering, you begin to cooperate with the current of evolution. This becomes voluntary evolution.

In voluntary evolution you cooperate consciously. In conscious cooperation you strive toward perfection to eliminate the hindrances on the path of evolution within you and within others.

This conscious and voluntary evolution is the path of initiation. On this path you expose yourself to the current of evolution, and you let it be active in you not only physically but also emotionally, mentally, and spiritually.

One of the goals of the evolutionary process is to prepare men and women who can use the energy of evolution on higher planes and help the current expand its usefulness.

Everyone who voluntarily and consciously uses the current of evolution becomes a part of the evolutionary current.

The path of initiation is the **current** of evolution in action toward higher dimensions.

Exercise

Do not be discouraged if you cannot gear immediately into these exercises, but a start is important. Approach these exercises in simplicity and sincerity. If you make yourself ready, you will go deeper into them and receive great benefit. These are multidimensional exercises, and you can gradually learn to do them.

This exercise must be done in a non-dreaming state of mind. You must be very realistic and practical.

1. Relax and close your eyes.

3. *Ibid.*, para. 111.

2. Visualize a higher state of consciousness, whatever this means for you, a state of consciousness which you wish you had.

People talk about higher states of consciousness, but they never try to experience them or actualize them. In this exercise we will make an attempt to experience a higher state of consciousness and see how we feel in it.

No one can tell you what that state of consciousness should be for you. It is you who has to visualize it, strive toward it, and experience it. You are your own measure of attainment. Now start visualizing a higher state of consciousness and try to experience it.

3. Visualize how that state of consciousness will change or may change the course of your thinking, feeling, words, relationships, and activities.

Every expression of consciousness brings in new standards. And every new standard introduces new changes into your thinking, feeling, and acting processes.

4. Try to see what new standards you expect to have in your new state of consciousness and what changes you expect to introduce into your life.

5. Some people do not yet know the difference between thinking and a state of consciousness. Try to discover it, and see how it affects your thinking.

For example, if you are a king, how will you act? Similarly, if you reach a higher state of consciousness, how will you act?

Your state of consciousness determines the mode of your relationship with the many sides of life. By visualizing a new mode of relationship with life, you can penetrate into that state of consciousness which conditions such a new relationship.

For example, you visualize that you want to relate to life through Beauty, Goodness, Righteousness, Joy, Freedom, gratitude, and sacrificial service, and then slowly you discover a hidden state of consciousness which is the cause of such a new relationship.

Striving is to occupy new territories in the realm of consciousness and to actualize them in your relationships on those planes. A new state of consciousness can be found only if you liberate yourself from the limitations of your former thinking, feelings, and actions.

There are nine major states of consciousness with nine divisions each.

Sometimes you feel that you are up against a wall. You are not. The wall is built within you because you have remained too long in your familiar state of consciousness. If you continuously persist in your efforts, you will make a breakthrough. Liberation from your past level of consciousness helps you make a breakthrough.

6. If you sensed a new state of consciousness, or if you visualized it as a possible future state of consciousness, try to visualize five kinds of actions which are the manifestations of your new level of consciousness.

7. Visualize five past actions that were not in harmony with such a state of consciousness and their effect on your health. Often, positive values are better understood by their opposites. One must have a confrontation with former states of consciousness *after he is above them.*

8. Try to translate your new state of consciousness in terms of new and more refined emotions. What kind of emotions can be named and felt? Find five emotions which you think can translate your new state of consciousness. Then think about their five opposites, and see how and why you were stuck in these past emotions. Be practical. Name these emotions, and see what their effect was on your heart.

9. Check your new state of consciousness. See if you are still focused there, and see if you can feel and experience it better.

10. After reassuring yourself that you are still in your new state of consciousness, try to translate it through five new ways of thinking. See these new ways of thinking as objectively as possible. Try to see five old ways of thinking, and try to realize how they affected your health in the past and also how they are affecting you in the present.

11. Open your eyes and record your experiences.

With every new and higher state of consciousness, you build new and higher standards. And when your level of consciousness moves to higher dimensions, you build new standards in your three worlds and create a new life for yourself.

Also, your effect on life increases. This produces reactions and responses. You learn from reactions, and you use responses to further expand your consciousness.

Expanding your consciousness is the best way to demonstrate your striving toward perfection. This is called the ladder of conscious and voluntary evolution. You reach a new level of consciousness, then build new standards in it, and shape your whole life on these new standards. Then you move ahead to a still higher state of consciousness and build higher standards, shape your life on these new and higher standards, and move ahead toward your ultimate purpose of life.

Your health is based on the state and level of your consciousness. An expanding consciousness eliminates all those factors in your nature that cause ill health. It is the expanding consciousness that sees the effects of the negative and positive elements of your nature upon your health.

Expanding your consciousness is like increasing your pure light and seeing things as they are and their possible effect on your physical, emotional, and mental health. When an expanded consciousness sees a negative element, eventually it gets rid of it.

The more expanded your consciousness, the more healthy principles and standards you have in your life.

The more your light increases, the less darkness you have.

In this exercise you slowly see that you are not a form, or you are not the form you visualized yourself to be, but a state of consciousness. Not many people have experiences of being a *state of consciousness*. The goal of this exercise is liberation from being a form into being a state of consciousness and still feeling that you exist.

Every achievement in a new state of consciousness must be supported by a new way of practical living, corresponding to that achieved state of consciousness, so that you are grounded and not lost in space.

If you have a new inspiration, manifest it to keep the balance.

2

The Constitution of Man

The development and unfoldment of the petals, permanent atoms, chakras, glands, and organs are orchestrated by the consciousness of man. The more the human consciousness advances, the more his mechanism on all levels advances. This is why great Masters of Wisdom advise that man must develop, unfold, purify, and expand his consciousness to be able to lead all his mechanisms into perfection.

Most people know themselves as bodies — a physical body with eyes, ears, hands, feet. If someone thinks about himself, he thinks about his body. What happens? When anyone thinks only about his body, his thought energy goes to the body and energizes the body. Because he does not know he has different bodies, he creates an imbalance in his constitution.

If you always think about one part of your life, you energize only that part; the other parts remain without food. The same thing happens to your health and well-being when you concentrate your thought energy on one part of your body or on one part of your life.

Let us say you are building a business and you are dedicated to it one hundred percent. That is wonderful, but your life becomes unbalanced if you do not have other fields of interest to channel your thought energy. Wherever you channel your thought energy, you create life there. In the same manner, if you are thinking only about your physical body or a specific organ, you are transmitting life energy into that part only. But because your constitution is not limited only to the physical body, you are creating imbalance as long as you are only thinking about your physical body. Other parts of your constitution are not receiving energy, electricity. Wherever you channel energy, that part is going to be energized and other parts will be out of balance. That is one of the reasons for ill health.

As one expands his consciousness and lives a more inclusive life, more parts of his nature receive energy — which helps to coordinate and balance his nature and life.

The constitution of man is like the constitution of Cosmos: man is built of seven layers of matter and substance.

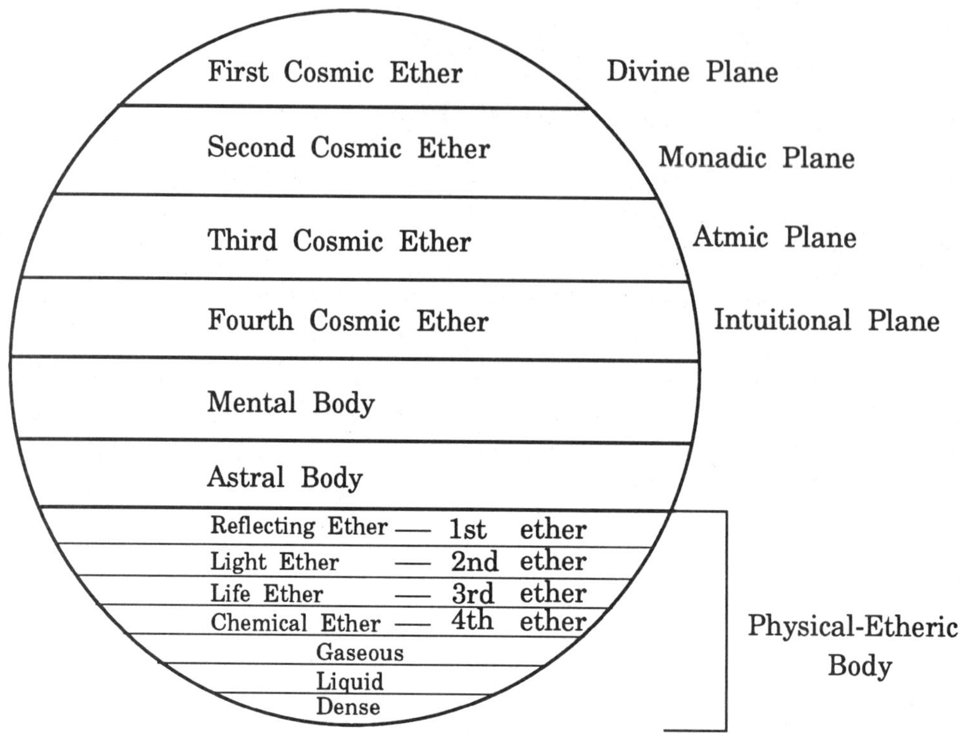

Diagram 2-1 Constitution of Man

The physical body is made up, at the lowest point, of a dense physical vehicle — flesh and bones. Then there is a liquid part, such as lymph, blood, and various secretions. Then there is the air or gas found in the ventricles of the brain, in certain bones, etc. Then we have the four ethers, the totality of which is our etheric or electromagnetic body.

After the etheric body we have the astral and mental planes, and then four higher vehicles which are called the Intuitional, Atmic, Monadic, and Divine Planes.

These four planes are also called the four Cosmic Ethers. This means, our four higher vehicles are built of these four Cosmic Ethers.

Our etheric body, formed by the four lower ethers, is a mechanism which receives energy from the Sun, assimilates it, and passes it through the etheric and physical spleen. Thus our body is energized.

The prana of the Sun is received by the specific centers on the head and shoulders and passed to three centers in the etheric body.

One of the three centers is found at a point between the shoulder blades. Another is found above the diaphragm, and the third one is the etheric spleen. When prana enters this triangle, it circulates in it three times, then goes through the etheric spleen and passes to the physical spleen, and then from the physical spleen directly into the blood.

Most health problems are related to the uneven circulation of this energy. The energy in the etheric body is called *active heat* or *solar radiation* or *prana.*

In the physical body there are two fires. One is called *internal vitalizing fire,* the source of which is the center at the base of the spine. The next fire is called *latent heat,* which is found at the center of every cell of the body. These fires are considered one fire, and they are named as one fire — *the fire by friction.*

The second major fire or energy is the fire of the mind, which is called *solar fire.* The third major fire is called the fire of the spirit or *electric fire.*

The health of the human being on physical, emotional, and mental planes depends on these major fires — through the right relations between the fires and their eventual fusion.

The first fusion is the fusion of the *internal vitalizing fire, latent heat,* and *active heat* or *prana.*

These three fires fuse with each other at a point between the shoulder blades. This is a great accomplishment which brings health and happiness to man.

The second fusion takes place between this first fusion and the fire of mind or *solar fire.* As a person engages in meditation, contemplative study, and creative work, the solar fire increases and pulls the fire focused between the shoulder blades up to the head.

During this process the three currents of fire coming from the base of spine, the Kundalini fire, mixed with the pranic fire climb and contact the throat center, which transmits the fire of mind.

As the Kundalini fire rises in the three etheric channels, it meets with the fire of mental substance as it radiates from the throat center, and climbs up to the neck until it contacts the fire of the mental triangle.

At the beginning of this process, the mental (or manasic) triangle is composed of

Throat center

Pineal gland

Pituitary body

But as the fusion begins between the two fires, the alta center replaces the throat center.

When these two major fires fuse in the manasic or mental triangle, the person radiates health and vitality because as the fire of Kundalini rises naturally due to the expansion of consciousness, it purifies all the etheric centers on the spine, and thus makes the centers transmit energy to each ductless gland of the body and to their corresponding organs.

The third major fusion takes place between the mental fire, the second fusion, and the fire of spirit or *electric fire.* This takes place in the head center, above the head. The fusion of these three fires produces a great Initiate, dedicated to the alleviation of the sufferings of the world.

Coming back to the four ethers, they as a whole form the blueprint and electrical system of the physical body.

The human etheric body has four dimensions. They are called from coarser to finer ethers: fourth, third, second, and first ethers.

The fourth ether controls the base of spine, generative organs, solar plexus, and spleen centers and it is called the *chemical ether*. The third ether is related to the throat center and is called the *life ether*. The second one is related to the heart center and is called the *light ether*. The first one is related to the head center and is called the *reflecting ether*.

The health of these four ethers depends on our actions, emotions, speeches, and thoughts. If these four actions are "right" or in tune with the Cosmic Intent, they will convey health and happiness to our physical, emotional, and mental bodies. But if due to impure conditions of the etheric network and incorrect actions, emotions, speeches, and thoughts they are burned or congested with the energy of prana, they will be sources of endless troubles for us. Thus the disorders in the etheric body accumulate through congestion or destruction of the etheric network.

Congestion occurs when too much prana is drawn into the physical body. Destruction of the etheric network occurs when the energy accumulated in the etheric body is used for self-interest or for the exploitation of others.

Congestion in the etheric body and the resulting destruction of the tissues of the physical body cause most of the diseases prevalent today.

The congestion occurs when the pranic centers absorb more energy than the body can handle. Pranic fire must be fused with the latent fire in the body in a right dosage to bestow health and energy on the body.

The destruction of the etheric network occurs when incoming pranic energy burns certain parts of the etheric body. This has its physical causes. For example, if a man is living in a polluted atmosphere, where there is no sunshine or hygienic conditions, he cannot have a healthy etheric body. Either it is congested due to the lack of circulation, or it is burned because of moral conditions.

When energy is misused by our actions, or wasted by excessive sex or heavy labor in polluted conditions, it burns the etheric network.

Burning occurs when the latent fire does not balance the pranic fire. This occurs when the latent fire is wasted or short-circuited. When the energy is congested in certain places, the corresponding organs have a foul odor and thicken and do not allow the circulating fire or prana to bring energy to various parts of the body. Also, when certain locations of the etheric network are burned, astral energy leaks into the physical body and damages the brain, nervous system, and glands.

Congestion and destruction of certain portions of the etheric network create abnormal conditions in which the human soul cannot contact the Higher Self and remains unprotected and not balanced by higher principles.

To have an uncongested and undamaged etheric body we need

To have clean air

To have a clean psychic environment

To practice virtues

To avoid playing with our centers

To live for the service of humanity

To avoid falling into ego, vanity, pride, revenge, greed, and separatism

Congestion can happen in any location of the etheric body. In such a state, the corresponding organs enlarge, for example the heart, kidneys, or pancreas, and are unable to absorb the excess energy. When the etheric network is burned in certain locations, the corresponding organs starve for energy and slowly weaken and degenerate.

Regulation of the breath and deep breathing in clean air brings great help. Also taking long hikes, especially climbing mountains, helps to put the etheric body in order. Massage of the physical body is very helpful to many people, as are mineral baths and swimming.

Our etheric body reflects like a mirror all the conditions of the physical body and vice versa.

Those who are involved in advanced photography and trying to photograph the electrical sphere or the energy field of the body are contacting the fourth lower ether. Study of their photographs will eventually prove that the ills of the physical body are the result of the ills of the etheric body.

The four lower ethers are related to seven etheric centers. The fourth ether is related to

1. Base of spine

2. Generative organs

3. Solar plexus

4. Spleen (etheric and physical)

The third ether is related to the throat center. The second ether is related to the heart. The first ether is related to the head center. This means that the four ethers, with their seven centers, directly control the corresponding ductless glands, organs, and parts of the physical body.

In order to be able to live a life of fulfillment, you must penetrate into all departments of your nature and use them. Most of us live here in the physical plane and are stuck in the physical body. When you start working in the emotional plane, you move a little bit outward on the path. When you start living in the mental plane, you are closer to your Self. When you are in the Intuitional Plane, you are even closer.

From the Intuitional Plane you control your three lower bodies. You emancipate yourself from your physical, emotional, and mental bodies. You realize that they are all devices for you to use to help reach your destination. The mental device is used like an airplane to go immediately here and there. The Intuitional Plane is used as instantaneous communication. The Atmic Plane is totally universal. As you penetrate into these planes you, at the same time, emancipate yourself from the devices, from the vehicles that you are using to communicate with corresponding levels in Cosmic planes.

In the emotional plane we have seven chakras. These seven chakras create in the emotional plane seven senses. When you die and enter into your emotional body, problems start. What are the problems? You do not have sight. You do not have the sense of smell. You do not have taste. You do not have hearing. They were not built. Where can you build them? You build them here on earth. If your seven chakras are active when you enter into the emotional plane but the corresponding senses are not developed yet, you have problems. Those who are active in the astral plane and know what is going on have independent power over their own machine. They are almost emancipated human beings because they are no longer earthbound. They can function in that subtle plane.

In the *New Testament*, an apostle said, "You have different bodies — bodies of glory, bodies of light." And then one apostle said, "I do not know what happened to me, but I was out of my body. I was listening and seeing things." This indicates that he had his emotional or mental body formed and its senses were formed.[1]

The mental plane is a very interesting plane, and it can be seen around your head. Around the brain you have an etheric brain exactly the replica of your physical brain. The color of the mental body depends on its development. Some mental bodies are very primitive, and the color is muddy green and lemon yellow. Sometimes grey and green are mixed with the lemon color, which makes it a mixed color.

As we advance, the color becomes clearer. The lower part is still green but clearer, and the higher part becomes clearer and clearer, eventually becoming totally lemon yellow. After the Third Initiation, the whole mental body shines in lucid colors of lemon yellow.

When the mental body forms and unfolds, it radiates twelve translucent colors which shine like a crown of precious diamonds.

The legends say that the first kings of humanity were Divine Beings Who came from a very advanced civilization from Space and guided and ruled

---

1. Please refer to *The Psyche and Psychism* and *The Science of Becoming Oneself*.

humanity. At that time people used to see etheric crowns on the heads of the kings or queens.

As these Great Beings left this planet after fulfilling their duties, human kings succeeded them, and because they were not advanced spiritually, they did not have their natural crowns. People built crowns for the kings with precious stones and colorful materials.

Again the legends say that the first priests who came from other civilizations in Space to lead humanity on earth used to shine with their etheric, mental, Intuitional, and higher bodies during the ceremonies. Ages passed, and they departed. To imitate them, human priests prepared colorful vestments as correspondences or symbols of their finer bodies.

All these higher bodies exist within us, and they are visible to a true clairvoyant. Everyone of us must do his utmost to unfold his higher bodies and strive toward perfection.

It is possible to enter into the mental plane. Many Initiates have witnessed that They entered into the mental plane and saw things that cannot be explained by human words.

The mental plane is divided into seven levels and has two main divisions, the lower mind — levels seven, six, five, and four — and the higher mind — levels three, two, and one.

On the fourth level of the mental plane, there exist along with the mental unit the four following centers:

1. Base of spine
2. Generative organs
3. Solar plexus
4. Spleen

Remember that these centers are not etheric but are built of lower mental matter.

The base of spine center in the lower mental plane provides the fire for the thoughtforms which the human soul builds. If that center is active, the thoughtforms of the human soul will be fiery, influential, and far reaching in their effects.

The generative organs in the lower mental body provide the positive and negative energies needed for creation of thoughtforms. Sometimes this polarity is kindled by those people with whom the creative person has spiritual ties. The generative organs in the lower mental plane are androgynous. They do not need outer stimulants, but in some cases, due to various shocks, they become dormant and need outer stimulants. The stimulation comes from close friends, wife, husband, teacher, etc.

The generative organs in the lower mental plane are fertilized by opposite polarities and kindled by inspiration and the creative process.

For example, the male and female organs are fertilized by the opposite organ of the person around us. But remember we are talking about mental creativity.

The solar plexus center in the mental plane is the center of higher psychism, controlled and balanced in the mental plane.

The spleen in the mental body provides the life energy for the thoughtforms. Thoughtforms live longer if the vital energy is put into them through the mental spleen.

The mental unit is the foundation on which the bridge of consciousness is built between the lower and higher mental planes. The extension of the mental unit toward the Mental Permanent Atom provides the first trace on which the Antahkarana is built.

This information shows how imagination — creative imagination and visualization — effect our health. Such practices bring a strong influence on the centers in the lower mental plane and create changes in the astral, etheric, and physical planes.

Following on these principles, many advanced exercises are given in this book which can create miracles if they are done correctly.

These fiery centers are related not only to the astral and etheric bodies but are also related to the network of energies which compose our Chalice in the higher mind.

On the third and second levels of the mental plane, we have a center which is called the Chalice or the Lotus. This Lotus potentially has twelve petals, or twelve flowers. But in average man it appears like a bud. As the person advances, the petals gradually open, and eventually all the petals become fully open. In the Core of the Chalice is found the human soul.

We have also certain foci of energy which are called the permanent atoms. At the root of the Chalice is found three permanent atoms:

Physical permanent atom

Emotional permanent atom

Mental unit

Then we have the Mental Permanent Atom found on the highest level of the mental plane, which is called the atomic level of the mental plane. The Intuitional and Atmic Permanent Atoms are also found on the highest level of their own planes.

It is wonderful to know that every organ and sense in our body is related to a chakra or center. Every chakra is related to a permanent atom. Every permanent atom is related to certain petals of the Chalice.

It is very important to realize that the development and unfoldment of the petals, permanent atoms, chakras, glands, and organs are orchestrated by the consciousness of man. The more the human consciousness advances, the more his mechanism on all levels advances. This is why great Masters of Wisdom advise that man must develop, unfold, purify, and expand his consciousness to be able to lead all his mechanisms into perfection.

3

The Etheric Body

The etheric body is related to the whole manifested Universe and is a vehicle of prana. The etheric body is the communication link between all parts of manifestation, and prana is the vivifying energy which keeps the manifestation alive.

In order to unfold our healing potentials, it will be helpful if we have a clear picture in our mind of the inner constitution of man and a real knowledge of the human body and human biology.

It is assumed that the student of this book already has a thorough knowledge of the human body as taught in colleges and universities but, in general, is not aware of the *etheric body*.

The etheric body is an electromagnetic field in and around our physical body. This etheric body is the blueprint of our physical body. It is exactly the shape of our physical body except that all its organs and all its structures are etheric. It penetrates the physical body and extends beyond it for one to two inches. Upon this etheric blueprint is built our physical body.

The etheric vehicle is formed by one etheric thread woven into the same shape as the physical body. This thread serves as a tube through which the solar life-giving energy, or prana, circulates. Prana is a fiery energy which permeates the etheric network. Prana is seen as a golden light, and when seen clairvoyantly, the whole etheric body shines out in flame-colored light.

The constitution of the physical-etheric body is as follows:

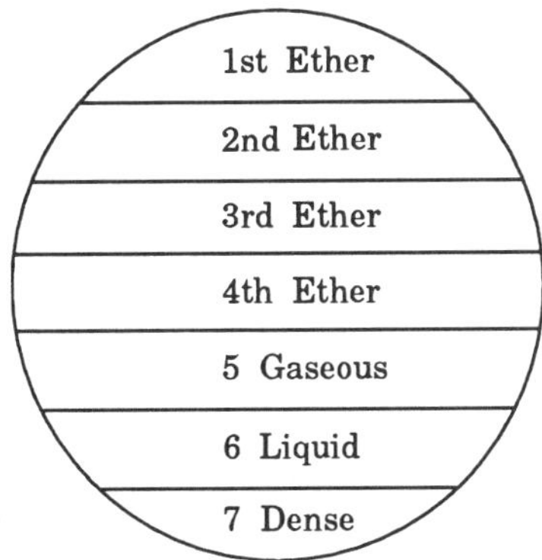

Diagram 3-1 Physical-Etheric Body

The seventh layer is the dense physical plane: the bones and flesh. The sixth layer is the liquid in the body: the lymph, blood, and various secretions. The fifth layer is the gaseous element found in the skull, in some bones, and in various organs. The fourth, third, second, and first layers comprise the etheric body and are also called the four lower ethers.

The four layers of etheric substance form the etheric body. The fourth layer has the coarsest substance, and the first one has the finest substance of the lower ethers. Each etheric level vibrates at a different frequency.

The constitution of man can be symbolized in the following diagram:

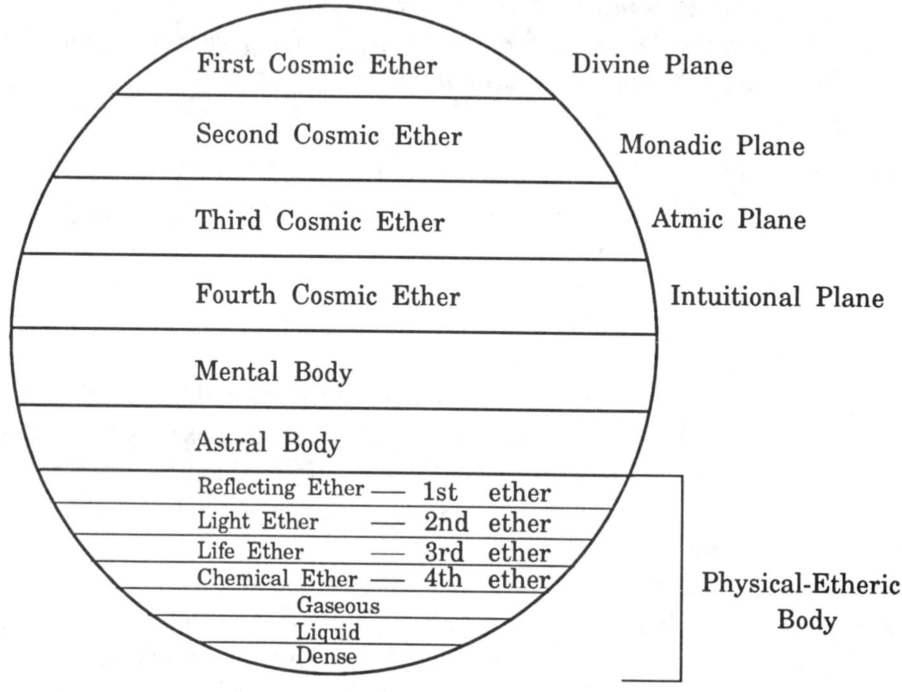

Diagram 3-2 Constitution of Man

The highest plane, Adi or Divine, symbolizes the Divine, Universal Life. The next three planes are called

Monadic	Will
Atmic	Purpose, Peace
Buddhic or Intuitional	Blessing, Pure Reason

These four planes, in esoteric language, are called the Four Cosmic Ethers. Below the Fourth Cosmic Ether, we have the mental plane; followed by the emotional plane; then the physical plane, composed of the four lower ethers which make up the etheric body and the gaseous, liquid, and dense physical levels.

The etheric body is related to the whole manifested Universe and is a vehicle of prana. The etheric body is the communication link between all parts of manifestation, and prana is the vivifying, vitalizing energy which keeps the manifestation alive.

The higher global Centers, Existences, Beings, and Karmic Lords reinforce the Law of the Sun through the etheric planes. For example, in our solar system the solar etheric body penetrates into the planetary etheric body, and the planetary etheric body penetrates into the etheric body of each living form. The Karmic Lords perform Their duty through this unified field of energy.

We receive impressions or energies from zodiacal sources or even higher constellations through our lower and higher ethers and especially via our higher centers. If certain centers are open within our subtle bodies, we will be able to synchronize with greater Centers, Hierarchy, Shamballa, other planets, or galaxies. We can tune to them and be impressed by their energy, direction, or message. That is why it is so important that our etheric body be purified and the etheric centers be synchronized and unfolded, so that we are in continuous contact with the whole existence. Actually, every man lives, moves, and has his own being in that electromagnetic field — the etheric sphere of manifestation.

The higher or Cosmic Ethers are particles of electrical fire. They connect man with the corresponding planes of planetary existence. The lower ethers have their roots in the higher ethers, and the evolution of man proceeds when the higher ethers gradually flow into the lower ethers and replace them entirely. As the higher ethers permeate the lower ethers, man contacts higher planes and receives higher wisdom and energy to further the Plan of evolution.

Even though the lower ethers originate from the higher ethers, they are slowed down in their vibration due to contact with the lower layers of matter. They are like water in comparison to steam. In some cases they are pure, and the prana circulates freely through them. In other cases they are polluted by various conditions of the physical, emotional, and mental bodies and also by environmental conditions.

The purity of the etheric body is essential in higher contact. This body-shaped etheric body can be purified and refined through a process of sublimation.

The first stage of sublimation is a result of the inflow of the Intuitional Light, or the inflow of the Fourth Cosmic Ether into the fourth lower etheric level. This lowest etheric level, the fourth, is called the *chemical ether* and is connected to four centers. If something is wrong with any of the related organs of these centers, it is probably caused by a disorder in this ether. If there is any blockage in this ether, energy cannot circulate freely and the organs as a whole suffer.

The chemical ether is very sensitive to colors, which often change into sounds in the inner ear.

When a higher percentage of intuitional substance or the Fourth Cosmic Ether penetrates and increases in the fourth etheric level you hear the colors and see the sounds. Also, your hear the thoughts of other human beings.

The next stage of sublimation is the inflow of the Third Cosmic Ether, the Atmic Plane, into the third lower ether, or what is called the *life ether*. This is the ether which enables a man to propagate his species as this lower ether is connected to the generative organs and seminal fluids. It is also the conductor of sound and has a close relationship to the eyes and vision. When the Third Cosmic Ether penetrates into the third lower ether, you develop higher clairvoyance.

The next step of sublimation is the inflow of the Second Cosmic Ether, the Monadic Plane, into the second lower ether called the *light ether*. The electricity of this layer supplies heat to the body. It is closely related to the nervous system and the muscles, and builds a bridge between the physical body and the outside world. When the Second Cosmic Ether's substance penetrates and increases in this second lower ether, a person develops divine vision and healing powers.

The last state of sublimation is the inflow of the First Cosmic Ether, the Adi or Divine Plane, into the first lower etheric level. This layer is called the *reflecting ether*, and the electricity passing through it enables the soul to control his vehicles by means of thought. This ether has the ability to store memories. When the First Cosmic Ether penetrates and increases in this level, it creates the power of pure Intuition and the memory of past lives. "...Light...has a close connection with, and uses, as a medium, the second ether. ...Sound functions through the third ether. ...Colour...is allied to the fourth ether."[1]

Eventually the Cosmic Etheric Planes totally replace the lower etheric planes and form the etheric body of an Arhat or of a Master. Through such a sublimation, the Self comes in contact with the Intuitional, Atmic, Monadic, and Divine Planes and associates with the life on these planes. Such a contact and realization expands a person's consciousness and awareness into the higher centers.

Continuity of consciousness is achieved on all planes when the two etheric portions of man, the higher and the lower, are fused within each other and the lower etheric body is the continuation of the higher, the Cosmic Ethers. Through continuity of consciousness, man becomes aware of the activities of various Ashrams existing on the Intuitional and higher Planes. He becomes aware of the activities taking place in the Hierarchy and in Shamballa.

When the etheric body is built by the substance of higher ethers, no sickness or disorder exists within it. A person then radiates healing energies into his environment. He radiates light, love, peace, serenity, and purifying, harmonizing, and uplifting powers.

People often think that perfection must be achieved in the subtle planes. But the entire teaching and the life of Christ are examples that demonstrate how

---

1. Alice A. Bailey, *A Treatise on Cosmic Fire*, p. 320. Also, electrical fire manifests as color in the Buddhic Plane.

perfection can be achieved here on earth. The transformation of man must be manifested while he is in his physical body. Death must be conquered in the physical body. Time and space must be conquered here on the physical plane. The Christ demonstrated that He could contact the Father in His physical brain, that He could resurrect Himself. He showed He could transfigure His bodies, heal people, and walk on the sea.

Some people feel that perfection is when they can enter into trances or into a hypnotic state and communicate with various elements. But that is not perfection. Perfected people do not need to channel; they do not need to enter into a trance or a hypnotic state. They are able to contact higher sources consciously, in a state of wakefulness, and are able to discriminate between the sources of contact and the quality of the contact. Etheric transformation brings exactly all these gifts with it.

The formation of the etheric body takes place as follows. As the rays of the Cosmic Ethers pass through the Solar Angel, they form a single ray which, as one thread, hits the physical permanent atom and serves as a film negative or a photographic plate. The content of the physical permanent atom is then carried out by this etheric thread and projected as the prototype of the etheric body. The etheric body is totally conditioned by the content of the physical permanent atom.

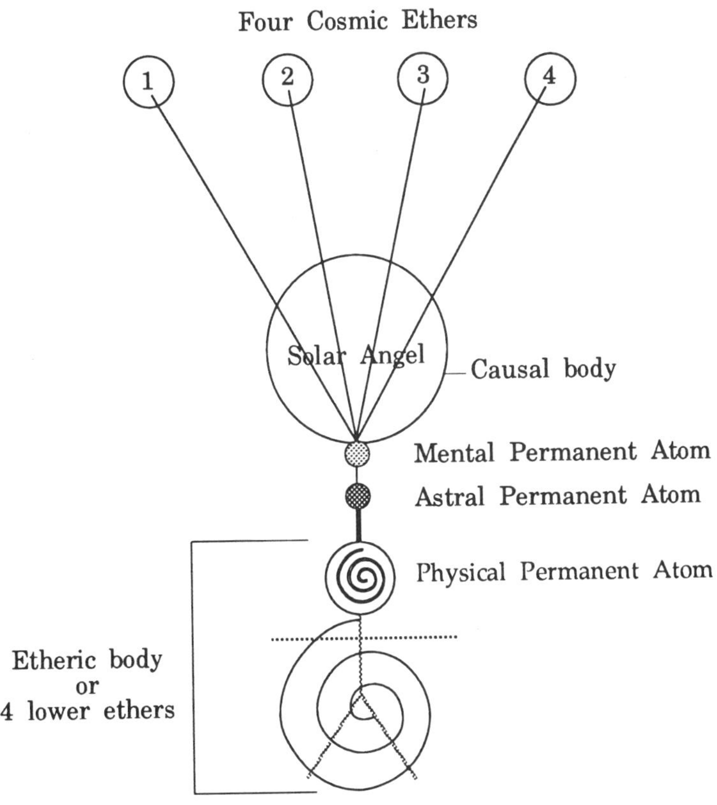

Diagram 3-3 The Relations of the Etheric Body

The etheric body of any form is responsible for the manifestation of that form. It is the blueprint upon which the physical form is built. The root of the blueprint extends into the realm of the Archetypal Plane, which in the Ageless Wisdom is called the Divine or Adi Plane, the highest plane of our Cosmic Physical Plane.

We are told that certain entities, called the lesser builders, weave the etheric thread into the etheric body. These lesser beings, or devas, are sometimes called weavers. Once the etheric body is woven from the etheric thread, it attracts elements which it condenses, forming the physical body as its shadow. The lesser builders weave the etheric body according to the contents of the physical permanent atom and according to the archetype. The etheric body is the mold upon which the physical body is built. The electromagnetic quality of the etheric body draws to itself the elements needed to form the physical body which eventually comes into being as a dense copy of the etheric body.

When we say physical brain, nervous system, or glands, we generally refer to the familiar substances of which they are formed. But let us remember that the elements or the substances that form the brain, nervous system, or glands of higher Initiates are not the same as the elements found in the bodies of others.

Substance and matter are materialized energy. As matter and substance become more energy and less matter, the constitution of the organs changes. A time comes when the physical organs become almost ethereal and extremely sensitive to higher impressions.

The freedom of the disciple from the etheric body and from the physical body opens great horizons of contact. The steps to freedom are composed of building the bridge — continuity of consciousness — between the Mental Permanent Atom and the mental unit. The mental unit is found in the fourth mental subplane (the highest level of the lower mind). The Mental Permanent Atom is found on the first level of the mental plane, the highest or atomic level. This level is the door to the plane of the Intuition, the Fourth Cosmic Ether.

We are told that three groups of Angels helped to build the human mechanism. It was the second group of Solar Angels who brought the mental unit and placed it in the mental body as an anchorage to be used later to influence animal man. This was an anchorage in mental matter. There is another anchorage, and this is the Mental Permanent Atom which is linked to the Spark. Between these two points the bridge must be built so that man becomes the human soul and leads himself into conscious immortality.[2]

If the mental unit is destroyed, the Solar Angel can never come back to that person. The mental unit is the Holy Mother, or the seed of active intelligence. The mental unit may be destroyed through extreme criminality or corruption. The mental unit can also be eliminated in a positive way, during the Fourth

---

2. For further information on the Solar Angel, please refer to *The Solar Angel* and *Other Worlds*.

Initiation, when the Solar Angel withdraws Its anchorage and, like a celestial ship, sails away from the shores of materiality.

After building the bridge between the mental unit and the Mental Permanent Atom, the human soul withdraws himself from the lower ethers and works in the Fourth Cosmic Plane, or Intuitional Plane. As he gradually anchors himself in the Intuitional Plane, the human soul withdraws his anchorage from the astral plane and eventually from the lower mind and achieves freedom on the Intuitional Plane as a living and free soul who can use the lower vehicles but is never trapped within them. When the human soul totally withdraws from the lower mind, the mental unit does not have any anchorage and the Solar Angel departs.

The Tibetan Master, speaking about the mental unit, says,

> *The mental [unit] is not a septenary permanent atom, but only responds to four types of force, and not to the entire range of vibrations. Herein lies a reason for tolerance. Until a man is coming consciously under the control of the Ego [Solar Angel] and is beginning to sense the vibration of the manasic permanent atom, it is useless to expect him to respond to certain ideals, or to grasp certain aspects of truth. The mental unit suffices for his need, and no bridge exists between it and the manasic permanent atom.*[3]

The first step in sublimation and transformation of the person is to bring more and more intuitional substance into the lower ethers, electrifying them with higher fires. As the person's contact with the Intuitional Plane increases, he simultaneously learns to free himself from his etheric body.

When the intuitional substance composes fifty percent of the lower ethers, the person releases himself from the fourth subplane of the astral body.

When the intuitional substance increases to seventy-five percent of the lower ethers, the consciousness of a person liberates itself from the fourth subplane of the mental plane and functions in the causal body, or in the higher mind.

When the intuitional substance forms one hundred percent of the lower ethers, the person receives his liberation from the physical, etheric, astral, and mental bodies and acts consciously on the Buddhic or Intuitional Plane. At this stage, the man is an Arhat, a Fourth Degree Initiate.

It is at the Third Initiation, the first major initiation or the Transfiguration, that the Initiate can escape from the limits of the lower ethers and function on the higher mental planes. At the Fourth Initiation, he escapes from these higher planes and destroys the causal body. At the Fifth Initiation, he functions in the Third Cosmic Ether, the Atmic Plane. At the Sixth Initiation, he functions in the

---

3. Alice A. Bailey, *A Treatise on Cosmic Fire*, p. 530.

Second Cosmic Ether, the Monadic Plane. At the Seventh Initiation, he functions in the First Cosmic Ether, the Divine Plane. He then escapes from the four Cosmic Etheric Planes and functions in the Cosmic Astral Plane. He has now graduated from the Cosmic Physical Plane.

We are told that Christ is progressing in the Cosmic Astral Plane.

As the higher or Cosmic Ethers penetrate into the lower ethers of the body, the pattern of the etheric lines crisscrossing each other changes. A primitive man has a square pattern in his etheric body. The etheric pattern of an advanced man changes into triangular formations. The fire of prana circulates more rapidly in a triangular formation than in the square formation. This starts from the first etheric plane and slowly penetrates into the second, third, and fourth planes.

The etheric body of a Third Degree Initiate starts changing from a triangular pattern into a circular pattern, and the fire then circulates even more rapidly and without any obstruction.

The change in the etheric pattern awakens all of our seventy-seven centers. Eventually, the man appears as a revolving wheel of fire of different colors and configurations.

To accelerate this transformation, we must begin by forming Triangles of Light.[4] A pure dedication to the work of Triangles helps to change not only the pattern of our own etheric body but also the pattern of the etheric body of the planet.

It must be mentioned here that the aura is not the etheric body. The aura is the radiation of the physical, emotional and mental bodies, and, if a person is advanced, the aura also has strong radiations of the Soul and Intuitional, Atmic, Monadic, and Divine energies. All these forces and energies form a field around the physical body. The aura has many colors, continuous fluctuations, and an egg-shaped form. Any thought, emotion, or action changes the colors and waves of the aura.

The aura also should not be confused with the halo seen around the heads of Great Ones. That halo is composed of the radiations of the head center. It expands beyond the head and forms a multicolored sphere. Sometimes the halo is the twelve-petaled Lotus on the higher mental plane; sometimes it is the vehicle of a great Spirit overshadowing the person.

Throughout centuries, people's attention has been drawn to the evolution of the dense physical body, but as etheric vision develops, people will realize that the evolution of the physical body, its refinement and transformation, depends on the evolution of the etheric body. The physical body is called the shadow of the etheric body. Any change in the etheric body reflects in the dense physical body.

---

4. Please see *Triangles of Fire.*

The evolution of the etheric body in turn depends on the mental and emotional currents of energy. If the mental and emotional activities are lofty and pure, the etheric body slowly fuses with the higher ethers.

In the Cosmic Ethers is found the archetype of the physical-etheric body. Archetypes are those forms which are built by the Solar Logos through visualization. Our physical body is an incomplete objectification of an archetype. The beauty of the archetype stands beyond the power of our imagination. As ages pass, through the activities of the Seven Rays,[5] human aspiration, lofty thinking, and striving, the archetype exercises more influence on the higher permanent atoms and produces a better reflection in the physical, astral, and Mental Permanent Atoms.

The permanent atoms have seven spirillae, but the mental unit has only four spirillae. The archetype has its reflection in the first spirilla of the permanent atoms, which in its turn is reflected on the lower spirillae. Often this reflection is distorted by the life a human soul lives on the three personality levels. The etheric body is the result of such a distorted image, and the dense physical body is the materialization of the etheric image. As the etheric body refines itself, our physical body will be a better replica of the archetype. Gradually, all physical ills will disappear, and the science of the etheric body will become a specialized field in the medical profession.

The refinement of the etheric body is carried out through the following:

— Meditation.

— Lofty aspiration.

— Right diet.

— Sunshine, fresh air, exercise.

— Striving toward perfection.

— The influence of the Seventh Ray. This Ray works to project the prototypes or archetypes more clearly on the physical plane, thus providing the etheric substance a better opportunity to be impressed with a clearer image of the archetype or prototype.

— Right relations with others as well as with Nature.

— The development of a closer relationship with higher devas, or angels. Such relations can be carried out on the intuitional levels after the Third Initiation of Transfiguration.

---

5. Please see *Cosmos in Man*, Chs. 6 and 7.

The refinement of the etheric body starts from the seven etheric centers. These seven etheric centers are found on the first, second, third, and fourth etheric planes. On the first etheric plane we have the etheric head center. On the second etheric plane we have the etheric heart center. On the third etheric plane we have the etheric throat center. On the fourth etheric plane are found the etheric base of spine center, the etheric generative organs, the etheric solar plexus, and the etheric spleen.

As the four higher ethers, or Cosmic Ethers, penetrate into the four lower ethers, the transmutation of the etheric body takes place and the reflection of the archetype becomes clearer and more accurate. It is after such a transmutation process that the transformation of the dense physical body takes place.

At the Third Initiation, the reflection of the archetype within the higher spirillae of the permanent atoms impresses itself on the etheric body with such an intensity of vibration that the physical body becomes radioactive within the downpouring light of the Cosmic Ethers. Such a state is called **Transfiguration**, when the earthly image of man changes into the image which God had in His Mind for man.

As more human beings enter into this state of Transfiguration, we will see greater numbers of people so refined and so beautiful that the beauty we see now will be like the beauty of a baboon compared to the beauty of a model or an athlete.

As the refinement proceeds, more people will develop etheric vision, and as a consequence the inhabitants of the etheric planes will be revealed to us. At this stage a new science will be given to humanity — the science of right relationship with the inhabitants of the etheric planes. Through this science, human beings will be able to have the cooperative help of devas and angels to solve their manifold problems on earthly planes and on the planes that are above the earth. Thus, a great breakthrough in human evolution will be achieved, and once more the traveler on the Cosmic Path will see the great Future awaiting him.

In all these processes of fusion of the higher and lower etheric planes, and in the process of impression of the archetypal image on the lower man, the Solar Angel acts as a fiery Agent between the lower and the higher ethers. All higher etheric currents focus themselves within the heart. All lower streams of etheric substance reach up to the heart. Through the fire of the heart, the transmutation process starts, and gradually the lower ethers are replaced by higher ethers.

At the Fourth Initiation the Solar Angel, like a fiery Magnet, takes the reflected image of the human Spark up to the center of the Lotus where, through a fiery application of higher etheric energies and through transmutation, the Solar Angel unites and fuses the "image" or "reflection" with the Reality.

In some legends we are told that the Chalice is the temple where the human soul receives his wings. The legend of the winged child in the Chalice is mentioned in many traditions. It is after one grows "wings" that the freedom of space is gained, and the appreciation of the beauty of existence is carried in his heart like a flame raised in gratitude. The winged child now functions in the sphere of Intuition.

At the time of death, when the human soul withdraws, it pulls out of the etheric vehicle through the head, heart, or solar plexus center. In the meantime, the etheric body withdraws from the physical body but stays attached to the body until the body begins to disintegrate. The human soul passes into the astral body but cannot detach himself from the dead physical body until the etheric body begins to disintegrate. Cremation of the body releases the human soul.

Cremation helps the etheric body detach from the dense physical body which, upon death, begins to disintegrate. Cremation also helps the etheric body to melt away into the etheric reservoir of the planet, and allows the astral body to sail away like a boat to the other side of the shore, carrying the Eternal Traveler.

The etheric body also separates or withdraws from the physical body during accidents, under anesthetics, during great excitement, while in a trance, or when in deep meditation. When the etheric body withdraws itself, the physical brain does not register any contact with the objective or subjective worlds unless the **bridge** is built.

The ancients knew how to perform surgery on organs and even on the brain by withdrawing the etheric body of the patient from the physical body. This was not hypnotism or mesmerism. It was done by the magnetic power of the healer who would slowly pull out the etheric body and then perform the surgery. In this technique, the life thread extending from the Spark to the heart was kept intact, but the consciousness thread was withdrawn from the brain.

The top of the head is related to the spleen. The etheric body is connected to the spleen through a cord, like the umbilical cord of an infant. This cord extends to the top of the head, and when the etheric body is withdrawn, it pulls on this cord and at the exact time of death this cord is broken. One can see clairvoyantly a silvery cord which is cut between the spleen and the departing etheric body at the time of death.[6]

There are three centers through which prana is absorbed: a center between the shoulder blades, a center above the diaphragm, and the spleen.

It is possible for the etheric body to withdraw only partially from the physical body. For example, at times it withdraws from the fingers, legs, or arms. When it withdraws, the organ or the member affected becomes paralyzed. The physical causes of paralysis are due to etheric causes. Often paralysis disappears along with its physical causes when the etheric conditions are corrected. Since the etheric body has a very close connection with the nervous system and glands, the first physical cause of paralysis appears in the nervous system and, later, in the glands.

---

6. *Ibid.*, Ch. 19, "The Process of Death and Life After."

Sometimes the spleen is damaged or removed surgically. In such a situation the other two centers and the etheric counterpart of the spleen carry the burden and transmit the prana to the body.

The etheric body is the dynamo around and within the body. Any action in any part of the body is performed by the electricity which the etheric body generates for the physical system. All seven senses work because of the etheric body.

Any weakening of the etheric body reflects in the physical body. We can say that death begins with the etheric body, and old age is the weakening or partial withdrawal of the etheric body from its physical counterpart.

The etheric body is like a bundle of tubes or tiny pipes through which prana runs. Any blockage on the path of prana creates complications. It sometimes happens that prana accumulates in a certain area of the etheric body and creates heavy congestion there.

The assimilation of prana is easier and more vitalizing when a person is full of love, thinks clearly, has willpower, and is motivated by sacrificial service. Those who have these qualities live a longer, happier, and more creative life.

Prana turns into poison in the three levels of the personality when the mind is distorted, when the heart is in apathy, and when the will is in inertia or made forcefully active to fulfill the distorted decisions of one's mind and heart. Such conditions create indigestion in the pranic centers, and that person walks like a contaminated body — mentally, emotionally, and physically.

The etheric body is a coil of wire. In certain areas, due to our negative emotions, wrong thoughts and harmful actions, it is weakened, blocked, or even to a certain degree burned. When an area of the etheric body is weakened, excessive prana causes destruction in that area. This excessive prana is accumulated through breathing exercises, through Hatha Yoga, through exposing oneself to the Sun for a long period of time, through agitation, and through premature revelations. When the coil is blocked in any area, prana accumulates and causes congestion there.

One of the main factors of etheric disorders is the result of loading the centers with solar prana. When one exposes his body to the Sun and very quickly absorbs a great amount of prana, it creates congestion in the etheric body and makes part of it swell. For example, the etheric body can swell whenever a great amount of prana is accumulated in the head, back, shoulders, or in any part of the body. This condition thickens the etheric body in those areas. The thickening of the etheric body affects the physical body in which a corresponding thickening process takes place. This creates a very undesirable imbalance in the physical organs, in the circulatory flow of the prana, and in the etheric body.

Wherever the congestion is, the physical body is affected and sickness gradually starts. For example, if some part of the etheric heart is hardened or swollen, heart trouble starts, such as an enlarged heart or an irregularity in the heartbeat. Similar things happen to the liver, kidneys, and other organs. Muscles are affected in this manner as well.

When the etheric body is burned, it means that the electricity in your "house" is turned off. If your refrigerator does not have electricity, whatever you have in it spoils. The same thing happens in your body. The wires are burned and your body has no electricity. All your organs starve for electricity, and if the current of electricity is not restored, the organs decay. Some degenerative diseases are the result of the burning of the etheric web.

We do not assimilate prana correctly when we pollute the etheric body through moral and spiritual distortions or through disorders in our mental and emotional bodies. Fear, for example, weakens the etheric body, and continuous fear exhausts all pranic energy and creates a blockage against a new inflow of energy.

The blockage in the etheric body can be caused not only from etheric disorders or from burning of the etheric web, but also from astral and mental trash pouring into the etheric body through the etheric centers. That is why there must be great emphasis on emotional and mental purity. It is also very important that the channels linking the etheric body to the astral and mental bodies be purified.

Disorders in the various bodies are the result of congestion in the centers. Mental disorders affect the lungs; emotional disorders affect the digestive system; and etheric disorders start manifesting themselves first through the kidneys.

Congestion in the mental centers is a result of

— The habit of negative thoughtform building

— Pride

— Destruction of thoughtforms, the remains of which block the centers

— Criminal planning against one's own conscience

— Mental crimes

— Hatred

— Separative reasoning

— Illusions

Congestion in the astral centers is the result of

— Glamors

— Attachments

— Negative emotions

— Fear

— Depression

— Jealousy

— Gossip

— Criticism

Congestion in the etheric centers is a result of

— Chemical poisoning

— Unclean sexual activities

— Tamasic food

— Irritation

— Unclean air

— Radioactivity

— ELF currents

— Drugs

— Alcohol

Actually, the Teachings of Krishna, Buddha, and Christ will be recognized in coming centuries as scientific prescriptions for health, happiness, success, prosperity, and joy. Love, patience, solemnity, magnanimity, silence, courage, purity — all these and other virtues keep the channels open in the threefold vehicles of the personality through which not only prana but also energies from higher planes circulate and help the person to bloom and unfold his spiritual beauty.

Because of the blockage of the channels, a person living in the physical plane cannot communicate with the higher planes, with the Higher Self, and with higher principles, and he loses his vision. He eventually falls into a condition of mental disturbance. Many mental disorders are the result of starvation from lack of higher light or lack of Soul contact. It is like running your engine without water and oil.

We are also told that a congested etheric body makes the physical body develop in an abnormal way. Certain parts or organs of the body grow abnormally and exercise great pressure on others and thus cause imbalance within the whole system.

If some areas of the etheric web are burned and destroyed, very serious consequences in the physical body will result. First, a great amount of flow from astral realms may be released, bringing many astral experiences and astral entities against which a person will find himself totally unprotected. Brain cells may be destroyed, causing paralysis in corresponding organs or leading the man to death through various mental and physical sicknesses.

Those people who use drugs and perform various unhealthy exercises to open their centers or communicate with higher forces are in danger of burning or congesting their etheric web. These people, after they stop using drugs and doing such exercises, must be very careful not to expose themselves to heavy doses of meditation or pranic emanations, and they must try to live a life of peace and relaxation for at least three to five years. Such people have probably weakened or burned their etheric web to a certain extent, and if they try to release powerful electrical prana into it, they will burn the web further and be caught in painful experiences or in mental disorders. Meditation and concentrated study of metaphysical books are forbidden for them until the web has regenerated itself, the astral contacts are totally eliminated, and the effects of the drugs are cured.

The radiations photographed through Kirlian methods are neither the etheric body nor the aura. They are pranic emanations. These pranic emanations project the condition of the organs, tissues, or any living form. When the living form has internal troubles, which eventually manifest as sickness or diseases of various kinds, the projection of the pranic rays shows distortion.

In Nature there are eight radiant signs of health:

Symmetry

Rhythm

Cycle

Harmony

Palpitation

Clear color

Clear sound

Sweet fragrance

To a higher clairvoyant, these signs must demonstrate the following on the person's aura as colors, pulsations, and currents of energy:

1. Symmetry, based on a certain design or archetype, must be present.

2. The pulsation must be rhythmic, and the light or color lines must manifest the rhythm.

3. Definite spacing and repetition, which must be cyclic as seen in cardiograms, must be present.

4. Harmony of lines, cycles, and colors must manifest.

5. The vibration must expand with the beat of the pulsation or palpitation, which is regulated by the heart or by the organism in its expanding and contracting motions.

6. The color of the vibration must be a living color, not a fading one.

7. The harmony of the sound of the subtle bodies can be heard as a sign of perfect health.

8. A sweet fragrance, which is the result of the vibration of the vehicles under the impact of higher ethers, can be detected through astral smell.

Projections or photographs of various forms of life expose the internal conditions of the etheric body and the organs six or seven months before the physical organs show the signs of deterioration. It will be a great medical help to detect such conditions and take preventive measures.

The etheric body has two systems: the outer system and the inner system. The outer system is composed of the three pranic centers — the center between the shoulder blades, the center above the diaphragm, and the etheric spleen — which receive the prana from the Sun and the earth. It also includes the three locations — the head and the two shoulders — through which the prana is channeled to these pranic centers. Through the three pranic centers, a person is linked to the etheric body of the planet and the solar system.

The inner system is composed of

1. The seven etheric centers

2. The life thread anchored in the heart

3. The energy lines coming from the astral and mental bodies and from the Solar Angel

4. The creative thread

5. The consciousness thread anchored in the head

6. The nadis

This inner system differs in color and intensity due to the quality and amount of energy coming from higher centers.

Through the seven etheric centers and the network of higher centers, a person focused in the physical and etheric body is related to the astral, mental, Buddhic, Atmic, Monadic, and Divine or Adi Planes. Because of this relationship, the etheric centers can register higher states of consciousness, especially when the *ida*, or solar energy in the base of spine, is circulating through the centers.

Nadis are the etheric counterparts of the nervous system. Nadis relate the etheric body to the nerves. They are mostly concentrated behind the spinal cord and the brain and around the major nerve ganglia. They pass the electrical impulse of the etheric body to the nervous system.

The system of nadis determines the quality of the nervous system. When the nadis relate to each other in a harmonious way, the health of the body reaches its perfection. Nadis are influenced by the Life or Spirit aspect. To keep them healthy, a person must strive to keep the channel of spiritual energy or psychic energy open and prevent any formation of imperil upon the channels of the nerves.

Imperil is a substance which accumulates in the nerve channels and makes the nerves unreceptive to the incoming life energy or electricity. When imperil accumulates, the nerves begin to degenerate. Imperil is caused mostly by irritation, and we are told that wormwood oil, rest, joy, and purification remove imperil from the nerve channels.[7]

The well-being of our five senses is directly related to the nadis. Our senses operate in perfect condition if the corresponding nadis in the etheric body do not have disturbances or decay in them.

7. Please refer to *The Psyche and Psychism*, Ch. 27.

4

Prana and the Etheric Body

It is prana that keeps the organs and the body working as an integrated organism. Without prana, the body would be a pile of independent cells.

Different kinds of rays emanate from the Sun. Those which are called solar pranic emanations stimulate the life in the cells and have a constructive effect upon the physical body — as far as man is concerned. Other rays, we are told, are destructive to forms. Still others produce accelerated motion; others produce retardation.

The solar pranic emanations work through the four lower ethers. Prana is solar radiation. It is a "vital and magnetic fluid which radiates from the sun."[1]

We also have planetary prana which emanates from the planet. Actually it is solar prana, absorbed by the earth and radiated out to Space.

The radiation of the Sun is received by solar devas who have golden hues. They assimilate and focus the Sun's radiation toward the man. The radiation then enters man through the etheric head and etheric shoulders, and reaches the center between the shoulder blades. Then it rushes to a point above the diaphragm and goes to the etheric spleen

The etheric body receives solar prana from golden devas and planetary prana from violet devas. The etheric body assimilates the prana, feeding the cells, organs, and atoms of the man, and charges them with vitality and with the rhythms of the Solar and Planetary Entities. It then transmits prana to lesser devas and animal or subhuman kingdoms. It is prana that keeps the organs and the body working as an integrated organism. Without prana, the body would be a pile of independent cells.

---

1. Alice A. Bailey, *A Treatise on Cosmic Fire*, p. 90.

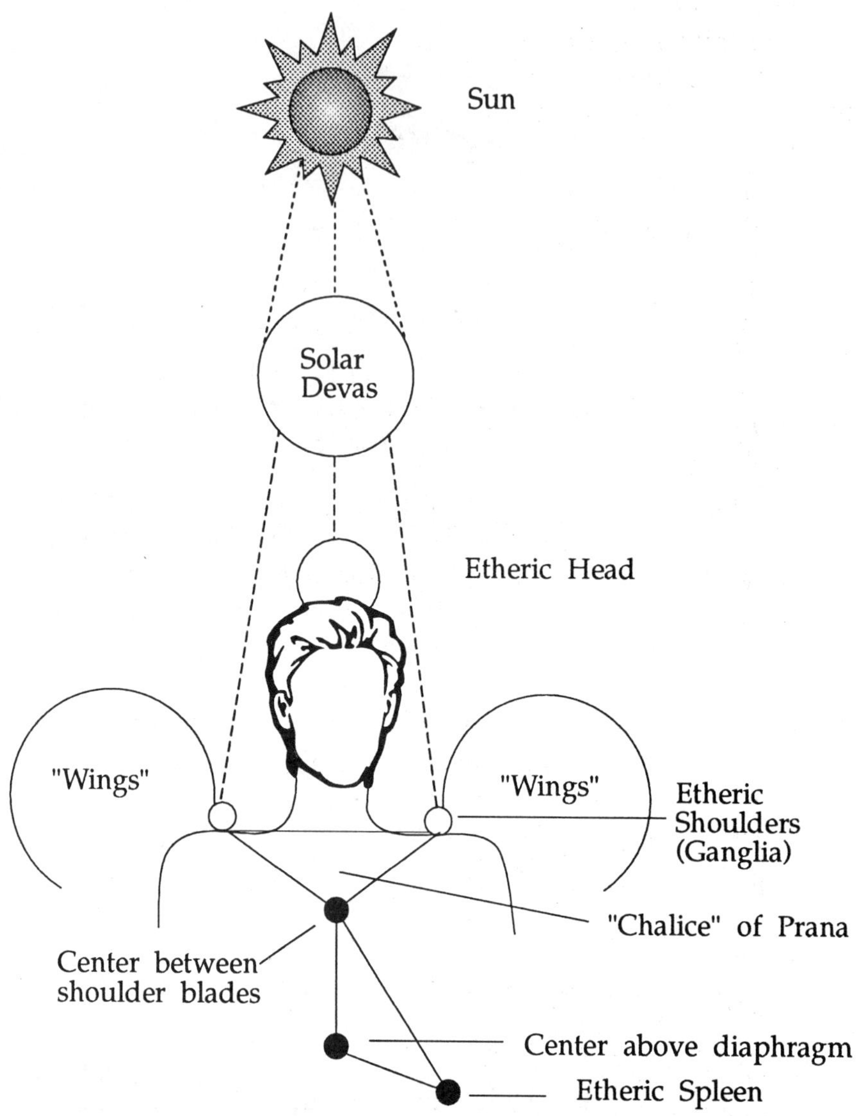

Diagram 4-1 Prana Flow

The etheric body is negative or receptive in respect to the rays of the Sun, and positive or expulsive in respect to the dense physical body. This can be explained with regard to sex: man's body is negative in respect to a woman's, and a woman's etheric polarization is positive in respect to a man's. That is why a woman produces more blood than a man. At the time of contact with a man, a woman gives abundant prana to him and he gives astral radiation to her.

We are told that at the fifth Round, human beings will work in their etheric bodies, much as they function now in their physical bodies.

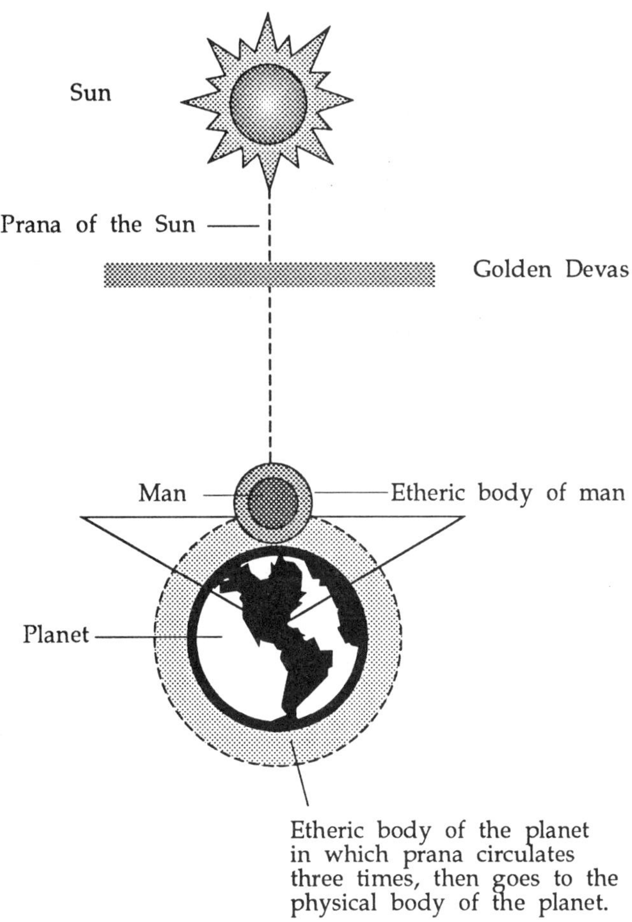

Diagram 4-2 Prana from the Sun to Man

Planetary prana, therefore, is solar prana which has passed throughout the planet, has circulated through the planetary etheric body, has been transmitted to the dense physical planet, and has been cast off thence in the form of a radiation of the same essential character as solar prana, plus the individual and distinctive quality of the particular planet concerned. *This again repeats the process undergone in the human body. The physical radiations of men differ according to* the quality *of their physical bodies.*[2]

2. Alice A. Bailey, *A Treatise on Cosmic Fire*, p. 92.

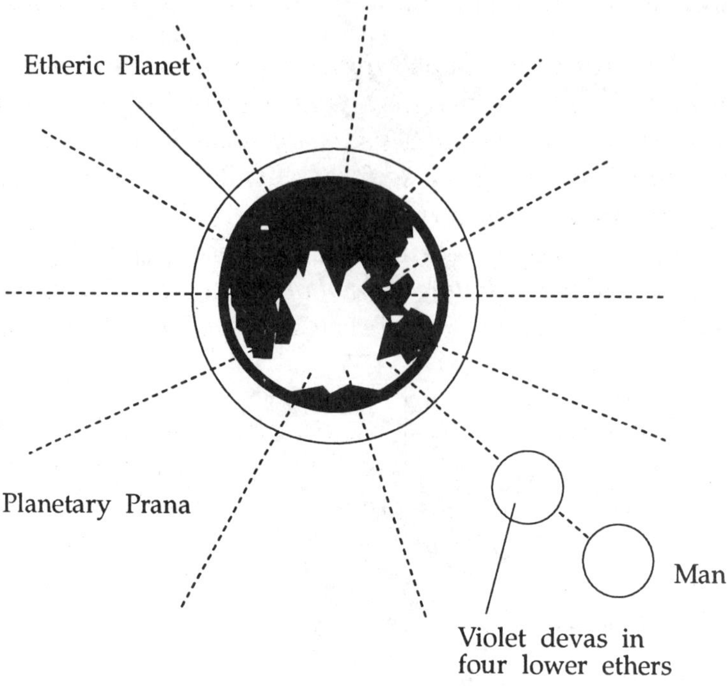

Diagram 4-3 Devas and Prana

Planetary radiation reaches a person through the agency of some devas who are slightly violet. They function in the four lower ethers.

The prana from man is carried to the animal kingdom by devas also.

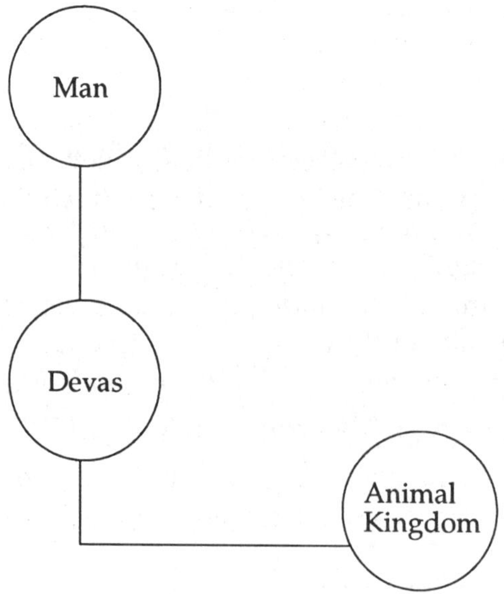

Diagram 4-4 Man and Prana

Then there is the role of the vegetable kingdom and the animal kingdom.

> *...The pranic emanations given off by units of the animal and vegetable kingdom (after they have absorbed both solar and planetary prana) are naturally a combination of the two, and are transmitted by means of* surface radiation, *as in solar and planetary prana, to certain lesser groups of devas of a not very high order, who have a curious and intricate relationship to the group soul of the radiating animal or vegetable.... These devas are also of a violet hue, but of such a pale color as to be almost grey....*
>
> *...The human form transmits the emanative radiations to a much higher grade of deva. These devas are of a more pronounced hue, and after due assimilation of the human radiation, they transmit it principally to the animal kingdom, thus demonstrating the close relationship between the two kingdoms....*[3]

In *The Bhagavad Gita*, there are very interesting references to devas. For example,

> *Through your sacrifice, you nourish the Shining Ones, the devas, and they, in their turn, nourish you. Thus, nourishing each other, you will attain the highest good.*[4]

The sacrifice here refers to those acts that are charged or fused with selfless thoughts and emotions. Our pure thoughts, aspirations, ecstasy, and joy produce in Space the nourishment the devas like. Our pranic emanations carry with them our emotional, mental, and spiritual vibrations or essence. Thus, our emanations either feed the devas or make them sick of us. If the etheric emanations of a person are sending out the fragrance of spiritual achievements, harmony, rhythm, mental nourishment, or emotional purity, the devas will love that man and will help him be in increasingly better conditions so that they may enjoy him as a fragrant and a colorful flower with rare qualities.

Great thinkers, great humanitarians, and great creative artists enjoy the company of devas who nourish them or receive nourishment from them. Emanations of creative thoughts, emanations of deep meditation and contemplation, are highly charged vitamins for the devas. But those individuals who are walking in base thoughts, stagnated emotions, and harmful actions smell like decomposing animal bodies. These people repel the devas of high order.

---

3. *Ibid.*, pp. 95-96.
4. *The Bhagavad Gita* 3:11

Eventually the higher nature of these people starves, and they fall into the hands of their animal urges and drives.

All virtues emanate fragrance; all vices emanate heavy, putrid odors.

Thus, the whole creation is a chain, and each kingdom and each living form is a link in it. Through this chain circulates the divine flow of life-giving energies. Each link takes in energy, adds its own qualification to the life, and passes it on.

Devas help in various ways when you nourish them with your pure essence, with your pure emanations. For example:

1. They fill your sphere with great magnetism.
2. They link your mind with higher clouds of knowledge and information.
3. They remind you of things from the past which can be used in your creative speech.
4. They carry messages from your friends and from their Souls.
5. They warn you of dangers.
6. They open opportunities for you.
7. They protect your aura from the thoughts of your enemies.

Aspirants, disciples, and initiates will cooperate more and more with devas when their lives reach great levels of purification. The devas will directly teach us; they will become links between us and greater centers. In rare cases, they will even supply those articles which we need — a book, money, or other needed materials.

Pranic Centers

> *The process of assimilation is carried on in this triangle, and the prana which enters into either centre, circulates three times around the triangle before being transmitted to all parts of the etheric vehicle and from thence to the dense physical body. The main organ of assimilation is the spleen — the etheric centre and the dense physical organ. The vital essence from the sun is passed into the etheric spleen, and is there subjected to a process of intensification or devitalisation, according to the condition, healthy or not, of that organ. If the man is in a healthy state the emanation received will be augmented by his own individual vibration, and its rate of vibration will be keyed up before it is passed on into the physical spleen; or it will be slowed down and*

lowered if the man is in a poor condition of health.[5]

We are told that at this time the center between the shoulder blades is "the main center of the reception of prana." The center above the diaphragm is not

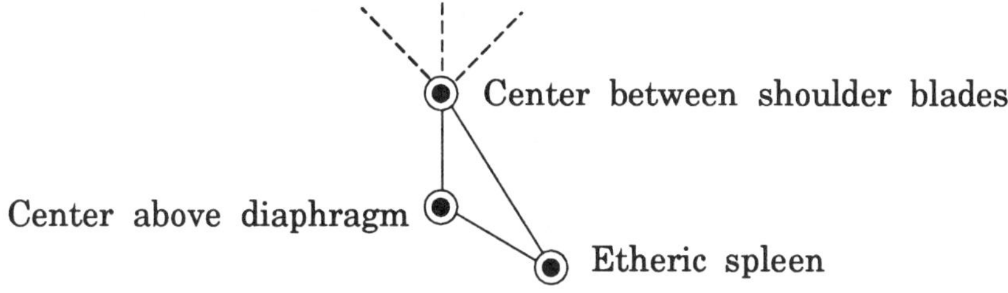

Diagram 4-5 Pranic Centers

truly active in most cases at this time.

The prana received by the centers circulates three times through the triangle of these three centers before it is transmitted to the etheric body. The spleen assimilates the prana through its etheric counterpart and physical organ and then transmits this energy to the blood stream.

These three centers — the center between the shoulder blades, the center above the diaphragm, and the etheric spleen — have saucer-like depressions, resembling somewhat the appearance of small whirlpools. These whirlpools draw within their sphere of influence the currents that come their way. The prana then enters into the etheric and physical body, revitalizing all parts of these bodies. This fluid "finds its point of departure for the entire system at the further side of the spleen to that at which the prana entered."[6] As the prana or fluid circulates through these three centers and the etheric body, it is affected by the quality and health of the centers, the spleen, and the etheric body.

The prana carries its work in three steps:

5. Alice A. Bailey, *A Treatise on Cosmic Fire*, p. 99.
6. *Ibid.*, pp. 99-100.

1. The prana circulates three times around the three pranic centers, which form a triangle, and is distributed into the body. Thus, it vitalizes the function of all organs.

2. The prana blends with the fire of kundalini, drives that fire gradually upward toward the head, and transfers the fire of the lower centers to their corresponding higher centers. These centers and correspondences are

   base of spine — head center

   solar plexus — heart center

   sacral center — throat center

   The fire of the kundalini finds its fusion point at the center between the shoulder blades where prana and the kundalini fire meet. The kundalini fire is threefold and prana is threefold as it circulates through the three centers. When they merge in a correct manner, the evolution of man proceeds rapidly.

3. The three major centers become active. They are the ajna center, the head center, and the medulla oblongata. These centers slowly become radioactive, and the fire in them expands into a sphere of fire around them, until they blend with each other, and the kundalini fire and pranic fire circulate within the triangle of the three centers. Kundalini fire increases their radiance, and pranic fire increases their rotation.

   The fire of matter and the fire of Spirit make the fire of mind burn in greater radiance. The fire of mind is fed by the fires of matter, and both these fires increase through the solar pranic emanations, which originate from the Cosmic Mental Plane.

   > *... It is this aspect of the manasic fire that develops under the forms of instinct, animal memory, and functional recollection which are so apparent in the little evolved man....*
   >
   > *The united result of this blending is the destruction...of the etheric web, and the consequent production of continuity of consciousness and the admission into the personal life of man of "Life more abundant," or the third fire of Spirit.*[7]

---

7. *Ibid.*, p. 125.

> *Should a man, by the power of will or through an over-development of the mental side of his character, acquire the power to blend these fires of matter and to drive them forward, he stands in danger of obsession, insanity, physical death, or of dire disease in some part of his body, and he also runs the risk of an over-development of the sex impulse through the driving of the force in an uneven manner upwards, or in forcing its radiation to undesirable centres. The reason of this is that the matter of his body is not pure enough to stand the uniting of the flames, that the channel up the spine is still clogged and blocked, and therefore acts as a barrier, turning the flame backwards and downwards, and that the flame (being united by the power of mind and not being accompanied by a simultaneous downflow from the plane of spirit), permits the entrance, through the burning etheric, of undesirable and extraneous forces, currents, and even entities. These wreck and tear and ruin what is left of the etheric vehicle, of the brain tissue and even of the dense physical body itself.*[8]

Immediately when the etheric body is built, the prana enters in and produces magnetism and vitalization. It is this magnetism that attracts the needed elements for objectification. The elements are built around and within the etheric body, an interpenetrated complete unit.

The etheric body, during incarnation, stands as a barrier between the astral plane and the dense physical body and protects the body from the astral force. But when we develop continuity of consciousness, we can eventually penetrate into the astral plane through some etheric doors and function on the astral plane as well.

Any premature penetration into the astral realms produces serious difficulties and disorders in the physical body and in the consciousness of the person. It may channel the influences of entities living in the astral realms; a person may hear their voices or see their forms and lose control over his own senses. Asylums are full of such people who penetrated into the astral realms through drugs, breathing exercises, Kundalini Yoga, great shocks, and unhealthy thoughts and living.

Astral force is fiery, and its frequency is more potent than the physical. When it flows into unready etheric centers, it creates excessive stimulation in the corresponding organs, creating overdevelopment or destruction of the tissues in the glands and organs.

Hatha Yoga was used many millions of years ago to create greater synchronization and attunement between the physical and etheric bodies. But because of the progress of the race in this direction, Great Ones discontinued

---

8. *Ibid.*, p. 126.

Hatha Yoga and even indicated that it would be harmful to the health of the individual if he continued to practice it. Hatha Yoga makes the physical body excessively cling and stick to the etheric body and hardens or crystallizes the astral body. People in such a condition will eventually have trouble with their health, emotions, and communication. At the time of death they will have difficulty in withdrawing from the physical and astral bodies.[9]

9. For further information, please refer to *The Psyche and Psychism*, Ch. 40.

5

The Three Centers of Prana

Assimilation of prana creates an urge for striving, an urge for improvement and perfection, an urge to create.

The first center of prana is located between the shoulder blades. The second one is located immediately above the diaphragm, close to the center of the body. The third center is the etheric spleen, located below the diaphragm and close to the stomach.

These three centers form a triangle. Master Djwhal Khul says,

> *...Owing to centuries of wrong living, and to basic mistakes (originating in Lemurian days) man's three pranic centres are not in good working order. The centre between the shoulder blades is in the best receptive condition, though owing to the poor condition of the spinal column (which in so many is out of accurate alignment), its position in the back is apt to be misplaced. The splenic centre near the diaphragm is sub-normal in size and its vibration is not correct.*[1]

The center above the diaphragm has been allowed to become partially dormant in man through the abuse of so-called civilization. It is situated slightly above the solar plexus.

The duty of these three centers is to receive prana, circulate it between the three points, and then pass it to the etheric body.

The quality of the prana will depend on the quality of these centers. If they are totally rhythmic, then the physical body is in the best of health. If the centers are in disorder and not synchronized, the fire of prana will pass into the etheric body in an unbalanced way. The three centers can be compared with the distributor in a car. If there is no synchronization between the distributor and the spark plugs, the car cannot run smoothly. If the centers are polluted, blocked, or in a process of disintegration, the prana passing into the etheric body will not be

1. Alice A. Bailey, *A Treatise on Cosmic Fire*, p. 106.

healthy, life-giving, or regenerating, and the etheric body will suffer and affect the physical body as a whole.

In our solar system, it is the Central Sun that receives Cosmic prana and radiates it to our system as solar pranic radiation. On our planet, the prana is received through a center which is connected with the location of the two poles.

We sometimes hear the term "health aura." The health aura is prana which circulates through a person's etheric body and radiates out. This surface radiation is called the health aura. It is a golden hue, and if it is clear and even over all parts of the body, the health of the body is perfect. But if it loses its radiance and fades away, or in certain parts totally disappears or mixes with grey colors, that location is not healthy and needs immediate attention.

The center between the shoulder blades is affected mostly by our thought currents. The center above the diaphragm is affected by our emotions. The spleen is affected by the quality of the air, by etheric emanations of other human beings, by the food we eat, by the water we drink, and by the general condition of the body. These centers, being responsible for the reception, assimilation, and transmission of prana, must be in very high order — clean and healthy — so that the incoming prana does not lose its life-giving, energizing, and integrating qualities but regenerates the body as a whole.

Thus, in order to absorb the prana, we must be careful with our thought currents and thought life, keeping our thoughts in a very high order and charged with inclusiveness. Our thoughts must be the vehicles of Beauty, Goodness, and Truth. As we strive toward such standards, the center between the shoulder blades demonstrates more activity and keeps the flow of solar prana circulating rhythmically.

The next step is to purify our emotions and guard our emotional reactions on tempting occasions. As we purify and raise the quality of our emotions, the center above the diaphragm will show greater rhythmic activity and will receive and transmit prana without polluting it with glamors and emotional intoxications.

The same procedure applies to the splenic center and to the spleen. Our food must be of high quality. We must have the needed rest in Nature. We must be very careful about our physical contacts with other people. The spleen is affected not only by the emanations of other people, but it can also be polluted by the disorders found in the etheric bodies of others. Even a handshake can affect the spleen, or an article which is charged with evil or negative emanations can pollute the spleen when we touch it.

Our food must be mostly vegetables and fruits, and no alcohol or tobacco must be used. Drugs, tea, coffee, marijuana, alcohol, and too much chocolate damage the spleen and create poisons in it. Then, when the prana is circulating in the spleen, this organ infuses its poison into the prana and transmits it into the etheric body. Subsequently, the etheric body lacks vitality and the physical body loses its joy of strength and health.

When a person is living in a smoggy city where various chemical emanations are fused with the air, the etheric centers will have a difficult time to receive, assimilate, and transmit prana. The same phenomenon occurs when a person is living in an atmosphere of emotional tension in which there is hatred, jealousy, anger, fear, greed, depression, and other negative emotions. All these emotional waves block, distort, and pollute the flow of solar pranic emanations.

The same situation appears when a person is living in an atmosphere of distorted, criminal thoughts and plans. The mental sphere does not allow pure prana to pass through it if that sphere is unrefined or is clouded with ugly, criminal, separative, distorted thoughts. The prana that passes through such an atmosphere is polluted, and this pollution is carried into the etheric body.

Sometimes our etheric body appears to be a stagnated, dirty pool. To have a healthy etheric body, we must have

1. A healthy mental body
2. Purified emotions, or purity of heart
3. Right motives
4. Right physical conditions
5. A balance between labor and rest
6. Contact with the right people and the right objects
7. Clean food and pure air
8. Avoidance of hallucinative drugs, tobacco, and alcohol
9. Economy of sex
10. Creative labor
11. Harmlessness
12. Use of right colors and right music

Let us develop each point further:

1. The health of the mental body can be achieved through right thinking and right meditation. Right thinking is a way of thinking by which the improvement of you and your fellow man is guaranteed and your evolution and progress are secured. Right meditation is thinking in the light of great spiritual and Cosmic principles. When we practice right thinking and right meditation, we develop the ability of clear thinking. In clear thinking, our illusions eventually vanish and we see things as they are.

Our thoughts have a direct affect on our health. Thoughts affect the etheric body, and the etheric body affects the physical body. When a person has wrong thoughts — thoughts that are harmful, negative, destructive, ugly, selfish, or not based on fact — these thoughts distort the rhythmic pulsation of the fires of the etheric body, creating blockages in the electrical wires of the etheric system and preventing the natural flow of prana. With every wrong thought, we create a blockage and disturbance in our etheric body which gradually penetrates into the dense physical vehicle and manifests as disease. The same thing applies to our negative emotions and wrong actions. When the fires of thought, speech, and emotions are used in a wrong way, it weakens or partially burns parts of the etheric body. These effects vary according to the intensity of thought, emotion, and action, and according to the level of evolution of the person.

Lofty thoughts, pure thoughts full of compassion and striving, have a great healing effect on the physical body. The etheric body absorbs all the energies of what the consciousness of man is focused upon and transmits them into the physical body through the spleen. This means that the composition of prana depends on the level and focus of your consciousness. If you are astrally focused, you pour astral energy into your system through the spleen. If you are focused and active in higher ethers, your prana is charged with great vitality. The day will come when we will be able to nourish our bodies with the substance of higher ethers.

All the above statements lead us to think that Beauty, Goodness, Righteousness, Joy, Freedom, and the Will-to-Good are tremendous sources of nourishment for our etheric and physical bodies.

When there is congestion or pollution of thoughts and emotions, circulation of prana does not take place regularly in the etheric body of the person, and parts of the body suffer. The signs of disorder are registered by the heart, brain, stomach, kidneys, and sex organs. The heart loses its regularity, or the tone of its beat becomes louder. The brain feels tired, and the conversation of the person becomes slower and less integrated. The digestive track suffers; acidity increases; indigestion slowly appears. The urine smells foul, and the sex organs lose their vitality. Hearing and vision are also affected. When prana is circulating freely and regularly, the eyesight is in perfect condition. When thoughtforms of fear, greed, and hatred are settled in the etheric body, the sight suffers considerably.

Worry has a very destructive effect on the etheric body. It blocks the channels with sediment and distorts the rhythm of the circulation of prana. People with a weak etheric body must be checked first to find out if they have a hidden source of worry which continuously poisons their system.

We are warned by great Sages to beware of psychic healers for several reasons. It may be that they are able to transfer prana to our etheric body and vitalize it, but if they have intoxicated states of emotions, mental complications, obsessions, and wrong motives, they pour their toxins into our etheric body through their prana. This can be done even if the healer has good intentions.

A negative self-image and self-criticism are other factors which cause our ill health. Distorted images about ourselves carry unhealthy currents into the pranic current and create an unhealthy chemistry. Harmful and hateful criticism can immediately change the chemistry of the prana of the person and poison his system.

2. Purified emotions are the flowers of a purified emotional body. Such a purification can be achieved through eliminating all harmful and negative emotions and filling one's life with love and peace.

The purification of the emotional body requires staying away from people or from areas which are contaminated by violent emotions such as hatred, jealousy, revenge, fear, and greed. This is because strong emotional waves are sticky, and they easily penetrate and take over our emotional body.

Purity of heart is defined as an attitude of total harmlessness.

3. Right motive must stand behind all our thoughts, emotions, words, and actions. Right motive emerges or exists when a person accepts the reality that in each form the Divinity abides undivided and complete; he accepts the fact that the sons of men are one; he acknowledges the truth that there is only God manifesting through all living forms.

Right motive exists when the urge behind all our actions on all planes is to respect, unfold, and release Divinity.

4. Right physical conditions are necessary. The absence of pure air, water, and food and the presence of polluting elements in our environment block the etheric tubes and also retard the ability of the spleen and the body to absorb prana. For example, when little children are exposed to cigarette and cigar smoke, they usually cannot absorb prana satisfactorily and may develop lung and brain diseases.

In a polluted atmosphere the lower fires cannot contact the higher fires, and they express degenerative impulses, base thoughts, criminal urges, hatred, and depression. The senses, especially the sight and hearing, suffer considerably. People also lose the power of striving.

Assimilation of prana creates an urge for striving, an urge for improvement and perfection, an urge to create. The assimilation of prana releases the fire of enthusiasm. Prana not only gives energy to the body, it also helps the brain increase its sensitivity to the inspirations of the inner creative center, the Soul.

Sunbathing is another important way to accumulate prana. We must often expose the whole body to the direct rays of the Sun. The duration of the sunbath must not last more than three minutes due to the decay of the ozone layer. After that, you damage your etheric body with congestion or by burning the etheric web. We are told to cover our head when we are walking or sitting in the Sun. Also, it is better if we wear white clothes while we are in the Sun.

5. A balance between labor and rest is necessary. Modern man does not know how to rest. The secret of rest is withdrawal from personality levels and entry into the Inner Sanctuary. Daily we must have such a rest. Weekly and monthly we must have such rests, and the major rest period must be the last ten days of the year.

Labor is also important for assimilation of prana. Without labor the etheric body loosens and develops areas of stagnation. The fire in the etheric body is best assimilated in rhythmic labor. But if the etheric body is weak, total rest is necessary in a secluded area in Nature.

6. Contact with right people is very important. Handshakes, embraces, kisses, and closer relations blend the etheric bodies, and the sensitive one can absorb the pollution in the etheric body of the other and be vampirized by that polluted vehicle.

Handling or touching objects which are magnetized with destructive or negative forces or have polluted thoughtforms and emotions attached to them can hurt one's etheric body and contaminate it. Places where crimes have been committed must not be visited, and objects with which crimes were committed must not be touched. Etheric emanations of such places and objects heavily contaminate the etheric body.

7. Clean food and pure air — how does one find them? They are still available and will be even more so if we demand them. Deep breathing in pure air has a tremendous purifying effect on the etheric and physical bodies.

8. Drugs, tobacco, and alcohol block the passages and the absorbing agents of prana.

9. Economy of sex is very important. Unhealthy sexual practices waste the energy of prana. Sexual fluid is mostly etheric. It is even possible to say that it is the condensation of prana and etheric force. Wasting this energy causes various mental sicknesses, destroys the nervous system, opens the doors for various germs, and leads a person to premature death.

10. Creative labor. The etheric body can be disciplined and brought under the total control of the mind through concentration on art, music, dance, movements, painting, and other creative works. Throughout ages, spiritual groups developed control over the etheric body through the art of making tapestries, china, pottery, works of brass and gold. In many Sufi schools or advanced esoteric schools, a member is required to pass through a lengthy training and show that he can carve, sculpt, and create with his hands.

All this must be done with intense attention, concentration, and focus. It is through these methods that gradually the person gains control over the etheric body and brings the physical body into alignment with the etheric and mental bodies.

The weaving of oriental tapestries or rugs was originally a concentration exercise with intense creative expressions. You can find many mystical and abstract ideas in the designs of oriental rugs in which a great teaching is imparted through a symbolic language based on color and design. Some rug specialists agree that the unique designs of oriental rugs have deep meanings. They say that a design cannot be translated completely unless the color of the design and the symbols are taken into consideration.

Great spiritual teachers trained a huge number of advanced disciples by making them concentrate their minds, hearts, and hands on a given labor such as creating designs and using colors to manifest an idea. In India and China this was done through woodcarving and the making of jewelry. In other places, such as Armenia and Egypt, they carved many magnificent symbolic and esoteric designs into the rocks. In Greece and Italy, they concentrated on sculpture, and it was by such trained disciples that the Notre Dame in Paris and hundreds of other magnificent cathedrals throughout Europe were built.

Etheric control can be achieved by hard labor. In this creative work, the secret is to penetrate into the great ideas, visions, and prototypes of the higher Cosmic Ethers, reflecting them through the mind onto the lower ethers and making them manifest through labor — hard, continuous, concentrated labor. Through this method, the higher Cosmic Ethers fuse with the lower ethers and replace them. As they replace the lower ethers, the radiant center of creative genius grows in man, and all the etheric centers turn into revolving lights.

For many centuries, wise people advised us to do whatever we are doing **with all our heart, mind, and being**. In some monasteries this discipline was given to neophytes in the form of physical labor. The neophyte must dig, build, cut trees, cultivate the soil, clean the stables, and collect wood with the utmost love of doing so and with the utmost attention. Such a wholehearted fusion with the labor organizes the etheric body, which in its turn vitalizes and organizes the physical body.

If these points are observed to a high degree, you will see an improvement in your health and an increase in your creativity, magnetism, and spiritual influence upon people. The purification of the etheric vehicle places you in contact with higher levels of consciousness and makes your centers unfold and bloom.

11. We are told that the most effective method to purify our etheric body and clear the blocked threads of the etheric web is to practice harmlessness. This is a harmlessness which is demonstrated on physical, emotional, and mental levels and also in our individual, family, and social life.

Harmlessness is an active procedure. It releases higher energies from higher planes and higher centers, and these energies gradually permeate our etheric body.

Harmlessness is an act of standing in the light of the Universal One Self and striving to make that Self successful on Its path of perfection and creativity. As you try to be harmless, the power of the One Self pours into you and through you and goes out to all that you contact. Thus, you open the channels of the circulatory flow of Divine Energy.

12. Purification of the etheric body can be further achieved through right colors and right music.

When you are in an area loaded with heavy pollution, or you are under a load of emotions, fear, negative thoughts, and depressions, you can help yourself by placing some pure, cold-pressed olive oil on the three pranic centers and massaging them gently in a clockwise motion. Soon you will feel energized, and your depression and negativity will probably disappear.

Most of the depressions that people experience are because they do not assimilate prana. This depletes them, fixes their attention on the present moment, and veils the future. A glimpse of the future brings rays of hope, and depression vanishes.

These three centers (between the shoulder blades, above the diaphragm, and the spleen) have a concentrated sphere of nadis. These nadis are the etheric nerves which carry energy to the nervous system from the etheric centers.

Olive oil is a good conductor of prana. That is why in olden times the kings, and later the bishops, were anointed and blessed with olive oil. Various churches also use olive oil in the consecration of priests, in baptism, and even in times of sickness to allow the vitalizing prana to penetrate into the system. During the time of Jesus, His disciples used olive oil to consecrate or to heal various diseases. The blessing energy, which is a combination of prana and psychic energy, flows through the oil and penetrates into the tissues. Psychic energy is the energy of the Self and the Soul which pours inspiration and power into the man.

6

Prana and the Sun

People of advanced spiritual faculties can draw more prana from a given location than people of corrupt morals and intellect. The reception of prana is equal to our unfoldment and state of purity.

The Tibetan Master says that those devas who transmit solar prana to man

> *... are of a very powerful order, and, along their own line, are further evolved than man himself. Unprotected man lies at their mercy, and in this lack of protection, and man's failure to understand the laws of magnetic resistance, or of solar repulsion comes, for instance, the menace of sunstroke. When the etheric body and its assimilative processes are comprehended scientifically, man will then be immune from dangers due to solar radiation. He will protect himself by the application of the laws governing magnetic repulsion and attraction, and not so much by clothing and shelter....*[1]

The laws of magnetic resistance or of solar repulsion can automatically adjust themselves in any given situation if

1. The three receiving centers are in good order
2. Assimilation in the etheric body is not hampered by the influence of illusion, glamor, and maya
3. The etheric centers are active and in harmony with each other
4. The radiation of the human soul is powerful enough to balance the radiation of prana
5. The personality is clear of combustible materials — materials which are not assisting in the evolution of the human soul

---

1. Alice A. Bailey, *A Treatise on Cosmic Fire*, pp. 90-91.

Most of our troubles are caused by friction. Friction comes into being as a result of the following:

1. When one of our vehicles absorbs energy or substance beyond its capacity.
2. When we are exposed to an energy or substance, while having in our bodies elements which create friction with the incoming energy or substance. Here the friction creates several problems:

   a. Often the elements are burned, causing pain and suffering.

   b. Often these elements reject or reflect the prana back or impede circulation.

Rejection creates friction. Friction creates short circuits or retardation of the electrical impulses. But when there is right assimilation, there is no friction.

When we stand in the Sun, there are elements which burn in our aura. There are elements which reflect back the prana or pollute it — hence, sunstroke. We are told,

> *...These golden hued pranic entities are in the air above us, and are specially active in such parts of the world as California, in those tropical countries where the air is pure and dry, and the rays of the sun are recognised as being specially beneficial....*[2]

We are also told that to assimilate prana requires refinement, purity, and unfoldment. People of advanced spiritual faculties can draw more prana from a given location than people of corrupt morals and intellect. The reception of prana is equal to our unfoldment and state of purity.

Disciples are advised to protect the crown of their head from direct contact with the Sun. Due to their increased receptivity, these disciples can absorb an excessive quantity of prana which causes congestion in their system until they learn how to control the pranic inflow.

Some etheric bodies even work as refineries. They absorb the polluting elements, burn them, and radiate amplified prana. Some people who are not yet powerful enough to purify and refine, absorb with the prana the ills of the other persons. This is one of the reasons for feeling very weak when in the presence of those whose etheric body is polluted.

When man becomes a Master, his physical body absorbs the highest and purest prana, and he is then able to live in his physical body as long as he wants.

In daylight we receive prana directly from the Sun and from the planet. At night we receive prana only from the earth. For this reason it is necessary to

---

2. *Ibid.*, p. 90.

reduce energy output by sleep. Those who work for a long time on the night shift eventually develop various etheric disorders and then physical disorders due to a lack of the energy from the Sun.

Great Initiates advise us to sleep early and to awaken early, even in twilight, so as to enjoy the benefits of prana from the Sun at sunrise. Such a life creates great balance between the two kinds of prana which, in turn, builds greater balance between the body and mind.

As the full moon approaches, the earth's radiation is increased, and man absorbs greater amounts of earth prana and solar prana. We are told that at full moon times we must not expose our head to the moonlight because it saps the prana from our etheric body. It also causes pranic congestion. We can expose ourselves to the light of the stars when the moon has not yet risen.

In the Agni Yoga literature we read,

> *It is good to be in the sunshine, but the starlit sky also brings harmony to the nerves. The moon, on the contrary, is not for us. The moon's pure light affects the prana. The magnetism of the moon is great, but for repose it is not good. Often the moon evokes fatigue, like people who devour one's vital energy....*[3]

Master D.K. explains the disorders of solar, planetary, and human etheric bodies which originate from various causes. He says,

> ...We will need to bear carefully in mind when studying this matter, that all the diseases of the etheric body will appertain to its threefold purpose and be either:
>
> a. *Functional*, and thereby affecting its apprehension of prana,
>
> b. *Organic*, and thereby affecting its distribution of prana,
>
> c. *Static*, and thereby affecting the web, when viewed solely from the angle of providing a physical ring-pass-not, and acting as a separator between the physical and the astral.[4]

The method of healing is then given as follows:

> *a. Microcosmic functional disorders.* These have to do with the reception by man, via the necessary centres, of the pranic fluids. We must always bear in mind, and thus keep the distinction clear, that these emanations of prana have to do with the heat latent in matter; when received and functioning through the

3. Agni Yoga Society, *Leaves of Morya's Garden II*, p. 32.
4. Alice A. Bailey, *A Treatise on Cosmic Fire*, p. 104.

etheric body correctly, they co-operate with the natural latent bodily warmth, and (merging therewith) hold the body in a vitalised condition, imposing upon the matter of the body a certain rate of vibratory action that leads to the necessary activity of the physical vehicle, and the right functioning of its organs. It will, therefore, be apparent that the A.B.C. of bodily health is wrapped up in the right reception of prana, and that one of the basic changes that must be made in the life of the human animal (which is the aspect we are dealing with now) will be in the ordinary conditions of living.

The three fundamental centres whereby reception is brought about must be allowed to function with greater freedom, and with less restriction. Now, owing to centuries of wrong living, and to basic mistakes (originating in Lemurian days) man's three pranic centres are not in good working order. The centre between the shoulder blades is in the best receptive condition, though owing to the poor condition of the spinal column (which in so many is out of accurate alignment), its position in the back is apt to be misplaced. The splenic centre near the diaphragm is sub-normal in size and its vibration is not correct. In the case of the aboriginal dwellers in such localities as the South Seas, better etheric conditions will be found; the life they lead is more normal (from the animal standpoint) than in any other portion of the world.

The race suffers from certain incapacities, which may be described as follows:

First. Inability to tap pranic currents, owing to the unhealthy lives passed by so many. This involves the cutting off of the source of supply, and the consequent atrophying and shrinkage of the receptive centres. This is seen in an exaggerated form in the children of the congested quarters of any great city, and in the vitiated anemic dwellers of the slums. The cure is apparent — the bringing about of better living conditions, the employment of more appropriate clothing, and the adoption of a freer and more salubrious mode of living. When the pranic rays can find free access to the shoulders, and to the diaphragm, the subnormal state of the average spleen will adjust itself automatically.

Second. Over-ability to tap pranic currents. The first type of functional disorder is common and widespread. Its reverse can be found where conditions of life are such that the centres (through too direct and prolonged submittal to solar emanation) become overdeveloped, vibrate too rapidly, and receive prana in too great an amount. This is rarer, but is found in some tropical countries, and is responsible for much of the troublesome debility that attacks dwellers in these lands. The etheric body receives prana or solar rays too rapidly, passes it through and out of the system with too much force, and this leaves the victim a prey to inertia and devitalisation. Putting it otherwise, the etheric body becomes lazy, is like an unstrung web, or (to use a very homely illustration) it resembles a tennis racket which has become too soft, and has lost its resilience. The inner triangle transmits the pranic emanations with too great rapidity, giving no time for the subsidiary absorption, and the whole system is thereby the loser. Later it will be found that many of the ills that Europeans, living in India, fall heir to, originate in this way; and by attention, therefore, to the spleen, and by wise control of living conditions, some of the trouble may be obviated.

In touching upon similar conditions in the planet, both these types of trouble will be found. More cannot be said, but in the wise study of solar radiation upon the surface of the planet in connection with its rotary action, some of the group rules of health may be comprehended and followed. The spirit of the planet (or the planetary entity) likewise has his cycles, and in the absorption of planetary prana, and in its correct distribution, lies the secret of fertility and equable vegetation. Much of this is hidden in the fabled story of the war between fire and water, which has its basis in the reaction of the fire latent in matter, to the fire emanating outside of matter, and playing upon it. In the interval that has to elapse while the two are in process of blending, come those periods where, through karmic inheritance, reception is unstable and distribution inequable. As the point of race equilibrium is reached, so planetary equilibrium will likewise be attained, and in planetary attainment will come the equilibrium that must mutually take place between the solar planets. When they attain a mutual balance and interaction then the system is stabilised and perfection reached. The even distribution of prana will parallel this balancing in the man, in the race, in the planet and in the system. This is but another way of saying that uniform vibration will be achieved.

b. Microcosmic organic disorders. These are basically two in number:

Troubles due to congestion.

Destruction of tissue due to over-absorption of prana, or its too rapid blending with latent physical fire.

We have a curious illustration of both of these forms of trouble in sun stroke and in heat stroke. Though supposedly understood by physicians, they are nevertheless altogether etheric disorders. When the nature of the etheric body is better understood, and its wise care followed both these types of disease will be prevented. They are due to solar pranic emanation; in one case the effect of the emanation is to bring about death or serious illness through the congestion of an etheric channel, while in the other the same result is brought about by destruction of etheric matter.

The above illustration has been used with definite intent, but it should be pointed out that etheric congestion may lead to many forms of disease and of mental incompetence. Etheric congestion leads to the thickening of the web to an abnormal extent, and this thickening may prevent, for instance, contact with the higher Self or principles and its resultants, idiocy and mental unbalance. It may lead to abnormal fleshy development, to the thickening of some internal organ, and consequent undue pressure; one portion of the etheric body being congested may lead to the entire physical condition being upset, resulting in diverse complaints.

Destruction of tissue may lead to insanity of many kinds, especially those kinds deemed incurable. The burning of the web may let in extraneous astral currents against which man is helpless; the brain tissue may be literally destroyed by this pressure, and serious trouble be caused through the etheric ring-pass-not having been destroyed in some one place.

In connection with the planet a similar state of affairs may be found. Later information may be forthcoming, which is at present withheld; this will show that whole races have been influenced, and certain kingdoms of nature troubled by planetary etheric congestion, or the destruction of planetary etheric tissue.

We have dealt with the functional and organic ills of the etheric, giving certain indications for the extension of the concept to other realms than the purely human. In the human kingdom lies the key, but the turning of that key opens up a door to a wider interpretation as it admits one into the mysteries of nature. Though that key has to be turned seven times, yet even one turn reveals untold avenues of eventual comprehension.

We have considered the reception and distribution of pranic emanations in man, the planet, and the system, and have seen what produces temporary disorders, and the devitalisation or the over-vitalisation of the organic form. Now we can look at the subject from a third angle and therefore study:

> *c. Microcosmic static disorders,* or a consideration of the etheric body in connection with its work of providing a ring-pass-not from the purely physical to the astral. As has been said, both here and in the books of H.P.B., the ring-pass-not is that confining barrier which acts as a separator or a division between a system and that which is external to that system. This, as may well be seen, has its interesting correlations when the subject is viewed (as we must consistently endeavour to view it) from the point of view of a human being, a planet and a system, remembering always that in dealing with the etheric body we are dealing with *physical matter*. This must ever be borne carefully in mind. Therefore, one paramount factor will be found in all groups and formations, and this is the fact that the ring-pass-not acts only as a hindrance to that which is of small attainment in evolution, but forms no barrier to the more progressed. The whole question depends upon two things, which are the karma of the man, the planetary Logos, and the solar Logos, and the dominance of the spiritual indwelling entity over its vehicle.[5]

Since our etheric body is a part of the planetary and solar etheric bodies, we often share the disorders or disturbances taking place on global and solar scales. These disturbances express themselves as various sicknesses having originated from the planetary and solar etheric bodies.

The overactivity of the solar plexus affects the etheric body and even leads it into inertia or negativity. Excitement of the solar plexus caused by the mass media, television, and newspapers also affects the health of the general population, rendering its etheric body relatively dull.

When the etheric body is not vibrant and rhythmic, the brain suffers, and the physical man cannot communicate with virtues or with his own conscience; thus he tends toward criminal or suicidal activities or heavy depression. In such cases where there is overexcitement of the emotional body, the physical body falls under the forces of emotions which cause various organic, glandular, and blood diseases. Most heart problems are caused by uncontrollable emotions and by solar plexus activity.

Epidemics attack those areas where there is etheric depletion resulting from astral overactivity. Due to the weakening of the etheric body, germs are transferred through the etheric substance and planted in the physical body.

---

5. *Ibid.*, pp. 105-111.

7

Fires in the Bodies

The etheric body, since it is related to fire, is itself fire in its various forms. This fire can be used for purifying, healing, and regenerating purposes.

Our body is built by the action of two fires. One fire is called *latent fire*, or *inherent fire*; the other is called *active fire*, or *radiatory fire*. These fires are brought together by the fire of the Solar Angel, or by the human soul after the Fourth Initiation. When these fires are separated, the form disintegrates.

Fire by Friction is active in the planes of the lower ethers. Electrical Fire is active in the higher Cosmic Ethers. These two fires are brought together by the Solar Fire. It is the Soul in man, the Solar Fire, that bridges these two fires — Fire by Friction and Electrical Fire.

Because of the existence of these fires, the purification of the bodies is very essential. Each of these three fires can be safely blended if the physical and etheric bodies are in a pure condition and if the astral and mental bodies are not polluted by glamors and illusions.

The Tibetan Master says,

> ...The more refined and rarefied the form, the better a receiver of prana will it be, and the less will be the resistance found to the uprising of kundalini at the appointed time. Coarse matter and crude immature physical bodies are a menace to the occultist, and no true seer will be found with a body of a gross quality. The dangers of disruption are too great, and the menace of disintegration by fire too awful.[1]
>
> 1. There is *Internal Vitalising Fire*, which is the correspondence to fire by friction. This is the sumtotal of individual kundalini; it animates the corporeal frame and demonstrates also in the twofold manner:
>
> First, as *latent heat* which is the basis of life of the spheroidal cell, or atom, and of its rotary adjustment to all other cells.

---

1. Alice A. Bailey, *A Treatise on Cosmic Fire*, p. 103.

Second, as *active heat* or prana; this animates all, and is the driving force of the evolving form. It shows itself in the four ethers and in the gaseous state, and a correspondence is here found on the physical plane in connection with man to the Akasha and its fivefold manifestation on the plane of the solar system.

This fire is the basic vibration of the little system in which the monad or human spirit is the logos, and it holds the personality or lower material man in objective manifestation thus permitting the spiritual unit to contact the plane of densest matter. It has its correspondence in the ray of intelligent activity and is controlled by the Law of Economy in one of its subdivisions, the Law of Adaptation in Time.

2. There is next the *Fire or Spark of Mind* which is the correspondence in man to solar fire. This constitutes the thinking self-conscious unit or the soul. This fire of mind is governed by the Law of Attraction as is its greater correspondence. Later we can enlarge on this. It is this spark of mind in man, manifesting as spiral cyclic activity, which leads to expansion and to his eventual return to the centre of his system, the Monad — the origin and goal for the reincarnating Jiva or human being. As in the macrocosm this fire also manifests in a twofold manner.

It shows as that intelligent will which links the Monad or spirit with its lowest point of contact, the personality, functioning through a physical vehicle.

It likewise demonstrates, as yet imperfectly, as the vitalising factor in the thought forms fabricated by the thinker. As yet but few thought forms, comparatively, can be said to be constructed by the center of consciousness, the thinker….

These dualities of expression are:

1. *Active fire* or prana.
   Latent fire or bodily heat.

2. *Mental energy* in the mental body.
   Purely mental thought forms, animated by self-engendered fire, or by the fifth principle, and therefore part of the sphere, or system of control, of the Monad.

These form an esoteric quaternary which with the fifth factor, the divine spark of intelligent will, make the five of monadic manifestation — manifestation in this case connotating a purely *subjective manifestation* which is neither altogether spiritual nor altogether material.

3. Finally there is the *Monadic Flame Divine*. This embodies the highest vibration of which the Monad is capable, is governed by the Law of Synthesis, and is the cause of the forward progressive movement of the evolving Jiva.

...Just as in the macrocosm the blending of the three essential fires of the cosmos marked the point of logoic attainment, so, in the blending of the essential fires of the microcosm, do we arrive at the apotheosis of human attainment for this cycle.

When the latent fire of the personality or lower self blends with the fire of mind, that of the higher self, and finally merges with the Divine Flame, then the man takes the fifth Initiation in this solar system, and has completed one of his greater cycles....[2]

Human latent fire, the heat interior of the human frame causes production of other forms of life, such as —

1. The physical body cells.
2. Organisms nourished by the latent heat.
3. The reproduction of itself in other human forms, the basis of the sex function.

Human radiatory, or active fire, is a factor as yet but little comprehended; it relates to the health aura and to that radiation from the etheric which makes a man a healer, and able to transmit active heat.

It is necessary to differentiate between this radiation from the etheric, which is a radiation of prana, and magnetism, which is an emanation from a subtler body (usually the astral), and has to do with the manifestation of the Divine Flame within the material sheaths. The Divine Flame is formed on the second plane, the monadic, and magnetism (which is a method of demonstrating radiatory fire) is therefore felt paramountly on the fourth and sixth planes, or through the buddhic and astral vehicles....[3]

The etheric body, since it is related to fire, is itself fire in its various forms. This fire can be used for purifying, healing, and regenerating purposes. The simplest form of using fire is a wood fire. Long ago disciples and initiates jumped over the open fire, or ran through it, or slept by it.

The etheric body is affected by an open wood fire. It is good sometimes to sit in front of an open fire and expose your whole body to the fire. Eventually you can do this for thirty to forty minutes, occasionally turning your body so that

2. *Ibid.*, pp. 45-47.
3. *Ibid.*, pp. 53-54.

all parts receive heat. Fatigue sometimes can be overcome through this method. Also, it is very beneficial for muscular aches or bruises. It also coordinates the etheric body, the nadis, and the nervous system.

8

Devas and the Etheric Body

Through reception, assimilation, and rhythmic radiation, your body is sustained and regenerated, and you are put in contact with the greater Universe.

We are told that there are some classes of devas who radiate the color violet, and they are very closely allied with the evolutionary development of the etheric body of man. It is these devas who transmit the solar and planetary prana to man. Solar prana is first received by these very high level devas. Their violet color is mixed with golden hues. They receive the solar pranic emanations, and

> *...pass them through their organism and focalise them there. They act almost as a burning glass acts. These rays are then reflected or transmitted to man's etheric body, and caught up by him and again assimilated....*[1]

The prana transmitted by these violet-golden devas passes into man's etheric body through his head and shoulders and is

> *...passed down to the etheric correspondence of the physical organ, the spleen, [via the two centers] and from thence forcibly transmitted into the spleen itself....*[2]

These violet-golden devas are in the air, especially in those places where the air is pure and dry. It is also stated that,

> *...These devas are of a very powerful order, and, along their own line, are further evolved than man himself. Unprotected man lies at their mercy, and in this lack of protection, and man's failure to understand the laws of magnetic resistance, or of solar repulsion comes, for instance, the menace of sunstroke. When the etheric body and its assimilative processes are comprehended*

1. Alice A. Bailey, *A Treatise on Cosmic Fire*, p. 91.
2. *Ibid.*, p. 90.

> *scientifically, man will then be immune from dangers due to solar radiation. He will protect himself by the application of the laws governing magnetic repulsion and attraction, and not so much by clothing and shelter....*[3]

The devas represent the feminine pole and man represents the masculine pole. The emanations of the Sun represent the masculine polarity.

After the prana circulates in the etheric body of man, the surplus prana is cast out in the form of physical magnetism. This magnetism carries with it the qualities which the person has as a result of his state of health.

The electromagnetic sphere which is called the etheric body has three functions:

1. It receives prana.

2. It assimilates prana and distributes it into each living cell and organ.

3. It radiates prana out into space.

Through reception, assimilation, and rhythmic radiation, your body is sustained and regenerated, and you are put in contact with the greater Universe. The prana is pumped rhythmically in and out of the body by the rhythm of the heartbeat. The lungs also play a great role in assimilating prana for the body.

Each of us has an etheric body which is different in appearance. This difference is the result of our mental, emotional, and physical activities. All our thoughts, emotions, plans, visions, imagination, and visualizations directly affect the ability to receive prana, to assimilate, and to emanate prana. And because we think, feel, and act differently, our etheric bodies are built differently and our physical bodies have different features. Consider the thousands of lives with different interests and different strivings, and you will see why our etheric and physical bodies are different from one another.

As initiates advance, they change into the form of the ideal man — Christ, the archetypal Man.

Devas are not human beings. They are living beings, but they do not have dense physical mechanisms. They live in the etheric body of the planet and are related to our lower etheric planes.

Let us study the following diagram:

---

3. *Ibid.*, pp. 90-91.

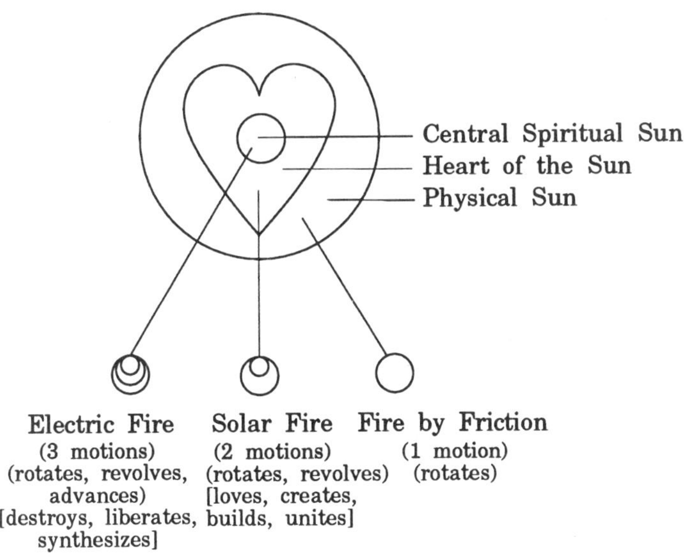

Diagram 8-1 The Three-Fold Sun

The Central Spiritual Sun emanates the Electric Fire. This is a destructive energy. It is also a liberating and synthesizing energy. It destroys limitations and hindrances in which the spirit is caught and liberates it, leading to a new synthesis.

The Heart of the Sun emanates the energy which we call love energy or Solar Fire. This energy creates, builds, and unites on all levels according to the Divine Purpose.

The third energy is the Fire by Friction which emanates from the physical Sun. This is the root of solar prana.

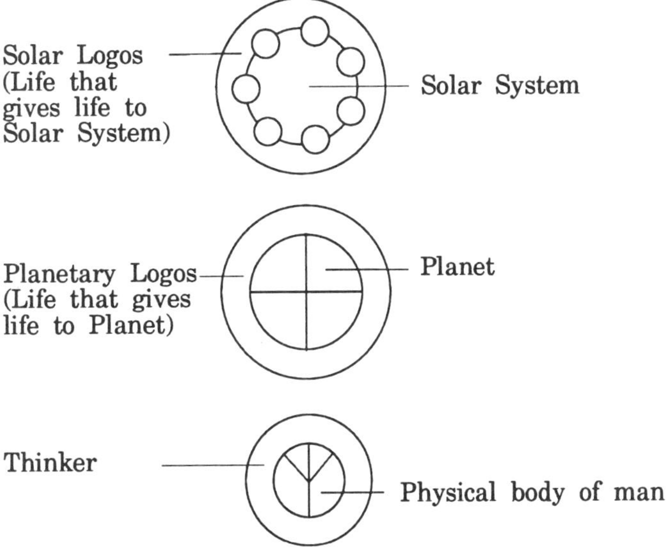

Diagram 8-2 Solar System, Planet, Man

The above diagram shows the Solar Logos or the greater Life Who ensouls the solar system and incarnates through the solar system. The Solar Logos is the Thinker in the solar sense.

Also shown is the Planetary Logos, or the Life of the planet. He is the Thinker in the planetary sense, and He incarnates through the planet.

Then there is the man who in his essence is the thinker in the individual sense.

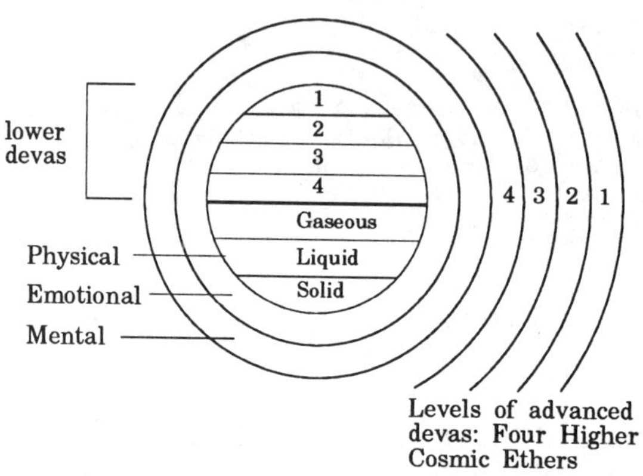

Diagram 8-3 The Planes Where Devas Live

The above diagram shows the planet and the etheric planes within which live devas who are directly related to human beings. Also shown in Diagram 3 are the higher Cosmic Ethers in which live advanced devas or Great Beings.

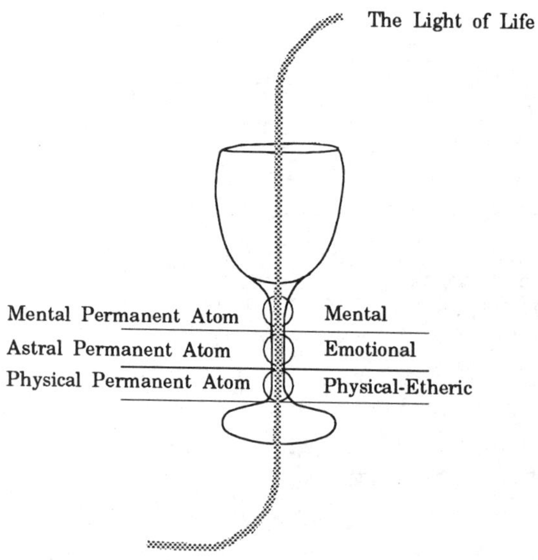

Diagram 8-4 Permanent Atoms and the Chalice

The above diagram shows the permanent atoms as parts of the Chalice. Permanent atoms are those seeds which accumulate within themselves all our past history, achievements, and failures. When we incarnate, these seeds serve as films or negatives through which the stream of Life passes and projects the contents of these atoms onto the physical plane — as the man in manifestation on the physical, emotional, and mental levels of being.

The permanent atoms are found on the life thread. In the permanent atoms, the resumé of all our past lives is found. When a man incarnates, the life-force hits the atoms as if they were a photographic negative and produces a person who inherits all that exists in the permanent atoms. This includes the many qualities, abilities, tendencies, and talents, plus new aspirations of future hope and vision and new possibilities of advancement — if they were planted in the past.

The permanent atoms are the conditioning factors in our incarnation. They condition our physical, emotional, and mental constitutions and also contain the possibilities for further advancement.

Note that there are planetary and solar permanent atoms through whose influence the great planetary and solar Lives take incarnation. However, their permanent atoms are not in lower etheric levels but rather in the Cosmic Etheric Planes.

The physical permanent atom of our Solar Logos is found in the Adi (Divine) Plane of the Cosmic Physical Plane; Adi is the First Cosmic Ether. The consciousness of the Solar Logos is focused on the lower mental plane of the Cosmic Mental Plane. We are told that He is working to bridge His Cosmic lower mind with the Cosmic higher mind. As our Planetary and Solar Logoi advance, human beings and all living forms receive a greater amount of prana from higher and higher sources through more advanced devas.

Initiations are a gradual expansion of your vision and creativity. For example, when you are not an initiate you are imprisoned within matter, just like a prisoner living in a dungeon. When you take the first initiation, you have another prison, but there is a little window through which you can see a portion of the real world. When you are a second degree initiate, you have a wider window and some skylight. When you are a Third Degree Initiate, you have a skylight, windows, and a door. As a Fourth Degree Initiate, you are out of your prison. As a Seventh Degree Initiate, you are at the summit of the highest mountain.

Initiations are related to the ethers. The first three initiations are achieved through the transformation of the lower ethers and through the natural unfoldment of the seven etheric centers.

The higher initiations are achieved within the Cosmic Etheric Planes. The Fourth Initiation is achieved when the Initiate penetrates from the higher mind to the Fourth Cosmic Etheric Plane, which is called the Intuitional or Buddhic Plane. At the Fifth Initiation, he functions on the Third Cosmic Etheric Plane, which is called the Atmic Plane. At the Sixth Initiation, he passes into the

Monadic Plane, which is the Second Cosmic Ether. At the Seventh Initiation, he dominates the First Cosmic Etheric Plane, which is called the Divine Plane or Adi, and then passes into the Cosmic Astral Plane.

As you expand your consciousness and increase your ability to create, you live a more sacrificial life for others. You become harmonious with life, instead of being a distorted note in the symphony.

Master Djwhal Khul, speaking about devas, says,

> *...The group of violet angels or devas who work on the four etheric levels will be especially active and they will work in the four main groups of men who are in incarnation at any given time....*
>
> *These four groups of angels are a band of servers, pledged to the service of the Christ, and their work is to contact men and to teach them along certain lines.*[4]

Please remember that this will happen when Christ reappears and brings with Him some of the great Angels. The Master continues,

> a. They will teach humanity to see etherically....
>
> b. They will give instruction in the effect of colour in the healing of disease, and particularly the efficiency of violet light in lessening human ills and in curing those physical plane sicknesses which originate in the etheric body.
>
> c. They will also demonstrate to the materialistic thinkers of the world the fact that the superconscious world exists....
>
> d. They will train human beings in the knowledge of superhuman physics so that weight shall be for them transmuted. Motion will become more rapid, speed will be accompanied by noiselessness and smoothness, and hence fatigue will be eliminated. In the human control of etheric levels lies the overcoming of fatigue and the power to transcend time....
>
> e. They will teach humanity how rightly to nourish the body and to draw from the surrounding ethers the requisite food. Man will concentrate his attention upon the etheric body and the work and health of the physical body will become increasingly automatic.

4. Alice A. Bailey, *Externalisation of the Hierarchy*, p. 508.

f. They will also teach human beings as individuals and as a race to expand their consciousness to include the superphysical...![5]

The deva evolution will...have much to do with the transmission of prana to units of the three higher kingdoms of nature, and this easier transmission (from the etheric levels of the physical plane) will parallel a correspondingly easier transmission of spiritual or psychical force from the fourth cosmic ether, the buddhic plane. The results of this pranic transmission will be more healthy physical bodies among the sons of men.... This...will only begin to be noticeable about three hundred years hence, when the incoming seventh Ray Egos will be numerically strong enough to be recognised as the prevailing type for a certain period. Their physical bodies, owing to their being built for seventh Ray force will respond more readily than the others, though first Ray Egos and fifth Ray Egos will benefit enormously from this influence. The etheric devas will build during a peculiarly favourable period, and the physical bodies then constructed will be distinguished by:

a. Resilience

b. Enormous physical magnetism

c. Ability to reject false magnetism

d. Capacity to absorb solar rays

e. Great strength and resistance

f. A delicacy and refinement in appearance as yet unknown

The etheric levels of the plane will be full of an increased activity, and slowly but surely, as the decades slip away, man will become conscious of these levels, and aware of their inhabitants. The immediate effect of this greater etheric energy will be that a numerically larger number of people will possess etheric vision, and will be able normally and naturally to live consciously on etheric levels. The majority of men only function consciously on the three lower levels of the physical — the gaseous, the liquid, and the dense — and the etheric levels are as sealed to them as are the astral. In the coming centuries, man's normal habitat will be the entire physical plane up to, though not including, the second subplane. The fourth and third etheric levels will be as

5. *Ibid.*, pp. 508-509.

familiar to him as the usual physical landscape to which he is now accustomed.[6]

Rays have a great effect on our system through their corresponding centers within our etheric body. The centers responsive to the Rays are

Head center to the First Ray

Heart center to the Second Ray

Ajna center to the Fifth Ray

Throat center to the Third Ray

Solar plexus center to the Sixth Ray

Sacral center to the Seventh Ray

Base of spine center to the Fourth Ray[7]

Through these etheric centers, the Rays influence the expressions of man and his relationship with man and Nature. As man develops, he has more sensitive responses to these Rays.

At the present, the Sixth and Seventh Rays are in conflict, and because the Seventh Ray is related to the sacral center, we witness a widespread interest in sex; we see a greater amount of sexual abuse and an increase in sex related problems.

As the race develops, the higher counterpart of this center — the throat center — will be a balancing and creative factor, and we will see great creative expressions everywhere.

The Tibetan Master says,

---

6. Alice A. Bailey, *A Treatise on Cosmic Fire*, pp. 473-474.
7. In *Esoteric Psychology*, Vol. I, p. 428, the centers and corresponding Rays are as follows:
Head center — First Ray
Ajna center — Fifth Ray
Throat center —Third Ray
Heart center — Second Ray
Solar plexus center — Sixth Ray
Sacral center — Seventh Ray
Base of spine center — Fourth Ray.
In *Esoteric Psychology*, Vol. II, p. 521, the centers and cooresponding Rays are as follows:
Head center — First Ray
Ajna center — Fourth Ray
Throat center — Third Ray
Heart center — Second Ray
Solar plexus center — Sixth Ray
Sacral center — Fifth Ray
Base of spine center — Seventh Ray.

> *A mysterious group of devas...are, at this juncture, swept into being, and they embody the fire of sex expression as we understand it. They are the impulse, or instinct, back of physical sex desire. They were peculiarly dominant in the fourth root-race, at which time sex conditions reached a stage of unbelievable horror from our point of view. They are gradually being controlled, and when the last of the Lemurian Egos has passed into the fifth root-race they will be slowly passed out of the solar system altogether....*[8]

The etheric body and its centers are conditioned by the type of energy that pours into them. The Seventh Ray influence is slowly increasing. The Seventh Ray facilitates the transformation of the etheric body through helping some devas bring the substance of the Buddhic Plane into the etheric body. It is the substance of buddhic energy which will reveal the nature of true love, bringing greater harmony within the etheric body and linking the man with the life more abundant.

---

8. Alice A. Bailey, *A Treatise on Cosmic Fire*, p. 677.

9

Color and the Etheric Body

To be utilized properly, colors must be used under clairvoyant observation or intuitive perception.

Colors have a great effect on the etheric body. If they are used in the right way, they

- Heal
- Purify
- Vivify
- Integrate
- Nourish
- Transmute
- Initiate

The etheric body is an electromagnetic sphere through which the solar and earth prana

1. Keep the body alive
2. Nourish the etheric centers
3. Enable the brain to register certain impressions
4. Nourish lower kingdoms and devas
5. Keep the man related to the solar whole
6. Enable man to contact higher centers
7. Help the Spark move on the path of initiation

To be utilized properly, colors must be used under clairvoyant observation or intuitive perception.

The colors of the rainbow are

— red

— orange

— yellow

— green

— blue

— purple

— violet

People can be categorized according to their auric color.

The higher ethers, when they are active, radiate living and fiery colors. The mental, astral, etheric, and physical bodies have their own colors. All these colors characterize the progress of man and his achievements.

The aura of the average man is chaotic and does not have vibrant colors. When the personality is formed, a person has a dominating color among the other colors. When Soul-infusion is achieved, many colors of the aura change into two dominant, harmonious colors. When the man penetrates into the Spiritual Triad, the color of the Monad releases Itself and the person changes into a rainbow dominated by the Monadic radiation, of which the personality color shines forth as a reflection.

Each mood, thought, emotion, word, and movement creates a color in the aura according to its sources and its alignments.

Colors have a great effect on our aura in general, and on our etheric body in particular. The intensity and effect of the colors are stronger if they are the living colors of Nature, such as the colors of the sunset or sunrise. These include the blue sky, the colors of the ocean, trees, birds, animals, insects, or colors of great paintings — the works of those artists who have Soul or Triadal consciousness. Artificial colors have their own effects when we wear them or use them in various ways.

It is very important to know that each sound creates a color, each word creates a color; and if a word is inspired from higher ethers, its color is superb. Thus, the speech of a Sage is a living symphony of colors which heals, uplifts, and energizes the whole being of a person.

Actually, mantrams are compositions of words expressed by very advanced individuals who were inspired by or anchored in higher realms. Because of their attunement with higher realities and the refined and sensitive conditions of their instruments, their every utterance was, and is, a mantram or word of power. That is why the speech of the Sages is more powerful in the original language in which it was spoken.

In using the original language of the Sages, you draw pure energy from the corresponding planes of your being. Sacred writings are composed in the light of higher planes, most likely in the Intuitional and Atmic Planes. They carry high voltage energy if approached with a pure heart and right motive. For these reasons, in many such scriptures we find warnings not to change their wording.

There is a book that was written in Armenian in the ninth century A.D. which is used even today for healing. Throughout ages, miracles have been performed by using that book. It is a book of mantrams, the reading and chanting of which create a tremendous upliftment, inspiration, and power. The book is entitled *Nareg* and has been partially translated into several languages. In these translations you have the meaning but not the power or the symphony of colors the words radiate.

In translating the words of Sages, the power of the charge is lost, just as when you use inadequate electronic tubes, you lose the clarity of your television picture. However, a translation can be approximated to the original wording if the translator has the same level of consciousness and is in contact with the higher planes from which the original inspiration came. In whatever way the Cosmic Ethers are used, you have the power of spirit, the psychic power.

Every time you channel energy from Cosmic Ethers to lower ethers, you sublimate, purify, strengthen, and electrify your nature. This can be done through coming in contact with highly charged literature, music, or art. Musical compositions of some great and spiritually advanced Initiates are like mantrams. They transform the life of the listener. But if the music is given by some unrefined and confused person with all kinds of discordant, nerve-racking noise, piercing moaning, and meaningless screaming, the noise will have a destructive effect on the nervous system, resulting in moral and spiritual degeneration.

Various races have a dominating color in their auras. Nations have their color. Continents have their color. Our earth and other planets have their own colors, and our solar system has its dominating color. For a clairvoyant, Space is a phantasmagoria of living and fiery colorful Rays and magnetic fields.

We are told that in the future man will be categorized according to his dominant color. Color will be used in a very advanced and specialized way to heal on many planes:

- To expand consciousness
- To create harmonious relationships
- To create success
- To attract special energies from Space
- To communicate with higher planes

The use of color will be an alchemical science, and colors and their frequencies will be calculated so as to bring the desired effects.

We can communicate with devas through colors. And when we radiate fiery colors, we nourish the devas or give them great pleasure or joy, and they in turn send us their celestial blessings.

In the future we will have a universal language based not on sound but on color. We will have the alphabet of colors by which we will communicate not only with each other but also with angels and devas. Devas will be able to read our writings, and they will communicate with us through colors which we will detect in Space by using certain types of very sensitive film.

In the healing art and the use of colors, one must know exactly the Rays of the personality vehicles, as well as the personality and Soul Rays. Each Ray has its own color, and knowing the Rays gives you the right key to use colors for healing and other purposes.

If the Rays are not known, the use of colors will be a dangerous experiment. That is why the regulation of colors must not be enforced for a long time. Careful observation can be made while using color for only short periods, but the subject must be isolated during the time of the experiment to prevent the mixture of other colors by physical contact. It is also necessary that the doctor have some similar colors in his aura and dress.

Centers in the etheric body have their own colors. Once their esoteric color is known, it will be possible to stimulate them, to retard their activities, or to unfold them. Such a task is a great responsibility, and only higher clairvoyants can deal with it without danger. Before the color is used, the colors and hues of the petals of the centers must be measured clairvoyantly and similar or mixed colors or different hues must be used for a strictly limited time and dosage.

The most potent effect of colors, if they are charged with intuitive and higher mental fire, is on the twelve-petaled Lotus in the higher mind. This Lotus has all the colors of the centers and the aura.

Some people use various color reflectors or magic boxes to project colors. This is a very dangerous game, and it leads to imbalance. It eventually distorts the equilibrium of the centers and creates different health problems.

The Tibetan Master, speaking about colors, says,

> *1.* Orange *stimulates the action of the etheric body; it removes congestion and increases the flow of prana.*
>
> 2. Rose *acts upon the nervous system and tends to vitalisation, and to the removal of depression, and symptoms of debilitation; it increases the* will to live.
>
> *3.* Green *has a general healing effect and can be safely used in cases of inflammation and of fever, but it is almost impossible as yet to provide the right conditions for the application of this*

colour, or to arrive at the adequate shade. It is one of the basic colours to be used eventually in the healing of the dense physical body, being the colour of the note of Nature.[1]

1. Alice A. Bailey, *Letters on Occult Meditation*, pp. 247-248.

10

Centers and the Etheric Body

Each of these centers represents a major virtue, and when the virtue is found and cultivated, the center unfolds naturally and releases creative energies.

Our glands are the physical manifestation of the seven major centers and other secondary centers. The seven centers of the etheric body and the corresponding glands are as follows:

1. Head center — pineal gland
2. Ajna center — pituitary body
3. Throat center — thyroid gland
4. Heart center — thymus gland
5. Solar plexus — pancreas
6. Sacral center — gonads
7. Base of spine — adrenal glands[1]

These *centers* are not in the physical body but in the etheric body, two to four inches away from the dense physical body. The *glands* are the physical mechanisms of the centers, and they are built according to the type of energy which radiates from the centers.

The Tibetan Master, speaking about the etheric centers, says,

> *...The centres can be in one of five conditions....*
>
> *1. Closed, still and shut, and yet with signs of life, silent and full of deep inertia.*

1. Note: The spleen center is counted as a center until the Third Initiation. The ajna center exists only after the Third Initiation.

2. *Opening, unsealed, and faintly tinged with colour; the life pulsates.*

3. *Quickened, alive, alert in two directions; the two small doors are open wide.*

4. *Radiant and reaching forth with vibrant note to all related centres.*

5. *Blended they are and each with each works rhythmically. The vital force flows through from all the planes. The world stands open wide.*[2]

The seven centers have the following characteristics:

The **head center** distributes the energy of the Supreme Self in man. It has twelve radiations which appear as flames or petals of flowers. Their color is a mixture of pure white with gold. Around these central twelve petals are arranged another nine hundred and sixty-nine petals which are the correspondences of all lower centers. That is called the thousand-petaled Lotus in the head.

The **ajna center** has ninety-six petals. The colors of the petals vary with rose, yellow, blue, and purple. The center resembles the wings of a bird spreading over the eyebrows — two main petals in which are found smaller petals resembling the feathers of a peacock. The energy that is transmitted is violet in color, and the petals are dominated by a white glow. These colors change according to the initiation through which a person passes.

When this center is fully awakened on the etheric plane, the person can see etherically. When it is linked with its astral correspondence, one becomes astrally clairvoyant. Higher clairvoyance comes when one functions on the higher mental plane and uses the ajna center with the third eye.

The **throat center** has sixteen petals and their colors are mostly purple mixed with silver. The energy passing through the petals radiates a blue color mixed with purple.

When this center is connected with the two astral centers near the ears, man hears astral and etheric voices. Higher clairaudience is achieved when this center is connected with certain centers in the fourth mental plane.

The **heart center** has twelve petals radiating a golden color. The energy passing through the petals appears mostly smoky blue in color.

The **solar plexus** has ten petals, and they are rosy in color mixed with green. The green flow of force comes from the spleen and then goes to the solar plexus.

2. Alice A. Bailey, *Esoteric Healing*, p. 81.

The organs connected with the solar plexus all receive the same flow of green force. They are the liver, intestines, and stomach.

The solar plexus is formed by two interlacing triangles, like a six-pointed star. The lower pointing triangle is the mechanism of lower psychism; the other is for higher psychism. The lower triangle is formed by the forces of the lower three centers, and the higher triangle is formed by the energy coming from the head center. The lower channels astral energy; the higher transmits solar energy.

The **sacral center** has six petals and they have an orange-vermilion color. The energy passing through the petals is pure white.

The prana acting in the sacral center — when economized and sublimated in chastity and in mental purity — turns upward and divides into three color rays. A yellow ray goes to the brain and vitalizes the brain centers and increases the sharpness of intelligence. A crimson ray goes to the heart center and to its correspondence in the head and creates a sense of responsibility and pure affection. A violet ray goes to the head center and becomes the vehicle of greater willpower.

The **base of spine center** has four petals. The colors of the petals are red mixed with orange. This is not the color of the energy which pours down from the spleen, but is caused by the rate of the vibration of the center.

There are three etheric channels originating from the base of spine center which pass through the spinal column. Together they are called *kundalini* fire. One of these three electrical lines sustains the health of the body and feeds it — that is the *pingala*. The next one is the *ida*, which is related to the consciousness of man. The middle one, the *sushumna*, is related to the Spirit aspect. It is this one that becomes active and is slowly raised as the person passes through the major initiations — through living a life of sacrificial service and meditation.

When the kundalini energy is raised prematurely, it stimulates and fosters the growth of the weaknesses found in the etheric, emotional, and mental bodies. For example, if a person prematurely raises this energy and he has the habit of imagining sexual affairs or sexual activities, the energy will rush into these thought patterns and will strengthen them to such a degree that the logic and sanity of the mind will fail to prevent the immediate demand or satisfaction of the resulting drive. Hundreds of people, otherwise controlled and balanced, become victims of their latent urges when they play with the kundalini fire without being watched by a real master of this science.

If the person has emotional and mental disorders, these will increase and control his life. Vanity, pride, shallow-mindedness, gossip, and other weaknesses will grow out of proportion and cause great distress to the person who, in most cases, assumes the role of both the doer and observer.

Master D. K. says,

> *...The kundalini fire will be raised and carried up into heaven* when *all the centres are awakened and the channels up the spine are unimpeded. This removal of all obstruction is the result of the*

> *livingness of the individual centres which, through the potency of their life, themselves are effective in destroying all hindrances and obstructions....*[3]

The human being who can do this in full consciousness is therefore an Initiate beyond the Third Initiation. He, and he alone, can safely raise these triple fires from the base of spine center to the head center.

Each level of development has its particular pattern of energy: square, triangular, or circular. As man develops and moves into the higher planes of existence, the geometrical forms of energy currents also change in the three vehicles of man. First, square formations predominate, then triangles, then circles. It is not always one kind of geometrical formation but mixed, or in a process of changing from one to another and then back again until esoteric stability is reached.

When man is controlled by the astral plane we are told that three centers are active and are related closely to each other, forming a triangular circulation of force. These centers are

- base of spine
- solar plexus
- heart

But if man is controlled by the mental plane, some of the centers are different, although they again form a triangular circulation of force. These centers are

- base of spine
- heart
- throat

When a man is Soul-infused, or an advanced human being, he has a different geometrical formation between the following centers:

- heart
- throat
- head
- base of spine

---

3. *Ibid.*, pp. 185-186.

- solar plexus
- ajna
- sacral
- alta major

A Third Degree Initiate uses

- heart center
- throat center
- the correspondences of the seven centers in the head

A Fifth Degree Initiate uses

- heart center
- seven head centers
- the thousand petaled Lotus

All these combinations create different radiations of colors, with different intensity and beauty. Seen from the subjective levels, an advanced man is an unfolding flower. Master Morya often refers to these flowers as the "flowers of My garden."

Each of these centers represents a major virtue, and when the virtue is found and cultivated, the center unfolds naturally and releases creative energies.

Some schools teach to sit and meditate on a particular center to raise it into action. Masters warn us not to play with the centers. They stress that a life of sacrificial service, a life lived in virtue and harmlessness, brings all the centers into activity and causes them to bloom at the right time.

Because of the progressive evolution of the Planetary and Solar Lives, stronger and more abundant energies are pouring down on humanity. These energies will either help humanity progress more rapidly, or they will create friction in the etheric centers if they are resisted and blocked along their path. This is why it is imperative that humanity refine itself, spiritualize its life, and create those conditions within which the sons of men can unfold their innate Divinity.

Nature has its ways to clean the blockages on the path of the Divine circulatory flow. Resistance to this flow will not only increase diseases but will also lead the planet into natural catastrophes. Disturbances in the energy system of the universe in one area will affect the rest of the world, and humanity will face great natural destructions. Assimilation of this energy flow is the key. This can be done through scientific meditation, sacrificial service, and a life of purity and striving.[4]

Groups can serve as healing agents when they are coordinated by love. They can render *radiatory healing* or *magnetic healing*. Radiatory healing is done when the group focuses all its *Soul energy* and concentrates on the center in the patient where the trouble exists. This must be done gradually so that the patient is able to assimilate and use the energy.

> *In radiatory healing,..."the healer must seek to link his soul, his brain, his heart and auric emanation."...*[5]

The group must be careful not to use *will energy.*

Radiatory healing can burn out all those etheric, emotional, and mental obstacles and hindrances within the sphere of the patient which prevent the circulatory flow of life energy from penetrating into all parts of his mechanism. By such removal of the obstacles, a new flow of energy starts to radiate from the Core of the patient's soul and, fusing with the radiatory energy of the group, it activates the healing of its own vehicles.

Magnetic healing is different. It is an evocative activity of the Soul energy of the group, which releases the fires of the patient's etheric, emotional, and mental bodies, revives them, and urges them to do the work of healing and purification wherever it is needed. It also absorbs those forces which are creating the diseases and passes them through the refinery of the group's etheric body, and thereby releases the patient.

The Ageless Wisdom teaches that there are Seven Rays which form the entire energy system of our solar system. We are told that these Rays are rivers or beams of light penetrating the whole Planetary Life and cyclically conditioning Its expressions. Our physical, emotional, and mental bodies respond to some of these Rays. Our personality responds also and has its own Ray; our soul also has its own Ray. Not all of the Seven Rays are in active manifestation at this time. Five great streams of energy primarily condition our life manifestation on the planet.

Each Ray has its own objective and subjective color.

Ray	**Objective Color**	**Subjective Color**
First Ray	orange	red
Second Ray	indigo with a tinge of purple	light blue
Third Ray	black	green

4. See also *Cosmic Shocks*, and *Earthquakes and Disasters, What the Teaching Tells Us.*
5. Alice A. Bailey, *Esoteric Healing*, p. 654.

Fourth Ray	green	yellow
Fifth Ray	yellow	indigo
Sixth Ray	red	silvery rose
Seventh Ray	white	violet

In healing with colors, it will be a great help if one knows what Ray colors the patient's bodies have. If the Ray of the vehicle is known, the healing group, through meditation, can use the same color to vitalize or purify the body or the organ.

The personality Ray color can be used for the three lower vehicles (physical, emotional, mental), plus the color of the vehicle in trouble. The soul color is not easy to find because in most people the soul is not as yet in active manifestation.

Using the combination of the colors of the Rays and centers, the healing group may render a good healing service for those who are in need.

In the Ageless Wisdom we learn that the base of spine center, the sacral center, and the solar plexus center are under the direct control of the first, second, and third lower ethers respectively. The heart center is controlled by the Fourth Cosmic Ether; the throat center is controlled by the Atmic Plane, the Third Cosmic Ether; the ajna center is controlled by the Monadic Plane, the Second Cosmic Ether; and the head center is controlled by the Divine Plane, the First Cosmic Ether.

The fourth lower ether assumes control of the three lower sacral centers which are the sacral center proper and the two sex centers — gonads or ovaries.

When the three personality vehicles are integrated, the lowest of the Cosmic Ethers, the Fourth, uses the head, the highest center, to blend the solar plexus and heart, leading to Soul-infusion.

The Will of the Central Life which is in man, in the globe, and in the solar system is impressed on the lives living in these three spheres through the Cosmic Ethers and the lower ethers. The action of these three spheres is checked by the four Lords of Karma through the higher and lower ethers.

The etheric body is the field of action and also the substance of action. We are told that the Plan of the Hierarchy is formed by the substance of the Fourth Cosmic Ether, and man will be able to understand and consciously work for the Plan when the substance of Intuition increases in the sphere of his etheric body. Even the impressions of Shamballa reach the human being via the Cosmic Ethers.

Continuity of consciousness starts when, for the first time, the etheric web which is separating the physical brain from the astral world is rent. Through this rent man comes in contact with subjective events and gradually becomes conscious on the mental plane; he comes in contact with his Solar Angel, and through the Solar Angel with his Master. Thus, one must build the bridge through the mental plane to be able to work consciously in the astral plane.

In the etheric body we have three very important centers which operate the whole sphere of human life, consciousness, and activity. They are the heart center, the head center, and the throat center.

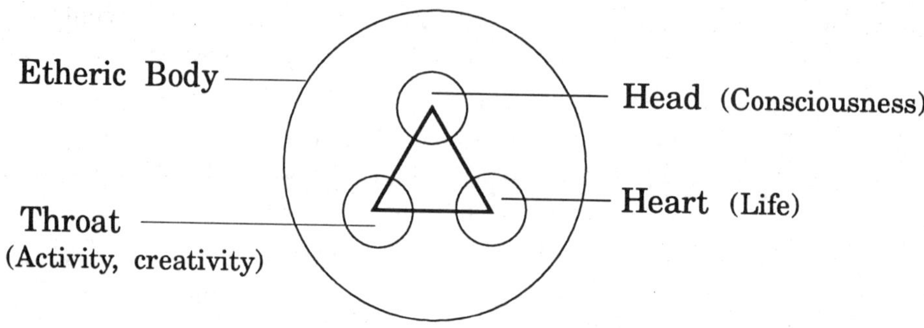

Diagram 10-1 Three Centers

These centers are the extensions and distributors of Monadic life.

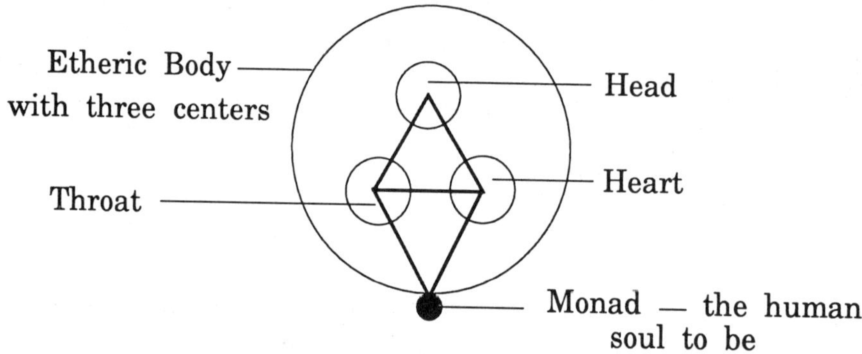

Diagram 10-2 The Monad and Three Centers

The Monad is identified with the physical body first. Then It progresses toward the astral, the mental, then higher bodies, and eventually It becomes Itself on the Monadic Plane.

The Monad is called the human soul as It journeys from the physical plane to the Monadic Plane. However, the Monad becomes a soul after a process of transformation which takes place when it fuses with the Solar Angel. In occult books this is called Soul-infusion, in which the human soul tunes in completely with the vision and frequency of the Solar Angel. This is called by mystics, "the marriage in heaven." We are told that it is the most powerful attachment of the human soul.

On his journey the human soul attaches himself to the physical nature, and this is a *tamasic* attachment.[6] Then he attaches himself to the astral body, and this is a *rajasic* attachment in which he is all motion and activity. The third attachment is with the Inner Guide. This is a *sattvic* attachment with all its beauty, glory, and ecstasy. Such an attachment binds the human soul for centuries. The only way to come out of this attachment is by the process known as **crucifixion**, a painful process which involves renouncement and isolation, like a forced separation from a most beloved one.

When the Monad is identified with the physical nature, It develops the **life principle** through the heart and through the heart center.

When the Monad is identified with the emotional nature, It develops **love energy** around the nucleus of life in the heart.

When the Monad is identified with the mental nature, It develops **intelligence** and creative energy around the nucleus of life and love.

In the same manner, when the Monad is identified with the physical plane, It develops **consciousness** in the head center.

When It is identified with the emotional plane, It develops **creative intelligence** around the nucleus of consciousness.

When It is in the mental plane, It develops **life energy** around the nucleus of consciousness and creative intelligence.

When these two centers — heart and head — are equipped with the threefold energy, Light, Love and Will, they create a fusion and project their united energy into the throat center. Thus the throat center receives

— a ray of life or will lighted by consciousness

— a ray of love energized by creative intelligence

— a ray of creative intelligence charged with the purpose of life

Through such a projection the throat center becomes the center of creativity in order to manifest the purpose of life — intelligently and with wisdom.

These three centers — the head, heart, and throat — with their threefold energies form the furnace of alchemy of the spiritual life. Later, as the progress of the Spark, or the human soul, emerges onto the Intuitional Plane, we see a change occurring in the centers. The head center pulls up the heart and throat centers, and a threefold head center comes into being with the heart holding the central power and position. The heart center becomes the heart center in the head, and the throat center becomes the throat center in the head.

---

6. For more information on the three gunas — *tamas*, *rajas*, and *sattva* — please refer to *The Science of Meditation*, pp. 130-136 and 158-161.

Through such a synthesis, the heart center in the head radiates willpower which reveals the Purpose of the greater Will of the Planetary and Solar Lives. The head center in the head radiates purposeful creativity charged with wisdom. The throat center in the head radiates purposeful activity charged with wisdom.

On the physical plane the three glands in the head — the pineal, pituitary, and carotid — serve as anchorages for the activities of these three centers in the head.

Thus, the Spark first projects lines or threads, and then travels from the physical to the etheric, from the etheric to the emotional, and from the emotional to the mental. Eventually the Spark, or the human soul, anchors himself in the twelve-petaled Lotus, where the process of fusion with the Solar Angel takes place.

This fusion is dissolved at the Fourth Initiation — the Crucifixion or Renunciation — then the Spark projects the higher counterparts of the previous three threads toward the three higher permanent atoms and forms a triad. He projects the life thread to the Atmic Permanent Atom, the consciousness thread to the Buddhic Permanent Atom, and the creative thread to the Manasic or Mental Permanent Atom. There, these permanent atoms form the Spiritual Triad, which is the higher counterpart of the twelve-petaled Lotus and which enables the Spark to establish deeper contacts with higher centers in Cosmic Space.

As the Spark, or the human soul, progresses from one level to another, from one plane to another, his healing power increases over his vehicles.

Our vehicles become sick because of outside pressures, pollution, and attacks and because of pressures coming from higher contacts. The healing energy released by the human soul is nothing else but a harmonizing energy. It harmonizes the bodies to the developing and increasing pressures of the Higher Worlds and builds a shield of higher frequency around the vehicles to protect them from outside, destructive, polluting factors. The success of the human soul in harmonizing the bodies with the frequencies of Higher Worlds brings health, happiness, and constructive creativity.

We must remember that the human soul is trained in his duties by the Solar Angel.

The human soul dwells in the heart. That is where the Self is. This heart is the etheric heart center. From the heart center the human soul operates the lower centers, such as the base of spine, the sacral center, and the solar plexus center, which are all in the etheric body.

It sometimes happens that the human soul identifies himself with material objects, sexual objects, food, drink, etc. At these moments he temporarily lives in these three centers. His presence overstimulates these centers and their corresponding glands and prepares the field of suffering and increases karma. He locates himself in the lower centers because of his lack of experience; because of the pulls of the body and pleasures; because of wrong education, the media, and wrong literature; because of his posthypnotic suggestions; and because of his debts.

When he is identified with the lower centers, the heart loses its virtues and goes through a process of slow petrification, resulting in criminal or crude actions for a long period of time. In such conditions the enslaved human soul functions against the laws of survival and compassion.

It is after long years of suffering and training that the human soul finally picks up the frequency of the Inner Guide and ascends to his throne in the heart center.

11

Coordination of Centers

..Nothing is permanent in Nature if it is not developed and unfolded under its own power, without any artificial stimulation.

As evolution proceeds, man comes in contact with higher and higher levels of consciousness. This is accomplished through unfolding his centers by means of meditation and sacrificial service.

The first centers that must be opened are the etheric centers. When the etheric centers open naturally and geometrically, man develops

1. Closer contact with the organs of his body
2. Closer relations with his family
3. Closer relations with his nation
4. Closer relations with humanity
5. Closer relations with global life
6. Closer relations with solar life
7. Closer relations with galactic life

Each unfoldment increases his joy and also increases his conscious suffering, according to the various conditions of life. One shares more as he advances. One's advancement makes him more inclusive, and inclusiveness carries him further forward.

When the person develops his emotional centers, he becomes influential emotionally. His emotional life reflects the emotional ocean of the nation, the planet, the solar system, and the galaxy. As his seven astral centers unfold geometrically, he becomes aware of

1. His own emotions
2. Family emotions

3. National emotions
4. Human emotions
5. Planetary emotions
6. Solar emotions
7. Galactic emotions

For example, we read in legends about the violent emotions of the gods of Olympus, or the marriage proposals of the seven Rishis to the seven Pleiades. Such events involve Cosmic anxieties, turbulences, excitements, or decisions. Such events also show how the decisions and events resulting from such events influence the millions of stars which compose the heavenly bodies. Even love waves between galaxies or solar systems create various conditions in Space!

Most human conditions are the echoes of the emotions of the Higher Worlds. We can have control over these spatial waves of emotions only when we focus ourselves in our Core and control our own emotional responses and reactions.

Evolution is based on the correct registration of impressions, the correct translation, the correct adaptation to our own level of understanding, and then living accordingly.

Each human center corresponds to a similar center within the planet, solar system, and galaxy. As the particular human center opens, it tunes to the corresponding higher center and shares its conditions. For example, as human beings have seven astral centers, a nation also has seven astral centers which are composed of different groups of people who collectively represent the astral centers of that nation. Thus in unfolding our astral centers, we tune ourselves to these centers.

We must emphasize that as our emotional centers open, we feel the joys and sorrows of people — whereas before we were limited only to our own joys and sorrows. We progress through joy and sorrow. We can control the emotions of the center only by focusing our consciousness on the next higher center. Then individual interests are lost in family interests, family interests are lost in national interests, and so on.

People wonder if the planet has emotions. It has, because the planet is the body of a psychological Entity. On Its own level, It has various emotions which originate from within or are imported from spatial events. For example, if a planetary Entity has a family relationship with another planetary Entity, known to It billions of years earlier, the first Entity will feel it if the second Entity is going through difficult times in Space. Also, It will feel joy if the other Entity is recording great achievements.

The life in the sky is the replica of the life of human beings, but it is a million times more intensive. It is only certain "blind people" who look at the stars and think they are fire balls or petrified elements thrown into Space for our amusement. For example, our planet is very closely related to Venus. What must Venus feel when the body of our planetary Life is eighty percent poisoned by so-called human beings?

We were not always unfeeling. I met a child who was crying over frozen fish. Another child did not eat his supper because his brother had broken a newly planted tree. Another child lay sick for a week when his lamb was slain. But when we grow, we shut off our centers, and even butchering people does not upset us!

It is not easy to unfold your fourth center — the heart center — if you are stuck to racism and nationalism. If you stay occupied too long with the third — the solar plexus — center, you turn into a source of trouble for humanity. The heart center never opens if a person does not overcome the emotions of separatism.

Between all seven centers, there are barriers. For example, if you are identified with your own emotions, you build a barrier, and you cannot identify with the emotions of your family. If you are identified with the emotions of your family and you are lost in them, it will be very difficult for you to pass to the next center and identify yourself with the emotions of your nation...and so on.

On every step of progress, there is a barrier that you must overcome. The barrier is the test. If you pass the test, you are in a greater life.

It is not easy to enter the next level, or to open your next center. There are things that must be left behind, things which you must renounce, and things you must build in order to be able to stand under greater pressures and greater responsibilities.

Many years and even lives are needed to pass from one center to another. Remember that centers are doors leading you to new conditions. Sometimes people, like a pendulum, fluctuate between the old and the new center before eventually settling themselves in the new condition.

There was a person who used to belong to a very fanatical church. It took him twenty-seven years to overcome his religious separatism, to read about and love other religions, and eventually to respect all faiths.

Many people are persecuted when their higher centers open. Sometimes society tries by all means to prevent the opening of your next center because, in their opinion, they lose you when you are subject to a higher influence which makes them uncomfortable. Of course, the interests of various groups are great barriers. It is not easy for them to let you go, just as it is not often easy for parents to see their children leaving home.

Many leaders speak about unity, but because their next higher center is not open, they still act in separatism. Of course they must talk more and more about unity until their being begins to accept the idea.

When the five centers are open, you sense planetary emotional states. When the six centers are open, which is very rare at this time, you feel solar emotions.

In one century only six or seven people are able to open the sixth center. Such people feel and register the emotional waves in the solar system.

The next center connects the person with the galaxy.

Let us repeat that as we open our higher centers, we enter into the pressure of emotions present in greater and higher fields of existence. This is why our personality vehicles must go through transmutation, transformation, and transfiguration so that we are able to stand under such pressures and are able to expand our consciousness and our field of sacrificial service.

All progress is achieved in acts of giving. You must give yourself to your family. You must give your family to your nation. You must give your nation to humanity. You must give humanity to the whole planetary Life. You must give the whole planetary Life to the solar system.... On each higher step, you sacrifice things that are uniting you, not with sorrow but with joy. Because the Cosmos exists within you, it is possible for you to climb toward the Cosmos.

The process of opening higher centers is the process of withdrawal of the human soul into the higher vehicles. When each center unfolds, it puts you in contact with a higher sphere of influence. The whole process of evolution can be formulated as follows:

Progress depends on your ability to contact and register the contact. It depends on your right translation of your registration and on your ability to adapt your life to your understanding of the registration.

People think that as you lose your lower interests and lower identity, you lose yourself; but the reality is that as you lose your former self, you enter into your greater Self. This is why to find your True Self you must always lose yourself. This process takes you through seven stages:

1. You have your Self.
2. You have the family Self.
3. You have the national Self.
4. You have the Self of humanity.
5. You have the global Self.
6. You have the solar Self.
7. You have the galactic Self.

You never lose your Self, but you find it in higher and higher planes or spheres.

The concept of the galactic Self is not easy to understand. One day a cell of the body asked the next cell, which was a little wiser, "What is man?"

The other cell answered, "He is a finger."

Then the finger asked the thumb, "What is man?"

"Oh, silly finger," he said, "Man is an arm."

Then the arm asked the next arm, "What is man?"

The arm said, "Man is a shoulder from which we are hanging."

Eventually the body asked its internal organs, "What is man?"

And the internal organs answered, "Man is a totality. You and we are man."

But they were not yet able to ask about the emotions, thoughts, soul, or creative powers in man....

The galactic Self can be understood only when we become that Self. Before that, we are cells, organs, members; body, emotions, and thoughts. Each unfolding center makes you conscious of the next stage of the Self.

You do not exist until you are conscious of your existence on a particular level. For example, when your astral centers are open, you can live on the astral plane as an astral entity.

The seven etheric centers have their correspondences in the head. The thousand-petaled Lotus is the sum total of the petals of all the etheric centers. Do not confuse the head centers with the centers of the mental plane.

When you begin to open your head centers, you go through similar changes in your consciousness. When the first head center opens, you become conscious of the thoughts of your Inner Guardian.

When the second head center unfolds, you become slowly sensitive to the thoughts of others. This is a great progress.

When the third head center unfolds, you are able to read the thoughts of a nation or the thoughts of groups in the nation.

When the fourth head center opens, you become aware of the thoughts of humanity and the thoughts of nations composing humanity.

When the fifth head center unfolds, you become aware of the thoughts of the One Who ensouls our globe. Of course this is a very advanced stage, and only a few people reach it in any century.

When the sixth head center opens, you become aware of solar or spatial thoughts.

When the seventh head center opens, you receive impressions from galactic sources. These impressions are mighty waves of thought. They do not exist for those who do not have their seventh center in the head open.

The centers in the mental plane are

1. Base of spine
2. Generative organs
3. Solar Plexus
4. Spleen

These along with the mental unit are located in the fourth level of the mental plane.

When all these centers are active, you can live as a mental entity in the mental plane.

Each registration of a thoughtwave creates reaction, action, assimilation, reorganization, expansion of consciousness, a little deeper understanding of life, synthesis, change of level, and opening of new centers. The ability to register thoughts from higher and higher levels is the source of many ideas, inspirations, and impressions coming from spatial sources.

People often think that the brain thinks or the mind thinks. In reality, neither the brain nor the mind thinks. The Thinker is either the Solar Angel or the human soul. The brain is the typewriter; the mind is the fingers.

When you are in the astral or mental plane, you do not need the brain. When you are in the Intuitional Plane, you do not need the mind because you communicate directly. Thinking is direct communication between the Solar Angel and the human soul. But if you want to communicate with the physical plane from the Intuitional Plane, you need the brain and mind, or you use the brain and mind of someone else.

Real thinking is an endeavor or an effort to harmonize your life with the life of the galaxy. If you are thinking thoughts (or speaking or doing things) that are not in harmony with the Purpose of the galactic Life, you are not thinking. Thinking should always be an effort to harmonize your being to the life of the galaxy.

If you are in harmony, you think in terms of pro-survival, Beauty, Goodness, Righteousness, Joy, Freedom, and fusion — that is, you think in harmony with all that exists.

Thinking is like playing an instrument which has seven strings. If this instrument is not in tune, you can try to play music but it comes out as noise.

These seven strings are

— Pro-survival thoughts, words, and actions

— Beauty

— Goodness

— Righteousness

— Joy

— Freedom

— Fusion or synthesis

If these elements are not in existence in your nature, your thinking is not thinking; your music is noise and abortion. You must see which strings are absent or not in harmony. Your instrument must be tuned to the principle of the galactic

Vision and the galactic Life. Thinking means to produce music on a tuned instrument.

You sit down and play a piano sonata, but the piano is out of tune. Are you really playing the sonata, or are you creating a terrible noise? The latter is what thinking is for the majority of humanity, including those who have graduated from sophisticated branches of learning.

People may ask, "Are not all scientists thinkers, and isn't science a product of thinking?" An honest answer to that question will be, "No."

There is no true science if the subjective and objective realities are not considered and related. Most thinking is abortive and without a soul. Our science still has no soul, and actions resulting from such a science pose grave dangers to human evolution, just as do children born without a human soul.

Suppose a person created some medicine which is good for the physical body but very bad for the mental body; suppose it strengthens the energy in the body but destroys the reservoir of energy in the spiritual body. Suppose one conquers a nation with an atomic bomb but puts in action a tidal wave which will come back and destroy that conquering nation.... What kind of thinking is this?

Present day science is blind. It has no enlightenment about the realities, laws, and principles found on the subjective planes. It is like a child who plays with the hands of a clock without considering the wheels and gears behind the hands. The conclusion is that we do not have yet a real science.

We must consider the coordination of the centers. What does coordination mean? Coordination can be defined as

1. **A cooperative relationship** between centers on one plane. Not all our centers are cooperative yet. This is why we have various ailments and technicolor disturbances on various planes of the personality.

2. **Attunement** with the Core Center, which is the Chalice.

3. **Synchronization** of the centers found on one plane with the centers found on various other planes.

We must consider that there is horizontal and vertical coordination. Vertical coordination is intended to coordinate the etheric chakras with the astral and mental chakras. Horizontal coordination is coordination of the centers on the same plane.

There is another geometrical form created when the solar plexus, heart chakra, and throat chakra of the etheric body coordinate themselves with similar or other chakras of the astral or mental planes. Other geometrical forms are created when they are connected with the petals of the Chalice. All these coordinations build the network of **sensitivity** for incoming impressions.

Coordination takes place either sequentially or in geometrical forms. The Soul organizes a geometrical procedure because of various needs and conditions of life and of the advancing human soul.

A geometrical procedure is not sequential. It connects various centers on one or several planes, building geometrical forms such as triangles, squares, or pentagons. For example, a geometrical form is created when the solar plexus, heart, and throat function as one unit for certain goals.

Sequential coordination goes from number one to number seven simultaneously on all planes, although number one is not the first center but, rather, any center that is more open — from past lives and so on.

Geometrical coordination takes place according to the need of the time and the responsibility of the human soul. For example, if you are going to act as a leader, you need three important energies — the energies of the First Ray, Fifth Ray, and Seventh Ray. You coordinate the head center, ajna center, and sacral center. Then you have the triangle of a politician.

You can add the heart center (Second Ray) and turn the geometrical form into a square. Or you can coordinate these configurations with other chakras on the astral and mental planes and make your leadership a really powerful and glorious accomplishment.

Coordination does not stop on the human level. You may coordinate your chakras with the chakras of your Solar Angel, your Master, the Hierarchy, the planet, the solar system, or the galaxy. Thus, coordination is an ever growing process until the Son is perfect in the Father.

The Rays, the seven fields of human endeavor, and the chakras can be tabulated as follows:

RAY	CHAKRA	FIELD
1st	head	politics
2nd	heart	education
3rd	throat	philosophy, communication
4th	base of spine	arts
5th	ajna	science
6th	solar plexus	religion, devotion
7th	sacral	economics, finance, rituals

The Seven Rays, the seven fields of human endeavor, and the seven chakras on the three planes must eventually be coordinated to produce a great server like Christ. Coordination of the centers gradually leads a person into higher and higher initiations. Higher psychism is an impossibility without coordination of the centers. Coordination provides the foundation for communication between the abstract and the concrete.

How does one coordinate the centers? There are three factors which assist in the work of coordination:

1. Purification of the chakras; using them purposefully and economically and avoiding pollution that contaminates their corresponding organs.

2. Expanding the consciousness; thinking more and more in terms of the whole; increasing your viewpoints and the viewpoints of others; spreading Beauty, Goodness, Righteousness, Joy, and Freedom in the world.

3. Developing virtues and applying them in a creative life and sacrificial service.

When these three methods are used intelligently, you will see that all your actions, words, and thoughts are charged with the energy of the etheric centers, with the emotions of the astral centers, and with the fiery thoughts of the mental centers. Thus every action of such a person will be charged by thoughts and emotions; every emotion will be charged by thought and experienced through action; every thought will be charged by emotion and experienced through action.

Every center has three functions:

— thought

— feeling

— action

In the mental plane, thought is prevalent. In the astral plane, emotion is prevalent. In the physical plane, action is prevalent.

Coordination of the centers makes our actions on any level powerful and influential.

People are either full of ideas, or they live in emotional dreams and excitement, or they are all action. Idealism is not only to have ideas but also to live by them. Coordination of the chakras heals this divided situation.

Coordination does not stop with the chakras; it goes on to synchronize with the senses. We have chakras, senses, and organs. It is a great achievement to coordinate these three on all planes. A Master is one Who has achieved this coordination.

It is also very important to remember that when all the etheric centers are coordinated with each other, the etheric body becomes one center. The same is true with the other bodies: the whole emotional body becomes one center; the whole mental body becomes one center. When coordination between these bodies reaches perfection, the personality — the mental, emotional, etheric, and physical bodies — becomes **one center**.

Thus we see three centers — the personality, the human soul, and the Solar Angel. Later, when evolution proceeds in the right way, the human soul melts away in the Self, the Solar Angel departs, and we have only two centers — the Self, and the personality acting as the mechanism of the Self. During such a coordinating process a person becomes fused with humanity, Hierarchy, and Shamballa — the three planetary Centers.

Let us look at the factors that assist the work of coordination in detail.

Purification of the chakras is the first factor in the coordination of centers, and this can be achieved by using them goalfittingly or purposefully. For example, the sacral center chakra is overused and polluted by wrong use; the throat center is misused by idle and false speech, through wrong communications, and through leading others and ourselves into confusion. Purification means to introduce into your sex life a better relationship; to use your knowledge in the right way and for the benefit of others; to use your words or the power of speech to increase Beauty, Goodness, Righteousness, Joy, and Freedom.

You must also economize your energies. Wasting energy is a great transgression against the Source of energy. Any waste of energy creates disharmony between the forces that give and those who receive. Wasting not only saps the energy of the center but also forces it to borrow energy from its higher or lower correspondences, thus overloading the activities of both and eventually burning them.

Avoiding pollutants is connected to purification. For example, sexual intercourse with people without discrimination and at the expense of higher responsibilities and tasks pollutes not only the etheric centers but also the astral and mental centers and even the Chalice. Contaminated persons can ruin not only your present life but also your future lives.

Sexual intercourse is the fusion between all the active centers. The fusion either uplifts your centers or pollutes and destroys them, with many psychological and physical consequences.

Even association or close contact with people who are polluted may affect your aura destructively.

The second factor in the work of coordinating the centers is expansion of consciousness. Any change in the centers on the three levels must start through our consciousness. Discrimination is the result of the purity of our consciousness. Understanding is the result of expanding the consciousness. Illumination is the result of raising the consciousness from one plane to another plane.

Conscious expansion of our consciousness starts from the lowest level of the mental plane, which is related to the physical body. Then it rises to the fourth level of the mental plane, which is related to the astral plane. Then it rises to the higher mental plane, which is related to the mental body, the Solar Angel, and the human soul.

A gradually expanding consciousness creates a psychic pressure upon the Core of the centers and makes them bloom naturally. The safest method to expand the consciousness is to meditate on virtues and try to actualize them in your daily life.

The third factor in the process of coordination is the application of virtues in a creative life and in sacrificial service. Conscious creativity is related to your sacrificial service used to spread the Ageless Wisdom, Beauty, Goodness, Righteousness, Joy, and Freedom and to uplift the consciousness of others. You can serve if your thoughts, words, actions, and creative expressions are spreading these principles.

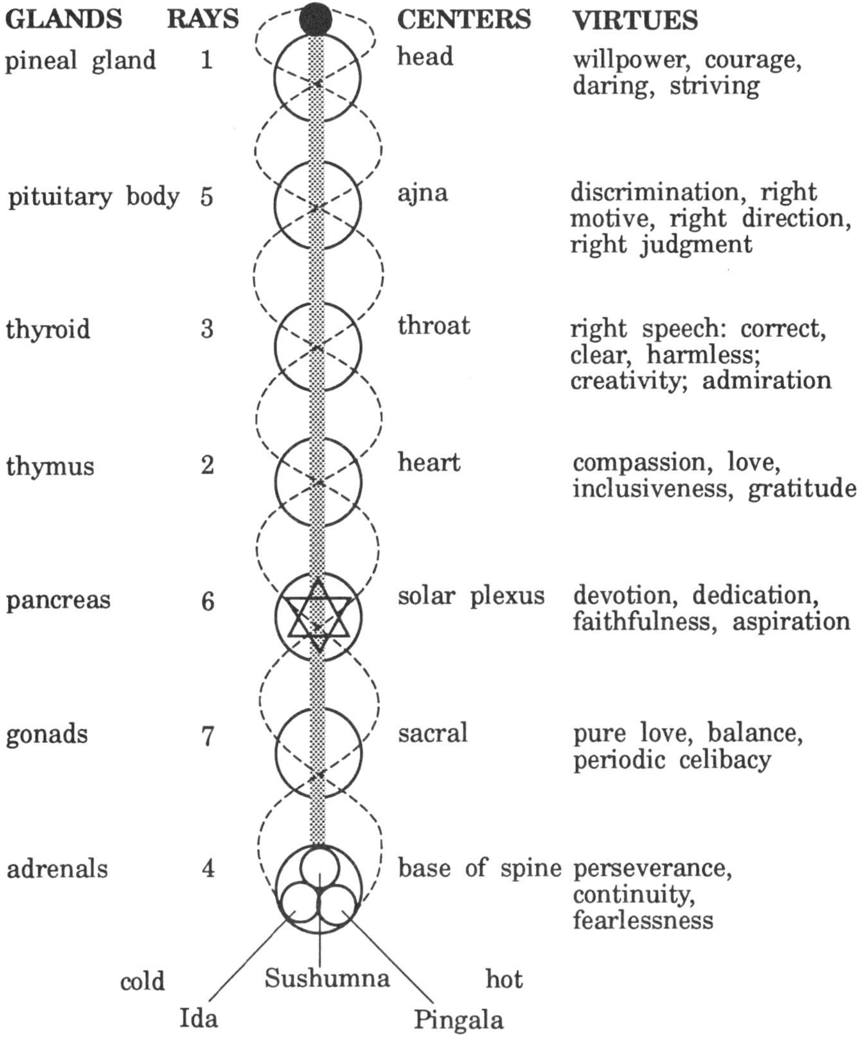

Diagram 11-1 Ida, Sushumna, Pingala

In the astral plane we have the exact replica of these centers which control our emotional life and emotional body and relate it to the etheric and physical bodies. On the mental plane we have a different arrangement.

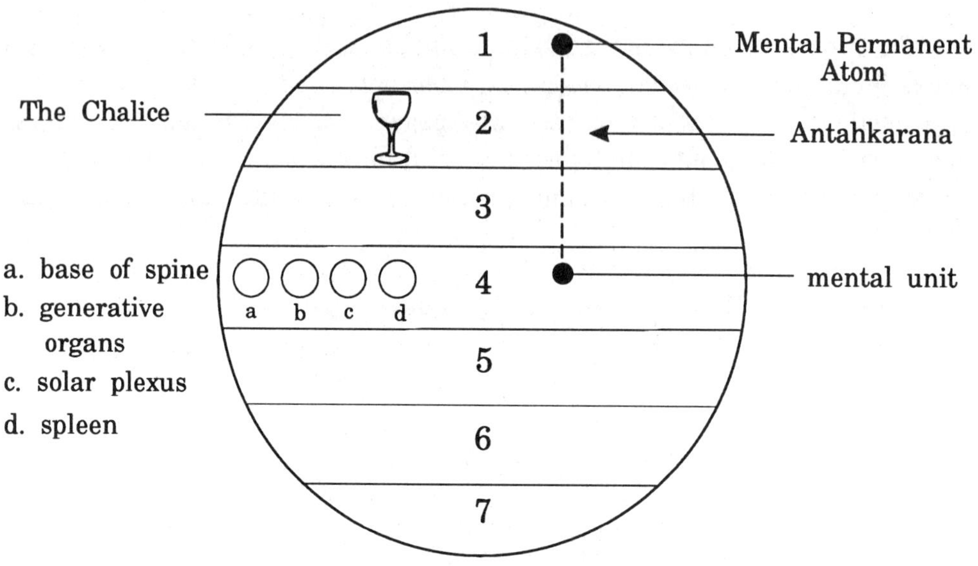

Diagram 11-2 The Mental Plane

What is the benefit of coordination? A machine can work with forty, sixty, or one hundred percent efficiency, according to the coordination of its parts with the source of energy. When a person's centers are coordinated, he has the most supreme instrument in his hand to enjoy

— health

— happiness

— communication with Higher Worlds

— creativity

— nobility

— joy

— beauty

— freedom

Such a person functions differently than the average person; all his thoughts, emotions, and actions are one current of energy. His physical actions have emotions and thoughts behind them. He has emotions in which he has thought and which are expressed with action. He has thoughts in which emotions are present and which are expressed intelligently through action.

Temple dances are a great means to create coordination between the centers if they are done with mental vision, with emotional enthusiasm, and with corresponding and proper movements.

One must know that centers cannot reach any coordination except when they are unfolded naturally, through the expansion of consciousness.

We have three modes of existence:

— havingness or knowingness

— activity

— beingness or rhythm

In the central point of each chakra a core is found which is rhythm or atomic substance, esoterically understood. When the consciousness expands and beingness increases, this core releases a fire which expands out like flames. These are the petals of the center. As the petals open, knowledge turns into action, then into beingness — because the atomic substance increases in the vehicles concerned and causes transmutation, transformation, and transfiguration.

If the petals are not open, knowledge accumulates and eventually forces man to act; but knowledge and accumulation of data and use of knowledge in various ways does not mean the transformation or transfiguration of man. If transformation does not take place, man uses his knowledge and possessions against his own survival and against his own progress.

Knowledge and possessions make a person eventually the enemy of others. A certain percentage of beingness may balance this situation.

The most important center which must be unfolded and developed is the heart center. Once the heart center begins to operate, it makes you sensitive to the needs of people and the hindrances in them. You become inclusive; you work and live for unity. The heart center puts you in contact with the heart of the planet, the solar system, and the galaxy and makes you sense the heartbeat of these centers. Through your heart circulates the flow of life of these centers, unifying your heart with the Cosmic Heart.

Gratitude is a very important activator of the heart center. As one develops gratitude, the heart center opens with eleven other virtues.[1]

---

1. Please refer to *The Psyche and Psychism*, pp. 905-1165, and *The Flame of the Heart.*

The head center puts you in contact with the Command Centers of the planet, solar system, and galaxy. Through this contact you find your **direction**. You have no direction if you are not in contact with the Command Centers within you, the planet, the solar system, and the galaxy.

Direction means to find the Path leading you Home. This Path is never found unless you come in contact with the Command Centers.

The ajna center uses the energies of the heart and head with discrimination, right motive, and right judgment. This is a great healing center which operates through the eyes, directing the energies of light, love, and power.

The ajna center unfolds as a result of our efforts in discrimination and right motive. When these concepts become part of our consciousness, the center opens. Any wrong sort of discrimination or wrong motive blocks this center.

The throat center is related to speech and creativity. Discipline to use right speech and efforts to be creative gradually unfold the throat center.

Any center is very sensitive to right energy and wrong force. Negative things close it; positive efforts open it. The center is damaged if hot and cold or right and wrong alternate continuously.

One must never directly concentrate upon the chakras until he passes the Third Initiation. The Third Initiation is the total transfiguration of the three vehicles of the personality. It is after the purification of the vehicles that the further unfoldment of the centers can be carried out directly, through meditation and visualization. Before the Third Initiation, any impurity in the environment of the centers creates **combustion** or severe health problems.

The throat center is also activated during admiration, ecstasy, bliss, and the appreciation of beauty and the arts. Those who are seriously concerned with unfolding their throat chakra must learn an aspect of the arts and try to be creative in it. It is also very important to economize the sexual energy because these two chakras are very closely connected to each other. Cyclic celibacy greatly helps the throat chakra unfold.

The solar plexus is composed of two parts — higher and lower. The lower triangle has been active for centuries. To minimize its disturbing influence and to open the higher counterpart, one should dedicate his life to a great service with intense devotion and aspiration.

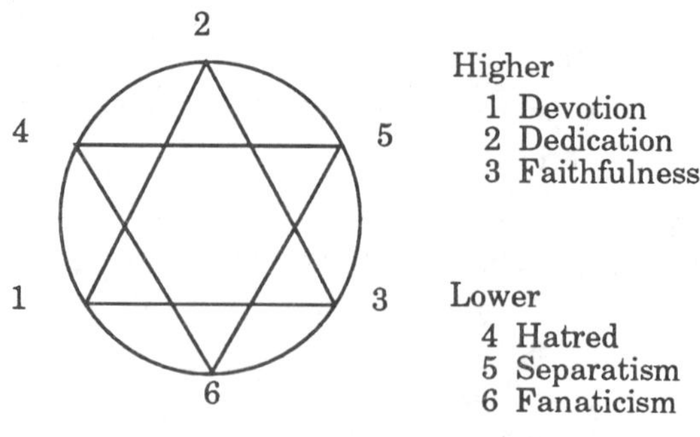

Diagram 11-3 The Solar Plexus

Faithfulness to your friends, family, and co-workers creates the needed tension to make the petals of the solar plexus unfold. Dedication, devotion, and faithfulness create a fiery sphere around the center, which gradually becomes magnetic and inflames the lives of those who are in any way related to you.

The sacral center is also wide open in general. One can modify the energy pouring through the petals and sublimate it by changing the desire for sex into aspiration and creative activity. Sex must be moderated with the virtues of chastity and purity and even with periodic celibacy. The Seventh Ray has a strong influence on this center. If the above virtues are exercised, the center becomes magnetic and a powerful source of cooperative energy.

The base of spine center must not be meditated upon (nor should the other centers), but instead one must develop and meditate upon

— fearlessness

— perseverance

— constancy

Every time we overcome a hindrance with a conscious effort, we help the petals of this center unfold. The petals are actually flames which form when the Central Fire in the center begins to flow out into the aura. One does not need to try to raise the kundalini fire. It climbs naturally by itself as the person lives a life of striving and overcomes the difficulties and obstacles of life. Naturally, it takes centuries, but nothing is permanent in Nature if it is not developed and unfolded under its own power, without any artificial stimulation.

12

The Kundalini Fire

The kundalini fire rises as the etheric webs slowly melt away, and the agelong accumulations in the channels are cleaned out. These webs melt away when each center becomes purified and fiery due to right living, right thinking, right meditation, and sacrificial service.

In the etheric body, around the base of spine center, there is the three-fold fire of the *kundalini*, or *serpent fire*. This fire is coiled within the base of spine center and provides life for the atoms of the physical body. The kundalini fire has three channels which rise upward along the spine to the head through the other centers on the etheric spine.

Between each of these centers on the spine there is an etheric web. There is one between the base of spine and sacral center; another between the sacral center and solar plexus; a third is located between the solar plexus and heart center; and a fourth is between the heart center and throat center. We have other webs in the head, and we are told that they bisect the skull horizontally and vertically.

Master Djwhal Khul says,

> *The three channels up the spine are responsive in their totality to the three major centres:*
>
> *a. To the solar plexus centre, providing thus the impulse of desire and feeding the physical life and creative urge.*
>
> *b. To the heart centre, providing the impulse to love and to conscious contact with ever widening areas of divine expression.*
>
> *c. To the head centre, providing the dynamic impulse of the will to live.*[1]

These three channels in Sanskrit are called

1. Alice A. Bailey, *Esoteric Healing*, p. 187.

- *ida*
- *pingala*
- *sushumna*

Ida is related to matter, or the intelligence aspect; *pingala* is related to the Soul or the love-wisdom aspect; *sushumna* is related to the Monad or the will aspect. We are told that the sushumna channel, the middle channel, is responsive to the head center. For safety reasons, we have no information about which centers are responsive to the other two channels.

The three channels are related to three Rays and also to the three stages on the Path. For example, the *sushumna* center is related to the Path of Initiation; the other channels are related to the Path of Evolution and to the Path of Discipleship.

This threefold fire climbs the spine in natural and proper geometrical order when the four lower ethers are in the process of transmutation; or in other words, when the higher Cosmic Ethers are replacing the lower ethers. As this process of transmutation takes place, the fire from the sacral center rises slowly and anchors itself within the three head centers: namely, within the alta major center, within the ajna center, and within the thousand-petaled Lotus or head center.

The blending of fire proceeds in the following way: The kundalini fire, which is a triple fire, rises through the etheric spine up to the base of the skull. The pranic fire and the kundalini fire, which are called the fires of matter, blend and fuse within the center between the shoulder blades. The next step is to lift this fire to the head where there is another triangle formed by the alta major center, pineal gland, and pituitary body. The united fire of matter approaches the skull and enters the triangle of the head via the alta major center.

We are told that there is a gap between the alta major center and the point on the spine from where the fires of matter will depart. This gap can be bridged by an etheric channel which will allow the fire to ascend into the skull via the alta major center. This bridge is built through meditation, dedication, and through intense striving. Once the passage of the fire is built, the fire establishes a continuous flow into the alta major center, and the etheric channel is no longer needed.

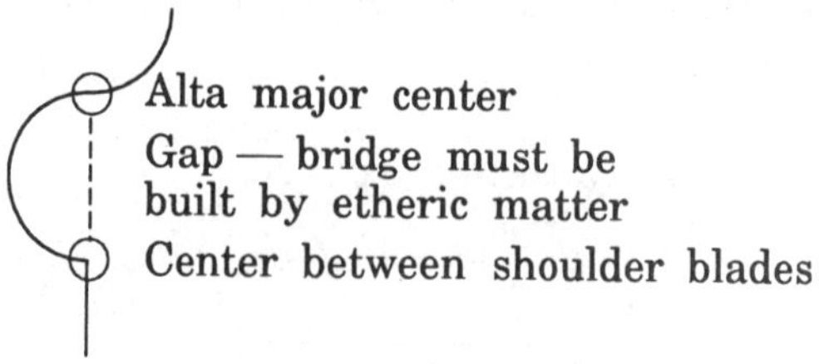

Diagram 12-1 Antahkarana

In the skull, and at the center of the triangle of mental fire, the second fusion takes place. The two fires of matter and the mental fire fuse and blend.

The next fusion takes place when these fires blend with the electrical fire of the Spiritual Triad through the thousand-petaled Lotus. These fires travel through the Antahkarana, the bridge which unites the lower mind, the Lotus, and Spiritual Triad via the Mental Permanent Atom.

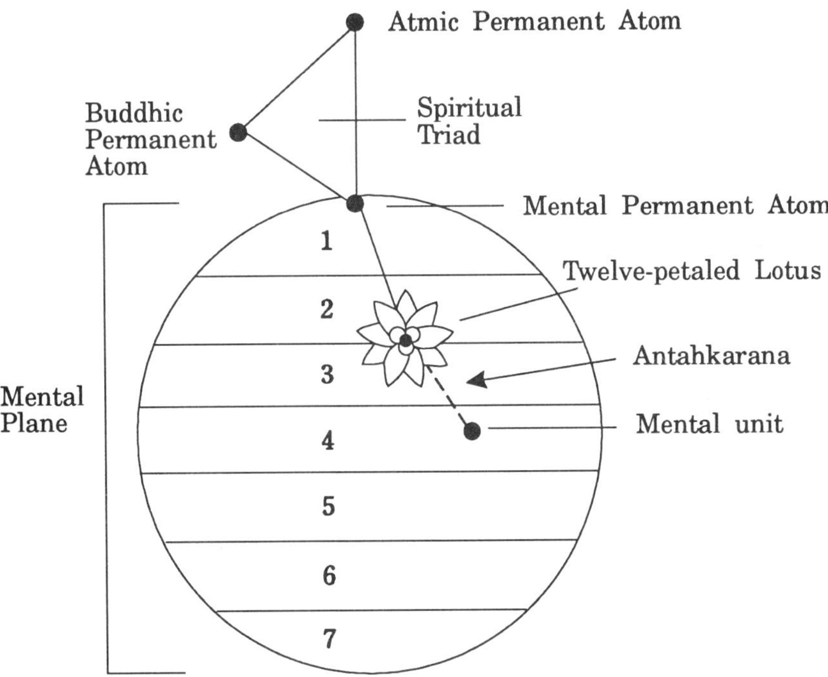

Diagram 12-2 Antahkarana

Soul-infusion is the result of the blending of the fires of matter and mind. Such an infusion grants good health to the body and provides abundant energy which is used for a great service carried out under all kinds of pressures.

When these fires blend with the fire of Spirit, Transfiguration is the result and the Antahkarana is complete.

The Master D.K. says the fire of kundalini

> *...is only roused into full activity by an act of the will, directed and controlled by the initiate. It is responsive only to the will aspect, and the will-to-be in incarnation is the factor which at present controls its life and produces its effects as it feeds and directs the life principle in matter and form....The true occultist in training has naught to do with the kundalini fire.... I must refrain from indicating modes and methods of arousing the*

> *activity of this centre, on account of the extreme danger involved in any premature work on the basic centre....*[2]

The three channels of the kundalini are the paths of the Supreme Fire which expresses Itself as *Electric Fire, Solar Fire*, and *Fire by Friction.*

Fire by Friction provides the heat for the cells and the atoms. *Solar Fire* provides consciousness and sentiency. *Electric Fire* provides the will. These three Fires can be raised and directed to their corresponding head centers through the "use of a word of power sent forth by the will of the Monad," and by the power of the Soul-infused personality. This is done only by a man who has already left behind the Third Initiation, the Transfiguration.

The kundalini fire rises as the etheric webs slowly melt away, and the agelong accumulations in the channels are cleaned out. These webs melt away when each center becomes purified and fiery due to **right living, right thinking, right meditation,** and **sacrificial service**.

In Sanskrit, this base of spine center is called the *muladhara chakra.* It has four petals and three colors: red, crimson, and orange. Each petal has a Sanskrit letter indicating its proper vibration. They are *va, sha, sha, sa.* At the center of this chakra lies the serpent fire, the threefold fire.

> *...When this process [of raising kundalini fire] is carried forward with care and due safeguards, and under direction, and when the process is spread over a long period of time there is little risk of danger, and the awakening will take place normally and under the law of being itself. If, however, the tuning up and awakening is forced, or is brought about by exercises of various kinds before the student is ready and before the bodies are coordinated and developed, then the aspirant is headed towards disaster. Breathing exercises or pranayama training should never be undertaken without expert guidance and only after years of spiritual application, devotion and service;... I cannot impress too strongly upon aspirants in all occult schools that the yoga for this transition period is the yoga of one-pointed intent, of directed purpose, of a constant practice of the Presence of God, and of ordered regular meditation carried forward systematically and steadily over years of effort.*[3]

2. *Ibid.*, pp. 181-182.
3. Alice A. Bailey, *Externalisation of the Hierarchy*, p. 18.

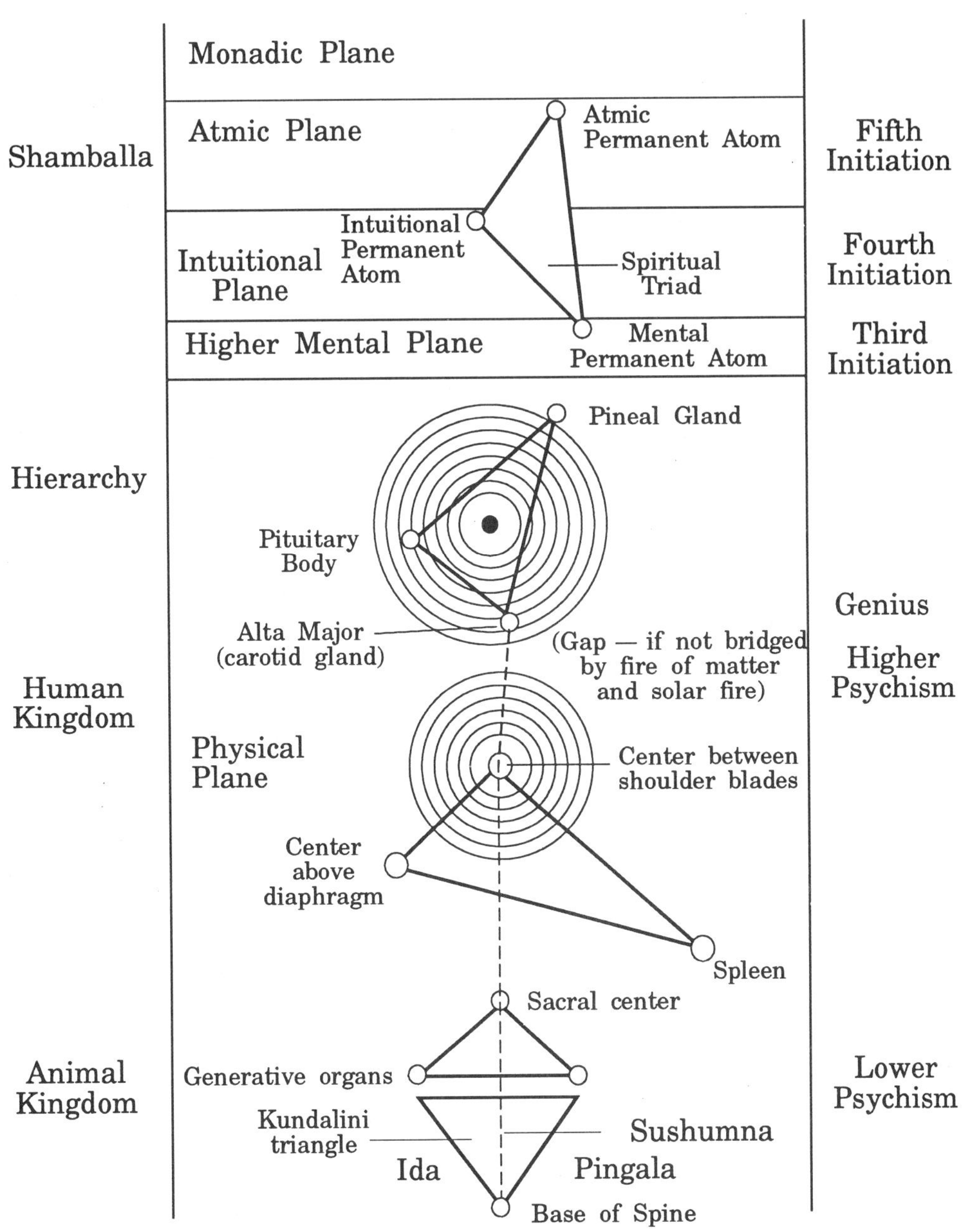

Diagram 12-3 Path of Kundalini Fire

As the aspirant progresses on the path of purity, service, and meditation, the triangle of the pranic center glows with a golden light into which slowly merges and fuses the rising fire of the threefold kundalini. This merging and fusing takes place at a center which is located between the shoulder blades. The kundalini fire and pranic fires are called "the fires of matter." As these fires fuse within each other, they energize and vitalize the cells and the atoms of the body, and the man radiates out healing and vitalizing energy through all his contacts.

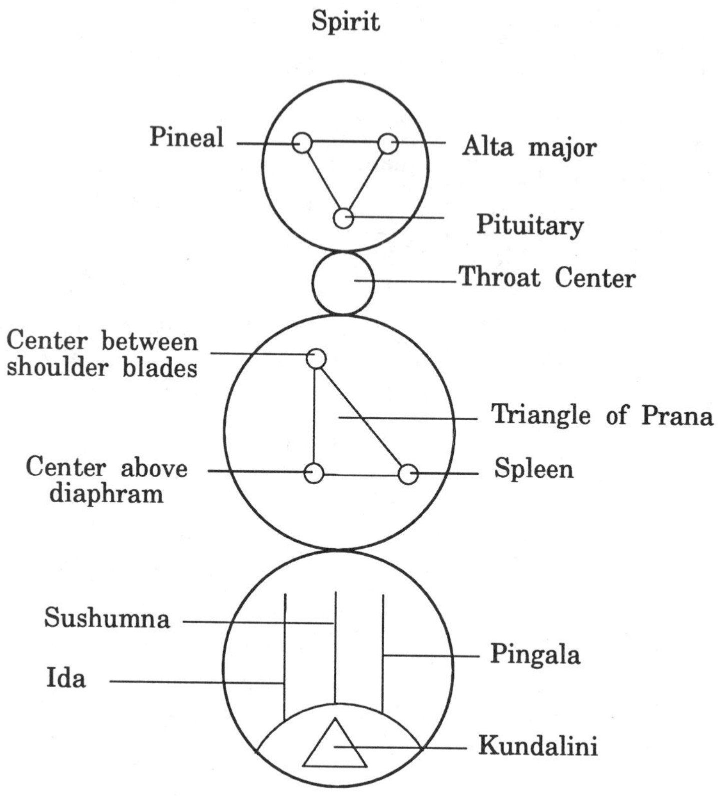

Diagram 12-4 Kundalini and Pranic Fires

The merging of these two fires attracts the third fire, the fire of the Spirit, which flows down into the man through the thousand-petaled Lotus. The thousand-petaled Lotus is the sum total, in the head, of the counterparts of all the seven centers. As the fire of Spirit descends through this center, all the centers in the etheric body are synchronized, vitalized, and energized. It is in the thousand-petaled Lotus that eventually all three fires meet and fuse. It is at this stage that higher psychic powers manifest.

As the fires of the kundalini climb up the etheric spine, they meet the fire of mind at the gate of the throat center, where the fire of mind burns. This contact leads the fires toward the pineal gland and the pituitary body. Once this linkage is accomplished, the alta major center comes into action and forms a triangle of fire with the pineal gland and the pituitary body.

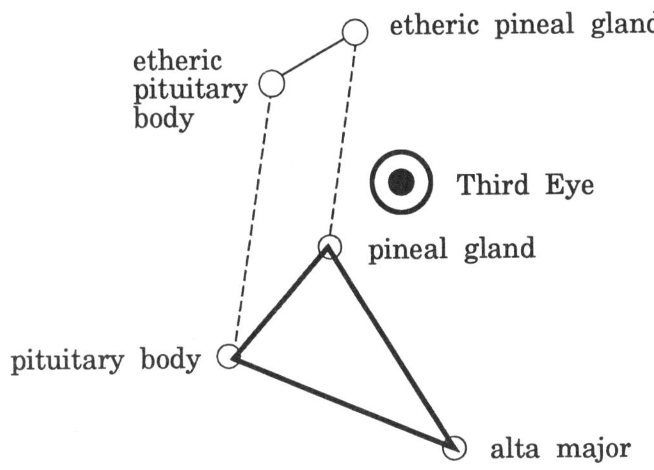

Diagram 12-5 The Third Eye

The throat center bridges, in a sense, the gap which exists between the alta major center and the point on the top of the spine where the fires of matter reach. The bridge in the etheric body between this point and the alta major center is built by the creative activities of man inspired by the unfolding throat center and the man's functioning in mental matter. Thus, the threefold kundalini fire, the three spheres of light of the three centers in the head, and the pranic fire blend and fuse within each other in rhythmic colors and waves.

We are told that this occurs between the first initiation and the Fourth Initiation, during which the etheric body is totally purified and the fire of kundalini can rise without hindrance and danger. The raising of the kundalini produces greater willpower, continuity of consciousness, and a deeper love to serve and sacrifice. As the synchronization of these centers progresses, the Initiate gradually comes in contact with the throat center of the planet, humanity. For the first time he sees humanity as one center and feels responsibility toward humanity.

Then the Initiate contacts his Teacher, the Ashram, and the second planetary center, the Hierarchy.

Eventually, as his initiations proceed, he contacts Shamballa, the head center of the planet. These closer and higher contacts result in more creative and sacrificial service.

We can better understand how a Master uses the heating and cooling systems of the kundalini by comparing them with the functioning of an electric refrigerator or gas stove. These fires produce heating or cooling, controlled by the central fire, or *sushumna.*

The etheric body is the vehicle of prana and the prototype of the physical body. It also protects the fires of the spine from premature contact with each other. In addition, the etheric body prevents the premature contact between the centers on the various planes, and keeps the pranic currents from mixing with the triangle of higher centers and the kundalini. Along with this role of separating and protecting, the etheric body relates all fiery systems to one another until the time when safe fusion is possible.

We are told that the three kundalini fires compose an etheric thermostat through which one can cool his body or increase its heat as the need arises. A Master is not affected by the cold on high mountains with elevations of fifteen or sixteen thousand feet because He can put His internal fire into action. A Master can also control His body heat by operating the cooling system of the kundalini. A Master feels the cold but is not affected by it.

Many people are already successful in fusing the fires of matter, or the kundalini and pranic fires. But the long-range goal is to fuse each fire of the kundalini with each fire of the pranic triangle. These fires are lifted up to higher fires only through

— self-discipline

— mind control

— purification of physical, emotional, and mental bodies

— dedicated, sacrificial service

— joy

We are told that when the kundalini blends with the pranic fire, the etheric centers become three-dimensional. They become four-dimensional when they fuse with the mental fire. They become six-dimensional when the fires fuse with the fire of Spirit.

Continuity of consciousness is the result of the destruction of the etheric webs on the etheric spine and in the head. Kundalini fire, through its increasing radiation, helps to melt away these webs. This implies that physical health and longevity can be achieved by fusing these fires which provide the best harmonious conditions for health. Actually, health is the result of increasing harmony between these three fires.

When the fire of kundalini is forced to rise up through the etheric channels, the following very dangerous conditions may be created:

1. The fire passes extra fuel to the center or centers involved and distorts the harmony between the glands, organs, and centers. When the gland and organ are not purified together with their etheric counterparts, the extra activity in the centers causes great damage to the glands and organs, burning them with a flow of energy which they cannot handle.

Many organic sicknesses come into existence because of an overflow of fire into the system. The overflow of fire first appears as overstimulation in the centers; then as an urge to satisfy the demands of the overstimulation; then the burning out of the organs starts with congestion, degenerative diseases, or partial or total paralysis of the organs.

The raising of the kundalini fire can be beneficial when guided by a great clairvoyant teacher who knows how to control the dosage of the fire and sees the conditions of related glands or organs. But the safest method is to purify oneself from the glamors, illusions, maya, or crystallizations within the threefold system through discipline, service, and meditation.

Purification, meditation, service, and discipline expand our consciousness. Only through the expansion of consciousness can we induce proper changes in our physical body. The expanding consciousness creates those conditions in which the etheric body refines itself and causes refinement in its physical counterparts. After such refinement, the fire can be turned on without danger. Thus, we can say that the degree of raising the fire should be proportionate or relative to the degree of purification of the threefold vehicles and to the degree of the expansion of consciousness.

2. When the centers are burned through premature release of the fire of matter, the pranic fire cannot reach the various parts of the body, and the rhythmic flow of prana is distorted. The whole engine eventually becomes out of tune. Such a condition affects the brain center, and man eventually loses his equilibrium.

3. Any impurity that exists within the personality vehicle serves as a fuel for the fire of matter and creates inflammatory conditions, not only in the physical body but also in subtler bodies.

4. It creates overstimulation in certain centers which were active and healthy but now overflow with energy and use the whole man for their own ends. For example, the sacral center takes over and uses the whole man for its ends. The man works, feels, talks, thinks, and creates mostly to satisfy that urge. It can be the urge to eat, to drink, to have sex, etc.

5. Glamors, illusions, and maya increase with the forced raising of the kundalini fire.

The faculty of discrimination must be achieved before a man tries to use the fires. Discrimination is the ability to see illusion, glamor, and maya, as well as the ability to choose the path which leads out of illusion, glamor, and maya.

Discrimination does not start until you use the hidden Light within your Inner Self. It does not start until you have the Light of your Teacher. Discrimination means to follow the viewpoint of the Soul, or of the Inner Light, and reject the viewpoint of the personality. Discrimination always requests sacrifice. When you choose to follow the Light within, you must sever your friendship with your illusions, glamors, and maya.

Maya in man is a state of consciousness which follows appearances instead of reality. Maya is created by the senses of impression. Because of their stage of evolution, the senses report the phenomena, not the reality. As man follows the phenomena, he misses the cause; he bases his life on phenomenal appearances, instead of making his life one with the cause. For example, you have some kind of skin disease, and it appears that you must be allergic to something. This is the phenomenon. If you do not find the real cause of the phenomenon, you will use the wrong medication and perpetuate the phenomenon. This is how one follows phenomena and bases his action on the phenomena.

Until such a state of consciousness is cleared, additional energy from the base of spine will feed the illusions, glamors, and maya and seal the door of liberation.

Kundalini fire, released prematurely, can nourish glamors found in the emotional body. The person eventually becomes the victim of his various glamors.

Glamors are those patches of emotional matter which have an automatic drive to control the man for their own satisfaction. They are mostly unsatisfied desires, strongly reinforced by experiences of pleasure or imagination. Most of the time they are controlled by the pressure of circumstances, but when the fire of matter touches them, they are stimulated and strengthened to such a degree that the man and the circumstances lose their control over the glamors and the man then becomes their victim. In such a condition, no moral, ethical, or social law can stop such a person until he destroys himself through his glamors, misusing money, position, talent, persons, and conditions for the interests of his glamors.

Similar things happen with illusions. Illusions are those truths or facts which are distorted by the logic of the lower mind, by the separative interests of the individual or society. These illusions grow out of proportion through the artificially released fire of matter and control the actions of man. This leads to the state of consciousness in which Hitler, Nero, Mussolini, and other such persons lived.

Illusions create unbearable fanaticism in religious and political fields. Everything that stands on the path of such illusions is thus destroyed. The inquisitions of all ages are the result of such stimulations. When one thinks that he has the whole truth and tries to impose his illusion on others, he produces those obstacles and hindrances which for a long time prevent the progress of humanity, a group, or an individual.

Illusions exist on the mental plane, within any field of human endeavor, as self-actuated units. They are often like a flood that carries away the sanity of man.

6. Without the ability for total concentration, the person can severely damage his body or his centers.

Masters, Who know how to use the kundalini fire, try by all means to teach Their disciples first the art of concentration. Concentration is the power to hold any image, vision, or vibration in the state of form, without letting it melt away in the energy field. For example, when you imagine a flower and hold its image in your visualization, in four seconds it turns into something else or it vanishes. This shows the lack of power of concentration. Or if you try to visualize an energy line connecting the centers, or contact some person through his image, or direct the fire to different parts of the body or centers, you need to develop great skill in concentration, or else you will either ruin your system or fail in your efforts.

Lack of concentration is more dangerous when you are playing with fire, even if your bodies are quite pure. I have seen those who were forcefully directing these fires to certain centers, but when they lost the focus of their concentration for one second, they damaged their vehicles or directed the energy to wrong centers where big problems were created.

To give a very common example, a boy was trying to raise his kundalini fire through some exercises. At the time of his exercise, in which he was leading the fire mentally to the heart center through visualization and concentration, he heard a noise which reminded him of a pleasure, a moment with his girlfriend, and for a few seconds his mind was occupied with his sexual center. There is a law in occultism which says, "Energy follows thought." The fire of kundalini rushed there and caused a large rent in the etheric web. From that moment on, his sexual center was overstimulated to such a degree that every time he sat for his kundalini exercises, the sacral center absorbed the major part of the energy. The result was disastrous to him physically, mentally, and morally.

One must develop perfect concentration of mind before he can direct the fires of matter. The energy can hit the solar plexus, the heart center, even the brain, when you lose control over it for even one second and wander in various directions because of memory associations or uncontrolled impressions.

The lifted but undirected fire burns where it is left, if even for one second. It may burn any part of the etheric body and thus prevent the free circulation of prana, which has dire consequences.

Even if one knows all about the kundalini, his knowledge does not qualify him to be a teacher. We are told that **no one is qualified to teach Kundalini Yoga unless he is a Third Degree Initiate, is equipped by the unmistakable light of Intuition, and can use his Third Eye not only for checking the conditions of the bodies and the centers but also the flow of energy.** The Third Eye has power over the fires, and it can control the flow and prevent any damage whatsoever.

Such Teachers and even Masters never work with the kundalini of their disciples except in rare cases when their evolution must be hastened to make them meet a special task at a given time. On that occasion, the Master personally watches the disciple and scientifically raises the fire through certain channels. Even if the needed substance is lacking in the vehicles, the Master borrows it from His own substance to enable the disciple to be ready for a greater service. A disciple, to be worthy of such help, would have to have had many lives of service, discipline, and purification. The presence of highly qualified Masters is necessary not only for instruction but also for protection. At the time of special preparation, the Master protects the disciple with His own aura during the whole period of training and exercises.

Because the fire of kundalini can attract invisible fiery beings, whose contact can be disastrous for the pupil, the Master's shield prevents such a contact. He also prevents the arrows of negative thoughts and spears of poisonous emotions from touching the disciple's aura. It is only in His protection and guidance that the special and urgent preparation of the disciple is carried out. Such a Master appears when we are ready for special, daring service for humanity.

A disciple not only must be ready to submit himself to such a task, but the Teacher must also be confident that after the student undertakes this discipline he will not damage himself through criticism, hatred, gossip, fear, greed, jealousy, negative thoughts, etc. because all these burn the etheric body to a certain degree and create a safety hazard. This is why those who undertake the discipline of raising the fires are isolated in remote places of mountains, far away from any possibility of worry, fear, or temptation of any kind, and are wholeheartedly dedicated to the task of self-development.

The physical, emotional, and mental environment of the aspirant can create a real condition of danger if it is polluted with criminal thoughts, anger, fear, hatred, etc. because all these telepathically influence his aura and make him fail in his task.

7. The premature raising of the kundalini fire also hurts and damages the weaker parts of the etheric and physical body. Before these areas are exposed to the fire, they can still do well and present no major problem. But as the fire goes to such places, they raise major problems through being burned or energized to such a degree that they allow the prana to rush through them and cause overgrowth in corresponding parts of the physical body.

Cancer is a phenomenon of the etheric body. It originates from the disorders of the etheric body. Its cure lies in the purification and harmonization of the etheric body. When the etheric body is "leaking" into various places of the physical body, it lets the energy of prana accumulate there. As the energy of prana leaks through the etheric body directly to the physical body, the area of leakage burns out and the astral fire rushes in. This causes the malignancy of cancer, which must be treated in the astral, etheric, and physical bodies.

8. Another great danger of playing with the kundalini fire is that it may damage the physical permanent atom and the mental unit. This is very rare, but those who have this experience delay their evolution for eons and cannot incarnate on the physical plane. Their Guardian Soul leaves them, and in occult literature they are called "lost souls."

Before any work is done with the kundalini fire, the physical, emotional, and mental bodies must be in a pure state of health. Many students of Kundalini Yoga had normal health before they engaged in such exercises. Their concentration was very focused, their emotional life was very pure, and they were very loving and serving. But as they did the exercises, they lost their health. My first question to them was, "How was the health condition of your physical body?"

"Well," said one of them, "I did not have any complaints, although my digestion was not perfect."

Another said, "My kidneys were giving me a little trouble."

This is where the danger is. Any weak organ exposed to the fire of matter gets worse because it increases the defects in it or stimulates the germs, microbes, or cancerous cells in it.

When the kundalini fire prematurely rises, it brings out all the defects in your physical, emotional, and mental nature in such a dosage or taxation that you cannot handle it.

With all these warnings, we must say that the kundalini fire exists, and safe methods to raise the fire exist. The great science of Kundalini Yoga exists. No one can deny this, but the right Teachers are very rare, and the prepatory work to make aspirants ready for such work is not yet available.

13

Thought and the Etheric Body

Thought, in particular, is very effective on our etheric body. We can vitalize our etheric body through elevated thoughts.

Thought affects the etheric body. The physical body is activated and influenced by the etheric body. Thought impresses the etheric brain, and the etheric brain puts the physical brain into motion.

It is from the mental realm that all our actions are controlled via the etheric centers. Proof of this is the phenomenon of the *stigmata*. People produce various physical phenomena through their thoughts. I have seen people who, while watching an enactment of the crucifixion of Christ, develop in their palms the stigmata of the wounds of Christ. The image in their mind is amplified by their thoughts and impressed on the etheric brain, which impresses it on the etheric body. Then the same impression appears on the physical body, almost identically.

Such impressions can come also from astral realms. Some people wounded in their dreams have the impression of a wound on their physical body. This phenomenon is called *repercussion*. This shows that our physical conditions are almost entirely the result of our thoughts and emotions, our visualizations and imaginations, or our decisions and emotional reactions. That is why in the esoteric Teaching the physical body is called "the shadow."

It is reported that a pregnant woman's imagination and thoughts have a great and decisive effect on the figure of the future baby. Some women, by concentrating their mind on certain pictures or statues, delivered children with almost identical features.[1]

In Armenia, grandmothers used to isolate their pregnant daughters to prevent them from seeing animals, ugly figures, clowns, or hearing depressing or destructive conversations. They used to say that a pregnant woman is like a magnet. She attracts the good and bad and impresses them both on the embryo. Pregnant women were provided with good music, companions of pretty girls and children, and told the heroic tales of outstanding world figures.

---

1. See also *Sex, Family, and the Woman in Society.*

Often you see in stores greeting cards of disfigured human forms. You like to take your children to see clowns or puppet shows. The impressions accumulated from such pictures or shows have a very degenerative effect on the etheric body.

The mind builds similar images or thoughtforms of these disfigured images and impresses them unconsciously on the etheric pattern which then becomes agitated. The etheric body rejects such figures because they are a violation of its progressive patterns. But if these images are repeated and admitted through the intermediary of certain thoughts and emotions, the etheric body eventually gives up and accepts these figures which can then start their degenerative work. Such etheric pollutions contribute heavily to the rise of crime in the world.

It is deplorable to see illustrations of disfigured human, animal, and vegetable forms in cultural and educational publications. The whole aura of a book of lofty thoughts is thrown out of balance and integrity through one ugly drawing.

People think it is funny and humorous to have disfigured illustrations of living forms. Let no one forget that the impressions received through the eyes condition our imagination and the etheric body. Every time we see a disfigured form, our etheric body passes through a great shock. It tries to reject the impression, but the imagination cannot easily rid itself of the impression and superimposes the impression upon the etheric body, which continuously tries to reject it until eventually it accepts a part of the disfigurement.

This acceptance creates a partial deformity and injury in the etheric body. If such impressions are continuously imposed upon the etheric body, the degeneration of the health of the physical body takes place. Many races have vanished because of their customs of disfigurement.

The same thing happens when people create ugly characters in their literature. Their creation eventually molds their etheric forces and produces similar forms. An actor played the role of a sick man. One month later he showed the same symptoms and passed away. Our thoughts affect the etheric body, and the etheric body conditions the physical body.

In all ancient nations there was an effort to keep the race noble and pure through mental, emotional, and physical purity. Joy affects the etheric body and charges it with great vitality. Gratitude, solemnity, and nobility have very healing and vitalizing effects on the etheric body. Harmlessness has a great purifying effect on the etheric channels. A man can live and enjoy life longer when he makes his mental, emotional, and physical life harmless.

Caricature is considered a great art and also a means to bring out and expose hidden qualities of people and events in a visual form. But can you imagine what the disfigured form will do to the true subject? Both the artist and those who see or study the disfigured image, like a broadcasting station, impose this image upon the mind of the subject himself.

The disfigured image will not only alter the etheric prototype of the subject, but it will also cause many psychological and physical disturbances in him. Any broadcasted, distorted image will be a discord in Space and, amplified by the minds of thousands of people, will affect the consciousness of the masses. Thus, in the name of artistry and art, distortion is promoted.

Malice, slander, and gossip run upon the same principle. They distort the image of the victim and cause great damage.

Our food and drink change the chemistry of our etheric body and our aura as a whole, creating different colors and hues in the aura. There are elements which help us to register certain impressions, while others block the impressions. Initiates know what to eat, how much to eat, what to drink, and in what location to live because they know that the food, water, air, and the aroma of trees, bushes, and flowers infuse different chemistries into the aura.

Pure water is important not only for the digestive system and kidneys, but also for the blood and for the vitality of the etheric body and the aura. Polluted water is a great danger for the human species.

Recycled water is very bad, not only for vegetables and trees but also for human health and sanity. The recycling process does not remove the psychic elements that were fused with the water as it passed through the human body. Psychic contaminations will slowly spread, and through water people's psychic sicknesses and disorders magnetically will pass to the vegetation and sometimes to those who directly use such water.

Water absorbs our emotional, mental, and also etheric qualities. Water absorbs the correspondences of germs or microbes that exist in etheric, astral, and mental matter and transplants them into plants and innocent human beings. A serious scientific study will prove that recycled water is detrimental to sanity and health.

The sewage of millions of people carries incredible amounts of psychic complications. Only Nature has the way to get rid of them through the processes of evaporation, solar fire, and electrical storms.

A sensitive aura can be blocked by a fragrance which creates a different chemistry in the aura. Even a contact with a person can change that chemistry. Thus, we can experiment and observe the degree of our sensitivity, creativity, and joy when we are in contact with certain persons or articles or visit certain locations. According to this information, it will then be possible to refine our psychic nature by choosing the right food, the right herbal tea, the right water, the right place, the right persons, and the right vitamins.

Nature is built on the law of chemical combinations. Once we penetrate into the science of metachemistry, we will be able to build radios, televisions, telephones, and broadcasting stations within our own aura.

The intake of proper elements can be very important from the standpoint of the objective world, but we must realize that the elements also exist in their subtle forms. These elements can be brought into use either in our higher nature or in our physical nature through various thoughts, emotions, and actions.

Many emanations of thought bring into existence some crystals, or salts, or other elements in our body. Actually, they first existed in vapor form, so to say, but our particular thoughts and emotions acted as magnets and condensed them.

Thought, in particular, is very effective on our etheric body. We can vitalize our etheric body through elevated thoughts. Thoughts that are expressions of Beauty, Goodness, and Truth are vitamins for the etheric body.

We can organize our etheric body through our thoughts, and meditation is one of the best ways to organize it. Meditation brings the etheric body closer to the inner spiritual world and helps it synchronize itself with the ideal in the subtle planes. Meditation also channels substances of the higher ethers and builds the chakras with higher etheric substances.

Meditation is a creative process for the etheric body. Master Morya says,

> *Friends, I repeat — hold your thoughts pure, this is the best disinfectant and the foremost tonic expedient.*[2]
>
> *...Small unkind thoughts generate poisonous gases.... But every kind thought and striving towards the Beautiful helps one to advance rapidly.*[3]

Healing thoughts, creative thoughts, thoughts full of love and light greatly affect the etheric body of those to whom they are directed. It is easier to heal a person etherically in the subjective levels than on the objective levels. The greatest factor in healing is impersonal love through which you direct the harmony of Cosmos into the coil of the etheric body.

It is also possible to be contaminated by those etheric bodies which are in bad condition. This happens if one's own pranic system is weak and psychic energy is almost nil.

It is better to refrain from the practice of subjective healing until you are able to be active consciously on the astral plane and can rise up and out of its influence into the mental sphere. Then you can try to heal the etheric bodies of others. For astral healing, it is better to be conscious on the mental plane in order to protect yourself from various astral attacks, since astral disorders are mostly associated with astral entities.

Some people like to imitate the behavior of other people, or pattern themselves after another's manners, or act as if they were blind, deaf or dumb, or were a robot. In such actions the mind is used intensely through imagination and visualization. Intense thoughtforms, imagination, and visualization force a new pattern upon the normal etheric body, and exercise a great pressure on it to be, for example, blind, deaf, dumb, or act like a robot. The pressure of a strange

---

2. Agni Yoga Society, *Community*, para. 23.
3. Agni Yoga Society, *Fiery World*, Vol. II, para. 55.

pattern impresses itself upon the etheric body patterns and causes great disturbances between the etheric and physical counterparts. As the disturbances increase, the following effects can be noted:

1. The etheric centers feel the pressure of change and react to such an artificial pressure, thus creating a dangerous tension within themselves.

2. The glands feel this disturbance in the centers and react with abnormal behaviors.

3. The corresponding organs may receive overstimulation or receive a decreased or disturbed, unbalanced, non-rhythmic flow of energy.

4. Pain, pressure, and weakness are felt in the area of the senses.

5. Emotional tensions and abnormal outbursts of feelings can be noticed in closer intervals.

6. The heart, the liver, and the pancreas show signs of disturbances.

7. If the imitation continues for a long time, with moments of intense identification with the thoughtform, it is possible that the pattern of the etheric body changes, even in this lifetime. In the next incarnation the person will have the very qualities he toyed with previously in his mind.

To dramatize this situation, let us create a dialogue.

The thoughtform will say, "I am blind."

Etheric body, "No you are not, everything is okay, normal, and natural."

Thoughtform, "No, I am blind. You see I am acting like a blind person, and thousands believe me."

Etheric body, "I will transfer the impression you are giving me to the glands involved."

Thoughtform, "I am blind...."

Etheric body, "I see some truth in what you suggest. I think you are blind."

Gland, "What is going on there? You are presenting a new pattern. I cannot change myself suddenly."

Thoughtform, "I am blind."

Gland, "I am afraid I am forced to believe and act accordingly."

Organ, "What is going on? I am uncomfortable. I am losing my power, my clarity, my joy. I am not blind. I can see.... See, I can see!"

Gland, "You can't."

Thoughtform, "You are blind."

Organ, "I believe I am."

This is the critical moment when deterioration starts in the subtle bodies, and if the thoughtform continues, the result will be detrimental.

It does not mean that impersonation or faking has an immediate result, but it has effects on the organ slightly at first, then heavily and continuously if the moments of identification with the thoughtforms are repeated and stressed for a long time.

Any progressive, evolutionary thoughtform generated by the mind acts on the etheric body as a vision and as a nourishment. Such thoughtforms, if sustained for a long time, create an intense aspiration within the etheric body. This aspiration unfolds and evolves following the creation of the vision and urges man to achieve the vision. Thus, for example, when a man acts as if he were a disciple or an advanced soul, he unfolds and evolves because the vision set in his aura urges him to meet the requirements of discipleship or of an advanced soul.

Let us not forget that the cells of our organs and glands, and the atoms of our etheric, emotional, and mental bodies are lives, entities, and they can easily believe us. If we tell them they can do things better, they will, because the expanding creative energy is within them. We are not violating their innate nature.

And if we say, "You are dead, dead, dead, dead," the cells and atoms will deteriorate because we are imposing a pressure that is contrary to the intent of the atoms. The blooming tree must not be forced to reverse its process and "un-bloom" itself.

14

A Protective Meditation

At the time of crises, natural catastrophes, earthquakes, revolutions, and anarchy, we see the energy pattern in the sphere distorted. This comes from the earth's magnetism and energy current trying to adjust itself to the solar and galactic currents.

Man as an atom is subject to these energy currents and he reacts violently with moral, physical, and mental disturbances. But he can escape such a danger by putting his consciousness in action through meditation. Meditation becomes a surfing process at difficult times.

Meditation balances you. It gives you courage and daring, fearlessness and energy.

To do such a meditation:

1. Sit cross-legged on the floor or with ankles crossed, if sitting on a chair.

2. Relax — physically, emotionally, and mentally.

3. Visualize a mountain.

4. Visualize that you are sitting on the top of the mountain under a tree.

5. Say the Great Invocation in a loud voice.

    From the point of Light within the Mind of God
    Let light stream forth into the minds of men.
    Let Light descend on Earth.

    From the point of Love within the Heart of God
    Let love stream forth into the hearts of men.
    May Christ return to Earth.

    From the centre where the Will of God is known
    Let purpose guide the little wills of men —
    The purpose which the Masters know and serve.

From the centre which we call the race of men
Let the Plan of Love and Light work out.
And may it seal the door where evil dwells.

Let Light and Love and Power
Restore the Plan on Earth.

6. Say three OMs.

7. Meditate on the following:

The love of Infinity is in me. I am God's love. God is my love.

The joy of the Infinite is my essence. Let joy radiate through me in all conditions.

Beauty am I. My beauty is the magnet of the benevolent forces of the universe. My beauty is the blossoming of the Infinite One. Let Beauty spread all over the world.

I am a fountain of enthusiasm. I am harmony, rhythm. I am flame. I radiate the rhythm of the Cosmic Heart. The Eternal in me always is and will be forever.

NOTE: These are the seed thoughts to be meditated upon successively. Use each seed thought for one week, then go to the next one. You may continue for three months or three years.

8. After meditation say

May I be led
from darkness to Light,
from the unreal to the Real,
from death to Immortality,
from chaos to Beauty.

9. Then visualize yourself sitting under a pyramid (which is your Spiritual Triad) having three sides instead of four and each side with a different color — crimson red, midnight blue, violet, and with a diamond point at the top.

10. Sit under the pyramid and let it spin around its axis three times until the color you started with comes back to its original position.

11. Say three OMs, raising both your hands up at a forty-five degree angle, palms facing out.[1]

1. Adapted from *The Psyche and Psychism*, Ch. 65.

15

Objects and the Etheric Body

When one has a healthy etheric body charged with golden prana, he can destroy any negative formation on any object if he concentrates his psychic energy through prayers and through concentrated thought power.

The etheric body can be affected by the objects with which we come in contact. Those objects which produce negative effects are

1. Any object handled by criminals, by those who were charged with negative emotions, or by those who were in depression, suicidal moods, hatred, greed, fear, or perverted sex. When we use chairs, pencils, books, or cars which were used by the above types of people, we draw the etheric sphere of those people into our etheric body or into our aura.

2. A handshake or intercourse with people who are polluted by drugs, crimes, alcohol, or tobacco transmits the seeds of their weaknesses into our aura and depletes our energy, joy, and creativity. We often lose our joy, energy, and creative impulse because of such contacts.

3. When we visit places where there is mass obsession, crimes, or mass hypnotism; whorehouses and nightclubs where sex and alcohol consumption is heavy; dance halls where one mixes with many kinds of auras; slaughter houses and battlefields where blood was shed, we naturally absorb many dark waves, pollute our etheric body, and fall into various physical, emotional, and mental traps and sicknesses of many kinds.

Spiritually refined and advanced people are more sensitive than those of average consciousness. We are told that in some royal houses people were advised

1. Not to shake hands with strangers and with those who were not of noble spirit and morals

2. Not to use circulated books, papers, or pencils

3. To build a new palace for the new monarch and fill it with new furniture

In these ways the royal house was kept pure and clear of any physical, emotional, and mental pollution so that the leaders would be able to lead the nation on a path toward a more spiritual direction.

Royalty used to think that an old palace was naturally crowded with many negative emanations, decisions, arguments, and even crimes. They wanted to make sure that the new monarch would start pure and clean, uninfluenced by the emanations of his ancestors.

Symbols also have a strong effect on the etheric body since most symbols are patterns of forces. These forces penetrate into the etheric body via the astral and mental body and cause various changes.

Symbols that are given by higher Initiates produce ideas in the higher mental planes when absorbed correctly. They create an emotional effect on the astral plane in terms of various responses. However, the force pattern of the symbol goes directly to the etheric body and fuses with the prana. Because of this effect, most of the great movements have a leading symbol to transmit energy or force and lead people into action.

Sometimes the ideas created on the higher mental plane by the symbols are not realized, but the feelings and actions are there. To bring these abstract ideas into realization, one must meditate and serve.

Symbols also can create negative reactions if for a long time they were associated with painful, destructive, and unpleasant thoughtforms, feelings, or actions. Such symbols evoke corresponding painful impressions and often activate them beyond control.

When a symbol becomes so dense that your intellect cannot penetrate into it, it turns into an idol. When it becomes transparent, the symbol changes into an ideal. When the symbol disappears in the light of your Intuition, the only thing that remains is the idea, the soul of the symbol.

Symbols become crystallized and materialized when they are used for greed, hatred, fear, and separatism. They are thickened by the materialistic forces with which we surround them, and they turn into the servants of our lower nature.

To keep a symbol alive, one must strive toward the ideals of the plane which gave birth to it.

Black magic uses various symbols, stones, or jewelry to affect people. Jewels worn by people of bad reputation or of low moral standards must not be used by innocent people if they do not want to pollute themselves. The thoughtforms and emotions associated with the object and its etheric emanations are very harmful and destructive, and disciples must always carefully choose the people from whom they buy or receive such objects.

Those people who are engaged in lower psychism, mediumism, and spiritualistic seances carry heavy pollution to their environment through their presence or through the objects they touch. Sometimes the whole character of a girl or boy changes through wearing the objects that were handed to them by lower psychics.

Of course, one can protect himself from such harmful emanations. Objects can be purified by sandalwood incense, prayer, and by the power of the cross. They can be purified by the energy of Christ or a Master, if invoked in a spirit of purity and by an elevated consciousness.

When one has a healthy etheric body charged with golden prana, he can destroy any negative formation on any object if he concentrates his psychic energy through prayers and through concentrated thought power. But one must always remember that sometimes it is too risky to play with degenerating emanations. Ancients, knowing the effect of emanations, used this knowledge in various ways. For example:

1. When their child was having psychological disturbances, they brought the coat or shirt of a holy man and made the child wear it for a while. Or they brought objects used by higher Initiates and made the child touch and use them in order to become charged with their harmonious waves or emanations and curative vibrations.

2. They used to take their sick relatives to those places which were highly charged by the presence of holy men. They arranged to have them blessed by holy men and drink water from their cups.

3. Often they took their patients to the lakes or rivers where a holy man was washing himself. They believed that water was an excellent conductor for the benevolent emanations released by holy men.

4. They would have their patient eat the bread which had been partially eaten by a holy man, or drink the water partially drunk by a holy man.

5. Great Teachers used to send their disciples various gifts to pass to them their electrical charge or blessings. They used to send flowers, pens or pencils, wood, incense, carved pictures or symbols — all carrying their emanations. Disciples would touch the objects and be charged by them.

In Asia, where we had a monastery, some of the boys used to go and meditate under the tree where our Teacher used to sit and meditate or speak. We would wait, at a distance, until he had finished his meditation or class, then run and sit under the tree and meditate. We were able not only to feel but also to touch the emanations of our Teacher, and our meditations were unusually deep, creative, and vitalizing. Sometimes so many ideas would reveal themselves in my mind that I almost felt I was standing in front of a limitless and bottomless ocean of ideas.

Once I spoke to our Teacher about our secret adventure. The Teacher smiled and said, “I am glad it was you and your few friends doing it. The emanations of my thoughts and ideas have charged the tree and that area and have built a sphere of light in which you can easily contact your Soul or the Mind of the Universe and draw new visions and new ideas. But for newcomers, it may create problems by overstimulating their etheric centers."

During his travels throughout the world, my Teacher never slept in the bed of another person. He used to carry his blankets or sleeping bag and sleep outside under the stars. Once he said, "Motel rooms or public places are not for disciples or sensitive aspirants. There can be accumulations of many harmful emanations there."

In the study and lecture hall, our Teacher had a chair on which no one but he was allowed to sit; it was strictly private. I had a chance to talk to him about the chair, and asked why another person was not allowed to occupy it. He answered: "Everyone has his own etheric frequency and auric emanations. The chair must not be mixed with various emanations if the flow of ideas or the stream of inspirations is to be kept unaffected by these emanations. The lower etheric centers heavily charge the chair with their emanations. If they are of low order, the teacher, no matter who he is, to a certain degree loses his intensity of focus as well as his alignment with higher realms."

Money is related to pranic energy, and as prana, it has the three characteristics of *tamas*, *rajas*, and *sattva*. This means that the money can be used or acquired through tamasic ways — through the means of inertia; it can be used or acquired through the means of motion — rajas; or through the means of sattva — rhythm.

The way you spend money has a great influence upon the construction and the material of your etheric body. If you are spending money in tamasic ways, you are channeling to your system tamasic energy, or inertia. If you are spending it in rajasic ways, you are absorbing rajasic energy. If you are spending it in sattvic ways, you are channeling sattvic energy into your system.

Similarly, the way you acquire money is very important. You may acquire it by tamasic means, such as by selling drugs or killing people. This brings you inertia, and your subtle centers close and eventually become inactive.

You may acquire money by rajasic means, for example, selling liquor, sex, or prostitution, or lying or cheating. This creates great force and conflicting energies in your system.

You may acquire money by sattvic means such as honest labor, creative arts, or by using your education and talent through honest means. This brings joy, rhythm, and harmony into your nature, and you enjoy the wealth you have.

Many people do not enjoy the money they accumulate. It becomes either a burden on their shoulders or a means for their moral and spiritual downfall; but when acquired by sattvic means, it brings peace, harmony, enjoyment, and unfoldment.

The money that circulates from hand to hand carries these energies. It is wise to bless money before you put it in your pocket because blessing changes the vibrations of the money and makes it more rhythmic when it is acquired by right means.

16

Telepathy and the Etheric Body

Distortions in telepathic reception, visions, and dreams occur when the etheric body and, in particular, the etheric brain are not in a healthy condition or if the physical brain is intoxicated with alcohol, tobacco, drugs, or negative emotions and thoughts.

Telepathy is communication between the Thinker and other forms of intelligent life. The mechanism of communication is the seven etheric centers which are connected to the lower and higher ethers. But since all centers are not active or operative, the Thinker, the Self, communicates with other life-forms through the center that is active and unfolded.

In telepathic work the factors involved are

1. The etheric body of man, the planet, and some life-forms
2. The human soul, or the Self, or the awareness unit[1]
3. The center
4. The etheric and dense physical brain and the mental body
5. The Antahkarana

Ordinary people communicate through their solar plexus center. Advanced ones communicate through the throat center. Initiates communicate directly, soul to soul. The Masters of Wisdom communicate with their disciples on the soul level or even on the intuitional level.

Communication is carried through the etheric substance in Space. If a man is advanced, he uses higher ethers; if he is average, he uses the lower ethers. The quality of his communication depends on the purity of his aura, including the network of the etheric body.

---

1. The Self is the human soul, but it is subjective. The human soul is a stage of growth of the Self.

All communication on all levels is transmitted through etheric substance which uses the electricity of the individual, planetary, solar, and galactic prana.

Distortions in telepathic reception, visions, and dreams occur when the etheric body and, in particular, the etheric brain are not in a healthy condition or if the physical brain is intoxicated with alcohol, tobacco, drugs, or negative emotions and thoughts.

There are many detrimental conditions that can occur in the etheric body, and all these following conditions affect the registration or recording system:

1. atrophy
2. agitation or storms
3. congestion
4. burning out
5. blockage
6. looseness
7. sapping
8. displacement

1. Atrophy is the hardening and crystallizing of the etheric body. Certain parts of etheric matter dry up and cause the degeneration of their physical counterparts.

2. Agitation or storms are created when too many forces are poured in — forces which are not in harmony with each other and with the prana. Many such storms are manifested as inner conflicts. Through such a stormy sphere, the impressions coming from higher sources have no chance to be registered accurately in the brain.

3. Congestion is the result of the reception of too much prana and the inability of the etheric body to circulate it. Congestion blocks the contacts with subtler planes.

4. Many wires or areas can be burned in the etheric body. This makes reception almost impossible. It is similar to a typewriter in which some of the characters are broken off and do not hit the paper.

5. Blockage is not congestion. Blockage is the result of psychic waste being thrown into the etheric network or tubes. This waste prevents the free circulation of electrical currents. Congestion is the accumulation of force in certain areas or centers, or even in glands.

6. Looseness is when the etheric body, the nadis, the nervous system, and the glands are not in gear. The result is that there is no contact, or very little contact, and the impressions coming from higher realms cannot be fully recorded. Most mediums have a loose etheric body, and entities are able to occupy a position between their etheric and physical bodies and use their mechanism, especially the throat center and the hands.

Advanced stages of looseness lead to obsession or possession. Most of the prophecies of destruction circulating in the world are the messages given by possessing entities who want to create confusion and mistrust and cause hatred, fear, and panic.

7. Sapping of the etheric body and the prana is a very common phenomenon. Those who have a loose etheric body sap the prana of others, and those who are obsessed or possessed draw part of another's etheric body to use as a vehicle of manifestation for the obsessing or possessing entity. This is why a great Sage suggests that we keep away from mediums and from those who are possessed.

8. Displacement is the phenomenon where parts of the etheric body shift their location. It occurs sometimes around the head and on the axis of the spine, causing various and mysterious troubles. In such a condition, the message goes to the wrong electronic tube and is lost forever. That is why etheric health is not only necessary for physical health but also for spiritual guidance.

Most materialistic people have partly atrophied etheric bodies, displaced centers, and hardened nadis. As a result, they cannot respond to any spiritual impulse or impression.

Etheric Phenomena

Many people, because of their mystic aspirations, pull their etheric body partially out from their head. It looks like a balloon above their head. If it stays there, they feel spaced out.

We have a physical brain and also an etheric brain. If this etheric brain pulls out of the physical brain due to intense devotion, worship, or admiration, the brain does not think but is flooded with impressions which it cannot formulate into common sense.

Ecstasy is sometimes caused by the suspension of the etheric brain. At the time of ecstasy, the brain is almost inactive but flooded with joy. The brain has no power at that time to translate the mechanism of ecstasy.

When the etheric body withdraws unevenly from our body, the etheric part that is withdrawn draws its physical counterpart toward itself. For example, when you are doing a mystical or devotional meditation, you observe that your head is going backward or sideways or forward. This is an unconscious action caused by the withdrawing part of your etheric body which is pulling the corresponding part of the physical body.

When a man withdraws from his physical body, he is not in the etheric body. His etheric body remains with his physical body, but he travels with either his astral or his mental body. Travelers in the mental body are very rare. Mostly we are found in our astral bodies and are in contact with the astral plane. Disciples and Initiates are privileged to be in their mental bodies and even their Buddhic bodies.

From the heart center of the etheric body extends the *life thread* to the heart center of the astral body, and the etheric body receives the life electricity through this thread. It sometimes happens that this cord is snapped, and the man can no longer reach his physical body.

You leave your physical body and enter the etheric body when you have an accident or die suddenly. You leave your physical body and are in your astral body when you sleep. When you meditate deeply, you leave your physical body and enter into your mental body.

When you are in your astral body, you have contact with your brain through dreams. When you are in your mental body, you contact your brain through visions. When you enter your intuitional body, your brain registers all your experiences in the intuitional world in proportion to the purity and serenity of the brain.

When you are thinking, your etheric body stays as it is with your etheric brain. In the process of thinking, the etheric body is geared to the physical brain. Otherwise thoughts are not transmitted to the brain. Thinking helps you keep your sanity.

Let us remember that the *consciousness thread* is anchored in the etheric brain and is connected with the pineal gland. The *life thread* is anchored in the etheric heart and is connected with the thymus gland. As long as the consciousness thread creates responses from the pineal gland and the brain, man maintains his consciousness. As long as the life thread creates responses from the thymus gland, the heart beats and the body lives.

At the time of astral withdrawal, both these lines are intact. At the time of mental withdrawal, the consciousness thread attains an extra luminosity, and the light in the head increases as the dweller in the mental body gathers experiences from the "Hall of Wisdom." This is why we are told not to be drowned in our emotions but first learn to purify our heart and then learn to **think**.

Great success waits for those individuals who know how to think in the light of their purified heart.[2]

2. For more information on the heart, please refer to *The Flame of the Heart*.

17

Etheric Centers and Their Coordination

The etheric centers transmit prana to all our organs. The deeper we breathe and the cleaner the air, the more vitality we transmit to the corresponding organs of our etheric centers.

We have a body, a real body that is called the etheric body. It is sometimes called the *etheric double* because our dense physical body is the exact replica of our etheric body.

In the etheric body we have seven etheric centers which are called, from lower to higher:

— Base of spine

— Sacral

— Solar plexus

— Spleen

— Heart

— Throat

— Head

There are also minor centers.

Each center is a whirlpool of energy.

The centers are related to our consciousness, thoughts, emotions, and actions.

We not only have seven etheric centers but also seven emotional centers, which correspond exactly to the seven etheric centers. We also have four mental centers, along with the mental unit, which are called, from lower to higher:

1. Base of spine in the fourth mental level

2. Generative organs in the fourth mental level

3. Solar plexus in the fourth mental level

4. Spleen in the fourth mental level

In humanity the most active centers, at the present, are the solar plexus and sacral centers. The solar plexus has two departments. The lower one is related mostly to negative emotions such as hate, fear, anger, jealousy, revenge, slander, malice, nosiness, depression, etc. The higher department of the solar plexus is related to lofty aspirations, healing, brotherly feelings, etc.

The overactivity of the sacral center in the world results in complications in the related organs and widespread sexually transmitted diseases.

The heart center is partially open in those who have loving understanding and compassion. The throat center is partially open in creative people. The head center is partially open in those who are in leadership positions, or engaged in scientific discoveries, or who, in their various fields, exercise pure reason, logic, and sacrificial service.

The switchboard of all centers is in the human consciousness. The more we expand our consciousness and the more we dedicate our life to the service of humanity, the more our centers unfold and bring into our aura greater currents of life, love, and light.

This is why the right way to open our centers is to expand our consciousness and not to use artificial means, postures, yogas, and exercises.

It is a drastic mistake to work directly on the centers. It may have grave consequences on our health and consciousness.

When our consciousness expands, it creates pressure on the mental switches and they let the energy of consciousness go into the centers, energize them, and cause unfoldment.

When we work directly on the centers, we stimulate them mechanically and we put their corresponding glands and related organs in great danger. Some of the cancers in the organs or glands are caused by overstimulation.

If in the past you tried artificially to open the centers, you will experience in this life mental and emotional disturbances and certain diseases.

In such conditions, your centers may still be in a state of overstimulation, or they may be damaged by the reaction of the stimulated organs acting in a reverse manner.

To cure such a condition is not easy, and only a high degree Initiate can handle such cases, if the karma of the subject does not prevent it.

Coordination of the centers is horizontal and vertical. Horizontal coordination is alignment of the centers existing in the same body and coordination with their switches in the consciousness. Vertical coordination is between centers on different planes such as the physical, emotional, and mental planes.

The switches of all centers on the etheric, astral, and mental planes are found in the fourth level of the mental plane.

The coordination process of the centers runs parallel with the purification process.

To unfold your centers naturally and safely, the steps to take are as follows:

1. Expand your consciousness.

2. Purify your nature of elements that prevent the unfoldment of the centers.

3. Develop the virtues related to the centers.

4. Use the energies of the centers economically and wisely.

5. Resign from activities on those levels that are harmful to the centers.

Expansion of consciousness is through service and right meditation.

Purification of the centers can be achieved by developing virtues and abstaining from activities that hurt the centers. For example, if the solar plexus is blocked and causing various health problems in its surrounding area, one needs to develop fearlessness, lovingness, inclusiveness, joy, peace, gracefulness, tenderness, etc.

There are specific virtues related to the centers. If you want to know what virtues are related to what center, you must find the Ray of each center and search for the virtue of each Ray.[1]

The energies of the various centers are different. For example, the energy of the heart center is love and compassion; the energy of the head center is willpower; the energy of the ajna center is direction; the energy of the throat center is creativity; the energy of the solar plexus center is healing and relationship; the energy of the sacral center is sex; the energy of the base of spine center is sacrificial labor.

Of course these energies can be named differently, but the main point emphasized here is that **one must economize and use his centers intelligently and not waste them by overactivity and overstimulation.**

Of course, those who are on the spiritual path may feel burning sensations in their various centers or connected areas in the body. Such pain often appears intensely, and then suddenly disappears.

When a new energy is poured into any center because of our spiritual progress, that energy burns the dross accumulated from the past or past lives. This is the cause of the pain. When purification is done, the body adjusts itself to the condition of the etheric center and the pain disappears.

We should also be concerned not to feed a center with negative elements. For example, let us assume that your solar plexus is open and you feel the fears,

---

1. For further information please refer to *Esoteric Psychology*, Vol. I, by Alice A. Bailey, pp. 200-212.

anxieties, and troubles of others and cannot stand it. What will you do? As much as possible, you must try not to feed your solar plexus center with fear, anger, jealousy, hatred, revenge, or greed. If you try to stop such destructive fiery currents from going to your solar plexus, you stop feeding your center and it slowly regulates or normalizes itself.

To regulate your throat center, the best step to take is to stop gossiping, lying, and slandering people and at the same time to be constructive and energizing through your words and speech.

When you have inflammable material in your pocket, it burns when you approach fire. Similarly, any pollutant existing in your centers burns when new energy is channeled to it. That is why it is necessary to give a rest to your centers before you start nourishing and energizing them.

When your centers are used to serve such things as

— hatred

— fear

— anger

— slander

— greed

— separatism

— jealousy

— revenge

— malice

— slander

they deteriorate and destroy not only your joy and happiness but also your body and even your business.

Misused centers become a load and a powerful burden on your shoulders for many lives.

There is another point that must be considered. Sometimes we force our centers to overwork, which creates friction between the center and its corresponding gland. Friction is the cause of many kinds of pain in your body.

Coordination of the centers proceeds mathematically. Every time an etheric center unfolds to a certain degree, its astral and mental correspondences feel the unfoldment and in some cases begin to unfold.

At the beginning, certain petals of the centers open sequentially. Then, when the person enters into the arena of so-called civilization, his centers open in non-sequential ways. But when he enters the Third Initiation, a certain order and rhythm appear in the unfoldment of the petals of the centers.

There is an arithmetical and geometrical sequence by which the centers open. The arithmetical sequence is related to the petals of the centers, and the geometrical sequence is noticed on the centers existing in the various planes, coordinating themselves to the rhythm of the unfolding petals of the Chalice.

Until the Third Initiation, you develop the centers according to your need and the labor that your karma brought to you.

But after the Third Initiation, you do not run from one post to another because your life is regulated and you live by the plan of your Inner Light.

At the second initiation, your wishful approach to the centers and your desire to use them for your pleasures stop.

At the Third Initiation you become an accepted disciple, and you no longer live inharmoniously with the whole of Nature but try to coordinate and harmonize yourself with the Plan of the Hierarchy.

There are not only individual centers but also group centers, national centers, and global centers. All these centers are under the same laws, and they unfold and open under the pressure of the expanding consciousness of the individual, group, state, nation, and humanity.

Bear in mind that a man must try to become, with all his various centers, one center in the body of a group. A group must try, with all its individuals and group centers, to become one center in the body of a nation. A nation must try, with all its individuals, groups, and national centers, to become *one* center in the body of humanity.

As we become a part of a greater body, our centers on all levels coordinate, fuse, and synthesize into one center. This is true for groups and nations as well.

During the coordination of the centers of a group, the group goes through various phases. First, the individuals try to manipulate the group entity; then they begin to serve the group; then fuse with the group and become a conscious part of it. At this stage, each party of the group becomes a part of one of the seven centers of the group.

For example, some members of the group represent the head center, others the heart center, others the ajna center, and so on. When coordination reaches the highest stage, then the group characterizes itself with one dominating center which will serve a larger group as one of its centers.

For the average person, in general, coordination with the higher centers of higher planes starts with the coordination of the lower centers with their higher correspondences.

For example, we have

Head

Throat

Heart

Spleen

Solar plexus

Sacral

Base of spine

The base of spine center corresponds to the head center.

The sacral center corresponds to the throat center.

The solar plexus center corresponds to the heart center.

The spleen center must be related to the physical and astral permanent atoms and to the mental unit.

Eventually the sacral, solar plexus, heart, and throat centers must come under the control of the head center.

As you may notice in the list of centers given above, the ajna center is not referred to. The reason is, first, the ajna center is considered a part of the head center. Second, the ajna center only comes into creative activity when the Antahkarana has been built.

People have the opinion that building the Antahkarana is related only to continuity of consciousness and to create a relationship with the higher world. This is correct, but it is not the complete reason.[2]

One of the main reasons to build the Antahkarana is to have viewpoints on various planes simultaneously — to draw wisdom, energy, and substance from these planes and use them to construct better vehicles, better relationships, and increase the joy of life in our own and others' hearts.

In the future, advanced Teachers will show how the Antahkarana can be used as a device to secure spiritual, moral, mental, emotional, and physical health.

The threefold Antahkarana is a communication device, and it is a far more complicated computer than we imagine. For example it does the following:

1. It puts you into communication with higher levels of consciousness or awareness, with higher centers, without abstracting your consciousness from corresponding lower centers.

2. It automatically compiles all information needed by you from higher sources and from your Chalice and even from your subconscious mind and memory disks.

---

2. Also see *Psyche and Psychism* and *The Science of Becoming Oneself.*

3. It measures the people's consciousness and allows you to speak only so much that they will understand and try to apply.

4. It correlates the time, the events, the people, the conditions, and your future plans and gives you a clear picture of how to act and what to convey.

5. It reveals to you the possibility of future attacks due to your past negligences and gives you a chance to escape the attacks or intelligently to confront them.

6. The Antahkarana reveals to you the plan of your life, suggested by your Solar Angel, so that you do not waste energy fighting against elements which carry the plan to fulfillment.

7. The Antahkarana always reveals to you the changeless in the changes, the Infinity in the finite, the ultimate victory in failure and defeat, the everlasting joy in sorrow and in pain.

In the healing process, the Antahkarana provides you with the things you need to do to your vehicles and the steps you must take to heal your vehicles or prepare to depart.

The computer of the Antahkarana even brings together all that you need for your plan.

If a healer's Antahkarana is built, the Antahkarana of the patient gives the true diagnostic information to the healer and helps him choose the right methods to heal the problem in whatever body it is found.

To repeat, in general the ajna center is not active, and it is considered only when one is dealing with more advanced human beings.

A similar process must go on individually in the astral plane. Then the astral and etheric centers must coordinate with their corresponding centers and with the Chalice in the mental plane. These two sets of centers must come under the control of the Chalice to be the channels of willpower, love, and light. As the centers express these three aspects of glory, man enters into a greater and greater degree of illumination.

When all the centers are coordinated with the unfolding petals of the Chalice, we say that the spider web is complete. The spider web is the device which attracts and catches impressions and inspirations coming from Cosmic Sources.

The Lotus is a key center in the mental plane. Throughout ages it provides the dynamism and creative energy for all the centers and for the bodies. It is actually the body of the Solar Angel in the womb of which the baby, the human soul, evolves and reaches maturity.

Mental centers bring in impressions related to the will or to the Purpose. Astral centers bring in impressions related to cooperation, love, and the Plan.

Etheric centers bring in impressions related to the light, knowledge, ideas, and creativity. All these centers function in the light of the consciousness.

Every center has its own fire. As the centers unfold, the fire from the core of the center radiates more intensely. It is this fire that opens the path through layers and planes of various elements.

Every fire has its own frequency and power of penetration. The intensification of the fires of the centers is caused by the unfolding Chalice, by the expansion of consciousness, and by the advancing of the human soul.

The most powerful manifestation of the fire of the centers is reached when the fire fuses with the fire of Space. The currents of the fire of Space can be used by the fire of the centers when the consciousness of the human being is advanced enough to stand in the pressure of fire. This combined fire can be used for constructive and purificatory reasons.

Fire creates, and also, if necessary, it destroys those obstacles which stand on the path of purification or on the path of evolution. It is possible for the fire of the various centers to use the fire of Space for great creative works. One advanced man or woman, who is ready to use his fires, can change the destiny of a nation.

The etheric centers relate the man to the *ida*; the astral centers relate man to the *pingala*; and the mental centers relate man to the *sushumna*. The *ida*, *pingala*, and *sushumna* are three channels of fire which exist in the base of spine center.

These three fires climb to the head center through these etheric channels.

The right channel is called *pingala* and corresponds to the solar system. The left channel is called *ida* and corresponds to the lunar system. The central channel is *sushumna* and corresponds to Synthesis.

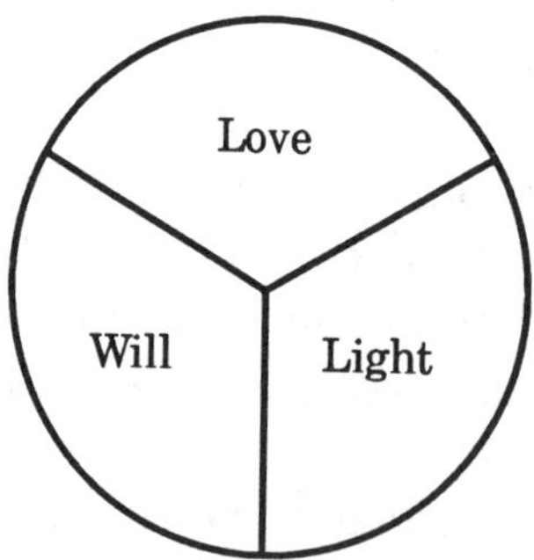

Diagram 17-1 Love, Light, Will

The etheric centers translate the Law of Economy; the astral centers the Law of Attraction and Repulsion; and the mental centers the Law of Synthesis.

Every center must first develop its love, light, and will portion if the man is to be kept out of trouble. The same thing in the group centers: First we must develop love, then light, then willpower if we want great success and a permanent opportunity to serve.

It is possible that you can shut off the right sequence of the unfolding portions of every center. For example, you love someone and the love portion of your center is stimulated. Then you try to exploit him and the light portion of that center is shut off, and if you try to force your will, the will portion gets the stimulation. Hence, we see how we disturb our centers by not acting along the lines of love, light, and will and misuse these energies.

Contradictions in your consciousness disturb your centers. For example, you say you love, but you exploit and force your will. Or you say you know, but you do not; you say you love, but you do not; you say you are strong, but you fall into inertia. Such kinds of contradictory states in your consciousness create conflicting situations in your centers and they lose their rhythm, health, and dynamism.

Every contradiction becomes more dangerous when your thoughts contradict your emotions and your emotions contradict your actions. This eventually leads to insanity, which is the result of the damage of the light portion of the centers or the centers related to light.

Every move in consciousness is a command to your computer. Wrong and negative moves eventually make you realize that your computer no longer is giving you any answers or meeting your needs.

Of course each center is related to a Ray. The predominant Ray of your vehicles makes it easy for you to unfold the corresponding center.

In the future, you will have the power to select your Rays and to influence the needed centers consciously.

Life after life we must try to coordinate our centers. Maybe a few lives are dedicated to developing the heart center and another few lives to the head center. Maybe another few lives to the throat center, then another few years to coordinate these three and pull up the three fires of the base of spine center.

Meditation and sacrificial service are the best means to expand your consciousness, and through it to unfold the many petals of your centers.

Each meditation must be organized in such a way that it affects your love, light, and will centers, first slowly, then speedily, until all your centers individually and collectively are coordinated. This is why meditation must be a daily discipline.

When your etheric centers begin to unfold, you become aware of your etheric body and eventually you can use it at will. When your astral centers begin to open, you become aware of your astral body and eventually use it for your subjective life. When your mental centers begin to unfold, you become aware of your mental body and eventually use it to contact Higher Worlds.

Lower bodies (physical, astral, mental) are built according to the development of the centers. The more unfolded are the centers, the better vehicles you have.

The ideal bodies have all these centers freely open and coordinated with the corresponding senses of the higher planes or bodies.

The centers are divided into seven rows. Each row corresponds to a specific part of the Chalice.

The first row of centers is

Base of spine — etheric Base of spine — astral Base of spine — mental	related to the sacrifice petals

The second row of centers is

Generative organs — etheric Generative organs — astral Generative organs — mental	related to the knowledge petals

The third row of centers is

Solar plexus — etheric Solar plexus — astral Solar plexus — mental	related to the love petals

The fourth row of centers is

Spleen — etheric Spleen — astral Spleen — mental	related to the physical and emotional permanent atoms and to the mental unit which leads to the Jewel in the Lotus.

The fifth row of centers is

Throat center — etheric Throat center — astral	related to the knowledge petals in the Lotus

The sixth row of centers is

Heart center — etheric Heart center — astral	related to the love petals in the Lotus

The seventh row of centers is

Head center — etheric Head center — astral	related to the sacrifice petals in the Lotus

The connections with the petals of the Lotus are established only if the petals are sufficiently unfolded.

In the personality vehicles, the first row of centers makes you individually conscious, conscious of what you are. The second row of centers makes you family conscious, or group conscious. The third row of centers makes you nationally conscious. The fourth row of centers makes you conscious of humanity. The fifth row of centers puts you in contact with the global Life, including all kingdoms of Nature. The sixth row of centers puts you in contact with the solar Life, and the seventh row of centers puts you in contact with the galactic Life. Thus, centers are doors and bridges leading you toward your expanding reality, your expanding Self.

But we must remember that as our higher centers open and progress one after the other, the higher always includes the lower and synthesizes it. Thus with the seventh row of centers, we contact the whole Universe in all its aspects of activity. Also we must remember that the Law of Correspondences is a Cosmic Law — "As above, so below."

The etheric centers transmit prana to all our organs. The deeper we breathe and the cleaner the air, the more vitality we transmit to the corresponding organs of our etheric centers.

The astral centers also transmit energy to the astral body and astral organs and senses, and gradually build that body to perfection.

The mental centers nourish the mental senses and mental organs. For example, there are many senses and many organs in the mental body which need energy and nourishment to build and grow.

We must remember that as we build our physical body throughout ages and eventually make it a *perfect* form, similarly we are going to build our astral and mental bodies and use them consciously and with great control in the corresponding planes.

As an example, we used carriages on land, which corresponds to our physical plane; then we used sailboats in the ocean, which corresponds to our astral plane; then we used airplanes in the air, corresponding to our mental plane. Each of our bodies must reach perfection if we want to be active in the corresponding planes.

We must remember that the etheric centers are vivified by correct, deep, natural breathing and by light. The breathing of the astral body transmits love energy, and the breathing of the mental body is inhalation and exhalation of ideas. Thus, breathing is threefold in all our three bodies.

If you are observant, you will see that various actions, various emotions, and various thoughts change the way you breathe. Your breathing is related to your consciousness, actions, emotions, and thoughts.

Thus, there are actions that either burn your etheric centers or build them. There are emotions which either burn or build your emotional centers. There are thoughts that either burn your mental centers or build them. Watch how you breathe when you love, when you have intercourse, when you hate or get angry, when you are creative or destructive. Your breathing and heartbeat shows you what is happening in your bodies.

Each row of your centers, when fully open, synchronizes with the corresponding centers of a group, nation, globe, solar system, and galaxy.

The greater the unfoldment of your centers, the greater the fusion you have with Greater Units. This means you share the problems, energy, and glory of the Greater Units.

When a certain row of centers are half developed, you enter into crises because you register the problems and troubles of the higher centers with which you are coordinated. But when your centers unfold and reach 60%, 80%, 90% development, you start sharing the victory, the joy, the glory of the Higher Units because of your coordination with Them.

Our centers put us in contact with the Greater Universe, and we realize Its existence, Its emotions, Its thoughts, Its plans, and Its purpose.

Man is organized in such a way that he can share the beauty of all that exists in the visible and invisible Universe.

18

Healing and the Increase in Disease

Many discoveries by science are the fruits of delusion, the mechanics of darkness, and the expressions of evil. Man will not be able to see this until he sees the difference between knowingness and beingness. Knowingness without beingness is an anti-survival factor.

We can definitely say that sickness and disease are increasing, and there are four reasons for this:

1. Man lives in cycles. We have a cycle in which the physical body is used the most, and the emotional and mental bodies are relatively dormant. Then a cycle comes in which we extensively use the physical and emotional bodies. After that, we enter a cycle in which we use our three vehicles simultaneously.

As we increase the number of bodies we use, we increase our problems. For example, if you have three new cars in your garage and you are using only one car, you can have only one car in trouble. If you are using two cars, you can have two cars in trouble; and if you are using the third car also, your expenses and headaches increase in proportion.

Of course, as we are using body after body, we are building them; but their building process is not a smooth one. Every time we do not use them properly, they create problems — physical problems, emotional problems, and mental problems. And as we proceed on the path of integration of these three bodies, the problems of each body are shared by the other bodies. This will continue until we start using yet another body, the intuitional body.

It is in this body that the human soul will achieve illumination, be able to use all his vehicles in harmony with natural laws and principles, and restore the health of the whole person. This means that the best way to escape diseases is to strive toward the sphere of the intuitional realms and reach illumination.

When we start to use our emotional nature, we eventually enter into the conflict of negative and positive emotions. Positive emotions raise our sensitivity and build a finer mechanism. Negative emotions cause great damage to this mechanism, which then reflects in the physical and mental bodies.

In using our mental mechanism, we mostly follow the path of our emotions. We often use our mind to secure the demands of our negative emotions, thus breaking the laws of harmony and health. When we use our mind destructively, negatively, and against the laws of survival, we create not only mental but also physical complications. These complications increase as we use our mind in wrong directions and create many poisonous gases, chemicals, destructive nuclear weapons, harmful pills, contaminated food, etc. and pollute our air, water, and land with smog, gases, and fallout. This is why sickness has increased at an unimaginable rate, and the best businesses and fields for exploitation have become the fields of medicine, surgery, drugs, and nuclear energy. At present, almost everything in Nature is contaminated with fallout, gases, poison, insecticides, and radioactivity.

Man, like a bull, is running toward his own destruction. This situation will continue for a while until man realizes his wrong direction and enters into a level of enlightenment, focusing his consciousness on the Intuitional Plane where he will see how he has distorted the life and what he can do to cleanse it and put it in order.

We have two kinds of scientists: the kind who exploit because of the desire of the masses or politicians, and the kind who have not only scientific knowledge but also love-wisdom. It is the first type of scientist who created most of the anti-survival factors. These people were inspired by dark forces or by their own hatred and greed. True scientists were, and still are, those who released their discoveries to negate the destructions and heal the damage done to humanity by the unwise scientists.

In these days, everyone speaks highly of scientific discoveries. Science builds an illusion in our mind that it is equal to truth, to survival. If science says anything, then it is the truth, and we accept science as the only real authority. This illusion will shatter as man enters into the domain of Intuition. Many discoveries by science are the fruits of delusion, the mechanics of darkness, and the expressions of evil. Man will not be able to see this until he sees the difference between knowingness and beingness. Knowingness without beingness is an anti-survival factor.

This lesson was given to humanity in the first pages of the *Torah*, where man ate the fruit of knowledge and was thrown out of Eden. Eden is the symbol of health, harmony, beauty, joy, and bliss. Man, because of his knowledge, was thrown out of Eden. Man chose knowledge, but his prime duty was to obey the **Will of God**.

We have knowledge, and we have the Will of God. Knowledge is havingness, the symbol of accumulation; the Will of God is the symbol of beingness. One need not know to be; when one is, he knows. And this is the knowledge which is Divine.

2. There is another main reason for ill health which can be called "human aspiration." Aspiration is an effort to raise yourself upward while many factors are pulling your feet down. This happens when you see Beauty, Goodness, and Truth and try to live in harmony with these principles, but many factors in your

system and in your environment pull you down. It is because of the tension created by this situation that many psychological and physical complications, disorders, and depressions are created.

This struggle leads us toward conscious suffering. We continuously submit ourselves to various kinds of suffering to pull ourselves out of matter and penetrate into the world of light and health.

3. When people are trying to heal the body without eliminating the roots of the diseases in the astral and mental bodies, they are making the roots stronger and more malignant. When such a man takes another incarnation, these roots violently come out and express themselves in the form of various kinds of disease. In the past, people did not have the ways and means to block the expression of sickness, as we do today, and the sickness would exhaust itself totally. Today, people can use artificial ways and means to keep a body alive even after the soul has already departed.

People who dedicate themselves to a life of Beauty, Goodness, and Truth complain that such a life has brought them "misfortune" and burdened their lives heavily with sorrow and suffering. Such a complaint may have a foundation, but the structure built upon it does not have true architecture.

When one increases his speed, he creates greater friction. When one increases his light, he sees the details, causes, and effects of events and objects. When one increases his knowledge and wisdom, he sees the greater needs of people and greater fields of service.

When a man increases his strength, he evokes stronger opposition. When a man increases the wealth of his virtues, karma demands larger and quicker payments.

When he increases the light of his Intuition, he sees exactly the boundaries and demands of battle, and he feels the urge to involve himself in the battle against dark forces.

This is how greater light, greater love, and greater power open greater fields of responsibility for the one who is striving toward perfection and service.

It is true that the opposing forces mobilize their agents against the traveler on the Path, but the spotlight of the Hierarchy gradually builds a shield around the traveler and follows his steps.

4. Another cause of sickness is malice. Malice attracts dark forces and opens the gates for them to attack various organs. Malice breaks the shield of the aura and creates ulcers in the etheric, astral, and mental substance. This attracts various forces and leads them to the physical body. Many obsessions take place through such cracks.

Malice also produces a poisonous gas which suffocates the living atoms of the aura and spreads out to harm the target of the attacker.

Malice creates organic and psychosomatic disorders, weakens the whole organism, and makes it prey to destructive forces.

The effects of malice can be eliminated by expressing increasing goodwill and benevolent thoughts, which cure the body and establish harmony and equilibrium.

Let us remember that the chemistry of the body is affected and often conditioned by the state of emotions and thought and the quality of the currents of energy we let loose into our aura through our words.

Malicious thinking penetrates like darts into the aura of the victims and causes infections. Many leaders and teachers suffer from such infections, the causes of which lie in the malicious thoughts of their "friends."

But every time the malicious darts hit a pure aura, that aura releases a substance of light which travels back toward the source of malice and burns the network of nadis around the source's body. This is why it is said that those who attack Holy Ones prepare their own destruction.

Nature does not tolerate actions which are based on separatism, self-interest, and hatred. The reaction of Nature does not appear at once, but the accumulated reactions work like gophers. The great pine tree appears healthy and beautiful, but it suddenly falls when all the roots are eaten or cut.

Malice must be eliminated from our lives as the most poisonous element because the consequences of malice require many incarnations to be cured.

Physical diagnosis is very important in order to take the right action in healing. But the emotional and mental diagnoses must also be taken into account, and all must work together. Unless the cause of sickness in the emotional and mental bodies is found, the diagnosis of the physical body will not bring permanent success in healing.

Malice is a very sneaky actor. It hides in the most unimaginable forms of expression and in the most beautiful garments. Malice opens the gates for infectious diseases.

People are of the opinion that microbes and germs exist only on the physical plane. In reality, there are emotional and mental germs which are more potent than their physical counterparts. Often it is possible to **curb** the activities of the physical germs and microbes, but the activities of the emotional and mental germs spread as if blown by the wind. Malicious people spread these germs and microbes, broadcasting them all over the globe.

Humanity instinctively and naturally wants to fight against such currents which cyclically attack humanity. Once malice weakens the subtle organism and exhausts the psychic energy, the human body falls victim to the hands of physical diseases.

It is said that malice is one of the great barriers on the path of human evolution and joy.

We are told that malice and cursing go together. Those who curse create very ugly thoughtforms which contaminate the sphere in which they live. This sphere is filled with dark formations of ugly thoughts and negative emotions. The beneficial forces in Nature run away from a man who curses.

Man does not live only by what he eats and breathes. Our aura is a great assimilator of subtle substances radiated out through the Sun and the Life of the planet. The vitality of the Sun and the planet cannot be assimilated by an aura which is full of the pollution of curses. This creates imbalance in our physical system, and our health degenerates. Every curse carries with it negatively charged particles. Like an exhaust pipe, it pollutes Space and attracts unwholesome guests.

Those who really want to be healthy must get rid of malice and cursing. Those who were slaves of malice and cursing appear with black faces in the Subtle World.

Healing must actually start from the soul of man. It can include the healing of the body, but even the healing of the body must be carried out in the interest of spiritual progress.

If you are healing the body for the sake of the body, for the enjoyment of the physical life, physical healing will create subtle complications and your body will suffer with different problems, in this life or in future lives. We must know that sickness is the result of a violation against the spirit, against Beauty, Goodness, and Truth. No matter how much you heal the body, if Beauty, Goodness, and Truth are not restored, you will continue having the same or heavier problems in this or other lives. Thus healing originates from the spirit, and when the spirit heals, no karmic seed remains anymore to make you sick.

Thus, all medicinal and various other kinds of treatments for the body must be done for only one purpose — to give the man an opportunity to spiritualize himself, to pay his debts and no longer violate the principles of life. That is why Christ said, "First seek the kingdom of God, and everything else will be given to you."

Thus, healing starts from the inside, not from the outside. It is in the Treasury of the Monad that the words of power are hidden, and you can have them when you enter into the Treasury of the Monad through your initiations.

People are anxious to be healthy. But individual health does not exist if one does not try to keep the planet healthy. Even this is not enough; one must try to keep his spiritual life healthy. Without spiritual health, the individual and planetary health will soon degenerate.

Individual health is the health of the whole body mechanism. The health of the planet is related to all natural resources such as the oceans, lakes, rivers, air, vegetation, forests, animals, trees, and earth, etc.

Spiritual health is related to our motives, thoughts, and deeds and to our harmonious relationship with the spiritual laws such as justice and compassion.

Health on the physical, emotional, and mental levels must be considered if one really wants to live a healthy life and prepare the world in such a way that the incoming generations live a healthy life as well.

Spiritual health is generated when a person lives in the light of higher virtues and in contact with higher, superhuman spheres of intelligence and wisdom. Without the guidance of these superhuman spheres and Cosmic Laws, health will not have a foundation or a real destination.

19

Various Healing Exercises

The exercises given in this section must not confuse you. Choose any one of them, according to your need. Whichever one you choose, stay with it for at least one month or one year. If it is a year-long exercise, it will have a great healing effect upon your entire nature. Be faithful to the given exercise, and do not mix it with others or add to it.

Most people are of the opinion that a healing process is a matter of a day, a week, or at the most a month. The real healing process is not related to such short time periods. It needs years of purification of consciousness and clearance. It may take lives to get rid of physical, emotional, and mental sicknesses. As a matter of fact, physical sicknesses that originate in the physical plane last for a shorter time than sicknesses originating in the astral and mental planes.

Purification of consciousness and the clearance of karma sometimes take ages. We die and reincarnate with the same seeds of illnesses. Some of them lie latent; others may become active. We need continuous efforts to purify our consciousness and to pay our karma patiently until the transformation and transfiguration processes take place within our constitution.

We are of the opinion that taking a few pills and a few injections will solve our problems. In reality this is not true.

Healing is not an outer phenomena only, but essentially it has to do with our emotions, thoughts, motives, expectations, aspirations, and attitudes. All these factors must be oriented toward the ideal, through the purification process and through the payment of our karma.

One must meditate upon the word "harmlessness" and make every effort to live a harmless life. Harmlessness is one of the techniques by which we create purification in our consciousness and immensely reduce our karmic debts.

Every impurity in our consciousness creates perpetual disorders in our vehicles and in our environment.

Every harmful act loads our karma. And with disordered vehicles and increasing karma, even if all the physicians come to us with their healing arts, we will not be able to enjoy good health.

Health or sickness are the threads of life going through all our incarnations. Our lives on the physical plane are the expressions of this thread. No matter how hard we try to heal ourself, we will again and again confront health problems if the health thread is not pure, due to our unclean consciousness and karma. This is why the most important factors of health are a purified consciousness and a clean karma.

In these exercises, you will find the methods I have collected throughout many years. Ponder on them, discover the spirit of them, and apply them if you really want to improve your health on many levels.

Healing With Beauty[1]

> *...The purpose of life, on any level, is the expression of Beauty....*[2]

PHYSICAL LEVEL:

1. Look at your body and find the parts that express beauty.

2. Find the parts of your body that are totally under your control to improve, and find how you could improve the beauty of your body. Work out very practical, gradient steps to improve the beauty of your body.

3. Do the same with your clothes. Go through your closet and pick out each piece that is beautiful. Separate them from the drab pieces of clothing that do not bring out beauty. Gradually replace your clothes until all are of beauty.

4. Go through your apartment or house, room by room, and do the same.

5. Do the same with your office, car, etc.

6. Continue until you have gone through all your physical possessions and replaced them with beauty. Finally you will be surrounded only with beauty.

EMOTIONAL LEVEL:

1. Assess all your emotional relationships with people, one by one — father, mother, brother, sister, lover, husband, wife, child, etc.

   a. Find the areas of beauty in each relationship. Then work out how you could bring one more aspect of beauty out of them each time you are with them.

---

1. Exercises are based on the book, *The Flame of Beauty, Culture, Love, Joy.*
2. *The Flame of Beauty, Culture, Love, Joy*, p. 1.

b. Do this first in your mind. Then actually go out and do this on a practical level when you are with them.

c. Afterward, review and see if you could have brought out more beauty.

d. Continue until you have brought out great beauty from within each of these people each time you are with them.

2. Assess yourself, and see how much more beauty you have brought out in yourself through these actions.

3. During the day, try to catch any negative emotions and change them into positive ones through imagination. For example:

    a. Change fear into courage.

    b. Change hatred into love.

    c. Change depression into happiness.

    d. Change nervousness into calmness.

    e. Change hiding into openness.

    f. Change crying into laughing.

4. During the day, try not to react to negative emotions expressed around you.

MENTAL LEVEL:

1. Assess your thoughts. Change all negative thoughts to thoughts of beauty.

2. If you find any difficulty with any particular thought, change it to beauty on a gradient scale.

> *Inspired men tell us that God sings, and all comes into existence as manifestations of His Song....*[3]

1. Find really beautiful and inspiring music. Sit and listen to each note.

2. Walk outside at sunrise and listen to the birds singing.

3. Watch the majesty of the sunrise.

---

3. *Ibid.*, p. 3.

4. See the beauty of the sunset.

5. Go for a walk and look at beautiful flowers or plants.

6. Find a flower, even if in a flower shop, and look at its beauty.

7. Find flowers that are fragrant and smell each of them.

8. Walk down the street and find people who radiate beauty to you.

...In beauty we are united.[4]

1. First start with yourself, then go to the family, then to groups, then to the city, then to the state, then to the nation, then to the international level. Find areas that are not united; then see how unity could occur through beauty.

2. Write or discuss your ideas with others, and work out creatively how you could introduce beauty to unite the particular areas.

With beauty we conquer....[5]

1. Go through your life and find situations you could conquer if you introduced beauty.

2. After doing this on a personal level, take up newsworthy items in your community and see how they could be conquered with beauty.

Approaching Beauty

Beauty is everywhere. To enjoy beauty and use it as an agent of healing, self-transformation, and self-actualization, one must be aware of it and fuse with it.

Beauty always has an effect upon a human being whether he is aware of it or not, but conscious contact with beauty is a direct method to receive the full benefit of the charge. To have a conscious contact with beauty, people must be trained in the following points:

1. The object of beauty, in whatever form it is presented, must be observed very carefully. If you can touch it, you must touch it

4. *Ibid.*, p. 1; quote from Nicholas Roerich, *Roerich Adamant*, p. 83.
5. *Ibid.*, p. 1.

with your fingers, palms, face, even with your lips. You must come in physical contact with it, observing every sensation you are receiving from it.[6]

a. Walk around the room and pick up something small and beautiful. Touch it with your fingers, palms, face, even with your lips.

b. What color is it? What is its temperature, its weight, its smell? Put it near your ear; what sound do you hear?

c. Continue this exercise, each time taking something larger.

2. If it [the beauty] is visual or auditory, concentrate your eyes or ears on the object in a deeply relaxed manner. See the shades of sound and color; the relations of notes or colors; the symbolic language they speak. Notice all your physical, emotional, and mental responses.[7]

Looking at something of beauty:

— See the shades of color, the relations of color.

— What is the beauty that this symbol speaks?

— What is your physical response to the beauty?

— What is your emotional response to the beauty?

— What is your mental response to this beauty?

Hearing something of beauty:

— Hear the variations and levels of sound. Listen for each different note. Observe the relations of the notes.

— What is this sound trying to say to you?

— What is the symbolic language of this music?

— What is your physical response to the music?

— What is your emotional response to the music?

— What is your mental response to the music?

---

6. *Ibid.*, p. 13.
7. *Ibid.*

3. Then absorb the beauty into your being. Focus yourself and see the beauty in an inner sense. Hear the music as if it were playing within you until the moment when you and the object of beauty fuse into each other.

4. ...Find the level on which the beauty originated. Uplift your consciousness to that level and try to find the real task of the beauty, the purpose for which it was created.[8]

Use the music or the same object of beauty as in the previous exercises.

5. ...Try to manifest the experienced beauty through your life expressions.[9]

Take what you have from listening to the music or looking at the piece of art and ask what inspiration you received. Try to formulate a way to bring this beauty into your personal life on the physical level, emotional level, and mental level.

6. ...Use your creative and inspirational moment as a means of service for humanity—radiating out the love, the beauty, the ecstasy, the light to all humanity—with the intention of healing the wounds of people; dispersing the clouds of hatred and separation; and creating right human relations, goodwill, understanding, and a transformation of your social life. This step can be called the projection of beauty to the world.

Listen to uplifting music and at the same time visualize it as if it were sounding all over the world, inducing great harmony and rhythm in human life. See great colors and inspiring forms and project the beauty to all places where disharmony and hatred exist. Visualize the exciting changes occurring in those fields.[10]

7. ...Endeavor to find a balance in color, sound, form, and movement in whatever field [you] live and work.[11]

a. Look at where you are living. Put everything, flowers, furniture, etc., in a balance of beautiful color. Work out sounds of beauty to go through your home. Look at the forms in your home, your furniture, drapes, etc., and increase their beauty.

---

8. *Ibid.*, pp. 13-14.
9. *Ibid.*, p. 15.
10. *Ibid.*, p. 16.
11. *Ibid.*, p. 17.

b. Do the same in your place of work.

..Let us remember that beauty is energy and people must be introduced to beauty gradually.

First they must learn to appreciate:

— the beauty of sound, the music of the streams, rivers, waterfalls

— the music of the wind and the breeze when it is passing through the trees, bushes, and fields

— the music of the birds at dawn and at sunset

— the beauty of the human voice and the melodies and symphonies of great masters

The next step is to introduce students to visual beauty:

— the beauty of colors, movements, forms, relationships or proportions, paintings, and other works of great artists

— the beauty of the mountains, forests, rivers, lakes, and oceans — the sailboat

— the beauty of the stars

The next step can be to introduce the beauty of the human emotions:

— love, all-inclusive love, respect, fearlessness, kindness, peacefulness, enthusiasm, and joy

All of these can be presented through dramatic performances with color and music.

Next, the beauty of great ideas can be presented to the students. Great heroes and great leaders and great geniuses in any field are those who are inspired by great ideas:

— ideas of freedom

— ideas of unity

— ideas of mastery of time, matter, space, human limitations

— ideas of great service and illumination of the masses

—*ideas of a world without crimes*

—*ideas of the brotherhood of humanity*

—*ideas of life after death*[12]

12. *Ibid.*, pp. 46-47.

20

Recharging and Healing Meditation

Have you ever thought, my brother, that just as there is a discipline of pain and sorrow, there may also be a discipline of joy and of achievement? This is a thought worthy of attention....

The Tibetan[1]

As with any of the preceding meditations and exercises in this book, you may use the following meditation to recharge your personality, to purify it of glamors and other hindrances, and to create a healing process in your body.

1. Relax your physical body.

2. Do the kneeling exercise, if you wish and are able to, as follows:

Kneel with feet apart. Now sit down, feet out to the side of your body. This is the first position. At first it may hurt, but later you will be used to it.

Now stand on your knees. Exhale slowly as you bend down to put the top of your head on the floor. When you reach the floor, stay in that position while holding your breath for 5 or 10 or 20 counts, which means 5, 10, or 20 seconds. Then slowly come back to your former position, in the meantime inhaling. Sit on your knees and exhale through your mouth, as if you were blowing out a candle.[2]

3. Align your three lower bodies.

4. Say the following Invocation:

Lead me, O Lord,

From darkness to Light,

From the unreal to the Real,

---

1. Alice A. Bailey, *Discipleship in the New Age*, Vol. II, p. 671.
2. *The Science of Meditation*, p. 80.

From death to Immortality,

From chaos to Beauty.

5. Visualize one of the following:

   a. An eagle of white light

   b. A sphere of pure blue light

   c. A five-pointed star in a glow of pure orange light twelve inches above your head

6. Raise your consciousness into the light and fuse with it, remaining silent, mentally and emotionally. This will take five minutes or less.

7. You will start feeling the light penetrating your mental body and cleansing it of many kinds of limitations. Meditate upon what the limitations are and upon the fact that the light is clearing them from the mental body.

8. Feel the light penetrating into your astral sphere and purifying it of many emotional problems. At this point you need not think or meditate; just visualize the process of purification as it is taking place in the body.

9. Feel the light penetrating into your etheric body and electrifying it, creating great harmony between the etheric body and the nervous and blood systems, recharging your whole body.

10. When you have done the above, immediately begin to visualize again; see the light of your Soul flooding all of your personality and radiating out into the room, into your office, to wherever you may be going.

11. Keep a minute of silence without imagination and thought.

12. Say the Great Invocation.

From the point of Light within the Mind of God

Let light stream forth into the minds of men.

Let Light descend on Earth.

From the point of Love within the Heart of God

Let love stream forth into the hearts of men.

May Christ return to Earth.

From the centre where the Will of God is known
Let purpose guide the little wills of men —
The purpose which the Masters know and serve.

From the centre which we call the race of men
Let the Plan of Love and Light work out.
And may it seal the door where evil dwells.

Let Light and Love and Power restore the Plan on Earth.

WARNING: Do not exceed fifteen minutes in doing this meditation. If, later, you feel some unpleasant sensations, discontinue the meditation for a few days. The incoming energies may create friction with the crystallized ridges in your subtle bodies and cause some unpleasant or uneasy feelings. This does not happen when your bodies are in a pure condition as they relate to each other, and when you avoid creating thoughts and emotions in opposition to the radiating light, love, and power of your Soul.[3]

3. Adapted from *The Psyche and Psychism*, pp. 699-700.

21

Radiant Health

Health is gained only by those people who develop their spiritual nature and charge their material nature with light, love, and energy.

When we study the art of healing in its various branches, we find three fundamental principles. **The first principle is Light, and any act against the Light of our conscience, against the Light of our Soul, against the Light of our True Self generates sickness.**

Action against Light creates inner conflict, irritation, tension, fear, and confusion. These conditions slowly expand within our astral, mental, and etheric realms and produce disease. If these inner conflicts end with the victory of Light, recovery is possible and the damage can be gradually repaired, if not in this life then in coming lives. If the act against Light gains momentum within the man, the destiny of that man will be pain and suffering for many incarnations.

We can say that those who bring more light and help for the victory of Light are the great healers of humanity.

The second principle is Love, and any act against Love is an act against good health. Any time a man acts against the principle of Love, he creates short circuits in his energy network. Love is life. Actions against Love are actions against life. This is true for an individual, for a family, for a nation, and for all humanity. Violation of the Love principle creates various disturbances, not only within our emotional nature but also within our mental nature and within our social and international life. Free circulation of the Love principle is the answer to most of our health problems.

The third principle is the principle of the spiritual Will, and any time we knowingly or unknowingly act against the spiritual Will, we sow the seeds of trouble throughout our psychological and physical systems.

Spiritual Will is an innate, sensitive mechanism which keeps us oriented toward the laws and directions of the Central Power in the Universe.

A subtle mechanism within us warns us when we are in the process of a wrong action, wrong thought, or wrong feeling. We feel that we are acting against the Purpose of life, and if we continue acting against it, we gradually enter upon the path of sickness, disease, and degeneration.

These three principles must always be observed in all our relationships if we want to have a healthy body and a healthy society.

When we are talking about Light, we are referring to the Light of Intuition which gradually penetrates our mind and expels all those thoughtforms which are based on illusions, ignorance, superstitions, prejudices, wrong motives, lies, and deceptions. Unless we clean out all these shadows of darkness, they will channel poisoned forces into our nature and make health impossible for us.

To increase the Light means to think clearly as much as possible, to search for reality, for facts, for the laws and principles of life, and to live accordingly. When a man lies for any reason, when he deceives or misleads people with false information, he is like a man who puts sugar in the gas tank of his car. Very soon his whole mechanism will reflect his unwise action.

Love must be increased in our life every day. All our thoughts, feelings, and actions must carry the energy of love. This energy will strengthen and purify our nature and dispel the poisonous accumulations brought in through all those thoughts, feelings, and actions which were the dark forces of hatred, fear, jealousy, revenge, and greed. As long as we are polluted with such accumulations, medical help will be superficial and will last only for a short while.

The spiritual Will must be active and must be used in all our expressions and relationships. It harmonizes all actions on all levels with the Divine Purpose. Even if we do not know anything about the Divine Purpose, we take the right direction when we follow the spiritual Will.

The Light principle creates radioactivity in our aura, harmonizes all centers on the physical, emotional, and mental planes with Soul intent, and destroys contaminated thoughtforms and illusions. The Love principle builds a shield around the aura, prevents hostile attacks from dark forces and destroys glamors. The spiritual Will galvanizes the aura with the energy of the fire which burns away all that slows down the progress of man. It also destroys the maya, the force which causes inertia, apathy, and depression.

These three principles can be used together for healing the entire man. If a man does not work against the Light and Love principles, against the spiritual Will, there is hardly anything that can make him ill. Our diseases and sicknesses, in most cases, are like taxes we pay for the actions taken against these three principles. These three principles can be translated into spiritual techniques which we can use to increase our health, happiness, and prosperity.

One of these techniques is called *gradient detachment*. This technique uses light, love, and willpower. If we want to live a longer and happier life, we must learn the techniques of detachment. Detachment is the ability to withdraw ourselves from the traps of the physical, emotional, and mental planes and enter into our own Essence.

All those objects with which you are identified sap your energy — no matter how lovely and charming the objects may be. Spiritual detachment enables you to dis-identify yourself from objects and come in contact with your deeper Self. Identification with the objects of your physical, emotional, and mental natures consumes your energy and time, prevents you from proceeding on the path of your spiritual evolution, and increases your fear and worry. Health is gained only by those people who develop their spiritual nature and charge their material nature with light, love, and energy.

Those who really want to be healthy must not attach to material objects. No material object belongs to us. Once you develop detachment, you may enjoy the objects without being enslaved by them. People are in fear and worry about their form objects — my ring, my gold, my account, my property, my business. Their belongings become a source of constant fear and worry. This affects their nervous system and their mind, changes their attitudes about life, and develops various sicknesses in them.

A detached man can have great wealth without identifying with it. He has no fear and no worry. If anything happens to his belongings, he keeps his serenity and striving. As long as we are attached to our belongings, we lose the most precious energy — psychic energy — because we are identified with non-reality. Identification with non-reality is an act of betrayal of our own Divinity.

The second step in detachment is detachment from emotional objects. Emotional objects are those objects which give us emotional security and pleasure. Emotional objects are our wishes, our desires, our vanities, hatreds, jealousies, our sex, our so-called dreams, ambitions, and show-offs. It is not easy to detach ourselves from emotional objects, even though we very often feel that they consume our energy. Detachment from emotional objects gives us a great release of energy and helps us enter into a greater equilibrium with the energies of Nature.

We must also detach ourselves from mental objects. Mental objects are our fanaticisms, our faith or traditions, our religion, our philosophies, and our political doctrines. When one is identified with mental objects he is condemned to insecurity, turmoil, inertia, crystallization, and conflict. These conditions are the causes of serious psychological and physical diseases.

When people are really stuck with their mental objects, most of their sickness originates from the mental plane. Wherever your identification is, there the trouble originates. If you are attached to physical objects, your trouble is going to start mainly from the physical plane. If you are attached emotionally, your trouble will start from the emotional plane. If you are attached mentally, your trouble will start from your mental body, but it will spread into your physical body and create various complications there. This is the reason why humanity is not healthy. Most of the influential people lead humanity toward greater attachment instead of greater detachment; attachment brings us all the suffering we see on the planet.

Fanaticism is the worst kind of attachment, and it can operate on physical, emotional, and mental levels simultaneously. Fanatics are infected by a contagious disease, so it is better to stay away from them. A fanatical person carries germs of destruction, separatism, non-tolerance, and hatred. Fanatics also develop brain tumors and heart diseases if their fanaticism is joined with violent emotions. Fanaticism ends with the destruction of its carrier.

Mental hospitals are full of people who identified with their mental objects to such a degree that they lost their sanity in the object of their identification. Slowly try to detach yourself from the objects to which you are attached. Try to detach yourself from your physical body and physical objects, from your emotional body and emotional objects, from your mental body and mental objects. Then you will gain greater health, greater energy, and greater power over your nature.

Use material objects without attachment; love without attachment; respect and enjoy without attachment; learn, know, and study without attachment. Do not be a fanatic; fanaticism is a mental cancer. No book, no teacher, no teaching should make you a fanatic if it is coming from the Most High. The Most High cannot limit Itself in any mental, emotional, or physical form. Your fanaticism is the fever of your limitation. Do not limit the Most High with the content of your mental nutshell. Fanaticism not only destroys a man with various diseases, but it also destroys cultural centers and civilizations.

It is also important to detach ourselves from so-called spiritual objects. This is very difficult to understand, but we have enough examples in the history of humanity which we can use to penetrate into this subject. For example, we are told that Lord Buddha renounced Nirvana to help humanity. Christ, we are told, left His Father's home to serve humanity. Great servers of our race are preoccupied with the well-being of humanity rather than with their own salvation.

Our salvation, our true path toward God, is only possible through a life of self-denial, self-sacrifice, and service for the cause of all humanity. Only those who work for the salvation of others can achieve freedom and liberation. Those who work and live only for their own salvation will most probably go to "hell." If we continue to drive people toward a selfish and separative search for salvation, toward a search for "heaven," for "paradise," and so on, we will lead them toward a great illusion, toward a greater self-interest in which man will desperately use all means to save himself. That is "hell."

If one wants to find himself, he must lose himself. One can lose himself only in seeking the salvation of others and sacrificing himself for the highest good of all humanity. If we continue our selfish path, soon our churches and colleges will be used as hospitals.

I remember one day my Teacher said to our class, "If a man dares to say that this is my God and that is your God, know that man does not have God because God cannot belong to separative interests." Imagine three groups involved in a conflict, each professing that God is on its side, and praying to God to help it in the conflict against the others!

We have gone so far away from God that we made Him "my God and your God." We have made Him an angry God, a vengeful God, a God Who hates and loves if He so chooses. And because we have such a God, we are not taken care of and suffering, sorrow, and the danger of total destruction are hanging over us.

As long as we are stuck with our selfish spiritual interests, we will be chained to this planet. Life after life we will reincarnate upon this planet, filling our karmic pool with our dirty actions in one life and then coming back again and trying to empty our pool in the next life. Graduation from this planet is possible only for those who work for the salvation of others. Working thus, they purify their lives forever.

So, detachment is a process of withdrawal into your innermost Divinity, your innermost Center of Light, Love, and Beauty. It is only from this Center that the energies of health, happiness, prosperity, inspiration, and creativity radiate out.

The next step toward health is *alignment.* Alignment means to bring all your life in harmony with the higher planes so that you create a continuous circulation of Life energy from the highest to the lowest.

We can align ourselves with the higher planes through concentration, meditation, contemplation, and prayer. By every act of goodwill, by every act of light and love, we align ourselves with the Sources of light, love, and the highest good. By any act of service to others, by any word of unity and synthesis, we align ourselves with the forces of reconstruction and with the forces of resurrection.

The human soul can align himself with the Inner Guide, with his Master, with the greater centers of beauty only through moments of intense prayer, dedication, and selfless service. It is in these moments of alignment that fiery energy comes from higher sources, purifies the vehicles and the environment of man, and radiates as the energy of healing and blessing.

Separatism and selfishness are the causes of disease. Alignment and unification are the foundation of health. We are advised in the Holy Scriptures to align ourselves daily with our inner God, with the Almighty Power, through regular meditation, prayer, and selfless service.

You can align yourself in the following way:

1. Sit comfortably and relax your whole body.

2. Feel deep joy and tranquility in your heart. Make your mind serene and clear of any thought.

3. Feel the rhythm of your heart, and with every beat of your heart, radiate energy to your physical, emotional, and mental natures.

4. Visualize your physical, emotional, and mental natures flooded with the light of your Inner Guide.

5. Then try to visualize above your head a shining star, and see a great stream of fiery energy pouring down and radiating out through your aura — purifying, healing, and energizing your whole nature.

6. After doing this for one month you can add another step, that of aligning yourself with those Great Ones Who guide the evolution of the planet.

Such an alignment process will gradually manifest itself as health, happiness, and creativity. Alignment is very important for spiritual groups so that they carry the power and inspiration from higher sources. Alignment not only makes a man whole but also unites people and groups and creates greater wholes. **Health is a direct result of alignment.**

The next step toward health is *deep breathing*. We are unaware of how badly we breathe. We fill only half or less than half of our lungs with air. Our lungs must be completely filled with air and rhythmically exhaled. Daily every two hours check your breathing. Try to breathe deeply, retain the breath, exhale, wait a second, and breathe again in the same way. You will be surprised what deep breathing does for you.

When you are in Nature, breathe deeply. This is not a breathing exercise. This is the way to breathe. Very soon you will notice how your sense organs are improving, how much more energy you have, and how much resistance is developed in your nature against germs and diseases.

Deep breathing revitalizes your etheric network and expands your aura. You come in contact with the vital force of the Universe which clears out the toxins accumulated within your system. Deep breathing not only purifies your etheric body but your emotional and mental natures as well. You can dispel most of your negative emotions through deep breathing. You can purify your mind and increase its clarity through deep breathing. Make your important decisions after deep breathing for at least two minutes, and you will see the result. If you are depressed or are under an attack of negative emotions, go outside and start deep breathing. You will probably conquer your negative emotions.

Those who are touchy, hateful, irritable, critical, and full of self-pity are those people who breathe very badly. When they learn how to breathe, they slowly conquer their miserable negativity and other vices. I remember a friend who used to have stage fright. One day before he went on stage, I made him breathe deeply for three minutes. He greatly improved his lecture and had great energy when he was speaking. You can use deep breathing before any creative performance and experience great improvement and success in your performance.

In deep breathing we heal our bodies, and often we burn germs and prevent future complications. Most of our mental, emotional, and physical problems originate from the congested and blocked areas of our etheric web. Deep breathing burns and clears out these blockages and restores health. It is recommended that you breathe deeply before you go to sleep. Also, there is a great advantage in running, as deep breathing rightly exercises the lungs.

The next step on the path to health is *relaxation*. Try to relax daily at least five to ten minutes with music or silence, or by sitting in a dark room where noise cannot reach you. Good music creates a rhythmic flow of energies. Silence makes your aura expand, and darkness relaxes your nervous system.

Light and noise create pressure on your aura. Electrical light puts a great pressure on your body and aura. One will be much healthier if he exposes himself less to electrical light, electric blankets, and hair dryers, which very slowly damage our etheric body and sap our energy. Humanity, after a long period of suffering and pain, is going to go back to Nature and live a natural life.

You can do the following exercise for relaxation:

1. Lie down on your back with your arms at your sides.

2. Try to push your body into the floor for two minutes.

3. Relax your entire body, starting with your toes and moving up your body, inch by inch, until you reach the top of your head.

4. After you feel the joy of relaxation, imagine a dark curtain in front of your eyes.

5. Then feel bliss all over your aura.

This should only take about five to seven minutes, and you will see how you can greatly improve your dynamism and health.

The next step toward health is *singing*. Daily try to sing for at least three to five minutes with all your heart, joy, or tears. Singing burns away accumulated ugly thoughtforms within the sphere of your mind. It burns away all negative, destructive, inharmonious, and separative thoughts accumulated within your aura, especially if you sing those songs which uplift your heart toward the Most High, or those songs which are dedicated to beauty, goodness, and unity. Actually, OM is the greatest song one can sing with all his being. It is the symbol of the Most High, and as one sounds the OM, he must release his heart to ascend toward the Most High.

You can sing while you are taking a bath. You can sing before your breakfast, or at sunrise or sunset, or before you sleep. Singing is a great method to increase health and happiness. Sing with all your heart. See how the birds sing. For the birds, singing is a healing process, a tuning in process, an act of assimilation of health-giving energies and creative forces, and you can use this method of the birds. Whenever you stop singing there is something wrong with you; clear it out by singing with all your heart.

The next step toward health is *dancing*. This may surprise you, but rhythmic dancing has a great influence on health and happiness. Your dancing need only take five to ten minutes, or even only three minutes, but choose a nice dance and dance in your own room or office whenever you have a few minutes to escape.

The important thing in such dancing is to create your own dance based on the music you choose. Try to make your movements meaningful, rhythmic, and beautiful and give your whole attention to them. Such dancing will bring greater joy into your life and greater vitality into your body. You will be more positive and happy.

You can even dance with your family before dinner or two hours after dinner. Hold the hands of your spouse and children and dance, forgetting all those worries accumulated in your brain from your daily labor and associations. You will increase the health and joy of your family.

Dancing releases those energies in your nature which respond to rhythm and motion. Once energy circulates in your system, all kinds of pollution accumulated in your aura are expelled. If you have privacy, you can dance naked after taking a shower. This facilitates the cleansing process of your aura which takes place when you dance.

Do not use the same music for more than fifteen days. Use different music with a different rhythm. However, you can use your favorite music cyclically after using four other dance pieces. After you dance once, you can try to improve it the next time and eventually create a dance which may translate your beautiful vision.

The next important point on the path of health is *not to nourish the viper of criticism in your heart.* This is very important for your health. An inner dialogue with a negative spirit disturbs your glands, and they secrete poison. Criticism that is the result of your hatred and jealousy, your separative and selfish spirit, or your fanaticism and ignorance is a viper in your heart, and sooner or later it will knock you down with ill health.

Women who have such critical attitudes are damaged mostly in their female organs. Men are damaged mostly in the brain. Absentmindedness, a "spaced" mind, and lack of responsibility come first. Then it hits the eyes, ears, and spine. One cannot afford to engage in the destructive and ugly exercise of criticism.

The next point on the path of health is *to beware of irritation.* Irritation blocks the life energy running through your nervous system and glands. It creates a gradual paralysis in your sympathetic nervous system. Many troubles related to your nerves originate from the poison produced by irritation. Wherever this poison settles in the nervous system, it eventually kills that nerve and penetrates into the bones.

Keep away from people who are continuously irritated. They radiate poison through their aura or through the objects they touch. Your health will greatly improve if you yourself keep away from irritation and the poison it produces and spreads. Also, try not to irritate people around you because they will create poison, and then they will spread it into your aura.[1]

---

1. For more information on irritation, please refer to *Irritation — The Destructive Fire.*

Another point on the path of health is *the elimination of jealousy*. Jealousy kills red blood cells. It affects the pineal gland and retards one's physical and spiritual metabolism. It distorts the regular circulation of the blood. Jealousy burns the health aura and creates a barrier between you and people, between you and objects, and charges them with a destructive force. The "Evil Eye" is the eye which is full of the force of jealousy. It rends the aura of other people and causes strong irritation.

Jealous people destroy their own future because jealousy causes irrationality in their mind and leads them into destructive actions. There is an ancient proverb which says, "Jealousy is like a strong viper which bites its container."

The next point is *self-pity*. Self-pity is the cause of many emotional and mental disorders. Self-pity develops when the unfolding human soul identifies himself with the weaknesses of the threefold lower vehicles. The cure is to withdraw oneself into the Light of the Inner Guide.

As far as a person is identified with his lower self and its weaknesses, he will perpetuate these weaknesses and draw low-quality atoms to his three vehicles. This will eventually create a barrier for the unfolding soul. This barrier will be the cause of many health problems. Self-pity and its brother, touchiness, consume psychic energy and utilize it for self-defense and for aggressive actions.

The next point on the path of health is *not to make promises easily*, neither to yourself nor to other people. Any time you make a promise, fulfill it. The expectancy of others builds various thoughtforms which may distort your thought processes and create conflict within your aura.

Sometimes we feel irritated without apparent reason. Irritation is a phenomenon of conflict in one or more of the personality vehicles. When two forces conflict, they create a tension which is called irritation. You do not have irritation if you do not have resistance.

A promise becomes a chain of thoughtforms in the mind of the one to whom you made the promise. In your mind you have the thoughtform of the promise, but it is neutralized by another thoughtform, your denial of your promise. The one who expects you to fulfill your promise continuously sends you his thoughtform demanding fulfillment. Your thoughtform of that promise agrees with his thoughtform and thus invites it into the sphere of your mind. Then the thoughtform of the denial of your promise fights with them and draws your consciousness into a turmoil because part of you demands fulfillment and part of you rejects it. Such conflicts may go on within your aura without your awareness and create conditions in which you are irritable without being able to detect the cause.

I remember a boy coming to me and asking if he could become a Master in three years if he followed my instructions. He was very sincere and very rich. It would have been possible to make a false promise to him and take his money. I told him, "Do not have faith in anyone who makes promises to you that you can become a Master in three years or even ten years. I can only tell you that mastery is the result of a never-ending process of striving and research and transmutation. You must depend only on your own labor and striving."

The boy was sad because he felt he was losing a chance to become a Master. When he was leaving I added, "Do not even make the promise to yourself because you are far away from your Self. Only your True Self can make a promise."

When you make any promise to your Higher Self, It demands the promise and even exerts pressure upon you to fulfill your promise, which leads you toward greater disturbances in your life.

The next point is very important. *Do not have close contacts or sexual relations with those who are obsessed.* Obsession is a very contagious disease, and sometimes you must escape to save your own skin. There are many signs of obsession, and some of them can be mentioned here:

1. If a person is addicted to anything, he has some obsession. It can be a partial obsession or a total obsession. For example, if he says, referring to his addiction, "I can't help it," "I can't stop smoking," "I can't stop using drugs," or "I can't stop wasting my sexual energies," be careful. Some force is holding his will in its hand and using his mind, and his defense system is giving up. If he is an alcoholic, stay away. He may have some invisible entities within his aura, and they may easily enter into your aura through any close relationship.

2. The eyes reflect the psychological state of a human being. When a person is absent from his own eyes and the eyes look like dull, empty orbs, you must be careful around such a person. Sometimes the obsessor uses the eyes to channel negative destructive force, lust, greed, or power in order to hypnotize you. You can be sure that such eyes can be dangerous to your life. Christ said that the eyes are the mirrors of the *soul*, or of the inner condition of the man.

3. Sometimes those who are obsessed have ever-changing behavior. They sit calmly for two minutes, then jump up without reason and feel nervous, or start to do something only to change, and then do something else a few minutes later. Their conversation takes on the same pattern; they start talking about a subject only to jump suddenly to another subject which is often accompanied with contradictory statements. They seem very happy for a few minutes, then they feel sad and miserable, then indifferent. And these changes happen continuously every half-hour or less.

4. The obsessed one has a different voice, different vocabulary, and different style of speech. You can easily observe this as he converses with you.

5. An obsessed or possessed person has a very deep-seated hatred which he often tries to cover up with artificial lovingness, but his lovingness is separative and is used only to mislead people.

Sometimes the hatred of an obsessed person is concentrated on those who render great service in their environment for human welfare.

6. Fanaticism is another sign of obsession. Fanaticism leads to various mental disorders and thus gives greater opportunity for the obsessing forces to act freely and to control the man more freely.

7. Uncleanliness is another sign of obsession. The body of an obsessed person smells. Their house, their bedroom, and their bathrooms are filthy. Although they use lots of makeup, you can still see the uncleanliness of their dress. They like to accumulate dirty dishes in their sink and dirty clothes which wait months to be washed. Their gardens are full of weeds and accumulated leaves. Obsessing entities hate cleanliness.

8. Obsessed ones do not like to smile. They have some kind of coldness in their face and actions. They do not smile at flowers, trees, and natural beauties. They have a sick smile only when a victory is won by the obsessed entity.

9. An obsessed person's nervous system is shaky, and when you touch his body he shakes or jumps as if hit by an electric shock.

10. Obsessed people have a strong tendency to force their will on others. They try to force their own ways and manners with moments of forceful showing off. Lord Buddha was very careful of those who would show-off. At the first sign of showing off, he used to dismiss the person from the brotherhood. Obsession is very contagious. Showing off is a sign that the obsessed one cannot hide and is trying to catch the attention of people.

11. Obsessed people are always in motion. They prepare to walk or do something, then continuously change the object of their attention. They use heavy drugs and are addicted to various vices.

To keep your mental and physical health, try not to react to such people emotionally. Handle the situation from the Soul level. This means without self-interest, fear, anger, irritation, or criticism. Obsessed ones always try to make you react. Reaction stimulates them and gives them the opportunity to relate to you. Indifference, calmness, and a loving understanding may save you from their attacks.

It is also said that one can protect himself from the attacks of obsessed ones by visualizing a blue and orange light around one's body and fixing one's mind on Christ.

The next step toward health is *to have a noble goal*, a spiritual goal which is beyond your selfish and materialistic interests. Have a goal that is related to human welfare, dedicated to the service of humanity, to the service of the planet and to its various kingdoms. Health increases in the spirit of inclusiveness. Have an inclusive goal for the good of all. Separative goals breed the seeds of sickness. Your goal must be a goal that is like a melody in a symphony. If you have such a noble goal, the whole existence will cooperate with you. The whole of Nature will nourish your physical, emotional, mental, and spiritual nature and increase in your heart the power of striving. Striving toward a noble goal attracts the fires of Space which create polarization toward the Highest in your system. Polarization creates rhythm, harmony, melody, and health within you.

The next step toward health is very beautiful. *Try as often as possible to sit by or under an oak, pine, or deodar tree and think about Nature's love for you and for all.* Sit a few minutes or a few hours, but put your back to the tree and feel it.

We are told that such trees are the transmitters of psychic energy. They transmit this psychic energy via your spine into your aura. Put your palm over the needles of pine trees and feel the energy flowing into your system. Sit by pine trees and read inspirational books...or rest. Pine needle tea is very beneficial. (Goats like to eat pine needles. They are smart animals.)

Increase your love toward Nature. True love does not create attachment. Real love is freedom, is pure reason.

The next step is *every day to have a few minutes of deep silence in the presence of Christ.* We must know that Christ is the Healing Center on this planet. Daily, we are told, He radiates healing rays, a healing symphony into Space to the whole world. These rays continuously fight to establish balance, equilibrium, and purity in the consciousness of humanity. Whenever we try to contact Him, we become the carriers of His healing rays and transmitters of His loving Fire.

All those who walk on the path of higher achievements are healers. Their presence and their looks carry healing energy. As a man expands his consciousness and contacts the spheres and dimensions where the Great Ones function, he becomes a transmitter of Their beauty. We are told that the Christ is building the bridge between Himself and the Father's Home. He is the greatest transmitter of those energies which eventually will bring to humanity greater beauty, harmony, love, cooperation, freedom, and health.

22

Sixteen Steps for Healing

A healing process is a liberation process. You cannot regenerate your vehicles as long as you are identified with them.

People think that the secrets of health are found outside of themselves, but actually the secrets of health are within. The potential for healing power within the man has very deep roots which as yet are not touched by him. Many modern healing arts deal mostly with the surface of the man. Various psychological methods deal with the emotional body or the lower mental body. But the time will come when healers will occupy themselves mainly with awakening the inner man and using his cooperation in healing the ills of the mental, emotional, and physical bodies.

We are told that in the etheric, astral, and mental bodies there are subtle centers which, when used creatively, can cure, heal, enlighten, strengthen, and vitalize our bodies for as long as we want. But these centers can only be used constructively when the awareness unit, the real human soul, is able to detach his identification from the physical, emotional, and mental bodies and focus himself in his own Essence.

One can use these centers, influencing them from the outside by physical, emotional, and mental methods, but such procedures do not evoke the help of the centers as long as the innermost man has not been contacted. It is only the owner of these centers who can use them safely to restore health, happiness, and strength.

The energy of healing will flow from these centers and purify and heal the bodies once the owner of these centers turns the key. The secrets of healing are within the etheric, astral, and mental bodies, but the keys to these secrets are in the hands of the human soul.

There are very simple steps by which you can gradually center yourself in your own Core:

1. *Have pure thoughts in your mind.* Thoughts condense and build your body. Thoughts create various substances in your body. Thoughts change the rhythm and the function of your organs. Thoughts create magnetism or repulsion in your aura. There are thoughts which attract germs; there are thoughts which

burn germs and repel negative currents of dark forces. With ugly thoughts you may poison all your system. Your entire energy network enters into great tension and crisis when your thoughts carry wrong motives.

Pure thoughts bring health, joy, and success. Pure thoughts are the formulations of those principles and laws which progressively help the human being unfold and proceed on the path of perfection, which always work for the survival of humanity and the beautification of life.

Any thought against the survival of humanity, against the progress and unfoldment of humanity, against beauty, and against health is an evil thought and carries destructive forces.

If one wants to be healthy, he must not allow his mind to produce any evil thought, accept any evil thought, or encourage any evil thought, but instead he must continuously make his mind create thoughts which uplift and transform life.

Those who want to remain healthy will be very watchful of their thoughts, and they must stop any thought when they feel that it is not a pure thought. Such people, in choosing and using pure thoughts, can save their life, their money, and their beauty. Thoughts of cheap criticism, full of vanity and hatred, must be ruled out. Thoughts that dwell on the weaknesses of others must be eliminated. With each thought we bring a force into our system, either for destruction or for construction.

Once a Sage said that ugly, dirty, and evil thoughts hang around a man and sap his psychic energy, his Light, his magnetism, and leave him like an empty bag.

The human body is like the earth; if the day is cloudy, the earth does not receive the rays of the Sun. The chemistry of the rays loses its beneficent quality if there are poisonous gases surrounding it. The same is true for a human being: if he is surrounded with evil thoughtforms or with polluted thoughtforms, the rays of his Soul cannot reach him and give him beneficial guidance, vitality, and strength. Instead, in mixing with his dark thoughtforms, they create toxins in the body — especially in the glands.

After you accumulate dark thoughts around you, you feel weak and become susceptible to various colds and sicknesses. Or you cannot operate your mind and brain as clearly, or solve your problems in the right way, or pass your exams.

We must remember that our etheric network, in most cases, is essentially healthy and harmonious in itself, but as we grow up we distort the harmony through our wrong actions, negative emotions, and evil thoughts.

The physical body is the shadow of the etheric network. If we keep the etheric body clear and harmonious, our body will be healthy and beautiful. But if we create distortion and disturbances in the etheric body by our acts, emotions, words, and thoughts, we create problems in our bloodstream, nervous system, glands, and organs. Thus the subtle body, the etheric body upon which our physical body is built and from which it absorbs its main nourishment, must be kept pure. And the greatest agent of purity is pure thought. When one has pure thoughts, he can purify his words, his actions, and his emotional reactions and, through the mental fire, cause transmutation in his nature.

Our mind is also conditioned by outer events. This is why we must avoid watching criminal and ugly events or actions as much as possible, so that we are not impressed by them and do not build thoughtforms because of them. This does not mean that one will escape from his responsibilities and duties if life brings events to him which are not beautiful and need to be handled or cleaned. Most of us cannot detach ourselves from an ugly event, but some of us act as surgeons and are not impressed or affected by the ugly conditions of life.

My grandmother used to say, "If you hear people talking or doing ugly things, do not stay with them; go away."

"Why, grandma?" I asked one day.

"Because ugly words and ugly manners or deeds stick in your imagination."

"What happens if they stick?"

"Eventually you tend to use the same words and do similar things. Imagination controls the behavior of man."

Some people see an ugly act or hear an ugly conversation or read a corrupt article and then go and repeat it in detail to their friends, either as information or because they want others to disapprove of it also. *In both cases they have served to distribute the ugliness.*

The power of ugliness is in its creators, buyers, and transmitters.

The mental body is composed of a very sensitive substance and, with every impression, the mental body builds a thoughtform which then lives in the mental sphere to do good or to do bad. The New Age is the age of seeing good things, doing good things, speaking good things, thinking and writing about good things. The more we think about good, the more it increases. The more we think about evil, the more evil increases. When we increase the good, we increase the health on earth.

2. *Have right motives.* When you have right motives, you think, you feel, you act, and you speak to increase joy, beauty, goodness, truth and bring in those conditions which help people grow and prosper. A wrong motive creates an inner conflict within your mental, emotional, and etheric spheres. A wrong motive is selfish, separative, full of vanity; it is sneaky and full of hypocrisy. Wrong motives create those energy waves within your system which create friction within you or between you and the energy field of your True Self. Wrong motives try to deceive other people and misuse them. Wrong motives create inner pressure.

In his essence, man is divine, harmonious, beautiful. Wrong motives create distortions, disturbances, and friction in the inner world of energies. These disturbances eventually distort the right functions of the etheric centers. The etheric centers control the ductless glands and the corresponding organs, and disturbances in these centers are reflected in the glands and organs and eventually cause various diseases in them. A Sage says that people enter into greater responsibilities only through their right motives.

Some people pretend they are channels, clairvoyants, psychics, or divine messengers, but their only motive is to collect money or satisfy their vanity. They mislead people; they present false values to them and eventually make them hate true spiritual values. When you study the lives of such "psychics," the first thing you notice is their bad health. They are irritable, touchy, critical, and aggressive because of a continuous conflict occuring under the surface of their consciousness — between their wrong motive and their own conscience. One must try to eliminate inner conflict as much as possible if one wants to live a long life and be healthy.

3. *Have a spirit of gratitude* throughout the day and throughout your life.

When you see a waterfall, turn your mind toward Infinity and say, "Thank you, Lord. What a beauty you gave me." When you watch the sunrise or sunset, express your gratitude in words of joy, in dancing, or in deep meditation and repeat, "Thank you, Lord." When you see mountains, lakes, rivers, birds, when you walk on the grass or swim in the ocean or lakes, feel that all is for you, all is for us; how fortunate we are to have Nature with all its living creatures.

Once I was taking a bath in a natural hot spring. It was so beautiful and pleasant that I started to sing, "Thank you, O Lord. What nice water you gave us to remind us of your Presence." I sensed the water. I smelled it. I drank it. I kissed it. I was in love with the water. We can develop that same spirit of gratitude for all those who work for us, who help us, who teach us, who inspire us, who protect us, who love us. We must not ever forget to express our gratitude for a cup of water or a cup of tea given to us.

Gratitude releases many accumulated tensions from our inner world, from our mental, emotional, and etheric bodies, and lets our body relax and feel happy. Gratitude releases psychic energy into our system and vitalizes it. A great Sage once said, "*Great is the healing power of gratitude.*"

Wherever you find a person, a family, or a group that is healthy and prosperous, you will see that a great spirit of gratitude is circulating in them. On the other hand, any failure is preceded by the spirit of ingratitude. Gratitude is the prelude to a happy, healthy, and prosperous life.

Often, because of various tensions, we fail to express gratitude; or because of negative attitudes toward us, we develop an aggressive attitude. Both these ways eventually lead us into disease. We can reverse such attitudes by reminding ourselves that we have more reasons to be thankful than reasons to be ungrateful.

4. *Develop goodwill.* Goodwill has a great power of healing not only physical ills but also psychological and social ills. In some regions in Asia, if a man feels sick, he distributes food, clothing, and money to needy ones. They say that such an act of goodwill has a great healing effect. I have seen many rich people distributing some of their cattle, sheep, goats, chickens, and the fruit from

their gardens to the poor. Some of these rich people, if they are capable, give free lessons in languages, the arts, and freely train the poor in certain jobs. This makes them happy and they feel useful.

One of my Teachers used to say that a man of goodwill is the extension of God. When one performs acts of goodwill, the energy of Good passes through his system and charges it, purifies it, and restores the health or prevents diseases. Goodwill can be exercised by doing a good deed every day with joy and conscious intent.

The Core of man is goodness, is divine beauty charged with goodness. It is a powerhouse of creative energies. When you release that Core, you flood your nature, your whole system, with healing energy. Those who have goodwill live a longer and happier life. The absence of goodwill leads us into depression, into apathy. The best remedy for depression and apathy is to get up and involve yourself in deeds of goodwill.

Once I asked a man of 117 years what made him live such a long and healthy life. What was his main food?

He smiled very beautifully, kept silent for a few minutes, then looking into my eyes said, "You are asking about outside things. Ask about things inside also."

"Well, what are the things inside of you which make you live such a long life?"

"I like to do good to everybody. I share my blessings. I like to make people happy. When I make people happy, I feel with a sensation of joy the Life energy penetrating into my body. I feel I am sharing the blessings of God with others, and I even help animals. Many wild animals come and eat near my home, and I have special arrangements for them...and every Christmas I send new shoes to fifteen or twenty children."

I do not know how long he lived, but I felt his healing energy. After our conversation I was a different boy. I remember as I was leaving him he touched my arm and whispered, "When you do good, know that nothing belongs to you. Secondly, do not encourage weakness; do not pity."

I learned through my experiences that you can render acts of goodwill by challenging people to stand on their own feet, by challenging them to strive and to educate themselves. To do good does not mean to encourage weakness, but to escape from an act of sacrifice is not worthy of excuses.

5. *Be joyful* in all ways and everywhere. Joy releases a healing energy into your system. Joy attracts vitality from Space. Joy clears the toxins found within your tissues, glands, and nervous system.

The greatest enemies of mankind are those who bring sadness and sorrow to humanity. The benefactors of humanity bring joy.

In a sacred brotherhood joy was called *the messenger of good*, and the members of the brotherhood used to sit daily under the trees or on the banks of rivers in great joy and ecstasy. We had a head cook who would also serve the dinner to all the members. His manners, words, and facial expressions used to radiate a deep, solemn joy. One day my Teacher said that the cook had learned the secret of life — to transmit joy to everyone through his every act.

The company of a joyful man has a great healing power. Only by increasing our wisdom can we increase our joy. Joy is the most powerful vitamin for our body, brain, eyes, and mind. And it has no tax!

Be joyful. Express a joy that comes from an inner realization, an inner achievement; a joy that comes through a contact with a beauty; a joy that comes through your acts of goodwill; a joy that comes through your sacrificial deeds for others; a joy that comes when you create peace and understanding; a joy that comes when you are creative and loving; a joy that comes when you overcome your weaknesses and gain victory over your problems.

Try not to exchange your joy for anything transient and futile. A joyful man radiates golden rays which expand and penetrate into Space and fuse with the song of the Universe. Each golden ray brings you blessings, power, and wisdom. Joy makes your sleep deeper and your subjective contacts higher and clearer.

Joy builds its foundation on acts of goodwill, on selflessness, sacrificial service, and inclusiveness. Wherever you go, take joy with you. Joy is a great psychic power which uplifts and heals.

Once I told a girl, "If you write a letter, put joy in it." One day I received a letter from this girl, and I felt deep joy in my heart upon opening it. The first word was "Rejoice!" It was a beautiful letter. I called her long distance and asked, "What did you do to your letter?"

"Did you feel the joy?" she asked.

"Yes."

"I wrote it and holding it to my heart, I charged it with my highest joy. I am glad you felt it."

After our conversation I made some experiments with flowers, letters, and different objects, and I am convinced that joy is a special substance which can be received and transmitted through any object.

I also experienced that joy disperses heavy layers of negative thoughts and emotions from our homes. Whenever you give something to somebody, charge it with joy; your joy increases as you give it to others.

Some objects are charged with destructive thoughts and emotions, and they carry poison with them. Once I received a letter in which the writer asked me to return a record that he had given me for my birthday. I was surprised. At the end of his letter he said, "When I came on Sunday to your meeting, you did not even see me."

I sent the record back and tried to write a letter that would not hurt him or be an expression of hurt feelings. It took me two or three hours to write that letter. First I tried to be joyful and radiate joy to him. Then I took the pen and wrote, "I send this record back to you, and it does not really matter whether this record is with me or with you because we are one in Spirit, and your joy is my joy, as my joy is your joy. Love...."

A week later, I received another letter from him. "Dear T., I can't conquer you; you conquered me and healed me from a sickness which was with me for a long time. You may call it touchiness, self-pity, or jealousy.... Your letter, in a flash, wiped it out. I felt great joy, so great that I cried aloud and was released from my sickness. Please forgive me for being so nasty."

Mechanical reactions, habitual reactions to life events, consume a great amount of energy. On the other hand, a soul reaction, a joyful reaction, brings abundant energy into our system.

When you react to a negative person, you let his negativity penetrate into your system with its poison; but when you react with joy and understanding, you reject his negative forces and even disperse them from his own sphere of life. That is why the greatest Physician, the Christ, said, "Bless your enemies."

6. *Cultivate a close friendship with Nature.* It is very important that we must occasionally be in Nature — hiking, climbing mountains, running along the seashore, swimming in the lakes, the rivers, or the ocean. Nature is a great healer if you come in close contact with it. Sit under the trees and enjoy Nature. Work in your garden; touch the flowers and talk to them.

Walking is one of the most precious gifts to humanity. Whenever you have a chance, walk under the trees, in the parks, in the mountains. Running is fantastic; it cleanses many toxins from your system and energizes your heart, lungs, and other organs.

Walking, running, and swimming are also very helpful to your emotional and mental natures. You feel more positive and think better thoughts. You see things more clearly.

7. The next step in healing is *not to eat after sunset or before sunrise.* In some mystery schools the Teachers say that the forces that aid digestion and assimilation are not active at night or after sunset. Our digestive mechanism uses different reservoirs to digest food eaten after sunset, and this wears out the digestive mechanism, resulting in many disorders in the system.

The Sun has a direct influence on our digestion and assimilation. Our health will be much better if we discipline ourselves not to eat after sunset. This will also help our sleep. Most of our silly dreams which keep us close to earth and to earth problems are the products of food eaten after sunset. Food brings many psychic influences into play which have a part in the formation of our dreams.

The process of digestion after sunset puts pressures on various organs.

During sleep we must be able to penetrate into the mental plane or the Intuitional Plane to receive new orientations, new instructions from our Soul or from the invisible Teachers. Food eaten after sunset keeps us in our etheric and astral bodies, and undeveloped entities use our bodies for their pleasures and often contaminate our bodies with their earthbound urges and drives.

The best way to sleep is to eliminate the waste our body produces, take a shower, read uplifting and inspiring literature, meditate and pray, and go to sleep.

Some people run, play tennis, dance, etc. before sleep. These are very beneficial exercises. It is during a good sleep that our physical body is repaired because our etheric body, which is a network of thousands of threads, rebuilds itself and establishes better contacts between glands, blood, and various organs through the etheric centers. In deep sleep the etheric body makes deeper contacts with astral and mental centers, and creates integration and harmony within the network of forces and energies in the human system. We may say that sleep is a harmonization process, and one must be careful not to distort it with food or by other means.

In some schools teachers recommend sleeping from 9:00 or 10:00 p.m. until sunrise. Those who are living near the north and south poles must adjust their lives differently. It is observed that when one sleeps after sunrise, his etheric body is sapped to a considerable degree by the rays of the Sun while he is in sleep. One feels very dynamic if he gets up early in the morning before sunrise. This also affects our mental attitude and capacity to think.

The food we are eating after sunset mostly affects our emotional and mental bodies, creating turbulences in them while we are asleep. Those who eat before sunset live a longer and healthier life, but those who eat only once a day live a much longer and healthier life and become very productive and creative people.

Those who eat a heavy meal after sunset or late at night often feel strong sexual stimulation, and usually they indulge in sex more often than those who eat once a day. The overuse of sex energy deprives a person of energy, and one usually spends more energy through sex than he can obtain from eating a heavy meal. Thus heavy meals eaten late work against one's own health in many ways.

8. The next step for health is *to set aside a proper time every day to contemplate a beautiful future for yourself and for humanity as a whole.* The future is a blank page. Create something beautiful on it. Visualize yourself surpassing your present level and your present limitations. Build a vision; pull yourself out of the present conditions and live in your vision, as if it were real and factual. Do not try to duplicate your past happy days but create future ones.

You will feel that your health is improving as days go by because when you free your mind from your own limitations and live in the realm of success, beauty, harmony, and joy you release health-giving energies from your inner resources and invigorate your whole system, even if your contemplation is done for only a short time.

Contemplation on the future can be done in the following way:

a. Sit and relax your whole body.

b. Feel calm.

c. Think about something very beautiful.

d. See yourself involved with that beauty. See yourself free from the limitations of time, body, money, and environment. See yourself in a state of liberation in which you can do almost anything you want.

e. See yourself free from your own weaknesses. Let your physical, emotional, and mental weaknesses be lost in the vision of your new achievements.

f. See what you can do for humanity so that humanity is more happy, healthy, prosperous, and cooperative.

g. See how you can eliminate crime, and in your vision try to eliminate it and show people the way to liberate themselves.

h. Think about your future in relation to time. First start with ten days; then take your contemplation beyond one thousand years or one million years.

i. Think about your death. Go beyond and see yourself incarnated in different places, in different nations, with better bodies, with greater talents, and with higher positions.

j. Think about your role in the ocean of time. What would you do if one thousand years were given to you? Start doing it, but remember that your progress will be real if you do not duplicate your present or past life and call it the future. The future is the progressive liberation from all that is blocking your path from spiritualization.

k. Think about those who achieved greatness and who can further surpass themselves.

By thinking in the future, you break all the etheric, emotional, and mental prisons and walls which you have been building for centuries and burying yourself in. A healing process is a liberation process. You cannot regenerate your vehicles as long as you are identified with them.

Do this exercise every day of your life. After a few years of doing it, you will not be the same person. You will be one hundred years ahead of yourself.

When they put Gandhi into prison, he asked for a copy of *The Bhagavad Gita*. *The Bhagavad Gita* is a book of the future. In contemplating the future through the visions presented in *The Bhagavad Gita*, Gandhi planned the future emancipation of five hundred million people, and he did it.

The future is composed of freedom, joy, progressive perfectionment, greater creativity, greater contact with the Universe, and mastery of time, space, energy, matter, and form.

9. The next step for health is *forgiveness*. Do not keep remorse or grief in your heart. Do not keep the image of wrong things done to you...or the image of the doer. As long as you keep them in your mind, they influence you, and eventually you do what they want you to do. They take your free will out of your hand.

An unforgiving man is in a constant tension. This tension in any area of your mental body crystallizes and forms tumors. You can have not only physical tumors but mental tumors also, which are more dangerous. Get rid of such a danger. Forgive and forget, and never turn back to the same subject.

Unforgiveness keeps your mind, emotions, and nervous system in a state of revenge. Revenge is a process of contamination. The mental tumor expands into the astral body, then into the etheric body, and expresses itself either by a crime or by some sort of complicated disease. Unforgiveness saps all your psychic energy and cuts your relation with your Soul.

People may argue, saying that they hated and were unforgiving but nothing bad happened to them. They cannot see the damage they did to their physical, emotional, and etheric centers. They cannot see the damage they did to their various organs, to their genes, to their future incarnations. We must never forget that Nature works slowly, and the weeds you plant today may become ripe in a future incarnation. That is why the great Physician strongly emphasized forgiveness and said, "Forgive one another."

10. The next step toward health is *alignment.* Daily align yourself and your vehicles with your Soul and feel the energy of the Soul flowing down to your vehicles, invigorating, energizing, and purifying them. This is called a spiritual shower. A few months later, align yourself with the Hierarchy. You can advance your alignment further with greater sources of energy as you make yourself ready for the increasing voltage of energy and use these contacts for your own perfectionment.

11. The next step on the path of health is *to stay away from lower psychics, pseudo-aura readers, astral clairvoyants, fortunetellers, mediums, automatic writers, speakers in tongues, pseudo-prophets, and all those who masquerade the divine realities and make people hate higher values*. Such people not only can contaminate your aura but also all your emotional and mental nature and mislead you on the path of your life. If they catch you, you eventually turn into a slave. You lose your free will and cannot achieve self-actualization in your life.

Necromancy is another very dangerous practice which must be avoided if one wants to be healthy.

People must not be led by the blind but must try to lead themselves by striving to increase their own light and to expand their own consciousness.

In many places in Asia, teachers warned us not to visit the homes of mediums, sorcerers, and black magicians because they contaminate the subtle vehicles and create obsession.

12. The next step is *to avoid liquor, smoking, drugs, marijuana, overindulgence in sex, and eating meat.* Whoever yields to these vices cannot expect health and happiness. The whole nature of man is to be the Temple of God, and it should be kept pure and clean.

13. The next step on the path of health is *to eliminate fear.* Fear is one of the worst killers of health. Avoid not only fear but also the causes of fear.

14. *Avoid pity.* Pity is identification with the weaknesses of people. Do not pity people. Make them stand on their own feet and pave their own way. Pity makes you absorb the weaknesses of the people. Through your own pity for them, they can contaminate you with their failures. Use your love not in pity but in making them help themselves. Even let them suffer in order to learn their hard lessons. Do not make them depend on you. It is observed that through pity one can transfer the sickness of other people into his own system.

15. *Do not come close to those people who hate others and gossip heavily, who are separative, who like revenge and are jealous people.* People with such kinds of attitudes emanate destructive rays from their bodies and disturb the harmony of your aura.

16. *Do not watch those television programs or films which advertise crime, violence, pornography, racism, fanaticism, or separatism.* And when you watch an educational program, sit twenty-five to thirty feet away from your television set. Do not watch television for more than thirty minutes daily. After thirty minutes, you are overloading your astral and mental bodies with heavy radiation.

Do not let children under twelve years of age watch television. It is detrimental to their health and sanity. Increasing crime and juvenile delinquency are proof of this. Leukemia is prevalent in those children who watch television for two to three hours daily and sleep in front of the television while their parent is out having "a good time." Radioactivity from television hits the pineal gland and the red cells and retards the harmonious development of health.

These sixteen steps will lead you on the path to better health. It may take a little time to adjust yourself, as well as a little effort, but eventually you will see the improvement in your health.

23

A Healing Meditation

To overcome anxieties, fears, worries, and doubts:

1. Sit relaxed and withdraw your focus of consciousness within the Spiritual Triad. See a triangle of colors — blue, orange, and fiery red — and at the middle of this triangle take your stand.

2. Inhale these fiery energies three times, expelling all fear and pollution from your physical-etheric, astral, and mental bodies.

3. Think that nothing evil can reach you and all that troubles you is associated with the three bodies.

4. See a door where you stand in the Spiritual Triad. Open it and enter into the Cosmic Presence and say,

    O Almighty Power, may Your peace

    pour into me and build a shield,

    and may Your power radiate through me.[1]

1. *The Psyche and Psychism*, p. 675.

24

Healing and Space

One of the main causes of the psychological and physical sicknesses of man is his limiting, contracting space.

There are three ideas which have great healing power if assimilated by our mind and put into practice throughout our life. They are

- Space
- Future
- Infinity

The human essence is a bottled space. The human essence is a concentrated fire. This human essence cyclically pulsates and expands, releasing energy, fire, and bliss into its system.

Often this effort of expansion meets hindrances, barriers, or obstacles built by the human personality in physical-etheric, astral, and mental realms. These hindrances, barriers, and obstacles are all those actions, activities, urges, drives, feelings, emotions, and thoughts that are based on separatism, limitations, and rejections.

Illness or sickness is the result of friction between the power of expansion and the force of contraction. The efforts or elements of contraction prevent the natural expansion of space, of fire, of bliss.

Any expression of limitation, any effort to prevent inclusiveness and expansion of love, beauty, goodness, and light generates the seeds of illness and disease. Limitation or contraction creates friction, breaks the free flow of energy, builds barriers on the communication lines, and produces imbalance. A distorted balance is the result of lack of communication and lack of awareness of the greater field of reality.

One of the main causes of the psychological and physical sicknesses of man is his limiting, contracting space. Primitive man had more space than civilized man. Primitive man's space was an unlimited physical space. He could sit anywhere and enjoy the sky, the mountains, the rivers, the ocean.

As this space was taken from him and he was given a limited space, he began to develop sicknesses resulting from contraction. His room had been a forest; now his room is a dark apartment from the window of which he can see the neighbor's wall. His garden had been the meadows; now his garden is the backyard or the balcony.

As his space became less and less, man identified more with his body, his emotions, and his thoughts and developed a life around the axis of his self — he became selfish. Selfishness is the absence of emotional space. As his emotional space became narrower or disappeared, man cultivated his mind only to serve his limited space, his self, his group self, or his national self.

The time came when any attempt to expand man's space resulted in violent reactions, not only from the emotional and mental natures of the man but also from his physical nature. This reaction created irritation and continuously poisoned his system.

Man can live a thousand years or more if he learns to expand his space, gradually, gently, and with utmost harmlessness. It will take a long time until this science is developed and practiced in the modern psychiatric hospitals.

Contraction of the space of man is caused by the following factors:

1. Deeds that were harmful to others

2. Emotions that were expressed to reject and to exploit

3. Thoughts that were based on separatism

These factors created limitations in the space of other people. Those who are not loaded with such factors are attacked by the tidal waves of such people and are deeply hurt and weakened.

One must not limit the space of other people with his wrong deeds, words, emotions, and thoughts.

Karma is limitation of space because it binds you to special locations, special conditions, special states of consciousness, and various health conditions.

People commit a crime by limiting others' physical, emotional, and mental space. When your physical, emotional, or mental space is limited, you can commit many sorts of crimes. Any limitation of space leads you away from your health, happiness, joy, and freedom.

Freedom is expanding space. But if your freedom is taken away, or you take away the freedom of others, you contract your space.

When the space of man is narrowed to such a degree that he cannot see beyond his nose, he starts wars and lives a criminal life. Wars and crime are the symptoms of dire disease in the emotional and mental natures of man. These actions cause the death of millions of people, pollute the earth, and cause widespread destruction.

Hatred and greed are techniques used to narrow one's space and the space of others.

As the space becomes narrower, man develops fear, irritation, and the ways and means for self-destruction. Self-destruction and suicide are the result of a logic blinded to the expansion of space. When the space reaches its extreme contraction, man becomes self-destructive and suicidal. Because of his blindness, he thinks that his space is rediscovered and expanded if the limitation, which is his body, is eliminated.

Hope is expansion of space; love is expansion of space; beauty is expansion of space.

Hopelessness is contraction of space. When space is contracted, one is led to death.

Hatred is contraction of space. When space is contracted, one turns into a criminal.

Ugliness is contraction of space. When space is contracted by ugliness, man loses his sense of self-respect, his solemnity, and his sense of value, and he leads himself toward vulgarity. Ugliness brings degeneration to the etheric body.

Primitive man's space was mostly physical, and those who are identified with their physical nature or matter have only physical space. Such people instinctively try to cure themselves by expanding their physical space. Taking a vacation is an effort to expand their space. Making more money and acquiring more property are efforts to expand their space. Greedy people are sick people, and to cure themselves from their sickness, they try to **have more** at the expense of others because greed blinds people and they do not see the right technique or the right means to cure themselves. Their cure will come in renunciation, benevolent distribution of their riches, or intelligent sharing.

Man added to his space the space of his emotions when he began to love Nature and form families, races, and nations. But those who identify with their emotions, whether on an individual or national scale, are on the path of contraction. Expansion of emotional space should be in having a greater inclusiveness of others. More love will expand emotional space. Labor done for others because of love will further expand one's space. **Healing will come to the emotional man through love, service, and inclusiveness.**

Man added another dimension to his physical and emotional space — mental space. Expansion of consciousness is expansion of space.

Knowledge is expansion of space.

Ignorance is not expansion of space.

Expansion of consciousness is a process to come in contact with the lives in other forms and help them expand their space. Expansion of consciousness is expansion of communication, then identification, and then fusion.

Expansion of consciousness is not an act of filling your mind with opinions, data, thoughtforms, or even with certain knowledge. Often the increase of knowledge limits our space. That is what has happened to our civilization; man contracted his space because of his knowledge.

Knowledge has enabled us to live in a more limited space with the illusion that we have more space. Thus, paradoxically, all our communication and transportation systems have made our space more limited. Our apartments, condominiums, and houses are built upon each other's shoulders, thus limiting our space.

Factories and complicated machinery took our space away from us. The less space we have, the less life we have. Space is life. With each limitation of space, our life is shorter because we are in essence a space.

Those who identified with their sophisticated mind, mental nature, or knowledge followed the same path of contraction of space.

Man has the delusion that he knows certain things, and his survival depends on his knowledge. We see now the end result of such knowledge. Systematized crimes, dangers of radioactivity, dangers from the vast pollution in our air, water, and soil, overcrowded and overpopulated cities — with these dangers man is cutting his throat with his own hands, with his own so-called scientific knowledge.

Knowledge did not expand the physical, emotional, and mental space, but it worked in the opposite direction. It limited the space and brought contraction. Limiting the space of man's mind is equal to his suicide.

When the physical, emotional, and mental spaces become narrower and narrower, we see the degeneration of the health of the planet.

Thus we have two kinds of space — the subjective space and the physical space. The subjective space is the space you occupy with your awareness and with your conscious influence. The physical space is the space you see and have control over; it is your room, your home, your street, your garden, or the mountains, rivers, oceans, or canyons. These two dimensions of the one space must expand if we want to restore health and sanity on the planet.

How can we expand our space?

It must start from both dimensions, from subjective as well as physical space.

The steps to physical expansion are as follows:

1. Have more mirrors and windows in your home.

2. Try to live in big rooms, with as little furniture as possible.

3. Often go to the mountains and enjoy the expanding view of hills and meadows.

4. Regularly go to the ocean and sit at the shore and enjoy the space.

5. Often lie on your back and look at the blue sky in the daytime, and at night watch the stars for at least fifteen minutes.

6. Observe the tall pines or the oak trees, watching their branches and the light through them.

7. Visit deep canyons and gorges and spend hours and days enjoying the space. Visit great mountain ranges in the world, great waterfalls and rivers, and spend time enjoying the space.

   You will notice a great change in your attitude toward life, a great improvement in your health, and an increase in energy.

8. Avoid all actions or activities which bring limitation to you and to others. Do not deprive people of their space.

   Actions based on selfishness, greed, hatred, fear, or anger diminish your space and the space of others; you cannot expand your space if you limit the space of others. Eventually you come to the awareness that space is one, and it can be enjoyed only in keeping it as one for everyone.

9. Any time you limit your or another person's space, **try to undo it** in any way possible. Health is the result of expansion of space. Expand your space, unfold yourself, and destroy the walls you erected within you, within your space, and within others.

Emotional space can be expanded through the following steps:

1. Increase your aspirations toward ideals which are holistic or inclusive.

2. Expand your love of human beings to those of lower kingdoms and even toward the stars and galaxies.

3. Purify your emotions.

4. Do not involve yourself in the negative and destructive emotions of others.

5. Increase the joy in your life. Joy expands your emotional space just as love does.

6. Develop detachment from objects, persons, and locations.

7. Learn to contribute to the efforts of those who are striving toward beauty.

8. Worship and pray to an embodiment of beauty, power, goodness, or compassion. This can be a daily ritual.

9. Use only constructive, uplifting, expanding, and inspiring speech.

Along with the efforts to expand your emotional space, you may exercise the thirteen steps of expanding your mental space. You can expand your mental space through the following:

1. Expand the field of your responsibility and service.
2. Think in terms of greater wholes.
3. Build bridges between subjective and objective values, between the spiritual and physical worlds, between abstract and practical life, between extremes.
4. Exercise psychic meditation or creative thinking.
5. Try to fuse with the Intuitional Plane.
6. Open your mind intelligently to the impressions coming from outer space.
7. Transmit the energy of light, or pure, clear thinking.
8. Think in terms of the future, in terms of Infinity, in terms of ever growing possibilities.
9. Expand your time concept.
10. Gradually destroy the ownership concept and the body concept.
11. Think in terms of energy and relating yourself to others and to objects as an energy flow.
12. Contemplate upon Infinity and the ever progressing achievements of the future.
13. Handle your knowledge, your traditions, your religion, your philosophy, and your faith like toys with which you play for awhile and then outgrow.

Through these thirty-one steps you will expand your space, and gradually you will become more space and less limitation. As you grow in space, you will grow in beauty, in creativity, and in power because you, in essence, are Space.

Your mental space is the limit of your conscious registrations of impressions reaching you from the living forms built in space. As your field of registration of impressions increases and expands, you expand your Beingness. The small self gradually fuses with the Self, the Space.

Our space is the field of our conscious influence. As our influence carries out a growing beauty, goodness, joy, and bliss, our space expands and we pass from one initiation to a higher one. As we expand our space, we come closer to our Innermost Self. The process of becoming our Self is the process of expanding our space.

Our personality vehicles, our senses, and the objective world limit our space and narrow it as we come down into material identification. But greater limitations and contractions of space occur when we formulate lies and build methods of exploitation. We further limit our space in building glamors and illusions.

Liberation from our own prisons depends on our efforts and striving to advance toward spiritual achievements, cultivate superhuman senses, and develop contacts with the Universe. Liberation can gradually be achieved in releasing our Self into space. The Self is the space, limited in personal, planetary, and solar karma and in matter and time.

As we go toward our inner Core, we become more space and less limitation.

Guard your space, and let no one limit your space or build hindrances and walls around it.

All brainwashing techniques, all fanaticism, all kinds of totalitarianism, all kinds of racism, nationalism, all kinds of separatism are efforts to limit your space and deprive you of your happiness. The enemies of human freedom are perpetuating the sources of the psychological and physical sicknesses of humanity.

Expansion of space takes you toward freedom, toward your glorious future.

A healthy world, a sane world can be built only by the hands of those who have dedicated their lives to expand the space and to lead you toward Infinity.

Exercise

Expansion of Inner Space

1. Sit quietly. Close your eyes.

2. Visualize where you are sitting.

3. Visualize the room you are in.

   Visualize the building.

   Visualize the city.

   Visualize the state.

4. Come back to your room.

   Push the walls out; expand them.

   Push the roof up; expand it.

   See a bigger room.

5. Now see the expanded building as clearly as you can.

   See the city.

   See the state.

6. Now see the world.

   Find your house.

   Find your room.

   Go back and see the world.

   Try to see it from all sides.

   See the lands, the oceans.

7. Now see your house, your larger house.

8. See the world from all sides.

   Try to see New York,

   London,

   Moscow,

   Beijing,

   Darjeeling.

   Try to see the whole world again.

   See the solar system,

   the Sun and the planets.

   Try to see their movements.

9. See our galaxy.

   See the solar system in the galaxy.

   See the earth.

   See your country.

   See your state.

   See your city.

   See your home.

10. Go back again and see the earth, the solar system, the galaxy.

    See the Cosmic Space.

Try to see millions and millions of galaxies.

Come back to your galaxy,

to your solar system,

to your planet,

to your country,

to your state,

to your city,

to your home,

to your chair.

11. Now visualize the room in your Self or in your head.

    Make a miniature room and see it in your head.

    Try to contain the whole building.

    See it from all sides.

    Remember it is in your head, in your Self.

12. Now see your city in your head.

    See your state, your country in your head.

13. Holding your country in your head; find your home, your room and your chair within your head.

14. Focus your attention on the country, then the whole globe within your head.

    See it as it turns on its axis and goes around the Sun.

    See the solar system in your head.

    See the galaxy.

    See the solar system in the galaxy within your head.

    See the galaxy again.

    See other galaxies.

    See the Creation all within your Self.

15. Holding the whole Cosmos in your inner space, focus your consciousness on the galaxy,

    on the solar system,

on the earth,

on your country,

on your state,

on your city,

on your house,

on your room,

on your chair,

all inside your head with your true Self.

16. Relax more. See your head expanding more than your room,

    more than your house,

    more than your city,

    more than your state,

    more than your country,

    more than your planet,

    more than the solar system,

    more than the galaxy.

    See the whole galaxy in your head.

17. See a small light in your head.

    Let the light grow bigger than your head,

    than your room,

    than your city,

    than your state,

    than your country,

    than the planet,

    than the solar system,

    than the galaxy.

    Try to visualize your light as the light of all existence.

    See yourself as the light filling all space.

    Visualize the stars, as many as you can, and let each star receive its light from you — the Light of Space.

18. Visualize the galaxy,
    the solar system,
    the earth,
    your country,
    your state,
    your city,
    your home,
    your room,
    the chair on which you are sitting.
    See that it is your body sitting on the chair, and you are the Light of Space.

19. Touch your chair,
    your hands,
    your knees,
    your nose,
    your head,
    your eyes, and rub them.
    Feel the chair.
    Imagine your room.
    Open your eyes.

25

Healing and the Aura

The health of the whole man is conditioned by his aura.

A good way to purify and heal our aura is to raise the level of our thoughts. Energy follows thought. Energy can be directed by thought, by creative imagination, and by visualization.

The quality and the function of thought, of creative imagination, and of visualization choose the type of energy that pours into our aura. It is also true that the type of our thoughts, the type of our creative imagination, and the type of our visualization have much to do with the frequency and voltage of the flow of energy coming into our aura.

The quality of thought decides the level of the energy. The type of thought decides the way the energy functions within our aura. The level of our thinking is raised through admiration, worship, and ecstasy.

To illustrate, let us take the following diagram. The central circle is the aura. The outer circles form the four higher ethers, the four higher reservoirs of energy.

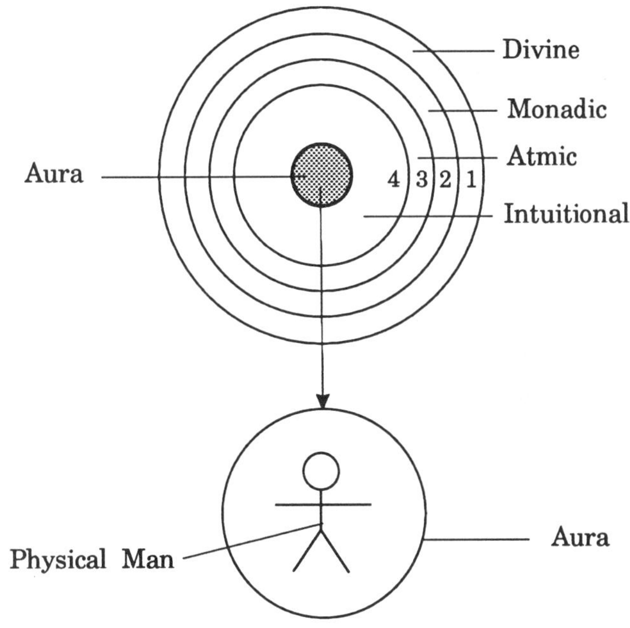

Diagram 25-1 Higher Reservoirs of Energy

When we are thinking lofty thoughts and visualizing lofty images, we are tuning into higher reservoirs and bringing their energy into our aura. When we are thinking and visualizing and imagining base thoughts, we are bringing into our aura low-level, involutionary, separative, destructive energy. On whatever level our thoughts are, we draw into our aura the corresponding energy from the reservoirs. The higher reservoirs are the higher etheric centers, astral centers, mental centers, the Lotus, the Spiritual Triad, the Monadic and Divine Planes. These are the doors of planetary, solar, galactic, and Cosmic reservoirs.

Whatever a man thinks, so he is. This is a law in our solar system. Thinking releases energy because thinking is a process of tuning in.

When you are tuning in to astral energy, your aura is filled with astral substance. When you are tuning in to Atmic Plane energy, your aura is filled with atmic substance.

When you are thinking on the physical-etheric, emotional, and lower mental levels in negative ways, you not only draw force into your etheric body from these sources, but you also draw illusions, glamors, and maya from other people.

Thinking is tuning in within yourself and within the Universe. When your thought is related to the Divine level, you are absorbing into your system Divine level substance. If you are thinking on the physical level, you are absorbing physical substance into your aura.

Your aura is built daily by the energies you bring into your system. That is why your thoughts are so important. Your thoughts are on various levels and are of various types. If they are separative, selfish, destructive, negative, or criminal thoughts, these thoughts will bring great pollution into your system through the substance of your three lower bodies which has become contaminated by your glamors, illusions, and maya.

If you have thoughts of Beauty, Goodness, and Truth or thoughts of beatitude, peace, and purpose, you will absorb energy from higher planes and build your aura accordingly.

Your aura, according to your thoughts, can be a muddy lake or a radiating sphere of many colored lights.

The health of your body depends upon what you eat, but the health of your aura depends upon what you think and feel. Without pure thinking and clean feelings, your body will never be healthy because your aura will be a stagnant pool in which your body floats.

The health of the whole man is conditioned by his aura. If the aura is polluted with many kinds of forces contradictory or antagonistic to each other, you have chaos in your aura, which prevents you from having a healthy body. But if your aura is a pure sphere of harmonious forces and energies, your body is healthy and radioactive.

Some auras are like lakes whose water is muddy and dirty because they are formed by the flood of the lower, base life. When you are watching television or a movie, or reading a book or magazine that is the product of lower energies, you are channeling them into your aura and polluting and poisoning yourself. When you are enjoying highly creative movies, arts, or books, you are charging your aura with those high-level energies which produced such an art.

This means that public health can really be endangered by movies and publications which channel low, destructive, involutionary, separative, and criminal substances. Conversely, public health can be improved by imparting manifestations of art which channel high-level energy into the aura.

There is also another very important point to consider. Pure, clean, and radioactive auras attract angelic and creative forces. Polluted auras attract dark forces which eventually destroy the vehicles they contact.

Your physical body, as well as your home and environment, must be physically clean. No higher force can approach you unless you are clean in your body, home, and aura.

Thoughts can be raised and purified by the fire of admiration. Although a variety of psychological methods are used in many parts of the world, the method of admiration is prevalent in the hearts of people. It is so simple that no psychologist has observed it and tried to utilize it as a potent method of sublimation or transformation. Little children heal and uplift themselves through the process of admiration. You can see this in the behavior of saints or holy ones. They have a childlike admiration for everything they contact, and this is a natural method of healing, uplifting, and transforming themselves and others.

Admiration heals the emotional body which has been wounded by negative attitudes, hatred, fear, and rejection. Admiration brings intellectual substance into the emotional body and throws away all that is not related to beauty, harmony, and the Divine.

To admire means to accept deeper values, to strive toward higher values, to attach oneself to the ideal, and to emancipate oneself from the slavery of crystallized values. Admiration is also a process of reception of something higher, such as accepting and fusing with something more beautiful. Note that some people flatter instead of express their admiration.

Worship is a form of admiration. In esoteric schools, teachers lead people into conscious admiration — to admire trees, birds, flowers, mountains, lakes, waterfalls, constellations, and the beauty of the body and faces. When contemplating and admiring these beauties, the heart center of the student opens and the Teaching is understood.

Admiration creates trust and cooperation. Admiration creates freedom in the one you admire. You create self-confidence and striving toward higher values in the one you admire. Admiration does not produce pride in an advanced person but, rather, humility.

Admiration helps the Soul influence the personality. This is because admiration is directed to the soul qualities and the spiritual qualities of a person or an object.

Admiration is a process of fusion with an object that transcends your present stage of evolution. You create Soul-infusion by admiring someone because you witness or affirm his soul value.

Admiration develops decentralization within you and dissatisfaction with the glamor of selfishness or self-worship. It cures your mental, emotional, and egocentric activities which block the divine circulatory flow and which create problems in your system.

Admiration opens the door of higher beauties because, through admiration, your sense of value grows. Admiration creates focus and integration; your etheric, emotional, and mental energies are focused on the article of admiration. This focus seldom occurs otherwise. This focus creates closer cooperation between the bodies, and when they integrate, your evolution proceeds.

Greater admiration or ecstasy is the moment when you lose your identity in a beauty and go through a process of transformation. One can advance faster if he has in front of him an object of admiration.

Those people who are unhealthy, separative, selfish, or aggressive are those people who do not have admiration. When they see a beautiful flower, they immediately concentrate on a petal that does not have the same beauty as the rest, and they say, "I don't like that flower....That music is not good because...." Beauty and greatness remind them of their ugliness and smallness, and thus they hate both beauty and greatness.

Admiration is stretching and expanding yourself to a lofty idea, image, or level of consciousness. You are stretching yourself toward the future of yourself. Through admiration you are integrating your physical, emotional, and mental being and bringing it into focus. This focused personality then enters into the new rhythm presented by the object of your admiration, which causes transformation within your being.

Admiration, worship, and ecstasy are stages of fusion with the object of beauty. Ecstasy is a form of admiration. It is a moment in which you are lost in the object of your admiration. When you are lost and identified with the object of admiration, you do not exist, but the object exists. And when only the object exists, then the object is in the process of transmuting your entire being with the voltage and frequency with which it is charged.

As a result of this transmutation, admiration leads you to such a degree of integration, alignment, transformation, sublimation, and transfiguration that your humanness is lost in your Divinity. Through admiration, people can heal themselves, expand their consciousness, and be led into greater light.

We must learn to admire because admiration is a process of tuning to the higher reservoirs of energy. Admiration of beauty techniques must be applied on a gradient scale. The object of admiration will be chosen according to the consciousness of the person, and then gradually it must be lifted to higher objects of admiration. Thus you expand the consciousness gradually and do not cause congestion, overstimulation, or destruction in it.

Admiration should be practiced in stages. Start with admiring a simple object; then go toward the admiration of virtues; then to the embodiment of virtues such as heroes or saints. Then go to objects that are planetary, solar, and galactic. Admiration should be a slow process and done on a gradient scale.

I remember once when my father brought me a butterfly and asked me to observe the great beauty of colors and forms on its wings. In the meantime he expressed great admiration for the butterfly until I really began to admire it. Later, the object of admiration changed and became more abstract and transcendental. Discover those movies, music, theatrical performances, dramas, dances, paintings, and architecture that create admiration in you.

Actually, admiration is the higher correspondence of the physical orgasm. On all planes you can reach the climax of your love, and this is done through admiration. Admiration can be on emotional, mental, intuitional, and higher planes, as long as it is a fusion with the subject of admiration. At the moment of admiration, a new substance precipitates from higher planes into your nervous system, highly nourishing and invigorating it. After each admiration, man has more creative power.

We must learn first the alphabet of admiration. Then we will build words of admiration, then sentences, paragraphs, chapters, sections, and books. First try to admire the individual. Then expand it until the whole creation is the subject of your admiration.

I had some children in my high school who were very critical and negative of other students. I wanted to start them on the first lesson of admiration, so I took them to the mountains to hike. I stopped every quarter of a mile and admired something. "Look at this flower...the five petals...the colors, the shape, the fragrance. Why is it so pretty and the fragrance so enjoyable?"

At first they did not pay any attention, but, when I persisted in my sincere admiration, they came closer and looked. "Yeah, it is beautiful," they agreed. By the end of the day they began to show me flowers, butterflies, insects, birds, trees, the sunset.... After a few days they learned to admire Nature. Then one day I directed their attention to their eyes, ears, nose, internal organs, and we admired these beautiful gifts. Then we went on to admire each other — as a real game — to find something in each person which we could admire. We found very interesting things to admire in each other.

Many months later, I would often hear them say, "Do not hate him because he has good qualities, too." "Why do you criticize him? He has his own beauty." They talked to their classmates in this new and beautiful way.

People who have admiration are the life givers of society. All great artists, scientists, politicians, and religious figures are great admirers.

Admiration is the moment of fusion with the mystery in beauty. Admiration is not formulations of the intellect, but rather it is the door of greater light. It is after true admiration that a great creative work is produced. First there is fusion and ecstasy, then an elevation of your level and consciousness within the beauty, then the formulation of beauty.

Nothing of great value can be created without admiration. Admiration cannot be entered into by mental modification but rather by Intuition. Your human soul is touched by a beauty and fused with it in great joy. After the level of admiration is achieved by your conscious evaluation, then creativity starts.

Once we went to a hermit in the mountains. He was a very old man, 115 years of age. The most important thing I saw in him was his spirit of admiration. He would see a bird and exclaim, "Wow, isn't that bird beautiful!" Then he looked at us, "Oh, my goodness," he said, "what a divine beauty you are. How did you climb this mountain? You are a real youth!"

Every time we said something intelligent, he admired us with words and gestures. When the sunset came, he made a sign for us to watch it. We sat for fifteen minutes in silence watching the sunset. Occasionally I watched his eyes and face — all admiration and ecstasy. When we came down from the mountain, we were full of energy, enthusiasm, and dedication.

One of us said, "It seems to me that the first lesson he wanted to teach us was how to admire."

The spirit of admiration forced us to climb that mountain of seven thousand feet again and again to see the hermit, who now had a new name — "The hermit of admiration."

On one occasion, this Teacher said that when a man admires, his features change and a great beauty descends upon him. When a man speaks of beauty he has the most beautiful lips. Those who advance on the path of their perfection have one sign — admiration — because they develop the spirit of beauty, the eyes of beauty, the heart of beauty.

The spirit of appreciation, admiration, and gratitude must increase in the world if we really want to enjoy life and expand our consciousness. Whenever there is no appreciation of beauty and no admiration of values and virtues, the human and spiritual relationship deteriorates. People need admiration without bribery and flattery. When you do not have any admiration for your husband, wife, children, mother, teacher, or student, he or she cannot grow in a healthy way. Rejected and unwanted children or persons are the sources of human problems in all walks of life. Rejection evokes negativity and egotism and creates aggressive, self-centered people who justify themselves in all their aggressive and destructive acts.

Admiration evokes soul qualities, develops trust and fearlessness, and creates cooperation and tolerance. Admiration allows you eventually to come in contact with the soul of people and with the Soul of the Universe.

Admiration is a highly needed nourishment for the developing, unfolding human soul. When a mother feeds her child on her breast, she looks at the child with the eyes of admiration and love. Such a child grows physically and spiritually in balance. The same is true for those with whom we are related —

our admiration feeds and nourishes them. No other nourishment is ever craved by a human being except admiration. Immediately when you give admiration, you see a change in the person. He glows and shines, relaxes and loves. He feels at home and vitalized.

When you admire people, you direct them to the right path of living, without the need for criticism.

Criticism fixes the attention of the person on the image that you are presenting through your criticism. Naturally, he hates you and tries to ignore the image presented by you. As much as he tries to ignore the image, he fixes even more attention on it to such a degree that eventually the image becomes absorbed by him. Thus, you may build other people according to what you think about them.

Admiration lets the person see his nature and his weaknesses from a level on which there is no identification with his weaknesses. Once a person sees his weaknesses, he tries to improve them without creating in himself a spirit of negativity and rejection. He feels secure and safe in the hands of admiration.

Admiration is contact between souls. Admiration is like watering a flower. Admiration is like opening a window to fresh air and sunshine.

The Sages say that we must eventually have soul relationships with each other more than personality relationships. A soul relationship is a relationship of beauty, respect, truth, admiration, and cooperation for the Common Good. Those who have soul relationships are those who lead humanity to a higher level of existence.

Jealousy is the opposite of admiration. Jealousy sees in beauty its own ugliness and hates that beauty and wants to destroy it. In beauty he sees a danger for his existence. Beauty reveals his lower self to himself. Jealousy wants only himself to be beautiful. The beauty of others is a threat to him. Beauty for him is a separate quality. It is not something that unites everything in everything.

All great Avatars and heroes became the victims of jealousy. They were killed, crucified, and poisoned because a great danger was seen in their beauty.

Jealousy can be healed if a person exercises admiration. Admiration is one of the petals of the heart center. This petal grows and unfolds when the heart center is active. The more you admire, the more you draw love energy into your heart center.

When one is jealous, one can see beauty intellectually, but the heart does not affirm it. This is because the sense of admiration is not active due to many reasons. Jealousy leads one to destruction; admiration leads a person toward construction. Jealousy is involutionary; admiration is evolutionary. Jealousy does not care; admiration is full of compassion and caring. Jealousy cannot feel the unity of life and works against it; admiration is the affirmation of the unity of life.

Admiration is not mental evolution, measurement, or comparison. It is a spiritual at-one-ment with beauty. It is beingness, not thinkingness; it is acceptance, not investigation.

Admiration is a form of self-forgetfulness. When you start admiring something you have done, immediately say, "It is the Life, the One Life that did it through me. I admire that One Life which is in everything, and all beauty is Its manifestation." When you remember this, you will not be trapped in vanity. Vanity has its roots in separatism.

Admiration has no expectation. You do not admire to please yourself, but it is a spontaneous, instantaneous outpouring of love and appreciation.

Admiration calls forth streams of joy from your heart and also from those whom you admire. Joy not only heals but also protects.

We are told that it is possible to create a shield around us through joy. Our aura is full of cracks, weak points, spots of agitation, and sores because of negative feelings and dark motives. When we release joy from our Innermost Core, it pours down into our aura and creates harmony in it, repairing the cracks, healing the sores, and establishing a rhythmic circulation of energy.

The energy of joy expands beyond the periphery of the aura and forms a golden sphere which protects the person from all kinds of attacks. This is what the shield is. When the shield is formed, a regenerative process takes place within the physical body. The energy increases, and the human soul begins to act more harmoniously with the Creative Forces of higher realms.

The shield of joy also acts as a magnet to attract currents of inspiration from powerful sources and gives a greater opportunity to the person for creativity. An aura magnetized by joy turns into a sensitive network for higher communication. Such an aura can attract very high-level currents and impressions of ideas, visions, and revelations. We are told that the Great Ones rejoice when They see that an individual or a group of people is able to build the shield of joy.

Such a shield is not only an achievement but also a service for the Great Ones because it is through such a shield that They can transmit Their message to the world and have dependable, strong co-workers on the earth.

It is noticed that people cooperate with each other and understand each other better when they are in joy. Great leaders inspire joy, especially when they are preparing their co-workers for a difficult labor. The joy in them turns into a source of continuous energy and understanding. They give to their co-workers the joy of vision, the joy of the future, the joy of possible great achievements, and then they lead them to daring labor. With joy, impossible tasks become possible.

Those homes in which the substance of joy is alive are more healthy, successful, influential, and creative than those where the joy is a wounded bird. We are told that the Ashrams of higher realms are spheres of joy. Those who have an opportunity to visit these Ashrams depart with a charge of great joy which not only heals them but also enlightens them and strengthens them on the path of their most difficult labor.

Things we use in our daily life, in our homes or offices, last longer and render a better service when used in joy. The flowers around us give more aroma because of our joy. The birds offer us better songs because of our joy. People send us pure love because of our joy.

Joy opens the gates of the future and paves the way for higher revelations. The shield of joy turns into a mirror on which the stars dance.

Visualization to Heal the Aura

1. Sit quietly and relax. Close your eyes.
2. Visualize a wheel in front of your eyebrows.
3. Visualize another wheel one inch behind the first wheel.
4. Make the first one turn clockwise. Start slowly, then gradually let it speed up to the highest speed.
5. Start the second wheel spinning counterclockwise, again starting out slowly, then spinning at the highest speed. Both must turn, one clockwise, the other counterclockwise. Try to control both of them, running in opposite directions.
6. As they turn, try to make them get bigger and bigger until they are at least twenty inches in diameter in front of your eyebrows.
7. Make them three feet big, and visualize them as fiery wheels. See that all negative elements in your aura are expelled out, creating a pure white aura, nine feet in diameter around you.
8. Turn both wheels inside out, unite them together, and let them radiate orange light into your aura.
9. See yourself at the center of the wheels for about ten seconds.
10. Inhale three times and increase the fire in the wheel for about ten seconds.
11. Radiate joy for one minute.
12. Relax. Feel your body, your face, and open your eyes.

26

Seven Major Exercises

There are many locked energies within our aura. There are energies which are invoked by us through aspiration. They are released from higher realms or from higher sources and accumulate within our aura. Due to a lack of means of expression, they stay there and exercise various kinds of pressure.

These pressures stimulate our etheric centers or cause depression in them. Stimulation and depression manifest in different ways through our mental, emotional, and physical natures.

Many kinds of overactivity of the glands, organs, emotions, and mind are caused by such pressures. Additionally, various kinds of depression and failures of organs, glands, emotions, and thoughts are the effect of excessive energy which paralyzes the system and leads it into failure.

Meditation, intense prayer, aspiration, forceful lectures, or contact with charged persons creates locked energies within our aura. The best ways to get rid of such accumulations are through

1. Regular and continuous creativity

2. Visualization

3. Living a life in harmony with our aspirations

4. Sacrificial service

5. Practical actualization of virtues

Many psychological and physical complications resulting from pressures can be handled successfully through these above methods.

Creative labor, when intensely carried on, eventually uses the blocked energy accumulated within the aura either in thoughts, emotions, or labor. If the creative labor is oriented toward expressing beauty as a means of service for humanity, it is a highly curative method.

Through visualization one can use the blocked energies and release them into Space and take away the pressure exercised on the centers, the nervous system, the glands, the organs, etc. Through visualization one can release the blocked energies and create those thought patterns which slowly transform one's nature and enable it to hold pressures and use them in creative activities.

To explain the procedure, let me take an example. A certain lady, forty years of age, visited me for help. Her complaints were

"I smoke."

"I use alcohol."

"I have so much energy; I am uncomfortable; I feel like bursting."

"I am restless."

"I can't concentrate."

"Occasionally I fall into depression."

"I like to fight."

What she was trying to say was, "I have so much energy; I don't know how to control it and how to use it."

Through experience I found out that acts of daring and courage consume a great amount of blocked and accumulated energy within our aura, if they are carried out through creative imagination, visualization, and identification. Actually, when an inner urge to dare and to be courageous is blocked by circumstances, an inner tension builds up and becomes trapped in the aura. Trapped courage or daring turns into fear, into hatred, into isolation, or into violent action. The method I used with the lady was as follows:

Week One — First Exercise

1. Visualize yourself standing in the light of your Transpersonal Self. Your Transpersonal Self can be visualized as a condensed light passing into your thought world, your emotional world, and your physical body and flooding them with rays of light.

2. Visualize a great radiance around your body.

3. Visualize yourself as beautiful as you can.

   Such a visualization develops self-confidence which is important for the progressive work of improvement. Self-confidence is an act of focusing oneself. The diffused, scattered rays of the Self draw back to the center and create a focus. This is self-confidence.

4. Imagine a big stage in a huge hall with thousands of people in the audience. See the colors of the curtain, the walls, the people, and the lights — all that makes it more real.

5. You are a singer. You are dressed in a very pretty, long blue gown. [If a man is doing the visualization exercises, change the clothing to a suit and tie, etc.]

6. Visualize a piano at the middle of the stage. See the curtain opening slowly to roaring applause from the audience. See yourself coming to the front of the stage and standing in the spotlight.

7. See and hear the continuing applause.... Now everything is quiet. You give a look to your pianist and he starts a simple, beautiful song, the one you love most.

8. See yourself singing with courage and daring. You feel no fear; you feel at home, happy, and beautiful. Your song flows out of your heart. You are in great joy.

   At the end of your song, see the audience applauding for a long time. Go offstage and come back again and let them continue applauding.

9. Sing your second song, a joyful, beautiful song. At the end of your second song, see the audience on their feet applauding and screaming. A few young boys and girls climb onto the stage to hug and kiss you.

   See tears in their eyes. Let a few drops of tears come from your eyes. Express gratitude and love to all the people present. Let the curtain fall, and see yourself alone on the stage.

   You are happy and relaxed, and you have the feeling of a great accomplishment.

10. Visualize an angel in a white dress and with eagle wings appearing in front of you and offering you a bouquet of flowers. Hug her; kiss her; express great joy for the recognition. Feel that your songs are accepted by the invisible hosts, too.

11. Let the angel disappear. Go offstage. Rest a few minutes and see the curtain opening to great applause.

12. Sing another song with all your love and strength.

13. At the end of the song, see people applauding for a longer period of time than before.

14. Let a girl bring you roses. Accept them gracefully...and let the curtain fall again.

15. See yourself on the stage surrounded by hundreds of people who express their feelings and admiration.

16. Hear at least ten clear, precise statements from the people on the stage. For example:

    a. "She is gorgeous."

    b. "Her voice transforms my whole existence."

    c. "This was the greatest day in my life."

    And continue hearing another seven compliments, those which you want to hear.

    See yourself departing in a car, and you are at home by yourself contemplating your success.

NOTE:

1. This exercise must be carried out very slowly. Ample time must be given to every detail as if the actions were occurring on the plane of reality.

2. The exercise must be repeated at least three times, increasing the duration of the exercise and making the person see more details in his or her actions with greater identification.

3. The above exercise must be carried out for at least three hours.

4. The subject must sit very comfortably, relaxed, and with eyes closed.

5. The room must be ventilated and, as much as possible, be quiet.

6. After the exercise is over the subject must touch his body and his face. He must visualize where he is sitting, the room, etc., and slowly open his eyes and sit quietly for ten minutes.

7. The subject must keep a detailed diary and record in it his feelings, thoughts, physical events, and conditions until the next session, at which time he must present his report.

Week Two — Second Exercise

1. Visualize the same stage. See how people are filling the chairs. See yourself dressed in the most beautiful dress, orange in color. [If the person is a man, have him visualize wearing an orange shirt.]

2. See the curtain opening. Walk out to great applause. Sit at the center of the stage on a beautiful, comfortable chair and tell the audience:

   "Today I will tell you about three of the most beautiful events in my life…."

   The subject will visualize herself telling about an event in detail, an event which was the most joyful, happy, and beautiful event in her life. There will be no hurry, no artificiality. The storytelling will be frank, open, humorous, and real. The retelling of the three events of the subject's life will last at least one hour.

3. After each story:

   a. great applause

   b. curtain coming down

   c. a few friends backstage congratulating you for your simplicity, beauty, accuracy, and humor.

   All this must take ample time. It must be visualized in detail and as realistically as possible.

4. At the end of the third story, carry out the steps presented in number 3, then:

   a. See the whole audience departing, and you are sitting alone on the stage in great joy.

   b. Visualize the same angel coming and this time giving you a necklace of pearls. Receive it with deep gratitude and let her disappear.

Often, inhibited desires, longings, and visions release themselves out of our aura through a creative visualization.

This second exercise will take, as a whole, two hours, after which the subject must repeat the exercise of the storytelling once more. This means that exercise two will last at least four hours.

If necessary, a ten-minute break can be given after the first exercise during which silence must be observed.

At the end of each session the subject must touch her body and her face and visualize where she is sitting, the room, etc., then slowly open her eyes and sit quietly for ten minutes. Repeat, following the notes given after the first exercise.

If the subject cannot visualize these exercises, they must be carried out in short durations and on a gradient scale. A gradient scale means that each exercise must be taken step-by-step, part after part. For example, if a subject cannot visualize herself dressed and ready for the performance, start in the following way:

1. Now put on your shoes.

2. Now find the dress.

3. Put it on.

4. Put on your makeup. Match it with your dress, etc.

5. See the floor of the stage, the walls, the curtain, the hall....

Expand the subject's vision gradually and with short periods of visualization. After each ten or fifteen minutes, give the subject a rest until she develops more concentration.

Make the exercises joyful. Create interest in the exercises and explain how they work. Increase the subject's faith in the exercises.

Week Three — Third Exercise

1. Repeat steps 1 and 2 of **Week Two — Second Exercise**, except this time wear a red robe.

2. Speak to the audience about your future vision, inspired by beauty, goodness, and compassion. Speak to them about your vision, and tell them how your vision will bring greater joy to humanity, greater health, greater righteousness, greater prosperity, greater unity and synthesis.

   Speak to them about your vision, and tell them about the futility of crime, war, tyranny, and exploitation.

   Speak to them about the victory of righteousness, beauty, and sacrificial love.

   Have three clear visions in your mind. Start with the first and tell about your vision in detail. Explain how it will manifest itself and what a great service it will do for humanity.

3. See people enthused with your vision. Hear voices coming from the audience — "We will support you and help you actualize your vision."

4. End the first session with great applause, reverence, and love pouring out of the audience.

5. Visualize an angel in a white dress with eagle wings appearing in front of you and offering you a bouquet of flowers. Hug her; kiss her; express great joy for the recognition. Feel that your vision is accepted by the invisible hosts, too.

   Let the angel disappear. Go offstage. Rest a few minutes and see the curtain opening with greater applause.

6. Start with your second vision. Repeat all the above steps.

7. Go to your third vision and repeat steps 1 through 5 above.

   Do not hurry. Hurry creates confusion, complications, and results in failures.

Week Four — Fourth Exercise

1. Visualize yourself achieving three great successes:

   — financial success

   — creative success

   — spiritual success

2. Visualize great obstacles and hindrances on your path to these three successes.

3. Overcome each obstacle with courage and daring and achieve your successes.

4. Make your mind think that each success is going to be a service for humanity.

5. See in detail how humanity is benefited by your successes and in what way.

6. Orchestrate all your activities in detail, with buildings, persons, machinery, and furniture.

7. You must have three great successes in three major fields:

   — financial

   — creative

   — spiritual

You must work out in detail:

a. the start

b. the development

c. the accomplishment

d. the fulfillment

8. At the end of each success exercise, you must repeat the steps given in the notes following the first exercise.

Week Five — Fifth Exercise

1. Visualize yourself sitting on a high mountain and watching a glorious sunrise.

2. See the colors, the Sun, Nature — birds, trees, rivers…. Make it real.

3. As you are sitting on the mountain, visualize a great Individuality taking form in front of you. This is the One you always wanted to contact. He or She can be the embodiment of art, wisdom, knowledge, success, love — Whoever He or She is.

4. Ask Him questions and try to formulate in your mind His answers.

5. See Him disappear into your aura and become your True Self.

6. As the Sun rises, you fly toward the Sun. As you enter the sphere of the Sun, see your physical body melt away. See your astral body evaporate. See your mental body fade away, and you stand in the Sun as a five-pointed star. Feel that you are pure light, beauty, immortality, and bliss.

7. For at least five minutes stay in the Sun. Then build a new mental body from the fire of the Sun.

8. Build a new astral body from the love of the Sun and a new physical body from the light of the Sun. Come back to the mountain where you started your exercise.

9. Visualize that the Sun is you. Visualize the Sun radiating out of your physical body, your astral body, and your mental body. Visualize the whole mountain full of light.

10. Stay in joy and bliss for another five minutes.

11. Visualize your room, your furniture, and your chair. Touch your body, your face, and sit quietly for a few minutes. Then open your eyes.

Repeat this fifth exercise three times. It must last at least one and one-half hours if correctly done. Go slowly through each step and do it as faithfully as possible.

Week Six — Sixth Exercise

1. Visualize yourself sitting on the bank of a river.

2. Visualize a five-pointed star at least one foot above your head. The color is blue.

3. Visualize the rays of blessings pouring down upon your head, body, and heart. Feel a purifying process going on through your three bodies. Feel a deep sensation of peace and serenity.

4. Visualize a diamond upon your forehead and two other diamonds above each of your breasts near your shoulders.

5. See a silver light forming a triangle between these three diamonds.

6. See three children playing in the river.

7. See yourself in the river swimming by the children.

8. Come out of the river and relax on the shore. Then suddenly hear the screaming of children. One of them is caught in the current, and two others are panicking and do not know what to do.

9. Jump into the water. Swim fast and reach the child in the current. With great difficulty take him to the shore.

10. As the children depart from the shore, close your eyes and see a vision.

    You are a little child, caught by a stream running into a waterfall. See your sister saving you.

11. Suddenly realize that the child you saved was your sister in a past incarnation.

12. Walk toward the forest. Meet a Great One and let Him bless you for your heroic deed. Looking into your eyes, let Him tell you:

    "My child, keep your body pure.

Keep your heart pure.

Keep your thoughts pure.

Keep your words pure.

Keep your deeds pure...."

And as He stands in front of you, sing a song of gratitude to Him.

13. Let Him embrace you.

14. Let Him bless you.

15. Visualize your room, your furniture, and your chair. Touch your body, your face, and sit quietly for a few minutes. Then open your eyes.

Week Seven — Seventh Exercise

1. Visualize a huge, tall tree and climb to the top.

2. Slowly come down.... Repeat this three times slowly.

3. Stand in front of a wall and pass through it to the other side. Repeat this three times.

4. See yourself giving a short message in three locations simultaneously. Repeat this five times.

5. Radiate joy to all humanity for five minutes.

6. Visualize a fire and stand in its midst. Feel the heat but do not be burned.

7. Visualize that you are one with the Universe. Do this for five minutes only.

8. Relax. Remember your home, room, furniture. Touch your body and face. Wait three minutes. Open your eyes.

These seven major exercises must be performed — one every week — for seven weeks. It is better if a friend leads you through these exercises, using a soft voice and reading slowly to you, so that each of the steps can be taken.

It is very probable that in seven weeks you will create a tremendous reorientation within you toward light, love, beauty, and joy and release the force accumulations within your aura, thus annihilating the seeds of future complications.

27

The Four Laws of Health

The secret of health is to strive toward the Soul and tune to the frequency of the Soul until the body radiates out the life of the Soul.

Esoteric tradition says that millions of years ago conscious, living fires came down from high places to help infant humanity. They led the steps of the human souls toward Beauty, Goodness, Truth, and Harmony by impressing the human minds with lofty ideas and visions. These conscious, living fires became the Inner Guides of infant humanity.

In modern psychology the Inner Guide is sometimes called the Transpersonal Self, and in esoteric literature It is called the Solar Angel, the Soul. Thus, in each human being, we have the guiding Soul and the personality vehicles or bodies, namely the physical, emotional, and mental vehicles. The duty of the Transpersonal Self or the Soul is to awaken the human soul and make him respond to the vision It is holding for him.

In the Ageless Wisdom we are told that illness, sickness, and disease are fundamentally the result of an inharmonious relationship of the bodies or vehicles with the Soul. When your physical, emotional, and mental bodies are not in harmony with the vibration or frequency of the Soul, no matter what you do externally, you will be sick. This is the first Law of Health.

The body lives longer once it is totally fused with the Soul and the life energy circulates within it without any hindrances and frictions. Of course, this is not easily achieved as we have many years or lives behind us in which we lived a life that was not in harmony with the Soul, and thus for ages we created causes for disease and sickness. But this does not mean that one cannot minimize these causes and eventually have a healthy body.

The secret of health is to strive toward the Soul and tune to the frequency of the Soul until the body radiates out the life of the Soul. Whether we stay on this road for a few years or for a lifetime, we must try again and again to build the foundation of our future health and strive continuously toward that goal.

In trying to synchronize yourself with the Soul, you will notice that, year after year, life after life, your health is improving because you are bringing your physical, emotional, and mental bodies under the control of your Soul's light, love, and energy.

You are the human soul, the real man, the essence, the Self. You are on the evolutionary arc, which means you are going toward unity, spiritualization, synthesis, and beauty; you are on the path of fusion with the Spirit of the Universe. But your physical, emotional, and mental atoms or elementals are at the point of transition from the involutionary arc to the evolutionary arc, and it is the human soul who must assist these bodies to make the transition, as the Soul tries to do the same for the human being.

Such a labor by the human soul is not easy because of the agelong tendencies of the elementals toward involution which creates a conflict between them and the human soul. The tiny lives of the bodies have the tendency to look back and draw the human soul with them.

We attracted them when our spirit was descending on the arc of involution. But as time passed during the Fourth Round in our globe, the direction changed toward evolution, and now all the lives are under the pressure of the evolutionary arc. But the tiny lives of our bodies cannot accomplish this shift unless we, as their redeemers, turn their direction toward evolution. This is the greatest labor of those who want to progress on the path of spiritualization. The battle must be won if one wants to be healthy and be a man of virtue and great creativity.

As we sublimate our three vehicles, our health improves. But if the vehicles carry us down with their involutionary direction, we will have more pain and suffering.

Humanity as a whole is engaged in such a conflict. All our social life is a reflection of it. This conflict is symbolized by the cross. The vertical arm is the spirit rising; the horizontal arm is matter. At the point where the two arms cross each other, a whirlpool of energy is formed which is symbolized by an unfolding rose.

The rose is the symbol of balance, equilibrium, and harmony between spirit and matter. It is this balance that produces health and beauty. As the horizontal line rises more and more upon the vertical line, creativity increases, and man goes through a Transfiguration process until the horizontal line reaches the "top" and turns into a circle.

All medical science and the healing arts are parts of the total healing effort, and all this effort is an action on physical, emotional, and mental planes.

All this is necessary for humanity, but there comes a time when the man gradually reverses the process of healing. Instead of trying to heal his personality vehicles — his physical, emotional, and mental nature — he works on his soul, and through his soul tries to create harmony and beauty in his vehicles of manifestation. "Working on his soul" means to take the emphasis off the vehicles and strive to radiate light, love, and spiritual bliss. This is done by trying to live a life of virtue, meditation, and sacrificial service under the inspiration of the Inner Guide.

Such a man works hard and tries, first of all, to be a soul, to be his own Self, and gradually assumes control over his personality vehicles.

The first step toward this accomplishment is to expand our consciousness and make it more inclusive. The second step is to try to transmute, transform, and transfigure our personality through our spiritual thinking and living. Thus gradually our physical, emotional, and mental natures are controlled, sublimated, and transformed under the light of our expanding consciousness and spiritual living.

The physical, emotional, and mental bodies do not like to be controlled. They try to react against any effort to control them. But, as the man strives toward spiritual realization, he eventually takes them under his control and changes their direction toward spiritualization. Thus the bodies, instead of living for their own sake, begin to live for the sake of the spiritual man. It is at this stage of development that the energy of the Spirit, the energy of Life, begins to circulate freely throughout the man's physical, emotional, and mental systems.

Health is the result of the free circulation of the Life energy within the vehicles of man. We can also say that health is the manifestation of the harmony of the spiritual realms.

All disease, all illness, is the result of hindrances in the vehicles of man where the circulation of the energy of Life or Spirit has stopped or created friction.

If the friction or blockage is in the mental body, the root of your sickness is in the mental body. Because of this blockage, the Life energy creates friction and disturbance there. This disturbance reflects in the emotional body and eventually affects the physical body in the form of disease.

If the blockage is in the emotional body, it affects the mental body and physical body simultaneously and manifests as a disease on the physical plane and as a mental problem on the mental plane.

If the blockage is on the physical plane, it creates physical disease and causes disturbances on other planes which eventually, in turn, increase the blockage on the physical plane. This is why in the future, people will be more active on these three lower planes and, awakening to the spiritual planes, their problems will be faced not only physically but also emotionally and mentally until the time when great healers appear and teach them how to heal their vehicles from the spiritual realms.

Every sick person is a point of infection in the body of humanity. And every healing is a healing process in the body of humanity. Healthy people are great gifts for humanity, and those who strive to create health on all levels are the great benefactors of humanity.

In the future, people will realize that great Teachers such as Buddha and Christ were great healers and great physicians, and Their Teachings were great formulas for healing. In all Their Teaching They tried to reverse the blockages and hindrances and establish a free flow of energy within our system, within the system of humanity, which would then create a harmonious relationship between humanity and the great power of the Universe. It is through such a contact that the creative Life energy will circulate freely throughout our system and bring to our vehicles health and beauty.

These great Teachers emphasized **love** as the most powerful healing agent. They taught us that love is life, and the life or love must not be blocked in our system, in humanity, in Nature. The blockage of love will have a drastic effect in the life of a man, in the life of a nation, and in the life of humanity. Any thought, any action, any feeling against love was condemned by Them because such actions would create blockages on the path of the circulatory flow of Life energy and cause diseases in humanity.

Thus, our prime duty on the path of health is to eliminate all hindrances and blockages within our nature. If a thought is not charged by love or does not benefit others, eliminate it. If an emotion is negative or separative, get rid of it. If an action is harmful, stop it. **The first Law of Health, then, is to remove hindrances on the path of the circulatory flow of Life energy.**

The second Law of Health states that a disease is the result of an ancient error.

Fifty years ago you may have used drugs, or exposed yourself to music created by a mentally sick and spiritually retarded person. These past errors may have created urges which were repressed by various means, but one day they may come into action again and create disturbances in your system. It may be that you committed mental, emotional, and physical crimes in the past or in past lives; they eventually come back to you in the form of disease or in the form of misfortune.

Great Teachers taught us that we can eliminate such past errors by living a sacrificial life, a life of love, and a life of selfless service and harmlessness.

People do not realize that a life lived at the expense of others will put a heavy tax on them and retard their own development. Total healing cannot be achieved by trying to erase the memories of past events or past errors but by actually paying them back with acts of love, sacrifice, and service. "The Eightfold Path" of Buddha and "The Sermon on the Mount" of Christ are the best prescriptions to avoid errors in our life, which then cannot act as seeds of trouble in our future.

The third Law of Health states that each man is a cell in the body of humanity, and he shares the karma of the deeds of humanity as a whole. We will understand this better and better as the world enters into the stage of greater unity and integration.

If your family, nation, or a great part of humanity is involved in crime or living a life contrary to spiritual evolution, you as a unit in the body of humanity will share the effects of the crime in various ways. If you are withdrawn into your spiritual realms and are living a life of harmony with the Divine Intent, then most probably you are going to share the karma of the greater unit in forms of great sacrificial service.

In this law we see clearly that the salvation of the whole is the way to save the unit, and vice versa. The so-called energy crisis has taught us a great lesson.

The pollution of the air, water, and earth is teaching us another serious lesson. It is evident that no individual or nation can live for itself alone. The world is becoming one world. At least we are becoming aware of the oneness of the world and all living beings in it.

It is better to arrange our life in such a way that we have less pain and suffering and greater happiness and joy as a result of our improving life.

Humanity is like a **man**, and every sense, every organ, every system of the individual should work for the total man to provide happiness, joy, and health to every cell in that body.

Those who are working for the unity of mankind are great healers. Any healthy organ works for unity, for the whole. Any sick organ in the body of humanity works for its own self. Health leads to unity; disease leads to death, to separation.

The fourth Law of Health is that our globe is a part of the solar system, the solar system is part of the galaxy, and each cell in the body of the galaxy shares the conditions existing in the galaxy. If a solar system or a globe is in the process of disintegration or explosion, it has its effects on each cell, each atom, each form, on any level of the Cosmic Physical Plane.[1] Some changes in the galaxy promote evolution. Some changes in the galaxy cause disturbances in the system of living units, and these disturbances express themselves as various forms of disease.

We receive various streams of energy from Space, from the stars and constellations. Each energy wave brings the influence of the conditions of its source. If a star is passing through a crisis, its energy brings the waves of crisis to the shores of human life. If the star is passing through states of harmony and joy, its energy brings to the living forms harmony and joy. Thus, in accordance with the Law of Unity, the parts are related to the whole and the whole is related to the parts.

The way to escape destructive influences is to enter deeper into the core of the Self and control your form by the principles of the Self.

Along with these four main laws, we have many rules which can be exercised with beneficial results.

The *first rule* is to try to contact the Soul through meditation, right speech, right thinking, right action, service, and harmless living. These are all ways and means through which you can gradually bring about Soul-infusion.

Daily meditation builds a strong link with your Soul, and Soul energy begins to flow into your system. Right speech allows your Soul to help in your contact with others. Right thinking allows your Soul to sublimate your mental mechanism. Right action opens the channels of your body to the flow of Soul

---

1. For an explanation of the Cosmic Physical Plane, please see *The Ageless Wisdom*, *The Psyche and Psychism*, and *Cosmos in Man*.

energy. Service brings the Soul in contact with life. Harmless living prepares those conditions in which the Soul can create in the light of the Divine Plan and Purpose.

The energies of the Soul first create friction as they meet hindrances within your nature, but eventually they purify your nature in rhythmic circulation. This is how health is brought into your whole system.

I remember a lady who had pains all through her bones. Physicians gave her every kind of painful test, but they could not find the cause or the cure of the sickness. I went to see her in the hospital, and she told me that there was no cure for her sickness.

"There must be a way to heal you," I said.

"What is it?"

"Come in contact with your Soul."

"With my Soul? How?"

"Find a way," and I left her. Three days later she called me and said, "I am cured; my Soul cured me."

"How did it happen?"

"After you left me, I really tried to come in contact with my Soul, but it was impossible. On the second day I tried harder and harder, and suddenly a warm electrical energy was released from the top of my head and spread all over my body, electrifying every part of my organs and bones. This took only two minutes; then it disappeared with all my pain. I walked to the doctor's office and told him that I felt totally cured and that I wanted to leave the hospital. He did not understand me; he did not ask any questions, and after a moment's pause said, 'Then you may leave.' Now I am at home. I know now that there is a Soul in us Who can heal!"

The Inner Guide, the Soul, is the healer. It can make you conquer all that is against health, happiness, joy, and success.

Many people in the world have had moments of contact with their Soul which have uplifted them, transformed them, expanded their heart and consciousness, and led them on the path of harmony and beauty. We must not forget these moments but make them a lasting experience throughout our life.

The *second rule* is to strive to contact the spiritual Will. To do this we must cast away our own desires, decisions, emotions, and thoughts and surrender ourselves to the electrical network of the Will which is in Space around us and within us. This is the power that makes everything new and whole.

Some people contact this Will in the critical times of their life and receive Will energy in order to regenerate, inspire, and strengthen themselves. This Will energy is very potent; it acts like lightning and purifies your whole system through burning all that is against your integration and health. This energy inspires you, makes your mind creative, makes your heart full of joy, and energizes your body. The first reaction to its inflow is an urge to dance, sing, play music, or to go out and serve; this energy releases the creative urge in you. This energy is contacted through discipline and sacrificial living for the sake of one humanity.

The *third rule* is to know one's own Rays, which are the conditioning energies of the physical, emotional, and mental bodies of one's personality and Soul. This is not an easy labor, but a great number of explanations are given about the Rays in a series of books by Alice A. Bailey. Knowing the conditioning energies of your mechanism helps you adapt your vehicles to the energies, find ways and means to receive more of them, and consciously and scientifically use them in your creative works and relationships with other people.

Each body has its proper and individual way of being healed, and when the right healing method is used, the body reacts more positively and heals much sooner.

The *fourth rule* is to have magnetic purity. This means that gradually we must purify our physical body as much as possible of any kind of pollution if we want to have healthy bodies. The same applies to our emotional system, which must be purified by the fire of aspiration, love, and dedication. The mind also must go through an intensive process of purification through right and altruistic thinking and right motives. Our whole system must be protected from anger, fear, hatred, jealousy, and all negative thoughts and emotions.

Every time you accept emotional and mental pollution into your system, you destroy the foundation of your health. Thoughts that are full of hatred, anger, and separatism must be cast out. Thoughts that are based on lies, deception, and illusions must be thrown out of your system. Thoughts that are based on crime or on the intention to destroy or paralyze the lives of other human beings must be washed out totally from your system. Every impure thought is a point of infection in your mental body which may contaminate your entire body and life.

The Teaching says that lofty thoughts have a great capacity to heal, to strengthen, and to integrate, and when one reaches such a stage of mental purity, he will be able to receive abundant energies without friction.

The *fifth rule* is not only to have pure thoughts or purity in all our vehicles but also to have thoughts that are universal. Thoughts that are concerned with the welfare of humanity, with the welfare of the animal and the vegetable kingdoms, attract a tremendous amount of healing energy from Space and from far-off worlds. To keep Nature healthy means to keep ourselves healthy.

Universal thoughts are all-inclusive thoughts which lead us to live an unselfish life for the benefit of all.

Universal thinking makes you a brother to the stars and galaxies, and thus you harmonize yourself with the great Whole and let the Life energy circulate throughout your system. The greater your integration with the Life, the greater is the amount of Life which circulates within your whole mechanism.

The *sixth rule* is to think always about beauty, in beauty, and for beauty. Try to observe beauty, touch beauty, hear about beauty. Beauty has a great power for healing. Beauty brings harmony and rhythm into your life.

I was visiting a family and we were sitting under the trees in their garden when their daughter, seventeen years of age, came and sat by me and wanted to ask me a question.

"What is it?" I asked.

"I have some trouble. My stomach does not digest well."

"Did you check with your doctor?"

"I did, but he could not find anything wrong."

After talking with her for half an hour, I said to her, "May I see your bedroom?"

"Why?" she asked in surprise.

"So that we can find a clue to your trouble."

"What does my bedroom have to do with bad digestion?"

"Let's see," I said, and she led me inside the house to show me her bedroom. On the walls of her room were pictures of clowns, deformed animals, and a picture from a movie in which someone was putting a spear into the stomach of a man. The rest of the room was in chaos.

I asked her, "Why do you have such pictures in your room?"

"What is wrong with them?" she asked.

"Can't you hang some beautiful paintings such as ones of rivers, mountains, lakes, or pictures of great heroes?"

"But what is wrong with these pictures?" she said, pointing to her walls.

"These pictures are controlling your energy system, your glands, and as long as you have these pictures on your walls, you will have trouble in various forms, especially this one in which the spear is being put into the body of the man. This is restimulating some absent memory in you and that memory is creating disturbances in your energy network."

"You know," she said, "I remember the time I bought this picture; I felt nauseated but I thought it was originating from something else. I am going to try it...."

She put all the ugly things away, decorated her room with beautiful colors and pictures and a few days later she was released from indigestion. I gave her a meditation on beauty and she meditated on it for several years. Now she is doing very well in her studies and in her life.

Beauty releases the energy of the Soul and makes it circulate freely.

28

How to Communicate with Your Soul

The Soul stands within the man as the principle of Beauty, Goodness, Righteousness, Joy, and Freedom. These form a five-pointed star. Everything that man does against these five radiant rays of the Sun creates an obstacle between him and the Soul.

The Soul within man is like the Sun. The Sun gives light, life, beauty, activity, and creativity.

Every beautiful thing that comes to our life is from this Source, and we have this Source within us. Just as Nature has the Sun, man has within his own nature a center which is called the Soul. In the Ageless Wisdom this center is called the Master within, the Inner Guide, the Solar Angel, the Inner Guardian, or the Source of Wisdom. This is the "Sun within" that gives light and love and creativity.

Many people are not in contact with this center. This is a very sad fact. If man is not in contact with this Source, he is like a child lost in the desert.

The Soul stands within the man as the principle of Beauty, Goodness, Righteousness, Joy, and Freedom. These form a five-pointed star. Everything that man does against these five radiant rays of the Sun creates an obstacle between him and the Soul.

If you do something against Beauty, you create a barrier. If you do something against Goodness, you create a barrier. If you do something against Truth, you feel that something is wrong within you. If you lie to a friend, a veil forms in front of your eyes. If you do something against Joy, if you hurt people and take their joys away from them, you create a barrier between the Source of light, beauty, vitality and yourself.

If you do anything against inclusiveness, unity, and synthesis, you again create a barrier. This is why millions of people do not have contact with their Soul.

If you do anything against Freedom, it creates blockages within you.

What does it mean not to have contact with your Soul? It is just like flying an airplane or navigating a ship without a compass — you do not have direction. What is direction? Direction is the way you live, think, feel, decide, and plan. If that direction takes you toward perfection, unfoldment, creativity, joy, and beauty, you have true direction. But if you do not have direction, you are lost like a creek that comes from the mountains and disappears in the sands.

It is imperative that we develop contact with that inner Source of Light. That Source is within us, within our aura, and we are going to create a contact and a communication with that Source. After communication we are going to marry that Source. This is the sacred marriage which we read about in the Bible or in the Sufi teachings.

In the Ageless Wisdom we are told that a man must marry his Higher Self. This is what is esoterically called **Soul-infusion**. When a man transforms his whole nature, he suddenly radiates light. We can read throughout history that certain great Initiates radiated light. How did this happen? The human soul fused with the Solar Angel and became radioactive.

There are twelve main ways and means through which you can establish Soul contact:

1. Do not do things that are not right or that really bother you or your conscience. People may say, "I know that." If you know that, it is good, but are you doing it? If something bothers you or your conscience, do not do it; or if you have any doubt, stop it. Doubt is like asking your teacher a question and having your teacher ignore you; there is no communication. If you continue doing what you are doing in spite of the warnings that you hear from within, you create a barrier between you and that Source of Light. This is so simple.

Who is it who annoys you and tells you that you are doing wrong? You may listen to this inner voice and stop doing it. This is an inner conversation, but you must be mature enough to have this conversation. Try to develop it and learn how to translate that communication into the system of your thinking, talking, expressing.

Any time you hear a warning telling you not to steal, not to lie, not to gossip, do not say, "That is none of your business," because this is the direction, and you will feel uncomfortable if you reject it. Every time you act against that Light, a cloud comes and obscures the Sun and you enter again into the shadow. You feel it; you feel the cold; you feel something departing from you. What is it, and why don't psychologists try to find it? What is it that leaves you? Why do you feel guilty or rejected? Try to find It, to know It, and to walk with It.

2. Do not hurt people. Your Soul grieves when you hurt people because people belong to Souls. If you hurt someone, how do you feel? You feel empty; you feel that some creative energy is cut, some inspiration is cut, some impressions are cut. Something is cut, in spite of all your rationalizations.

You are going to be alert to see these things happening. Immediately when you hurt someone you are not the same person; your joy is gone. You wanted to hurt that person, but then why is your joy gone? Why is something lacking in your system? Why has some integrating, fusing factor departed from you?

3. Never be unrighteous. If you borrowed five dollars, give it back with interest. If you observed some event, do not exaggerate it; do not tell lies about what happened. Be totally righteous. Righteousness is a great quality of the Sun within you.

When Mohammed was dying he suddenly called one of his disciples and said, "Come quickly. One month ago I borrowed a chicken from my neighbor, and I forgot to give one back. I cannot die until I repay him."

Do not enter into the Subtle World, the next world, loaded with unrighteousness, with burdens on your conscience. You do not know what suffering will be waiting for you. People collect millions of dollars by unrighteous means. How are they going to face the other world with such a load, with such a burden?

With deception, lies, exploitation, and monkey business people say they are living a beautiful life. Wait until they see the storm on the other side.

Unrighteousness builds a wall. The Soul says, "My goodness, what is he doing? For ten dollars, he is lying. Look, he is exploiting. Look, he is stealing.... Well, I do not want to watch this man anymore." And your Soul is grieved.

These things are so simple. Try to live a righteous life.

One day I visited a friend. At six o'clock he started to panic and became very nervous. I said, "What is wrong?"

"You know, that woman.... This is the third day now that she is coming home late."

"I know your wife," I said. "She is wonderful. Why are you acting this way?"

"You don't know; this is America. You don't understand these things."

"Be righteous whether this is America or China," I said.

The woman came home half an hour later. He opened his big mouth and cursed his wife. My goodness, I was ashamed. She said, "Well, my dear, I had a flat tire again."

"Everyday a flat tire, he said. "I am sick of flat tires!"

"Then buy her a good set of tires and take care of her," I said.

Do not be unrighteous. Unrighteousness will obscure the inner Sun, and you will lose your protection and guidance.

4. Every time you have a problem, do not immediately seek counsel from your lawyer, your priest, or your friends. Ask your Inner Guardian. Sit down in silence and say, "What can I do? Please tell me." You will receive an immediate answer, but you must try to catch it and listen to it.

Sometimes the answer humiliates you; sometimes it demands labor and sacrifice; do it just the same. Just sit in a corner and say, "What can I do?" Talk with your Soul as if It were in front of you.

In the darkest hours of your life, the first one you are going to contact is your Soul. Shall I keep this date? Shall I do this? Shall I take money? Shall I give that money? What do I do in this condition? When you are really sincere, a beam of light will come to your brain. The idea will be so clear, but remember that throughout ages you built millions of barriers.

As you start to become clearer, more beautiful and pure, the inner guidance will increase. Then it will be so easy for you to call on It and say, "Inner Lord, I want to give a lecture. Can you help me?" And It will say, "Of course, I will help you." The Soul inspires you, gives you energy, gives you joy, strengthens you, and heals you...and you do not have to pay for it!

5. Do your daily meditation. Meditation is a very beautiful way to come in contact with that great Source of Light. The Tibetan Master says in *A Treatise on White Magic*, "The Soul meditates and goes deep into meditation to come in contact with the man." What does this mean? It means that the Soul tries to find ways and means to catch that goat. Man is like a goat. He runs here, there, jumps — he does not know what he is doing — but the Solar Angel tries to catch him and discipline him.

When the contact is created, you have the best advisor, the best source of energy within you, and the best source of health.

When the Soul heals, the healing lasts ten or fifteen incarnations. When the hospital heals you, the healing has a short life. It is the Soul Who must heal you. The Soul is that Divine Presence within you, the Messenger of God within you.

Every day do five minutes of meditation. Think of a seed thought, for example, a saying that a great Sage gave us. This is meditation. Read the *New Testament*, the *Bhagavad Gita*, the *Dhammapada*, whatever you like to read. Find a jewel of a seed thought or a topic and think about it. Through thinking you purify the atmosphere between you and It, and suddenly you see that the impressions reaching you are from Space, and you start registering them.

After meditation you start behaving better, talking better, relating with people better. What happened? The smog and fog that was created between you and the Soul lifted. You have more light now; more light is coming to you. When the light is coming to you, you have guidance; you have energy; you have health; you have inspiration.

This is why daily meditation is so important. Not one hour, ninety minutes, or two hours — you do not need that. You need only five minutes, at the most fifteen minutes, but not more than this. It is not the time that counts but the speed and intensity that are important; it is the focus that is important. You receive two or three words, just at the time of need, and what you receive is better than opening a dictionary and reciting it.

Five minutes of meditation every day is essential to making Soul contact. It is so beautiful. Do not sit and hallucinate.

6. Go into seclusion one day a month and seven days per year. It must be real seclusion; sit in a lonely place and say, "What am I doing here? What have I done?" Look at your past, present, and future. Look at how you can improve yourself. Look at all the crazy things you are doing and all the beautiful things

you are contemplating and see what the ratio is between your actions and contemplations. Make a plan to renew yourself, inspire, and challenge yourself. Charge yourself and say, "Now I am coming out of my seclusion."

If humanity has something beautiful in life, it is because Great Ones went into seclusion and brought back wisdom. We know that They were always in the deserts, in the mountains, in the caves. When They came to the people, They were dynamos because They had undergone silence, loneliness, and isolation. In that isolation They were able to make better contacts with the Divinity within Themselves and within Nature.

7. Respect the freedom of others, as long as they do not violate the law. Never violate the personal freedom of others. This one wants to pray this way. Good. That one wants to pray that way. Good. He likes to read this way; he likes to read that way. It is not your business to put your nose into his business and say, "Read my way; your way is not good." Do not violate his freedom because everyone does things according to his karma. Do not violate anyone's karma.

Fanaticism is the fire of Satan; it destroys. Do not be a fanatic; be cool-headed.

Once I saw a minister on television saying, "Unless you do this you will burn in hell. Finished!" I said to myself, "My goodness, don't do that. Speak good things. We love you, but don't hurt people. Give them freedom; let them learn; love them. Do not express anger and violence; just love them. It is your love that will make them bloom and find the way. Give them space and inspire them; they are your children; you cannot threaten them."

Threatening creates fear, and fear creates rebellion. This is so basic, so simple. Do not create fear in people. Fear will react and oppose you. Once a fearful man finds freedom, he will really get back at you.

Leave people alone. This is very important because your Solar Angel, your inner Soul, will not like what you are doing to other people. God has millions of ways to act.

One day a boy came to me and said, "I am doing these wrong things. What do you think?"

I said, "Maybe that is your way to learn. I told you three months ago these things were no good."

"Well," he said, "you didn't emphasize your words too strongly."

"I am emphasizing them now. **Don't do it!**"

So he went and did these things again, and he was shot in the leg. He was in the hospital for three months. One day he called me and said, "I am changing my thinking. I will never do those things again."

"I see you learned your lesson," I said.

He did not learn from me; he learned from his own mistakes. This is why Christ said, "Do not judge people." But we say, if we do not judge, what are we going to do with our tongues?

8. Do not waste your time, energy, and life. Do not waste. What did you do for humanity, for the future? What is humanity leaving for its future children? Smog? Radioactive waste? Poison? Waste materials? Atomic bombs, hydrogen bombs, gases? If this is what we are leaving for our future children, our poor children, they will come fifty years later and say to us, "Daddy, mommy, thinkers, and creative people, is this what you gave us? We cannot find any water to drink!" Seventy years later they are going to sell you air in bottles.

What are you doing? Do not waste your time, energy, and life. Do something beautiful for the future generations, for your country, for the world.

There was a great king called Akbar. When he was sixty or sixty-five years of age, he ordered ten thousand people to plant trees. Some people came and said, "Your Highness, these trees take thirty years to grow three feet, and you are already sixty-five."

"You self-seeking people," he said. "I am not planting them for myself. I am planting them for future generations so that they can enjoy the trees. I am thinking about the future."

Your Soul loves you when you think about the future. The Soul is the future.

You are lying now — what affect will it have on your future? You are spending your money, energy, life, sex, everything now. What will remain for the future? Think about it.

9. Everyday for three or five minutes sit alone and talk with your Soul. Say, "How are you? You know, yesterday I was really mad. What do you think about that? You don't like it? Okay.... You know tomorrow I am going to do this.... What do you think about it?"

Create this rapport. This is what the saints, holy people, and holy fathers used to do. What was the Source of the power they were receiving? It was that Inner Presence, the **Sun** within them which radiates light and wisdom.

10. Always use clean language and do not curse. Cursing creates a tremendous obstacle between you and your Soul. Always use pure, loving, clean language. A Sage says that when you curse you create a storm of dust in the Subtle World which upsets the inhabitants of the higher spheres. You create dissonance, disturbances.

We must not pollute Space with our ugly tongues. If we want to be in contact with our Soul, we must take care of our mouths.

A great prayer says,"My Lord, always keep Your watch in front of my lips so that they never insult Your beauty in Your presence." In another book it reads, "And suddenly the angel came and put the fire on my lips and my mouth was purified."

Purify your mouth. It is not so difficult. You do not need psychology, philosophy, or biology to purify your mouth. Just use your common sense. If you control your tongue, you will be the beloved one of the Soul.

It is not by knowledge that you grow; it is by doing things that you grow. There are many mules that carry gold, but they do not know what gold is. Some people have lots of teaching, but they never learn how to actualize that teaching in their lives.

11. Keep your body, emotions, and thoughts clean. There is a story about a mountain man who had a very beautiful wife. A stranger once came and asked if he could stay one night with him. The mountain man said, "Why not? We have one room. This is my wife. We can all sleep together in this room."

"Well," said the visitor. "That's good."

Before sleeping, the mountain man took a basket and filled it with water and hung it above the stranger's head. Then they went to sleep. The water in the basket had been magically contained, but soon it began to drip on the head of the stranger. "Drops of water are falling on my head!" shouted the stranger.

The host said, "Correct your thoughts!" The stranger had been imagining the host's wife. The host continued, "If you correct your thoughts, drops will not fall on your head."

Clean your thoughts.

This story is an example in the Ageless Wisdom which demonstrates that if you start thinking in wrong ways, with dark and distorted thoughts, something drops on your head; something "funny" happens to you to prove that you are not thinking in the right direction.

Try to purify your thoughts. When you think about your friends, about anybody, think beautiful thoughts because your thoughts will go and mold them. If your thoughts are ugly, you will influence your friends negatively. If you think ugly things about a man or woman for three years, that man or woman will appear ugly because you forced that idea with your own thoughts. Thought is energy; it molds people.

I once ran a school of several hundred children. Some of the children were not doing well. They were smart, nice children, so I thought, "What is the reason?"

One day I took three or four of the children and counseled them. I asked them what was happening. Eventually I found the cause of their failure. One girl told me, "My mommy always tells me I am stupid. It is so stuck in my mind that I want to be stupid to please my mother." Others said that their parents also insulted them.

For a few weeks I spoke with them and proved to them that they were essentially very clever, intelligent, and loving people. I found many beautiful examples in their lives and drew their attention to beautiful qualities that they had. Within a few weeks they changed to a remarkable degree.

One day I gathered them together again and taught them how to change their parents' attitudes. I told them that if their mother tells them they are stupid, they should go to her and in a loving voice say, "Mother, I am doing so well in school.

Everybody loves me, and you will be proud of me. Please tell me something beautiful."

"What for example?"

"Well, tell me that you love me and that I am beautiful, I am smart...."

Some of them told me that through such a contact their mothers, with tears in their eyes, hugged them and said, "I never want to hurt you." Thus they not only did well in school but also established right relations in their home, and they became very successful in life.

By repeating ugly words to your children, making insulting remarks to them, you hypnotize them and make them the way you want them to be. Once you take their self-respect away from them, you will have increasing problems in the future.

Take a woman and tell her, "Your color is fading; you are losing weight. Who knows what is happening?" She will go home and lie down and be sick, or feel very uncomfortable.

So clean your mouth, clean your thoughts, and clean your emotions because in cleaning them you will create a rapport with your Soul.

12. Serve and sacrifice. Every day do something or sacrifice something for someone. Can you do that? The most pleasant experience for the Soul is to serve and do something.

I knew a very disturbed boy. One day we were walking with three or four other students, and suddenly he saw a blind man about to cross the street. This boy immediately ran and held the hands of the blind man and led him across the street. He came back to us and said, "I feel so good."

Look what happened. The boy felt a great joy; his Soul smiled at him because he did something good.

Your joy is the smile of your Soul.

If you love someone and she smiles at you, what do you feel? You feel so beautiful. Every day, try to do something for your husband, wife, boyfriend, girlfriend, neighbor, anyone — do something good. Suddenly if you remember at ten or eleven o'clock that you did not do something good, call a friend and say a few good words, "I love you. You are so beautiful. I saw you walking. You were just darling...." But say these words with your heart.

You will sleep better if you sleep with a memory of a good deed.

There are seven important things which the Soul does:

1. If you come in contact with your Soul, after you pass away It will lead you to the right destination. Those who do not contact their Soul but create tremendous obstacles between their Soul and themselves feel very desperate after they pass away because there is no compass, no guide. There is no protector, and they do not know what to do in that infinite Space.

Let your Soul be your guide.

2. Your Soul protects you from dark forces. If a man has contact with his Soul, no dark force can affect him. Spirits and ghosts cannot come to him. If a house is full of ghosts, spirits, or entities, immediately when a man with Soul contact enters they all escape because darkness cannot stand Light, and the Soul is Light.

In the olden days when people had continuous nightmares, they would call a holy man to stay in their home for a few days, and the nightmares would disappear. The radioactivity, the rays emanating from the Soul of the holy man, dispersed the darkness.

3. Your Soul inspires you with great ideas and courage. A man who has Soul contact is so courageous because he knows that his Guardian Angel is always there to protect him in very subtle ways.

4. Your Soul always leads you in the right direction. For example, someone calls you and says, "Hello, would you like to have dinner with me?"

"Yes," you say, but then you have a little doubt. But it is a dinner; it's a young boy or girl; it's fantastic.... Maybe you will be taken dancing. But at the last moment your Soul says, "No, don't go." Or, "Go...."

Your Soul leads you in the right direction. If a journey is going to be fatal, the Soul may warn you through direct impressions or dreams.

Once a friend of mine felt a strong urge to visit a friend in the hospital. When he returned home, he found things had been stolen. He was very upset and said, "I wish I had not obeyed my Inner Voice."

"What would have happened," I asked, "if the thieves came and found you home and killed you?"

He opened his eyes wide and said, "I guess I must listen to the Inner Voice."

5. In your darkest hours the Soul fills your heart with joy, courage, and inspiration.

The best things that Gandhi did were not shown in the film about his life. He was in the Himalayas for one month, praying and fasting; then he came back to the multitudes. Millions of people were waiting for him. He took the *New Testament* and read the Beatitudes and then said to the people, "Go and live accordingly."

When he was in prison they asked him what he wanted. He said, "Give me *The Bhagavad Gita*. I want to study it." And he translated it, day and night crying, translating that book. Then from prison he wrote to a friend, "From the inspiration I received in reading the *Gita*, I found the courage and power to remove the British Empire from India."

Why did we not see these things in the film? Let the leaders of the world know that reading such books and living in the inspiration of God may lead them to great victories. Do not have faith in your bombs. Instead have faith in Almighty God. This is what the Great Ones do.

6. The Soul gives you freedom to think and contact higher ideas and visions.

7. The Soul brings you co-workers and loving hearts. If you establish contact with your Soul, you become magnetic and beautiful, and people love you and want to help you to shine the Light within you.

Using the twelve ways and means, we establish contact and enjoy the Light of our Soul.

I know many people whose lives changed when they came in contact with their Soul. I have known prostitutes, alcoholics who used to drink day and night, drug users. When I worked with them and they had one minute of Soul contact — they were changed.

This is what you will do. The most important thing is to come in contact with the Source of Light within you, the Sun within you, and receive light, truth, goodness, beauty, synthesis, and joy. Contact your Soul, your inner Sun.

29

Exercise on Freedom

...The petals of freedom slowly unfold and spread the fragrance of love, sincerity, respect, gratitude, harmlessness, sense of responsibility, creativity, service, sacrifice.[1]

1. Take each of the virtues named above and define it clearly.
2. Work out how you would incorporate these virtues in your own life, the life of your family, your race, your nation.
3. Then work out hypothetically the projects you could do that would incorporate each of these aspects in the fields of

- government
- education
- philosophy
- art
- science
- religion
- finance

...The highest freedom is total sacrifice, and total sacrifice is absolute communication.[2]

Look at areas where you would feel safe in sacrificing totally. Do so in your mind, and become one with that area so that communication is total.

---

1. *The Flame of Beauty, Culture, Love, Joy*, pp. 169-170.
2. *Ibid.*, p. 173.

...The highest freedom is total communication. Whenever you have a communication gap, that is your obstacle to freedom. Erase that obstacle and you are more free.[3]

1. Go through the following areas and see where you have communication gaps:

— mineral kingdom

— vegetable kingdom

— animal kingdom

2. Work out ways to bridge those gaps in order to have total communication.

3. Do the same with all the people you know.

4. Then do the same with higher thoughts, mathematics, etc.

True freedom is the ability to choose the wisest way to act, to feel, to think, so that you increase the chance of survival, success, and prosperity of all that exists.[4]

1. Go through your life and look at actions in which you are engaged that will benefit the whole of humanity.

2. Cease any actions that are only for yourself or for just a few. Replace them with actions that could aid the whole.

---

3. *Ibid.*, p. 173.
4. *Ibid.*, p. 174.

30

The Solar Angel

Persist and be patient; one minute of contact with your Angel is equal to many lives of experience and richness.

Great is the healing power of the Guardian Angel within us.

The Guardian Angel is called by various names. It is the Solar Angel, a radiant Being, the Meditator Who is in continuous meditation trying to come in contact with the human soul. It is also called the Integrator, the bridge-builder between the human soul and his future glory.

The Solar Angel is a very advanced Entity Who, after going through a great spiritual development, was called to help the animal man: to individualize him and help him progress on the path of evolution.

The Solar Angel has many duties toward the human being. The first one is to integrate the personality. It tries to harmonize and align the threefold vehicle of man so that it functions as one unit. First, It tries to make the physical body respond to emotional impulses, then to make the emotional body respond to the mental body, then to make the mental body be impressed by the emotional and physical bodies. When these three bodies are highly integrated, we say that man is a personality.

The second duty of the Solar Angel is to tune this integrated personality to Its own note and rhythm. This stage of evolution is called the Soul-infused stage of man.

The third duty of the Solar Angel is to inspire the blooming human soul, who begins to emerge from slavery in the three bodies and to radiate his own light.

The fourth duty of the Solar Angel is to impress the Hierarchical Plan on the human soul so that the human soul eventually synchronizes and tunes himself to the intent of the Hierarchy. When the human soul is impressed by the Plan, he feels uncomfortable and often irritable because he feels an inner urge to live in certain ways but does not yet see the Plan clearly.

The fifth duty of the Solar Angel is to reveal the Plan to the human soul and, in a few seconds, make the human soul feel the reality of the Plan by his own means. Revelation of the Plan takes a second or two, during which the human soul receives great inspiration, and he then dedicates himself more to the Plan.

The Solar Angel waits for moments of great ecstasy or moments of great tension to reveal a part of the Plan to the human soul. This revelation takes place when the Solar Angel bridges the soul's consciousness with the Intuitional Plane and gives a rare opportunity to the human soul to see or sense the Plan.

The sixth duty of the Solar Angel is to bring impressions from zodiacal signs or from Great Beings to the human soul at the time of new and full moons. That is why it is suggested that at the time of the new moon and full moon one must exercise certain disciplines and be open and watchful for certain spiritual impressions.

At the exact moment of the full moon, the Solar Angel impresses the human soul and charges the whole personality, evoking a new spirit of striving. These impressions expand our consciousness, enable us to see things in different dimensions, and help us reorient ourselves more clearly toward the Plan. Every month this is repeated, but most human beings receive the charge and waste it through various activities and excitements.

The seventh duty of the Solar Angel is to see that the karma of the man is not violated. The Solar Angel acts as an agent in man for the Karmic Lords, or for the Law of Karma. It is the Solar Angel who decides where, when, and how you are going to pay your karma. The Solar Angel has a psychic computer system, and in a moment It can do all kinds of calculations and make you pay your karma of the past ten thousand years, or of yesterday. Your karma is not only the result of your deeds but also of your thoughts and emotional reactions.

The Solar Angel watches all your actions on all planes, but It does not prevent you from doing wrong. It feels great compassion for you if you do wrong things, but in the meantime It lets you win your own battle by your own merit.

The Solar Angel is also called the Reporter. It reports your failures and successes to your Master through Its computer system; It comes in contact instantaneously with all that is related to your spiritual evolution. If you do well and pass into the stage of discipleship, your image is built of etheric matter in one of the offices of the Hierarchy. This image presents every change going on in your nature.

After your image is built, on rare occasions, the Solar Angel consults with your Master and sometimes brings messages to you from your Master. At the beginning, these messages evoke a strong urge within you to strive, to dare, and to be courageous on the Path. Then they are felt as goals and new visions. Later you hear the message as it is, and you cooperate with the Plan of your Master. Every time the Solar Angel contacts you, or every time your Master directs His eyes on your image, you feel charged, you remember your responsibilities, and you feel the need to take new steps on the path of your evolution. You want to strive; something magnetically calls you to action. It is also possible that these spiritual touches make you withdraw from actions that are not in harmony with your spiritual destination.

The contact of the Solar Angel and, later, the indirect contact of the Master through your image pass through different stages. First, you register them as an impression. Second, you register them as direct messages or events. Third, you hear Their voice and then see Their form.

Usually, it is your Angel Who appears to you first and speaks to you about your duties, responsibilities, and service. It is possible also that, if necessary, It reveals to you your past lives, those lives which are necessary for you to know. The Solar Angel keeps the records of your past lives, and the only accurate way to obtain information about your past lives is through your Solar Angel.

After you have a definite, conscious contact with your Solar Angel, your Master tries to contact you for world service. It is important to note that your Master takes permission from your Solar Angel to contact you. This is a very important point in the Teaching.

People have many contacts with certain entities or beings, but these are violations. Any violation is directed by wrong motives. Dark forces, for example, violate this rule and come in contact with the human soul to deceive him and to mislead him.

It often happens that an entity possesses a man's mental body and contacts some powerful entities on the left-hand path, giving the impression that the man himself is in contact with higher forces. And because these dark forces are full of power, the man appears powerful and dynamic and even performs miracles. The truth is that an enemy is occupying his control tower and is in contact with the forces of destruction.

The contact of the true Master starts with His special fragrance, then with His voice and His appearance. Before the Master appears, we are told that you feel His radiation in the form of a tension within all your aura. You do not feel fear but a pure expectancy to meet Him. If He feels that you are not able to receive Him in an unusual condition, He meets you in a very usual way, as Christ met His disciples or as the Master of H.P. Blavatsky met her in London.

A Master does not praise you, although He encourages you for greater tasks and responsibilities which He reveals to you and which will challenge you. A true Master never praises your personality. He invites you to work harder and harder. As you engage yourself in greater service and go through greater pressures and crises, He becomes happier. Your Solar Angel and your Master know that crises, difficulties, and tensions bring you to your senses and develop in you persistence, stability, and striving. These three virtues will be used for your higher evolution.

Inertia, slavery to pleasures, satisfaction with your level, and contentment with luxurious living are called coffins which take you to the grave. An easy life is the grave of the soul. That is why your spiritual Teacher feels happiest when you go through crises and through the joy of victory over crises.

It is interesting to note that in certain times when you are in a crisis, your *heart* feels joy, and often you do not understand it. You think you are crazy to be happy in a crisis, but you are. Often your joy is the reflection of the joy of your

Teacher, and at other times it is the joy of the human soul who sees things from a detached perspective.

One may ask, "If the Solar Angel is in the higher mental plane, why is the contact registered in the heart as joy instead of as a mental exhilaration?" The answer is that the heart is the most sacred center among all the etheric centers. The heart is the translator and the center most sensitive to the Solar Angel.

We must understand that the life principle dwells in the heart. The Self is within the heart. In lower dimensions the heart is shown as being away from the Self. But in higher dimensions the diagrams and illustrations usually shown do not work. In higher dimensions it is the heart that is in the central position and contains the Jewel.

When we say, "Om Mani Padme Hum," in higher dimensions we translate it as, "The Self is in the Heart." And here the Self is both the individualized Self and the Cosmic Self. This is how the heart is the Temple of the Cosmic Self.

The mind is an interpreter and most of the time a troublemaker. The head center is a mechanical center; it is the typist which works in its best conditions under the inspiration of the heart.

The ninth duty of the Solar Angel is to protect you at the time of your transition and at the time of the birth of your body. At the critical time of your transitions, the Solar Angel induces a certain vibration into your blood — via the heart — and your nervous system, and before you pass away you feel a deep ecstasy. This happens in natural death. In suicidal death you pass through a heavy crisis, and the protection of your Solar Angel is almost withdrawn. In natural death you may hold the hand of your Solar Angel or of your Master and walk away from the body.

At the time of birth, the Solar Angel protects you from many attempts of possession. Birth is a more dangerous moment for the human soul than the moment of dying. In death you are in the process of birth in higher planes and higher realms with a greater possibility of higher contacts. In birth you are in the process of dying. Your freedom, your space, and your light is narrowed, and you are put into a little mechanism in which you are almost helpless. The Solar Angel is the most protective at this stage of your life.

People will be surprised if they gather all the miracles that happen to infants and children and see the protective hand of an invisible Entity. Once Christ said, "See to it that you do not despise one of these little ones; for I say to you, their angels see the face of my Father in heaven." [1]

In the Ageless Wisdom birth is considered death. That is why the Lord Buddha advised His Arhats to try harder to work out their own salvation and thus be able to avoid returning any more into incarnation, into the death of birth. Those

1. Matthew 18:10

who lived a life of Beauty, Goodness, and Truth and sacrificed their lives for the Common Good see the victorious smile of their Angel and pass on in joy.

At the time of birth the human soul usually loses the vision of the Solar Angel, and that may be the reason for the first cry of the newborn baby. But we must remember that life does not end with death and does not begin with birth. Life *is*. Life is permanency, continuity, and duration — beyond time and space.

The tenth duty of the Solar Angel is to warn us, to guide us through dreams and visions and through the voice of conscience.

Always have a spiritual diary and write down your dreams. Observe them, analyze them, but do not identify with your interpretations. This is difficult, but one must learn to escape certain traps.

If you have a direct warning from your Soul through your conscience or through a vision or pure dream, try to obey it. If you obey it, you establish closer contact with your Soul. If you negate the warning of your Solar Angel, you build a greater barrier between you and your Angel. When this barrier becomes thick enough, you lose your contact, although It watches you. The sad thing is that you do not hear any more of Its warnings and Its guidance, and you sell your rights to thieves; for you the right or the wrong does not make any difference. When you do not use your inner ears to hear the voice of your Angel, they eventually become insensitive and petrified.

We are told that even in very hopeless conditions the Solar Angel tries to reach you, and often, when you suddenly turn your heart to your Angel, all accumulated barriers melt away in the love established between you and the Angel. To stay in contact with your Angel continuously, you must obey your conscience and listen to Its warnings. This does not mean that your life is totally controlled by the Solar Angel and that you do not develop any personal merit nor prepare to be an independent human being in the future.

The Solar Angel, like a mother, leaves your hand free at the time of many crises to develop in you the spirit of initiative, courage, daring, and striving. It is only on the edge of the abyss that It again stretches Its hand to you. Its whole intention is to make you free when you grow enough. But even when you know how to live, you may profit from Its wisdom accumulated throughout millions of years.

The Solar Angel rejoices when you do sacrificial service and try to live on the path of renouncement and isolated unity because it is on this path that the steps toward higher liberation are taken.

Sometimes your Angel flashes a suggestion into your mind in daring conditions and watches your response. For example, when you face a need, the Angel suggests that you meet it with joy. When there is an opportunity to exploit, to misuse people for your interest and pleasure, the suggestion comes to stand in your spiritual light and solemnity.

Thus, try to watch not only for guidance but also for warnings. Guidance and warnings are the moments of crisis and test for us. The Solar Angel expects an increasingly strict, austere, joyful, and blissful life from us, and tries to challenge us toward higher and higher victories.

The Solar Angel expects you not to sell your conscience, your soul, or your heart for money, for pleasures, for praise and flattery, for recognition and positions. It expects you to live in solemnity, with your heart, with your conscience.

The sleeping man says, "Take my heart or my conscience, but do not take my money or my positions. I do not care what happens to others. I care for my pleasures." Such a man is like the man who was busy drinking and loving while the whole house was burning.

Your Solar Angel does not care what group you are related to, what books you have, what books you have read, what spiritual showing off you do, to what extent your reputation grows and spreads, or what gurus or Teachers you assume you have. The Solar Angel is only anxious to see that the flame of life is growing in your heart, putting you in deeper contact with Its light, with the wisdom of Christ, and with the direction of the Cosmic Captain and thus making you a sacrificial server of the race.

It is also very interesting to know that the Solar Angel rejoices when you renounce your pride and when you stand indifferent while people praise you or disapprove of you, while people recognize you or ignore you.

The eleventh duty of the Solar Angel is to precipitate on your mental plane new ideas. New ideas open new directions, new goals, and lead you toward new labors. Each idea is a plan for a new activity. Each idea is a seed for future harvest. These seeds can be received through meditation, nourished by the love of the heart, and matured through service and actualization.

As you become more sensitive to ideas, you establish a greater relationship with your Angel. Eventually you arrive at such a state of sensitivity that on rare occasions the Solar Angel looks through your eyes, speaks through your voice, and acts through your hands and feet. At this stage, the Solar Angel opens the doors of your treasure-house where all the beautiful jewels of experience and the wisdom of thousands of incarnations are accumulated. Your wealth is now under your possession because you can use it intelligently and with wise appropriation.

When the doors of your treasury are open for you, you are inspired continuously because the treasures of your temple are the seeds which bloom as the flowers of the future, revealing the mystery of higher dimensions. As you use the treasure of your spiritual wealth, one day you come in contact with the Treasurer — and you find out to your great surprise that the treasure was your real Divine Self, serving within you as an eye for the Solar Life. This is the narrow door to the treasury which leads to a life more abundant.

The twelfth duty of the Solar Angel is to impart to you *creative inspiration* from the Hierarchy, from the Tower of Will, and from still higher sources.

Inspiration is like an energy current which reaches you and galvanizes all your being and, like a strong wind, pushes you into heroic action. Inspiration is the transmission of the energies of ideas, visions, and directions of great Centers, great Initiates, and great Lives. Such inspirations are transmitted to you via your Angel at the time when you are between the Third and Fourth Initiations.

Inspirations, if received consciously and expressed in creative labor, put you in contact with higher Centers, and you eventually find yourself in the company of higher Beings. Your life becomes a flow of creativity. You create beauty in whatever you touch because inspiration from higher sources reveals the essential Divinity in all forms.

The thirteenth duty of the Solar Angel is to put you in contact with those who will help you proceed on the path of your evolution. These people can be pleasant people or very unpleasant people. Pleasant people come to you to enrich your treasury, and unpleasant people come to you to make you aware of your past failures and karma. Both work for your own good. The unpleasant ones are disguised as friends to invite you to be more vigilant and watchful on your path.

The Solar Angel even leads you to places where you find greater wisdom to evolve or to learn a few needed lessons.

Once a nurse named Mary was visiting my mother. I was about twelve years old, and that day I came home early from school for some reason. I had with me a little poem, and I put it on the table and suggested that my mother read it. After my mother read it aloud, the nurse came and hugged me and said, "Tomorrow I will be here to take you to some people who will enjoy talking with you."

The next day she came wearing her white uniform and took me to a young girl and boy — twenty-five or thirty years of age. To my surprise they received me with great respect, and the nurse said, "Goodbye."

They asked me various questions. I was never aware that I knew the answers to all their questions. It surprised me more that these beautiful people were very solemn and very simple.

The one question that I remember most vividly was this:

"Do you think that plants have awareness?"

"Well," I said, "I know they are aware. They can contact us and they can talk with us and they feel the pains of our life. They try to help us through their beauty and fragrance…."

"How did you learn all this?"

"Do I need to learn?"

"Well…."

"Yes," I continued, "they are the forms of elevated beings, but unfortunately we slaughter them."

We had other conversations, and then we came to the Solar Angel. They asked, "Do you think you have an Angel?"

"Yes, I do."

"Why do you think so?"

"Because…. I can't tell you." At that moment I felt that I was too scared to talk about such a mystery.

Later they became my Teachers, and they led me to Blavatsky, to the Tibetan Teacher, to esoteric contacts. It was amazing how I was led through a simple poem to a nurse, Mary, and whole new contacts opened for me.

I remember also when I was in Jerusalem and wanted to meet a friend. I was guided to go to a certain place, only to find him there waiting for me.

The Solar Angel, like an airplane, sees from above and with Its light guides the physical man into certain locations or to certain persons.

It is important to know that *the Solar Angel does not lead you into temptation.* On the contrary, It warns you when you are inclined to go in the wrong direction. In all conditions the warning is there, but often the ears lack hearing.

The fourteenth duty of the Solar Angel is to supply psychic energy to give vitality, enthusiasm, and energy to the human soul to serve, to talk, to create, to sing, to compose and play music, and to penetrate deeper into the mysteries of Nature. Psychic energy gives you perseverance and concentration through which you never forsake the plans you made for service and the development of your spiritual life.

There is an energy in Space which is called psychic energy. This is the energy of the Ray of Compassion pouring from the Cosmic Chalice. This energy is everywhere in Space, but it is found in condensed form in the Seven Rays, in the form of seven rivers of energy. Furthermore, this energy is condensed in the Zodiac as a whole and directed into twelve streams of psychic energy.

On the human level this energy is absorbed and amplified by the flame of the heart and used as the energy of creativity, purification, healing, and contact with higher worlds and dimensions. As the flame of the heart grows in its beauty and radioactivity, it absorbs more and more psychic energy from the Cosmic Ray of Compassion.

The Solar Angel in man is also a depository of psychic energy. Psychic energy keeps the man in tune with the greater Universe and with the direction of the Cosmic Magnet. Psychic energy creates equilibrium, serenity, and mastery. It annihilates the danger of the subterranean fires and builds a fiery shield around the disciple against the fiery darts of the dark forces. If psychic energy weakens in man, the citadel of the heart falls into the hands of adversaries which destroy the form of man.

In natural death, psychic energy builds the golden bridge through which the human soul passes into higher dimensions.

Psychic energy is the greatest healer of almost all diseases. It is the electrical energy which purifies the etheric network and the astral and mental planes and burns all that is a hindrance to health in your physical body.[2]

---

2. For more information on psychic energy, please refer to *A Commentary on Psychic Energy.*

Withdrawal of the Solar Angel

The Solar Angel withdraws from a man when the man tolerates obsession and possession, when he becomes criminal, or when he works deliberately against the higher laws and principles. This withdrawal is gradual. First, the Solar Angel "keeps silent." Then It "turns Its face away from you." It withdraws Its protective shield — but always thinks about you. In the worst cases, the Solar Angel leaves you, and this is called the greatest disaster that can befall a human soul.

We are also told that the Solar Angel keeps a thread of contact with you if a drop of goodness still abides in you.

The Solar Angel leaves you when you make a pact with the devil and "sell your soul" to evil. It withdraws slowly when It sees you are engaging in crimes, drugs, or prostitution. Crimes, drugs, or prostitution burn the communication network between you and the Angel. It withdraws when you consciously falsify the Teaching of the Great Ones and fill your mental, emotional, and etheric bodies with the trash of deception, delusion, and illusion. It withdraws when you consciously work against the Plan and against the Head of the Hierarchy.

Whenever the Solar Angel begins to withdraw, your eyes lose their brightness of spirit; your criminal, separative tendencies increase; you become more selfish and destructive; you fabricate more lies and produce more delusions.

People think that advancement of knowledge or an increase of knowledge is a sign of spiritual progress. This is an illusion. Advancement is not an increase of knowingness but inclusiveness. Advancement is an act of increasing your beingness. You must be careful to increase your love for all beings and to increase your enthusiasm to serve them by all possible means. These are the golden rules which bring you into closer contact with the Solar Angel.

Contact with the Solar Angel

We can establish closer contact with the Solar Angel through

— meditation

— evening review

— service

— renunciation

— the exercise of gratitude

— prayers

— spreading the real Teaching

— serving the Great Lords

— loving

— living a harmless but active, creative life in our words, deeds, feelings, and thoughts

— being an example of sacrifice

Sacrifice is not an action; it is the name of the substance of the Monadic Fire. Whenever this fire is present, there is sacrifice. When any act on any level carries this fire, we can say that act is a sacrificial act.

The Monadic Fire has three flames: will, love, and light or Beauty, Goodness, and Truth. All three must be present in our acts if we want to be sacrificial.

As the fire, or the substance of sacrifice, pours down from the Central Core of the human being, it nourishes the petals of the Lotus through which the Solar Angel tries to reach the human soul — the echo or the reflection of the Monad in time and space. The flow of sacrificial fire gives the Solar Angel opportunity and facility to come closer to the Personality, the human soul. The Solar Angel almost always is in deep meditation. That is why It is sometimes called the Lord of Meditation. Through meditation It tries to impress the Personality, the human soul.

When the fire of sacrifice begins to flow down through the Lotus, the Solar Angel receives greater joy and finds greater facility to contact the human soul. The substance of sacrificial fire makes it easier for the Solar Angel to contact the heart of the human soul, as the fire releases and carries with it the accumulated knowledge, love, and power of thousands of incarnations. The human soul receives abundant nourishment through the release of the treasury of the Chalice. He receives inspirations, visions, great ideas, and spiritual impressions which nourish him and enrich his life of creative living and striving.

Let us remember that the Solar Angel is striving toward Its own Monad, as the human soul is striving toward his own Monad, his own Real Self.

The Solar Angel does not release will energy to the human soul. It releases only light and love energy. It is the human soul who, through his labor and striving, must draw the energy of the will from his True Self. When he draws more will energy from his True Self, he facilitates the task of the Solar Angel. That is why the Solar Angel eventually leaves the human soul when the innermost petals of the Lotus release the sacrificial fire, the fire of the will of the Monad.

It is important to mention here that at this time Christ is the Teacher of all Solar Angels Who are trying to make man proceed on this path of perfection. All Solar Angels are fed by Christ. He is called "the nourisher of little ones."

The Solar Angel does not release will energy because it would prematurely carry the man to contacts for which he is not ready. The Solar Angel waits until man masters himself through light and love and then by his own merit releases the will energy.

The flow of will energy brings a metamorphosis in man. If man is not ready and is forced to go through the process of metamorphosis, he fails on his path.

The Solar Angel is called "an Initiate of all degrees." The word "all" refers to the first five Initiations. The Solar Angel is a Fifth Degree Initiate, and because of Its great sacrifice and compassion, It is called a Solar Angel. "Solar Angel" is the name of the office.

Will energy is released only in group formation and for group use. When the human soul becomes group conscious and acts as a member of a group which is dedicated to furthering the Hierarchical Plan and Divine Purpose, he is allowed to call forth will energy which, in expression, turns into the substance of sacrifice. As the man transforms his life and dedicates himself to the service of greater and greater wholes, the will energy releases itself through acts of sacrificial service.

This gives a deep joy to the Solar Angel. It is the release and activation of the will energy that opens the path of the human soul and thus releases the Solar Angel to return to Its Cosmic labor for Its own evolution.

How to Invoke the Help of the Solar Angel

I. The First Two Days

To be able to create a closer contact with your Guardian Angel, it is necessary to begin by going into seclusion for a week or two. In your seclusion, for two days read the *Bhagavad Gita* or the *Upanishads*. Eat little and rest in Nature.

II. The Third Day

1. Light a candle and burn some sandalwood incense. Sit cross-legged on the floor, if possible, or on a chair. Relax and say the following invocation:

   O Thou Who watched me since my cradle

   and shed Your Light upon me,

   accept my gratitude

   and love for You.

2. Keep silence for a few minutes, thinking about the words you said.

3. Sound three OMs.

4. Repeat the invocation:

O Thou Who watched me since my cradle

and shed Your Light upon me,

accept my gratitude

and love for You.

5. Maintain a few seconds of silence in expectancy to feel the response of your Angel, which may reach your mind as a wave of joy, peace, light, or energy.

6. Sound three OMs.

7. Say this invocation in deep concentration:

O Thou Who waited for me throughout ages

to come in contact with You,

shed Your Light upon my path

so that I follow Your Light

that leads my steps into Your presence.

8. Sound three OMs.

9. Then continue saying:

I see on the mirror of my mind

all the obstacles I created

through my thoughts, words, feelings, and actions.

All these obstacles,

in the form of illusion, glamor, and maya,

made me insensitive to Your guidance and call.

But always I felt Your watchful eyes.

I want to disperse these agelong accumulations

and contact You directly.

I need Your permission.

I know my approach will be gradual.

But I want to make a commitment to avoid

all thoughts, words, and actions

that You do not approve.

I want to make a commitment to love,

to forgive, to stand in Light.

I want to make a commitment to protect Nature,

to protect the innocent,

to protect children,

to serve those who stand for unity,

purity, expansion, and synthesis.

May I be led

from darkness to Light,

from the unreal to the Real,

from death to Immortality,

from chaos to Beauty.

10. Rest for five minutes and take a walk in Nature.

III. The Fourth Day

1. Light a candle — preferably a beeswax candle.
2. Sit relaxed.
3. Breathe deeply.
4. Visualize a five-pointed star above your head. Visualize a soft blue light emanating from the center of the star and forming a sphere of light around you.
5. Sound three OMs.
6. Say:

O Thou Who watched me since my cradle,

hear my voice and turn Your eyes upon me.

I am ready to have closer contact with You.

My intention is to be a mature servant

and fulfill Your expectations to serve,

to sacrifice, to radiate light, love, and energy,
to fulfill the Will of the Almighty Power
in the Universe.
Here I am,
with all my humility
and with all my commitment.
I will not create any more barriers
between You and me.
Let Your Light inspire me.
Let Your joy fill my heart.
Let Your glory strengthen my arms and feet
to work and walk on earth
as a fiery servant for the Will of God.
Accept my commitment,
O my Angel of Love.

7. Sound the OM seven times and then rest.

IV. The Fifth Day

1. Light a candle — preferably a beeswax candle.

2. Burn some incense.

3. Relax.

4. Breathe deeply.

5. Visualize a mountain on which you see a temple. Knock on the door five times with all your desire to see it open.

6. See it slowly open, and enter in great solemnity and humility. See an altar on which is a shining sphere of light.

7. Kneel in front of the light and say:

You are the Light shining upon my path.
I walked the path of Your Light,

and now I am within the sanctuary

of my Inner Lord.

Let Your Light permeate me.

Heal my physical wounds.

Heal my heart and emotions.

Heal my mind and illuminate me,

as I stand in front of You as a flame of Light.

8. See the Light increasing in intensity and volume, building a sphere of Light around you.

9. Go deeper into your Self and think for fifteen minutes, five minutes on each of the following:

   - Compassion
   - Sacrifice
   - Synthesis

10. See the Light penetrating more and more into you, and think about joy, bliss, and freedom for five minutes.

11. Say in deep concentration:

    I solemnly and with all my being

    commit myself

    to spreading the joy of transformation

    and renunciation,

    the bliss of sacrifice,

    and the freedom of purity.

12. Sound seven OMs.

13. Relax.

14. Sit quietly for five minutes.

15. Later, write an article about joy, bliss, and freedom. Read it at night, make the needed changes, and go to sleep.

V. The Sixth Day

1. Relax.

2. Say the first invocation:

   O Thou Who watched me since my cradle
   and shed Your Light upon me,
   accept my gratitude
   and love for You.

3. In your visualization see three diamonds forming a triangle at the center of which is a golden Chalice. In the Chalice see a blue flame.

4. Say with deep concentration:

   O Thou Who art a fiery Angel,
   a flame in the Chalice,
   burn all impurities from my mind,
   my heart, my lips, my senses.

5. Visualize three blue rays extending from the flame and hitting the diamonds which are radiating a silvery blue light.

6. Say:

   O Flame of my journey,
   let Your Light
   consecrate the diamonds
   of my contact with the Universe.
   Let Your Light, pouring out of the Chalice,
   unfold the potentials lying within my diamonds.
   Let Your Light create the fiery field
   between the diamonds,
   and at the center let my eyes perceive
   Your glory, Your beauty, Your power;
   to be inspired by Your glory, beauty, and power;

to live a life of glory, beauty, and power

for the Lord of the Universe.

7. Visualize an electrical sphere forming between the three diamonds. At the center of the sphere, see a blue light. See that the blue light is changing into the pupil of an eye. Accept the eye as your eye, which is unfolding and opening to see — first, "as though in a mirror; then face to face."

   Look at the Chalice and visualize the most beautiful symbol of your Angel, or the most beautiful form of your Angel, radiating beauty, power, and glory.

8. Say:

   My eternal gratitude

   for the opportunity to contemplate,

   to visualize Your presence.

   It is the time of contact.

   It is the time of conscious cooperation.

   It is the time of commitment to sacrificial service.

   It is the time to pave the way

   for the coming Avatar.

   Gratitude to You for the awareness that I have.

9. Sound seven OMs.

10. Relax.

11. Record your experiences.

VI. The Seventh Day

1. Relax. Light a candle and incense.

2. Sound seven OMs.

3. Say the Great Invocation.

4. Visualize the three diamonds, the Chalice, the Flame, the three rays, and the eye.

5. Looking at the eye, the Flame, or the glorious symbol or form in the chalice, say:

   O Great Warrior of light, love, and beauty,

   I am ready to renounce my will.

   I am ready to follow the path of Your instruction.

   I will try to keep silent

   so that You impress me

   with Your instruction.

   Grant me, my Elder Brother,

   Your Will.

6. Keep total silence mentally, and in great tension of expectancy feel a real transforming power passing throughout your nature. Feel great joy; feel great bliss; feel great freedom, and wait patiently — maybe fifteen minutes, maybe thirty minutes, maybe two hours.

7. If your commitment is sincere, if your renunciation of your will is sincere, if your decision to serve is valid, you will have a signal of Its approval and contact. The signal can come as a flash of light — with colors — as a voice, as an appearance, as a symbol, as a touch, as a fragrance, as an energy, as an expansion, as a destruction of all links of attachments, as a sense of freedom.

8. Express your gratitude and say,

   My gratitude to You.

   I will persist to come

   closer and closer to You

   until the day in which Your Glory

   will shine in my eyes

   and in my life.

9. Sound seven OMs.

10. Relax and go to your bed and sleep.

11. Upon awakening, write down your experiences.

The disciple must know that this is a progressive approach to the Angel. You can repeat these steps in seven days every six months to the end of your life. Some disciples will have easy contact; others will wait many incarnations until the Angel decides if closer contact is safe and will serve the Hierarchical Plan or Purpose. Even a one inch approach toward your Angel is a great success because your future is based on these contacts.

It is possible that your Angel will introduce you to your Master, Who will instruct you. Or your Angel will lead you to one of the Ashrams where you will receive instructions. Or your Angel will help you to attain spirit-knowledge.

Spirit-knowledge means the knowledge that comes from your true Core, from your innermost Self, because you, in your essence, are a door to the Almighty Presence in Space.

Persist and be patient; one minute of contact with your Angel is equal to many lives of experience and richness. Try to stand closer to your Angel; feel Its presence. Ask It when you need It. Live in It.[3]

3. For further information about the Solar Angel, see *Cosmos in Man*, Chs. 1 and 2; *The Hidden Glory of the Inner Man*, Ch. 3; *The Science of Meditation*, Ch. 3; *The Psyche and Psychism*, Ch. 48; *Other Worlds*, Ch. 59; and *The Solar Angel*.

31

Angel Visualization Exercise

Visualize a mountain. Sit at the foot of the mountain. Look at the summit. See how high it is.

Start climbing up and up to the summit.

Sit on the summit under a tree and look down at the fields.

Visualize an Angel beside you Who will tell you that you are going to leave your body and be taken to the stars.

Lie down and visualize that you are coming out of your body. See the Angel holding your hand and taking you to Space. Let the Angel lead you to the galaxy, to one of the planets where flowers walk and talk, where trees sing, where the human beings are like angels.

Look at the earth as a distant planet, dark and enveloped in smog because of the moral corruption.

Go into a pool of water. As you bathe yourself, see that you are receiving a golden aura. Let the Angel tell you that with this golden aura you will carry a strong charge of energy to earth, bringing honesty, beauty, nobility, and righteousness to earth.

Now let the Angel take your hand and fly back to earth, seeing all other planets and stars on your path.

Come to your home and see how your light is shining in the room and everything else is reflecting your light.

See how you are transforming people around you, giving them more joy and light and healing their hearts, minds, and bodies.

Visualize a great Master coming to your room and saying to you,

"My child, always stay in Light, and the powers of the Universe will protect you and make you a servant of Light."

Kiss His hand and let Him disappear....

Take three deep breaths. Rub your hands, and open your eyes.

32

The Chalice and the Seeds

The cause of our psychosomatic illnesses is often found in the three permanent seeds simultaneously. Medical or psychological treatments often fail because they are used to eliminate only one part of the cause.

The mental plane, with its seven subplanes, is like a cloud around your head and body. Gradually, as your consciousness unfolds and as your experiences become richer, the mental plane organizes itself and seven colors appear, one for each subplane. These colors slowly become clearer, and you notice a vortex of energy which in esoteric literature is called the mental unit. Then, just as the moon emerges out of a mist, a point of light begins to appear on the higher subplanes. This is called the Mental Permanent Atom or seed.

The development of the mental plane continues, and one day there can be seen a faint outline of a Chalice. Centuries pass; the Chalice becomes clearer and clearer, with a rare beauty of fiery colors and the radiation of twelve streams of energy. More centuries pass, and the time comes when the Dweller in the Chalice is released and passes into Cosmic evolution.

What are the permanent atoms? We are told that the genes in the human body are "hereditary determiners." They condition the development of an individual and the characteristics of his body. They are transmitted from generation to generation. Thus, a gene is the living or permanent record, the nucleus of the body, which is kept throughout successive generations, slightly changing and modifying itself according to the combination of the parents. The important point is that the gene contains a record of all past characteristics, and it will be the seed of the future body. Therefore the characteristics are not lost, although they do undergo changes due to the pressures of education, environment, daily living, and other influences.

This may be true in regard to the physical body, but what about the "hereditary determiners" of our emotional or mental bodies or states? In esoteric psychology these are called permanent atoms, seeds, or stones. We have six permanent atoms: one physical, one astral, two mental, one buddhic, and one atmic. All of our experiences on these levels or planes are registered in these permanent atoms or seeds, whether we are conscious or unconscious of the impressions.

The Mental Permanent Atom registers all mental impressions; in the emotional permanent atom all emotional experiences and impressions are registered; the physical permanent atom registers all physical level experiences and impressions. Our permanent atoms are like "memory cells" or storage rooms in which is stored all that we have done or expressed and all that has been impressed upon our three levels of human endeavor.

All that we do physically, all that happens to us on the physical level, enters into the seed and forms a complex record. Even our "unconscious" experiences are registered in our physical, astral, and mental permanent seeds. But the mental unit registers only when we are not in an "unconscious" state of mind. In our conscious states we are impressed largely by what we do, feel, and think, but in our "unconscious" moments we are impressed by what others do to us. The body eventually perishes, but the permanent atoms remain in the subtler vehicles. Then, when an individual begins to prepare for another physical expression, another birth, the physical permanent seed, working through the etheric centers, builds the etheric body according to the content of the seed, and around the etheric web the physical body is built.

The emotional permanent seed contains all of our emotional reactions and impressions, conscious or unconscious. Long after we leave our physical body, our emotional body dissolves; but registered in the emotional permanent seed are all of our emotional life experiences, and each registration is a conditioning factor in the seed.

The mental body lives longer than the physical and emotional bodies, but the time comes when it, too, goes through a process of disintegration. The Mental Permanent Seed, however, contains all life experiences and impressions of the mental life. When the human ego prepares to return to physical plane life, the Mental Permanent Seed and the mental unit will vibrate; the building of the mental body will begin and proceed according to the recorded "notes" of the Mental Permanent Seed.

All three bodies are built in this way, according to the content of their permanent atoms or seeds, but it must be stressed here that the bodies or vehicles are not built at once; the building is a gradual process. As the physical body achieves its maturity, the emotional body continues on toward its maturity; the mental body continues to develop even after the emotional body has reached its maturity.

Thus, we have in our temple the permanent records; they are the "Book of God" in which everything is registered. Our whole life is primarily conditioned by the contents of these permanent seeds. Not only do the physical, emotional, and mental bodies grow from these permanent seeds, but also their future qualities, their potentials, and their possibilities for development are determined by the permanent seeds.

We react, we are impressed, we express according to the quality of our instruments. We cannot see a distant star with a toy telescope. We cannot play a symphony on a trumpet; we need other, more refined instruments. The permanent seeds furnish us with whatever we have put into them in the past, plus current experiences. In brief, they condition the range of our sensitivity, the range and quality of impressions, and the form and extent of our expression on the three levels of human endeavor. In the permanent atoms we find our complete past, with its good and its bad records. All that we have been in the past is in those permanent seeds, and from those seeds will grow our future. The past conditions the future, and thus we may say that our past and our future are in the permanent seeds.

We cannot change the past, but we can change the future in the present by living a conscious life and planting good qualities in all three of our permanent seeds. Wrongs done intentionally on the mental plane in our past lives are there, and if by some means they are stimulated and released, they will come down slowly, express themselves in our emotional and physical bodies, and affect our lives in many ways, with many forms of problems.

We must also consider that the content of the seeds is not always negative. On the contrary, you will find in them the best that you gave to your family, your friends, and your nation. These are the seeds which condition your well-being upon the three planes. They are the flowers, the water, the food, and the energy for your long journey back to your True Self.

In these seeds is recorded the degree of development of your three bodies. When you are ready to take the three vehicles for your next life, they will continue in their development from the point where they left off in your past life. Suppose your physical body reached a level of twenty-five degrees in development. The next time it will start its development at the twenty-fifth degree level. The same holds true for the emotional and mental body development.

There is a very important point to be made here, however. The bodies start to grow from the point where they left off, providing that "dark records" do not interfere as they do in the following example. Suppose you had a strong and healthy body, but before you died you committed a very cruel act which caused someone to suffer deeply. It is possible that in one of your future lives you will have a strong, healthy body and then develop a serious illness. Another result might be that you will be born physically defective.

The same example may apply to the other vehicles. A wrong done in any vehicle extends simultaneously to the others, and the result may express itself through one, two, or all three vehicles simultaneously.

When we use the terms right and wrong, or good and bad, they are not the echoes of the words of religious fanatics or devotees. In every man there is a sense which we call the conscience. It is the conscience which a man uses to make judgements.

The physical body is rooted in the physical permanent seed. The switchboard for the blood system, the nervous system, and the glands is in the physical permanent atom. The person has a new physical body, but the latent causes of trouble are in the seeds. Whenever these records are stimulated by various means, the switchboard works automatically and mechanically. It begins to affect the other bodies according to the records there.

On the physical level the permanent seeds work as follows: An event occurs which has a corresponding similarity in the records of the physical, emotional, and Mental Permanent Atoms. The records vibrate through the Law of Resonance and project an energy which is translated as a mood or an inner state or attitude. The emotional counterpart and then the mental counterpart of that event tune in with the physical records. The man is not aware of what is going on in his inner world, but his thinking, feelings, and actions are controlled; he has no power over himself. He has fears and new urges and drives, the intensity of which is determined by the degree or depth of tuning in one body to another.

In the New Testament this information is presented in a symbolic parable concerning a debtor who was put into prison and not allowed to be released until he paid all his debts. Esoterically, dark records are our debts. A lie is a debt; a theft is a debt; an act of cruelty is a debt. On the other hand, an act of love, service, or compassion is a credit, a seed of light.

The whole mechanism of cause and effect resembles a computer which, by the pressing of a few buttons, adds, subtracts, multiplies, and performs many other mathematical calculations. So it is with the human mechanism. We press a few buttons and the "machine" starts to work. In a short time the physical, emotional, and mental organs, the seeds, and the thoughts begin to work, and eventually the result appears. We do not see the activities of the thousands and thousands of cell-organs in the "machine," but we see the results, the effect. Fortunately, we are not computers, and there is a way to release and annihilate the dark contents of the seeds.

All therapists are unconsciously directed to those sources of trouble. They often restimulate the contents of the seeds without being able to erase them, and the condition of the subject becomes worse.

They sometimes lock the tiny doors or channels through which the trouble wave is trying to exhaust itself. Just as our outer nature does not like to keep dead matter in the "bodies," so it is with our inner nature. It pushes such matter out to clear the channels and purify the system. The energy that controls this eliminating process is symbolically called the *Fire in the Chalice.*

The cause of our psychosomatic illnesses is often found in the three permanent seeds simultaneously. Medical or psychological treatments often fail because they are used to eliminate only one part of the cause. For example, they may eliminate the physical cause, but this is only one part of the total cause in which all three bodies — physical, emotional, and mental — are involved simultaneously. An effective treatment will be directed to all vehicles or seeds so that the root of the problem is erased forever.

It is important to remember that our physical and emotional permanent seeds register all that happens to us in our "unconscious" moments because most psychosomatic problems have their origin in our emotional permanent seed. A great Master tells us that the permanent atom

> *... serves as a nucleus for the distribution of force, for the conservation of faculty, for the assimilation of experience, and for the preservation of memory.*[1]

Beyond these permanent seeds there is another vessel which is called the **Chalice**, or the **Lotus.**[2] This Chalice is formed of twelve different fiery petals of energy, like the petals of a rose or tulip. Three of these petals form the core of the Chalice.

In the average man, this Chalice is practically nonexistent, but as a man progresses on the Path, as he develops his knowledge, love, and sacrificial nature to some degree, a small bud appears, slowly grows, expands, and takes the form of a Chalice. In this Chalice are accumulated the real treasures of man. All achievements of the centuries, the essence of his love, true knowledge and service, are accumulated in the Chalice.

A Master Mind says,

> *... Of course, the treasury of the spirit is the Chalice, and that treasury also guards matter, because the powerful impulse of sacred Fire is laid in it....*[3]

> *... From the Chalice issue all creative laws and in the Chalice are gathered all cosmic manifestations. Therefore, the enrichment of the Chalice affords realization of all cosmic plans. The foundations are gathered in the Chalice, and each energy can be a creator. Thus, creativeness is molded by the law of containment.*[4]

> *The center of the Chalice gathers all creative threads. Therefore, each cosmic vibration resounds within the Chalice....*[5]

> *... As a synthesized center, the Chalice preserves the most essential, indescribable accumulations.*[6]

> *... The Chalice is the repository of everything loved and precious. Sometimes, much that has been gathered into the Chalice remains concealed for entire lives, but if the concept of*

1. Alice A. Bailey, *A Treatise on Cosmic Fire*, pp. 69-70.
2. For more information please refer to *The Hidden Glory of the Inner Man*, pp. 51-54.
3. Agni Yoga Society, *Infinity*, Vol. II, para. 34.
4. *Ibid.*, para. 192.
5. *Ibid.*, para. 152.
6. Agni Yoga Society, *Brotherhood*, para. 463.

Brotherhood has been impressed upon the Chalice, it will resound in both joy and yearning in all lives....[7]

...Untold treasures are accumulated in the Chalice. The Chalice is one for all incarnations. The properties of the brain are subject to physical inheritance, but the properties of the Chalice will be determined by self-exertion.

In the Chalice lies the winged child....[8]

... make for yourselves ***purses*** *which do not wear out and a treasure in heaven that does not run short, where the thief does not come near, and moth does not destroy. For where your treasure is, there also will be your heart.*[9]

In the cults of Zoroaster there is represented the chalice with a flame. The same flaming chalice is engraved upon the ancient Hebrew silver shekels of the time of Solomon and of an even remoter antiquity. In the Hindu excavations of the periods from Chandragupta Maurya, we observe the same powerfully stylized image. Sergius of Rodonega, laboring over the enlightenment of Russia, administered from the flaming chalice. Upon Tibetan images, the Bodhisattvas are holding the chalice blossoming with tongues of flame.

One may also remember the Druid chalice of life. Aflame, too, was the Holy Grail. Not in imagination; verily by deeds are being interwoven the great teachings of all ages, the language of pure fire![10]

... According to your growth shall you yourself gather pearls. By your own hands shall your match them. By your own hands will you develop dynamic power.[11]

In esoteric literature, heaven is the mental plane where the Chalice is found. The treasure is in the Chalice. It was symbolized as the Holy Grail sought by the Knights of the Round Table. It is in the Chalice that our true Guide exists, but our Guide cannot express Itself until the permanent atoms or seeds are cleansed, purified, and the Chalice is in full bloom, filled with the elixir of life.

---

7. *Ibid.*, para. 464.
8. Agni Yoga Society, *Agni Yoga*, para. 627.
9. Luke 12:33-34
10. Nicholas Roerich, *Altai Himalaya*, p. 33.
11. *Ibid.*, p. 43.

The purifying process is the result of the contemplation of the Solar Angel within us. The Solar Angel vibrates in higher octaves, and these notes act as purifying streams of energy which throw out all that does not fit into the plan of the human soul. The act of meditation is a process of conscious assimilation of these energies.

The Chalice is built primarily of the substance of the Solar Angel. The human soul makes himself ready to wear it as "the robe of glory." When this body, the Chalice or the "robe of glory," is woven or built, the emotional sea disappears and the astral body disintegrates. Thus the man enters into direct communication with the Intuitional Plane. Here lies the source of true and direct knowledge.

This was hinted at in one of the parables of Christ, when He spoke about the man who had no proper wedding garment to attend the feast.[12] One may ask how the man who was refused entered the feast. Some people enter into the higher levels of consciousness through the means of drugs and breathing exercises, but if they are not ready to wear the "robe of glory," they suffer in many ways.

In the Bible we are told about grace. Students of the Bible and religion have had great difficulty in finding the real meaning of grace, but it is very easy to understand the meaning of grace when you know about the Chalice. Grace is the essence, the content of the Chalice. It is your savings account, accumulated throughout centuries, and when you are in dire distress, it meets your needs. It saves you from great danger; it gives you light, illumination, beauty, attractiveness, and energy. You wonder where these precious gifts came from. They came "by the grace of God" — from the treasure of your Chalice. You may feel yourself to be unworthy of the great help you receive, but it is yours; it is paid to you from your savings account at the right time and in the right place.

The Chalice is the body of the Solar Angel. Its voice is your conscience. Nothing can enter into the Chalice which is against the Divine Plan, Purpose, and Will. Everything in the three levels of human endeavor which is in accord and in tune with the essence of the Chalice gives you great inner joy, energy, and inspiration. Anything you do contrary to the essence of the Chalice makes you poor and miserable, and you feel the soft, small voice of conscience warning you of your wrong action. The Chalice is the vessel of pure wisdom, the vessel of true love and knowledge, of beingness and realization.

The twelve petals of the Chalice are divided into four sections. The three outermost petals are called the *petals of knowledge*. They extend their influence upon the physical, emotional, and mental planes.[13] The higher impressions of light-knowledge pass through the Mental Permanent Atom to the knowledge petals, to the mental unit, to the generative organs on the mental plane, to the

12. Mathew 22:11-14
13. These are petal number 1, 2, 3 respectively.

astral throat center, to the astral generative organs, to the etheric throat center, and to the etheric generative organs.

The second three petals are called the *love petals* on the physical, emotional, and mental planes.[14] The love energy passes through the Intuitional Permanent Atom to the love petals of the Chalice, to the solar plexus on the mental plane, to the emotional permanent seed, to the heart center of the emotional plane, to the solar plexus center on the emotional plane, to the heart center in the etheric body, and to the etheric solar plexus center.

The third three petals are called the *petals of sacrifice*, each extending to the physical, emotional, and mental planes.[15] The spiritual will passes through the Atmic Permanent Atom to the petals of sacrifice, to the base of spine on the mental plane, to the head center on the emotional plane, to the base of spine center on the emotional plane, to the physical permanent atom, to the head center on the etheric plane, and to the etheric base of spine center where the Serpent Fire rests.

The three innermost petals are "the synthesis of knowledge, love, and sacrifice."

The permanent seeds function in the substance aspect of an existence. The nine petals of the Chalice deal with the consciousness or psychical aspect of the existence, while the three innermost petals are the expression of pure Spirit.[16]

The fire in the Chalice cyclically stimulates the permanent atoms, and gradually the spirillae come into action. Their unfoldment brings new urges, new drives, new understanding and growth, new creative currents, new motivations, and new impulses. As a result of these incoming energies, the bodies respond, and they become more sensitive to inner and outer impressions. These incoming energies may also create problems in the bodies if obstacles or friction exist.

The currents which come through the physical permanent seed are currents of regeneration, vitality, transmutation, and growth. These currents use the medium of the blood system, via the head center and the base of spine center.

The currents that come through the emotional permanent seed are currents of love, compassion, and peace. These currents mainly reach the glandular system via the heart and solar plexus centers.

The currents that come in through the Mental Permanent Seed may be called inspiration, Intuition, and vision. They come down to the nervous system via the throat and sacral centers.

But very often these incoming streams of energies, rays of power, inspiration, and love are obscured in the seeds themselves by the past accumulations, which are the micro-records of painful experiences, fears, losses, wrong actions, negative emotions, wrong decisions, thoughts, prejudices, superstitions, etc. Any

14. These are petal number 4, 5, 6 respectively.
15. These are petal number 7, 8, 9 respectively.
16. For further information, please refer to *The Science of Meditation*, pp. 220-225.

time a man acts against the principles of love, freedom, beauty, and goodness, he throws a dark shadow into the seeds. These obstructions, hindrances, and distractions always color incoming energies and condition them. When these higher energies pass through the moods or states of the mental and emotional atmospheres, they create different reactions.

A negative emotional state can poison the incoming energy, and a corresponding organ or system becomes influenced or affected. Thus many diseases appear on the physical level due to improper or negative reactions to the incoming energies. This fact was hinted at by a scientist, Edward Bach, M.D., when he said,

> *"Bodily health is entirely dependent upon the state of the mind,"*

and

> *"Disease is a kind of consolidation of a mental attitude, and it is only necessary to treat the mood of a patient and the disease will disappear.*[17]

These moods or attitudes are the effects of the inner contents of the seeds, and sometimes they are thrown out to the surface by the incoming energies or impressions. People should not approach the inner light in meditation or worship while negative or harmful thoughts are in their mind or while they are subject to poisonous moods.

In the past, only the physical permanent seed was active. The physical permanent seed was responsible for man's body and for its reactions and behavior. At the present time in evolution, the emotional permanent seed is active along with the physical permanent seed, and in the majority of people these two are conditioning the physical and emotional life expressions and problems of man.

Slowly the Mental Permanent Seed is entering into the field and affecting the threefold vehicles of the human being. This is why our mental problems are gradually increasing and we are building up a complicated response apparatus which is difficult to repair by physical or psychological means alone.

In the majority of cases, our conscious mind is not aware of and has no control over the physical and emotional permanent atoms or the Mental Permanent Atom. We are usually polarized in the conscious mind or in the mental unit, which is a separate unit in the mental plane. Around the lower mental plane are found all our thoughtforms, daily experiences, and the center of our daily activities.

---

17. Bach, Dr. Edward, *The Medical Discoveries*, p. 57.

But gradually the unfoldment or the development of the Chalice takes place. The physical permanent atom becomes radioactive. Then the emotional permanent atom becomes radioactive, and then slowly the Mental Permanent Atom is organized, unfolding the seven planes of the mental plane.

This unfoldment builds a bridge between the mental unit and the Mental Permanent Atom. Eventually the physical, emotional, and Mental Permanent Seeds come closer and their electromagnetic auras fuse with one another. This stage is called the phase of the Soul-infused personality. The permanent atoms gather themselves around the cup of the Chalice and they transmit the goodness, the truth, and the love of the Chalice to their corresponding bodies.

As a result of this transmission, the bodies pass through some serious crises, and then emerge into purity and golden health. This is the Transfiguration. All physical level urges and drives are exhausted; the body is built up with higher physical plane substance. The emotional body is cleansed from all negative emotions and becomes a peaceful source of love and compassion. These two bodies come under the control of the mental unit, and the reactive mind is washed away completely.

The bridge which unites the Mental Permanent Atom with the mental unit becomes a radiant line of light, brings down to the human level the treasures of the Chalice, and opens an infinite horizon of wisdom to the conscious mind.

Now the human consciousness becomes a unit. It contains not only the consciousness of the seven physical subplanes but also the consciousness of the emotional subplanes and the mental subplanes. Such a man is called an awakened man, a man who does not sleep in any of his twenty-one subplanes of the personality and has continuity of consciousness day and night. The glory of the Chalice expresses Itself more rhythmically as creative splendor, beauty, inspiration, leadership, invention, holiness, etc., and the man becomes a shining light for future generations.

The glory of the Chalice becomes more and more radioactive. The Central Fire blazes forth, and one day when It reaches Its summit of glory, the Chalice is set aflame and vanishes and the Dweller is released from the control of the wheel of life and death. He is an Arhat now. He has control over earth, water, fire, and air.

The Tibetan Master gives individual names to the nine petals of the Chalice. The three knowledge petals He calls

Petal of civilization

Petal of culture

Petal of illumination

When the first of the knowledge petals opened and unfolded on the physical level, "it brought a measure of light to the physical plane consciousness of humanity." This happened in Lemurian times, and a materialistic civilization came into being. In Atlantean times the second knowledge petal was unfolded on the astral plane. An emotional, religious culture was started, and man became creative. In Aryan times the third petal opened on the mental plane and created a mental illumination or knowledge. We are told that the Teaching of Buddha helped to accelerate the opening of the knowledge petals.

These knowledge petals are formed of three types of substance:

By the mental substance on levels 1, 2, 3

By the mental substance on levels 4, 5, 6, 7

By the mental substance found in matter itself

The knowledge petals correspond to the *Law of Service.*

The second tier of petals, the love petals, are called

Petal of cooperation

Petal of loving understanding

Petal of group love

We are told that the Teaching of Christ tremendously helped these petals to unfold and flood the heart of man with love energy.

It is evident that when the first petal of love opens on the physical plane, man becomes cooperative. The opening of the second petal on the astral plane makes him a man of loving understanding in whose presence you open your heart and bloom. Such a man becomes a great artist. The opening of the third love petal makes a man group-conscious. He lives and works for the group which we call humanity. Great humanitarians belong to this category.

These love petals correspond to the *Law of Magnetic Impulse.*

As the six petals unfold and open, they will affect the petals of sacrifice, and, with the help of the incoming new energies, these three petals will also be opened.

The three sacrifice or will petals are called

Petal of participation

Petal of purpose

Petal of precipitation

When the first sacrifice petal is unfolded, the individual or the group actively participates in the Hierarchical Plan; all the members of the group dedicate themselves to understand and work out the Plan. When the second sacrifice petal is unfolded, the individual or the group becomes united with the will of group disciples and touches the Purpose standing behind the Plan. When the third sacrifice petal is unfolded, the individual becomes one with the group of Initiates Who work for the precipitation of the Plan. We are told that the will or sacrifice petals correspond to the *Law of Sacrifice.*

Again, the great words of Hermes, "As above, so below," apply. A Master of Wisdom explains that our Planetary Logos is a twelve-petaled Lotus, a Chalice of energy, which sustains the planet. Our solar system forms a twelve-petaled Lotus on the Cosmic Mental Plane of the Solar Logos. Three of these Logoi represent the three knowledge petals; three others represent the three love petals; the remaining three are the will petals, the petals of sacrifice; and the innermost ones contain the Central Fire, the Jewel, which is the Solar Logos Himself.

Om Mani Padme Hum[18]

From this Chalice, the life of the Solar Logos pours down to all that exists in Its ring-pass-not, as the life-giving blood of the Cosmic Christ pours from the great Holy Grail. The petals are transmitters of energy. The Central Jewel in the Lotus is the source of the highest energy in man. This energy is the life of the physical, emotional, and mental bodies. The petals open, and more life flows into the bodies. As a prism refracts light, producing a display of rainbow colors, so do the petals act upon this energy, changing it into the energy of knowledge, love, and sacrifice. The petals are not only transmitters and transformers of energy; they are also translators, or interpreters, of the Solar Angel.

The knowledge petals formulate energies and high impressions into ideas and thoughtforms. These ideas and thoughtforms are gradually absorbed by the higher and lower mental levels until the brain is able to register them.

The knowledge petals are closely connected to the physical permanent atom, to the throat center, and also to the generative organs. These petals act as a magnetic center to sublimate and transfer the lower energies into the corresponding higher centers. For example, sex energy is sublimated and transformed into the throat center in the mental body, thus producing a very high-level creativity.

If there are aberrant contents in the mental unit, in the Mental Permanent Atom, and in the lower mind in general, a state of turbulence is created in the mental sphere and the flow of knowledge energy is turned into illusions. This is why in olden days the Masters urged the purification of the mind before transmitting higher ideas to aspirants or opening the window of the knowledge petals.

The love petals are connected to the emotional permanent atom, the heart center, and the solar plexus. They transmit the energy of attraction, affinity, understanding, and, above all, Intuition. When the energy of the love petals flows

18. Salutations to the Jewel in the Lotus.

through the astral body and meets negative emotions there, it creates glamors. A glamor is a distortion of love energy by a negative emotion.

The will petals bring will energy from Atmic levels and make it available to the three personality levels as fuel for the activities of the bodies. If the etheric body is infected with illusions and glamors, they strengthen the illusions and glamors in the mental and emotional bodies and create maya in the etheric body. Glamors and illusions create blind and uncontrolled urges and impulses which control the etheric centers, creating in man an ever-burning desire for sex and material possessions. His dominating center in this case is the sex center. He is like a man caught in a whirlpool of maya, and all his thinking, aspirations, and desires are controlled by the forces of that whirlpool. He is identified with his urges and with his mechanism. This identification is the greatest cause of maya.

The petals of will or sacrifice eventually dissipate maya, creating an ever-progressing indifference and detachment and transmuting desire into aspiration, intention, and pure will.

In the permanent atoms or seeds are built the patterns of our behavior, habits, and convictions, whether positive or negative; they are there and they are inherited. They affect the genes of the cells, and throughout many lives these behavior patterns continue. The inheritability of these behavior patterns does not refer to the traits passed down from generation to generation; man inherits what he has built within himself at one time or another. This does not mean that there are no side effects and other influences on him through his parents and associates. There are, but the main source of his beingness is himself — as recorded in the seeds and stored in the Chalice.

In cases of hypnotic trance, one can see how a subject awakens if a suggestion is against the pattern of principles in his seeds. At that time, an electric charge comes out of the entire unit and reestablishes the consciousness, rejecting the suggestion. Most hypnotic healings are very dangerous. They block the drainage of a wound which is in one of the permanent seeds. Medicine often does the same thing. With paper walls it blocks the presence of fire. It often succeeds in putting out the flames, but the embers are there and they will flame up at another time, through a different vehicle, in a different form, and perhaps in a future life.

If a healing is temporary and occurs in one vehicle only, it is not true healing. It is not a true healing if the healer cures a patient for a Friday only, or for a week only, but forgets the coming years, centuries, and lives through which the individuality will pass. If the hidden, true cause of a sickness cannot be reached, it is better in the long run to leave the expression of the illness free. Let it exhaust its resources. Let Nature clean its own house. Once the seed is truly cleansed, the patient will be immune to a recurrence of the ailment.

Is there a way to approach the seeds and purify them, cleanse them from the past accumulations, engrams, and records? Some master minds know the technique of how to reach them and exhaust the negative contents. "Your sins are forgiven," said Christ, and the man was cured. This sentence is an outer symbol of a complex inner technique.

All dark records in the seeds are sins, something done against love, truth, beauty, and law in the past, perhaps centuries ago, and the record is still there. As long as that record or debt is not erased, it will express itself eventually. Besides the dark records in the seeds, there is also much static in our minds. This static not only interferes with the inflow of the light from the Chalice and from the Spark, but sometimes it even cuts off the current of energy coming to the vehicles and organs.

What is this static? Static is like dust devils which are formed by opposing currents of air. They are what in common words is called sin. A so-called sin is committed by a particular part of the man, by the power of resistance of that part. But it does not cause static until the opposing current is there. The opposing current is the moral code of fear that the individual has incorporated from his family, from what he has read, from his church, his religion, his government, or his way of thinking. These are all impressed in the seeds, and these impressions resist everything that does not agree with them. The content of the seeds acts here as a judge or as an automatic rejector, refusing everything that is against the implanted conduct.

The conscious mind can play a role in solving these "sins" by creating buffers in difficult cases. Some so-called sins are the result of superstitions and man-made, obsolete codes of behavior. In this case, the "mind" can solve them and create peace in the inner space of the mental plane and reestablish the outflow and inflow of mental, emotional, and intuitional currents. The conscious mind can do this if it is disciplined enough to detach its thinking process from the common thought, or from the common code, and think in a wider space and periphery, but always tending to the highest good.

If the thinking of the man is in accord with the fire of the Chalice, the man is released more and more into freedom. But if his limited thinking is creating veils and buffers, then the lower life will gain control and the progress of the man will be delayed for centuries. He needs then to unveil himself, step by step, from the nets he has woven and is caught in, creating a real prison for himself. The Tibetan Master says,

> *...When mind becomes unduly developed and ceases to unite the higher and the lower, it forms a sphere of its own. This is the greatest disaster that can overtake the human unit.*[19]

The permanent seeds are not only containers of our activities or impressions on the three planes, but also they are pure seeds, each of which develops its corresponding vehicle.

---

19. Alice A. Bailey, *A Treatise on Cosmic Fire*, p. 261.

Each permanent atom has seven spirillae. It takes centuries to develop these spirillae. When the seventh (or lowest) spirilla is active, it contains only very rough impressions and builds a body corresponding to that level of vibration. When the third (counting from above) spirilla is active, the body is of a higher order, built of finer substances, and correspondingly the content of the seed is more complex, more inclusive, and has higher ranges of impressions. Only after building our bodies with the third level substance can there be a true channel of light, love, and power for the inner man. When the first spirilla is active, the man is divine and one with the Will of God.

Each spirilla is connected to the corresponding subplane of that particular plane. Seven spirillae serve the seven mental subplanes, seven for the emotional subplanes, and seven for the physical subplanes. As was stated, the higher planes of any vehicle become active when the higher spirillae of the seeds are active.

To the extent that the spirillae of the seeds become active and the corresponding subplanes are formed and organized does the content of the Chalice become richer and of higher quality. Even the form, the color, and the radiation of the Chalice become more beautiful and more luminous, and proportionately the horizon of the field of your consciousness becomes larger and larger. When it is fully developed you can see nine flames, like petals of a rose, forming the Chalice. Therein are observed three electric-blue flames which eventually will burn the Chalice and release Its fiery essence.[20]

The Chalice and the Influence on the Bodies

We are told that each permanent atom has seven spirillae, except the mental unit which has only four spirillae. These spirillae are not always active. Some spirillae of the permanent atoms sleep for a long time until they are activated by the expansion of consciousness. The more spirillae that become active, the more the human soul enters into greater enlightenment and creativity.

The Lotus petals in the higher mental plane have a very close connection with the spirillae of the permanent atoms. For example, when the knowledge petals open fully, they help the first three spirillae of the physical permanent atom to function, and as they function they transmit more vitality to the physical body.

Similarly, when the love petals open, they affect the astral permanent atom and assist the first three spirillae in the astral permanent atom to be active.

The four spirillae of the mental unit become fully active when the seventh petal of the Lotus, which is the knowledge petal of the sacrifice petals, fully opens.

The sequence of the unfoldment of the petals does not always follow this order. They differ according to

20. Reprinted in part from *The Science of Becoming Oneself*, Ch.12.

The person's Monadic Ray

The person's karma

The person's service

It is clear that the unfoldment of petals affects the activation of the spirillae of the three permanent atoms.

The spirillae of the permanent atoms are related to the seven centers, the Seven Rays, and even to the seven sacred planets.

As the spirillae begin to function one after another, the human soul proceeds on the path of greater communication with the Universe, on the path of greater creativity and service.

The activation of the spirillae is very important because they provide health and purity to the corresponding vehicles and release the energy of the cells and atoms of the vehicles, tuning them to the Jewel in the Lotus.

Thus, the physical body becomes charged and is able to live a long and healthy life.

33

Lotus Exercises

A.

1. Relax your body.
2. Take three deep breaths.
3. Keep the spine erect but relaxed.
4. Visualize a rosebud one foot above your head.
5. See it as clearly as possible.
6. Try to see a spark five feet above the rosebud.
7. Focus your attention on the rosebud.
8. Now look at the spark which has the color of deep electric blue. A few seconds later visualize the spark turning into a blue star.
9. Visualize a beam of light coming from the star and hitting the rosebud.
10. See the petals of the rosebud slowly unfolding and forming a Chalice as the light from the spark is hitting the bud.

    See the blue light filling the Chalice with light which is then radiating out and penetrating into your etheric, astral, and mental bodies.
11. Again see the star, the thread of light, the flow of light into the Chalice, and then the radiation of light passing through your threefold bodies and purifying them of maya, glamors, and illusions.

    NOTE: Do not identify yourself with your bodies. Stay away and direct the procedure.
12. Try to see a sphere of lemon-yellow light, pure and stable, around your head. This is your mental body.
13. From your neck to your solar plexus see a light blue starry sphere. This is your astral body.

14. All around your body see a violet sphere. This is your etheric body.

15. Now focus your attention on the rose and visualize yourself sitting in the rose and looking down at your body — the violet light, starry blue, and lemon-yellow spheres, the golden rose, the thread of light, and the electric blue star above your head.

B.

1. Relax again, breathe deeply, keep spine erect but relaxed.

2. See the golden rose, the beautiful rose. Touch the petals. Smell it, etc.

3. See the star.

4. See the thread of light,

5. See the rose.

6. Let the energy flow down to the rose, filling the rose with blue light.

7. Let the energy penetrate into your mental body, which is a lemon-yellow color, and purify it of all illusions.

8. Let the energy penetrate into your astral body — a starry blue — and purify it of all glamors.

9. Let the energy penetrate into your etheric body, purifying it of all inertia and crystallizations. Let the violet color become pure and stable.

10. Locate yourself in the rose and observe the harmony of your three vehicles and their colors.

11. Try to stand out of your body and watch it from outside, five feet away. Observe the bodies, the rose, the thread, and the star.

12. Stand ten feet away from your body and direct the blue light toward those places which need purification. You must do this very fast. No organ or physical part must be concentrated upon. The light must hit *only* the etheric, astral, and mental bodies.

C.

1. Repeat the same procedure as in sections A and B.

2. Relax.

3. Make the rose bigger. Smell it; touch it.

4. See the thread of light.

5. See the star with a white diamond in it.

6. See the etheric, emotional, and mental vehicles with their colors (violet, starry blue, and lemon-yellow).

7. See the beam of light from the diamond. Let it pour down to the bodies.

8. See yourself standing in the center of the spark.

D.

1. Repeat A, B, and C.

2. Relax.

3. Think about your True Self as a focal point of energy.

4. Flood your physical, emotional, and mental bodies with a blue-violet light. See a great harmony in them. Feel serenity in them, joy in them.

5. Think about beauty. What do you think beauty is? Enumerate ten component parts of beauty and visualize an object of beauty with all these ten characteristics.

6. Relax for fifteen minutes.

34

Elementals

Thus, seven lives are developing through our seven planes. They are there to help us; we are there to help them. The harmony between their lives and the human soul brings happiness, joy, and bliss.

In esoteric literature we read about some life-forms which are called *elementals*. As far as the human mechanism is concerned, we have three elementals — the physical elemental, the astral elemental, and the mental elemental.

The physical elemental is the sum total of all the lives of the cells in the physical body. The astral elemental is the sum total of all the lives of the astral body. The mental elemental is the sum total of all the lives of the mental body.[1]

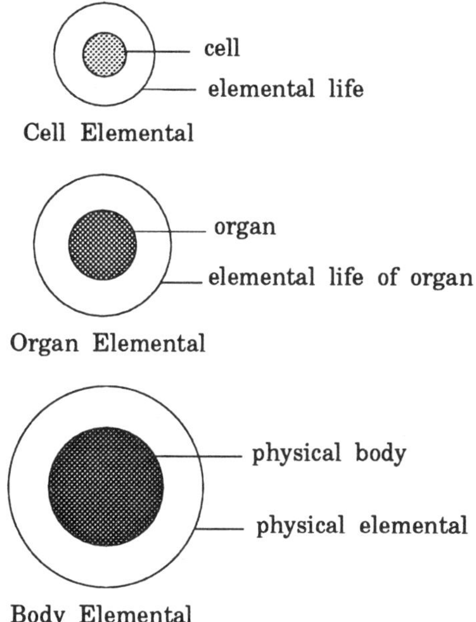

Diagram 34-1 Cell, Organ, and Body Elementals

1. For more information on elementals, please refer to *The Psyche and Psychism*, Ch. 17.

The physical elemental is the spirit of the physical body, separate from the individualized spirit of man.

In the first diagram, we have the elemental of the cell. The second diagram shows an organ which has its own life. This separate life is an elemental which controls the organ. The third diagram indicates the elemental of the body, or the life of the sum total of all these cellular lives. This is the elemental of the physical body.

For example, we have a group and a man. Let us assume that each member of the group is an elemental, and all the members of the group form the body of a man. An elemental is the life of the atom. An elemental is also the life of all the cells combined. Through the sum total of all physical cells in the body, a separate entity is in the process of evolution as a physical entity.

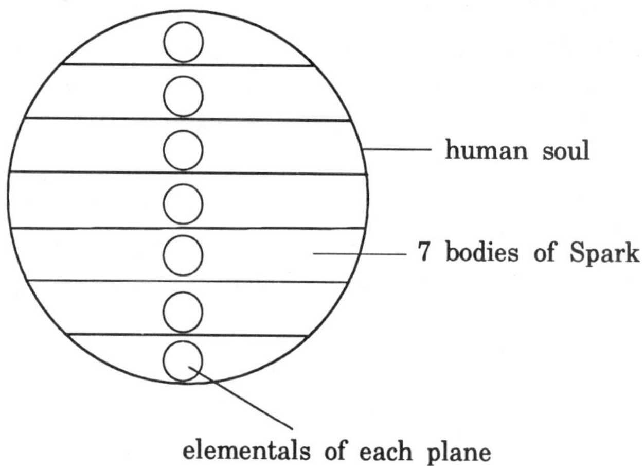

Diagram 34-2 Elementals

To explain further, there are seven planes. The big circle is the human soul. He is progressing on the path of his evolution. In addition, through each vehicle of the person, another entity or group entity is developing. For example, our physical cells are developing, our astral atoms are developing, our mental atoms are developing, and so on; they all have their different evolutions. Our evolution helps them to evolve, or our actions may retard them. Their evolution in turn helps us evolve.

Elementals evolve within the sphere of our aura. That is why we must be very careful with them and try not to pollute them. For example, if we do anything wrong with the physical elemental, it protests through pain. We have no right to destroy our elementals. On the contrary, as advanced intelligent beings, we must live in a way that right conditions are created for their evolution.

It must also be remembered that a portion of the elementals are involutionary lives, and great and intelligent discipline must be exercised and sustained so as not to let them go further into involution. We should aid them in initiating a movement toward evolution. H.P. Blavatsky once said that "man is a life plus lives." All these little lives are progressing through man, in the atmosphere of man, and man is acting as a liberator for them. Anything harmful to the evolution of these elementals, or to the three bodies, must be prohibited.

Thus, seven lives are developing through our seven planes. They are there to help us; we are there to help them. The harmony between their lives and the human soul brings happiness, joy, and bliss. This will be easy to understand if we imagine that we are a captain and we have seven groups of soldiers under our command. If they do their best as individuals and as individual groups, then we can do our own job better. The understanding and harmony between the group members, the groups, and ourselves guarantee the success of the command.

Some groups even do an extraordinary job and bring great help to the others. And if our various elementals are in an advanced stage, they bring us great success.

It is very interesting to note that a man's consciousness is identified with the elemental that is either spoiled or acting crazy. If our body is sick, we are identified with it. If our emotional body is upset, we are identified with it. But if our elementals are in harmony and in rhythm with our progress, they do not bother us and we do not even feel their existence. This means that the liberation of man from the elementals requires the person to sublimate, transform, and transfigure them.

It is possible that the elementals come and occupy the same bodies again and again in each incarnation.

The harmonious development of man is the harmonious development of all the lives that construct the vehicle of manifestation. When we develop one part of our nature, we create a temporary imbalance, and then we are forced to work upon the other elementals who were not given attention. There are people who do not take care of their bodies but develop their minds or are devoted to spiritual practices. This creates an imbalance. All parts of the vehicle of manifestation, the seven planes, must be developed harmoniously. To play divine music on our sevenfold instrument, all the keys must be in tune.

Elementals graduate from their own plane and enter into a higher plane. A physical elemental, when refined, becomes an astral and then a mental elemental. As the fire in them is awakened, they proceed on their way of evolution. Do not forget what H.P. Blavatsky said, "All in Nature tends to become Man."[2]

It is beautiful to think that each cell, each atom within your sphere, in billions and billions of years will eventually become a human being. Actually, you are a galaxy. Your etheric body, your aura, your seven vehicles, all the atoms and cells, are like stars in one galaxy. You are a galaxy, but you do not have that expanded consciousness in you. You think you are just a chemical body, but this is not true.

---

2. H.P. Blavatsky, *The Secret Doctrine,* Vol. II, p. 170.

Man eventually will find out that not only is he a galaxy, but all humanity is also a galaxy in which each person is a cell or an atom.

You can speak to the elementals of your bodies to inspire them toward certain activities and encourage them toward certain directions. But another person has no right to suspend you — the human soul — and make suggestions directly to the elementals of your bodies. That is what hypnotism does.

The mental elemental is influenced by sound. It is very sensitive to sound, and mostly it is controlled, advanced, or related to through sound. Cures in the mental body are accomplished through sound.

The emotional elemental is influenced by color. Color brings changes in the reactions and responses of the emotional elemental. Cures in the emotional body are carried out through color.

The physical elemental is influenced by movements. Rhythmic movements, drumbeats, geometrical movements, ceremonies, and rituals affect the physical elemental.

Remember that sound, color, and movement are related to each other like ice, water, and air. A certain movement creates a certain color and a certain sound. A certain sound creates a certain color and motion. A certain color creates a certain sound and movement. Thus a movement is color in the astral plane and sound in the mental plane.

Similarly, sound in the mental plane is color in the astral plane and movement in the physical plane. This is why these three bodies affect each other.

Along with the sound, color, and movement are created fragrances or odors. Harmony with higher spheres in sound, in color, and in movement creates fragrances. Disharmony creates odors.

The healing of the physical body elemental is performed through movements, dances, running, swimming, climbing, etc., but all should be rhythmic. When the sound, color, and movement are coordinated in proper ways, it brings great healing for the whole man. This is why the ancient ceremonies were organized and processions were a daily routine, not only for religious purposes but especially for healing purposes.

The ancients used sound, color, movement, and rhythm more scientifically and goal-fittingly than contemporary composers or producers, who are more interested in the income than the effect of the art.

Some people are sick because of the colors they wear, because of the music they hear, because of the movements they make or observe. If the right color is scientifically found for different types of people, they will recover from their emotional tensions and sicknesses. If the right music and the right pitch of voice are heard by them, they will advance mentally and their mental troubles will gradually vanish. If they observe right movements, and if they move with right motions and submit themselves to right labor, most of their physical troubles will vanish.

This is why one must be careful about wearing certain colors, hearing certain sounds, and observing or making certain movements. In fact, all sounds, colors, and movements, even if proper, can be harmful if the wrong rhythm accompanies them.

If people observe their behavior and their mode of creativity and health while changing the colors of their clothes and environment, while changing the music they listen to or even their movements or dances, they will eventually learn the effect of these three factors and use them more intelligently.

The forms of clothes, too, have their effect upon us. Change the dress of a girl and observe the change in her psychology. Unfortunately, most of the fashion designers are more interested in their income than in the psychological and beneficial effects of their products. One can stimulate the public with certain fashions and make them spend more money for the benefit of fashion designers.

Music affects the entire life of a person because it affects the mind. In the future it will be possible to educate people in how to change their voice in conversations and bring health and happiness to themselves and others.

For uneducated people, color has more influence than sound. For materialistic and earthbound people, movement and rhythm have more effect than color or sound.

In the future it will be possible to build bridges — by using sound, color, movement, and form — between our present consciousness and those levels of consciousness which are related to the solar, galactic, and Cosmic mysteries. All these bridges must be built on the foundation of occult meditation and esoteric thinking.

Leadership in the future will not be based on politics alone but on the **science of effects**. Leadership will encourage all music, color, movements, and various programs that raise the health, sanity, and living standards of people and prevent those conditions which bring failure and crime. It is easy to formulate laws against crime, but laws will never help if the source of the crime is not controlled and prevented.

A healthy and prosperous city is turned into a city of crime and failure because of a new music, because of a new form of dance...and the law was not able to prevent the increase of crime.

Future leadership will prevent those influences which bring public degeneration. The healthier, more educated and more prosperous are the public, the easier it is to rule.

A city made prostitution and gambling legal to lower income taxes. But the authorities were forced eventually to spend more money to deal with the increase in crime. And to keep their positions, they increased the taxes more and more. Thus they created a vicious cycle!

Of course, there is a great danger of totalitarianism if the leaders control the life, but such a danger is eliminated if things are approached in a scientific spirit by organized committees who are specialized in different fields and are acting under wise leadership. The government must not only have committees to investigate the effects of insecticides, chemicals, and radioactivity but also committees that investigate the effects of music, color, dances, movements, sounds, tones, and literature.

The government must not be only a party that rules, but it must also be a party that is deeply responsible and concerned with the health, sanity, and progress of the people.

35

Diseases on Many Levels

We now know how the physical body functions, but with all our medical inventions we are not able to end pain and suffering in the world. The main reason for this is that only one part of the human mechanism is considered important; the astral body and mental body are left out.

There are various kinds of sicknesses — physical, emotional, and mental. People are interested mostly in physical sicknesses, but we are told that all physical sicknesses have psychic origins, or emotional and mental origins. When things go wrong in the emotional and mental realms, the body develops various troubles according to the problems occurring in the other realms.

Every physical sickness has a correspondence in the emotional and mental bodies. For example, cancer is found on the physical plane, but there are also astral cancers and mental cancers. Such kinds of cancers are not recognized in the astral and mental bodies as serious problems, but they are the ones that eventually prepare the physical body for cancer.

Emotional cancer is caused by the feeling of separatism because every form of separatism is a cancer. Separatism weakens the healthy atoms of the astral body and gives the sick atoms the chance to multiply. These atoms eventually destroy the astral vehicle and descend to the physical plane in the various forms of cancer known to the medical profession.

If real research is done on cancer patients, it will become clear that the cause of some cancers is astral, and the principle cause is separatism in its multiple forms.

Mental cancer is caused by building the ego in oneself or by egoism, which is a mental form of separatism. When a person feels that he is separate from other human beings and all others are not part of him but created to nourish his ego and separative interests, he himself becomes a cancer in the body of humanity.

Egoism is a form of malignant tumor on the mental plane. It says, "I am the best; all must serve me. I am hurt. I am touchy. I am great; there is no one who can be compared to me," etc.

This mental tumor infects the whole emotional and physical body. Eventually it attracts corresponding astral atoms and physical cells, and the cancer starts in the body.

Sometimes this process takes a few lives, but it manifests especially when outer pollution and radioactivity weaken the vital cells and sap the psychic energy from the body.

Those who have mental cancer often come together and demonstrate certain characteristics, some of which are

— fanaticism

— separatism

— exploitation

— racism

— criminality

— totalitarianism

— oppression

— greed

It is not easy to heal mental and emotional cancers by psychological surgery, but Nature knows what to do.

Sometimes the physical body cancer is the last manifestation of the subtle cancers. Sometimes it is just the reflection of what is going on upon higher planes.

The important thing is to educate people and eventually eliminate all seeds of separatism and egoism, if people want to get rid of this dire disease. The remedy is to develop the sense of unity, the feeling of unity. Unity is power — in man and in the human body. Every separative direction ends with destruction, pain, and suffering. Egoism is mental separatism.

Separatism on emotional and mental levels is more destructive than on the physical level. One can live on a mountain alone, but emotional and mental separation destroys families, nations, and eventually the whole humanity. One must know that there is only oneness and unity as the foundation of all existence. Violation of unity creates heavy consequences. Anything happening anywhere in the Universe affects everything, everywhere.

Anything that happens in your mental centers echoes in your astral and etheric centers. It even affects the corresponding centers in the planet, the solar system, the galaxy, and beyond. A whisper for our physical ears is a trumpet for those who have astral ears and a roaring tornado for mental ears.

Similarly, when human sound travels in space, a whisper turns into a trumpet in the astral plane and a roaring tornado in the mental plane. The noise rising from the planet at this time is unbearable for astral and mental inhabitants and for numberless angelic forces living in the subtle planes.

Man, in his folly, increases the noise on the planet as if it were a sign of his progress. But human sound and mechanical sound go to a certain plane and then come back to the planet in the form of pressure and tension. It is this pressure that creates lymphatic disorders, heart diseases, and other various ailments and natural disasters; and man thinks that he is not responsible for the calamities coming to the earth age after age.

One can introduce infection into a planetary center. It is also possible to cause paralysis in planetary or solar centers through massive madness, but the reaction comes back in the submergence of continents and other natural calamities.

The ancients used to say to live a good life so that you do not upset the equilibrium of the earth. This may sound like a hallucination to some of our sophisticated scientists and especially to our sophisticated politicians.

Every separate life-form is like a computer. It accumulates all data, all that is going on anywhere. Thus, every atom is affecting life as a whole. How carefully one must try to live in order to increase the benevolent recordings in Nature. As above, so below. As here, so there.

It is also true that human problems and difficulties originate from different galaxies. When certain formations collapse and disintegrate in a galaxy, the destructive wave reaches us many centuries later; and when it hits the human consciousness, it can be translated as an urge toward war, or we may have epidemics or natural catastrophes.

The ancients used to speak about the Heavenly Man. With this word they referred to the idea that planets are like human beings, solar systems, or greater Heavenly Men. Galaxies are great, great Heavenly Men. Whatever happens in one part of Their body affects the other parts of Their body.

People have no idea about thoughts and emotions. A certain thought can act like a poison; other thoughts act like thorns; other thoughts act like various kinds of germs. The same is true for emotions.

One must remember that a germ in the physical body is less contagious than a germ in the astral or mental body. The emotional body of an individual flows into the astral body of humanity. The mental body of an individual is part of the mental body of the planet. Any germ in the bodies multiplies and spreads everywhere.

There are medicines and injections for emotional and mental germs. They are moral purity and intellectual honesty. This is actually what religions teach, if they are accepted spiritually. The Ageless Wisdom and the Teaching about karma and reincarnation can provide very helpful cures for certain mental and emotional ailments.

People must learn about their emotional and mental bodies as they learn about their physical body. Even in universities people must learn about the anatomy of the soul. We are late in learning these sciences, despite the fact that these sciences were given to humanity ages ago. The *Mahabharata*, the *Upanishads*, the *Ramayana*, and the *Vedas* are especially full of such information. The Teaching of Christ is not a religion but a super-medical prescription.

People concentrated only on the physical body and forgot the rest. Such a separatism has created its consequences. We now know how the physical body functions, but with all our medical inventions we are not able to end pain and suffering in the world. The main reason for this is that only one part of the human mechanism is considered important; the astral body and mental body are left out. This attitude is just like a man who, being released from a mental hospital, came home and took the motor out of his car. When his wife asked why he did it, he answered, "I need the car, not the motor. Do you understand?"

"Of course," said the woman with tears in her eyes. "Yes, I understand. You only need the car...."

We are slowly realizing that man is not only a unity in himself, but the whole Universe is a unity. For example, when man is in fear, many organs of his body are affected. Also, when there are emotional disturbances in the planet, solar system and beyond, many people, planets, and solar systems are affected as if they were the organs in a body.

Of course, if good things happen in greater bodies, such happenings are opportunities for the expansion of man's consciousness or for spiritual achievements. It is also possible that many mental disturbances or advancements occurring in planets, solar systems, or galaxies affect smaller life-forms such as plants, animals, or human beings, for good or for bad. Man has no control over them unless his consciousness is beyond the plane where the events are occurring.

Astronomers claim that certain galaxies explode, spreading their debris for many billions of miles. Of course, such events occur far from us, but we are affected by the pressure and the subatomic elements such an explosion radiates. Such explosions manifest as diseases, social problems, and economic problems. We must find the source of the problems on the earth, in the stars, or in different planes.

If the causes of many diseases originate from solar and cosmic sources, does this mean that man has no control over them? The answer is that man can have control over them in three ways:

1. He can accumulate an aura charged with creative thoughts, with the energies of love and compassion, and with psychic energy. These three energies build a shield around the physical body and strengthen the astral and mental bodies in such a way that they function like a shock absorber and a shelter for the physical body.

2. He can protect the body from spatial tensions and pressures by eliminating irritation. Irritation not only creates poison in the body, but it also cracks the aura and invites destructive forces into it.

3. He can use mechanical methods, like living under an earth covered or tile covered roof, or underground. The source of the pressure in Space can be prevented by living underground or under a well insulated roof, especially at times of electrical storms in Space.

Houses built of stone are better than wood. Of course stone, earth, and tile cannot prevent many currents of energy from pouring into our world, but certain pressures can be prevented.

Your clothes should be made of cotton or wool. No synthetic material must be used. Shoes should have rubber soles, or one must walk barefoot if he is sure that the earth on which he walks is not contaminated.

Salt water is a great protection if one jumps into it during times of cosmic catastrophes. Two hundred years later we will have special forecasters who will daily forecast the pressures, tensions, calamities, and storms occurring in the solar and galactic space. According to these forecasts, man will conduct his daily life, as he does now according to the daily weather forecast.

Pressure builds more in valleys and canyons than on high ground. Pressure is a wave of force emanated or originated from galaxies or stars which are in the process of disintegration. It also originates from various waves when they hit each other in Space, releasing a tremendous amount of energy.

Pressure also originates from the friction of stars or galaxies when their electromagnetic spheres touch each other. The faster they rotate, the greater the amount of energy they release in Space, which gradually turns into a pressure wave in Space.

As one advances in his initiations, his protective shield grows. Eventually he can protect himself with the right diet, right relationships, elevated emotions, and pure thoughts.

It is very interesting that, in general, spiritual ideas have been thrown out of hospitals and only science and money rule there. This can even be seen in hospitals which are controlled by various religious organizations. Most doctors and nurses do not believe in anything supernatural. Their training is limited to technical data. Of course, some materialistic psychology is given to them in their training, but not the real psychology which deals with the transcendent values existing within the patients.

In general, doctors and nurses do not handle patients with faith. A patient is a case for them; he is not an immortal soul facing a journey to the Subtle Worlds or passing through a crisis of paying his karmic debts or adjusting his body to the new, incoming energies and forces or breaking through the layers of certain crystallizations. In most cases a patient is a source of income for doctors and hospitals, or he is a case for study and research, but he is not a soul with hopes and karmic obligations.

When a patient is handled in such a way, his soul feels the despair of ignorance. It is not enough to have a priest come and say a few nice words, hear a confession, or prepare the patient for the transition. The whole attitude of doctors and nurses must change. All those who are engaged in the healing practices must have faith and a sense of the supernatural. They must have a connection with the Higher Worlds. It is such a faith and contact that charges them with psychic energy, leads them into sacrificial service, and makes them handle their patients as a soul.

The healing process will be immensely improved when doctors and nurses are charged with psychic energy and with the feeling of the supernatural. The Supermundane World can even guide those who are open to supernatural energies and forces. Combined with modern scientific techniques, psychic energy will produce better healing and will put doctors and nurses in contact with the Higher Worlds, from which will come miraculous help and assistance to the healing profession.

Hospitals, doctors, nurses, and the rest of the healing profession must not be limited or blinded by their own religious beliefs and superstitions or try to impose them upon their patients. Rather, they must have the sense of transcendence. The sense of transcendence is an intuitive awareness that man has a soul, that beyond this life an eternal life exists, that the soul will be conscious in Higher Worlds, and that every soul must be cherished and taken care of, even if he has different beliefs or is from a different faith, race, or nationality.

Religion is not the collection of our beliefs, dogmas, and doctrines. It is, in reality, a connecting link with the Supermundane World. The ancient healers were also priests, and the priests were also healers.

In the future, doctors and all those who are engaged in the healing arts will develop the sense of transcendence, and all our scientific labor will be enlightened by the light pouring down from the Supermundane World. Glory to those doctors, nurses, and healers who approach their patients as immortal souls, Sparks of the Divine Fire, and co-travelers on the Path.

Our patients of today will be our doctors of the future.

36

Diseases and the Planes

Every deviation from the direction of the Cosmic Magnet causes the phenomena called pain, suffering, catastrophes, and calamities in the individual and Cosmic sense. Any readjustment with the direction of the Cosmic Magnet is a recovery, a moment of equilibrium, health, joy, and happiness in its spiritual sense.

Diseases are not only on one plane but are on other planes as well. For example, you can have a mental, astral, or physical-etheric disease. You can have a disease that is spread in all of them or in two of them.

If a physical disease spreads into the astral and mental planes, after you leave your body you face similar problems in the astral or mental bodies. If the astral and mental bodies are the originators of the sickness, then you will repeat the sickness in your physical body, incarnation after incarnation, until it is exhausted.

Some of our physical sicknesses are the termination of astral and mental sicknesses. They come down and exhaust and clear themselves, and thus man is freed of them.

Some mental and astral diseases originate from the physical plane, generally when we misuse our energies, our tongues, and our mental mechanism to exploit and deprive people. Thus, our acts, words, and thoughts — when expressed against Beauty, Goodness, and Truth — create astral and mental wounds which eventually turn into diseases and are used by dark forces in the mental and astral planes to retard our progress.

Most of our mental diseases are cured through a life of dedication to higher ideals, through sacrificial service, through a compassionate life, and through dedication to higher ideals.

Meditation, discipline, repentance, and a sacrificial life are great tonics for our subtle bodies. Beauty is the greatest antibiotic. Joy is a spiritual vitamin.

In olden days the great Sages emphasized the higher virtues such as patience, simplicity, courage, daring, and honesty as medicine for our subtle bodies. A truly virtuous man lives a long, creative life, not only here on earth, but he enjoys the subjective planes, too, without being attached to any of them.

There are also abnormal conditions which are not the effect of germs, microbes, or accidents. For example, certain pains in various parts of the body, swellings, even hemorrhaging can be caused by the contact of a higher voltage of energy coming from the soul or from spiritual realms. Usually such phenomena disappear without any trace.

There was a girl whose body was in pain. All medical examinations showed nothing wrong. They could not find any reason for her pain. One day, suddenly the pain disappeared and the health of the girl was restored.

Sometimes even our senses are affected when energies of a spiritual nature contact them. The abnormal reaction of our body is due to the poison accumulated in it through food, air, or various contacts.

Sometimes such happenings are called *crises of adjustments* to which many servers are subjected, especially those whose environment is polluted by physical, emotional, and mental emanations.

People boast and become excited when they speak about their free will. It is often revealed that free will is not an advantage or a sign of progress but a disadvantage and a retrogression. Those who think that they have free will are the slaves of their blind urges and drives, their glamors and illusions; they are even the victims of mass hypnosis.

Some people, when they stand against Beauty, Goodness, Righteousness, Joy, and Freedom and oppose all higher principles, think that they have free will, but in reality they are opposing the Divine Will, or the One Will. Standing out of the One Will creates an enormous subjective tension which eventually hits the physical, astral, and mental bodies. The goal is not to have "free will" but to strive toward the vision of Christ Who said, "Not my will, but Thine be done." In renouncing His free will, Christ obtained the Divine Will, which led Him eventually into Resurrection. To have free will means to live according to the will of the highest Good.

All success, health, and prosperity, all expressions of beauty, power, and love are gained only by renouncing our free will to the Father's Will. This means the ability to synchronize with the direction of the power of the Cosmic Magnet. Every deviation from the direction of the Cosmic Magnet causes the phenomena called pain, suffering, catastrophes, and calamities in their individual and Cosmic sense. Any readjustment with the direction of the Cosmic Magnet is a recovery, a moment of equilibrium, health, joy, and happiness in its spiritual sense.

Free will can be gained through achieving victory over all those wills which are not part of the Divine Will. The "wills" of men are the expressions of their blind urges and drives, their desires and intentions, their interests and plans. All these wills must be conquered to have free will which is *the moment when one's own will disappears in the Will of the Almighty Power, the Cosmic Magnet.*

We have the impression that when a man passes away he

— goes to heaven or hell

— goes to purgatory

— is annihilated

— gains his freedom and advances to Infinite Light

— is born again

There is a certain amount of fact in these five points. The Trans-Himalayan Ashrams teach that after a man passes away, he leaves his physical-etheric body and enters into a new world which has many names. The name that is often used is the emotional world, or the astral world. This astral world is a replica of the physical world. There he has the same emotions, the same joys and sorrows, the same hatred and love, the same urges and drives, the same spirit of possession or renouncement. The only advantage, or disadvantage, of this sphere is that whatever he desires, he has.

First the man does not realize this, but eventually he finds out that the moment he desires something, that desire begins to take form. That is why the astral plane is the most dangerous trap on the path of Infinity, and a man must realize this fact and find ways and means to leave the astral plane without delay.

We are also told that in the astral plane you do not have fear of death like you have on earth. There you know that you can be born again, but here you are not sure that you can continue your life in the astral plane. In the astral plane you know that the Great Ones really exist. Here you are not sure of that.

The astral or mental life is the continuation of the physical life. You do not change your nature; you are the same as you were on the physical plane.

Your physical life has advantages over your astral or mental life in that on the physical plane you can advance in your beingness and knowledge. In the astral or mental world you can collect knowledge, but you cannot change your beingness. To change your subjectively gained knowledge into beingness, you must come down here to the physical plane and test your knowledge. This continues until the Fourth Initiation, after which things change.

You cannot progress on the astral plane if you did not prepare yourself here on earth to be detached from the astral world. People are caught there for centuries, and they even avoid the time of their rebirth.

In the astral plane there are also battles and wars. People carry with them their hatreds and greed and prepare themselves to take revenge on each other. Such wars sometimes involve the physical world, and then you have physical plane wars. This happens when the battling astral groups exercise a severe pressure on the related people on the physical plane and lead them into war. Often the pressure is so unavoidable that people start war for some reason which they themselves do not believe in. Like a tornado, the subjective war also involves the earthly nations.

The most interesting point is that those who are victorious in a war on the physical plane strengthen their enemies on the astral plane, and those who are successful over their enemies on the astral plane strengthen their enemies on the physical plane. Those who die here on the physical plane continue their battle in subtle levels, and those who are defeated in the subtle level continue their battle on the physical level. This insanity continues age after age in the name of money, land, religion, sex, food, patriotism, etc.

It is also observed that many of "our" enemies incarnate in "our" nation, and "we" incarnate in the nation of "our" enemies. When this is the case, the leaders of "our" nation create all those conditions in which "our" defeat is unavoidable. "Our" enemies incarnate in "our" nation and progress into higher levels and prepare for our destruction. This is seen in the history of humanity, when so-called "national heroes" led their nation to final destruction.

Many times we read in the scriptures of the world about the wars in heaven. Such wars, like a fire, slowly penetrate into the earthly domains and poison the minds of the people, block their thinking, blind their reason and logic, and bring them into the strong current of hatred and disaster.

This does not mean that man is an innocent victim. Man responds to the subjective wars if his nature is full of combustible materials, such as hatred, fear, jealousy, greed, anger, the spirit of separatism, totalitarianism, and materialism.

Before the earth catches the fire of war from the Subtle World, we see widespread crimes, degeneration of morals, the spirit of ugliness, injustice, exploitation, hatred, and fear. Then slowly the fire penetrates into the hearts of those who are related to the warring sides in the astral world. This condition creates widespread diseases, epidemics, earthquakes, and natural disasters with all kinds of health problems.

A Great Sage, referring to such problems, once said,

> *Sickness rises from sin — says the Scripture. We say that sickness comes from the imperfections of past and present. One should know how to approach the cure of sickness. To the regret of physicians, the process toward perfection is the true prophylactic measure. It can be understood that the process toward perfection begins with the heart....*[1]

Man advances through earthly life and through the astral world only by striving toward perfection. It is this striving that saves him from the traps of both worlds and their agonies. It is through this striving toward perfection that eventually our physical, emotional, and mental sicknesses will disappear and we will be qualified to finish our earthly evolution and pass to the path of solar perfection.

---

1. Agni Yoga Society, *Heart*, para. 96.

It is very beneficial to remember that "the process toward perfection begins with the heart."

37

Pressure and Tension

The damage of television on coming generations will be detected very clearly. Television, sound, and electric waves are causing irreparable damage to the genes of the new generation.

Pressure is one of the causes of disease; it affects the cells and organs of any living organism. Pressure affects the growth of vegetables, plants, and trees; it distorts the mechanism of the cells which absorbs certain energies and produces a certain chemistry in their bodies. Pressure blocks the sensitivity of cells, atoms, organs, and centers from pulsating in rhythm with the pulsation of the Cosmic Heart and thus creates cleavages in organisms and in Nature.

Pressure has various causes, but the main cause is the accumulation of sound waves in Space. Such an accumulation eventually will be so tense that it will shatter the living forms on the planet through degenerative diseases.

People do not pay attention to the noise generated by computers, machines, guns, cannons, bombs, explosions; to the sound of television, radio, and wireless; to the sound of human speech all over the globe. Parallel to the noise accumulated by mechanical means, we have the greater danger of the destructive words that come out of the human mouth. The Teaching says that words spoken in revenge, in hatred, in cursing, and in blasphemy have very destructive effects, and their accumulation in the lower strata of the etheric and astral planes creates heavy poisons which are eventually breathed in by human beings. These poisons are responsible for diseases of the throat, heart, lungs, and brain.

The human voice amplifies sound waves and charges them with destructive qualities of hatred, revenge, anger, and cursing. Such accumulations are disastrous not only for individual human beings but also for entire countries.

All these sound waves fill the Space and bombard the bodies of all living organisms, thus disturbing the natural conditions, chemistry, and evolution of the organisms and their biological tasks.

One of the greatest tasks of science will be to create a noiseless world. Noise pollution is more dangerous and is producing more destructive effects than anything else in the world.

Sound waves block telepathic communication between people and between higher sources and earthly beings. If we had less noise, we would be able to have clear thought communication with the subjective world and with Great Ones. Sound waves distort the energy waves reaching our planet from great constellations and thus deprive us of their supply of precious energy. No wonder the prophets of olden times sought the peace and serenity of the wilderness or mountains to come in contact with higher forces.

The damage of television on coming generations will be detected very clearly. Television, sound, and electric waves are causing irreparable damage to the genes of the new generation. The effect will be discovered only in one hundred years. We will have more physical, emotional, mental, and spiritual retardation and, as a result, more crimes and more expenses.

Those who are working in airfields or traveling on airplanes for joy and pleasure will see the damage they have done to their genes and to the genes of their descendants. Modern science, when it awakens from its vanity, will apply itself to undo the things it did to humanity.

People are satisfied with the present and do not worry about the future. But the future is something from which there is no escape. One can escape from the past, but the future will catch him.

Parallel to the danger of sound waves in Space, we have another danger which is the blood transfusions performed daily in hospitals. Of course many lives are saved, which means some people, because of their transfusions, live a few years longer. The tragedy is that the blood carries the psychic energy and the aura of the person from whom it is taken, and it passes to the one into whom it is injected.

There are three things that must be cleared before blood transfusions are made:

1. The physical properties of the blood. This is done successfully in our hospitals.

2. The psychic factors. This is not done yet. The psychological and psychic conditions of the donor of the blood are not taken into consideration yet.

   Blood is charged with the subtle psychic conditions of the donor, and these psychic conditions are planted in the patient. Imagine what chaos is created in the patient's aura when a foreign and disturbing psychic influence begins to grow in his psychological sphere.

   One must follow for a few years the steps of those who were subjected to blood transfusions. Such investigations will open great secrets to scientists.

3. The next element is the karma of the donor. Blood carries the karmic element, and through transfusion it becomes the karma of the patient.

A physician may laugh at such a statement, but in the future more dedicated physicians will discover the fact that after a transfusion of blood, the patient begins slowly to live a life to which the donor was subjected. They will see similarity in both lives. This does not mean that the karma will always be painful or disastrous.

Let us not forget that our medical system is young yet. Maturity will come slowly.

Another factor that the future physician will discover and reveal is the effect of gases and pollution of the air on the living organisms and on the soil. As the pollution of air, matter, space, and soil continues, disease will increase to such a degree that the planet will be uninhabitable. This condition can be avoided only if great cataclysms — as in the past — occur and wipe away our modern civilization, with its noises, fumes, gases, poisons, and pollutions, together with billions of people.... Such disasters are not an impossibility if we remember that the earth is an Entity and Its tolerance has a limit.

This is a gloomy picture, but one must face it and mobilize the forces of Beauty, Goodness, and Truth to take action before it is too late.

The next great danger is thought waves in Space which are charged with hostility, malice, hatred, and revenge. Such thought waves are as real as the bullets released by a machine gun. The only difference is that bullets have a limited time and distance to fly, but thought waves penetrate Space, surround the globe, and eventually form ulcers in Space.

These dark spots or space ulcers are very dangerous sources of poisoning. The energy coming from luminaries, when transmitted through such ulcers, creates various epidemics, not only physical but also emotional, mental, and moral. Many organized crimes are the result of such ulcers in Space directly influencing people who are receptive to their poisonous waves.

People have the opinion that they breathe air through their lungs. This is true. But they forget the fact that our emotional nature breathes in the emotional sphere, and our mental nature breathes in the thought sphere of the planet.

As it is forbidden by law to throw rubbish into your neighbor's garden, it is similarly forbidden by spiritual law to throw the thoughts of your hostility, hatred, and revenge into Space and let the winds carry them to far-off victims. In the coming age the great physician-philosophers will advise people not to throw their psychic rubbish into Space — for their own and for their neighbor's welfare.

Hostile thoughts irritate the mucous membranes. If you are a hated leader, you will have symptoms in your throat, ears, eyes, and nose...and you will eventually see the degeneration of your health and morals.

Love, respect, forgiveness, and gratitude are called the panacea of the healing arts.

When Space is polluted with hatred, hostility, revenge, fear, and crime, the life-giving rays of the Sun are considerably altered. The higher impressions coming from spiritual sources are hindered. The direction of the Cosmic Magnet is distorted. This is the condition in which humanity loses its direction, and only the blind forces and elements of the earth, like huge waves, lead the ship to the rocks of destruction. The planet can be saved by a Universal Figure Whose heart bleeds for humanity, Who is the embodiment of Beauty, Goodness, Truth, and Power.

If humanity produces such a figure, this humanity will be saved, provided that human beings prepare His way in spreading right human relations, goodwill, and respect for life.

38

Cosmic Sources of Illness

It is stated in the Teaching that some of our illnesses are the result of the disturbances going on in Space, within and even beyond our planet and solar system. The disturbances are electrical in nature, and these electrical charges come from decaying comets, moons, meteors, solar systems, and galaxies.

People have thought that all illnesses are the result of

germs

radioactive materials

accidents

poisonous gases

malnutrition

wrong eating

overeating

eating meat

drinking alcohol

using excessive sugar and oils

exhaustion

inertia

Or they thought illnesses came from emotional disturbances, even mental distortion, wrong thinking, or living an unvirtuous life.

All these and many other mundane sources have proven to be true all over the world. But people have not yet investigated the sources which are of Cosmic origin.

It is stated in the Teaching that some of our illnesses are the result of the disturbances going on in Space, within and even beyond our planet and solar system. The disturbances are electrical in nature, and these electrical charges come from decaying comets, moons, meteors, solar systems, and galaxies. Beyond all these electrical storms or disturbances we have disturbances which emanate from entities living in the etheric, astral, and lower mental worlds with distorted motives and activities. These distortions create disturbances in the mind and result in emotional reactions and distorted activities. Eventually, people are put out of harmony and balance and finally led into various illnesses.

It is probable that some of our ways of thinking and acting have no earthly origin at all. However, this does not allow us to excuse ourselves for the distortions, disturbances, and destructions we do impose upon the planet and upon humanity as a whole.

For a long time people thought that our earth was the center of the Universe. For a long time people have also thought that they were living in an insulated manner in the Universe. The first stage did not last long. The second one is almost disappearing. But people are still stubborn in their refusal to see that every form in the Universe is tied to all others through electrical lines, and that all forms are in the One Space which holds all forms as parts of one organism.

Most people do not register these influences but are affected by them. Some people feel Cosmic disturbances with their etheric centers. Those who register them are ones with sensitive natures; they suffer a great deal with unusual pains and have psychologically strong mood changes. There are other people who try to remain immune from Cosmic disturbances by harmonizing themselves with the Cosmic Magnet.

One may ask what the average man can do to protect himself from Cosmic disturbances. The answer is that one must strive for purity — purity in thoughts, actions, and emotions — and harmlessness. Purity and harmlessness are shields which repel most of the attacks of destructive currents coming from Space, especially when we, as souls, are linked with the Invisible Guardians of the planet. Such a linkage draws a great amount of psychic energy which protects man and his environment from Cosmic attacks.

What a great treasure of information will be revealed to us when systematic research is done on the subject: "Maladies from Space."

Besides material causes, we also have causes which are related to the realm of massive emotions and massive thoughts. It is often observed that psychic explosions occur in Space when great accumulated tensions of thoughts and emotions suddenly are set ablaze by benevolent Cosmic energies or by accumulated human thoughts and emotions. These explosions create a tremendous tension in all those who are conditioned to the formations by their will, negative emotions, and destructive thoughts. Of course, they in their turn carry their infection to those people surrounding them.

Thus, spatial accumulations heavily damage those who were associated with them or contributed to their formation. Each particle of the exploded emotional or mental elements carries with it the voltage of energy which destroyed it. Often the elements return to those who gave birth to them.

Very often we think that the only sources of sickness are physical, emotional, or mental or based upon spatial disturbances. However, there are other causes which do not fall into these categories.

For example, an intense striving toward higher spheres of awareness; a contact with those who are in their advanced stage of evolution; a sudden revelation of a higher mystery; a sudden act of transmission of a high-voltage current from Great Ones; contact with objects which are charged with an intense vibration; a journey in subjective spheres with one of your subtle bodies; a sudden impact from an overflowing source of beauty — all these can contribute to various kinds of diseases. One of the major effects is felt by the *heart.* The heart manifests various disorders under such tensions. The kidneys, generative organs, and the thyroid gland are affected later. Certain tensions affect the eyes, ears, and teeth.

If the tension of higher spheres is great and evokes the fire of matter, man will have various pains in his body, the reasons for which will be very obscure. These are called *sacred pains*.

There are also pains which one feels when masses of people are under distress because of natural catastrophes, wars, and crimes. The intelligent reader will ask, "What can we do to protect ourselves?"

The greatest protection is steady progress toward perfection through the spheres of trials, attacks, and confusion. Many things are unavoidable because of the world situation, but the fearless in spirit will walk triumphantly onward, and in each confrontation he will gather knowledge, wisdom, power, and joy.

There are also causes of disturbances which come from even more distant sources. These causes are seven streams of energy, sometimes called Rays. These seven Cosmic energies or Rays can cause various problems for those who do not have the suitable preparation to absorb these Rays, or to withdraw from their influence.

Each Ray is connected to one of the etheric centers. When a Ray is in operation, it brings great tension to the corresponding centers in man, in the planet, and in the solar system.

When a Ray is in the process of withdrawal, the corresponding center loses its energy or tries to grab onto the withdrawn energy. These two main conditions create various glandular and organic problems and difficulties.

At this time, for example, the Seventh Ray, which controls the sex center, is in the process of establishing or anchoring itself on the physical plane. The sex center is therefore in a state of overstimulation. There is a widespread increase of the sex drive everywhere, from the lowest to the highest, from the youngest to the oldest. This stimulation is creating the present sexual chaos and its related problems — diseases, overpopulation, and other complications in the family and in society.

The Sixth Ray controls the solar plexus, which in its turn controls important related organs. As the Sixth Ray energy is withdrawing, many complications are arising in the solar plexus and related organs, especially in people who have in their nature strong Seventh Ray energy or who live in places that have a great focus of such energies, as the Seventh Ray energy creates direct conflict with the Sixth Ray energies.

Those who are focused in their sex organs will create many problems for humanity, not only physically but also politically, because the Seventh Ray is closely related to the First Ray of politics.

Those who are focused in their solar plexus will affect not only their related organs but also the world economy, food, and other material objects. Sex and material possessions will present the greatest problems to humanity at this time.

Curiously enough, the Sixth Ray is related also to religion and the Seventh Ray is related to money.

It is very clear that all these areas present a very challenging problem to those who are in leadership positions in all fields of human endeavor.

In sum, there are many sicknesses, the origins of which are outside the solar system. The only way to escape these tensions and pressures is to refine our nature and purify it to such a degree that we do not create friction with the fires of the Rays but absorb them intelligently and use them in our creative living, with a corresponding state of consciousness.

At the time of the inflow of Ray energy and of the withdrawal of Ray energy, the corresponding centers must be put into right conditions or one will have numerous frictions with the Rays. For example, the sex center must be refined, drawing its energy into the throat center. As much as possible one must abstain from sexual imagination and reading and watching pornography. Purity of sex must be practiced intelligently through normal relations.

Another help for the sacral center is sports. A life dedicated to sports, in its various forms, eliminates many problems of the sacral center.

The solar plexus can be controlled through living a life of tolerance and generosity and through living in a state of peace.

There is another mysterious cause of sickness which comes from planetary centers. If any planetary center, because of the progress of its members, is highly stimulated and is radioactive, it exercises a tremendous pressure on those life-forms which cannot assimilate and use its radiations due to their own retardation or inertia. These forms of life, which create a great friction with the radiation of those centers, slowly disappear and become extinct.

Average people create friction with incoming energies because of their state of unfoldment. Advanced people are also in danger if their consciousness is not in harmony with the *tonality* of the incoming Ray. Each Ray brings its own tonality. For example, the Seventh Ray's tonality is *synthesis.*

Those advanced human beings who are separative in their thinking and selfish in their motives and activities will have a very difficult time with their health. They will suffer primarily from heart and spinal problems. But if they clear their mind and begin to live within the tonality of synthesis, their sicknesses will disappear because they will not create friction with the Ray but instead will transmit it. Let us not forget that man, above everything else, is an electronic transmitting tube.

This situation will be critical after the year 2175 when the full power of the Seventh Ray will descend upon earth.

It is suggested that medical professionals develop foresight and take steps to protect people from the incoming dangers of the future, planning and implementing those steps which will lead the consciousness of humanity toward synthesis and brotherhood.

The Sixth Ray will go out of manifestation or will withdraw in the year 2025. Its withdrawal will affect the solar plexus, and the solar plexus will collapse. This center transfers mostly lower astral energy to the body. It has a higher counterpart which transfers soul fire or enthusiasm to the body.

Those bodies that are nourished by lower astral energy, such as fear, anger, hatred, jealousy, and various lower desires, will be cut off from their supply of energy and will go through a process of petrification.

The solar plexus is the only center which has two nuclei of dynamic points. Other centers below and above the diaphragm each have only one dynamic core.

The petrification process will hit the liver, the pancreas, and related organs and produce mysterious sicknesses and burning pains. Healers must prepare humanity to confront such a situation. The way out of such a complexity is to cut the supply of fear, anger, hatred, and jealousy flowing into corresponding organs through the lower solar plexus center and, instead, create an intense devotional urge and aspiration toward great values and virtues. Such an aspiration will create integration between the two dynamic points in the solar plexus and will begin to feed the organs with the energies of love, tolerance, forgiveness, and gratitude.

The organs sooner or later must learn to digest such higher food. The period of adjustment is the period in which widespread troubles are anticipated, especially for those people whose solar plexus is wide open and whose lower core dominates the destiny of the man, group, or nation. This period will start in the year 2025.

Often we are told that a pure spiritual life is not only a beautiful and inspiring life but also a life of health, happiness, and success.

Very little attention is given by physicians regarding the influence of the stars upon the health of humanity.

There is no scientific body to investigate the changes of chemistry in Space or to discover how these changes are affecting not only the health of people but also their emotions, thoughts, and even motives.

When we talk about chemistry, we think about chemical elements and their various combinations. But we have not yet thought about the laboratory of Space where every Ray from the luminaries is in the process of producing new combinations in Space.

Our earth, which is an atom in the Cosmos, is a chemical factory emanating not only millions of tons of gases and chemicals but also emotional and thought chemicals into Space.

The sounds of music, singing, praying, chanting or the sounds of lamenting, mourning, wailing, weeping, crying or the sounds of Nature, animals, and birds or volcanos and waves — all these are agents creating chemistry in Space. Poisonous gases created by various kinds of explosions are also creating chemistry in Space.

Our earth is a factory which is actively engaged in creating a new chemistry in Space, either to promote pro-survival or anti-survival.

Of course, every human being — with his thoughts, emotions, sounds, actions, and labor — is a chemical factory contributing to the world chemistry.

The changes of chemistry in Space, or the quality and quantity of chemicals in Space, determine the quality of the civilization, culture, and in general the life of this and other planets in our system.

Physicians have not yet investigated the chemistry of human thoughts and emotions which have a direct effect on human health.

The whole Universe, in its physical, emotional, and mental phases, is a chemical process. It is a laboratory which has a direct effect on human health and human activities.

Often human beings are victims of a chemistry created in Space. The extinction of many species of animals, flowers, and trees is the effect of such a chemistry.

People are occupied in destroying each other with chemicals, with biological weapons, and with atomic, hydrogen, or other kinds of bombs instead of trying to discover ways and means to create a healthy chemistry in Space which will guarantee the survival of the planetary life.

It is true that whatever you give, the same you receive.

Our survival or destruction depends upon what we give to Space — with our thoughts, emotions, words, and actions.

We can see the future by seeing what we are not giving to life. Our future is conditioned by what we give to the chemistry of Space.

"Malice is a condenser of heavy chemism."[1]

Various vices and habits, crime, murder, and wars are condensers of poisonous chemism.

The health of humanity can be secured only in a holistic labor to create a new chemistry in Space through understanding, love, compassion, spiritual enlightenment, righteousness, relationship, cooperation, and a sense of responsibility. M.M. says,

> *...One may regret that so much energy is wasted in quarrels and mutual belittling. But if it be asked to what extent such thoughts of the Subtle World are chemically harmful, one can only say that small unkind thoughts generate poisonous gases.*[2]

One can imagine the immensity of the danger that is accumulating in Space. Future generations will have difficulty surviving.

1. Agni Yoga Society, *Fiery World II*, para. 19.
2. *Ibid.*, para. 55.

39

The Law of Karma

No one can be healthy without caring for the health of others.

The ancients traced a fundamental law in Nature and called it the Law of Karma, or the Law of Cause and Effect or of action and reaction.

The ancients saw that when they planted potatoes, potatoes were produced. When they planted beans, beans were produced. They saw that a fig tree brought figs and not cherries. This was the key which opened the door of the fundamental law of life, the Law of Karma.

Gradually, intelligent people observed that this law is effective also in the moral and spiritual life, and they found that good deeds bring good results; bad deeds bring bad results. Throughout the ages people penetrated deeper into the mysteries of this law, and at present this law is also called *The Law of Righteousness, Balance, and Equilibrium.*

Our life is almost the replica of the life which we built for others. Our life is conditioned by what we do for others, by how we live, think, speak, and act. Our every action, every word, every emotion, every thought is a building block in the construction.

The spiritual, moral, and psychological effects of our thoughts, emotions, words, and actions are instantaneous upon us, but the physical effects take a shorter or longer time to manifest. For example, in causing blindness to a person, you destroy your etheric and sometimes your astral and mental sense of sight, and years later or in the next life you are born without physical sight because you had destroyed the trees that bear the fruit.

When you commit a crime, the physical result may come days or weeks later, but you cause an immediate crack in your etheric brain. The damage of a wrongdoing is done instantaneously to your subtle mechanism. You already damaged the picture on the film, and the projection will reveal the damage.

Karma never punishes anyone, nor does it reward. It is the law that creates righteousness, balance, and equilibrium.

One day a teacher showed us a scale, a balance. He put one stone in each of the cups of the balance. Then he added a few stones, always trying to keep the equilibrium.

Then he took a stone from one cup and asked us, "Who can restore the equilibrium, and by doing what?"

A boy took an identical rock from the lower cup and the balance was restored.

"This is how the Law of Karma works," he said. "If you add precious stones to one of the cups, the Law adds precious stones to the other cup. Thus the balance is kept with fuller cups."

Karma functions simultaneously in the physical, astral, and mental planes. Life is a continuum. No matter where you are — in the basement, in the kitchen, or in the tower — karma is always with you.

It is surprising that the spiritual, moral, and social manifestations of the Law of Karma are not studied scientifically. We do not have any college or school which studies this fundamental law in our solar system and enlightens people about the effects of not considering it. I trust that in the future this law will be investigated in all its aspects, and we will use the discoveries as the foundation of all laws.

People have lost their direction. They think that they can make themselves enlightened, rich, progressive, beautiful, healthy, and joyful in working for themselves alone; whereas the truth is that no one can be enlightened if he does not enlighten people. No one can be rich if he does not make others rich.

No one can progress if he does not help others progress. No one can be beautiful if he does not make others beautiful. No one can be healthy without caring for the health of others. No one can be joyful and successful if he does not make others joyful and successful.

People have ignored such concepts, and now they see the accumulating chaos above their heads. Behind all our endeavors must stand the motive to serve, to elevate, to transform people's lives.

In the future, people suddenly will be enlightened to the fact that their identity and survival are guaranteed in others only. In the future, others will be more important than you and yours, and you will have more love even for your enemies than you have for yourself. These are very hard concepts for the mules who brought our civilization to the brink of total destruction.

Only a public enlightened to the Law of Karma can create right human relations and create those conditions in which the survival of humanity becomes possible.

Your life reflects exactly what you did for others. If you are beautiful, healthy, free of fear and greed; if you are successful and prosperous; if you have a clear conscience and live in the presence of higher values, you prove that your life reflects the things you did for others. You have only those things which you gave to others. This explains why karma is not only disciplinary but also highly instructive.

Disciplinary karma takes your freedom away from you. It takes first your mental freedom, then your emotional freedom, and eventually your physical freedom.

Instructive karma brings you greater freedom, greater creativity, and greater light.

During disciplinary karma you feel as if you were in prison; you feel you are limited. You sit in your prison and see a great urge in you to be free, to be creative, to be pure; but life's circumstances prevent you from all this. Life's circumstances are exactly the result of your negative and separative or selfish thoughts, emotions, words, and actions. You limit your own life.

During instructive karma you feel as if you were the freest person. You feel that all existence loves you, and you feel the ability to create, to help, and to serve. You see and witness that everywhere, and all the time, you meet co-workers and helpers to further your good plans. You created exactly the life you gave to others.

People have the opinion that karma cannot be changed. This is not true. Karma can be changed, although you need to spend more energy than the amount of energy you used to create the karma. For example, a true change in your motives, a true renunciation, a true penance, a real decision to change your conduct, a real and deep dedication to a great humanitarian cause, a heroic and sacrificial act can transform your life, minimize your past karma, or even totally annihilate it.

The Law of Karma corresponds to the laws of physics, chemistry, and space dynamics. It is found not in the domain of hallucination but in the domain of science.

You can overcome your karma by raising the level of your consciousness and working hard to repair the damage you did to others. You can increase your beauty, goodness, light, joy, and freedom and overcome a certain amount of your karma. Striving toward the summits of beauty and freedom breaks heavy layers of your karma.

Spreading the knowledge of karma wherever you can takes away an amount of your karmic taxations. Meditation and prayer help you reduce to a great degree your disciplinary karma. Your karma can be lightened if you never encourage people to increase their karmic debts. Your karma can be reduced to a great extent if you do not join or associate with people who are full of hatred, separatism, selfishness, and greed.

There are eight factors which create beneficial karma, or instructive karma.

1. Living a life of beauty in your thoughts, motives, words, emotions, and actions.

Trying to spread beauty yields high interest which can be used in the dark hours of your life, eliminating or balancing the intrusion of a bad deed performed ages or years ago.

It is also possible that your beauty hurts the feelings of others and causes jealousy and antagonism toward you. But all such reactions work for your own advantage, first, by increasing your radiation and, second, by paying your former debts.

Sometimes great people accumulate the karma of others and suffer for them; they give them a chance to be free from the limiting forces of their bad karma.

Doing this, these great people shine like stars in the Subtle World and attract the attention of the Great Ones.

2. Living a life full of goodness creates beneficial karma and prevents the possibility of bad karma.

When you charge all your motives, thoughts, words, and deeds with the spirit of goodness, you create a symphony around your existence.

The Law of Karma, in its disciplinary aspect, does not exist if you do not violate the law. Generally the law exists only for the violators. And living a life of beauty and goodness makes the disciplinary karma non-existent.

3. Try to be always righteous and to act righteously, and you will not create painful karma. Your joyful karma increases as your righteousness increases and spreads through all your relationships.

People sometimes build mansions on an unrighteous judgment and, accordingly, create a great amount of painful karma. When you think righteously, you improve the capacity of your mental machine; it functions better. But if you act unrighteously, your mental computer acts as if a few wires and tubes were broken in it, and you always reach an answer which is not favorable for your survival.

Your brain and mind are like your engine. If you put contaminated or unrefined gas or oil in your engine, it does not run properly, or it will not run at all. This is like a mind into which one continuously dumps ugly, bad, destructive, low-quality thoughts.

Righteousness is like the right gasoline put into your mental machine, and as you fill it with the thoughts of righteousness, your mental mechanism functions better and better and brings into your life great rewards.

Righteousness brings harmony into your mind. Harmony spreads over your body, nervous system, glands, and bloodstream and creates harmony in them. The result shows as your good health.

These are statements that are easy to read, but one must strive with all his heart to make them actualize in his life.

4. Joy is another factor which does not create painful karma.

Joy, love, light, and freedom increase within us if we give them to others. This is a strange fact which can be tested in our daily life.

Joy within our aura increases when we make other people joyful. And the joy within us becomes an inspiring source of energy and wisdom.

5. Freedom is the next factor.

One may argue about freedom and ask, "What about if I give freedom to others and with their freedom they violate my freedom?" This may happen if you are giving freedom to those who are the slaves of their emotions, fanaticism, hatred, prejudices, and vanities. Real freedom is achieved only if people are free of selfish interests and emotional and mental hang-ups.

You can give freedom to others only through liberating them from their own limitations. Such a freedom will never act against true freedom.

6. The next one is responsibility.

Whenever you escape from your responsibilities, you create karma. Responsibility is an active manifestation of your sense of righteousness.

The sense of responsibility is the process of making your righteousness manifest through all your relationships. The sense of responsibility only exists on the foundation of righteousness. If you are not righteous, you do not have the sense of responsibility. Only in facing your responsibilities do you avoid creating painful karma.

When you are meeting your responsibilities toward your family, friends, partners, and the world, you dissolve the accumulations of your past painful karma. Every time you escape from your responsibilities, painful karma follows your steps.

7. The next one is unity.

Living for unity, synthesis, and for one humanity makes your life joyful and dissolves the sediments of painful karma. No one can escape painful karma if he violates the Law of Unity, the Law of Oneness of Life.

Karma is the law that works to keep unity, balance, and equilibrium in the Universe. Through the study of the Law of Karma, one can really understand the oneness of life.

When we violate the unity and oneness of life, we sow the seeds of painful karma throughout our lives. But if we think, speak, and act in terms of oneness, we never create painful karma. It is true that people who are against the idea of unity can mobilize their efforts to bring us pain and suffering, but we must not be fearful. They will work to make evolution speedier and spread our ideas more widely than our friends could do.

8. The eighth one is trustworthiness.

Those who understand the Law of Karma try to be trustworthy and also to trust other people. Trust creates nobility in others, and trustworthiness manifests as the spirit of nobility.

Trustworthiness never creates painful karma. You even trust people who try to misuse your trust and bring difficulties into your life. They will work for your own advantage, and later they will serve your cause.

A wise man once said, "I try to make people indebted to me, so that whenever I am short of something, I can ask from them." Sometimes in fighting against our noble principles people make themselves indebted to us.

Painful karma has a heavy influence over our life. Here is a list of things that painful or disciplinary karma does:

1. When you increase your bad karma it delays your evolution; it prevents you from enjoying your life and expanding your consciousness. For example, if it would normally take one hour to get to your destination, you get there in eight days and through many troubles.

To delay your evolution means to have more pain and more suffering.

In the Core of the human being there is a timetable for his evolution. For example, in this life he must reach the summit of that mountain when he is twenty-one. At age thirty-five he must reach a higher peak. At age forty-two he must reach the summit of an even higher mountain. At age sixty-three he must reach a certain initiation. If this timetable is not met, he will meet many difficulties, complications, and sufferings to keep going and meet the timetable of his evolution. And if he cannot reach it, his karmic tax increases for the next life.

When you plan your life intelligently with short-range and long-range goals and try to meet these goals, you evoke the timetable of your evolution from your Soul. Eventually you become aware of this timetable and try to work accordingly.

You must remember that without the permission of your karma, you cannot be initiated; it is your merit that initiates you.

2. Bad karma creates diseases, accidents, and even death. People must not blame life or others if bad karma hits them. Whatever we sow, we reap.

Grace, which is a result of the contents of your Chalice, diminishes bad karma, protects you from many dangers, and prevents dark attacks. Dark attacks reach you through the cracks that your bad karma created.

3. Bad karma destroys your magnetism, your attractiveness. People begin to leave you alone. Your helpers and co-workers disappear. People reject you and ignore you because your magnetism is wiped out through your bad karma.

People come to you as a response to your magnetism. Your magnetism nourishes them and gives them joy and happiness. Once your magnetism is gone, they feel as if you were a dry fountain.

Increase your magnetism with good deeds, and you pave the way for your prosperity and health.

4. Bad karma weakens your intelligence, your creativity, your insight and foresight. You slowly become mentally blinded.

Creative people notice that whenever they act against their conscience the source of their inspiration weakens or even dries up. Creativity is the flow of the light of your intelligence that builds forms through which people progress and achieve. When you use your life destructively, the source of your inspiration withdraws.

5. Bad karma results in depression. Depression comes when you *deprive* yourself of Beauty, Goodness, and Truth and violate the Law of Karma. Those who are depressed have a memory of a deed which weighs heavily on them.

Any time you are depressed, try to find out how and when you violated the Law of Karma.

Depression is an automatic revenge that one takes upon himself to punish himself for his own hidden acts. You can dispel your depression if you bring to the surface the image of the act which is bothering your conscience and decide to clear it with your good deeds.

But through depression you do not pay your karma. Depression is the effect of your karma.

6. Bad karma leads you to suicide, and suicide is the most stupid effort to escape your karma. Karma weakens when you face it; it strengthens and multiplies when you try to escape it.

Bad karma makes you miss opportunities. Opportunities pass in front of you, but you do not see them. You hear things, but you do not listen to them. You observe things, but you do not understand them.

7. Bad karma prevents you from coming in contact with higher spheres, higher realities.

8. Bad karma delays your liberation.

9. Bad karma prevents you from meeting your Inner Guide or your Master.

You create a very heavy and complicated karma when you are engaged in the following activities:

- When you force your own will on others
- When you make people your blind followers
- When you interfere consciously and deliberately in the karma of others
- When you are engaged in mediumistic activities and past life readings
- When you interfere with the private lives of others
- When you engage in sexual relations with those who have a large amount of bad karma and pollution
- When you cheat on your wife, husband, or partner in business
- When you are jealous

We are told that an intelligent man will never throw himself into such traps.

A good deed is like a grain of wheat. One grain gives birth to a thousand, and a thousand produce millions of grains of wheat. The benevolent effect of good deeds goes from generation to generation.

Karma is often considered as only acting in one dimension, whereas it has a three-dimensional activity. Causes and effects are not limited to the physical dimension only, but they also extend into emotional and mental dimensions, and there they create effects as real as those on the physical plane.

It is very interesting to note that karma often interferes. On certain occasions it blocks our consciousness, and on other occasions it enlightens our consciousness. For example, if an intelligent man is going to fail because of his karma, he misses an important point in his plan, and because of that point he fails. On the other hand, when the future of a success seems dark, he is inspired to take certain steps which brings total and surprising success to him.

This is also seen in different situations. For example, because of his karma a man's time has come to die and, although he may be very healthy, he gets into a situation where he becomes angry, has a heart attack, and he passes away. On the other hand, if karmically it is not his time to die, even in a very dangerous condition, he receives help and does not die.

Sometimes it even happens that the Inner Guide, knowing that the man will pass away or will fall into a great difficulty, inspires him to make certain arrangements for his work or possessions. Being healthy, the man never thinks about his death, but anyhow he makes the arrangements "for the future" and passes away in a few days.

The awareness of the Inner Guide is sometimes not registered in a man's consciousness due to his preoccupations or his dream-like state of consciousness.

It is necessary to observe the behavior of people to find out if they are unconsciously following the Plan of the Inner Guide without noticing any difference in their own behavior. A keen observer can distinguish between the operation of the Inner Guide and the operation of the human consciousness, both working through the personality.

Very often our future is reflected on the mirrors of our higher bodies, but our consciousness is not yet trained to reach them and translate them. Sometimes karma is hidden from our consciousness so that we do not follow a path against it.

If, for example, a man knows that he is going to die half an hour later in an accident because of his karma, he will not drive his car, and he will try to escape. But if his karma wants him to be alive, either he is not hurt in the accident or he arrives upon the scene of the accident a few minutes late.

One of my Teachers knew that he was going to pass away on a certain date. A few days before that date he fell ill. My father took his medical bag and hurried to the Teacher's home. My Teacher was waiting for the right time to leave his body. In spite of all the advice and pleas of my father, he refused to take any medicine or an injection. A few hours later he raised his right hand and held the hand of an invisible visitor. He said it was Jesus, and he passed away.

There are many other cases such as this in which one works consciously with the Law of Karma. King Akbar used to do very dangerous things. When once he was asked why he was risking his life, he replied, "Nothing will happen to me if I am protected by God. If not, let it happen."

It is possible to expand our consciousness to such a degree that we become aware of our karma and cooperate with it in full measure. It is also possible that once we reach the state of knowing our karma, and if absolutely necessary, we can change our karma through our fiery thoughts.

Karma then can be changed through spiritual striving, through fiery thoughts, and through transmuting our consciousness. Such a change is introduced or induced not because of fear, not because of personal interests, but because of a dire need for sacrificial service. This does not mean to break the law but to meet the law in a different way.

At the time of great cataclysms, one can see how karma programs every detail for every man. Often those who know about the hour and location of the cataclysm cannot utter a single word to those who karmically are going to perish. This is one of the tests of initiates. They cannot interfere with the law. Sometimes they are even ordered to stay at the location of natural cataclysms, so as not to make people follow them and escape their own karma. The majority of people, even if warned, are too busy to heed the warning. Their consciousness is blocked by their deeds.

It is through the expansion of consciousness that you will be capable of cooperating with the laws of Nature. The decisive factor in your karma is not what you know, is not what you have, but *what you did and what you are.*

Karma can be exhausted only on the physical plane. Karma created on the physical plane will have its effects on the astral and mental planes when the human soul leaves his physical body and enters the astral and then the mental planes. It is his karma created on the physical plane that will determine his condition on the astral and mental planes. But the karma will not be exhausted while in these planes. The person will come back and pay his past debts on the physical plane itself.

Once all our karma is paid on the physical plane, we will be free not to incarnate again. Of course, it is possible to come again to the physical plane with a physical body, but it will not be by the pressure of the karmic forces but by our free will to serve the Plan of the Hierarchy and the Purpose of God.

Many Great Ones come to the world just to serve. Their life does not create karma because They live a harmless and sacrificial life.

Karma cannot be created in the subtle and fiery worlds.

When we pass away it is not karma that punishes us but the accumulated flammable elements within our subtle bodies that really cause us pain and suffering. Karma waits for us in the physical world, and when we incarnate, it "gets" us according to its own laws.

Many religions have the opinion that we will be punished after we pass away for our many transgressions, for breaking the Law of Love and Unity, and that after we are punished, we will be ready to enter paradise. It is true that we will pay, but not after we pass away. We will pay after we reincarnate in the physical world!

The suffering and pain that we will be subjected to in the Subtle World are caused by combustible materials that we carry with us while we journey toward the Subtle Worlds. These materials come into being when we live in hatred, fear, anger, jealousy, treason, malice, slander; or when we exploit and manipulate people for our greed and separatism; or when we become the victims of our vanity, ego, and self-deception; or if we try to deceive others, flatter or bribe them, and hinder their evolution.

These combustible elements also come into being when we are attached to physical, emotional, and mental objects, or mislead people to secure our selfish and separative interests.

These combustible elements settle in our astral and mental bodies and, as we go deeper into the astral and mental planes, they catch on fire and begin burning for a short or long time, according to the amount of accumulations.

We also suffer when we see the sufferings that we caused others, as we see the video tape of our criminal actions again and again. But all these do not exhaust our karma.

The Karmic Law awaits us on the physical plane until we appear again. It is only on the physical plane that we pay our debts and get free of our karma.

Some people think that our suffering in the Subtle World will eliminate our karma, and we will not have karma when we return. This is not true. Karma operates exactly like the law in our mundane daily life.

A criminal kills a few people, robs them, and disappears, and the law cannot catch him. But this man passes through suffering and pain and eventually makes his life miserable. His inner conflict and guilt and fear increase to such a degree that he chooses either to surrender, to commit suicide, or to suffer forever with his conscience.

It is after the criminal's surrender that the law will decide what to do with him. This is why many Great Ones, before They pass away, pay back all that They can to others and even ask their forgiveness and blessing.

Before you enter into the gates of the Subtle World, make your accounts clean and your heart and mind enlightened with the joy of harmlessness.

We must remember that with all our transgressions and mistakes we have also days of sacrificial service and caring for others. We have days of light, love, and beauty; days of constructive activities; days of high aspirations and lofty thoughts. These also create an element in our subtle bodies which, classically, is called "bliss." It is this element that will counteract the flammable elements in our subtle bodies, even overrule them and make our passing very enjoyable.

Of course, on our journey we will see pockets of fires, but the bliss not only will protect us but will also extinguish these fires, or render them pleasant for us. Blessed are those who have the great treasure of bliss with them when they cross the subtle threshold.[1]

The bliss referred to here was the oil of the wise virgins in the parable of Christ.

In conclusion, if you want to be healthy now and in the future, plant seeds that will flower later as health and happiness.

1. For more information about the Subtle Worlds, please see *Other Worlds*.

40

Dangers of Hypnotism

When posthypnotic suggestions gather associated links and form a chain, they appear as if an entity were possessing the person.

Hypnotism allows the physical, emotional, and mental elementals to take the man under their control. Posthypnotic suggestions are carried out by these elementals which, instead of working under the direction of the man or the human soul, take actions independently from the human soul. The curious point is that when the human soul once again gears himself with the brain, he responds to the demands of the bodies as he used to do before, but without realizing that his bodies are under the will of another mind.

Drugs and narcotics have almost the same effect as hypnotism.

In advanced schools of spiritual discipline the students are taught a method of withdrawal from the physical, emotional, and mental bodies, leaving the bodies insensitive to outer stimuli. In this case the elementals are left alone to keep the mechanical functions of the vehicles operating without interruption.

There are two important factors in achieving this state. The first one is that there is an electrical line which must be built between the lower and higher mind, and between the higher mind and the Self. The second one is that man must practice first focusing his eyes on the tip of the nose, then concentrating his mind between the eyebrows and slowly collect his scattered Self from the bodies so that he can enter into a contemplative state similar to Samadhi. Through these two techniques a person is able to withdraw himself from his body, even to the point of having surgery performed on him, because he has withdrawn himself from the area of pain and suffering.

Many Eastern and Western yogis put all their attention on the tip of their nose without first being able to build the cable between the lower mind and the Self. Because of this, very little success is achieved, or many complications are encountered. The building of this electrical line is done in the field of consciousness through striving, service, and sacrifice. All our spiritual attainments are based on sacrificial service and conscious striving toward the highest.

Our etheric body, which controls the conditions of the body, nervous system, brain, and blood system, is by nature electromagnetic. Electricity and magnetism are in balance within our etheric system. If one or another is in excess, the physical man is in trouble.

Hypnotism increases the electrical contact in the etheric body and decreases the amount of magnetism. When hypnotism is used frequently, the subject is in danger of losing all his magnetism.

Magnetism creates the medium through which the human soul comes in contact with the physical mechanism. Electricity is the substance through which the etheric body influences the nadis and nervous system. The increase of electricity gradually paralyzes the organs as the electrical current floods them. Absentmindedness, forgetfulness, loss of focus and direction, and spacing out are signs of flooding our brains with the flow of electricity. It is possible to balance the system by increasing the magnetic current in the etheric body. H.P. Blavatsky once said,

> *...There is the danger of black magic, into which all the world, and especially America, is rushing as fast as it can go. Only a wide knowledge of the real psychic and spiritual nature of man can save humanity from grave dangers.*[1]

In the same article she says,

> *...Do you not see the tremendous evils that lie concealed in hypnotism?...*
>
> *...Hypnotism and suggestion are great and dangerous powers, for the very reason that the victim never knows when he is being subjected to them; his will is stolen from him.... These things may be begun with good motives, and for right purposes....Whoever lets himself or herself be hypnotized by anyone, good or bad, is opening a door which he will be powerless to shut; and he cannot tell who will be the next to enter!...*[2]
>
> *...In hypnotism the nerve-ends of the sense-organs are first fatigued and then by continuance of the fatigue are temporarily paralysed; and the paralysis spreads inwards to the sense-center in the brain, and a state of trance results. The fatigue is brought about by the use of some mechanical means, such as a revolving mirror, a disc, an electrical light, etc. A frequent repetition of this*

1. H.P. Blavatsky, *Collected Writings*, Vol. VIII, 1887, p. 406.
2. *Ibid.*, p. 407.

> *fatigue predisposes the patient to fall readily into a state of trance, and permanently weakens the sense-organs and the brain. When the Ego [the human soul] has left his dwelling, and the brain is thus rendered passive, it is easy for another person to impress ideas of action upon it, and the ideas will then be carried out by the patient, after coming out of trance, as though they were his own. In all such cases he is the mere passive agent of the hypnotizer.*[3]

There is a great difference between hypnotism and *mesmerism*. Mesmerism is not mechanical, is not a technique, but the use of so-called auric fluid — the electromagnetic force of the etheric body. H.P. Blavatsky says,

> *...He may thus, in the case of sickness, regularize the irregular vibrations of the sufferer, or share with him his own life-force, thereby increasing his vitality. For nerve-atrophy there is no agent so curative as this, and the shrivelling cell may clairvoyantly be seen to swell up under the flow of the life-current. The pranic current flows most readily from the tips of the fingers, and through the eyes; passes should be made along the nerves from center to circumference, with a sharp shake of the fingers away from the patient and the operator, at the end of the pass. The hands should be washed before and after the operation, and it should never be undertaken unless the mind is quiet and the health strong. The loss of vitality should be made good by standing in the sun, with as little clothing as possible, breathing deeply and slowly, and retaining the breath between each inhalation and exhalation as long as is convenient, i.e., not long enough to cause any struggle or gasping. Five minutes of this should restore the pranic balance.*[4]

Mesmerism can be as evil as hypnotism. But if it is used by a knower and by a man of high integrity, it can be very useful.

Suggestion in reality is mesmerism. In suggestion, as in mesmerism, one channels Soul energy or psychic energy, or the will to harmonize the defective bodies or parts of the bodies, to give strength to the original cells or atoms and enable the body to fight and conquer.

There is also another difference between suggestion or mesmerism and hypnotism. Hypnotism prepares the body for obsession or possession, but suggestion keeps entities away from the body. Hypnotism weakens the mental

---

3. H.P. Blavatsky, *Collected Writings*, Vol. XIII, 1890-1891, p. 362.
4. *Ibid.*, pp. 362-363.

body and makes it lose its control over the emotional body and over thought currents. Being free from control, the power of imagination takes over and the person slowly becomes the captive of his imaginations, the content of which changes according to the stimulation of his various centers.

Imagination is a great source of physical and emotional illness. Imagination is like making furniture or any other form in astral matter. These forms stay a long time within the aura, and if not nurtured they disintegrate and cause astral pollution. If they last a long time on the astral plane, they eventually create crystallization and hardening in the astral body. This affects the astral body, affects its senses and centers, and affects the liquid part of the human mechanism. Astral centers mostly control the flow of the lymphatic glands, ductless glands, the blood, and any kind of secretion in the physical body.

Imagination directly affects the glands and their corresponding nerve centers and organs. Our imagination is mostly composed of

— sexual images

— images of food, dress, and drink

— possession of various objects or properties

— images of fear and various ambitions

All these images, with their various forms and colors, build barriers in the astral body where the circulation of psychic energy becomes impossible. After the psychic energy is withdrawn, one may expect every kind of trouble and attack.

With self-hypnotism it is even possible to create stigmata. I once saw sisters exercising intense devotion and hysterical ecstasy in front of a crucifix, and a few days later the signs of the wounds like those on the hands of Jesus appeared on their hands. The intense concentration on the picture allowed the picture to impress itself on the mental and astral body and eventually on the physical body.

It is also possible to achieve the same result through hypnotism. But this time it is the hypnotist who suggests the image and impresses it on the astral and mental bodies, forming in them imaginative thoughtforms. It is these thoughtforms that will eventually manifest in the physical body.

It must be stated that posthypnotic suggestions can also be defeated by the human soul and eventually thrown out as dead materials, if the human soul is strengthened by moral and spiritual values and virtues. As the human soul is nourished by higher ideas, visions, and virtues, he gradually develops a very sensitive power of observation and discrimination. Eventually he discovers the impressions that were not admitted consciously and casts them out as materials foreign to his nature and to his plan. As the light of the soul increases day after day, the impressed suggestions melt away and disappear. One of the greatest freedoms of the human soul is the moment when he liberates himself from posthypnotic suggestions.

It is also possible to make oneself immune to hypnotic suggestions by developing intense watchfulness, observation, and an awakened state of consciousness.

People think that it is only the professional hypnotist who hypnotizes people. This is not entirely true. The practice is widespread. It is used in politics, in education, in religion, and in churches. People one day will be surprised when they awaken to the fact that churches in general have used heavy hypnotic suggestions on congregations for ages, keeping them as their slaves, and thus creating fanatics, zealots, and an insane psychology in them. There are only a few churches that are free of hypnotism. These churches work to awaken people into the light of true facts and reality, and protect them from the attacks of the whip of hypnotic deception and slavery.

It is very difficult to convince the average religious man or fanatic that he is under continuous, heavy, posthypnotic suggestion, that he is not allowed to see things from various viewpoints, and that his free will is chained to ideas and thoughts which are not received by him consciously and with his free will.

Hypnotism in churches has kept humanity away from freedom. Thus the Divine Will — the carrier of which was, originally, the church — has been blocked, distorted, and mutilated. Once churches began to yield to hypnotism, the destructive forces took over, and the result is the present situation all over the world.

Science is the path in which hypnotism has the least control, but unfortunately hypnotic suggestion has had a heavy influence on the application of scientific discoveries.

H.P. Blavatsky once stated that to save humanity from the danger of hypnotism people must be educated about the brotherhood of humanity and led to higher spiritual freedom. Healing must start from the Core of the human being. As the human Core, which is the Divine Presence in man, is released, its rays will dissipate all obstacles to health and purify the vehicles of man.

Real health is eventually obtained through a process of awakening into the reality of one's essential inner Divinity and letting the power of that Divinity rule the life of the bodies. The inner Core of man is reached through striving toward spiritual perfection, through meditation and sacrificial service, through compassion and inclusiveness, through discrimination of values, and through a life of detachment and renunciation.

One hundred years ago, people used to think that hypnotism was the same as mesmerism, suggestion, "psychology," charlatanism, transference of psychic energy, animal magnetism, and so on. Some teachers encouraged the study and application of hypnotism, but hypnotism for them was the art of directing psychic energy to people and helping them heal themselves.

Modern hypnotism has nothing to do with psychic energy, animal magnetism, mesmerism, etc. It is a mechanical technique to induce sleep and inject posthypnotic suggestions into the subconscious mind of the subject. It is a technique to take control of the mind of the subject.

There are two factors necessary to induce hypnotism: one is the knowledge and the skill of the hypnotist; the other is the cooperation of the subject.

It is thought that hypnotism is a state of sleep, as *hypnos* in Greek means "sleep." *Hypnos* is a different kind of sleep. In natural sleep the consciousness thread is still anchored in the brain, though the human soul is out of the body, or withdrawn. In hypnotism the consciousness thread is taken away and suspended, and the human soul is pushed out. The consciousness thread is the contact point of the soul with the brain.

In natural sleep, the link between the human soul and the brain is intact. In hypnotism, the mechanism of the brain and the astral, etheric, and physical bodies are abandoned by the soul temporarily, and sometimes forever.

In sleep, the senses are withdrawn; in hypnosis the senses of the physical, astral, and mental bodies are alert and sensitive to a certain degree, but the synthesizer or analyzer is absent. One can reach outside stimuli, but he is not conscious of them, and his reaction is mechanical — or physical, astral, and lower mental. The hypnotist can suggest any conclusion from any stimuli and the subject will register it. Thus, you can be professionally deceived by your own five senses.

The "animal magnetism" of the mesmerizer has nothing to do with the techniques of present day hypnotism. Animal magnetism was considered to be a subtle fluid, a kind of force or energy, which comes from the Sun and the stars. It can be accumulated in a human being and directed to objects and human beings to influence them properly and heal people of various ailments. In esoteric books this subtle fluid is referred to as psychic energy, which is used by suggestion — not hypnotic suggestion — while the subject is awake.

In suggestion, esoterically understood, there is a flow of energy to the subject. In modern hypnotism, this is not the case. The hypnotist does not know that his thoughtforms, motives, feelings, and even habits can stick in the mind of the subject as stronger posthypnotic suggestions than his verbal suggestions.

In mesmerism, it is believed that sicknesses are the result of distortion in the flow and circulation of magnetic fluid in and around the body. The subtle flow — called animal magnetism — is made to pass into the electromagnetic field of the body, which restores a harmonious circulation in the magnetic fluid and thus heals the body.

Hypermnesia is the act of making the subject remember his past through hypnotism. This is not a great mystery; all that man experiences is recorded in the permanent atoms and in the Chalice. As one can tie up the owner of a house and steal precious things from his home, in the same way the hypnotist pushes the human soul away and lets the hidden records be given out by the physical, astral, and mental elementals. The danger is that the human soul still believes that these memories are hidden and acts accordingly and is perplexed when he realizes that all is out in the open.

We forget things for various subtle reasons. We can remember them, if necessary, through conscious acts of searching. There is no need for hypnosis.

When we forget certain things, Nature covers them with certain strata of matter to prevent pain and suffering for us. When they are forcefully brought out to the surface of the mind, without the subject *remembering* them after hypnosis, they carry with them a great amount of disturbances which later manifest in the form of various difficulties and even illnesses. The human soul will never tolerate others to expose things which he thinks must be buried for a certain period of time.

There is also the belief that all that the subject says under hypnosis is factual and true. But sixty percent of the time they can be lies, and often the rest is mixed with information that comes together only through association. Only five to ten percent of the memories can be depended upon. The subject can even talk about the things that the hypnotist is expecting or anticipating from the subject. **Do not forget that!**

In hypnosis, the hypnotist is fused with the mental mechanism of the mind of the subject, almost acting as if he were the soul of the subject. It is very possible that at the time when the subject is "remembering things," many hypnotic suggestions are being planted in his mind.

It is possible to make man unfold and be his own master. This is a long path, but it is the shortest path in comparison with the "achievements" that hypnotism promises. All that we achieve through hypnotism will accumulate and become the hardest obstacle on the path for our future success, sanity, and health. Nature does not like shortcuts. Those who violate the laws of Nature pay heavily for their violations.

Hypnotism is wrongly used in business and in advertising. If this continues, we will have zombies on our streets and no one, not even the hypnotist, will be able to control them.

We must use different methods to affect others if our intention is to serve, transform, and heal. We must develop the technique which will make people contact the source of Beauty, Goodness, and Truth within themselves and allow these three energies gradually to release and transform their lives.

One must achieve through his own merit and right. Hypnotism weakens the will for ages. Nature works to create and strengthen the will. Nature wants everyone to be his own director; Nature does not want people to be slaves to each other. Once the will is weakened, it is easy to use that man for almost any purpose.

The new technique will be to build the power of the will in man.

Of course people need assistance, but not obsession and possession. True assistance is to help a man become his own master, to contact the beauty within his Self, and to try to manifest it throughout his life.

I was listening to a program in which a man was explaining how people are learning new languages through hypnosis. He was saying that the subconscious mind is the seat of learning and through hypnosis the new language goes into and accumulates in the subconscious.

It is true that our consciousness is not always aware of things going on on various levels of the mental plane, but there is no such thing as the subconscious plane. Subconsciousness is not a separate thing from the mental plane. The areas that are not in the spotlight of consciousness are termed *subconscious*. Everything impressed on the mental plane *not* through consciousness is a problem in the consciousness. This is because things registered by the consciousness have been accepted by the consciousness. Things *not* impressed through consciousness are not accepted by the conscious mind and do not belong to the consciousness. The difficulty is in how to bring these things out and have the consciousness accept them as if it had received them.

Language is not learned only in words but also in sentences. Thus, every sentence learned using hypnosis is a posthypnotic suggestion in the subconsciousness. Things learned by conscious effort are not registered as posthypnotic suggestions. If it happens that two sentences received by the consciousness and subconscious mind are in conflict, then there will be a tremendous amount of pressure created on the mental plane. This can result in a state in which man will have moments of "unconsciousness" — which will also be moments in which he receives other posthypnotic suggestions.

For example, a man tells me hypnotically to eat an apple. This goes into my subconscious. Then the man tells me not to touch the apple when I am conscious. Here, a conflict results.

Thus the conflict between the two parts of the mind will eventually lead a man to the asylum, and things received through hypnotic means will never be erased from his mind.

People think that to be hypnotized one must be made unconscious. This is wrong. One can be in a hypnotic state even when he is going to a lecture or playing music or doing manual work or talking with others. Most people do not even need to be hypnotized; they are already asleep, and any suggestion impresses them as a hypnotic suggestion.

Suggestopedia is a technique used to "awaken" the consciousness. However, a truly awakened consciousness can learn faster than learning by suggestopedia. A great difference exists between the two. The consciousness of the awakened man expands, but the consciousness of the man submitted to suggestopedia grows in tension because as the mind swells (so to say) with the rapidly accumulated knowledge, the consciousness cannot assimilate it. The result is that the consciousness and the mind eventually separate, and this is where the danger starts.

Once the mind gets free from the control of the consciousness, it goes toward destruction using all the knowledge it has.

People already live as programmed tape recorders. To hypnotize them is to push them into a dream state even more deeply.

There is no doubt that the technique of super-learning works and produces results, but it is at the expense of future progress, and at the expense of the higher vehicles. This is very different, if not impossible, for such practitioners to understand because higher bodies do not exist for them.

The Hierarchical Teaching does not work for commercialism such as making chickens lay eggs twice daily. Such an egg and such a chicken are no longer eggs and chickens but factories. Evolution must proceed naturally, with the effort and striving of the people. An artificial development in one's life sets one back for one hundred lives.

This will also be very difficult for some "scientists" to admit or even to understand. What is gained naturally by one's own efforts stays with him for ages and develops progressively. Nature does not tolerate exploitation. That is why one must not use drugs to contact higher states of consciousness. *Hypnopedia* and super-learning methods are not much different from drugs because they also violate Nature.

For a long time people will value super-learning, but learning will not change man or life. Those who know more will control others more, or people will want to be controlled by them. Thus a severe imbalance will occur in Nature which will result in disasters.[5] The Teaching does not exist to increase learning at the expense of moral values. Even wise ones will slow their own progress to help others grow.

Artificially forced learning remains only in the corridors of the brain. It is only by your conscious labor and assimilation that you gain power over the things you learn. Through such learning, your consciousness and mental mechanism stay in harmony.

Things you learn by super-learning lead you into directions toward which you were not supposed to go. You are forced to do things you were not supposed to do. This may sound ridiculous, but what would happen if the foot wanted to be a different shape than what it was *supposed* to be? The word "supposed" indicates that there are preordained plans and patterns which things must follow, and if one wants to change them, he must create causes consciously and by his own efforts and labor.

Things accumulated in super-learning are almost impossible to unlearn; and if you try to unlearn them by super-learning, you will have a greater inner chaos.

We may ask, what would happen if a person taught the science of crime to people through super-learning? What laws would prevent its use, and how?

---

5. See also *Earthquakes and Disasters, What the Ageless Wisdom Tells Us.*

You grow in right or wrong ways. You grow in the right way only by your conscious efforts and experiences. Then when you learn, you have power over the things you know.

The etheric brain relates the mental body to the brain.

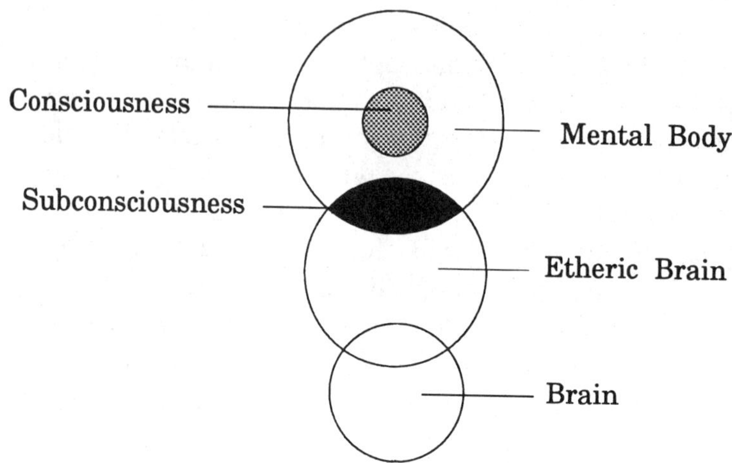

Diagram 40-1 The Etheric Brain

In super-learning, it is through the brain via the etheric brain that the mind is impressed. The natural method is through the mind — consciously accepted — to the etheric brain, and then it is registered in the brain. In the natural method of learning, the consciousness is in power. In *artificial* methods of learning, the etheric brain is in power and becomes the field of conflict between the knowledge and the inner plan.

By the word "artificial" we mean not the natural method — using an accelerated or retarded speed; excessive pressure or sub-weight pressure; not in right relation with the rest of the person's development, etc.

One can eliminate brain records but not etheric records where hypnotism is carried out. The subconsciousness is part of the etheric brain attached to the lower mental body.

Through super-learning, the data is accumulated in the brain and becomes available for use most of the time. But gradually it gains control over your mind and becomes an independent force. Eventually it totally controls your life and can even obsess you.

Through hypnotism you can eliminate hindrances, repeated "failure" images, "low appreciation" images, "I can't do it" images. But the elimination of such images is not real. They still exist, but you act as if they do not. Because of these conditions, you become divided or stay divided in your consciousness.

It is good to eliminate "failure" images by natural methods and challenge someone to strive to improve himself. But why take a hypnotic image and put another in its place?

Affirmations such as

— "I can do it"

— "Now I am achieving my goals"

— "Learning and remembering are easy for me"

— "My memory is alert; my mind is powerful"

are not only ridiculous but also extremely dangerous. Let us take each affirmation separately.

a. "I can do it." If you are not capable of doing it and you really think you can do it, you will be like the man who thought he could fly and he jumped from the window. Instead you can say, "I will try to do it."

b. "Now I am achieving my goals." Goals are achieved because of previous labor and preparation. What if a fool says, "I am becoming the President of the United States." Do you know what will happen if by chance he achieves his goal?

c. "Learning and remembering are easy for me." What if learning and remembering are not easy for you? Your inner opposition will clash with an affirmation that is not true, or you will feel humiliated when you cannot learn and remember. You can say, "Let learning and remembering be easy for me. Let me achieve them by my labor."

d. "My memory is alert; my mind is powerful." What a pressure will be created if a person who has a weak memory and a dull mind suddenly assumes the opposite. Instead say, "Let me direct all my efforts to create in myself a good memory and a powerful mind with my labor and striving."

It has been written that "tests showed that after super-learning experiences, people become steadily less suggestible and less likely to be taken in by misleading statements." If they continue to test ten years later, they will find that the practitioners themselves have turned into "zombies."

Through hypnotism one can "cure" certain vices or weaknesses in the victim; this is not a real cure but a suppression. The roots of the vices or weaknesses still exist in the subtle bodies of the person and create various pressures on his mechanism to express themselves. Actually, such suppressed elements manifest themselves in the next incarnation as powerful urges and drives or obsessions.

When a hypnotist gives hypnotic suggestions, the suggestions contained in his etheric, astral, and mental substances enter the aura of the victim and take positions there. They become satellites in the aura of the victim and affect him any time and for whatever reasons the hypnotist and victim are keyed into each other or to the elements of the suggestion.

The hypnotist puts himself in serious danger by hypnotizing other people. The portion of his aura that is put into the aura of the other person will be contaminated by the defects of that person, and, when the person dies, the part of the aura that belongs to the hypnotist will come back and pollute the hypnotist as a possessing entity.

A hypnotist does not know that he can hypnotize a person on many levels — such as physically, emotionally, and mentally — making certain areas of these bodies (or entities) enter into a state of hypnosis. But this is not the whole story.

During the process of hypnosis, the hypnotist himself is open to hypnosis. The subject unconsciously projects back to the hypnotist the package of vices, thoughts, and emotions that are the target of the hypnotist. The hypnotist is not aware that he also is deeply influenced and hypnotized by the subject during the session.

If a scientific study is conducted, it will be proven that the hypnotist will begin to develop, for example, a habit that he is trying to eradicate in his subject through hypnosis. Many hypnotists contaminate themselves in trying to help their subjects. This contamination involves the projection of habits, physical illnesses, emotional or feeling patterns, thoughtforms, and character defects. During hypnosis, the hypnotist is open to the unintended projections of the subject. He has no protection against them.

In addition, a person who prepares subliminal suggestions eventually becomes the slave of the suggestions he releases electronically by visual and audible means. His thoughtforms of subliminal suggestions act as magnets which draw to him the suggestions that he released for others.

Such facts can only be observed if scientific research is done on the life of hypnotists in relation to their subjects, or if an honest hypnotist observes himself objectively and discovers the facts himself.

The effect of the projections from the subjects on the hypnotist does not necessarily surface immediately. The time element varies. It may take a week, a year, or a lifetime, but the hypnotist cannot escape the effect of the suggestions that he planted in the subjects, nor from the effects of the unintended projections of the subjects.

I did some observations on hypnotists and discovered that their inner world was so complicated by projections that they either planned to commit suicide or continuously enacted the projections of those whom they hypnotized.

Nature has a principle that cannot be violated without suffering and pain. This principle can be expressed in many words, but, simply put, Nature does not tolerate interferences nor imposition. It encourages individual efforts for self-determination and self-realization. Nature encourages those who assist people to achieve health, happiness, success, enlightenment, and prosperity by their own efforts to the degree that their karma tolerates. Nature encourages people to save themselves by their own hands and feet and "be a refuge for themselves."

Once a wise man was asked how to give light to others, how to make them healthy, how to make them happy and prosperous. His answer was: Be a light unto yourself, and people will have light. Strive toward perfection, and you will minimize all health problems. Radiate joy and try to meet your needs in a righteous way and not at the expense of others.

Your light cannot be received by others until they develop their own light. Your light, your love, your energy must not be imposed but present a challenge. Those who secure their interests at the expense of others create confusion and sow seeds of future suffering and pain. People must realize that it is only through individual efforts and striving that they can reach the summit of higher achievements.

Hypnotism is not always done by individuals. Groups, even nations can act as hypnotists. Such actions eventually bring calamity to their groups and nations. These groups and nations try to impose their will, their thoughts, their actions to secure their own interests. But the laws of Nature act otherwise. Imposition creates a violent reaction and turmoil in the consciousness of the imposer, and he absorbs all the ugly elements that are found in the subject — individual, group, or nation — under imposition.

Freedom is not a state of life only; it is a law which is not understood yet. All actions based on freedom have a chance for perpetual success.

Whatever you do against your conscience creates cleavages in your mind.

A leader must not make serious decisions in a depressed mood or when sick or worried because he may make wrong decisions under such circumstances. Important decisions must be postponed until he is out of depression or exhaustion. Many times decisions taken under depression are proven to be wrong.

Affirmations are not hypnotic suggestions if they are done in a state of awakened consciousness and with right understanding. For example, I say, "I am beautiful," but I understand that in my essence I am truly beautiful, although in my personality life I do many ugly things. These ugly things prevent me from actualizing my beauty, but in essence I am beautiful.

Because I am beautiful in essence and I understand the value and effect of beauty, I must work hard to bring my affirmation of beauty into actualization. Thus my actualization helps me to know that I am beautiful in essence even though I do many ugly things in my expressions. Then I try to find the reasons why I cannot manifest my beauty through my daily relationships.

Affirmation is an announcement that the goal, the last station where I want to go, really exists. But I must make every kind of effort to reach that goal.

If affirmation is done unconsciously or mechanically, you split your mind and create confusion, or you turn into a hypocrite. A hypocrite is one who acts as if he were in his ideal condition while in reality he lives an obnoxious life.

Suppose I hypnotize a person and say to her, "You must be beautiful." She gets the hypnotic suggestion to be beautiful. But, first of all, she does not know what beauty is. Second, she did not work for it; she did not prepare herself to carry the voltage of beauty in herself; she did not aspire for it; she did not prepare the ways for the actualization of beauty. My posthypnotic suggestion will not have her conscious cooperation, and she will even have opposition from her nature against the actualization of beauty. But she will force herself to be beautiful, without knowing what beauty is, what beauty demands, and what dangers it evokes. If the plan of her Soul is not to lead her toward beauty at that time, she will be in turmoil as she strives toward beauty.

Any imposition creates reaction, and the worst reaction is created when one imposes posthypnotic suggestions.

The plan of your Soul works very closely with your karma. Hypnotism violates these two important factors. Hypnotism is interference without the permission of your Soul and your karma. In hypnotism you are programmed to do certain things, and you are unaware of the program. Your airplane flies against the flight plans of your Soul, but you are unaware of it and think you are still going in the right direction. A thief, the programming, is controlling your whole life, giving you the impression that you are running your life.

You can do things wrong in two ways: unconsciously under the power of hypnotism or consciously. If you are doing wrong things under hypnosis, you have almost no chance to change it. But if you are doing wrong things consciously, you have almost every possible chance to change your direction, once you realize the danger.

A drunk or hypnotized man walks with a conscious man. The conscious man says to him, "You know, we are walking on loose ground; let us turn back."

The hypnotized man says, "That is okay. This is where we should go."

Hypnotists would never practice their art if they were not really hypnotized to do it. We must try by all means to de-hypnotize them so that through a labor of self-actualization they can get rid of the posthypnotic suggestions to practice hypnotism which have been forced into their nature.

On the physical plane, the hypnotic suggestion takes the control in its own hands and pushes away those causes which the hypnotist thinks are undesirable. In this way, the hypnotist creates an artificial and temporary unity in the psyche of the man. Sometimes these repressed causes try to find doors to escape through various complications, or they may even fight against the hypnotic suggestion if the suggestion is not strong enough.

In the Subtle World, also, a conflicting duality appears. The suggestion and the suppressed cause fight against each other to dominate the man, who cannot decide which of the two fighters has the right to own him. Sometimes the fight is so serious that the man cannot advance in the Subtle World, and he periodically swings between the fighters.

In the next incarnation this duality is born with the man, and he has a split personality; he is a psychiatric case. Thus the posthypnotic suggestion does not end with the death of the person. It continues on the other side of life, with the suppressed cause releasing itself from the power of the suggestion and fighting against it. The suggestion turns into a cause and conditions the body in the next incarnation.

The ancients used to say that you should be careful when inviting strangers into your home; they may try to be a part of the family.

Can you imagine the confusion of a man in the Subtle World who has hundreds of hypnotic suggestions? What a battleground his life will be in the Subtle World and the physical world!

Most of our unconscious drives are the reactivation of posthypnotic suggestions received in the past.

The Core of man periodically, and with great tension and distress, eliminates the strangers from its field. The Core tries to solve its own problems, in its own ways, because its nature strives to be itself. The ultimate achievement of man is carried out only with his own hands and feet.

Most of our posthypnotic suggestions continue to exist in our subtle bodies after we die. There is even the possibility that one can be hypnotized in the astral plane if he accumulated posthypnotic suggestions while he was on the physical plane. Such people, due to their weakness and their readiness, can be hypnotized by astral plane black magicians while they are preparing to take their next incarnation.

When posthypnotic suggestions gather associated links and form a chain, they appear as if an entity were possessing the person.

Children born with double personalities (though actually with one soul or one entity) are not really possessed by an entity but by the hypnotic suggestion or the hypnotic chain of suggestions which is acting as an entity. The child is born in one body, but he has two command posts. One is him, his soul; the other one is his hypnotic chain of suggestions. When this chain is stimulated and activated, his individuality fades away, or it heavily influences the operation of his soul, interfering as often as it is stimulated. It is very difficult to disperse this chain of associated suggestions and release the soul from the nightmare in which he is living. The only method that is successful is daily, rhythmic meditation.

The kind of meditation to which we are referring is a mental process which operates on causes to find the effects, or on effects to find the causes. In the process of meditation, the person has a question and tries to find the answer or answers, or he is aware of a need and tries to formulate a way to meet that need.

In such a meditation, the person works on a seed thought. This seed thought can be related to any field of human endeavor. For example, let us take the following seed thoughts:

1. What is an ideal government or leadership? How can such an ideal government be brought into existence?

2. What is the purpose of education? How can we prepare ideal education?

3. What does it mean to communicate? What is the meaning of "meaning" or "significance?"

4. What is beauty? How is ugliness created?

5. What should science actually do?

6. What is the cause and the purpose of religion?

7. What does it mean to share?

Think daily for fifteen to twenty minutes on one of these seed thoughts for three months and take notes. You may also wish to formulate your own seed thoughts.

If you are faithful in your meditation, slowly your conscious mind will grow and become stronger, and your hypnotic "entity" will have less opportunity to interfere.

If you continue for six to seven years, your hypnotic entity will slowly dissolve and you will feel that you are the king of your kingdom. This is a slow process, but it is the best way to deal with such "hypnotic chains." During these several years of meditation, as the light of your intellect grows, you will learn a great deal about the secrets of such accumulations, and this in turn will help in their disintegration.

If this chain is not counteracted, broken, or dispersed, there is the possibility that the victim will carry the will of the black magician into the world, turning into a cause of destruction or pollution.

Once a great Teacher said that one can fight against a giant easily, but it is so difficult to fight against fleas. Thus small, negative, poisonous suggestions, like termites, destroy the foundations and make it impossible to create a new civilization.

Not all posthypnotic suggestions (given through television, newspapers, books, and radio) are detectable. They are highly subliminal. They work over a long period of time, but they do their destructive work nevertheless.

How can we heal such persons before they are born? How can we prevent such children from entering the womb?

The answer to the first question is that if you can function on the astral plane consciously, you have a chance to heal them, provided that you know how to do it. If you cannot function on the astral plane, your prayers can help, leading such people to an advanced soul who can take care of them.

There are also many invisible servers who try to help, but as it is here on the physical plane, people in the Subtle World also cherish their psychic trash.

The answer to the second question is that sexual intercourse must be performed between highly advanced people with due preparation and upliftment, so that during the act of intercourse they are able to build a bridge into higher planes and allow only higher souls to walk the bridge to the womb. Meditation, prayer, purity of life, righteousness, creativity, joy, and a spirit of gratitude all help us build this bridge during sexual intercourse.

Souls contaminated with hypnotic suggestions cannot approach a bridge or a magnetic field which is built of the substances of prayers, aspirations, Beauty, Goodness, Righteousness, Joy, and Freedom. Such entities can only be attracted to those who present an easy access with their low sphere of vibration.[6]

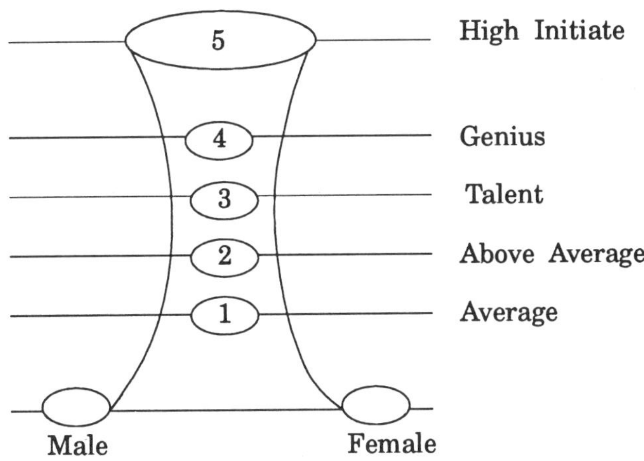

Diagram 40-2 Levels of Beingness

Wherever your bridge reaches, from that very sphere the entity will be "fished." The higher you are, the more advanced will be your baby. Your academic or social position and your knowledge are not the decisive factors. It is your beingness *at the time of intercourse* that is the most decisive factor in choosing the baby. Of course, such a beingness and readiness is rooted in the aspirations, motives, and long-range preparation in this direction.

Beingness is mostly the sum total of the love you have for Beauty, Goodness, Righteousness, Joy, and Freedom. Many simple people have a far more advanced beingness than those who are in the spotlight of television, the press, or public adoration. Those who are righteous, those who have the sense of beauty and responsibility, those who have pure love and feel joy in the gifts of Nature

6. See also *Woman, Torch of the Future*, and *Sex, Family, and the Woman in Society*.

sometimes have higher "bridges" and beingness than those who boast of their accumulated knowledge and social positions.

At the time of pregnancy, the mother and the embryo are very sensitive to suggestions, especially between the third and fourth months and the eighth and ninth months. The pregnant woman must be careful not to watch violent, criminal movies or read books which are negative, painful, or full of sensationalism. On the contrary, as much as possible she must be provided with a very pleasant environment. She must talk and relate with people who are joyful, optimistic, and happy. She must read or listen to beautiful poetry, legends of nobles, and so on. Bad news and upsetting events drastically affect the baby and condition it with bad health and a confused mind in the future.

At the time of pregnancy, it is imperative that the mother keep herself conscious, occupying her mind with constructive and creative objects in order to avoid any unconscious state of mind in which hypnotic suggestions are planted. During pregnancy, a woman must not allow anyone to hypnotize her. Hypnotism can have lasting and disastrous effects on the embryo, and later, on the baby.

A man and a woman can reject those souls who are ready to incarnate but are loaded with hypnotic suggestions in the astral plane by raising their consciousness as high as possible and having intercourse consciously with the intent of bringing into the world an elevated soul.

A higher consciousness requires purer and healthier bodies. This is why the Ageless Wisdom suggests that parents must have pure and healthy vehicles on all levels.

41

Visualization Exercises

Visualization is the translation of impressions which pour down from higher realms into visual symbols. Visualization is the ability to see things as they are and the ability to improve, harmonize, and relate them to higher sources of energy. Visualization is conscious control over mental substance and thoughtforms. Thoughtforms come under control only through visualization. Visualization brings in currents of inspiration to the mental plane. In meditation, these inspirations are used and formulated into thoughtforms.

Visualization develops slowly. First it is creative imagination, then pictorial visualization, which means really to see with your mental eyes the objects that you visualize. In advanced stages the ability to visualize develops another faculty which is called the ability to translate impressions and make them accessible to our mental body or to our five senses.

Thus, visualization is the ability to translate impressions, inspirations, thought currents, and ideas into plans, into thoughtforms, into a picture or a voice on the screen of our mind, just as our television tubes translate broadcasted radio waves into pictures, colors, and voices.

Visualization in its advanced stage is the greatest creative agent because it makes the abstract impressions tangible, the prototypal ideas objective, and the transcendental realities perceivable by our five senses.

A. Visualization Exercise

1. Sit in peace and joy.

2. Relax your body, calm your emotions, and fill your mind with serenity.

3. Say the Great Invocation.

    From the point of Light within the Mind of God
    Let light stream forth into the minds of men.
    Let Light descend on Earth.

    From the point of Love within the Heart of God

Let love stream forth into the hearts of men.

May Christ return to Earth.

From the centre where the Will of God is known

Let purpose guide the little wills of men —

The purpose which the Masters know and serve.

From the centre which we call the race of men

Let the Plan of Love and Light work out

And may it seal the door where evil dwells.

Let Light and Love and Power restore the Plan on Earth.

4. Sound the OM three times.

5. Visualize seven candles in seven colors on a table. Touch each of them and arrange them in various forms. Build a triangle, a circle, a wavy line, a semi-circle, a circle and a point, and other forms. Do at least ten forms. Try to visualize clearly your hand moving the candles and placing them in various positions.

6. After you arrange them in various forms, visualize around each flame a few concentric circles expanding and contracting. The circles must have the same colors as the candles.

7. Let each group of concentric circles expand and contract. In this process try to see all the separate colors and their movements. As they move, "hear" a music which controls the movements of the circles. You can visualize circles moving in rhythm with the music individually or in group formation with different but harmonious rhythms.

8. After a few minutes smell the "aura" of each candle as if it smelled like a rose or a jasmine or a carnation. Try to smell seven different fragrances.

9. After you smell the fragrance of each candle, try to taste the flame. Assume that the flames are like petals of flowers and touch them with your lips and tongue and taste them. Try to taste in them seven different tastes.

10. Think for five minutes about the symbol of the candles, circles, and flame-petals.

11. Visualize yourself as these seven flames, and in silence open yourself for the reception of the intuitive light. When an idea or a revelation dawns in your mind, keep in peace, and let it penetrate into your soul.

12. Say the Great Invocation with great gratitude.

13. After three minutes of silence, write down your experience in your spiritual diary.

The entire exercise must not exceed twenty minutes. You can do this meditation for one year, ten to fifteen minutes daily, in the meantime keeping yourself busy studying this book. On Sundays only, you may try another meditation suggested in this book instead of your regular meditation, but always keep the rule of safety: *slow but sure*.

B. Visualizations to Receive Spiritual Energy

1. Visualize a rainbow with seven distinct colors around your head. Do this daily or once a month; you choose the frequency. The rainbow will bring a great amount of energy to you from higher sources. Each color corresponds to a note in Space and keys in with a corresponding plane from which it draws energy into your system.

After doing such an exercise for a few months, add the symbol of a five-pointed star just above the top of the rainbow. The rainbow and the star will give you a tremendous amount of psychic energy if you visualize them clearly and with proper colors. You can visualize the star as a reddish-orange or blue color. Eventually this thoughtform will become a mechanism of contact with higher realms and a means to transfer powerful energies into your activities.

In all the exercises be sure to have the right motive — which is to receive energy in order to use it for the liberation of humanity. Selfish utilization of energy weakens your system and blocks the source of energy.

2. Visualize yourself every Monday morning standing under a waterfall. Feel the water; feel the air; enjoy the beauty of Nature; let the water pour on you and through you, and feel a deep joy. This exercise will bring in all those evoked energies standing in suspension in your higher planes and release them into your etheric, astral, and mental planes.

Let the water pour through your mental, emotional, and etheric bodies and purify them of all that is causing you trouble. Let the water cleanse your illusions, glamors, maya, and any kind of disorder or disturbance. As the water descends upon you as you stand under the falls, visualize the process of purification of your nature.

3. Visualize two mountain peaks and a beam of light connecting them. These are huge mountains almost two miles apart. Visualize yourself standing on one

of the peaks and walk on the beam of light toward the other peak. Do not hurry and do not have fear; you are a Spirit and you can do it.

After doing it a few times, look down at the cities, highways, and factories, but keep going toward the other peak. It may take time to be able to do this without fear, but in doing it you will conquer many kinds of fear within you.

Energy can descend and accumulate in a person when there is no fear in him. Fear prevents the flow of energy, or if the energy pours in, it gets polluted.

As you do this exercise, hidden fears will melt away without you being aware of them. There are many fears within us which sap our energy but which have no identity in our conscious mind. That is why they sap our energy and leave a great vacuum in our heart.

4. Once a day sit for a few minutes and visualize moments of great joy and glory for yourself. Make them as real as possible. Visualize meeting a great man, a great woman. Visualize a great victory, a great glory for yourself, a great service in which thousands are helped. Visualize your talents bringing creative results. Visualize thousands of people respecting and loving you. See yourself in front of a great audience. See how they are standing and applauding your talents, your beauty. Visualize things that give you joy. Joy is energy. A one minute visualization of an event of joy and glory will disperse any darkness in you. That is how disciples increase their joy and energy and become able to serve in daring conditions.

5. Have someone in your mind every day and send him your love, compassion, energy, and thoughts. Dramatize your visualization. See him sitting depressed and give him courage; see him rising, smiling, and talking with you, then dancing, running, and working. See yourself opening a path for him, removing an obstacle on his path, holding his hand when he is in fear, or inspiring him with great courage and daring. If he does not immediately receive your energy, he will eventually, especially when he is asleep.

The law is this: You increase your energy if you use it in the right way. To those who give, it will be given. This is what Christ said. This is a great law. No one can advance by taking and not giving.

C. An Advanced Daily Ritual

1. Visualize a sphere of light above your head and a diamond at the center of the sphere radiating the seven rays of seven colors in the sphere.

2. Visualize you are the diamond, and you are radiating the seven rays of the seven colors.

3. Think about beauty, and let the seven rays of the seven colors form a symbol of beauty.

4. Think about joy, and let the seven rays of the seven colors form a short dance.

5. Think about love, and let the seven rays of the seven colors play a symbolic dance of love.

6. Think about gratitude, and let the seven rays of the seven colors express their gratitude to the seven sources of Beauty, Goodness, and Truth. Try to find out what these sources are.

7. Think about enthusiasm, and direct these rays to some great work to be accomplished with fiery labor.

   During all these steps, try to identify yourself with the diamond.

8. Visualize your physical body, and flood it with the seven rays; make it pure, healthy, and beautiful.

9. Visualize your emotional body, and flood it with the seven rays and purify it; make it a body of registration of higher joy.

10. Visualize your mental body, and flood it with the seven rays and purify it; make it a mechanism of higher impressions. Then say,

    I am a point of light within a greater Light.

    I am a strand of loving energy within the stream of Love divine.

    I am a point of sacrificial Fire, focussed within the fiery Will of God.

    And thus I stand.

    I am a way by which men may achieve.

    I am a source of strength, enabling them to stand.

    I am a beam of light, shining upon their way.

    And thus I stand.

    And standing thus revolve

    And tread this way the ways of men,

    And know the ways of God.

    And thus I stand.[1]

11. Sound seven OMs.

---

1. Alice A. Bailey, *Discipleship in the New Age*, Vol. II, "Affirmation of a Disciple," p. 175.

12. Sit for ten minutes in silence.

D. Visualizations to Expand the Consciousness

To expand our consciousness further and to stimulate its faculty to synthesize and regenerate itself, we can use the technique of visualization. In this technique we visualize a certain symbol and in the meantime meditate on the meaning and the purpose behind it.

The following symbol is chosen to be used by individuals and groups:

If done seriously over a period of three to six months, it will expand the consciousness of the group or of the individual and synchronize it with higher creative centers found within the group and within the planet.

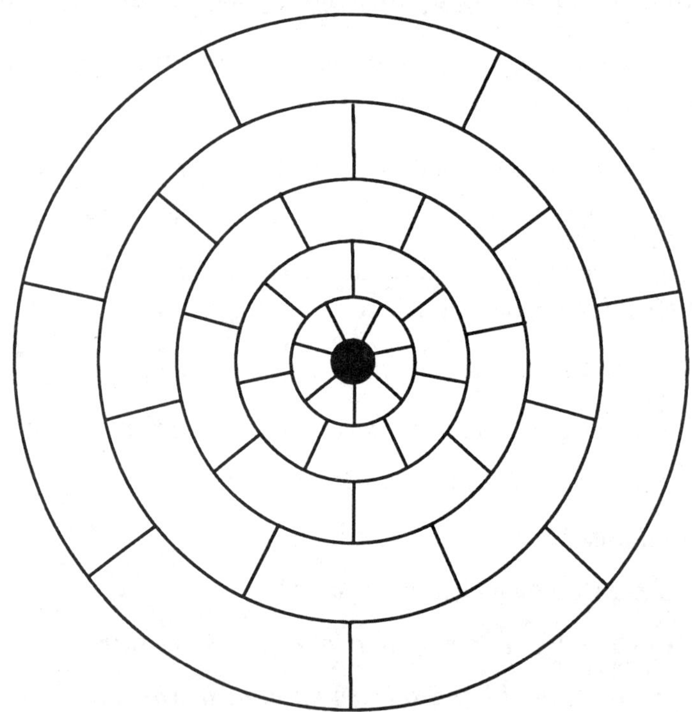

Diagram 41-1 Symbol

The steps of the visualization and meditation exercise are as follows:

1. Sit comfortably. Relax your body, calm the emotions, and rest your mind in peace.

2. Visualize the central circle which has seven spokes or seven radiant rays.

Start with the central point, which is the hub. From the hub send out seven radiations toward the rim of the first central wheel.

The success of your visualization is in direct proportion to your relaxation. Relaxation does not mean sleep; it means to free your mind from any strain or tension of the physical, astral, and mental bodies.

Start from the central point. Then try to see the seven spokes, then the rim around them, visualizing in color if you wish.

3. After a short time pass to the second circle, and make that first circle the hub of the second circle...and so on, until you reach the fifth one. As you do this exercise, you will feel energy flowing into your body, charging you with joy and vitality. Do not focus or direct energy to any location of your body. Just do your visualization, and the rest will take care of itself.

4. Start again now with the central point, and repeat the exercise.

   a. Visualize the central point.

   b. Project seven spokes.

   c. Start building the rim.

   If you cannot see it as a picture in front of your eyes, do not worry. Just try to use your creative imagination.

   Start the second circle.

   a. Use the first circle as the center, the hub.

   b. Project seven spokes from it.

   c. Now build the bigger circle or the rim around the rays.

   d. Try to visualize the second circle.

   e. Now try to see both of them in different colors.

   Now try the third one.

   a. See the seven spokes coming out from the second rim.

   b. See the rim around them.

   c. Then try to see the three together in different colors.

To the degree you are able to use your visualization or creative imagination, to that degree you are putting your mind in order. Even if you are only partially successful, it is good and it is very beneficial for your health.

Now start the fourth one.

a. Radiate seven rays from the fourth circle.

b. Build the last rim.

c. Visualize all five circles and their rays in different colors. Try to see them all at once.

5. Visualize yourself as being a flame in the center of these concentric circles and say OM five times, radiating a blue light toward all five fields of the circles and beyond to Space.

   OM. OM. OM. OM. OM.

6. Feel your body or chair. Touch your face with your palms and open your eyes very slowly.

The formation and fluctuation or changing of the symbol indicates the corresponding conditions of your mind. If you have conflicting currents in your mind, the symbol will not stay in its proper shape. It will change its color or form. Some parts will be clear, some diffused, but it will still create a better condition in your mind.

Later the group or the individual can do various experiments with this symbol. For example, the first wheel will turn clockwise, the second counterclockwise, and so on. Then you can see the symbol as a cone or as a funnel. Complicated revolutions of the wheels going in different directions can be added.

Always start from the center whenever the symbol fades away. Regarding the color, it is up to you to choose your own color for the rays and circles. But let us remind you that if you find the right colors in relation to each other, you can have greater results. Just as music has its own laws, there are laws of color. This means that certain combinations can create harmony while others create noise.

The law of harmony also exists in color formations. We sometimes use the right colors instinctively and receive great benefit. When this is the case, we are probably ready for an inflow of energy. If we do not use the right colors, we are not ready for an inflow of energy, which is a safeguard for us.

Visualization takes place on the electromagnetic field formed between the pineal gland and pituitary body. It is also related to our Ray type. Certain Ray types will have difficulty in visualization, but by persistence they can succeed.

Through visualization one can handle energy on the mental, astral, and etheric planes. Through visualization one can concretize energy and build forms in etheric, astral, and mental matter.

Sometimes people have cracked their etheric body and need to bridge or patch it. If they are left unpatched, some unpleasant forces flow through the cracks and contaminate their system.

Such gaps can be bridged through visualization. For example, you can suggest to a person that he visualize a sphere of light around his body, and if you see that in certain areas of his body he cannot visualize the sphere, you discover that these areas contain gaps or cracks. These cracks can be patched with an easy technique. You suggest to the person that he visualize building a bridge over the gaps and make it more and more substantial. If he has difficulty in building, then he must visualize that you are building it for him; thus he is cooperating with you in the building process. In this way, through visualization, the proper matter is brought from Space and changed into etheric matter to patch the gap.

Visualization gives you an opportunity to control your mind and create harmony within it. Sometimes, when you visualize a stick and you see that it is fluid, changing shapes and colors, it means that you have no control over your mental plane or mental substance. For example, if you are painting with some kind of color that is spreading like ink on blotting paper, you cannot create the form you want. A similar thing happens on the mental plane, and you cannot hold the object of your visualization steady. It flows away. This is a sign that you need to exercise your mind more in order to master it.

Sometimes you may feel pressure or tension while you are visualizing. The reason for this is that you are straining your muscles, rather than concentrating your mind. Concentration of the mind must start after total relaxation of the muscles. If they are not relaxed, your visualization will be weak, even dangerous to your body.

Through visualization you can direct energy, creating peace, harmony, understanding, and so on. Visualization is closely related to the science of energies. Energies in the higher realms are put into activity and direction through visualized forms. As your mind is organized with proper symbols, so your life will be similarly organized due to energies and their harmonious inflow into your system.

Let us remind you that the colors with which you visualize are related to the vibrations of your vehicles and, most interestingly, to the tonality and note of your voice. Every different vibration creates a different color or hue in your subjective vision. Those colors that have some painful association for you do not appear, even if you try to visualize them.

E. A Visualization to Put Your Mind in Order

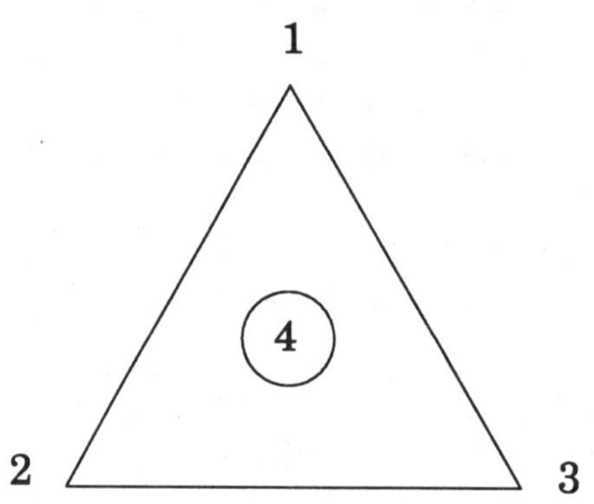

Diagram 41-2 Symbol

1. Visualize yourself as number 1, and try to see numbers 2 and 3.
2. Visualize yourself as numbers 1 and 2, and at the same time try to see number 3.
3. Then try to become numbers 1, 2, and 3, and watch number 4.
4. Then become number 4, and watch numbers 1, 2, and 3 on the triangle.

This exercise should not take more than three to four minutes. This is a very good visualization exercise which puts your mind in order and affects your aura constructively.

Often the mental body is dislocated. Dislocation occurs in sudden shocks, fears, disillusionments, depressions, and in various failures and losses. A dislocated mental body only occasionally obeys the will aspect of the man. The dislocation must be repaired before clear visualization is achieved. If the lens of your camera is dislocated, it is difficult to focus it. It is the same with the mind.

Through this triangle exercise you can gradually cure the situation. When you clear and focus your mental body, you can have right thinking. Your aura becomes stable, vibrant, and magnetic. Such an aura synchronizes itself with higher and greater centers and brings deeper wisdom and spiritual revelations. The condition of the mind not only affects the aura but also the senses. The senses are very important. They must be in their optimum state of clarity to be able to use the incoming energies properly.

F. A Visualization Exercise

1. Visualize a sphere of yellow light around your head. This is the mental body.

2. Visualize a sphere of silver light around your body. This is the astral vehicle.

3. Visualize a pure violet sphere around your body. This is the etheric vehicle.

4. Visualize a golden sun above your head, and see how the golden rays are penetrating into these three spheres and washing away all hindrances.

When these three vehicles are flooded with light, they will not react to outer negative conditions and will not create inner disturbances in the spiritual flow.

42

Psychic Energy in Healing

One can improve his health by having trust in his own psychic energy, trust in his own Solar Angel, and by developing thoughts of health about himself in his mind.

Psychic energy can be transmitted by direct suggestion to the human soul through the mind.

Direct suggestion is a soul-to-soul contact. The human soul at the time of crisis or sickness identifies himself with the conditions of the body and suffers with the problems of the body. To release the soul and give direction and energy to him, direct suggestion is used and, through the suggestion, psychic energy is transmitted. Thus, involuntary or forced acceptance of conditions by the soul is destroyed and the integrity of the soul is reestablished.

Psychic energy transmitted through suggestion to the soul makes the soul reevaluate his attitude or release himself from his "sleep" or identification. Suggestion made to the elementals of the bodies may conflict with the karma of the human soul. Thus, to suspend the soul in order to reach the elementals is a violation of the law of the soul.

Those who are exercising suggestion must have psychic energy. Psychic energy can reach the soul despite accumulated barriers in the mental, astral, and etheric bodies of the person. Suggestion without psychic energy does not reach the soul but creates eventual conflicts and disturbances in the threefold mechanism of man.

In cases when the soul is suspended as a result of accidents and cannot reach his mechanism, psychic energy transmitted through suggestion by an advanced Initiate can help the human soul re-engage himself with his mechanism and begin to repair it. *Let us not forget that the human soul has all potentials in him; the suggestion is done only to reactivate and engage him with his mechanism.*

Sudden shocks can separate the human soul from the body. Intense fear, acting as an escape mechanism, can also cause separation.

It is possible to reach the soul of the subject through direct suggestion. The brain of the subject may not respond, but that is not a problem. The human soul will receive the suggestion and in most cases return to his responsibility.

The average hypnotist is not aware of psychic energy. One does not need to hypnotize a person to pass a suggestion to him. If the hypnotist has psychic energy, he does not need mechanical procedures; through suggestion he can contact the soul of the subject and put him into action if karma allows him to do so.

Suggestion, if done by an Initiate, is very powerful. But in such a suggestion, there is no imposition and it does not violate the karma of the person. Posthypnotic suggestions are a direct violation of the karma of the person and the law of the human soul. For example, if one is smoking cigarettes and the hypnotist wants to help him stop smoking, he will put the person under hypnosis and tell him, "You will no longer desire cigarettes, and every time you take one in your hand you will reject it."

But direct suggestion uses the following procedure: The person making the suggestion will first visualize in his mind the subject free from the habit and then, directing psychic energy through his suggestion to the soul of the person, will say, "You can conquer that habit because you know you do not need it."

Hypnosis imposes action on the bodies and the soul. The soul, through identification with the personality, was carrying a posthypnotic suggestion in the form of the habit. Now he will abandon the habit but will follow the command of the hypnotist. The hypnotist has not released him, and the person is still subject to a command.

With direct suggestion, without hypnosis, there is no imposition but an affirmation that the human soul does not need to subject himself to the habit of smoking, and, because of this awareness, the soul will control the habit of smoking. Direct suggestion cannot help karmic conditions and alleviate them, but it strengthens the soul and makes him act intelligently, with courage and joy in his karmic conditions. Our karma increases if we fight against it, but it exhausts itself if the soul cooperates with the karma.

Hypnotism suppresses the outpouring forces which then try to find other channels through which to manifest. Hypnotism tries to prevent the payment of karma.

Master Morya, speaking about hypnotism, says,

> *...The weakest hypnotist can compel one to experience the effect of drowning. He can even order one to die on a definite date. Such cases have been recorded.* [1]
>
> *Even under hypnosis people rarely speak about the Subtle World. An earthly will cannot force one to say anything about the Subtle World....* [2]

---

1. Agni Yoga Society, *Community*, para. 168.
2. Agni Yoga Society, *Brotherhood*, para. 157.

The Subtle World mentioned here refers to the higher mental and Intuitional Planes.

Hypnotism can be used for crime; it can be used to exploit people and make them slaves for selfish and separative interests. It can make a nation act like sheep and manipulate it for the interests of a few. It can destroy the urge for freedom. Through hypnotism one can take away the identity of a person and lead him into actions he never dreamed of doing.

Through hypnotism you can make people work against their own survival. You can lead the human soul into the labyrinth of materialism and make him reverse his path of evolution for a long time. Through hypnotism it is possible to lead people into insanity, obsession, depression, and suicide.

In writing about the importance of suggestion, Helena Roerich made the following statement:

> *Suggestion, if applied with force for the purpose of gain [self-interest], is not only interference in karma but is plainly criminal.*[3]

Suggestion applied for self-interest is a criminal misuse of the energy contained in the suggestion. Misuse leads to the danger of obsession. It increases the tendency to dominate and exploit other people and violate their will. For all these and other reasons, the practice of hypnotism must be prohibited except for scientific research.

Hypnotism can be a very dangerous weapon in the hands of those who are walking on the left-hand path.

To protect people from the attacks of hypnotism, they must be awakened into their birthright of freedom. It is very difficult to hypnotize a person who is awake and wants to keep his free will and not subject himself to the will of other people.

Hypnotism can be practiced under many covers: through advertising, through subliminal methods, through propaganda, through religion, and through education. Hypnotism creates fools, especially if it is practiced with wrong motives.

If suggestion is done in silence using thought waves, the conscious mind of the subject may not record it, but his soul registers it and uses it. In hypnotism these two factors — the conscious mind and the human soul — are bypassed, and the command is directed to the elementals of the vehicles. As a result of this hypnotic state, when the soul returns and re-engages himself in the mechanism, he will have an internal conflict; he will not understand why things work differently and will try to change them into the previous condition. This will create tension and pressure which will be the cause of other problems.

---

3. Agni Yoga Society, *Letters of Helena Roerich*, Vol. II, p. 29.

Hypnotism is only safe in the hands of a high degree Initiate who has the power to see through the three vehicles; who has the power to contact the records of the karma of those whom he wants to serve; who has the purest motives; who understands the complexity of the mental mechanism. An Initiate has the power to insulate his bodies at the time of practice and not infect people with influences that will not be helpful to them. In these cases, hypnotism can be used as a psychological surgery to put the person's mechanism in order and to remove things which prevent the health and creativity of that person.

But when one develops his skill in hypnotism, the temptation to misuse it is so great that it is possible to develop a huge ego with mountains of vanity. The most curious thing is that when one has all the qualities of an Initiate, he does not need to use hypnotism at all because he can do his psychological surgery through suggestions, through psychic energy, or through the use of his pure willpower. For an advanced Initiate, hypnotism is an obsolete tool which he does not need to use at the present time for present-day human beings. Humanity now needs far more advanced techniques than hypnotism.

In the future, hypnotism will be replaced by another technique, which may be called *the technique of contact with greater realities on higher planes*. As man achieves greater contact with higher centers and higher planes, he can attain things through greater awakening instead of through sleeping. Instead of submitting his will to the will of a hypnotist, he can submit his personality to the Divine Will within himself and achieve greater success without violating his nature or inviting great danger to his evolution.

One must realize that every human being is constantly under the flow of hypnotic suggestions, and he is constantly acting them out. One cannot avoid this fact. Especially in moments of pain, great excitement, illness, or great success, one momentarily transfers his consciousness out of the body or focuses it in the astral and lower mental spheres. These are the moments in which posthypnotic suggestions from various sources penetrate into our bodies. This is why it is so important to stand guard, not only to prevent ourselves from planting posthypnotic suggestions in others when their consciousness is asleep to a certain degree, but also to protect ourselves from those who consciously or unconsciously plant hypnotic suggestions into our minds.

The ancients strongly emphasized *watchfulness*. They wanted their disciples to develop wakefulness and to be conscious. It is only in such states of mind that one can prevent the flow of posthypnotic suggestions and control his own expressions.

It will be almost impossible for a person to be himself if he is constantly under the influence of others. Evolution directs us toward freedom and toward self-realization.

Suggestion does not need verbal formulation. A glance, a gesture, an exclamation, a smile can transmit the suggestion and psychic energy. But the most powerful suggestion is built through intense visualization which carries psychic energy.

The operator, the one who uses suggestion, can visualize things the way he wants them to be and then make a direct suggestion. For example, "You are healed. Depart in peace." The operator can do this if he never doubts the power of his suggestion.

What is the difference between receiving a suggestion while one is asleep and while one is fully awake? The difference is that when one is sleeping, the suggestion bypasses his conscious mind or does not have the permission of his soul. On the other hand, when one is awake, he has his free will to accept or reject the suggestion. The soul is in gear, and the mind has its power of discrimination.

Hypnotism is imposition, while suggestion is received by acceptance or agreement, and with the permission of the soul. After a hypnotic suggestion, the subject is unaware of the suggestion, which operates in his house as an independent entity, while in suggestion nothing is hidden and the man is always aware of the suggestion and consciously appreciates the effect of it.

The Solar Angel uses suggestions through dreams, visions, and other psychic experiences. If the man understands the suggestions, he finds the right path and the path of health and happiness. The Solar Angel also impresses Its suggestions on the brain of the person and watches the responses.

Suggestions may come from persons around us, from higher beings, or from higher spheres, and they create certain responses and reactions from our vehicles and centers. Generally, those who are in spiritual training are advised to be very cautious in making suggestions. The reason is that a suggestion carries a certain fiery substance and the energy of willpower, and those who receive it without being ready to contain these elements can be burned and damaged by them. Before making a direct suggestion, one must see, feel, or know that the other person is in a receptive state and can contain the energy and make a favorable response. Much damage is done through suggestions if they are not done properly.

People think that suggestions can be done only to human beings. This is a limiting concept. One can make suggestions to animals, plants, birds, or to any living form. One can make suggestions to invisible beings, to the lives who form his own bodies, to spiritual builders or to destroyers.

It is possible also to use suggestion with inanimate objects. You can contact and relate to your furniture, the articles you are using, your clothing, your shoes, or even utensils and tools. You will be amazed how these articles respond to suggestion.

Through such a practice you sharpen your power of observation, learn the secrets of the technique of suggestion, and build a favorable atmosphere around you in which living forms, beings, and objects cooperate with you and help in your creative labor.

Many people project their anger, dissatisfaction, complaints, and curses through their suggestions. This creates an unwholesome atmosphere around them and leads them into conflict and failure. Respectfulness toward the whole life and gratitude to all opens the gates of joy, health, and prosperity.

In suggestion we have willpower, psychic energy, and the exact diagnosis of the condition. It is stated that those who want to use suggestions must be at least physicians or Initiates of a high degree. It is also stated that one must not attempt to heal infectious diseases by will and suggestion, although one can radiate psychic energy.

In the Ageless Wisdom we are given another method to heal certain conditions. It is called "the command of the will." This is different from hypnotism or suggestion. The command of the will dissipates some force formations in the vehicles of man which act as push-buttons and make the man a victim of their activities. The command is directed to the human soul to enable him to take action; in the meantime the force formation is hit by the command making it easy for the human soul to overcome it. The command of the will can cure alcoholism and many other vices of the flesh. Also, it can cure the tendencies to crime.

The command must be given with full power by an Initiate Who possesses willpower. The command must be direct and amplified with solemnity, decisiveness, and a tonality of voice which will carry to the man the conviction that the command cannot be avoided. It is possible also to use suggestion and the command of the will together to cast out entities who are possessing people and leading them into various crimes.

When a suggestion or a command of the will is artificial, pretentious, or done without faith and trust in oneself, it is very dangerous and may create conditions in which the possibility of a future cure is prevented.

One must know what suggestion is and how it must be done. One must know what willpower is and how it must be directed by a command. One must know what psychic energy is and how to project it outward. All this cannot be learned through schooling and lectures but through spiritual achievements and transformation of one's life.

These sciences are taught on intuitional levels, and we must qualify ourselves to penetrate these planes and learn the techniques. The techniques will unfold themselves within us and release an abundance of wisdom to use them correctly. Intuitional levels are available to those who demonstrate in their life pure striving, intense meditation, readiness to serve and sacrifice, and strict discipline of speech. These techniques do not yield themselves to money, self-interest, or titles.

The most important element to have is psychic energy. No one can drill a well of psychic energy within us. We must be ready and sensitive to release it from our own Core and accumulate it from Space.

Psychic energy is a condensation of fire in Space. As water is a liquid fire, so psychic energy is an electrical current, a flow of fiery substance. Because of its essential fiery nature, it repels certain destructive fires and assimilates or absorbs the "fiery surplus." As one can penetrate a burning forest protected by the water from fire hoses, in the same manner one can penetrate the planes of fire or spheres of fire protected by psychic energy.[4]

Certain fiery emanations from people or fiery emanations from luminaries are spread in Space. If these emanations are not assimilated by people, they cause fiery suffering. Only people who have psychic energy can assimilate the fires in Space or balance the power of these fires. Thus fire meets fire.

A person's health is affected by auto-suggestion. One can improve his health by having trust in his own psychic energy, trust in his own Solar Angel, and by developing thoughts of health about himself in his mind.

There are many people who think they will die young or they will have a bad sickness or a life of suffering. Most of these thoughts are imported suggestions and impressions from other minds, or even traces of memories from previous lives; the person often has no reason to think negatively about his health and success. But anyhow he does, using auto-suggestion in a negative way. Thus auto-suggestion eventually becomes a powerful posthypnotic suggestion and controls his life.

Instead of using auto-suggestion in a negative way, one can think optimistically, with trust and confidence, that his health is going to improve, that he is going to live long enough to serve and help people, and that all healing power is within him. Such a trust creates immediate effects on the health of the person, and in a short time great improvement can be seen not only in the body but also in the psychology of the man.

Think optimistically. Have trust that you are going to make it; you are going to stay healthy. It is your right to be healthy, to be joyful, to be successful, to be creative.

Trust that you have a great warrior within you, and often he will defeat your obstacles and hindrances before you are aware of them. Trust that all around you there are thousands of healing devas who can repair your body and repair your subtle bodies. Trust that in the darkest hours a beam of light will shine, and at the edge of the abyss you will see the presence of the protecting hand.

There is an energy which can be used for healing purposes. This energy is a combination of three fires:

— Life

— Love

— Light

---

4. See also *A Commentary on Psychic Energy*.

But the quality of love is superimposed over the other two. It is possible to increase and condense this love energy through meditation and sacrificial service and then direct it to people who need healing. This energy is highly equipped with a power which is called the *automatic ability to discriminate the situation and, within an awareness of karmic conditions, the decision to direct the right voltage of energy.*

M.M. speaking about heart energy says:

> *...Do not confuse the heart's energy with external magnetism and so-called hypnotism. Both of these manifestations are artificial and, hence, temporary. The heart's energy is not applied forcibly, but it is to be transmitted by contact with the current. If, prior to all physical means, the physician and the patient would simultaneously think about the energy of the heart, in many cases the reaction would be instantaneously useful and healing.*[5]

The heart energy is the part of psychic energy channeled through the heart center. The same energy can be transmitted through different centers, but the source is psychic energy.

Heart energy not only heals but also creates right motive in people with whom it comes in contact. It inspires them toward the right direction in life and enables them to renounce paths that are not approved by the standards of Beauty, Goodness, Righteousness, Joy, and Freedom. Heart energy also awakens the man to the existence of the Plan and the Purpose.

There is also a power which is called "thought-creativeness," or *creativity through thought.* In advanced esotericism thought-creativeness is considered superior to hypnotic command, which is sometimes translated as suggestion.

M.M. says,

> *...When We spoke to a certain sahib about permeating his dwelling with Our Aura, We naturally had in mind thought-creativeness, and not suggestion, which We willingly leave to petty hypnotists.*
>
> *Thought-creativeness is far more powerful than any suggestions. First of all, suggestion is transitory; it strikes the aura and creates karma, whereas thought-creativeness saturates the aura and does not interfere with independent action. In fact, space saturated with thought-creativeness concentrates the fiery power. The inviolability of karma remains one of the subtlest conditions of all. To give, to assist, and even to guide, without*

5. Agni Yoga Society, *Fiery World*, Vol. I, para. 53.

> *infringing upon the personality — this is a difficult task. Each one must confront this solution. Thought-creativeness, devoid of self, provides the way out of these labyrinths. Kindness, cordiality, and cooperation likewise help, but the fog of unsteadiness is a particularly poor guide.*[6]

Thought-creativeness is the ability to provide a most bountiful garden of flowers of ideas, visions, and knowledge, and leave people free to sublimate and elevate themselves in the aroma, color, and sound of beauty.

Thought-creativeness is the condition in which you provide creative thoughts, beautiful thoughts, thoughts of success, striving, daring, and courage and fill your room, your office with such thoughts. You can even send these thoughts to the locations where you want to present an opportunity for people to be inspired by your thoughts. The important point in thought-creativeness is that you do not impose either yourself or your thoughts on anyone, but you create an atmosphere of sunshine and beauty, with a pure, detached attitude.

On higher fields of service one does not use hypnotic commands or even suggestions. M.M. referring to this fact, concludes,

> *Indeed, the leaders of the spirit do not practice suggestion nor hypnotism, and great faith in Hierarchy is not illusion but the life of the Subtle World. The manifestation of followers and pupils is a consequence of the magnet of the spirit of the Hierarch....*[7]

---

6. *Ibid.*, para. 135.
7. Agni Yoga Society, *Fiery World*, Vol. III, para. 58.

43

Evening Exercise Before Sleep

After you change out of your daily dress and wash your body, sit in a quiet place at your home in a relaxed position and do the following exercise with concentration and visualization.

First Step:

Say the following:

"May the light in Cosmos illuminate my mind

and purify my thoughts."

Visualize a beam of light flooding your aura, bringing light into your mental sphere and transforming all those thoughts which are negative, separative, destructive, and ugly.

As you do this day after day, you will notice that your thoughts will engage in a fight against the incoming light because the light will expose and force them out of their hidden spheres. Such a fight is necessary in order to see exactly what condition your mental sphere is in. Continue your exercise and you will see that gradually you will cleanse your mental sphere and develop a new way of thinking.

People have an inclination to hang on to their negative and ugly thoughts, feeling that their sense of identity or ego will vanish if they get rid of these negative thoughts. People build a self-image with their vanities, with their negative, destructive, and ugly thoughts, and they do not wish to get free of these thoughts because they nourish their ego.

Second Step:

Say the following:

"May the love of Cosmos purify my heart."

Visualize a stream of love pouring into your aura and purifying your motives and emotional attitudes. Let all negative emotions go. Hatred, grief, fear, jealousy, greed, ill-feelings — you do not need them because they are dangerous for your health and are hindrances on your path of success.

Everyone must purify his mind and heart before sleep if he wants to enjoy the wisdom of the Higher Worlds.

See the energy of love transforming all your emotional nature, and stand in a pure golden light.

Visualize your mental aura and your emotional aura in harmony and rhythm, breathing in light and love.

Third Step:

Say the following:

> *"May the energy of constructive and creative fire*
>
> *purify my etheric and physical body."*

Visualize a violet colored energy purifying your etheric body of maya crystallizations and restoring its harmony and the good circulation of vitality. Visualize your whole body tuning in and harmonizing with your etheric body, correcting any disturbances in any organ or part of your body. See your body as energetic, healthy, and beautiful. See how light, love, and energy radiate out of your aura in a great magnetic field. Feel a deep joy within all your being, emotions, and thoughts, and let the currents of joy flow out of your aura in all directions.

Fourth Step:

Visualize a globe in Space, and see it surrounded with webs of light and love energy, and say the following:

> *"Let peace penetrate into the hearts of men and*
>
> *manifest as goodwill and right human relations.*
>
> *Peace, peace, peace to all spheres."*

Sound the OM three times, and go to sleep after totally relaxing your body.

After such an exercise you will enter into higher spheres and share the light and love energy and peace of higher spheres. Keep a diary and note in it your dream experiences and also any changes happening in your life.

44

Dreams

Through the scientific study of dreams, our race will find the path leading to higher sources. It will find the thread leading to higher planes, and it will see the first glimpse of the dawn of Immortality.

Dreams are a means of communication with the world unseen, with the subjective and supermundane world. This is the world which is not recorded by our five physical senses.

This world has many dimensions. After we sleep we usually enter the etheric plane. Then we pass on to the astral, mental, and higher planes if we have the appropriate vehicles to travel to higher spheres. Each sphere has its own

— Inhabitants

— Laws

— Events

— Turbulences

— Way leading to higher spheres

I. Inhabitants

Let us first take the *inhabitants* on the *etheric plane*. On this plane we find many trapped discarnate souls. This is the closest sphere to the earth and to the life on earth.[1] Many of the inhabitants are those who passed away through committing suicide. They usually stay on that plane the number of years they were going to live on earth had they not committed suicide.

Those who passed away in wars are instantaneously crowded into the etheric plane and are in great confusion and agony. Most of them are not aware of what happened to them, but they know that their life is different from that on the

1. For more information, please refer to *Other Worlds*.

physical plane. Often they are full of revenge, hatred, and passion, and they continue their fight on this plane in a continuous nightmare.

Most of the war dead obsess or possess those who led them to war or those who fought against them, or sometimes those who fought with them in order to encourage and increase their revenge and hatred against their enemies. Many of those who return from wars physically unharmed have deep troubles in their psychological systems and are never the same as before. War not only destroys bodies but also paralyzes the human psyche for a long time.

On the etheric plane are also found those earthbound people who are tied to the earth through their possessions, hidden treasures, or attached relationships. They wander around those living on earth who are deeply attached to material forms and other living beings attached to others to enjoy their etheric or emotional emanations. Often they try to possess living beings just to satisfy their own cravings for material objects, possessions, and positions.

On the etheric plane can also be found many kinds of beings who are called nature spirits, or devas of mountains, rivers, flowers, and trees.

The inhabitants of the *astral plane* are made up of many who are out of their bodies through sleep or because they left their bodies in death.

There are also astral corpses in that plane.[2] These are the astral bodies of those who left them behind and passed into the mental plane. These corpses degenerate and create various problems in the astral plane. Decomposing astral bodies can even create a bad odor if they come in the vicinity of our homes as a result of some sort of association.

You can also meet on the astral plane the phantasmagoric forms created by human imagination, by the deceased or living astral entities, or created by some tragic movies depicting human emotional life. The astral world is full of astral forms which last a few days or degenerate and disappear into other forms without cessation.

On this plane, among the changing colorful forms of human imagination and desire, you can also see the activity of the dark forces. They appear grey and dark. Their duty is to keep people on this plane busy with their desire life and to make them continue to run after the reflections of their physical desire life. On this plane a wish is a form, a desire is a deed, and people are caught in their created forms as in the arms of an octopus.

Most of the dark forces enter into the astral corpses immediately when the human entities vacate them. In this way they cover their identity and mislead astral or physically alive people.

In the first case they mislead the astral friends or relations of the astral corpse. In the second case they come in contact through dreams with the living people who are asleep. In the dream they give many messages, covering their intention

2. See also *Breakthrough to Higher Psychism.*

with half-truths, and thus mislead people. Or they come in contact with physical people through mediums. Most of the "guides" of mediums are those dark forces who, having the astral bodies of astrally dead people and being specialized in their particular field of interest, try to mislead the victims of mediums.[3]

Most pseudo prophets, channels, and mediums contact dark forces living in the astral plane. These entities are extremely clever and persistent, and they try to utilize any means to inject their poisons into the veins of living people in order to arrest their evolution. Sometimes they even know how to cover their diabolical activities with an artificial radiance.

Those who are out of their bodies and visiting etheric or astral spheres meet all these various phenomena, plus the emotional dramas, tragedies, and comedies of their own lives. If a person can bypass the etheric and astral planes by the power of his unfolding mind and spiritual orientation, he may save himself from many troubles.

After sleep you may penetrate into the *mental plane*, which is a world of its own. You see there the mental formations of all those events which are in the process of manifestation, actualization, or objectification. You can see some Teachers or senior disciples who conduct group meetings to instruct people in the art of thinking, planning, and creativity.

On higher planes you can see advanced scientific, psychological, and philosophic work going on continuously. Students in and out of incarnation attend these classes, just as they attend our colleges and universities.

On the other hand, there are a large number of distorters in the mental plane who use the illusions of human beings and try to impress upon people, who are as yet new in the mental world and can easily be deceived, their own interpretations. On this plane you sometimes witness great battles between forces of light and forces of darkness who fight using the force of thought power. Sometimes Great Ones can destroy an army of evil forces with one arrow of a thought.[4]

People do not realize that the mental plane is often a field of battle where the future of the culture and civilization of mankind is decided. Great Ones continuously emphasize the need for right thinking, cultivation of a thought life, meditation, concentration, and contemplation. When a disciple passes away, his thoughts and his power to think, meditate, concentrate, and contemplate will be his greatest shield, protector, and weapon through which he will pave his way toward higher planes and inspire people on earth with dreams, ideas, and visions.

Anyone who knows how to have pure thoughts is a future soldier in the Army of Light.

---

3. See also *Other Worlds*, Ch. 37, and *Breakthrough to Higher Psychism*, Ch. 8.
4. See also *Other Worlds*, Ch. 24.

On the mental plane there are the mental devas, Solar Angels, and Initiates who serve the Plan. They bring inspiration to the mental population from higher spheres. They appear as fiery beings. You can also find on this plane thoughtforms that are projected from higher sources. These thoughtforms are treasures for the future development of the human mind.

There are also millions of thoughtforms projected from living or mental beings. Some creative artists stay for a long time on the mental plane to plan for their future creativity on the foundation of a more intelligent approach — a creativity that is not only beautiful and meaningful but also useful and helpful for human evolution.

It is very interesting to know that on these three planes you see many animals, birds, and flowers built of the corresponding substances of the planes. Advanced animals such as whales, cats, horses, elephants, and dogs appear on the lower mental levels. Other animals can be seen on the astral levels, such as bears, lions, and tigers. On the etheric plane you see some snakes, gophers, wolves, and other types of animals.

All these planes are the fields of our dreams, and our dreams are formed by the objects and events in these planes and by our reactions and responses to these objects and events.

Above the lower mental plane you rarely see any animal forms, except if they are intentionally created for certain reasons.

II. Laws

Each sphere has its own inhabitants, plus its own *laws*.

The Etheric Plane Laws are

— The Law of Economy

— The Law of Right Relationship

— The Law of Rejection

The Law of Economy is the law of right use of energy and matter. The Law of Right Relationship is the law of influence, reaction, and response through which striving and progress are inspired and service is challenged. The Law of Rejection is the law of right discrimination, right choice, and right adaptation. Through these laws the entities living on the etheric levels are instructed to find their way, either to the astral plane or toward the proper incarnation.

Those who can penetrate into these planes can use these laws and liberate many souls.

The Astral Plane Laws are

— The Law of Attunement

— The Law of Formation

— The Law of Detachment

The Law of Attunement is used to attract the proper guidance on the astral plane. One must raise the level of his beingness or frequency to attract higher frequencies. The Law of Formation is the law by which every desire, every wish, every aspiration takes form in astral matter. Our voice and words immediately become visible with certain moving and living forms which either obscure our vision or form the steps of a ladder for our ascent.

The Law of Detachment is the law by which the human soul keeps himself aware so as not to identify himself with the existing and ever-forming phantasmagoria of astral life. Using the Law of Detachment, the human soul throws away his astral vehicle and all those phenomena which are attached to it.

The Mental Plane Laws are

— The Law of Synthesis

— The Law of Creativity

— The Law of Control and Mastery

The Law of Synthesis is the law of seeing unity in diversity and the law by which diversity is used for a unified purpose. The greatest difficulty on the lower mental planes is diversity. Diversity prevents the development of focus, and without focus and concentration one cannot proceed to the higher mental plane.

Dark forces create diversity and separatism and try to prevent synthesis.

The Law of Synthesis is used on the higher mental plane to create not only focus but also *certainty* and *clarity.*

The Law of Creativity is the law by which the Divine Plan is formulated into blueprints for the coming events on earth. This is done in advanced classes where the energies of the Rays are properly used. Timing and conditions are taken into consideration, and transmitters are carefully chosen to project through them the creative currents into the minds of men.

The Law of Control and Mastery is the law through which the mental entity, whether an inhabitant of the mental plane or visitor from earth, not only learns to control energies coming from higher sources and forces active on the mental plane but also controls and masters the power of the thoughtforms. This is the mastery through which he can penetrate into the sphere of the Intuitional Plane.

Only a few people, in comparison to the multitudes on earth, can penetrate into the Intuitional Plane. We are told that in the Intuitional Plane are located the Ashrams of the Great Ones, and it is where the great disciples and Initiates further Their education and purpose in the light of the Seven Rays and in relation to the seven fields of human endeavor.

III. Events

Each sphere has its own inhabitants, its own laws, plus its own *events.*

Etheric level events

The etheric plane reflects all that happens on the physical plane. The inhabitants there find it very difficult to isolate themselves from world events.

In the physical body we can cut ourselves off from many events occurring on the physical plane, but on the etheric plane this is very difficult to do. Our astral body on the etheric plane is always agitated or excited by the happenings of the earthly plane. The confusion is multiplied because the astral body is involved not only in earthly events, but also in the events happening on the etheric plane where powerful forces, urges, and drives are constantly active.

There is a third factor of confusion on the etheric plane because higher events from the astral and mental worlds are constantly reflected on the etheric plane. The journey of the entrapped human soul becomes very difficult, and we are told that the suffering of the human soul on these levels is great.

There are also bright phenomena on the etheric levels. Ceremonies and rituals of various kinds create beautiful configurations on this plane and often awaken and encourage souls to advance further on the path.

Life is a unity. We share everything, and as we evolve we become conscious of our sharing and strive to offer a greater gift to all. Actually the greatest blessing that one shares with others is the unfolding Divine Presence in his heart.

Astral level events

These originate from our fears, hatreds, anger, greed, jealousy, desires, and glamors. These seven are the most influential actors in the astral plane. In the astral plane we have the entire dramatization of these forces.

We have also distorted reflections of the mental and Intuitional Planes which, if taken as realities, will mislead us and create many complications in our life. For example, on the astral plane is reflected the movie of our past reincarnations, distorted and mixed with the millions of movies of the lives of other beings. Once we tune to these films, we think that they are the movies of our past lives, and we create certain thoughtforms about them and crystallize them on our mental plane. Such a crystallization is very dangerous because it controls our present and future life and misleads us; a film that belongs to others or a film that is mixed with various events gains control over us and directs our life.

This is how we begin to build our future on the wrong blueprint. Those who are reading past lives, those who lead people to contact the memories of past lives, do great damage to their victims.

In our dreams it is possible that we will come in contact with various events and often identify ourselves with them and translate such events through our wishful thinking.

There are great and continuous activities on the astral plane. A group called the *invisible servers* enters this plane after going to sleep and helps people find their way to higher planes.[5]

Mental plane events

On the higher mental plane, many groups are busy with various ideas and planning various goals. Many groups and individuals are busy studying the laws and principles of building thoughtforms and the effects of thoughts upon the three worlds. There are advanced classes especially on politics, education, psychology, and finance. There are also classes where one learns how to destroy superstitions, prejudices, and fanaticism.

Those who are astrally oriented cannot penetrate into such classes, and they come back into incarnation with their old dogmas and doctrines and cause additional troubles to the security of humanity.

On the lower mental plane occur events which have originated from the sense of separatism, prejudice, superstition, illusion, and selfishness.

One of the obstacles to progress through the mental plane is *egotism.* All negative events on the mental plane rotate on the axis of egotism.

All the events occurring on these three levels are recorded consciously or unconsciously by the etheric brain and eventually penetrate into the physical brain. These recordings affect our life at least eighty percent of the time. People do not realize that most of our life events are reflections or echoes of the events going on upon the subtler planes.

Intuitional Plane events

The Intuitional Plane is like a bright and clear sky in comparison to the chaotic and turbulent sky of the lower planes. On this plane are events connected to solar and galactic influences. The great Ashrams of the Chohans with their Initiates are extremely busy penetrating into the domain of the Solar Purpose and formulating It into laws for the kingdoms of our earth. This planning is carried out under the influence of the Seven Rays and through the seven fields of human endeavor, such as politics, education, communication, arts, sciences, religion, and finance.

On the Intuitional Plane you see the ideal forms of cultures and civilizations and the developing potentials of human beings. You can also see those who

---

5. For more information on this subject, please refer to *Other Worlds*.

penetrate into that plane through their contemplative meditation and are able to enjoy the beauty of the Intuitional Plane and return inspired, enriched, and purified to spread right human relations, goodwill, and wisdom. These are the only means by which humanity can be led from darkness to Light, from the unreal to the Real, from death to Immortality, from chaos to Beauty.

All these events can be contacted and translated as *dreams*. Dreams are the recordings of real events or mixed events, through a clear or a confused mechanism of communication.

IV. Turbulences

Each sphere has its own inhabitants, its own laws, its own events, plus its own *turbulences*.

Turbulences on the *etheric plane* are caused by physical plane wars, revolutions, strikes, natural disasters, epidemics, famines, civil disobedience, atomic radioactivity, pollution, and the destruction of the animal and green life of the planet. Great turbulences in etheric matter occur when forests are destroyed and animals are wiped away in massive quantities.

Most people register these turbulences not only in their dreams but also through their health and state of consciousness.

Astral plane turbulences are caused by organized crimes, depressions, hatred, and revenge. Many of these turbulences are registered through our dreams and sensed in our life through our nervousness, irritation, and by the resulting ill health, pain, and suffering. Because of the turbulences on the astral plane, people cannot record the rays coming from the Intuitional Plane. The Intuitional Plane is the plane of guidance, and the astral plane is the mirror which can reflect the Intuitional Plane. When the astral plane is in turbulence, the guidance is lost in chaos and man is left without protection.

Dark forces, knowing this, create conditions in which people are irritated, hateful, revengeful, greedy, and unstable. It is through such turbulences that man is cut off from the source of wisdom and direction.

Another cause for astral turbulence is a petrified heart. When a man's heart is petrified, he becomes a victim in the hands of destructive forces.[6]

All these astral disturbances affect our dreams and our sleep. Our brain cannot recharge itself during sleep and, as a result, begins to develop various complications.

Turbulences on the *mental plane* are caused by actions originated by insanity, separatism, egotism, vanity, pride, and also by electrical storms of hateful thinking, drugs, and mental obsession.

---

6. See also *The Flame of the Heart.*

Turbulences also occur on the mental plane when powerful thoughts are projected from higher spheres or centers and meet resistance in the mental crystallizations. Cyclically these projections occur to speed the progress of humanity. But the majority of human beings experience great turbulences and confusion in their lives because of their mental crystallizations and attachments.

Mental disturbances seriously affect our dreams and, through our dreams, our lives. Let us not forget that dreams are a form of communication, and communication to a certain degree is a fusion. Earthly currents mix with mental currents, and the result is either turbulence or a new expansion of consciousness.

Turbulences on the *Intuitional Plane* operate differently. On the Intuitional Plane, Cosmic winds and electromagnetic storms are registered, not as turbulences, but as opportunities for major breakthroughs.

V. Way Leading to Higher Spheres

Each sphere has its own inhabitants, laws, events, turbulences, plus its own *way leading to higher spheres.*

Our etheric body has seven senses, seven centers, and the three doors which lead to the astral plane: the head center, the heart center, and the solar plexus center.

Our astral body has seven senses, seventy minor centers, plus counterparts of the etheric centers. The two doors leading to the mental plane are the heart center and the head center.

Our mental body has seven senses, four centers and a mental unit, and one door leading to the Intuitional Plane — the Mental Permanent Atom.[7]

From the Intuitional Plane to the Atmic Plane there is no particular opening because the Mental Permanent Atom and the Intuitional and Atmic Permanent Atoms form a united field of fiery energies, and all information from these planes is available to all planes once the human awareness is focused within that fiery electrical field, which in esotericism is called the *Spiritual Triad.*

Your dreams are related to you in the following ways:

1. To your own past, present, and future activities and goals

2. To the activities of others who are related to you

3. To the activities of those with whom you have a certain affinity

4. To the events of the world

5. To the guidance coming from your Inner Guide or from other sources

---

7. See also *The Psyche and Psychism.*

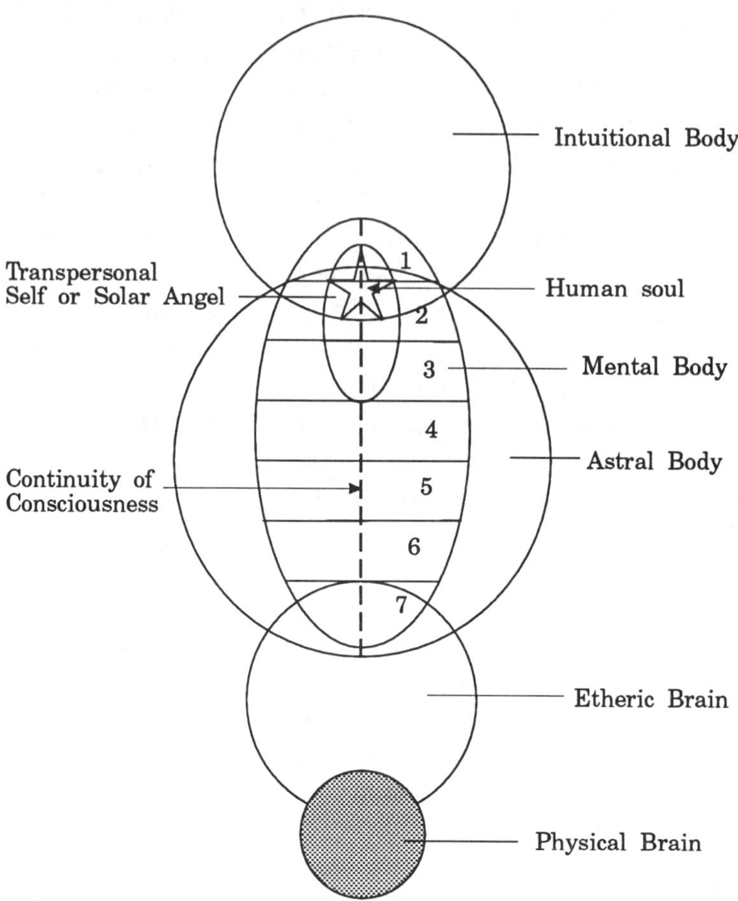

Diagram 44-1 The Mechanism of Dreaming

Note that the etheric brain is in contact with the astral, mental, and intuitional bodies via the mental body. The brain can register all that is going on in higher spheres through the etheric brain.

All our vehicles are in the process of formation and change. This means that the conditions of their corresponding spheres continuously change.

After sleep there are five possibilities for the human soul:

1. He may enter into the etheric sphere and remain there.

2. He may enter into the astral sphere if he has an astral body and either stay there or pass into higher spheres.

3. He may enter into the mental sphere if he is developed mentally. He may stay in the mental sphere or pass into higher spheres if he has higher bodies.

4. He may enter into the Intuitional Plane and be active there.

5. He may enter into higher spheres through his own right to enter, or be led by his Teacher.

In all these cases the dream is clear if the vehicles are pure and the senses are developed in the astral, mental, and higher vehicles.

Another important factor is the focus of your consciousness. Where you focus your consciousness determines where your clear registration is found. If your consciousness is focused in your physical nature, you will have difficulties registering higher impressions and translating them accurately.

The impressions collected by the senses assume meaning through the focus of consciousness. There is your astral sphere, or your astral body with all your desires, glamors, emotions, and the astral objects of your desires. Also, there is the astral world in which the world as a whole lives and moves.

There is your mental sphere, or your mental body with all your thoughts, thoughtforms, illusions, etc., and also the mental world in which most of humanity lives. The mental sphere and the mental world, like the astral body and the astral world, are divided into seven sub levels. Four of these sub levels in the mental sphere are called the lower mind. Three of them are called the higher, or abstract, mind.

Then we have the etheric brain which registers impressions from the astral body and the astral world, from the mental body and the mental world, and even from the intuitional body via the mental body. The intuitional body is in contact with higher spheres and with the three lower bodies of man — if the continuity of consciousness is established between the lower and higher mind.[8]

In the mental body one can see a star; that is the symbol of the human soul. But the consciousness of the human soul is not necessarily focused on the first, second, or third mental levels. Actually, this is very rare. Most of the time our consciousness is focused in our physical body, our astral body, or in advanced cases in the lower mental plane. Only an Initiate's consciousness can focus itself on the higher mental or Intuitional Planes.

In the diagram above, the line going through the mental body is the symbol of the continuity of consciousness which, when built, makes man conscious of things on the astral, mental, Intuitional, and Higher Planes.

A dream is a registration of events or impressions occurring on the Intuitional, mental, astral, and etheric planes. At all times, there are activities and impressions on all planes, but you can record or register them only on the plane in which you are active. If your senses are active on a given plane one-hundred percent, your

8. See *The Psyche and Psychism*, Chs. 46 and 47.

dreams will be recorded as actual events. If your senses are active only twenty to thirty percent, you will dream, but your dreams will lack clarity and unity.

Your vehicles must be mature and your senses active to have better registration. For example, if your astral body is refined and mature, your consciousness will function on the higher astral plane and be in contact with the higher levels of the astral world. If your mental body is advanced, your consciousness will work on the higher levels of the mental plane and register higher information, or record higher impressions coming from higher levels of the mental world.

If there is registration during your sleep in your brain consciousness, you are having a dream experience. If there is no registration, there is a contact but there is no dream.

There are *negative conditions* which must be avoided if we want to have better dreams. These conditions are

1. Negative physical conditions which chain us to the physical plane.

2. Negative emotional conditions which chain us to the emotional or astral plane.

3. Negative mental conditions which prevent entrance into the mental plane. But if by chance we enter higher planes, we see everything through the glass of our fears, anxieties, worries, base thoughts, etc. and sometimes are violently kicked back into the physical plane.

4. Sleeping in hospitals, asylums, or motel rooms where low-level, painful imagination, planning, and conversation have transpired will disturb our sleep to a considerable degree. Because of physical, emotional, and mental disturbances, the core of our dreams will be distorted, as if we were seeing a flower reflected in agitated waters.

VI. Sources of Dreams

We divide the sources of dreams into seven sections:

1. Dreams caused by higher forces

2. Dreams as the effect of physical, emotional, and mental conditions

3. Telepathically transferred dreams

4. Dreams caused by outer conditions such as noise, odors, movements, wind, storms, etc.

5. Dreams caused by past memories

6. Dreams as a result of our aspiration and dedication toward future glory

7. Dreams caused by massive thoughtforms

1. *Dreams caused by higher forces*. These are mostly guiding dreams. They are the result of projected thoughtforms coming from our Inner Guide, from Angels, Devas, Great Ones, Solar and Galactic Intermediaries, etc. Those Forces Who guide human destiny periodically send thoughtforms to the people of the earth to speed their evolution and to organize their lives in harmony with the Divine Will.

Such thoughtforms create various dream responses in people in different stages of evolution and evoke in them an urge to progress and strive for higher values. Some great movements to improve the life on earth in various fields of human endeavor are direct results of such dreams.

These great helpers are advanced Beings Who guide the destiny of humanity despite the denials of millions of people. These Beings are interested in our evolution. Some of Them are from our humanity; some of Them are from the different evolutions. No matter who They are, They want us to keep on the path of perfection.

If we see our children close to river rapids or about to fall into an abyss, we try to save them. We say, "Hey, stop! Turn back! Follow the other path!" And if they listen, they save themselves.

These great Beings do the same thing. They do not force Their will. They do not violate our karma. They do not expect more than we can do. But through dreams and visions and teaching, They guide us...if we want to be guided and do not refuse Their guidance. The history of humanity is full of such guidance.

Impressions coming from higher sources reach our vehicles continuously, but the average man cuts himself off from higher impressions during the daytime, and during sleep he cuts himself off from the impressions coming from the five senses. In both cases, the higher and lower impressions are always there. It is through the focus of consciousness that one or the other field of impressions is neglected.

At the present, the majority of human beings are focused in their emotional or astral consciousness. This is where the average man usually goes after he leaves his body in sleep.

Impressions coming from astral, mental, and higher sources pass to the etheric brain, and there they are registered during sleep. Immediately when the man awakens, the etheric brain engages the physical brain and passes the registration to the physical brain. This is how man in his physical consciousness remembers his dreams or his contacts or experiences.

It is possible that for some reason the etheric brain does not engage the physical brain. At that time, man in his physical consciousness does not remember his dreams, but he remembers them when he enters into higher planes.

For example, a mental experience that was not registered by the physical brain can be remembered on the astral and mental planes.

Actually you are active in your sleep for about three to eight hours daily, but you remember only one or two short dreams. Most people do not recall in brain consciousness their life on subtler planes. However, some people see it, and they witness their activities and record them in their dreams.

2. *Dreams as the effect of physical, emotional, and mental conditions*. The state of the physical body affects our dreams. If the body is sick or uncomfortable or going through certain strains, these conditions reflect in our dreams.

The state of our emotional body has a great influence on our dreams. Sometimes our dreams are direct reflections of our emotional life — with its glamors, desires, aspirations, failures, and successes.

The state of our mental life also has a very great influence on our dreams. Usually it is the mental conditions that bring all the physical and emotional elements together and characterize them with certain colors and certain meanings. The mental conditions act as a magnet to polarize the physical and emotional elements. In certain cases, if the emotional vehicle is in great agitation, it runs the show; but, again, the direction of the dream is controlled by the mental conditions.

Physical conditions provide the elements of the dream. The emotional conditions create the coloring and movement of the dream. The mental conditions provide the direction and significance of the dream.

Thus each dream can be analyzed through these three elements.

Many dreams that we dream in the astral plane have no connection with us at all. These dreams are just events which we witness, like the accidents we see on the freeway. By trying to relate them to our life, we mislead ourselves. Sometimes through pity and fear we even identify ourselves with the person in our dreams and assume that the dreams are related to us, but in reality there is no relation at all.

As we develop our astral and mental senses and exercise detachment, our dreams become clearer.

3. *Telepathically transferred dreams* are not rare. A person with a strong charge can transfer his thoughts, emotions, and imagination telepathically to many people who are in tune with him. This is how similar dreams are experienced by many.

It is possible to dream a dream and later to broadcast it intentionally or unintentionally while one ponders on the dream. Let us remember that people share the space with us on all planes, especially on the mental plane. Thus one can render a great service to humanity by trying to broadcast pure thoughts and great dreams.

4. *Dreams caused by outer conditions such as noise, odors, movements, wind, storms, etc.* Such elements, through the Law of Association, create various dreams according to the content of the human mind and emotions or even aspiration. For example, a wind in the window will make you dream about a military attack, a disaster; or it may create a dream of a symphony, or a dance; or it may create a dream of pine forests.

The factors involved in the creation of dreams are

a. the stage of evolution of the human soul

b. psychic elements in the aura

c. immediate urges or goals

Let us also remember that not only earthly conditions but also the conditions in the solar system and galaxy affect our dream life.

5. *Dreams caused by past memories.* It is possible that past memories which have been strongly impressed on our mind show themselves in our dreams again and again with multiple variations. There are also locked memories within us which occasionally escape the security measures of our conscious mind and manifest as dreams.

If our consciousness is advanced, some of our past lives manifest, mixed with present associations. Such dreams are not rare, and often we lose our present personality as we dress ourselves in the image of an old personality that we had centuries ago. If the personalities conflict, we will need mental care.

Deposits of memories often find release in our dreams. When our memory deposits are released, they mix with the events occurring on certain levels. The memory deposits are located within our permanent atoms, in our Chalice, and also temporarily in our cells and atoms. All these deposits, in certain cycles or conditions, release some sealed memories through association or because of necessity. Nature periodically releases accumulating inner tensions by letting some memories escape through dreams.

Certain memories from the Chalice give us great inspiration. The accumulations in the Chalice are the collection of experiences of achievements and heroism. Dreams can form through such released memories.

6. *Dreams as a result of our aspiration and dedication toward future glory.* Through their imagination, people form future images for themselves. One thinks he wants to be a Holy One, a great leader or a humanitarian, a hero, a saint.... Year after year, the particles of such aspirations crystallize and build the dream.

Sometimes such dreams, when not balanced with our real progress and transformation, suddenly capture us and we lose the reality in our life and begin to play the role of the image of what we were dreaming. Usually when such aspirations are produced by healthy thinking and accompanied with striving and discipline, they transform our lives gradually, and we eventually embody the image toward which we were striving.

Such dreams are not rare, and they give us hope for the future and inspire us *to be that which we are in our essence.*

Through dreams we can come in contact with the Inner Guide. It is true that the Inner Guide is always watching us, but if we uplift ourselves and try to communicate with the light of Its wisdom, we gain greater beauty and energy to live a better life. Such a conscious contact is made through meditation, or in our dreams, if we have the proper preparation and right to do so.

Free from the troubles of the body, free from the agitations of the emotional world, free from the barriers of the lower mind, the human soul can come in contact with the Inner Guide. This contact is registered first as a dream, but as the experience continues, man notices that he is having a real contact with a source of wisdom and beauty. This is the beginning of the experience which is called Soul-infusion or the marriage in heaven. Great creative inspirations and guidance are given to the human soul by this creative Center in the human being.

When people learn how to sleep, they will *awaken* on higher planes. When people are awake on higher planes, they will not go into sleep, but they will go to bed and rest their bodies. When people are not awake on higher planes, they are always asleep, even if they think they are awake.

In the creative experience some artists can transfer their consciousness to higher planes, tune to the beauty exposed on these planes, and formulate it into their art. This is similar to dreaming, but it is consciously controlled and worked on.

Often the Inner Guide tries to align, integrate, and transform the man's expressions through high-level inspiration. A lecture is sometimes a period of intense training in which the Inner Guide tries to make the man register Its impressions and express them through his own words. The Inner Guide releases core ideas and thoughts into the mental plane, and the speaker almost instantaneously picks them up as available sources of information and delivers them through his speech.

The training continues for a long time until the human soul finds the way to use the inner treasury of the Chalice and, via the Chalice, to tap greater and more inclusive sources of wisdom.

7. *Dreams caused by massive thoughtforms.* These massive thoughtforms are built through propaganda, advertisements, television, radio, publications, and speeches. Millions of people are affected, and strong impressions contribute to the building of group thoughtforms.

These thoughtforms are often mixed with various elements or are solo thoughtforms. They live and move in Space and, like a satellite or a news station, influence our dream life. Many dreams are the result of such massive thoughtforms which may have no foundation in our life nor the right of existence at all.

Dreams of any kind affect our life and affect the life of the planet as a whole. Every dream is a condensation or crystallization of a force of some kind, and this crystallization exists in Space and affects human life.

People think that they are not responsible for their dreams. Man is responsible and eventually will be conscious of this responsibility. Not only his actions, words, and emotions but also his thoughts and dreams have a tremendous effect on human life, for good or for bad. The esoteric Teaching warns us to keep the pool in which we swim clean; to keep our air clean because all of us breathe it; to keep the Space clean because we live, move, and have our being in Space. The day will come when we will realize that we are either condemned or promoted through our dreams.

Before you enter into sleep, you must observe the rules given in the chapter on sleep.[9] One of the rules you must never forget is to raise your consciousness through the concepts of

- Timelessness
- Infinity
- Space
- Future
- Transitoriness of life on earth

You may enter into sleep thinking about the above concepts through visualization or creative imagination. These concepts will help you uplift yourself easily into the subtle and fiery spheres of the Higher Worlds and attract beneficent forces around you.

There are four phases in the registration of dreams:

1. Contact with the existing impressions as far as your equipment allows
2. Dramatization of the impressions, associating them with your past experiences and future dreams or through revelations from higher sources
3. Registering or taping of the dramatization with your etheric and physical brain
4. The analysis or conclusion of the registration

9. See also *Other Worlds*, Ch. 20.

The third phase is very crucial; it needs a clear physical brain and a serene etheric brain. If the brain is not clear and if the etheric brain is in agitation, your dreams are like the reflection of trees in an agitated river.

The analysis of your dreams must be reached by your own Intuition, experience, and logic. Do not depend on common symbols and their interpretations. Every person is unique, and every one of us must interpret his dreams independent of ancient symbols.

The events on higher planes impress our etheric brain more clearly than the events occurring on lower planes. The higher our consciousness goes, the deeper the registration on the etheric and physical brain. Also, if the consciousness of man is active on the higher mental levels or in the Intuitional Plane, he can bypass the interferences of the astral plane and register the impressions clearly on the etheric and physical brains.

Our lower mechanisms are more sensitive and pure if we are focused on higher planes. One cannot reach higher planes without purifying his lower vehicles. Also, the higher we go, the greater our shield against the distortions coming from lower planes.

Regular, daily meditation is an effort to penetrate higher planes consciously and gain control over the mechanism of the planes. Meditation is also a means for the purification of our aura.

When we sleep, we are forced to go where our urges, drives, glamors, and illusions or our aspirations, intentions, and visions lead us. If you are entering sleep through blind urges and drives, you will probably be drawn to levels or places where your urges and drives seek satisfaction. Or you will draw yourself to all those who will satisfy your urges with their load of urges and drives. You will be accompanied by those who have similar urges and drives, and all these experiences will be dramatized as dreams.

When you go to sleep with your desires, cravings, hatreds, fears, anger, greed, and jealousy, you will attract phenomena related to your conditions, or you will be led to those spheres or places where similar emotions are violently active. Your greed for money, for example, will take you to those who are full of greed and those feelings which nourish greed.

If you sleep with cravings for sex, you will very probably be drawn to those spheres where you will find satisfaction, or you will experience total rejection due to different associations with sex life. Your craving will lead you to different positions in the astral world, and there you will have all that you want to have.

The astral world is a self-formative world; every desire and emotion is an object. You may attract so many objects of your desires that they literally possess you and fundamentally upset your life. Of course, you can also have lofty aspirations and dreams which will lead you to higher levels of the astral plane where there is much beauty.

When you enter sleep with great mental focus or interest, you will be drawn into those spheres where there are similar interests. These interests range from organized crimes to the most lofty interests to help humanity and serve the Divine Plan. Those who are service oriented are drawn to one of the human endeavors:

— Politics

— Education

— Philosophy

— Art

— Science

— Religion

— Finance

There are thousands of groups and thousands of thoughtforms related to these fields. During dreams the human soul on the mental plane learns, experiences, and renders great service on one or several fields of human endeavor.

In our sleep, we not only go to the subjective centers of our interest, but we also go and relate ourselves to the objective centers of our interests, relating ourselves to the thought world of those who are actively working on the physical plane.

Our dreams are also affected by the massive thoughtforms existing in Space. When people broadcast their thoughts and build thoughtforms through creative imagination or visualization, these formations go and accumulate in Space according to their frequency and objective.

The nature of these thoughtforms is various. Some of them are of very high order and available only to a few. Some of them are average and available to the masses. Some of them are ugly and degenerative and are surrounded by pollution and evil intent.

In our dreams, we come in contact with such formations. Sometimes a picture in our mind creates a connection, and we come in contact with the formations in a sudden shock. Or we may come in contact over a longer period of time and register these contacts as dreams. Usually we come in contact with these massive thoughtforms through the thoughts that we contributed to build the massive thoughtform further.

Our thought world relates us to one of these massive thoughtforms which affects our daily life and especially conditions our dream life when we contact it in our sleep.

It is also possible that you dream the thoughts of others.

During your sleep you have the opportunity to do the following:

1. Meet your Inner Guide

2. Meet your Teacher

3. Meet your co-workers

4. Become aware of the Divine Plan

5. Learn how to live in Beauty, Goodness, Truth, and Joy without the sense of separatism

6. Clean the causes of future troubles built by your thoughts, emotions, words, and deeds

7. Confront people and encourage them to strive and advance on the path of perfection

There are many people who have lost their beloved ones. Those who are on the subtle planes and those who are on the physical plane need comfort. If you are conscious on the astral plane, you can organize a meeting between those who have lost each other and explain the situation. For certain reasons people may not be able to contact each other, and they need someone who knows how to arrange such a contact. Some of the reasons for the inability to make contact follow:

1. The intense emotion of missing each other may become a barrier.

2. The departed one needs to adjust his consciousness and understand the situation of death.

3. The imaginary agony and fear that persist in the departed one can be a barrier.

4. Former unpleasant karmic relationships reveal themselves and build a barrier.

5. Certain past misunderstandings grow out of proportion in their consciousness and force them to repel each other.

6. The basic intentions of their lives lead them to different levels or different directions.

7. The real level of beingness of both parties leads them to different planes.

8. Former lies and behavior based on hypocrisy and exploitation can form a barrier between the living and the "dead."

9. The damage done by past attachments and "love" can form a barrier between two persons.

10. "Love" based on selfish interest creates repulsion on subtle planes.

11. Barriers are also built when one is far ahead in his evolution and passes on to higher planes.

One who is conscious on subtle planes can possibly arrange a meeting between two parties, overcoming the obstacles and helping them confront each other and free each other from the ties of grief and anxieties.

In sleep, it is also possible to guide people to the right doctor, the right place, the right person, the right job, as far as their karma allows.

People often do not remember the service they render in subtle planes.[10] They live two different lives, but as their evolution proceeds, the two different lives lived on subjective and objective levels unite and become a continuation of each other.

There are many kinds of dreams.[11] They are as follows:

1. Dreams as a result of physical conditions

2. Dreams as a result of registration of events on the astral plane

3. Dreams as a result of psychological conditions of people associated with you

4. Dreams as imposed dramas from dark forces

5. Dreams as causes in the process of manifestation

6. Dreams as reactions (astral and mental) to events taking place on higher planes

7. Actual happenings on any of the three planes

8. Disciplinary dreams

9. Dreams as the result of guilt

10. Dreams as the result of aspirations and desires

11. Entertaining dreams

12. Creative dreams

13. Test dreams

---

10. For information on invisible helpers, see *Other Worlds*, Ch. 6.
11. *The Psyche and Psychism*, Ch. 31.

14. Challenging dreams

15. Dream experiences of the past

16. Dreams of astral plane actualities

17. Instructive dreams

18. Dreams reflecting higher events

19. Healing dreams

20. Dreams preparing us to face or meet a difficult situation

21. Revealing dreams

22. Daydreams

23. Series of dreams similar to each other

There are other kinds of dreams. The first category of dreams may be called *guiding dreams* through which one is guided on:

- Where to go
- Where to stop
- What to eat
- How to heal himself
- Whom to marry
- How to escape certain dangers
- What to read
- How to speed his evolution
- How to lead people into the right direction

When we consider the thousands of guiding dreams, dreams that help us grow and improve, naturally we want to ask, who is guiding us? No matter who is guiding us, certain things are clear:

— He knows the future.

— He knows us and the conditions related to us.

— He is able to communicate with us.

— He loves us.

— He has superior intelligence.

— He is watching us.

— He is not forcing us.

— He wants us to evolve and be healthy and beautiful.

Who is he? Is he the one who lives within us and in many traditions is called the Inner Guide? Is he our Master? Is he an angel? Is he the one we worship? Who is he?

Whether we know him or not, he knows us, and one thing is certain — he exists.

People sometimes think that it is the subconscious that guides them. Most people do not clearly understand what the subconscious is. It is clear that merely having questions does not automatically create answers unless there is someone who provides the answers and extends his help.

Guiding dreams are clear proof that some intelligence higher than we are exists within or around us. Guiding dreams often reveal to us higher mysteries about man and the Universe. They reveal scientific discoveries and formulas and expand our consciousness to higher dimensions.

Guidance can be better followed and understood if people cultivate their mind and keep it open to higher possibilities. Without a developed intellect and an expanding consciousness, one can easily fall into the traps of prejudice, superstition, or fanaticism.

Here is an example of a dream:

A man neglected his regular daily meditation for a while. One day he dreamed that he was sitting with two men and one man was asking the other, "Is it necessary to do meditation regularly everyday?"

The other man, looking at the one who was dreaming, said, "What do you think?"

And the dreaming man began to explain and say, "It is very important to do regular meditation because it is cumulative. If you miss one day, the link is broken and the accumulated psychic charge disappears. Then you must start all over again."

After awakening the man remembered what he had said to the two men in his dream. It was an instructive dream dramatized in such a way that the subject, through his own words, advised his own self to do regular meditation.

One wonders how such instructive dreams come into formation with such artistic and intelligent dramatization.

There are many dreams which can mislead people if the intellect is not exercised and pure reason is not used.

There are also dreams fabricated by dark forces which build a thoughtform of a dream and project it to you as an active drama while you are on subtle levels. Such dreams usually lead you to self-hypnotism, failures, and ill health. They may complicate your daily life and create vanity, pride, or depression. We call such dreams *psychic attacks.*

The second category of dreams may be called *revelatory dreams*. These dreams reveal the future. They reveal the consequences of your thoughts, words, and actions. They reveal your past lives. They reveal the causes of your suffering or the causes of any condition.

For example, a rich lady had a servant who used to work almost eighteen hours a day, but the lady used to pay her very little and showed no appreciation for her servant's labor. Her money was everything to her, and she never helped anyone. On the other hand, the servant used to help her friends and poor children with the little money that her mistress gave her.

One night the rich lady dreamed that a gentleman was taking her to a town in the mountains. After passing forests and rivers, they came to a beautiful home with excellent gardens, waterfalls, and birds.

"To whom does this house belong?" asked the lady of the gentleman.

"This house belongs to your servant."

And they continued to walk. As they were walking the lady thought, "If my servant has such a gorgeous home, what must *my* home be like?"

After passing a river they came into a valley, and they saw a little hut without a roof. The walls were crooked, and there was an accumulation of trash around it.

"To whom does this hut belong?" she asked her guide.

"That is your house."

She felt very angry and asked, "Why?"

"Lady, our future lives are built by what we do here on earth, by what we speak and think, and especially our future is built by our hearts. Your heart is poor; your servant's heart is rich, and she has the best house."

And while the lady was protesting in anger, she awakened.

The story says that the dream changed her life, and she began to help not only her servant but also many people who needed her help.

Such dreams are revelatory and have a great effect on our consciousness. One may wonder how such dreams come into being.

Another dream involved a great professor who had a private student from a very rich family. He used to teach the student various subjects without noticing any improvement in his character and consciousness. One day the professor dreamed that he was carrying buckets of water from a nearby fountain and trying to fill a basket held by his student.

The poor professor tried until morning to fill the basket, but every time he came with a new bucket of water he found the basket empty...and, complaining loudly, he awakened.

The next day the meaning of the dream was clear to him, and he no longer wasted his time and energy teaching someone who was like a basket.

There was a man sixty-five years of age who had five girlfriends and was keeping them under his control through his abundant resources of money. One day he dreamed that he had a pool in his garden, and the girls were carrying the water away with their jars until not a drop of water remained in the pool. The man concluded that the pool was his energy resource, and the girls were sapping him.

Why was the advice given through such symbols, and who gave the advice? Is it possible that he was feeling guilty for his behavior and trying to convince himself in his thoughts, and the dream was the exact reflection of his thoughts? Or was there a watcher who was projecting a warning through some symbols that he would understand?

No matter what the answer is, one thing is clear — the person involved had a clear-cut guidance and revelation.

Physical deeds and emotions produce their results. If one is conscious on the mental plane, he can see the consequences of his actions and feelings dramatized and take a closer look at his life. In all cases, there is the person who is warned by an outer agent, or by his own Self.

The third category of dreams is related to our *health problems*. A man dreamed that he was trying to pass through a pipe, but the pipe was narrowing and the man was having difficulty getting through. Six months later it was found that he had a blockage in his bowels and surgery was necessary to remove the blockage.

Another person dreamed that his car was backfiring with a big explosive noise as he was driving. A friend of his suggested he check his heart, which revealed a serious problem.

Another person dreamed that a bug was entering his brain. Later a tumor was found in his brain.

A great hero, fighting to protect some innocent people from injustice, dreamed that a fly was sitting on his forehead and he could not make it fly away. Two days later he was shot in the forehead.

One of the kings in the Middle East told his friend that his father came to him in a dream and took his coat away from him.

"What is the explanation of your dream, Your Highness?" asked one close to him.

He said, "The coat is my body. My father died long ago. Today I may be shot if security is not well organized."

In the afternoon a man shot him in the mosque.

What is the source of such warnings? Is it in man or outside of man? Does it really make a difference?

If we know how to sleep well and withdraw the focus of our consciousness to higher planes, greater guidance, greater revelation, and greater protection will be ours. As we penetrate into higher planes, we will render greater service to humanity, greater service on the physical, emotional, and mental planes. We may protect people from crimes, warning them in their dreams in dire times. We can protect them from dangers, from destructive involvements, because as we go higher we can

1. See things that are going to happen more clearly
2. Mediate higher commands to people through a language more familiar to them
3. Put them in contact with their Inner Guide
4. Put them in contact with higher guidance
5. Explain to them the consequences of their actions on these planes

Those dreams that give us *guidance*, through direct or dramatized ways, are indications that there is a factor within man which has foresight, which cares for him, and which tries to direct his steps to the right path.

Mechanical arrangements do not reveal the higher plan and purpose.

When *instructive* dreams are registered, it means there are instructors; there is an organized plan to lead man to higher dimensions. When higher instructions are received, it means that the human soul can be aware not only in the physical world but also in higher dimensions.

Dreams also show that man can penetrate into other minds and see the effects of all causes.

Certain dreams give us the experience of being free from the physical body. We call them *flying dreams*. Flying in dreams is very natural. Actually, when you leave your body in sleep you do not walk but fly. You fly on the etheric and astral planes, as well as on the mental plane, all the time. But you cannot experience it until your etheric brain registers the motion and your own experiences together.

When you are in the airplane of your mental body, you register things going on upon the mental plane, but you do not register a flying airplane. The subjective world — beyond the physical — is not registered directly by our five physical senses but by our senses in the astral, mental, and higher bodies. If the subtle senses do not exist yet, the impressions reach the brain through the subtle vehicles themselves. In this case they are very much distorted. But if the wireless system of centers, nadis, and subtle senses is built, the impressions come in exactly as they are and are registered in detail.

What helps us to register our dreams more clearly? Suggestions follow:

1. Increase your joy, especially at the end of the day.

2. Love more and be more inclusive and full of charity.

3. Do not nourish the spirit of denial. Reject fanaticism in any form or color.

4. Try to build the Golden Bridge.[12]

5. Increase your psychic energy through self-forgetfulness, harmlessness, right speech, and sacrificial service.

6. Minimize irritation.[13]

7. Cleanse your aura:

   — by rejecting any criminal thoughts

   — by protecting yourself from obsession and possession[14]

   — by rejecting vanity, lies, and hypocrisy

   — by integrating and aligning your bodies in the light of your Soul

How can one be aware that he is dreaming?
Let us look at this diagram.

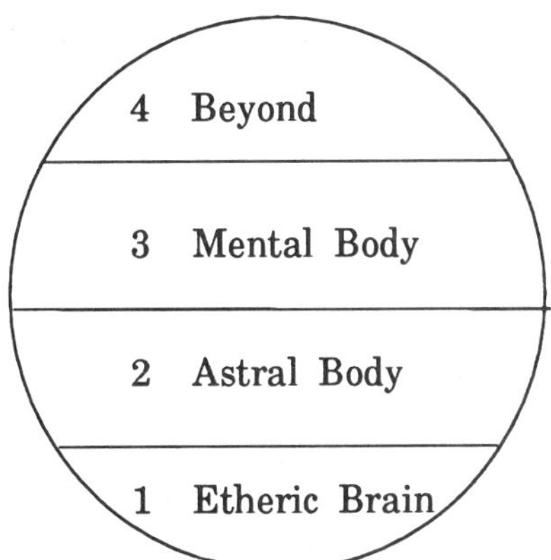

Diagram 44-2 Planes and Dreams

---

12. See *The Psyche and Psychism*, Chs. 45-47.
13. See *The Psyche and Psychism*, Ch. 27.
14. See *The Psyche and Psychism*, Chs. 32, 33, and 39 .

If you are focused in number one and registering number two as happenings or events, you know you are dreaming. When you are on number two and registering a higher plane, you are dreaming but you have no control over your dreams. But if you are on the mental plane and registering the lower planes, you are aware of your dreaming and you have control over your dreams.

For example, you are dreaming that you are falling from a rock on the astral plane. If you are on the mental plane, you control the dream, and instead of falling, you fly. But if you are on the physical-etheric level, you awaken while falling. You have no control, but you were aware of your dreaming.

What about if one is mixed up with urges and drives, with strong desires, and with intelligent interests? He will go from one to another, collecting images for his film, and at the end he has a picture which is a total mixture, or nonsense.

Why do we not remember our dreams, or why do we not dream? These conditions occur for the following reasons:

1. Sexual overspending deprives the etheric brain, which is the energy source of the physical brain. Wasting our sexual energy deprives us of certain elements which bridge the etheric brain with the physical brain. These elements are necessary for registration of the dream.

2. Gaps may be in existence between the etheric brain and the astral body.

3. If a person sleeps only on the etheric level, he is stuck with the physical body.

4. Worry, depression, and grief kill the sensitivity to higher impressions reaching the brain.

5. Certain centers of the brain may be damaged by a form of materialistic living.

6. It is possible that for certain reasons, when one enters into higher planes, the etheric brain becomes incapable of registering high frequencies coming from those planes.

It is very interesting to note that the unfoldment of the Self is equal to the development of a person's vehicles. Only the unfolding and developing of the vehicles allow the human soul to live and function on higher spheres.

Sometimes people ask why our beautiful dreams fade away very rapidly, or why we remember only parts of them. The answer is that our contact with events taking place on higher realms depends on our mechanism. The mechanism is our physical and etheric brain, our nervous system, and the mechanism of our emotions and thoughts. If we have stormy weather in our aura, the Sun does not shine long or clearly.

The same thing happens to us if we have agitation in our aura. We easily lose the impressions or receive them in a distorted way. Purity and calmness of the vehicles are necessary for better communication.

When the threefold personality is purified and transformed, the sleep experience is not the same as it was at your former level. In an advanced state, sleep is consciously entering into a new field of activity without breaking the line of your continuity of consciousness.

It was never reported that Great Ones dreamed. Christ, Buddha, or other Great Ones never dreamed because They were always awake in both dimensions. Once you are awake, your dreams disappear. Once you understand, words disappear.

Dreams are means of communication. When you make direct contact, you do not need this type of communication.

Visions are different from dreams. We see them in our waking consciousness, but on higher planes. They are sometimes thoughtforms of advanced souls consciously projected toward us. They have a special message, and a special voltage of energy.

Visions are sometimes events. Sometimes they are symbols with colors and sound. They can also be future consequences of present causes which can be seen by our Inner Guide and held out for us in our vision.

Hallucinations are the mistranslation of the events of the inner planes, due to the distorted conditions of the mind and brain, caused by various disturbances in the body mechanism. They reveal hidden causes of disturbances, and if they are manifested in waking consciousness, the subject is either possessed or loses the control of his mechanism.

It may even happen that past memory banks break out and mix with the present life and create chaos in the life of the person.

Revelations may be accompanied by a vision, or be without a vision. Revelations can be received in dreams or in a waking state of consciousness. Revelations take away the veils of the plane where the focus of consciousness is and open higher planes to the eyes of the subject. They reveal the future. They reveal the secrets related to evolution. They reveal principles and laws of higher dimensions.

The higher planes are revealed through the process of reflection or through a temporary bridge. An advanced soul, who will help in this event, will locate himself on the plane where the subject is and make him see the future events reflected in the advanced soul's being. Or he may build an antenna between the level of the subject and the level of the source of the revelation and help the subject communicate with the projected revelation.

Nightmares may be organized and planned attacks by dark forces, or they may be the results of ill health and improper conditions of sleep. Nightmares mostly occur when the subject is either on the etheric plane or trying to enter the astral plane. Some of the nightmares reveal deep psychological disturbances concealed in the person.

VII. Symbols and Dreams

We are told that there are twenty-one symbols through which greater messages are transmitted from higher sources. At the present, the most active symbols are the cross, the five-pointed star, the lotus, the torch, and the diamond.

These symbols have different meanings on different planes, or different meanings for those who have their focus of consciousness on different planes. The interpretation of the symbols is related to the level of consciousness of the person and to the position he has in society.

In the Aquarian Age, we will have another fourteen symbols, totaling thirty-five. These thirty-five symbols will be recognized as the hieroglyphic language of dreams and even for visions and telepathy. These symbols will be given in the mental plane, where esoteric psychologists or psychiatrists will penetrate and learn the language. Once this language is learned, a person will be able to determine the origin of the dream.

The first seven symbols belong to the Lemurian consciousness. The next seven belong to the Atlantean consciousness, or to the emotional or astral consciousness. The next seven belong to the Aryan consciousness, or to the mental consciousness. The next fourteen symbols belong to the Aquarian consciousness, to the future, or to intuitional awareness.

Let us not forget that although we have set symbols, we do not have set interpretations due to our

— level of consciousness

— experiences

— education

— level of beingness

— social status

— future goals

All these factors interfere, and thus the translations of the symbols vary. This will continue for a long time until the thirty-five symbols are given to esoteric psychiatrists and their meaning on all levels is explained to them.

Each symbol is interpreted differently due to its

- form
- color

- movement
- radiation

Through the scientific study of dreams, our race will find the path leading to higher sources. It will find the thread leading to higher planes, and it will see the first glimpse of the dawn of Immortality.

45

Morning Exercise

After washing yourself and before your daily meditation and breakfast, stand erect and close your eyes.

1. Visualize a small blue light in the center of your head.
2. Visualize a blue star ten feet above your head, and connect your blue light with the star.
3. Visualize streams of light pouring down into the light in your head and spreading throughout your aura in rainbow colors.
4. Visualize the light penetrating into your body and purifying, energizing, harmonizing, and healing it. Do not concentrate on any special part of your body, but visualize the whole body being penetrated by the light.
5. Still standing, sing or say in a whisper,

   More radiant than the Sun.
   Purer than the snow,
   Subtler than the ether
   Is the Self,
   The Spirit within my heart.
   I am that Self.
   That Self am I.

6. Sound three OMs.
7. Relax for a few minutes.

46

Healing and Fire

One day we will understand that all physical, emotional, mental, and social sicknesses, all distortions and confusions in the world are nothing else but the result of the violation of the Law of Love.

Part I

When Sages were talking about fire, they were referring to love. When Sages were talking about love, they were talking about the *energy* of love, the energy of compassion. We are told that God is burning fire and God is love. Everything in the Infinite Space is fire or the manifestation of fire.

As we go into spiritual realms and shift our direction from matter toward spirit and inclusiveness, love increases within us and fire increases in all our expressions.

Love manifests as creativity. Truly creative people are those people who have great love and have been deeply loved.

As we climb the ladder of evolution toward fire, we find that love, joy, bliss, and enthusiasm increase within us, since these are all parts of the one fire.

The greatest obstacles on our path are formed by those thoughts, emotions, and actions which are against love. One day we will understand that all physical, emotional, mental, and social sicknesses, all distortions and confusions in the world are nothing else but the result of the violation of the Law of Love. As soon as a person does anything against love, his conscience bothers him. His light goes out instantaneously, and he feels it.

Gossip creates short-circuits in the electrical systems of our aura and in Space which reach even to far-off worlds. Criticism, hatred, fear, anger, jealousy — these forces deprive us of our fire and change us into charcoal.

A joyful man radiates colors. When he starts to gossip hatefully, his aura darkens; the palpitating lights dim or go out, and his whole aura begins to turn grey and black.

Thus, less love is less life; more love is more abundant life. If we want to live a longer, happier, more prosperous, and more successful life, always full of joy, health, and creativity, we must work and live on the path of love.

Violation of love is the greatest crime and the greatest trap from which we cannot escape through our knowledge. Betrayal of love is the greatest transgression.

Space is fire. Fire is the Presence. The Presence is that which exists in everything. That is fire; that is love.

Whenever you do anything physically, emotionally, or mentally against fire, you are putting out your fire to a great extent. The fire of Space comes and tries to fill the vacuum in your aura, but because, through the exhaustion of fire in your aura, the corresponding centers in your various vehicles are petrified or crystallized, the fire of Space rushes into them with a great voltage and burns their petals, partially or totally, and makes them unable to function. Once the centers in the subtle bodies are burned, it takes only a short time to see the destructive result in the physical body in the form of various degenerative diseases.

Irritation extinguishes the fires of the centers, blocks parts of the network of the etheric body, and prevents the circulation of fire through that network. Irritation is mostly the result of breaking the Law of Love.

Hatred puts out the flame in the heart center.

Greed blocks the head center.

Fear damages the solar plexus and base of spine centers.

Jealousy burns two very important chest centers.

Anger attacks mostly the throat and heart centers.

These enemies of mankind are called the extinguishers of the Fire of Life.

There are five substances which kindle and inflame the fire of the centers and increase the life energy:

1. gratitude
2. love
3. joy
4. bliss
5. enthusiasm

These are the remedies of the future age for almost all diseases. They conduct the fire of Space and put the fires in man in contact with the fire of Space.

Through every movement man releases fire.

Thinking is movement.

Feeling is movement.

Talking is movement.

Acting is movement.

The emanating fire from your actions assumes various colors according to the reservoir of fire to which they are connected. For example, if your words are charged with the fire of the Intuitional Plane, they have a silvery-blue color. If they are charged from the Atmic Plane, they have red-orange colors. These colors are in addition to the individual hues of the entire person.

If your speech is negative, you damage the corresponding center, and your speech mostly resembles a fume with red flames burning up the resources of your fire.

Healing thoughts, emotions, and actions channel the fire of love which is a violet-gold fire. When fire is properly used, fire increases in the centers and in the corresponding organs. This is how love heals. One who loses fire through his ugly speech eventually lacks fire, magnetism, and attraction and becomes a failure in the world.

We are told that when a man passes away without carrying fire with him to the astral world, the fire of Space rushes into him. This is what "hell" is in reality.

There is another very interesting phenomenon which is called "exportation of red fire from the black lodge." The black lodge carries a great amount of destructive fire. This is the fire of matter, which they transmit to their agents through obsession and possession. The agent feels happy in his destructive work until the time when the members of the black lodge see that the fire in their agent is almost on the verge of exhaustion and they abandon him to his awful fate. Two great examples of this were Adolf Hitler in Germany and Enver Pasha in Turkey; they massacred millions of people and then died in extreme agony.

Fire beams out of the eyes. The eyes carry fire, either destructive or constructive. One can heal through his look. One can impart a great amount of energy through his eyes. Blessed are those who radiate love, joy, bliss, and enthusiasm through their eyes.

If you do not have fire in your eyes, you are like a car with burned-out lights trying to drive in the darkness. When the fire of your eyes is exhausted, your eye problems start. Those who are born blind are those who wasted their fire through their eyes with jealousy, hatred, pornography, and other destructive, negative motives. Our eyes will endure to the end if we continuously channel through them the fire of love, gratitude, joy, bliss, and enthusiasm.

Imagine how much negative force we direct through our eyes to others. Lies obscure our vision. Hypocrites expose themselves to many kinds of attacks. Lies and hypocrisy consume the fire of the eyes.

When the eyes are pure and rich with fire, then creativity, aspiration, striving, and sacrifice bloom within you. Your look can focus the fire of your eyes and cause healing. Your eyes can channel the fire of spirit and the fire of matter, which are both needed for the magic of healing. The eyes transfer joy, love, bliss, and enthusiasm. This idea must be repeated until it is totally impressed in our minds.

Joy clears your vision. Sadness and depression weaken your vision because they consume fire, not only within you, but also within others.

When you speak, try to channel the fire of love, the fire of truth, and the fire of beauty.

Hatred arouses the fire of matter in people and leads them into destructive actions. It consumes the fires of the higher vehicles first and then deprives them of contact with the Higher Worlds — with the worlds of reality, Intuition, and subtle values.

People become matter when they lose the fire and when their contacts with the world of living values are cut.

When your speech is full of hatred, fear, gossip, and dirty talk, you are putting exhaust fumes into your aura and polluting it. This is why vitamins will not help you replace the lost fires. Fires cannot breathe in an aura full of pollution.

Christ said that whatever comes out of your mouth is more important than what you put into it. Whatever wrong things you eat will only hurt your physical body, but when you are polluting your aura through evil talk, you are destroying or endangering your etheric, astral, and mental bodies and creating an awful future for yourself. When you damage certain centers in your subtle bodies, you must know that when you are born once again, you will come with corresponding damaged organs in your body.

How careful must a man be so that his look, his words, and his behavior always radiate love, joy, bliss, gratitude, and enthusiasm. Such a man is a great healer, a great magnet, and a pure source of inspiration.

There are motives or movements which radiate the fire of love when they express lofty thoughts and ideas, visions, and joy. There are also motives which spread gloom, depression, and fear. A handshake is a fusion. It is an electrical phenomenon. When you hug someone, there is a tremendous mixture of auras. If you are negative and lacking fire, you will sap the other person of his fire and pollute his aura.

When one sings, he can precipitate life-giving fire. When one plays music, he can radiate fire and nourish and kindle the fires of others. His fire reaches the higher centers of the audience if his song or music is channeling the fire of his own higher centers.

A song or music that is coming from the realm of great ideas, visions, and revelations or from inner fires fills Space with rainbows, flashing diamonds, and multicolored flames and flowers.

If your song or music is coming from dark thoughts, from your solar plexus and sacral centers, you will inflame these centers in others, make them consume their higher fires, and eventually lead them into a miserable state of existence. This is why people build barbed wire fences around themselves, imprison their soul, and then begin to fight and complain against the limitations of their life.

The Fiery World is the electrical Space. Concentration of mind, concentration of life on a lofty idea, causes the flow of fire.

Meditation and prayer absorb fire and assimilate it.

Contemplation is a period of fusion between the fire of mind and the fire of Intuition.

The lower etheric planes are the reservoir of the fires of matter and prana. The higher Cosmic Ethers, or our Intuitional, Atmic, Monadic, and Divine Planes, are the reservoirs of four higher fires which we call

1. The fire of enthusiasm
2. The fire of bliss
3. The fire of joy
4. The fire of love

The fire of love is actually a synthesis of all the fires and includes affection, love, and compassion.

The fire of mind is the transmitter of these higher fires to the lower ethers. When this transference is successful, eventually the lower ethers are replaced by the higher fires, and the man is called an *Agni Yogi*, a fiery being who is one with the fires of higher realms.

The mental plane must be kept pure if you want to transmit the fire and transform yourself into a fiery being. For example, if the mental plane is not polluted with degenerated thoughtforms and destructive, separative motives, a flash of the fire of enthusiasm comes through the mental body and charges all your system with fiery enthusiasm. A flash of enthusiasm brings with it purpose, vision, and revelation.

When one drop of bliss falls into your aura, you become fragrant. When one drop of joy falls into your aura, you become radioactive with rainbow colors. When one drop of love falls into your aura, you become magnetic.

Why deprive yourself of such blessings?

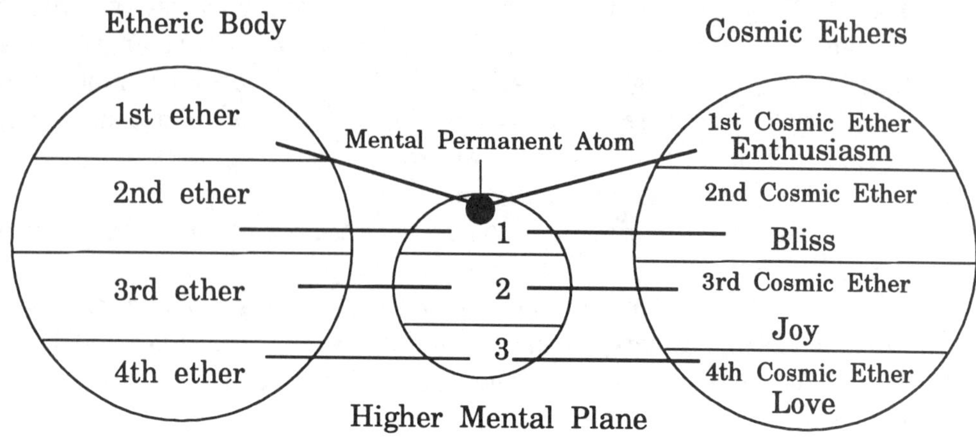

Diagram 46-1 Fires and the Etheric Body

As shown in the above diagram, the fire of enthusiasm hits the Mental Permanent Atom and rushes into the first ether and permeates the etheric body. The fire of bliss hits the first level of the mental plane and passes to the second ether and permeates the etheric body. The fire of joy hits the second level of the mental plane and passes into the third ether and permeates the etheric body. The fire of love hits the third abstract level of the mental plane and passes to the fourth ether and permeates the etheric body.

As the amount of higher fires increases in the lower ethers, man passes through the process of transmutation, transformation, and transfiguration. When the physical body passes through a process of transmutation, the emotional body undergoes a process of transformation, and the mental body enters into the process of Transfiguration, or Enlightenment. This is how the higher fires purify the person of all sicknesses, illnesses, diseases, and disorders and make him a temple of the Spirit of God.

The fire of the heart is a fused flame of all higher fires. That is why we are told that in the flame of the heart the whole existence is reflected.

Any movement which conflicts with the rhythm of the celestial bodies, with the rhythm of the heartbeat, or with the rhythm of the pulsations of your centers is a movement which lacks creative fire. Remember that the movements of the celestial bodies, your heartbeat, and your centers echo in the waves of Space and make the movements of these centers ever present in Space. Any movement that does not harmonize with the heartbeat of Cosmos or the rhythm of the Cosmic Heart does not generate fire.

The movements of Initiates and Their sacred dances are based on the law of the rhythm of the Cosmic Heart. Their chanting and movements are synchronized in such a way that They create a linkage with the Cosmic Source of fire and transmit the fire to earth — to enlighten, to purify, and to heal.

Start your day with love, joy, bliss, enthusiasm, and gratitude and continue it until you go to bed. You will see the miracle of the fire in your life and in the lives of others. Psychic energy is the ever-healing, ever-purifying, ever-creative fire, and we live, move, and have our being in fire.

Be fiery; open your centers to the fire in harmlessness, in selflessness, and in right speech, and you will turn into a flame on the dark path in the life of millions.

You can generate fire using the four techniques of love, joy, bliss, and enthusiasm. When you express love in your actions, emotions, and thoughts, you generate fire. When you express joy in your relationships, you generate fire. When you express bliss you kindle the fires of your higher centers. When you express enthusiasm you create a whirlpool of magnetic flames around you which evokes the fire of striving and spirit.

As you express fire you build closer communication with the fire of Space. We are told that the fire of Space conveys to you the highest measure of wisdom, makes you aware of the events taking place in higher spheres, and opens the path for you to Infinity. When the fire of Space accumulates in your centers, you become a radiant healer and a creative person of the highest quality.

When you do not live a life of love, joy, bliss, and enthusiasm but try to run your life on a path of hatred, gloom, cursing, and apathy, you break your contact with the fire of Space. From that moment on, the darkness grabs you and you gradually become a servant of darkness with a fearsome future.

There are two wheels in your generator of fire: one releases fire, the other cuts the circuit and leads you to darkness.

Every day, early in the morning, decide to increase your fire. The tests will come to you every moment to put your fire out or to exhaust your fire. Be careful and watchful, so that you do not shift your gear in the wrong direction.

People are used to gloomy faces. A face radiant with fire is a healing source of energy. Even our joy purifies Space and increases the life-force, the prana.

The patterns of fire existing in your aura condition the manifestation of your body. The patterns of fire in your aura come into existence through your actions, emotions, thoughts, and motives. If your actions, emotions, thoughts, and motives conduct fire, you produce fiery patterns in your aura which in turn condition not only your physical body but also your physical life.

The healing process is nothing else but an interplay of fire between a fiery aura and an aura which is losing fire and is in a state of disturbance.

In healing, you can transmit fire through your eyes, your hands, and your touch. But you must be very careful that you transmit fire only to those centers which are in need of fire. You must also know how much fire must be transmitted for healing. If a higher voltage is given to the fading petals of certain centers, you may disturb them and cause them to burn totally. This is why healers must naturally have not only higher clairvoyance but also a highly cultivated Intuition.

We must remember that values are expressions of fire. Ideas are patterns of fire. Visions are focuses of fire. When you speak about vision, you transmit fire. When you speak about the future, you transmit fire. When you are creating aspiration, you are igniting bonfires in the hearts of people. When you are creating discipline and striving, you are putting the fires in action. When you are spreading inertia, depression, and fear, you are pouring water on the fires.

Thus one must create future, enthusiasm, aspiration, and striving, and the wheels of evolution will bring greater love, joy, bliss, and power.

Our aspirations are trails of fire extending toward the future. Without aspiration and vision, one will resemble a boat about to go over Niagara Falls.

People are travelers on a fiery path toward Infinity. Often not only their path is blocked by the charcoal and ashes of past deeds, but also their fiery etheric web has many blockages through which the fire cannot circulate.

The best ways to open these blockages are through

1. Fiery striving

2. Manifesting Beauty, Goodness, and Righteousness

3. Creative efforts

These are the three main techniques through which the blockages are cleansed and the circulation of fire is restored.

Striving is the ability to concentrate and focus the fire. Whenever fire is focused, it burns and cleanses. Striving is a process of cleaning and wiping out obstacles on the pathways of the creative fire.

Living in Beauty, Goodness, and Righteousness demands a great effort, but it brings the supermundane fires from higher spheres of your nature into your environment.

Creative efforts open the channels of fire from higher to lower levels and eventually restore the circulation of higher fires in man.

Some artists have had real experiences of having their creative fire fade away when they act against the higher expressions of fire. When they put things right, they found that the creative fire again began to circulate and expand their awareness of higher values.

Thus the beams of enthusiasm, bliss, joy, and love must be focused on our vision through our aspiration, striving, and creative efforts. Only through such a focus will the striving human soul transcend himself and enter into the path of superhuman evolution.

The flame of enthusiasm is kindled the moment the human soul responds to the challenge of Cosmic labor. The flame gradually fills all his being, and the vision of the Cosmic labor leads all his actions.

The flame of enthusiasm inspires the fires of bliss, joy, and love and charges man with a greater urge for expanding service and creativity. In each creative action the presence of these fires keeps the action in tune with the Cosmic Intent.

47

Healing and Fire

Without increasing the fire in your centers and in your fiery Essence, you cannot create transmutation, nor destroy those obstacles that exist in your vehicles.

Part II

It is written that transmutation takes place through the agency of fire. Fire functions in three ways. These three functions are present everywhere and are called

1. The fire that destroys or purifies
2. The fire that nourishes or sustains
3. The fire that builds or unfolds

The fire that builds or unfolds is carried by fiery elementals, fiery devas, or fiery angels. They build the form according to the blueprint. All flowers, trees, and shrubs are the works of fiery beings. They build the form according to the blueprint to enable the expanding consciousness of the life to express itself and take part in the building of the Purpose of the Great Life.

The nourishing and sustaining fire makes the constructed form live and enables the ensouling life to manifest itself in a given period of time. This fire provides the communication between the entity living in the form and the form itself. This fire is the mediator in all forms, atoms, and galaxies.

The next fire is *the fire that destroys or purifies*. It destroys the crystallized form when the form can no longer express the intent, the purpose, the plan, and the frequency of the achievement of the expanding awareness of the inner entity. Thus the form is destroyed to enable the indwelling entity to be equipped with an advanced, more suitable, and progressive vehicle. This fire also destroys accumulated hindrances within the form itself and facilitates the circulation of the energy of Life.

The human soul, or the entity who is the owner of the human form, adapts the body to his expanding awareness and radiation through the agency of fire and through the process of transmutation, transformation, and transfiguration.

It is the fire that builds a body. It is the fire that purifies the body, causes transmutation and transformation in the physical and emotional vehicles, and eventually raises a man into the glory of Transfiguration.

Without increasing the fire in your centers and in your fiery Essence, you cannot create transmutation, nor destroy those obstacles that exist in your vehicles.

Actually, part of the role of the destructive fire is to cleanse the accumulated trash in the body, in the blood, in the nervous system, and within the etheric, astral, and mental nature and let the sustaining fire freely circulate throughout the vehicles of the human being.

These three processes of fire have been observed throughout ages and are related to all forms of existence. It is through these fires that the evolution of life continues perpetually.

These fires must be used or operated intelligently. It is very important to know that fire increases when it is used consciously and with wisdom.

In human nature we have four fires that the human soul can use for his own evolution, for his own creativity, and for the service of humanity. It is through these fires that the transmutation, transformation, and transfiguration process is carried out throughout the Cosmic journey of the human soul.

The first fire is called the *fire of love*. Love is fire. Love is energy emanating from the Intuitional Plane, or from the Fourth Cosmic Ether. The Intuitional Plane is a reservoir of energy and a transmitter of Cosmic love energy. Love is fire, or a fiery substance in the Intuitional Plane.

When one loves, he radiates fiery substance throughout his aura. Love can be received and accumulated in certain centers of man and then used as a very rare substance.

Love kindles the etheric, astral, and mental centers. Love makes the etheric body inhale in fire and exhale fire. This fire purifies the vehicles; when it reaches a certain frequency or amount in the system of man, it purifies, cures, and heals.

A kiss, a hug, or a handshake is a phenomenon of the exchange of fire. When there is no love, sincerity, and right motive, love does not flow from one person to another; the transmission of fire cannot proceed. If you hate someone but shake hands with him, there is no exchange of fire. It is like two dead wires touching each other without emanating a spark. But if you love someone and he responds to your love with his love, then the fiery essence of love builds a rainbow between you and him. This rainbow evokes or calls forth spiritual values from both of your Essences and causes blooming within your natures. Every time such people touch each other, a flash of light emanates from their contact.

Through real love you not only transmute your lower centers, but you also transform your vehicles and adapt them to the advancing life of your Essence.

As one loves more, he brings more fire and more love substance within his nature, and this increased love or fiery substance does not let the destructive elements settle themselves in his system.

People say that love is an emotion. Love is not an emotion. Love is a fiery substance. When you love, you bring into your system more love substance, and you charge and purify your physical, emotional, and mental vehicles with fire. It is through this fire that your physical, emotional, and mental centers begin a process of transmutation and transformation.

This process is like the smelting of iron ore or gold ore. Put a piece of ore in the fire, and soon you will obtain pure gold or pure iron. The gold or iron is purified, and the dross falls to the bottom of the pot.

The same thing happens when you increase the fire of love within you. It purifies your physical-etheric body; it purifies your emotional and mental bodies and liberates the human soul from those attachments which were holding him down and causing him to identify with false values.

To increase the substance of love, we must love someone — a wife, a child, a brother, a sister, a Teacher, a mother, a father, anyone — with intense love, without attachment, with pure motive, and without self-interest. Such a love generates love, generates fire, generates the fiery substance of love. Such a love will be unconditional and unending.

Part of the purpose of life-forms is to generate love, to produce love, and to bring the substance of love to this planet. That is why one must learn to love and love to the end, with the intention of letting the Inner Glory of the loved one manifest in Its whole beauty and grandeur.

To love means to transmit the fiery substance of love through the following:

— acts of sacrifice

— acts of dedication

— acts of worship

— acts of at-one-ment

— acts of service

It is through increasing the love substance that one approaches his own Essence and the Essence of others; one approaches closer to the Source from which he is emanated.

It is through the fire of love that one is able to pass through the doors of initiation. Unless one accumulates or generates within himself the energy of fiery love, he will not be able to break through the barriers of the evolutionary path, transcend his own level, enter into a higher dimension, and obtain a new level of awareness.

When the smallest obstacles on the path turn you away from the path, make you indifferent to a beloved one, make you an enemy, this proves that the substance of love does not exist within you yet. But when you strive to increase your love, you eventually make a breakthrough. Symbolically speaking, if you do not have seventy pounds of pure love, or a 5000-volt love energy within you, you will not be able to penetrate through the doors of initiation. That is why love is emphasized so much in all the Ageless Wisdom literature.

When you do not have the fire of love, you remain a piece of ore mixed with clay and other materials. This means you cannot cause transmutation in your nature, and all the efforts of others to transmute your nature eventually prove a failure.

People, through intense lovingness, channel a great amount of love to others. Those who really keep loving, in the deeper and deeper meanings of love eventually realize that they are a *wave of love*. They are love. They are the embodiment of love. Such Great Ones do not say, "I love you." They say, "*I am Love.*"

"Father, forgive them; they do not know what they are doing." These words were announced by a Soul Whose body was bleeding on the cross.

When the love energy increases in our system, an alchemical change occurs within our bodies: the motion of the atoms of the etheric body become four-, five-, six-, or even seven-dimensional. The atoms of the etheric body become intensely radioactive, and then they become astral atoms. When love increases more, the motion of the astral atoms enters a higher and higher dimension, and they begin to change into mental atoms. When love increases even more, the motion of the mental atoms enters a higher and higher dimension, and they begin to change into intuitional atoms. And when a sufficient proportion of mental atoms vibrate with the same frequency as the intuitional atoms, man enters into the glory of Transfiguration or Enlightenment.

Enlightenment is the moment when the human soul realizes that he is a drop of fire, a drop of love in the ocean of all-pervading love. It is through such a love that man brings transformation into the world.

If we did not have those Great Ones Whose lives were a radiation of pure love, we would still be in the savage stage in which men used to eat each other. One wonders how much love we will need to prevent the savagery going on in all areas of international relations. To prevent hatred, separatism, and war, we need to increase the fire of love. Love transforms not only our nature and our life but also our environment.

The Great Ones Who lived as the embodiments of love taught us how to increase the fiery substance within us and bring more of it from higher and higher sources. Actually, prayer is a way to ask for the fire of love. Religion is the bridge between man and the fiery source of love. And these Great Ones, through Their achievements, penetrated deeper and deeper into the ocean of love and brought that fiery substance to our planetary life.

Love is a substance of fire. Unless we have an increasing amount of love, we will not be able to sustain our vehicles and hold humanity together for a planetary breakthrough.

When a man is loving, he is generating love energy and, in the meantime, penetrating into deeper layers of greater love and channeling it to others. Such people not only charge their friends but also nations and continents. What a great love was brought down to humanity through Krishna, Buddha, Christ.... It is through such love that cultures and civilizations come into being. Great Ones blaze the path with Their fire, and we see, for at least one second, the Purpose of life, the North Star of our existence.

The Great Ones are great because of the great love They demonstrate. They appear like fiery comets and bring tremendous fiery transmutation into our sphere of being. Every Great One brings with Him a supply of love to endure at least three hundred years. His disciples try to increase that amount another two thousand years through their own sacrificial lives. Then a Great One, like a comet, reappears to bring a new supply of love for all kingdoms.

This first fire, the fire of love, works mainly for the transmutation process. Transmutation is a process of expanding your consciousness from one level to a higher level. Through transmutation you free yourself from lower attachments and are able to function on higher dimensions with full awareness. This is why love is needed for all progress on the Path.

St. Paul expressed the importance of love when He said, *"If I know the language of angels and know all sciences, but if I have no love, I am nothing."*

When you say, "I love you," think about the fiery substance that is pouring out of you, trying to cause transmutation in the whole nature of the one you love.

"I love you" means: "I am giving you the fire that will cause transmutation in your whole nature, and if you love me your fire will increase my fire and further help the transmutation of my nature."

A pure flow of love goes and hits seventy-seven fiery centers in your nature and kindles them.

I saw a great play once in a monastery. A man, in the form of a flaming heart, came onto the stage and lit seventy-seven candles. Years later I thought that love is the flame of the heart which sustains the nourishment of all centers and corresponding glands and organs.

Knowledge cannot change into wisdom except through the agency of the fire of love. Remember that the Masters of Wisdom are called the Masters of Compassion. One will never have wisdom without the fire of love. Love urges us to improve ourselves and our life. To improve means to be more inclusive. Improvement means to expand both vertically and horizontally. Improvement means to come closer to your essential Self.

Inclusiveness demands a greater capacity to understand, to relate, and to cooperate. The more it is called forth, the more one strives to answer the call. Inclusiveness is the ability to work on ever-expanding planes of higher and higher spheres of reality.

Improvement is the increasing capacity to create, utilizing energies and visions exposed on each stage of inclusiveness. The improving human soul, in his early stage of being, is a separated being. As he advances, he thinks and lives in terms of the whole, in terms of the fire of love.

The next fire that causes transformation in our whole nature and in society is called the *fire of joy.*[1] Many microbes and germs are carried by people who are depressed, in inertia, in gloom, or always in a negative mood, or angry, hateful, separative, and resentful. Such people are carriers of physical, emotional, and mental microbes and germs.

Experience proves that a joyful man's aura radiates a certain fire which, like a shield, surrounds the body and penetrates into the man's emotional and mental nature, thus preventing germs and microbes from penetrating into his whole system.

Joy opens the channels of energy between the personality and the Soul and transmits the fire of the higher solar plexus center to the heart center.

A joyful man also radiates love.

Joy makes you sensitive to the Plan. As you increase your joy, you see a greater goal in your life. It is only in joy that you find a real direction for your life. It is in joy that you make healthy, inclusive decisions.

Often young people come to me and say, "We do not have a goal in our life. What do you think we must do?"

I do not talk about their goals. I speak to them about joy, and often I give a certain form of meditation about joy. A short time later they call me and say, "I decided to be a lawyer, a physician, a psychologist, etc.... It works.

Aimless and goalless children come from homes where there was no joy. Instead, there was fighting, depression, or negativity.

The fire of joy purifies and clarifies the mind and thus creates more sensitivity to the Plan of your Inner Guide. Whenever you have a contact with your Inner Guide, or your Transpersonal Self, you see your goal and your destiny. It is the fire of joy that enables you to carry on your labor to achieve your goal.

Whenever a man loses his joy, he turns toward matter, and frustration traps him. A man without joy is a potential danger in society. Increase the joy of people and you will eventually annihilate crime.

Thus, joy is the expression of fire, a very rare substance which must increase in our nature if we want to come in contact with higher realities.

A symphony is the improvement of a melody due to greater inclusiveness.

Christ said, *"Rejoice! I overcameth the world."* The world, your nature, can be overcome through the fire of joy. You have increasing joy when your spirit is striving toward the future.

Faith and joy are two sides of a flaming sword. Faith is the ability to see your victory in the future. When you realize the victory which you are going to achieve in the future, that realization is your joy.

---

1. See also *Joy and Healing* for further information and exercises on joy.

Faith is the flame of joy. This flame can move mountains; mountains of difficulties and hindrances can be moved by faith. Faith is your victory in the dimension of the future. It is this victory gained in the future that appears in the present as your factual faith.

Joy increases your faith; faith radiates the fire of joy.

Joy makes you transparent, free, open, frank, direct, and clear. When you have joy, you think clearly. When you are without joy, you hide yourself behind your words, your manners, your expressions. A person without joy saps your life energy and creates darkness around you. A joyful person brings light, love, faith, and hope. Joy is a substance more precious than diamonds.

How can one obtain joy? ...Only through renouncing the objects of his identification and his vanity.

The next fire is the *fire of bliss*. The first stage of bliss is experienced through what we call ecstasy. Ecstasy is the ability to go beyond what you are. Those people who are stuck to their past and present self and its measures, to their images, identifications, and the thoughtforms of their personality, cannot reach ecstasy because ecstasy is reached in a moment of losing oneself and being fused with a greater vision of beauty. This vision of beauty grasps you like an eagle and takes you out of your former self. Sometimes this is called a true "peak experience."

The second stage of bliss is beatitude. This happens when you awaken to the reality of the grandeur of the mystery of the Universe, and you do not try to translate that experience, feeling that your translation will relate you to your former self.

Bliss is a very rare substance in the Universe. Those who have bliss are benefactors for the human race. Bliss is the panacea; it is the healing substance. It is the fire which creates universal harmony and calls forth the treasures of the Spiritual Triad to precipitate upon the person and upon his life and environment.

Transfiguration of the personality takes place through the agency of the fire of bliss, which gradually opens the greater head center and makes man the recipient of the fire of bliss. Bliss is related to the Purpose, to the motive power of what you want to be or what you want to do.

The next fire is the *fire of enthusiasm*. Enthusiasm is the king of fires in the human being. It is sometimes called the spirit in man or, rather, the God within man. In Sanskrit it is called *Raj-Agni*, the King Fire.

It is the substance of enthusiasm that opens the gates to Cosmic impressions, builds a communication network in the hearts of multitudes, and polarizes them to the same Purpose.

Enthusiastic men and women are like rivers of energy; they spread life and cause blooming, achievement, and victory.

The fire of enthusiasm not only dispels the germs of disease but also burns away glamors, illusions, and inertia and protects people from psychic attacks.

The fire of enthusiasm does not let the dark forces obsess or possess you. The fire of enthusiasm is the best tonic for the growth of the human soul.

Enthusiasm puts a human being and, in turn, all his expressions and activities into a state of resonance with the Cosmic Intent. Thus man becomes the outpost of the Divine Intent. This is the state in which the Victorious One says, *"I and my Father are one."*

Enthusiasm brings the realization that you are no longer lost in the wilderness of existence but you are now in contact with your Source, and the fiery energies of love, joy, bliss, and enthusiasm pour through you because you are fused with your Central Powerhouse. It is the fire of enthusiasm that eventually creates a conscious bond between you and the Cosmic Heart.

It is possible to awaken this fire within you. It is the fire burning within your True Self. Every time you come in contact with your True Self, you feel this fire descending to your head center and radiating throughout your aura. You can evoke this fire if you try to put all your heart and strength into the work you are doing as a service for humanity.

There are three kinds of people:

1. Those who have fire

2. Those who are in the kindling stage

3. Those who are either darkened or extinguished, as they never received fire

These three kinds of people are everywhere. Those who have fire are working for the purpose of humanity. They spread the fire of God — love, joy, bliss, and enthusiasm — and pave the way toward a glorious future.

Those who are in the kindling stage are producers of problems. They are the ones who are in a battle between darkness and light.

The third ones are the burdens, the problems of humanity. Whenever they see a flame, they pour cold water on it through all their expressions and behaviors. It is in these people that the germs and microbes multiply as they do in stagnated water.

These three stages also exist within the individual person, and the human soul must be watchful and keep the fire going. As one raises his fire, he proceeds further on the path of victory and helps all the living atoms of his vehicles to progress and enter into their next evolutionary path.

The purpose of life is not what you are now but what you are going to be tomorrow, in the future.

These four fires must be increased day after day, year after year, if a man wants to proceed toward his goal of perfection.

48

Healing and Fire

When any fire in your vehicle is fading, in any part of your nature, you have a problem there. Thinking and living in terms of higher fires sets your fires aflame and helps you to be healthy and energetic.

Part III

Man is an electrical phenomenon. The human being is a fiery coil of electricity. Life is a flow of fire, and all forms are related to each other through fire.

Form building is a process of individualization and appropriation of fire. All that man does or expresses, all his responses and reactions are a contact with fire. Fire is related to all motion.

Individualized man, the human soul, comes in contact with any object through the agency of fire. The seven senses are vehicles which are contact points with fire.

All messages and impressions are translated through fire. The body, especially the nervous system and the etheric nervous system — the nadis — is the electrical network of the inner, fiery Core to contact the whole Existence.

Breath is fire. Sound creates the most fantastic phenomena in Space if it is released by the fire of higher centers.

When you touch an object, there is an interchange of fire. Even your look flows like a beam of fire; it can heal or destroy life-forms.

All life is fire and all motion in the Universe is a dance of fire. Fire can be impressed on objects, and sometimes, according to the intensity of the fire, the flame stays impressed on an object for ten to twenty years, or even twenty to thirty centuries.

When you hold an object with physical interest only, you impress that object with your physical fire. When you hold that object with emotional and mental interest, you impress on it a greater flame. When you hold an object with your soul, with all that you are, the flame you impress on the object lasts for centuries. It is even possible to increase the fire in any object by looking at it.

Thus a man is a flame living in a sphere of fire.

People want to keep the articles used by advanced human beings. They keep their houses, furniture, musical instruments, brushes, hammers, even clothes...because all the things they used are flooded with the fire of their creative genius. In the future it will be possible to measure the fire accumulated in articles while they were used by human beings.

Loving, kissing, and shaking hands are exchanges of fire.

You kindle in others either greater fires or lower fires. Those who kindle higher fires in others through the touch of Beauty, Goodness, and Truth help their evolution or help them release greater fires from their Core.

People must begin to think of themselves as seven flames in one fire. As one changes his opinion about himself and thinks in terms of fire, his evolution will go forward with greater speed, increasing his love, joy, bliss, and enthusiasm.

Man for long ages identified himself with his body, emotions, and thoughts to such a degree that he almost thought or almost felt that he was his body, he was his emotions, or he was his thoughts, and nothing beyond. This identification can be detected in the vocabulary that contemporary man uses. He says, "I am sick, I am hungry, I hate, I am afraid, I need rest," etc. You, as the Divine Essence, cannot be hungry, cannot be sick, cannot hate, nor be afraid.

The real you does not need to rest; your body needs rest. It is your physical body that can be sick or hungry. It is your emotional body that hates. It is your mind that develops fear. You, as an essence of Divine fire, are beyond sickness, hunger, hatred, and fear because you are one with the Life in all forms.

When you are identified with your vehicles and their problems, you lose your own selfhood. You forget your *individuality* as a part of the Divine Identity. When you think that your body is your Self, you separate yourself from the Universal Whole. You build a mental fence around yourself, and you think, feel, and accept that you are a separate being. When such an attitude continues within you age after age, you build a thoughtform around you like a shell and imprison yourself in this shell, thinking that you *are* the body. And because you are identified with the body and because the body is continuously subject to changes and problems, you also become identified with the changes and the problems of the body.

This identification with the body reaches a stage where you, as a body, become the victim of various emotions and thoughts generated by you or by others.

As you advance you also identify yourself with your emotional body, then your mental body. Eventually you come to the conclusion that you are a separate existence apart from the whole that *is*. This stage is the ego stage.

An ego is a self-centered being, and it tries to use the existence as much as possible for its own ego-interest only. In this stage it develops intense selfishness and separatism. It criticizes, attacks, exploits, and acts under fear and hatred. The man himself becomes the victim of his own ego.

There are four identifications and their resulting hindrances which eventually must be overcome through striving, observation, and detachment.

In the first stage, when we are identified with the physical body or matter, we develop the first blockage in our system. This blockage is called *inertia*.

When we are identified with the emotional body, emotional objects, or the objects of our desires, we develop *glamors.*

When we are identified with our mental body or mental objects, we develop *illusions.*

When we are identified with our ego, with the thought that we are a separate being, we develop a heavy obstacle on our path which is called the *Dweller on the Threshold.*

These four obstacles are the enemies of our progress.

Our vehicles are like electrical coils: the fire radiates out of our body and flows into the fire of Space, and the Spatial fire fuses with the fires of our body. When we are identified with our body — our bones, flesh, and blood — we cut ourselves off to a great extent from the fire of Space, the all-pervading electricity of Space.

This is how inertia is created. We slowly lose our contact with the fiery rhythm of the great Nature.

Inertia is that state of your body in which the fire of your body does not flow into the fire of Space and fuse with it. You create a whirlpool of fire around yourself, and you cut off your communication with the fire of Space and stagnate "yourself" with your own pollution. When you create a whirlpool around yourself, you no longer join in the rhythmic pulsation of the Spatial fire. You then live only on the reservoirs of fire given to you by Nature which may last only fifty to seventy years.

Inertia is a physical-etheric disease because it slows down or prevents the flow of Spatial fire into your body and prevents your fire from flowing into Space. When you stop flowing into Space, you isolate yourself and awaken repulsion from the Spatial fire, and you find yourself in inertia. It is this inertia which is the cause of many diseases.

When there is no exchange and fusion of energies in a needed rhythm and dosage, the body develops various illnesses such as depression, apathy, lack of interest, etc.

Your emotions are electrical phenomena. Any time you express an emotion, your emotional electricity is in action. Feeling is electrical; you cannot develop emotions without producing a fiery phenomenon. Your emotions have their own wavelength, frequency, and intensity of color.

When you touch an object, your emotions flow into the object. If you touch an object which is heavily charged with emotion, that emotion flows into your aura without being exhausted. This is one of Nature's secrets. There is a continuous exchange of emotional fire between you and other objects, living creatures, and human beings. There is also a mutual flow between your astral aura and the planetary astral aura. If you try to insulate yourself from such a continuous exchange or flow of fiery emotions, you create a glamor.

Glamor is developed when you identify yourself with the object of your emotions and emotionally withdraw yourself into the object. You thus turn into a whirlpool of currents which flow into your astral body, into "yourself."

A glamor is an emotional disease. It paralyzes the emotional flow and exchange with the fire of Space. Friction is created when the astral body hardens through identification. When an emotion turns on itself and identifies with the object of the emotion, you have glamor. Glamor is the root of many emotional evils; touchiness, nosiness, hatred, greed, jealousy, anger are all like ulcers in the emotional body.

Your thoughts are electrical in nature. Your thoughts must flow outward instead of being self-centered, separative, and negative.

There is a systemic mental fire. Your thoughts must flow and fuse with that fire, but if you direct your thought into your body and emotions, into your own ideas, opinions, and thoughts as if you were your own ideas, opinions, and thoughts, you create illusion. Your thoughts are going to flow into the systemic mind. You are going to open your mind to the Mind of the Universe.

When you think that your thoughts, opinions, and ideas are the reflections of total reality, you create illusion. Illusion is developed when you think that your interpretation presents the ultimate reality and you try to force it on others. When you, as a separate being — body, emotions, thoughts — become the interpreter of the Universe and its laws, you fall into illusion.

Illusion is distortion of reality in a separated being. Reality is distorted when you allow your own emotions, knowledge, and thoughts to be the whole interpreters of reality.

Illusion is the root of mental diseases. When you are turning into your own limitation, you no longer flow into the fire of Space, and your flow turns on the axis of your own tiny existence. When you thus block yourself from the ever-refreshing, ever-illuminating flow of the Cosmic fire, you become a pool of stagnated water, fit only to feed germs of various kinds.

Flowing into and fusing with the mental fire of the Universe gives you the opportunity to come in contact with higher mental currents of the Universe which are carriers of greater revelations and visions. In Space there are the mental currents of planetary, solar, and galactic Entities. Illusion prevents you from coming in contact with these currents. Because of its egocentricity, illusion provides continuous confusion and mis-translation of the incoming impressions.

The path to reality is found when you unite yourself with a greater existence. Reality is lost when you cut your contact with the greater Self and imprison yourself within your pitiful self. You will never find the path to reality as long as you are identified with your opinions, traditions, religion, dogmas, doctrines, nationalism, and so on.

There are various mental diseases such as insanity, obsession, and fear. From these flow the urges to commit crimes of destruction and of self-annihilation.

The fourth obstacle is developed when you come to the conclusion that you, as an ego, are a separate being. This fourth obstacle is called the *Dweller on the Threshold.* It is formed when you lose your intuitive or instinctive sense of oneness with the Self of the Universe. Such an identification with your self-image creates your ego, which, as if a real existence, sits on the threshold of your higher possibilities and prevents you from achieving new breakthroughs into deeper mysteries of your inner Universe.

When ego is created you become an independent self by itself instead of being a part of the whole body. You carry the deceptive thought that you are a separate existence and do not have anything to do with the life of the whole body. Such a state of being creates the hardest shell around you. You become crystallized; you become the prison and the prisoner; you become your own obstacle and enemy. The living fire which is within your ego cannot exercise its oneness with the flame, with the fire which is found in all forms on all planes.

When your ego evaporates, you begin to feel that you are one with the One Cosmic Self. The Dweller on the Threshold vanishes, and you enter into a higher dimension of existence closer to your Central Reality.

The vehicles of the Spark are fiery spheres. There is the fire of the etheric-physical vehicle. There is the fire of the emotional body, and there is the fire of the mental body. This latter fire is divided into two parts — the lower fire and the higher fire.

Then we have the Intuitional fire — love; Atmic fire — joy; Monadic fire — bliss; Divine fire — enthusiasm. Each of these fires is connected to corresponding planetary, solar, and galactic fires.

The Spark is learning how to use these fires, how to orchestrate these fires, and how to fuse Its own fires with greater spheres of fire. It is learning how to be a part of a greater system of fires and secure the following:

1. Health
2. Peace
3. Knowledge
4. Experience
5. Creativity
6. Expansion
7. Stability

The first fire (love), the second fire (joy), and the lower part of the third fire (bliss), can be used for destruction — to eliminate obstacles or to destroy the forms that prevent progress. Here is a further explanation of the fires:

Physical fire is the fire of the etheric centers, the heat of the cells.

Emotional fire, when in flow, creates inclusiveness, sympathy, givingness, sharing, radiation, etc. When stagnated, this fire creates jealousy, hatred, possessiveness, greed, anger, etc.

Lower mental fire, when in flow, creates simplicity, exactitude, search, concretion, carefreeness, etc. When stagnated, this fire creates pride, vanity, fanaticism, separatism, fear, etc.

Higher mental fire creates universality, synthesis, creativity.

The higher fires — the Intuitional, Atmic, Monadic, and Divine — are fires of love, joy, bliss, and enthusiasm respectively.

These higher fires are flames around the Jewel, the Self, which burns but does not consume Itself. The Self is the Divine in man, the door to Infinity. The task of the Self is to emancipate Itself from these fires and use them as an extension of the *Will* of the Greater Life in which It lives, moves, and has Its being.

As you think in terms of fire, you make your higher fires penetrate into those locations in your body where the fire has been extinguished, resulting in various diseases and problems. When any fire in your vehicles is fading, in any part of your nature, you have a problem there. Thinking and living in terms of higher fires sets your fires aflame and helps you to be healthy and energetic.

When fire circulates in your bodies and is in continuous fusion with the corresponding fires of the Universe, you will always be healthy and creative. This is what the Great Ones are. These Great Ones are called *Agni Yogis*, which means "people who have fiery union with the one fire in the Universe." Fiery unity with the fire of the Universe creates Masters. A Master is a person Who is one with the system of the fiery web of the Spatial fire and is fused with it, a person Who has become totally harmonized with the rhythm of the Spatial fire. Microbes, germs, and distortions can no longer exist in His system because the fire purifies all that is not being absorbed and transformed into fire.

Start thinking that your emotions and thoughts are fiery waves. Your thoughts either burn and destroy or build, purify, and nourish according to the motive behind them.

Thus, you will be very careful in using these fires. You will think how to act, how to feel and respond with your emotions, how to think so that your life becomes a symphony of fire that purifies, uplifts, transforms, and spiritualizes others.

Whatever fire comes out of your system first qualifies the substance of your aura. You either burn your aura or enrich it with higher fiery substance. After the fire leaves your aura, it reaches those to whom it is directed, and it either helps them glow and shine or darkens them.

Think about your Inner Self as a flame in a big bonfire. You are a flame, and when you really begin to consider yourself as fire, you will see that your physical, emotional, and mental bodies will have more creativity, health, and beauty and more contact with the fiery Selves of all other beings.

The four enemies of human progress, the four main sources of our psychological and health problems — inertia, glamor, illusion, and the Dweller on the Threshold — can be annihilated through the intelligent use of our higher fires.

Again, the higher fires are

1. Love — pouring out from the Intuitional Plane

2. Joy — pouring out from the Atmic Plane

3. Bliss — pouring out from the Monadic Plane

4. Enthusiasm — pouring out from the Divine Plane

Glamor can be dispelled by the fire of love, or by the fire of "analysis, discrimination, and clear thinking."

Illusions are dispelled by the fire of joy and by the fire of Intuition.

Inertia is annihilated by the fire of bliss, or by the fire of inspiration and willpower.

The Dweller on the Threshold, or the ego, is cleared away by the fire of enthusiasm or by the fire of the Solar Angel using the highest Divine fire.

Love energy, or the fire of discrimination, must be used throughout all your expressions, thoughts, emotions, and words if you want to clean your system of glamors. To use the fire of love or discrimination means to do nothing, to speak and think nothing that is against love. Anything you do against love creates short-circuits between the fiery system of love and the emotional body.

With discrimination you will be able to choose all those activities and expressions that are against love, and you will stop them. Harmlessness is the key word. Harmlessness eventually annihilates all obstacles on the Path.

In the same manner you will use the fires of joy, bliss, and enthusiasm.

- Identification with matter is inertia.

- Identification with emotions and objects of desire is glamor.

- Identification with thoughts is illusion.

- Identification with your own ego is the Dweller on the Threshold. You become a dead-end for yourself.

All your actions, emotions, thoughts, words, and motives must radiate all these four fires. When you learn how to operate these fires, you will develop health, happiness, success, continuity of consciousness, and creativity, and you will clear your path by burning the four obstacles.

Love means universality, oneness with all existence, with no discrimination or separatism. Glamor is identification with one object. When one object becomes everything for you, you lose everything else in the Universe, or you separate yourself from everything else. This is how you fall into glamor. Love energy is light, and only through this energy can you solve problems. Only through love can you understand people.

Hundreds of statesmen cannot solve a problem if they are not activated by the fire of unity or of love. The problem will never be solved as long as they hate each other or think about their own separate interests. But bring love energy into them and the problem will be solved. For example, an "intelligent" wife and a "smart" husband have a problem. They sit together and until morning they fight and are not able to solve the problem. But if suddenly real love awakens in them, the problem is quickly solved.

Identification with objects creates petrification in your aura or whirlpools which block your fusion with the Spatial fire. The disappearance of these whirlpools or petrification allows the fire to circulate in your system and fuse with the fire of Space.

Love helps you to be one with the ocean of fire. Love naturally expands, and any identification with something on lower planes is against love because it creates cleavages in your system of fire.

Identification with any object creates glamor, no matter what that object is. Even identification with your self-image is a great trap for you. Identification with your reputation and your public image is as bad as identification with your money and furniture.

Recognition of the values of other realities opens the energy of love in you and enables you to free yourself from your own self-made prison and expand your vision into the universal unity. This is love. Love makes you like a drop of fire fused with the ocean of fire; you become one with that fiery ocean.

Once a boy came and said to me, "I want to kill myself."

"What is the matter?" I asked.

"My girlfriend is going with someone else."

"Big deal! You can find a better girlfriend, or you can make yourself better so that your girlfriend does not want to leave you."

"But I love only her...."

We had a good conversation. I explained to him that when his love is stuck, it turns into a glamor and becomes a dead-end street for him.

I told him that God has many millions of flowers, and he can find one that suits him. And when he finds the one he really loves, he can think about her as the symbol of beauty in which all are unified. One can love someone but not be stuck with her form if she is taken as the symbol of beauty and love which encompasses all his visions and responsibilities.

When you want to destroy illusion, you must use the fire of joy. Illusion is identification with what you know and the assumption that what you know is the absolute truth. It is a mental deception.

People say, "This is the only way to fly," or "This is the only truth," or "This is the only religion, tradition, ideology. This is the only doctrine or dogma which will save the world." When you think in this way, you are in illusion. You are mentally sick, and that sickness in the mental plane slowly will descend to the emotional plane and appear as fanaticism, intolerance, and hatred. Then it will go to the physical body and create many distortions there in the form of diseases.

Thus man cooks himself with his own lower fires.

Man can destroy illusion with the fire of joy. Joy expands the consciousness and makes the mind receptive to greater lights, to greater ideas. Joy helps the man synthesize and see things from many viewpoints and come closer to reality.

Man erroneously tries to create a symphony with only one note. Man needs to love other notes and relate to them properly to have a melody — or a symphony.

What you know now is nothing in comparison to that which you will know in the future, if you strive toward greater Light.

Illusion is the source of misery, fanaticism, fear, wars, and destruction. Joy dispels illusion and expands your consciousness. Joy sheds a great light into your mind and helps you see greater issues, greater plans, and better ways to relate to them.

When you are in joy, your mind is clearer. When you are sad, grieving, or depressed, things will reflect in your consciousness in a distorted way because sadness and grief are identification with your body and with those objects which are related to your body or emotions, or even to your mind. Whenever you are identified, the screen of your consciousness is not clear, and you distort new images with the existing images with which you are identified.

Joy cleans the screen of your consciousness. Joy expands your space and makes you see others as they are.

Joy gives freedom to others. Joy makes people express themselves as they want, *as they want to be*. Joy makes you understand them and their motives.

In the absence of joy, people hide their true nature. They live in the image of their illusion and build different masks all the time. They feel restricted by the absence of joy. Joy destroys illusions.

Then we have bliss. Bliss destroys inertia. The fire of bliss kindles the vitality of the cells and atoms of our vehicles and puts them in harmony with the rhythm of higher spheres.

Inertia descends on people when they do not receive fire from the Monadic sphere. Inertia is crystallization of the vehicles. Crystallization stops the sensitivity of the vehicles to the impressions coming from higher sources.

The electricity of the Divine Purpose and Divine Plan must circulate and polarize all lives into greater harmony, labor, and striving. The fire of bliss vitalizes the vehicles and inspires them for labor.

The Dweller on the Threshold can be overcome by the fire of enthusiasm, which often is called the king fire. The kingly fire is the radiation of your Essence.

This fire destroys all your attachments to the lower self and its interests and leaves you free to live a rhythmic life, in tune with the Life of the Universe.

This fire destroys the ego formed by the physical, emotional, and mental images and puts you in contact with the Universal Self. You have a body, emotions, and mind, but you feel that they are your tools, your mechanism to make your light shine into the three worlds. You become aware that you are the Self — one with all Selves. It is after such a realization that greater virtues appear in your life, and your life becomes a life of service and sacrifice. You walk as a healer and as a beauty, and you stand as a path through which men may achieve.

Thus, live in fire; express fiery words, emotions, and thoughts. Reject all that is not Love, Joy, Bliss, and Enthusiasm because things that are not fiery will be obstacles on your path. Live a life of love. Be love; be joy; be bliss; be enthusiasm. Be fiery, and darkness will not live within you or around you.

We can also send a strong current of love, joy, bliss, and enthusiasm to others in the following way:

Visualization

1. Visualize a satellite in which you are sitting and broadcasting a sentence to our globe:

   The fire of love purifies all that stands on our path of unity and synthesis.

2. See the fire of love spreading in every heart.

3. Again visualize a satellite and, sitting in it, broadcast around the globe the following words:

   The fire of joy uplifts and transforms all our life with an urge for regeneration and creativity.

4. Visualize again as above, saying,

   The fire of bliss transfigures the whole existence, all living forms, and makes their Divinity shine forth.

5. Visualize again and say,

   The fire of enthusiasm keeps us in tune with the strivings of the stars and galaxies. Through enthusiasm we tune our hearts to the Heart of the Universe.

I remember a drama performed in one of the temples of a brotherhood in Asia. The drama was called the Five-pointed Star Dance with Nine Fires.

On the floor of the stage was drawn a huge five-pointed star:

There was great music — mostly flute, oud, and drum.

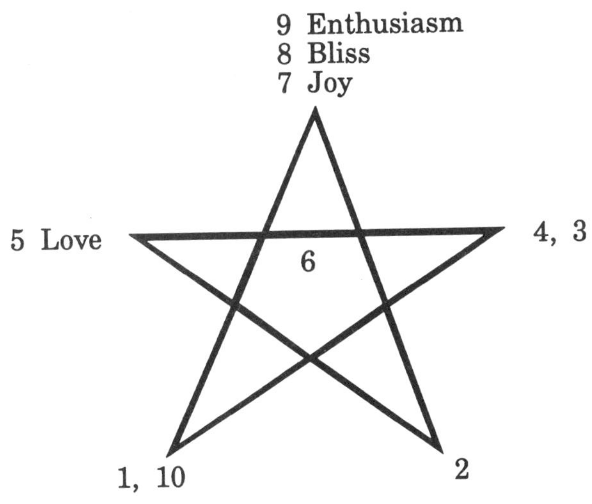

1 physical body
2 emotional body
3 lower mental
4 higher mental
5 Intuitional body
6 Solar Angel
7 Atmic
8 Monadic
9 Divine
10 Spark, diamond fire

Diagram 48-1 Star Dance I

First, three girls appeared on the stage wearing long robes and with flowers in their hair. With rhythmic movements they danced for a while, and then they each took their places at the points designated as 1, 2, and 3 on the star. They were dressed in violet, white, and green, respectively, and they had unlit candles in their hands.

Then an angelic figure appeared, dressed in a yellow robe and with a torch in his hand. He danced for a while with symbolic movements, and then took his place in the center of the star, shown as number 6.

Three beautiful figures with long hair followed him. One was dressed like the person at point number 3, but he wore two colors, green and yellow, and stood at place 4. The one who stood at 5 was dressed in silvery blue and had a sword in his hand. The one at point 7 was dressed in red and held a sword in his hand. These three occupied their places after performing symbolic movements.

Then three other figures appeared. One was dressed in midnight blue. He took his place at number 8. The other, at number 9, was in crimson red. Each was holding a sparkling sword.

The one at number 10 was dressed in pure white, holding a sword with a sparkling diamond on the point, like the head of a spear. His two companions, 8 and 9, went to their places with symbolic and fiery movements. When 10 came closer to them, they took him down, with symbolic movements, close to number 1 where he fell asleep.

The music continued for a while as this very special ceremony took place. The middle one, number 6, lit the candles of 1, 2, and 3. These three were symbolizing the physical-etheric, emotional, and mental vehicles. As he was lighting their candles he said, "Let this fire sustain you and your integrity."

He repeated this three times. Then addressing the three he said, "Let your fire lead the diamond fire forward to its throne. Be destructive to enemies. Be responsive to the pulsations of the diamond."

Then number 7, Joy, hit his sword against the sword of 10 and wanted him to awaken.

Then 10, the diamond, walked to the emotional fire. The emotional fire became aflame and danced very excitedly.

Then Bliss, 8, the Monadic sword, hit the diamond and the diamond walked from the emotional body to the mental body, and the united bodies became one. Then 9, Enthusiasm, hit the diamond, and the diamond walked from the mental body to the center.

Every time Joy, Bliss, and Enthusiasm hit the diamond, Love-Intuition first hit swords with them.

Joy said, "Be led from darkness to light."

Bliss said, "From the unreal to the real.

Enthusiasm said, "From death to immortality."

When the diamond reached the center, the Angel said, "You are led from chaos to Beauty," and they hugged each other.

A moment of darkness.

A moment of light.

The Angel disappeared, and the diamond shone more and more, with greater radiance. Fiery music and chanting ensued....

Then Love, Joy, Bliss, and Enthusiasm held their swords on the head of the diamond sword carrier, 10, and said, "O Self-revealing One, reveal Thyself in him."

And the diamond began to shine and walk to Love, to Joy, to Bliss, to Enthusiasm.

When he reached Enthusiasm, there was a moment of darkness and then a moment of great light.

Then we saw a different configuration. Number 6 was no longer there. The five-pointed star had changed into two triangles.

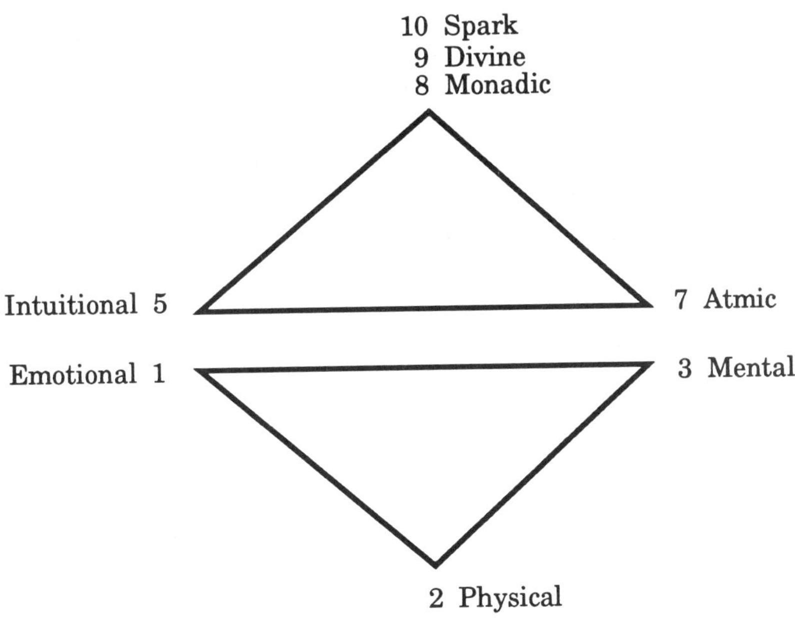

Diagram 48-2 Star Dance II

Numbers 1, 2, and 3 were holding their lights in a pyramid above their own heads. Numbers 5, 7, and 8 were uniting the points of their swords. Number 9 was holding his sword over the head of 8. Number 10 was holding his sword vertically toward the Space above.

During this time approximately one hundred people were chanting the following words with rhythmic movements:

"The diamond gained its victory."

"Enthusiasm, Bliss, Joy, and Love paved the way to the throne."

"I am the diamond."

"I am the way."

"I am the traveler."

"I am the goal."

"I am on the way of glory, glory, glory....

"Glory is achieved in radiating and giving."

The secret of how to increase these four fires is very simple. It is a secret because it is very simple. The secret is that these four fires only increase when you give them to others. The more love you give to others, the more you increase the love in your system. The love that you have is the amount of love that you give to others.

Fire increases only by burning and giving itself.

The more joy you give, the more joy you have. Do not wait for people to give you joy. What you receive will not stay with you. What you give belongs to you.

Bless people; be a blessing for others. Live in bliss, and your bliss will increase tenfold.

Give the fire of enthusiasm to others, and the king fire will increase within your system, increasing your beauty, health, prosperity, and creativity.

When there are radiations of love, joy, bliss, and enthusiasm in your home, microbes, germs, dark thoughts, and negative emotions will have a very difficult time surviving because fire burns all that does not serve the purpose of the Central Flame within you.

Keep these four fires alive within and without you, and you will be a blessing for the world.

The absence of these fires brings destructive forces into operation which hinder your progress.

These fires increase your magnetism. Your success depends on your magnetism. Your magnetism is nothing else but the combined sphere of these four fires.

The key to success is love, joy, bliss, and enthusiasm. It is these fires which electromagnetically organize and guide your life. Without this magnetism, you do not register the higher calls, and you remain deaf to the directions of your Inner Self and to higher guidance.

As you have your own electrical sphere which puts the right cells in the right places, similarly there is the network around the planet which guides the human being "cells" to the right places, if they are magnetically sensitive to the guiding energies. Many people were led to safe places by a Divine guidance when cataclysms and disasters were on their way.

When your own electrical system is integrated as a whole and functions in harmony with the electrical network of the Planetary Life, you have guidance, you have protection, and you are inspired and guided in all your life.

You are a flame in the ocean of fire. It is time now to think in terms of fire instead of in terms of matter and form.

Think about your True Self as being a flame. Think about your vehicles of expression as flames surrounding the Central Flame — the Jewel in the fiery Lotus — which is the mechanism of contact with the whole Existence and beyond. The whole purpose of life is to bring that Central Flame into harmony with that whole, universal, fiery symphony.

This realization is achieved through transformation. For centuries we have heard people say, "I love you," but it did not work. You can have love only by *being* love.

People say, "We have joy in our hearts." In the future they will say, "We are Joy; we are Bliss; we are the fire of Enthusiasm Itself."

Only by being fiery can one fulfill his destiny in this fiery Universe and become a healing, uplifting, enlightening, and guiding source for other flames.

Once we were sitting in a shelter during a very stormy and rainy day. A great Teacher passed in front of us. We forgot all about the rain and the storm because

Love was passing; Joy was passing; Bliss and Enthusiasm were walking in front of us.

You evoke the fires in others and awaken the flames in others only when you are fiery, only when you are a radiating flame. Expel from your nature everything that is not love, everything that is not joy, everything that is not bliss, everything that is not enthusiasm because all that is not love, joy, bliss, and enthusiasm is dead matter in your aura.

Bring living fire into your system, and be alive with fire!

49

Silence and Health

Your speech, carrying your thoughts, emotions, and urges, is related to the parts of your body, to the glands and chakras of your body from which it originated or toward which it is directed.

People have paid very little attention to the effect of speech on their health. Our speech is very closely related to our physical, emotional, and mental health. It is possible to say that right speech creates those conditions within our aura which contribute to our general health. Ill speech pollutes our aura, and, combined with our thoughts and emotions, it creates heavy barriers on the path of our evolution. These barriers manifest themselves as dark webs within which man is caught.

There are millions of webs surrounding the globe. Some of them are like dark webs without a design or pattern. Others are luminous with different shades of color, with various patterns and designs. Each web is produced by the words or speech of a person. We call them webs of the human voice, amplified and colored by the person's thoughts and emotions.

Some of these webs are close to the earth. Some of them extend toward higher spheres like spirals. Some of these webs carry waves of love, light, and power in various degrees. Others carry poison, pollution, and waves of degeneration and destruction.

Every human being builds his own web. Remember the caterpillar and how threads come out of its mouth. Remember also the spider. It is from the human mouth that the threads are projected into Space to build either a prison for the person's soul or a highway toward infinite progress, toward Higher Worlds.

Some of the webs are earthbound, earth-fed, and earth-feeding. Others are sky-bound; they are like energy channels transmitting life from higher spheres. Some of the webs are icy and dull. Others glow with warmth and fire.

All these webs have their individual frequency. Each web is different. Each web has its source — a human being, alive or dead. The human being weaves his web, age after age, every time he comes into incarnation or goes out of incarnation. When he is out of his body, these webs are woven further through his imagination and thoughts.

It is these webs that condition a person's vehicles in the physical world and subtler worlds. The vehicles of man are directly influenced by these webs. His etheric, astral, mental, and higher bodies are formed, age after age, with the influence of these webs which are built by his words, thoughts, emotions, urges, and drives.

We are told not to pollute Space. In comparison with the chemical pollution of Space, the pollution of human speech and thought is far more dangerous and more catastrophic. Such pollution makes it difficult, if not impossible, for certain devas to work with the human, animal, and vegetable kingdoms. Such pollution also cuts the guiding influence and energy from higher sources.

Each dark web of speech and thought prevents the free circulation of life energy. Any word that does not carry Beauty, Goodness, Righteousness, Joy, and Freedom builds the coffin of the human soul and creates the network of dark threads which spread poison, cruelty, and pollution into Space. Such pollution is not limited to any area or location. It spreads all over the globe and often works as a transmitting station to those who in some way tune to it.

The threads of the webs are of various colors. They are of different thicknesses and forms. Some threads are smooth. Some of them are wooly. Some of them are branched with thorns like radiations. Others have loops. Sometimes they are twisted with other threads of various colors and density. Sometimes they go parallel to others. Sometimes they crisscross each other.

Each time a man or woman mixes his or her aura with another person through sex, their threads become twisted and mingled. Sometimes they add to the beauty of the patterns in the aura of the person. Sometimes they distort each other's patterns, as if a child with a black crayon were distorting a beautiful drawing.

The threads that twist with each other often create a complicated situation. In esoteric expression this is called "tangling," or "tangles." These tangles present points of crisis when a person takes an incarnation. They affect the person, life after life, and create physical, emotional, and mental turbulences, with their various consequences, until they are untangled slowly or violently through shocks.

This is one of the reasons for the attachments, crises, and then detachments which people experience in their lives at various times. Untanglement takes time and requires painful cooperation between the weavers of the threads.

It is true that man builds his own future. Man gives birth to himself. Man has a "free will" to build or destroy himself, but he cannot escape from the consequences of his words which carry out to Space, in a definite frequency, his urges, drives, emotions, thoughts, and motives.

The health of our vehicles mainly depends on the condition of the webs. To a certain degree man is a puppet hung by the threads of his own self-made webs.

Dark webs transmit misfortune and maladies to the vehicles every time a man takes an incarnation. Dark webs mislead him on subtler planes or in subjective realms, bring disharmony within the vehicles, and plant seeds for future complications. Webs of light, scintillating with Light, Love, Power, Beauty,

Goodness, Truth, Joy, and Enthusiasm spread life energy and good luck and cause creativity, heroism, and nobility.

There is a very close relationship between the nature of the webs and various parts and organs of the human body. Your speech, carrying your thoughts, emotions, and urges, is related to the parts of your body, to the glands and chakras of your body from which it originated or toward which it is directed. For example, if you are talking about your sex life or about the sex life of another person with malice, lies, hatred, or harmful criticism, the web you create is related to your sex organs; and because you are building the web with the poison of malice, lies, and hatred, the web will slowly influence your chakras, your glands, and your sexual organs and lead you into trouble.

This is called the Law of the Boomerang.

The intensity and the effect of the reaction of your organs differs and is related to the intensity of the malice, lies, and hatred with which you charged your expression. Most heart diseases, for example, are counter-effects of your speech or of webs built by your speech carrying cruelty, hypocrisy, lies, and malice.

In the future it will be possible to study these webs more closely and find out when, where, and how a tangle or a dark portion of the web will strike a man, a group, or a nation. Sometimes many lives are spent to untangle the twisted threads and undo them. Nature often provides opportunities for us to meet those persons with whom we created complicated tangles. If we approach each other wisely, many tangles can be solved through the principles of detachment, renouncement, forgiveness, and sacrificial service.

A Great One once said, *"Hatred is not dissolved by hatred. Hatred is dissolved by love."*

My Teacher used to say that blood cannot be washed by blood; blood can be washed by water.

To undo the webs built by cruelty, crime, malice, hatred, anger, fear, greed, and jealousy, one must continuously pour out of his heart the fires of love, sincerity, trust, purity, and gratitude and live a life of virtues.

Often we find "strange" Teachings given by Great Ones. They say, for example, "If one wants to take your coat, give him also your shirt." Or, "If one hurts you, pray for him and bless him." Such kinds of advice are very esoteric, and one can understand their depth only when he realizes that such moments are moments of crisis in which some tangles can be dissolved, if the damage done in the past is paid back with understanding and humility.

Very often thieves and criminals are created by us, and we owe them all that they demand from us.

It is possible to undo our individual threads by increasing our goodwill, right human relations, service, and sacrificial deeds. Threads built by such fiery energies eventually consume the dark threads and build a network of beauty and light for our soul.

Every one of us can build his own symphony or his own prison — dark and cold. All construction is carried out by our tongues, by our speech, and by our silence. The greatest panacea for our ills does not come from pharmacies and hospitals but from our *words* charged with our sacrificial, heroic, and enlightened thoughts, motives, and emotions.

Man is born from his own mouth.

Throughout centuries Sages emphasized *silence.* Silence does not mean to zip the mouth and not communicate. Silence was recommended to warn people about their speech and to decrease the pollution from their speech.

Silence is physical, emotional, and mental. It is possible to keep silence with our mouth but talk mentally through our thoughts. It is also possible to be inactive in our thoughts but active with our mouth. It is also possible to be in silence within our True Self and watch the mental, emotional, and physical speech going on. In true silence, it is the Voice of the Silence that talks. It is the Self who talks.

Most of our speech originates from our physical, emotional, and mental elementals, from our urges and drives, from our glamors and illusions. This is what is commonly called speech.

Silence originates from the Self.

It is possible for man to detach himself from the utterances of his lower self and enter into silence. It is in such a silence that man can stop and check if any statement is issued from his lower self which will produce future obstacles in the creative expression of the Self. In such moments the Self can check if the utterances are true and correct and full of beauty and love.

Silence is entered into to observe the reactions of the centers, glands, and organs to the spoken word. Silence is entered into to check the effect of speech on the network of our words and thoughts. Silence is entered into to detect the motive behind the words. Silence is entered into to prevent those kinds of speech which originate from glamors, illusions, fears, hatred, greed, anger, and jealousy.

Silence is entered into to see if the words uttered are breaking right relations between parties concerned or building the network of light. Silence is entered into to see if the words are carrying the fires of beauty, wisdom, and joy.

Silence is entered into if your words are not constructive or comprehensible to your interlocutor. Silence is entered into when no one can pass your message to others in its entirety.

Silence is entered into when there is the danger of flattery, exaggeration, and lies.

Silence is exercised when you want to check any of your expressions on the emotional and mental planes. You can literally stop your emotions and your thinking process when you see that they were not put into action by you but by various factors such as vices, entities, or posthypnotic suggestions.

Silence is observed by advanced souls when their dear ones cause them pain and suffering and do not understand the great responsibilities and labors these souls have undertaken as a sacrificial service for humanity.

Throughout history, betrayers pierced the hearts of their Teachers or the ones who loved them most, and the spirit of ingratitude petrified the betrayer's own heart. Such people were defeated only by the silence of their Teachers or by the silence of the one who loved them deeply.

The wounds caused by our friends can only be borne through a deep-rooted silence, and even by a smiling silence.

An aspirant talks and expresses himself without responsibility. A disciple feels responsible for his expressions. An Initiate watches his every expression. He knows what to talk about, why to talk, where to talk, when to talk.

It is through our expressions that we are measured. Our progress on the Path is not measured by what we know and by what position we have, but it is measured by the degree of our mastery of our words and expressions.

With his carelessness, an aspirant creates disunity or breaks relationships between people. A disciple tries very hard not to cause any cleavage through his words and expressions. An Initiate creates right relationships and bridges cleavages through all his words and expressions; he reveals and dispels the causes of cleavages and encourages both sides to work for unity and synthesis.

Man is judged by his expressions. Every expression, especially speech — using etheric, astral, and mental forces — builds the web. Every man has his own unique frequency. He has his keynote, and in subjective levels it is possible to review the web created by a human being and see what is going on with him.

This web controls us throughout ages. It is hooked to our aura, and every minute it interferes with our expressions and makes our expressions follow the same patterns as the web. That is why it takes heroic efforts to break our habits of talking, feeling, and thinking.

Many, many times we feel that we are again entering a wrong path of conversation, but for some reason we continue. Later we feel badly, but it is already done. It is difficult to observe our emotions and thoughts and watch their automatic flow. When we are closely identified with our emotions or thoughts, it is more difficult for us to observe them.

Watchfulness starts with the power of detachment. Detachment is a process of entering into silence.

Most of our respiratory diseases and diseases connected with related centers and glands are the result of foul speech.

Heart diseases are closely related to our speech and expressions which create conflict and turbulence in our conscience and consciousness. The heart functions on the foundation of harmony. Any expression that upsets the harmony of the heart leads the person into trouble. Hypocrisy, lies, flattery, and foul speech are called the poisons of the heart.

The kidneys are also affected by our speech. When hatred, anger, and fear are verbalized, they carry a destructive poison to our kidneys and urinary system.

It is also very interesting to note that foul speech accumulates fat in our bodies if it is charged by an intense desire to possess and control.

Any time you feel that you are on the wrong track in your speech or expressions, take a break; take a moment of silence and observe yourself.

Initiates use silence on various occasions, for example:

1. When They are confronting an imminent beauty, a Cosmic vision, or grandeur.

2. When Their inspiration cannot be formulated into words because of its volume, power, and depth.

3. When people around them cannot contain the fire charging Their words.

4. When They want to reinforce Their words or commands by thought, or when They want to speak mentally to conclude Their speech.

5. When They want to announce an important statement, They do so in silence — mentally. Before They speak to the higher nature of the audience, They prepare them to understand Their words.

6. When They want to impress an idea without mixing it with the noise of the physical voice and emotional and mental formulations.

7. When They want to announce an important message, They keep mental and emotional silence so as not to make these bodies interfere with the purity of the message coming from Their Self.

8. When They want to conceive a powerful plan for the evolution of humanity. Great visions and ideas are born in silence. Similarly, great complexities and puzzles are solved in silence.

9. When They need to heal Their vehicles, They abstract Their consciousness into the Self, where silence is found.

10. Silence is also used after a great creative labor to reach the source of inspiration and have deeper insight.

Inspiration coming from higher sources can be translated and formulated on many levels according to the level of the consciousness of the artist at the moment of creativity. We are told that after their labor, great masters of art go deep into silence to renew their understanding and to reach, as much as possible, the source of inspiration. Recharged by such a close contact with the source, they often create a greater beauty, or see a deeper meaning and significance within their own creativity.

Inspiration can be translated on many levels and in many forms. The creative artist sometimes is able only to translate a little part of his inspiration. But through silent contemplation he can penetrate deeper into the stream of his inspiration and create better works.

It also happens that inspiration manifests itself through the artist without his full, conscious participation. It is only through silence that the depth of the creative labor is unveiled to him.

From childhood people must be trained in the discipline of silence. They must learn the science of speech and silence. Greater mastery is achieved in life when we do not waste our breath and voice but use them only to enlighten, guide, protect, uplift, and communicate with people.

Helena Roerich once wrote:

> *..Let us practice severe discipline of speech. Let us consider every word and remember that the "consequences of a word cannot be destroyed even by an Arhat." Let us broadly apply the indication that "each word should be like a ray of light and not a nail in the coffin." Know in your spirit when it is goal-fitting to tell the truth, even if it is bitter, and when it is better to be silent. But flattery and exaggeration, as well as belittling, are inadmissible.*[1]

> *..."The dreadful knife is not in your pocket but, verily, on the tip of your tongue...."*[2]

> *...When we sit in silence the bond becomes stronger.*[3]

> *...Speech must be beautiful, clear and deeply meaningful.*[4]

One of the greatest healing factors is a silence experienced in the presence of a Cosmic beauty. Admiration is a moment of silence. Ecstasy is a period of silence. Exaltation is a duration of silence. It is in such a silence that psychic energy finds a way to flow into your whole system and revitalize and purify it.

We call these moments the shocks of silence, the shocks of beauty, glory, and grandeur. The real essence of beauty is silence. The True Self is silence. Only vehicles talk. The Self is silence.

Formulate your decisions after a long silence. Write your letters after a few moments of silence. Start your lecture after a moment of silence.

Answer the attacks of your enemies with silence. Let them receive the whole blow of their own speech. Let them trap themselves in their own network.

Heal your bodies by keeping silence.

---

1. Agni Yoga Society, *Letters of Helena Roerich*, Vol. I, p. 50.
2. *Ibid.*, p. 130.
3. Agni Yoga Society, *Leaves of Morya's Garden*, Vol. II, p. 161.
4. Agni Yoga Society, *Agni Yoga*, para. 106.

Accustom yourself to keeping silence at least one hour every day, and one day every month. Start with the silence of your mouth. Then try to silence your emotions; then work on mental silence. It is in silence that the creative energies of Nature penetrate into your system. Silence is a progressive entrance into your Divine Self and into the One Self of the Universe.

It is through silence that your consciousness expands and your True Self manifests as a rare beauty.

Silence helps one concentrate and deepen his thinking. Silence makes man surpass the sphere of thinking and penetrate into the domain of Intuition. Silence makes man see the causes of events and the future effects of these causes.

Awareness of the Inner Dweller is achieved in silence. Only in silence can man prevent the clouds of forms from obscuring the vision of the Self.

Silence is serenity, purity, clarity, simplicity, direction, communication, and fusion.

The Voice of Silence speaks. When a man speaks as the Self to the Self through human lips, to human ears, we say that silence speaks. Such speech is verbal, but within each word there is the immensity, the grandeur, and the bliss of silence.

The Voice of Silence is not limited to words. It can speak through the eyes, through acts of renouncement, through love and compassion, and through blessings of the Soul.

Esoterically, when the Self manifests in Its beauty, wisdom, and joy, we say that the Voice of Silence is expressing Itself. When the vehicles are chattering for their own interests, we say that the silence is broken by the noise of the personality. Silence is a symphony. Speech is noise. Both are expressions, but the first one brings the beauty, power, and wisdom of the Self and fuses with the Selves of others. The second one is related only to the personal interests of man.

We must know that absolute silence means annihilation of form on all levels. We are told that the voice of the great AUM reverberates in every form.

True silence is the process of harmonization and fusion with the *Word*, with the purpose and plan of the innermost Self. The songs of wisdom and all creative sound stream forth from the Core of the Self.

When the symphony of the Self is expressed through the vehicles without distortion and alteration, we say that man has achieved *silence.* He is no longer controlled by the activities of the vehicles, but he is the source of all his actions.

50

Identity and Healing

If people want health, they must create conditions in which there is stability and certainty. As long as we do not have stability and certainty, our physical, emotional, and mental health will suffer. Our relations will be tense and destructive, and our growth will lead us into more pain and suffering.

In the ever-agitated ocean of human emotions, aspirations, thoughts, suffering, and pain; in the ever-changing ocean of human opinions, beliefs, judgements, and vanities; in the ever-changing phenomena of life, one must have an anchorage so as not to lose his stability, balance, and sanity.

Many sicknesses start when a man physically, emotionally, and mentally becomes a tiny boat in the hands of the ever-moving waves of life. People have known about this, and since the beginning of human consciousness they have tried to find ways and means to equip man with an identity, as we equip a boat with an anchor. For example, people gave names to each other. They called each other John, James, Susan, etc.

To expand your identity people gave you a surname, a title. You belonged to a family, to a nation, to a race, to a group, to a school. You developed a personality. You became a hero. You became a leader.

Further, you strove to prove your identity by trying to know yourself and be your Real Self. All these steps are efforts to have an identity and to keep an identity.

Throughout ages you noticed that every time you identified yourself with any object, you weakened your identity. Often you even lost your identity in your failures and mechanically performed actions, feelings, and thoughts.

Every time you exercised detachment and mastery over objects of the senses and over your urges, drives, glamors, and illusions, you built and increased your identity. The search for identity is the process of affirmation of your eternal, divine Self, without which you would resemble a dry leaf at the mercy of the winds.

Identity gives a man his existence; without identity he vanishes.

There are two forces in Nature. One force tries to dissolve all identities and melt them into one ocean, into one earth, into one Space. The other force in

Nature tries to build identities such as gems, flowers, trees, animals, human beings, and angels.

These two forces battle against each other everywhere, in everything. One force destroys your physical body; the other force saves you with your emotional identity. One force dissipates your astral body; the other force saves you with your mental identity and finds a way to make you incarnate to continue building your identity.

The constructive force gives you another body to continue your existence. The constructive force tries to develop not only your spiritual identity but also, eventually, identities from your physical body, from your emotional body, and from your mental body. In each of these are found the permanent recorders, which are protected by the constructive force to be used as seeds for the next cycle and to provide a better body.

Your physical body eventually will be an entity of its own. Your emotional body and mental body will graduate into their own form of entities.

In this conflict many people temporarily lose their identity, especially when the destructive hand of the first force hits hard, creating confusion and loss of vision, hope, and faith.

It is in this period of darkness that identity is lost temporarily, and the disintegrating force predominates in our lives, leading us into sickness, disease, and various kinds of failures.

People try to fight against the force of destruction by building physical identities such as possessions, positions, power, and reputations.

Emotional identity is given by one's own faith or religion, or even by his loved ones. To be loved means to have identity. Indifference toward you weakens your identity. It is strange that hate creates identity in people, but such an identity can seldom grow and mature. Faith, hope, friendship, love, and respect create a true identity.

On the mental plane man tries to create identity; his conclusions build his identity. When you recognize the value of a person and appreciate him, you build his identity. When you confuse him or ignore him, you weaken his identity.

If you fill the mind of a child with contradictory ideas, thoughts, or opinions, you destroy his identity. If you say you are fearless and act fearfully, you weaken his identity. If you tell him to love people but you hate people, you weaken his identity. Every time you weaken his identity you weaken his intelligence, his morals, and his potentials for survival and success.

In all our social life these two forces — destructive and constructive — are in continuous battle on the fields of our physical, emotional, and mental life.

There are people living without identity, and they are the most dangerous human beings. Criminals developed when their identity was under constant attack.

There are also groups and cities that failed to build their identity. There was much confusion of language, for example, at the Tower of Babel; they did not succeed in building their identity.

Identity is built on spiritual levels by living a life based on the standards or principles of Beauty, Joy, Goodness, Freedom, and Light. Any activity against such principles brings confusion and weakens the identity.

Efforts to achieve synthesis are noble efforts to expand identity without violating the identity of others.

Spiritual identity is reached through the recognition of the identity of others and through developing the sense of synthesis within you. Spiritual identity is not your differentiated body, not your emotions, aspirations, religious differences, dogmas, or doctrines. It is also not your beliefs, opinions, titles, or positions. *It is your experience of Self.*

The true identity is your Self, Whose light guides your steps from birth to death toward the inner Tower, the inner anchorage, the inner identity.

It is interesting that this inner identity is achieved by dissolving or detaching from all those elements in which one's *identity* is stuck — creating identification.

To protect your identity you must be alert to reject or not accept any attacks against your identity. For example, a nasty, belittling criticism, gossip, malice, or slander must be immediately rejected by your thoughts in an atmosphere of indifference. Also, the same must be rejected if it is directed toward any human being because such attacks sometimes are directed to you through other human beings. The destructive force often does not attack you directly but uses the paths of suggestions through literature, dramas, movies, etc.

Never accept attacks on human dignity because weakening the identity of others weakens your own identity.

Your identity is also weakened through the manifestation of ugliness. True identity is against ugliness. Ugliness is chaos and disintegration. Ugliness is confusion, and it weakens your identity and self-image. The image of God within you is your identity, your Self-image, not your personality image.

To weaken your identity, people try to make you the slave of your needs, to take your freedom away from you, to take your joy away from you, and to violate your human rights.

To weaken your identity, people create confusion in your mind — one by one knocking down the values that you have cherished for many years. If you love a hero, they make him into a joker. If you worship certain principles, they associate them with clowns, until they destroy the pillars which inspire in you the idea of identity.

Worship is a search for higher identity. If the object of worship is taken from you, your identity is weakened and even destroyed.

To weaken your identity, people try to make you doubt your own worth. In all such cases the traveler on the path of perfection should be firmly attached to spiritual principles which are very clear and simple. We can formulate them as follows:

1. Man is essentially divine.
2. Man has a great value.
3. There is always a way to master and to be successful.
4. The Self is beautiful, pure, and inclusive.
5. Love overcomes all evil.
6. Evil destroys itself.
7. Light, truth, and beauty always conquer.

These are the principles which, in your darkest hours and times of various attacks, hold you firm in your identity.

The diamond within us is built throughout centuries by the assistance of the two apparently conflicting forces. The destructive force wipes out all pseudo identities or identifications. The constructive force nourishes the identity so that it grows.

A wise man utilizes these two energies and never falls under the destructive force. In other words, he is not carried away into the abyss with his boat; instead he jumps out at the right distance from the drop and saves his identity.

If people want health, they must create conditions in which there is stability and certainty. As long as we do not have stability and certainty, our physical, emotional, and mental health will suffer. Our relations will be tense and destructive, and our growth will lead us into more pain and suffering.

Stability has a very deep esoteric meaning. Stability is the ability to adjust oneself to the changing conditions of the world. If the change is too wild and unexpected and the adjustment is slow and partial, the mechanism of man receives a setback and disturbances follow. If the person can foresee the changes and prepare himself for the changes before they come, he wins the game.

The second phase of stability is to make life conditions change following the progressive expansion of human consciousness. Instead of the changes in life imposing change in the consciousness, the advancing consciousness evokes changes in life. When the consciousness evokes change, there is always stability for that consciousness. But if life imposes change, man loses his stability unless he adjusts himself with conscious agreement.

Most of the changes in life are not the result of conscious activities but rather the outcome of unconscious reaction to the forces of Nature, an outcome of urges, drives, glamors, illusions, prejudices, superstitions, and violent negative emotions. These are the main factors of agitation and change.

Change which is rational leads to stability. Change which is irrational leads to uncertainty.

To create stability and certainty, some people develop the power to stand above the agitated waves of matter, emotions, and thoughts if they cannot control them. This is done through prayer, meditation, contemplation, detachment, and through the technique of spiritual indifference.

Our identification and liberation proceed on three dimensions: physical, emotional, and mental. Cyclically the destructive force takes away the body provided to us by the constructive force. The constructive force gives us a higher body to continue the process of building our identity, and we live in an astral body. Then our astral body is taken away from us by the destructive force, but a mental body is given to us by the constructive force.

After the destructive force annihilates the mental body, the constructive force starts a new cycle and builds a better physical body out of the records registered in the physical and astral permanent atoms and the Mental Permanent Atom.

These cycles follow each other until the spiritual man or the human soul eventually liberates himself and passes to the Intuitional Plane, where the destructive force has no power over his identity. The diamond is now formed and no force can destroy it. We call such people *diamond souls.*

The best groups and hierarchies are formed by such diamonds. Unless a man develops identity, he cannot contribute to the group activity. The process of building identity purifies his nature, makes him selfless, giving, and sacrificial. No symphony is formed until each note has its pure sound.

This is why so many communes and groups end in disaster. In the best cases, they find within themselves nothing beyond what common humanity has, except that they become more selfish, fanatical, and destructive.

Every healthy group is formed around a plan of striving and service. Every healthy group must have an example to prove to the members of the group that attainment is possible. Through the virtue of attainment, a person stands as the leader of the group, not to impose his will but to act as a forerunner for the entire group.

Even a herd of cattle has its leader.

Identity is the cornerstone of the group, and the one who is far ahead is the leader of the whole group. The leader achieves leadership only through his own advanced maturity, his intense dedication to serve, and his intuitive understanding of the conditions of the members. His identity or individuality does not mix the group into a colorless mass but evokes identity from each member and harmonizes them into a multi-dimensional rainbow.

An advancing spearhead creates challenge and polarity. It is only after a polarity is formed that the Law of Attraction operates. The Law of Attraction elevates the spirits of the progressing units to the one who expresses higher virtues of the spirit.

The leader in a homogeneous group acts as the anchorage of the group, and if the group is successful, all members develop their identities to such a degree that the group stands in a greater whole as an anchorage of hope, vision, and future. Thus, group leadership becomes a possibility.

In human beings, identity and non-identity are in conflict. Non-identity can be defined as all those human beings or all those elements in a man which are not in harmony with the progressive transformation of the human soul. These elements can be physical habits, negative emotions, mental crystallizations, or obsessive entities within the sphere of man. These elements can also be found within a group, personified in group members who fight against other group members.

Non-identity creates obstacles and hindrances for the identity and tries to prevent the further formation of identity.

Identity is the progressive human soul on the path of becoming himself. If the identity is strong and wise enough, he will be able to use all non-identities as steps for his progress and evoke from them the sleeping Spark to proceed forward and begin to build identities.

A group is more constructive if it has increasing numbers of identities. An increasing number of identities brings greater harmony between the group members and the leader. Conflict arises only from those who are stuck with their non-identity, or their non-identity saps the identity in process of formation. Any time the identity is sapped by non-identity, the degeneration of values and morals appears, bringing with it sickness, diseases, and insanity. One can clearly see the situation of a national entity in the light of the above viewpoints.

The loss of identity on individual, group, and national levels means identification with things you are not, with things that retard your progress and limit your expansion. Every time you identify with the things that you are not or with things that retard your progress and limit your expansion, you lose your balance, your equilibrium; you loose your physical, emotional, and mental health and your sanity.

Any identification with non-identity lowers your value. For example, take a man who identifies himself with the dollar. He will be as unstable as the value of the dollar on the international market, and he will put all his faith and trust in it. If in a moment of total identification with the dollar the dollar falls in value, he will pass away or commit suicide because he is lost into the disappearing non-identity.

When we identify with forms, with the body, etc., the destructive forces of Nature destroy the forms or the pseudo values with which we are identified, just to help us proceed on the path of building our identity.

Those who have lost their identity can be healed only by having a contact with an advanced identity. This is what history shows. The appearance of a Buddha or a Christ creates a new civilization, health, sanity, and culture because, like a great magnet, these Identities polarize all those who have sparks of identity and They inspire them with the spirit of progress, transformation, and resurrection.

Resurrection is an experience of withdrawal from global non-identity into solar identity.

People who have no identity often have the tendency to make people around them *nobodies*. The greatest damage one can do to another human being is to strip him of his identity.

You can lead a man, a group, or a nation into crime by taking its identity away.

Building identity in others promotes group, national, and international harmony, balance, prosperity, and understanding. Building identity is a universal service; destroying identity is a great crime.

If one tries to make a person a nobody, that nobody by his own right will try to do anything negative to be *somebody*. A man who feels that he is somebody can do something constructive. But if he feels he is a nobody, he wants to see everyone around him as nobodies, too. This is why he becomes destructive toward the existence of others.

Once when a criminal was asked what he was, he said he was "the greatest criminal." He had built an "identity" for himself to have the feeling that he existed.

To understand someone, to acknowledge his rights, his essential divinity, and his constructive goals is to build an identity in him and lead him into sanity.

Building an identity creates those states of consciousness within you which produce pro-survival functions in your glands and organs. It polarizes them toward a goal-fitting activity.

The ancients had their divine kings and their gods as the supreme examples and visions of identity. Today, people have their movie stars. Who knows how long it will take, if time is granted, to build visions once again in our consciousness and build heroes within our souls!

Action, feelings, and thinking are three means to create identity. When you work for yourself, you create identity. When you feel about yourself, you develop identity. When you think for your own interest and well-being, you create identity. But when you meditate, you try to respect the identity of others while trying to build your own identity.

Those who do not know how to use their mind become the servants of those who know how to use their mind. Actually, meditation is a process of searching for oneself. Meditation is an architectural activity, a labor to create a better self, a better identity.

People express their thoughts through words, gestures, and movements in order to communicate with each other. Very often, thought cannot be expressed entirely through such vehicles, and its strength weakens as it "dresses" itself in order to manifest.

The thought that is not put into words retains its power and is more effective than manifested thought. It keeps its strength and its integrity and is absorbed by the sphere of the mental fire. Those who have the ability to contact and register such thoughts have the sense of straight knowledge, or direct understanding, without the medium of words and other means.

This is why meditation is a very effective technique to spread greater light into Space, knowing that every thought expressed from our mind will sooner or later be assimilated by many fiery spheres.

Man builds his identity from the inside to the outside. Building one's identity means to bring out into manifestation the image he has in his being. Man builds this image through his deeds and expressed emotions and especially through his thoughts. Every thought brings out into manifestation one of the facets of the inner diamond.

Man is the manifestation of his thoughts and the manifestation of his identity.

Words crystallize the thought and limit it to the boundaries of language and interpretation. Pure thoughts radiate into Space without having elements of restriction, limitation, and possible distortion. Such a freedom allows them to exert their power more intensely and multiply in Space.

A better identity is created not by our spoken thoughts but by our silent thoughts or pure thoughts. Our silent thoughts manifest the real side of our essence and build the real identity more than the thoughts expressed by words because very often the spoken thoughts carry not only the limitations of language but also our hypocrisy, flattery, artificiality, concerns, vanities, fears, expectations, and excitements. When this is the case, our real identity cannot manifest in its purity.

An identity manifests, as the result of pure thoughts, as a source of continuous energy because, due to the multiplication of thoughts, the identity becomes a recharged source of radiation. It renews itself continuously and turns into a source of strength and creativity.

One can improve his identity by making himself ready to contact fiery thoughts sent by Great Ones. Such thoughts not only are the source of great inspirations and creativity, but they also have the power to build a superior identity.

Straight knowledge, or direct understanding, is the ability to come in contact with such thoughts and the ability to assimilate them into the fiery sphere of our mind.

Communication through silent thought is sometimes called the language of fire. Through the language of fire one contacts higher possibilities. It is through such a contact that the manifested identity renews itself, perpetually transforms and transfigures itself, and manifests as an ever-glowing transmitter of inspiration to the world.

51

Creating Identity

Psuedo identity is the main cause of inner conflict, and this inner conflict is the cause of many sicknesses and physical, emotional, and mental disturbances.... Inner conflict is eliminated by strengthening the real identity and weakening the pseudo identity.

Trust creates identity. When you trust a person, you build an identity in him or you reinforce his identity. If you do not trust him, you weaken his identity. If one is not trustworthy, it is because his identity was always under attack. Such attacks eventually destroy his identity and develop a non-identity in him which is characterized by

— greed

— fear

— over-protective psychology

— aggressiveness

— criminality

— lack of honesty

— a tendency to use people and things for his pleasure

Non-identity is the denial of the true identity. Once the true identity is inactive, man loses his self-respect.

Observe how parents name their children. Usually the name of a famous person, of a hero, or the name of a much beloved person is given to the child. Instinctively parents try to build an identity in a child by naming him after one who had or has an identity.

You can see this even in some prisons. When the criminals arrive they are assigned a number. They are told, "You are number twenty-seven." The criminal has a new name now; he is number twenty-seven. He has an identity. Although he lost his identity, he now has a new identity, and he tries to preserve it by creating trouble. He wants recognition. A criminal may try to escape in order to maintain an "identity" that he had.

The greatest crime is to take the identity away from someone. Watch a person when he talks about his father and mother, how much wealth they had, their great reputation, etc. Through all this he is trying to build an identity.

Flattery is a way to build a pseudo identity. Those who do not have identity are immediately trapped in the net of flatterers.

One day a rooster was trying to eat a piece of cheese while sitting on the branch of a tree. A fox passing by saw the rooster and the cheese in his mouth. Since the fox could not climb the tree, he used psychology. He said, "You are so beautiful, and I know your brother. He has a very beautiful voice. I know how beautiful your voice is and how everyone admires it. Can you sing just a little so that I can hear your voice?"

Puffed up with this flattery, the rooster opened his mouth and sang, but it was too late. The cheese fell down, and the fox disappeared with the cheese.

A pseudo identity works against the best interests of a person because it blocks the influence of the real identity.

Thinking is a method whereby you stay with your real identity. Thinking is the process of actualization of identity. Your identity manifests through thinking and meditation.

Meditation is pure thinking. It is through meditation that your greater identity finds ways to influence your life. Through meditation you give birth to your true identity.

It is possible to build a pseudo identity through manipulated thinking.

Pseudo identity is the main cause of inner conflict, and this inner conflict is the cause of many sicknesses and physical, emotional, and mental disturbances.

To eliminate these disturbances, you must eliminate the causes of the inner conflict. Inner conflict is eliminated by strengthening the real identity and weakening the pseudo identity. Sometimes this is done like surgery. It is a painful process.

Sometimes due to circumstances, we lose our identity and live as a non-identity.

Although we go to school, graduate from universities, create reputation and fame, we do so without feeling *identity*. We eventually destroy whatever we built on the foundation of non-identity because we feel that such a construction of our life is a process of the burial of our identity.

In such cases we must search for a person who has identity, and integrity, one who can be trusted. It can be a living person or a mythical one; it does not matter. We must find a source of identity and draw new inspiration from him. This can be done through actual search or through visualization. Things can be factual and real if we find the way to key in to them.

If you find someone who radiates identity and individuality, he may be able to help you. He will first destroy the accumulations of non-identity within you, then affirm your essential identity, your True Self. Then, step-by-step, he will bring the identity to the surface of your consciousness. This is why the relationship between the disciple and the Teacher is so sacred.

It is very interesting to note that pain and suffering also create identity. But if pain and suffering continue, they begin to build a pseudo identity or wipe away the true identity. This is due to the fact that man tries to escape from an identity that causes him suffering. Some people change their name just to escape their former identity.

We sometimes say about a person, "He is showing off." People show off because they want to nourish their identity or strengthen their identity.

You always need an identity to be successful in whatever you want to do. A non-identity has no success because that person does not exist in his consciousness.

People even get sick so that they can find an identity by attracting the attention of others. To attract the attention of other people is a way to make them build an identity in you. Sometimes the identity they build does not even fit you, or it is bigger than you expected. Such an identity serves you for a while, but sometimes it becomes a burden and you want to get rid of it.

Sometimes people build a big identity about you to satisfy your ego, but often you disappoint them because you cannot handle such a big identity; and when you do crazy things, you lose your reputation or your identity given by others.

Through thinking and by trying to reject your non-identity, you can raise the level of your identity from the physical, emotional, and mental planes. Thinking cannot *find* your true identity, but it helps it to manifest.

Thinking tries to define the nature of identity, but it cannot. Instead, thinking helps you *to know what you are not*. Selective thinking dissolves the non-identity and helps the true identity reveal itself. Thinking cannot define what you really are in your essence, and since it cannot do that, you are tempted to conclude that you do not exist as an identity.

Through the formulation of thought, one cannot reach the Self. It is through realization, awareness, and beingness that the Self is actualized. One can never know the Self, but he can become the Self.

It is possible to speak about the Self, but it will not make any sense to those who do not have a certain degree of experience of the Self, or Self-actualization.

There are seven methods through which the Self, or true identity, can be revealed. One must do extensive study on these seven methods and really understand their nature in order to reveal his own true identity and then use these methods as a great means of healing.

These seven methods are based on the following seven words:

- Self
- Beauty

- Joy
- Courage
- Love
- Harmlessness
- Gratitude

In identifying and gaining a true understanding of these words, we develop the methods by which a true identity is found and true healing is practiced. Thus, by knowing what is the Self, we learn to use the method of the Self in finding identity and in healing. The same holds true for the others. For example, in having a true understanding of the word love, we find an essential aspect of our identity and can then use love as a method to heal.

These seven methods then become a means of great healing carried out on the physical, emotional, and mental planes as well as in individual, family, group, social, and global fields.

Through these experiences, you gain control over those forces which try to dissolve your identity and gain mastery over those which protect and build your identity. When you succeed in controlling and mastering these two kinds of forces, you can then use these methods in your own life and in your relations with others to destroy the factors which attack an identity and provide those conditions in which a true identity grows.

In exercising these seven methods, you may create a state of consciousness within you in which the chemical balance in your body is kept normal and effective.

A negative state of consciousness disturbs the balance of the chemistry in your body and such a disturbance creates chaos in your glands, feelings, judgements, and thinking.

If you pay close attention to the wisdom that the Great Ones gave, for example, in the *Dhamapada*, in the *Bhagavad Gita*, in the *New Testament*, you will see that all their efforts were directed to create elevated states of consciousness in man.

Prescriptions of chemicals or herbs, physical exercises, or breathing exercises will never be truly effective without first having an elevated state of consciousness.

The Great Ones knew clearly that an elevated state of consciousness could heal, energize, or regenerate. Any other artificial help would not create an elevated state of consciousness. Such a state is the door through which man can continue his evolution and proceed toward perfection.

The root of our health, happiness, success, and joy is found within our consciousness. It is equally true that the root of our diseases, accidents, misery, pain, and suffering is programmed within our consciousness. In addition, karma programs our consciousness and we act according to that programming.

These seven words are seven states of consciousness. It is the state of our consciousness that conditions not only our health but also our behavior, our responses, and our reactions.

The state of our consciousness is responsible for the chemical changes going on within our body. When we learn how to change our consciousness, we will be able to control the chemistry of our body. We will be able to keep the chemical balance within our body.

We have not only a chemistry of our physical body but also a chemistry of our emotional and mental bodies. All this chemistry is controlled by the state of our consciousness.

People pay attention to the results, but the causes of the results are found in the consciousness. Unless the causes are changed, the results will not change.

Every human being has a gear box within his system. The gears do not work properly if they are not synchronized. A non-synchronized gear box makes the car stop. Non-synchronization in our nature starts when we fill our consciousness with different kinds of conflicting programs.

For example, if there is a command to start and then to stop, the machine within us wastes energy trying to find a way out. These are the moments when we do crazy, unexpected things as a way of escape. Elevated states of consciousness create synchronization, and our physical, emotional, mental, and spiritual gears do not gear in to wrong speeds and create chaos in us.

Artificial physical exercises, such as yogic asanas, breathing exercises, and other artificial means try to make our body run in fourth gear, for example, while our consciousness is engaged in first gear. That is why in all true disciplines, we must remember the necessity of harmonious development, and this starts from the consciousness.

In the future, people will increasingly work on developing the consciousness rather than the body. Sometimes, to heal a body means to clean the accumulated waste which the consciousness is continuously producing. The originating source must be handled properly if we do not want continuously to clean the waste in the body.

Consciousness affects the chemistry of the body, the circulation of the energy, the relationship of the organs, glands, etc. The chakras are very sensitive to the state of our consciousness. The chakras are the electrical system behind the glands.

Consciously built or manufactured thoughts directly carry to the centers the frequency of the state of consciousness and condition them. By changing, refining, and transforming our consciousness, we start a great process of healing within our whole system. This process produces physical health, increases our positive emotions and joy, clears our vision and logic and understanding, and creates integrity within and between our vehicles.

These seven words are seven states of consciousness. We can even have higher states of consciousness. However, these seven are a very powerful basis on which to create brighter, stronger, and clearer states of consciousness.

Exercises on the Seven Methods

We are going to take these words and try to change, elevate, and sublimate our consciousness.

1. The Self

The first word is the *Self* — or the *true identity*. The first procedure for the physical body is as follows:

1. Totally relax.
2. Close your eyes.
3. Try to feel that your whole being is full of bliss.
4. Direct your attention to your body. Think of your body and say,

   This is my body.

   These are my clothes.

   This is my shirt, my shoes, etc.

   These are my legs, my arms, my head.

   These are my ears, my eyes.

   This is my nose, my mouth.

   This is my heart, my stomach,

   my bowels, my lungs, my liver, etc.

   (Go over all of them, one by one, slowly.)
5. Then ask: "Is this what I am? Am I my body?"
6. Look at your face in your imagination and ask, "Am I my face?" Go over the body and each time ask, "Is this me?"

   You may go over your body again and again up to seven times, each time being more serious with the exercise and more involved in what you are doing. Do not forget to go into the body and see the internal organs. Direct your attention to each one and ask, "Is this me?"

Do not dwell more than ten seconds on each organ, but also do not rush.

7. Visualize yourself as a sphere of pure, white light, two to three feet above your head. Radiate pure, white light to every part of your body, but do not concentrate on any part.

   Flood your body with white light, with fiery, white light.

   If you have any problems in your body, visualize that the problem is dissolving and vanishing away. See how the light is penetrating your body and pushing out all the pollution accumulated in your system.

   You are taking a shower inside and outside simultaneously.

   Do not wander into other thoughts; just keep your mind on the procedure.

The next procedure is for the emotional body:

1. Again relax.

2. Take three deep breaths.

3. Close your eyes and think about your emotional nature. Visualize your emotional nature. Try to find five major causes of your troubles — namely fear, hatred, anger, jealousy, greed, and depression.

4. Now try to see fear in your emotional nature. Find out what kinds of fear you have. Try to find at least three major fears which may be hidden within your emotional body, creating poison there.

5. After identifying your fears, make a symbol which represents your fears.

6. Visualize your True Self, located one foot above your head, as a sphere of light.

7. Visualize taking a hose in your hand, and, instead of water, visualize fiery light coming out of the hose. Direct your hose to the symbol which represents your fear until you see it burned up and totally vanished. You may create three symbols for three fears, doing the same for each symbol.

   It is possible that after your symbol has vanished it may try to come back. Again direct your hose at it, and burn it again and again until the image is totally cleared away.

   Fear is the source of many psychosomatic sicknesses. It eats your body very slowly without you knowing it. This method is a very powerful means to clear your fears.

8. Now take anger, and make a symbol of your anger. See a picture presenting real anger. Anger is a poison and it damages your *nadis*, which are the subtle counterparts of your nervous system.

9. After you build the symbol of anger, hold your fiery hose in your hand and burn it into ashes. Let it vanish or dissolve completely.

   If during the burning of your anger, fear comes again, burn it again until both disappear.

10. Now take hatred, and make a symbol representing hatred. A symbol is very important because it synthesizes in itself all your hatreds which are accumulated within the symbol; and when you burn the symbol, you really burn the roots of your hatred. One can totally eliminate hatred from his system if he does this exercise daily for a period of three months. A psychological pattern builds in the emotional body which rejects any hatred automatically.

    Remember that every time you hold the hose in your hand to burn the symbol of your negative emotions, you visualize yourself as a sphere of light standing above your head.

11. Now take jealousy, and make a symbol representing your jealousy. Make it real and concrete.

12. Visualize yourself as a sphere of light and hold the hose in your hand. Start to burn the symbol until it is annihilated.

    You can make this feeling real if you imagine a few circumstances when you experienced fear, anger, hatred, jealousy, and greed.

13. Greed is the next emotion or vice which must be annihilated from your nature. First feel greedy. Then see in what areas you are greedy. Build a symbol representing your greed.

14. Now burn the symbol with the fiery light from your hose until it vanishes.

    Greed is a very dangerous emotion and it creates many diseases in your body. Once you clean them from your system, you feel a tremendous release. Your whole body, heart, and mind will feel different, and in this way you will prevent future diseases in your body.

15. Now take depression, which darkens your inner light and gives a chance for germs and microbes in your body to attack you. Make a symbol of depression, and burn it to pieces with a song on your lips.

These six emotions create poisons in your astral body which spread to your physical body and plant various seeds of complicated problems. They especially attack the heart and distort the rhythm of the heart. If you annihilate fear, anger, hatred, jealousy, greed, and depression, your heart will function in a perfect condition. When the heart is in a perfect condition, it radiates psychic energy all over the body and almost heals any disease in the body. But when the heart loses its dynamism and is polluted with the above mentioned sources of poison, it cannot pump psychic energy, although it tries to provide blood for the body.

You must work every day on one of these emotions or even take one for a week and try to dissolve it.

People think that psychological analysis helps. It does not. The best method is to impress your mental body with the imagery of burning your negative emotions. It is not just symbolic. It is real. Your Real Self is trying to annihilate your enemies through its fiery energy which is actually your psychic energy.

In doing such an exercise you dissolve the formations, the crystallizations within your aura. You disintegrate and destroy the formations of fear, anger, hatred, jealousy, greed, and depression and restore the free circulation of energy within your aura, in and out of your dense physical body.

Breathing is not only a physical phenomena. Every time we breathe, we breathe physically, emotionally, and mentally and we absorb different elements through our physical, emotional, and mental lungs. Every time we exhale, different pollutions are expelled from the three vehicles.

When you are breathing, remember to breathe consciously in three dimensions. The Sun provides three different elements of vitality for your three bodies.

Subtle breathing is possible when your physical, emotional, and mental bodies are not flooded with negative emotions. When any one of your systems is flooded with obstacles, that system cannot breathe, and the breathing process is not simultaneous and rhythmic. This creates imbalance in the three-dimensional breathing apparatus, with bad results.

Purification of the bodies facilitates the breathing and assimilating of the triple energy of the Sun.

The following emotions affect the various glands and organs:

Fear — is related to the base of spine, to the adrenal glands, and to the kidneys.

Hatred — is related to the pineal gland. Hatred retards the metabolism and hinders the circulation of lymph.

Anger — is related to the thymus gland and the heart.

Jealousy — is related to the solar plexus, to the pancreas, and to the intestines.

Greed — is related to the thyroid gland, the pituitary body, and also the gonads.

Depression — is related to the gonads, the liver, and the spleen.

Frustration is not depression. Frustration draws the energy of the throat center down into the sacral center and depletes the man.

The next exercise is for the mental body. We must remember that there are many factors in the mental body which keep us as prisoners and hinder higher energies from reaching the lower vehicles. These factors are

— vanity

— crystallized thoughtforms

— separatism

— hypocrisy

— insincerity

— illusions

These are cloud formations in the sphere of the mind, and they affect our life to a great extent. Those people who carry these elements in their mental body do not enjoy health.

Here is the procedure to annihilate them from your mental body:

1. Relax.

2. Take a few deep breaths.

3. Visualize that there is a seven-pointed star above your head, shining like a diamond with seven colors: *red, orange, yellow, green, blue, indigo, and violet.*

4. Visualize your mental body as a pure *lemon-yellow* sphere.

5. Try to find vanity in that sphere. Try to find a few vanities within your mind.

   Vanity is a false self-image which creates conflict within you. It blocks your mind with the images of the things you do not possess.

6. After you find a few kinds of vanity, make symbols of them.

7. When the symbols are formed, take your hose and burn them with a *red* colored flame. See the destruction of the symbols, and feel joyful and free. Watch how the mental sphere is gaining a pure color of *yellow* as the flame is destroying the symbols of vanity.

   Take personal, national, racial, and religious vanities and destroy them.

8. Do the same thing with crystallized thoughtforms. Crystallized thoughtforms are those convictions which have no foundation. Fanaticism is one of them. Dogmas and doctrines in any branch of human endeavor are other crystallized thoughtforms. We also have prejudices and superstitions. These elements weigh heavily on the mental body and block its space like icy clouds in the sky; they create various diseases in our circulatory system and glands; they affect human relationships and create complications in our life. They must be cleansed.

   Find a few of them; form a symbol to represent each one and dissolve and burn them with a *red-blue* flame. Do not hurry because you are doing an important work. Go slowly. The destruction of crystallized thoughtforms will change your entire life and your future.

9. Next take separatism and all thoughts of separatism. Try to find at least three main thoughts of separatism and burn them with a *white* flame.

   Use the same standard technique given above, but pay attention to the change of color of the fire.

10. Now take hypocrisy, and see in what manner you use hypocrisy and are a hypocrite. Do not think that you are free from hypocrisy. Try to find it and use the above technique to burn it with a *green* flame.

    Hypocrisy is a deceiving mechanism.

11. Next is insincerity. Burn the symbol with a *violet* flame.

12. Now take illusions. This will not be easy, but if you did the previous ones intelligently and seriously, you will find things that are distortions of truth within your mind. Illusions imprison the Self and block its progress and freedom.

    Always use the standard procedure given above, but use a *yellow* flame to burn your illusions. You will feel a great sense of freedom.

    After you are through with the burning process, visualize your mental sphere as a pure yellow sphere. Visualize your emotional body as pure silvery blue around your body. Visualize your etheric body vibrating with a violet and golden color. Visualize your physical body as pure, healthy, and beautiful.

    Direct seven rays with seven colors to your physical, etheric, astral, and mental bodies, and visualize them as a transparent unit. Hold your rays for a few minutes on the vehicles. Now enter into your head and radiate a pure white light pouring out from all your bodies. This is transfiguration. Sit for fifteen minutes in silence and the exercise is over.

The above exercises are called "contact with the Self."

2. Beauty

The second word is beauty. This exercise is an exercise on beauty for healing. The standard procedure is as follows:

1. Sit and relax.

2. Close your eyes.

3. Take three deep breaths.

4. Relax and focus your attention in your head.

5. Visualize five beautiful objects which you can touch or experience with your five senses. Create something beautiful. Take your time — five to fifteen minutes — to create.

6. Observe three ugly things and then transform them into beautiful ones just by looking at them.

7. Visualize your body and make it as beautiful as you want.

8. Meditate on the word "beauty." What does beauty mean to you?

9. Sit for five minutes in relaxation.

Using the same procedure as outlined above, create five emotional beauties. Dramatize these five emotional beauties as if they were part of your emotional nature. Relax for five minutes.

Take five mental beauties (ideas, visions, etc.), and dramatize these five mental beauties as if they were a part of your mental nature. Relax for five minutes.

Visualize five spiritual beauties, like heroes, saints, sages, Saviors, Avatars, or Universal Cosmic Visions, and try to act as if you were the embodiment of spiritual beauty. Now relax for five minutes.

Every thought and impression of beauty has a harmonizing and healing effect upon your nature.

The following visualization exercise on beauty can be done for half an hour:

1. Relax.

2. Then do something beautiful with your hands for three minutes.

3. Speak something beautiful to someone you love for three minutes.

4. Make a person feel beautiful for three minutes.

5. Make a person think beautiful thoughts about you.

6. See an ugly situation and create beauty in it.

7. Control an attack with beauty.

8. Recall an ugly situation in your life, and change it into beauty.

Feel, realize, and think that you are really beautiful, inside and outside, and beautiful in all your relationships. Visualize yourself being as beautiful as you can. Visualize how you walk, talk, feel, and think beautifully. Observe yourself as a beautiful person.

You can repeat this daily and witness the amazing changes within you. During the day try to

— think beautifully

— speak beautifully

— act beautifully

— be beautiful

Beauty releases sealed sources of energy within you which help you heal yourself.

3. Joy

The third word is joy. The standard procedure in using joy will be as follows:

1. Relax.

2. Create a state of joy in your consciousness for two minutes.

3. Feel or experience in your visualization a pure physical joy. Use your senses to touch, taste, see, hear, and feel. It should be a physical pleasure, pure physical joy. Try to find five physical pleasures.

   Feel these pleasures deeply; identify with them.

4. Relax and feel the continuity of joy in your body.

Now use joy on an emotional level.

1. Visualize someone and make him or her emotionally joyful. Try to keep this joy only on an emotional level. No sex, food, drink, or touch is involved; it is a pure emotional joy.

   For example, visualize a feeling of gratitude, a feeling of love, solemnity, purity, and truthfulness; a feeling of friendship or of being together with someone you admire. Try to recall such experiences, and if you do not have any, try to create them in your creative imagination.

2. Watch to see if you feel an increase of energy or an expansion in your being.

3. Visualize yourself singing something very beautiful near a lake, in a forest, on a mountain; singing with all your heart and expressing your joy to all creation.

4. Relax.

5. Open your eyes and smile.

Anger, fear, hatred, jealousy, and greed distort your face, your heart, and your brain. Joy brings your physical beauty out, makes your heart healthy and striving, and your mind clear and creative.

When a woman is beautiful, loving, and joyful, she is herself. When she is angry, jealous, fearful, or greedy, her charm and grace disappear with her true identity. When one loses one's identity, one loses one's health. As we go away from our True Self, we become sick. As we go closer to our True Self, we become whole.

Those who lose their identity lose their health. Joy brings the true identity into manifestation.

As you increase your joy, your body becomes more energetic, your emotions more positive, your mind clearer, and your direction faces toward Beauty, Goodness, and Truth. Joy is not a feeling; it is wisdom. It is the light of the Intuition felt in your personality.

A joyful man is a transmitter of energy and wisdom.

These exercises are lifelong exercises. They bring gradual development, improvement, and transformation. As you see greater improvement, give a little more time to these exercises until you see that the flowers are blooming within you.

Do not start by doing exercises all day. Start with five minutes, and increase it gradually to thirty or even forty-five minutes.

Now we will use joy on a mental level.

1. Find five kinds of mental joy. What are they, and how can you identify with them mentally? For example, a discovery is a mental joy. An understanding of something deeper is a mental joy. Revelation, knowledge, and creativity are mental joys. Try to find other mental joys.

2. Observe how your body and emotions respond or react.

3. Relax.

Next we have an exercise using spiritual joy.

1. Find five spiritual joys which are shared by your physical, emotional, and mental bodies. Spiritual joys are different from all the former joys. What are they? Service, sacrifice, heroism, transfiguration, initiation, meeting the Master, the ability to serve Him, contact with an Ashram — all are spiritual joys. Try to find them or visualize them, and feel them with all your being.

2. Radiate this joy into your personality.

3. Radiate it to the world.

4. Realize that no one in any condition can deprive you of such joy. Circumstances can change for the worse all around you, but this joy remains forever. Why? Ask yourself this question.

5. Visualize your three lower bodies absorbing your spiritual joy and passing through a transformational process.

6. Relax.

4. Courage

The next element is courage. The standard procedure for courage follows:

1. Relax.

2. Take five deep breaths, filling all your aura with a golden light.

3. Visualize a courageous person — physically courageous, emotionally courageous, mentally courageous, and spiritually courageous.

4. Find out the differences between these four.

5. Visualize yourself performing a courageous act. Speak something out of your courage. Think something courageous. Visualize a complicated and dangerous situation and be courageous.

6. Remember a moment in your life when you were courageous. Remember each courageous moment in your life.

7. Visualize yourself trying to jump from a high cliff into a lake. Every time you jump, climb higher and higher up the cliff. Make it as real as possible.

Once someone asked, "If my mind does not like me to jump, shall I still try to jump?" The answer is yes. The routine formation of your thought patterns must be broken. That is how crystallizations are broken. It is our past failures that prevent us from doing daring, courageous things. This failure pattern must be broken within our mind, and an image of success must replace it. There is a great difference between an image of failure and an image of success and achievement.

The failure image freezes the circulating energies; the success image polarizes them toward greater achievements.

A failure image is a crystallized image. A success image is an image of flowing energies, like an image of a tree or a rock reflected in streaming water.

It happens often that we cannot control our visualizations when failure images interfere. This is why we must repeat the exercise until visualization and creative imagination obey the success image.

For example, when you are diving from a cliff into the lake but instead you land on the shore on your head, this is an indication that the failure image is controlling your visualization and imagination.

You must be able to imagine and visualize the way you want. If you want to fly, you must be able to fly; if you want to dive, you must be able to dive. When you are able to visualize the way you want, this means you have destroyed many crystallizations. Every inner success becomes a success in your outer life.

Your visualization or creative imagination must follow your will, your thought. You think about jumping from a two-hundred foot building and landing very safely, and if you cannot do this in your visualization, it means that thoughtforms are controlling your intention or decision and you have crystallizations in your aura.

Courageous acts destroy these crystallizations. Often our logic is the crystallization of our failures and weaknesses. Once I told my students to visualize a car with square wheels and to drive the car. After ten minutes I asked them what happened.

Here are some of their replies:

"I put my car on top of an icy hill and slid down."

"I changed the tires and drove."

"I imagined my car was on a train, and I was moving fast."

"I imagined I was driving on the square wheels. It was bumpy but as I went faster and faster, it smoothed itself and became very comfortable."

The mind must be able to visualize things that are impossible or difficult in order to break crystallizations and not build patterns of escape.

Visualize impossible things that your heart desires, and you will be closer to reality than before.

Remember that to travel to the moon was an impossibility because of the images people built about the future. Someone broke that image, and the journey to the moon became possible.

For billions of people, the only reality from which no one could escape was death. But someone thought about resurrection and made it possible. It is now a challenge for humanity.

Courage has an important mission. Courage destroys many crystallized forces within your aura formed during the time of your failures. Any time you fail, you crystallize a force in your aura. Continuous failure leads you to the grave.

When you are going downhill in your life, try to do the exercises on courage so that you loosen your aura and melt away the crystallizations. Crystallizations freeze the circulation of energy in your system. Failure is an icing process. Success is a melting process in the aura. Crystallized particles of aura travel and block the interrelationship of the centers or enter into the centers and distort their natural function. Courage has a potent effect on crystallizations. It melts them and causes the circulation of forces in the organism.

5. Love

The next element is love. The procedure for love is as follows:

1. Experience physical love, the way you understand it.
   a. in terms of physical contact
   b. in terms of active protection, help, etc.
2. Experience emotional love. Visualize the event you want to experience using emotional love.
3. Experience mental love.
4. Experience spiritual love.

5. See the differences between them.

6. Visualize those moments in your life when you really loved physically. Visualize those moments in your life when you really loved emotionally, mentally, and spiritually. Try to re-experience these moments deeply and with as much detail as possible to release the energy locked in your system.

7. Think: What does love do for me?

8. Think: What does love do for others?

6. Harmlessness

The next exercise is on harmlessness.

1. Sit and relax.

2. Breathe a few deep breaths.

3. Think about how you can be harmless

   a. with your thoughts and motives

   b. with your words and in conversations

   c. in writings

   d. in the way you live

4. Try to remember five occasions in which you could have been harmful but you became harmless.

5. Can you find out what harmlessness is and why it is a healing agent?

6. Try to find a plan or decision in you, or a tendency in you, to hurt someone and reverse it. Change it into an intention of harmlessness.

7. What relation does harmlessness have to your karma?

8. Visualize a problem between you and another person, and solve the problem with harmlessness.

9. Do this exercise at least thirty minutes to be able to release the energies accumulated in your nature from those moments of your life when you were harmless in a challenging situation.

7. Gratitude

The next exercise is on gratitude:

1. Sit and relax.

2. Take three deep breaths.

3. Explain to an imagined audience the meaning of gratitude.

4. Express gratitude to the oceans, lakes, rivers, to the birds, animals, trees, flowers, and to life in general.

5. Express and feel gratitude toward your family, friends, teachers, and the Teaching.

6. Feel grateful for the difficulties and disciplines through which you have passed, are passing, or will pass.

7. Sense the feeling of gratitude within your heart.

8. Remember ten events in which persons were grateful to you.

9. Remember five events where you really were grateful.

With these seven methods you can bring in a great amount of harmony and health and energy into your system. You can do each one every day for one month, or you can do them successively forever.

After you have gradually built up the time from five minutes, the time limit can be between thirty to forty-five minutes. It will be easier for you if someone else guides you without interfering with your inner privacy.

Through these exercises you can create a new personality, a new life for yourself. Remember that nothing can seriously change in your life except when you change, transform, and expand your consciousness.

These seven exercises may change, expand, and transform your consciousness if they are done wholeheartedly, with dedication and joy.

One more point regarding identity must be brought up at this time. There is a phenomenon which appears and reappears again and again in the history of humanity. You can see it occurring at different times, in different places: masquerade parties, shows, festivals, dances, ceremonies, etc., in which people use disfigured masks, animal figures, satanic images, or they paint their faces to make them look ridiculous, outrageous, ugly, and so on. People have felt delight and pleasure in such festivities without knowing that the degeneration of human morals, health, labor, and striving begins with such festivities.

Historic research will clearly prove that before great failures, degeneration, increase in crime, and destruction, such festivities took a prominent place in the life of nations. The reason for such a destructive effect on human morals, existence, and health is as follows:

Through masquerading, one tries to build an identity beyond his real, essential identity. If one has an identity, he introduces into his identity a strange identity and creates disturbances and distortion in his essential identity. If he has no identity, he adopts the identity of the mask and his consciousness works within the programming received through the mask.

In our etheric, astral, and mental bodies there are found the prototypes of the form we have. For example, the etheric body is the model on which the physical body is built. Masquerading is an effort to introduce changes in the prototype and condition it to create a form in which we can mask ourself.

The prototype can gain and grow in power with any improvement, but it suffers and creates great tension when imposed upon by lower forms and inharmonious figures.

Such a distortion first damages the spirit of striving, improvement, and harmony; then the degeneration of the person and the group starts.

Your real prototype is the basis of your identity. Trying to create a lower form in your consciousness is an effort *to dissolve your identity.*

Every human being is a seed, and he must try to make his seed bloom. Any effort to make a rose bloom as a weed is involutionary and retrogressive. You must bloom as the seed you are.

Masquerading is a forceful imposition on your prototype — the blueprint — and a cause of inner confusion. Actually, confusion is the first sign of losing your identity.

The crimes that are continually presented to us by our television programs and movies will create non-identities because the real, non-criminal essence of the human soul will adopt a new identity in the form of a criminal, and his evolution will retard for ages.

The conflict between your true identity and the false identity imposed upon you will result in sickness, diseases, crimes, depression, confusion, and suicide. That is how a person, a group, and nations end. Once your imagination is forcefully impressed by the ugly image, your imagination will try to manufacture you according to that image.

The real blueprint is the "image of God" in which you are created. It is a force, a source of energy, an urge, and it wants you to bloom into it.

Any force distorting that blueprint ends in disaster.

It is very interesting to note that our physical body may enjoy masquerade parties, clowns, etc., and we may also enjoy them emotionally and try to justify their existence philosophically, even politically. But all these positive responses do not prevent the danger of distortion, disturbances, and confusion in our prototype. Rather, these positive responses invite, attract, and make us fuse ourself with the presented ugly image and imprint it strongly upon our consciousness.

Once the image is allowed to reach your inner chambers, the conflict will start within you, and eventually your positive responses will change into painful reactions.

The ugly images, distorted faces, masks, and clowns carry with them a subliminal, powerful suggestion for degeneration. This is a fact not noticed to this day by our prominent politicians, psychologists, and educators.

Once I asked a woman who was in love with an ugly character in a popular film, "Do you want to be in that shape?" She screamed, "No, no, no.... My God!"

"Why not? You love it so!"

"No...."

"But that image is a part of your consciousness. Can you trace the subtle influences it exercises on you and on your life?"

Sometimes we fight for a lifetime against imported and ugly images and waste precious energy. Sometimes we escape, but sometimes the bad example or the image molds us, and we become that repeated image. Why do we want to import such a danger into our consciousness?

When the Watergate scandal was revealed, an ugly image was impressed upon the consciousness of the youth of the whole world. The evolution of the consciousness of the youth was retarded to a certain degree by that image, an image we broadcasted day and night.

Images of great success, nobility, and heroism will move the world on the path of perfection. These are the images which must be impressed upon the consciousness of humanity.

A person becomes like the one that he loves. This is true physically, emotionally, mentally, and spiritually.

When you want someone to love you, you dress beautifully, you act beautifully, you speak beautifully because you know in your heart that he or she loves beauty. Beauty builds your identity and the identity in others and assists in your success.

52

Co-Measurement

Co-measurement teaches you how not to prevent the progress and blooming of others with your actions, thoughts, and words. You measure everything that you are going to do before you do it.

Co-measurement is based on balance, on righteousness. A righteous man is a balanced man. Co-measurement is balanced and righteous action. One takes in the measure that he gives. There is a balance in what he takes and in what he gives. Whatever one receives from Nature, he returns to Nature. Whatever he receives from people, he returns to people.

Co-measurement develops in you the awareness that you belong to all that exists. People think that they belong to themselves, or to their family, nation, race, or country. This is a great illusion in which people are trapped.

Co-measurement teaches you that you belong to the whole existence, and because you belong to the whole existence, all your actions, words, and thoughts must be in agreement, in harmony with the good of all. Your individual existence must glorify the whole by the way you live.

Of course, the whole is not a smooth flow on which you can stand. It is a choppy ocean, and you must find your balance in this ever-moving ocean. This is co-measurement.

Your real spiritual awareness develops when you lose yourself in the vision of the whole existence. One cannot find his Real Self unless he detaches from the little self with which he is identified as his "I" or his self. Losing your little self is finding your True Self, which is the Great Existence, the whole.

When your individual worth grows in your eyes beyond proportion, watch the midnight sky and think about Infinity. It helps you to co-measure your existence.

Responsibility has a very close affinity with co-measurement. Responsibility dawns in your heart when you identify yourself with the rights of others, with the aspirations and strivings of other people, and find the point of balance between the need and your response. Co-measurement teaches you how not to prevent the progress and blooming of others with your actions, thoughts, and words. You measure everything that you are going to do before you do it.

One may ask, "On what will our measurement be based?"

Of course we have many standards built within ourselves through our traditions, religion, and education. Some of them are languages from past lives. If all these are used as standard measures, we are lost. We are going to measure by Cosmic standards: Beauty, Goodness, Truth, Perfection, Holism, Synthesis, Oneness. These are seven Cosmic standards.

Co-measurement is not one-sided action but a balance between all that exists, as a point of inspiration, hope, and vision.

Your inner measures are often distorted. The right measures are found in your consciousness, in your soul.

Once I saw a man telling his son to go and take apples from two other boys who were about to eat them. He said, "Go get them. Take the apples from their hands and you enjoy them."

"I don't want to do it."

"You coward."

"I am not."

"Then go get them."

"No."

"Why not?"

"Because when they eat the apples, they will feel pleasure. They are two. Two boys will feel pleasure. I am one. One pleasure is less than two pleasures!"

Co-measurement is an increasing contact with the manifestation of life and a right relationship with it. Co-measurement leads to completion, ring-by-ring on the spiral.

> *Those who criticize or flatter people have lack of co-measurement. They criticize because they are stuck with a characteristic of another person which they don't like....*[1]

How do we eliminate criticism?

1. Take people you know, and find the areas in them of which you are critical.

2. Confront the same areas within yourself.

3. Work out a plan to bring these areas into beauty.

> *...They flatter someone if they think that flattery will help them obtain their self-interests.*[2]

How can we find this within us?

---

1. *The Flame of Beauty, Culture, Love, Joy,* p. 105.
2. *Ibid.*

1. Review the times you flattered people.
2. See what self-interest you were trying to obtain.
3. Work out a creative way in which you can obtain the same goal — not just for the self but for the whole.

Take an act you performed and examine it. Why did you do it? How did you do it? What kind of influences preconditioned your actions? Thus keeping your act at the center, you find many factors related to it. Such an expanding field in your consciousness develops co-measurement.

How to Develop Co-Measurement

I. *Exercise*

Choose an object, such as a pencil, paper, chair, table, or lamp, and try to find all the possible stages the object passed through to become what it now is. Do this for one month.

Then try to imagine the various uses of the object you considered. Do this for one month.

In the third month, try to find the ways you yourself used the object.

After three months you will see a considerable change in your consciousness. You will have a broader scope of thinking and a greater ability to relate and adapt.

After three months you can choose an abstract subject such as beauty, solemnity, responsibility and do the same thing as you did with your concrete subject. Thus, try to find in your meditation how these words and ideas came into being, how they originated, and how they developed. You do not need to look in an encyclopedia to find your answers. They are right within your soul — bring them out.

In the second month try to see the various ways in which these concepts, ideas, and words were used.

In the third month try to find the ways you used these concepts in your creative and practical life.

In the next three months you can take a very abstract subject such as "motion" and try to find the relationship of motion to the motion of various objects in your body, in your city, on the planet, solar system, and beyond. Try to find a relationship between all of these motions or movements.

Through such exercises you prepare yourself not only for executive positions but also for higher leadership. People think that positions can be grasped by artificial means. This is possible, but it brings many disadvantages with it. Rightful positions come to those who are ready for them. When you are ready, your position will not be a burden for you or an occasion of failure but a cycle of great joy, spiritual service, and satisfaction. Co-measurement is an ever-expanding relationship.[3]

II. Exercise

There is another exercise which can be done individually or in group formation. This exercise is called "questioning."

A group can sit together and choose a subject. Then the members ask you questions from various viewpoints, for example, "Harmlessness." The questions you might be asked may be from a political, educational, philosophical, artistic, scientific, religious, or economic viewpoint, and you will try to answer as best you can. Such an exercise discloses all your weaknesses and brings you to the realization of where you stand regarding that particular subject. This gives you a chance to try to expand the field of your information, to cultivate greater ability to think and formulate and see your object from as many viewpoints as possible. Such an exercise cultivates the faculty of co-measurement.[4]

III. Exercise

If a man or any living being or form wants to go back to the Source, there is only one way — to be a living love. No matter on what plane love operates, it produces or creates forms to further the evolution of the spirit.

There are seven levels of expression of love:

1. The first expression of love is sex....

It can be physical sex, in human or lower kingdoms.

It can be emotional sex.... In this stage, instead of thinking only of your pleasure, you think of the pleasure of others.[5]

---

3. Adapted from *The Flame of Beauty, Culture, Love, Joy*, pp. 103-104.
4. *Ibid.*, p. 104.
5. *Ibid.*, p. 110.

Discuss how a person could have emotional sex with others — how he could think of the pleasure of others and not of the self. Consider:

— Different members of the family

— Work

— Close people in your environment

— Country, group, nation

> *Then we have mental sex....*
>
> *...Many great visions, ideas, projects, and plans are created when two or more people put their minds together and inspire each other, as a mental-level sex activity....*[6]

a. Review your life and discuss when you have had, with one or more people, mental sex. What was the vision, idea, or project that was created?[7]

b. Then think of anyone at present with whom you have good mental sex. What projects are the result?

c. With whom in the future could you create plans, visions, projects? What kinds of projects would you like to create?

> *Man is a drop of fiery love fallen into matter. Our responsibility is to release ourselves and bloom in all dimensions....*[8]

a. Go over areas where you need to release the Self and love more, areas where you need to manifest and be love.

b. Work out ways this could be done in your relations with others.

c. Work out how you could be a fiery love that is in full bloom.

> *2. The second expression of love is* goodwill. *You will good for others. To will good for others means to meet their needs and prepare them in a way that they eventually meet their own need and the needs of others....*[9]

---

6. *Ibid.*, pp. 110-111.
7. See also *Sex, Family, and the Woman in Society*, Chs. 1 and 24.
8. *Ibid.*, p. 111.
9. *Ibid.*

a. Go over how you could meet the needs of others.

b. Then go over a way you could help them learn to meet their own needs.

c. Finally, discuss how you could help those people learn to meet the needs of others. Find five examples.

> *Think good for others. Any time any negative thought or image comes into your mind, reject it, and in its place immediately express a positive thought.*[10]

a. Review ten instances in the past when you have had negative thoughts. Replace each with a positive thought.

b. Discuss the present. Find all areas of negative thoughts and immediately express a positive thought in their place. Be thorough. Look for all areas in the self, the home, family, work, etc.

c. Go over what to do in the future when a negative thought or image appears.

> *Do the same with your feelings. Any time a negative thought or image comes into your emotional nature, replace it with a loving feeling.*[11]

a. Go over ten instances in the past when you had negative feelings and replace them with loving feelings.

b. Go over the present and view any negative feelings in life. Replace them with loving feelings.

c. Go over an imagined future at home, work, etc., and see how you can change negative feelings in your emotional nature into loving feelings.

> *Also, if you are ready to take an action which is harmful, criminal, or destructive, immediately stop and reverse it. Express a positive, benevolent action toward the one against whom you were ready to take harmful action. In this way you release that love energy and eventually feel that you are love itself. And because you are love, you can only love and will good to others.*[12]

---

10. *Ibid.*
11. *Ibid.*
12. *Ibid.*, pp. 111-112.

a. Go over ten instances in the past when you did harmful, criminal, or destructive acts toward another. Each time see a positive, benevolent action you could have taken toward the person.

b. See if there is anyone today you want to take destructive action against.

c. Work out an imagined future where this might happen, and see yourself reversing the situation and taking a positive, benevolent action.

> *3. The third expression of love in the human kingdom is* right human relationship....[13]

> *...Greater love helps you endure the pain of the present caused by your past deeds....*[14]

a. Discuss any pain you have in the present, and see how with greater love you could endure it more easily.

b. Continue with this until you see how all of the present could be endured if greater love were being expressed by you.

> *...Greater love makes you tolerant and forgiving of the acts of human beings who consciously or unconsciously try to hurt you.*[15]

a. Go over the past and review, one at a time, any acts of others who consciously or unconsciously tried to hurt you.

b. Then with greater love, forgive each and every act and also the person.

c. See the beauty of the person.

d. Work out a creative situation where you would have brought that beauty out.

e. Do the same with the present.

f. Do the same with five imagined future events.

> *When we try to show another human being how ugly, short, unwise, or unsuccessful he is, he hates us and tries to belittle us to prove that we are not better than he is. But when we see his*

---

13. *Ibid.*, p. 113.
14. *Ibid.*, p. 114.
15. *Ibid.*

beauty, he realizes his own shortcomings, silently improves himself, and respects our beauty because we raised him up to the level of beauty.[16]

Consider people you have known in both the past and present and do the following steps for each person:

a. Take a time when you tried to show another his faults.

b. Then reverse it. Take the same person and show him his beauty, not his faults.

c. Imagine how different the result would have been.

d. Take situations around you that you know might come up in the future, and see yourself bringing out the beauty instead of the faults of others.

The hindrances to right human relationships are five in number:

a. Imposition of one's own will on others

b. Greed

c. Unrighteousness

d. Uncooperativeness

e. Pride

...When you impose your will *on others, you are making right human relationship impossible.... Imposition of your will may take many forms. You can impose yourself by your physical force, money, power, position, fear, bribery, flattery....*

If you have something beautiful, you must not force others to admit its beauty, but you must educate and raise their consciousness in such a way that they see the beauty through their own efforts....[17]

a. Find the times that you have imposed your will on others. What force did you use? Was it

---

16. *Ibid.*
17. *Ibid.*, pp. 114-115.

— physical force

— money

— power

— position

— fear

— bribery

— flattery

b. See how you could have educated instead.

c. For each time you forced your will, work out an imaginary time in the future and see how you could educate and raise people's consciousness instead of forcing your will.

..In greed *one makes himself the center of the universe and uses others to feed his glamor.... It is an unsatisfied thirst for material possessions....*[18]

..If you really want to regain your joy and peace, use your accumulated money to create right human relations, more education, more health....[19]

Right human relationship is based on the idea that a man must live in a way that all the rest can profit from the life he lives, and because of the health of all the rest, he remains healthy.[20]

a. Observe the times when you were greedy. See where you could have used your accumulated wealth for right human relations.

b. Look at the present and see where you could be using your accumulations and money for right human relationships, not just for yourself. Go over your budget and see how you can help. Work out how much you can give and where it would be most effective.

The next hindrance is unrighteousness....

---

18. *Ibid.*, p. 115.
19. *Ibid.*, p. 116.
20. *Ibid.*, pp. 116-117.

Criticism has been forbidden for ages because in criticism we are always unrighteous, since we look at things not from the viewpoint of others but from the viewpoint of our interests.[21]

a. Take each situation where you were critical in the past and present, one at a time.

b. Then look at the same situation from the other person's viewpoint. If more than one person is involved, take each person separately and see his viewpoint.

c. Work out how everyone could have won by marrying all the viewpoints. Be creative.

d. Expand this to a newspaper. Read it; find several viewpoints.

e. Expand this to nations; see all viewpoints.

f. Then imagine yourself in five situations in the future where you feel critical. Stop. Then see the viewpoints of all concerned. Then work out a positive handling where all win.

The next obstacle is uncooperativeness.

Cooperation is the ability to see a common interest and the willingness to help others share in that common interest....[22]

a. Find times in the past and the present when you were uncooperative.

b. Look at the situations and see where there is a common interest.

c. Then work out a way to help others share in that common interest.

d. Look out beyond yourself. Look at people you know who are uncooperative in a situation; then look at groups, then nations.

e. Look at these situations and see where there is a common interest.

f. Work out a way to help others share in that common interest.

The fifth obstacle is pride.

---

21. *Ibid.*, p. 117.
22. *Ibid.*, p. 118.

Pride is a crystallized mentality in which one thinks that he is an object of worship and beauty, and the rest of the people are obliged to praise him every time he moves....

Pride does not allow him to see the value in others. Right human relationship grows and develops only in a consciousness which can see beauty, value, and merit in others.[23]

a. Take situations in the past where there was pride.

b. See the people in the situation. Discuss their value.

c. Discuss their beauty.

d. Discuss their merit.

e. Then take people in your life today. See their value and their beauty.

f. Then look at the value in

- government
- education
- business
- art
- science
- religion
- economics

g. Then look at the value of your nation; then the planet.

4. The fourth expression of love is service carried out in a great humanitarian project.

..In such service you are above your self, group, or national interest and are now entering into the field of pure human interest, with your project having a global meaning.

23. *Ibid.*

People who are dedicated to such a service will see their love increasing to such a degree that they often will feel as one spirit in many bodies, and eventually they will feel that they are living as streams of love.[24]

Every time you try to do something for humanity, you transform yourself into love and tune in more with the divine harmony.[25]

a. Think of a great humanitarian project to which you would like to contribute your services.

b. Research and see if such a group already exists.

c. Volunteer some time. Donate some money.

5. *The fifth degree of the expression of love can be defined as follows*. The vision of the future of humanity can be fulfilled through the divine Plan, *which indicates the way of survival, creativity, and manifestation of the beauty of mankind.*

...When we come in contact with the Intuitional Plane, we touch that dimension of love which penetrates into all living forms in Nature.[26]

...You sense the unity with all living forms.[27]

a. Take ten living forms and see what your commonness or unity is with each form. Do this with minerals, vegetables, animals, and humanity.

b. Take your company or business and see what unity it has with five other companies or businesses.

c. Take your family and see what unity it has with five entirely different kinds of families.

d. Take your nation and see what unity it has with five other nations.

e. Discuss the unity you have with all living forms.

---

24. *Ibid.*
25. *Ibid.*, p. 119.
26. *Ibid.*, p. 120.
27. *Ibid.*, p. 121.

6. The sixth expression of love is contact with the Will of Shamballa.

It is at this stage that love reveals to you the vision of the Purpose of life....[28]

a. Go for a walk. Look at the flowers, plants, trees.

— Ask yourself what the purpose is of each.

— Pick up rocks and objects from the mineral kingdom and do the same.

b. Remember a favorite animal. Ask yourself what is the purpose of that animal's life.

c. Go through each of your personal relationships. Ask what is the purpose of each.

d. Look at your group or your work and ask what is the purpose.

e. Look at your nation and ask what is the purpose.

f. Look at our earth and ask yourself what is the purpose.

g. Look at the sky and ask what is the purpose.

h. Look at or remember a time you were at the ocean and ask what is the purpose.

i. Look at or remember a mountain and ask what is the purpose.

j. Look at or remember a sunrise, then a sunset. Ask about each, what is the purpose.

k. Look at your own life and ask what is the purpose.

— See if you could work out a better plan to achieve that purpose.

— Discuss or write yourself a plan to achieve that purpose for one day, one week, one month, one year, five years, then the rest of your life.

7. The seventh expression of love is the stage in which you become the embodiment of the Ray of Cosmic Love.

---

28. *Ibid.*

> *...It is in this degree of achievement that a man realizes himself as a stream of Cosmic Love and becomes a radiant Son of God.*[29]

a. See yourself in your mind as a stream of Cosmic Love.

b. See yourself coming to earth and penetrating all living forms.

c. See yourself streaming through all troubled areas on our planet.

d. Go through all your personal relationships and see yourself as a stream of Cosmic Love bringing the beauty out of each relationship until it blooms into a flower with its own original color.

---

29. *Ibid.*

53

Occult Breathing

Thus, we are told, we spread subtle diseases through our breath, or we radiate healing currents through our breath and words or through our speech.

When we talk about breathing, we do not refer to breathing exercises, pranayama; but we refer to deep, regular, rhythmic, harmonious breathing.

Man breathes with only half or a quarter of his lungs. This has drastic effects on his health and consciousness, and, considering the polluted air he breathes, the effect can be disastrous.

What is breathing really for? Breathing is the ignition process for the centers of the three personality planes. The centers in the etheric, astral, and mental planes are ignited every time you breathe. This ignition makes them operate or receive mental, astral, and etheric energy — prana — to absorb and assimilate it and pass it to the body, glands, organs, and senses on the etheric, astral, and mental planes.

Breathing supplies fuel to the mechanism of the senses on all planes. It charges each cell, each atom, and each center and coordinates them with each other so that the whole mechanism is integrated and is under the command of the human soul. The light of the human soul cannot operate in the three planes unless one breathes.

One not only breathes physically but also emotionally and mentally. There is a three-cycle breathing: first the physical inhales, then the astral, then the mental. The mental body exhales, the astral body exhales, and the physical body exhales. This is why hurried breathing and irregular breathing do not allow time for the astral and mental "lungs" to do their part. This is also why any mental or emotional tension or crisis affects the physical breathing.

When breathing is not done properly, the consciousness becomes foggy and blurred and eventually fades away. It is the breathing that rhythmically makes the light of the consciousness pass from center to center, from one sense to another, from one plane to another. If coordination is achieved between the etheric centers and the higher centers, the electricity and light increase in them to such a degree that man becomes aware of his entire mechanism. This is accomplished at the Third Initiation during which his light evokes a response from the centers functioning on higher planes.

Continuity of consciousness is the result of right breathing on the three planes and of coordination with the Intuitional Plane and higher planes.

The control tower of breathing is found in the mental plane. The human soul breathes intuitional light. His breathing puts in motion the mental, astral, and etheric centers which control the breathing process on these planes. But the physical, emotional, and mental hindrances distort and disturb this process and create disharmony and a broken rhythm in the flow of breathing.

These hindrances are wrong actions, negative feelings, and separative and harmful thinking. These elements create pollution in the aura and make the breathing unrhythmic, irregular, short, and inharmonious on all planes.

When the centers, senses, glands, and organs are deprived of their regular share of fire which breathing brings in, they create various disorders and the health on these levels deteriorates.

The important point is that before the health deteriorates, one can see a deterioration of morals and of the thinking and consciousness. Health, morality, and consciousness are affected by wrong breathing.

The soul pulsates like a ball of light, receives energy, and radiates energy into the human aura. The physical-etheric, astral, and mental bodies synchronize themselves into this process of rhythm and receive, assimilate, and distribute their share of light, fire, and consciousness. Thus our breathing is directly affected by our actions on all planes, our emotions, our motives, our thoughts, and our speech.

Speech can directly distort all actions on the three planes and carry poison to the aura if it is used destructively for selfish and separative ends and for the distribution of hatred, malice, lies, and ugliness.

When a person speaks, you can see in the breath etheric, astral, and mental elements. Science has not yet researched the human breath. In coming decades, an electronic analyzer will be built to analyze the human breath and identify the etheric, astral, and mental pollutions spreading not only into the aura of the person but also into Space. Thus, we are told, we spread subtle diseases through our breath, or we radiate healing currents through our breath and words or through our speech.

Memory is very closely related to the coordination of the breathing process. When memory is lost, it is because the coordination of breathing is lost and cleavages are created between the mental, astral, etheric, and physical breath.

People will never forget anything if the breath is coordinated between the planes. If one forgets where he put his keys, in that moment there was a gap between the breathing mechanisms.

Moments of high creativity, inspiration, and reception of subtle impressions are the moments in which a pure coordination is achieved between the breathing of the three bodies and the soul. It is such a coordination that creates a great magnetic field in the aura which sensitively attracts higher currents of creative fires or higher currents of light.

The first practical effort should be to learn breathing on all levels, allowing time to make all the gears synchronize. To do this, take a few minutes for deep breathing. As you inhale, pause a while and visualize your astral, then mental breathing following after each other.

As you exhale, visualize a similar process in these bodies. When this is learned, you will try to shift your consciousness from the physical plane and realize that you are the soul, and then make your bodies follow the rhythm in which you are breathing.

Of course, this shift of consciousness will take time, but when you learn how to be the soul, you become a healing agent for the bodies through your breath.

Remember, once Christ breathed out, saying, "Receive the Holy Spirit." He was literally making all His disciples inhale His breath, which was a current of light coming from higher spheres. The disciples were absorbing that light into their lungs on three planes, transforming not only their consciousness but also their lives.

Right action on three levels and deep breathing not only make the centers unfold but also help the consciousness to expand. Right action on the physical plane is living in a way that you do not hinder the progress of other pilgrims. You do not mislead them or distort their thinking or use them for your own separative interests.

Right action on the astral plane means generating feelings and emotions not contaminated by fear, hatred, anger, jealousy, greed, revenge, and malice.

Right action on the mental plane is the generating of thoughts not contaminated with vanity, ego, separatism, and illusions.

If you begin deep breathing, you will see how a process of purification is taking place in your three planes. As you try consciously to purify your actions, to that degree your breathing on three levels improves.

The moments of seeing yourself as you are, are the moments when your consciousness is lit with the sudden synchronization of breathing.

Our breath has a tremendous power to create or to destroy. It does not matter if the breath if formulated into speech or not; it carries the electrical and fiery elements coming from the three planes.

Right action is not only things you do right but also things you do not do which would be harmful. Actions on three planes follow the rhythm of breathing until the soul takes control of the mechanism. After that, actions follow the rhythm of the breathing of the soul.

Every right action is a nourishment for our centers on all planes.

Average people must train themselves for physical right actions. Aspirants must train themselves for right action on the physical and emotional planes. Emotions are influential actions, even if they are not pronounced by words.

Disciples must train themselves for right action on the physical, emotional, and mental planes simultaneously. The thoughts one has in his mind, even if they are not put into words, are as effective as swords.

Right action on the three planes is the result of right breathing on the three planes. Wrong action on the three planes is the result of wrong breathing on those planes. Each wrong action pours a poison into your aura. When the poison accumulates, it kills the possibility of growth of your subtle centers and senses which need right nourishment to grow and bloom.

We are warned to be extremely careful with our breathing. First of all, no breathing exercise is allowed if the person's character is not pure and he is full of physical, emotional, and mental pollution. In such cases, any breathing exercises forcefully increase the pollution and create very unhealthy conditions in the body.

We are advised to practice only deep breathing, and even in deep breathing to concentrate our mind on lofty ideas and visions so that our negatively oriented centers do not receive any stimulation.

My Teacher used to exercise deep breathing by looking at the stars or the sunrise.

At the time of breathing, either the thought or the will directs the energy of the thought. If the thought is related to lower centers, negative emotions, or harmful, separative thoughts, it energizes the corresponding centers and makes them produce poison in the human body. This is why during deep breathing one must concentrate his mind on thoughts of Beauty, Goodness, Righteousness, Joy, and Freedom and focus his mind in light.

Right breathing nourishes your sense of direction, and you begin to coordinate your breathing with the breathing of the kingdoms of Nature and the breathing of the earth and the Sun. This is how you open the channels of communication between you and higher spheres and expand your consciousness to use your higher contacts creatively.

We must remember that every chakra or center on the three planes has three departments: acting, feeling, and thinking. Every act echoes in every center and produces effects. Right or wrong action on any plane is registered in every center. Similarly, right or wrong emotions and thoughts are registered in corresponding departments of centers on three planes.

Thus a wrong action on the physical plane damages the corresponding parts of the astral and mental centers and vice versa.

Every action on each plane must use the whole center if one wants to keep balance between the three departments of each center. For example, when you act on the physical plane, you must feel your action, you must think about your action, and you must not act mechanically. When you are feeling, you must act and think. When you are thinking, you must feel and act.

People use only one part of their centers and thus create disharmony in their centers and in their vehicles. Your expressions have a tremendous power when they are charged by the three departments of the three centers. Expressions which are supported by only one department of your chakras carry imbalanced substance and confuse the people you contact or create imbalance in their nature.

Good breathing makes your centers function in these three departments as one. And when they function this way, they make your organs and senses function properly, kindling their fuses to do their job. They make your kidneys work right. They make your sexual organs work right. They make your digestive organs work right. They make your heart, lungs, and brain work right. They make you sane. Sanity is the result of the proper functioning of all your glands and their corresponding chakras.

If you do not breathe in the right way, you create cleavages between the centers and between the three parts of each center, and you become confused physically, emotionally, and mentally. If you learn how to breathe etherically, astrally and mentally, you can retain your consciousness on these planes after leaving your body in death or when you consciously withdraw from it.

Your physical organs depend on your etheric organs or on higher organs. For example, if your eyes are not healthy, the cause can be found in the etheric eyes, or in the related center in the astral body or mental body. Through right breathing on the level where the trouble is, you can correct the situation and remove the cause of your bad eyesight.

The ancients used to make their decisions in an open field, under the trees, around a bonfire, near lakes or rivers, or at the sea shore, rather than in a room polluted with smoke, gases, poisons, and fumes. Right decisions cannot be arrived at if the atmosphere is full of pollution. In a polluted atmosphere, your mental lungs cannot breathe, and your sense of direction fails to operate.

Great decisions must be made in clean air and through deep breathing. Breathing is a process of fusion with "the One in Whom we live, move, and have our being."

People think that breathing is only a process of supplying oxygen to the blood. This is an old story, and we all know about it. The new story is that air carries not only prana — vitalizing energy — to the body, but it also carries particles of love to the astral body and rays of wisdom to the mental body. Great Beings Who brought a higher culture and higher directions to humanity were Those Who lived mostly in the open air, breathed pure prana, and exercised deep emotional, mental, and spiritual breathing.

How can we breathe in the right way? This will not be easy, but eventually we will learn.

Physical Breathing

I. *Exercise*

1. Choose a clean place to walk.

2. As you begin walking, exhale the air from your lungs.

3. Walk eight counts while breathing in.

4. Walk eight counts while holding the breath.

5. Continue walking and exhale for eight counts.

6. Continue walking and hold your lungs empty for eight counts.

Repeat the exercise five times. Then try to breathe deeply during the day. Do this exercise for at least three months. It becomes more effective if you use the following technique:

Inhale, thinking on each count:

May

Beauty,

Goodness,

Righteousness,

Joy,

Freedom

inspire

me.

At the interval of holding the breath, think and feel about what you said. While exhaling say with each count:

I am

charged

with

Beauty,

Goodness,

Righteousness,

Joy,

Freedom.

At the interval think and feel about what you said. Repeat this five times. Soon you will perceive that you are becoming more careful about your actions, words, expressions, and thoughts. You will notice the increasing clarity of your mind. You will also notice that you have more energy and more control over your actions, emotions, and thoughts.

II. *Exercise*

Lie on your back and relax.

Exhale through your mouth all the air you have in your lungs.

Slowly breathe in, with the three sections of your body: First, fill your abdomen and let it swell with the air. Then inhale into your lower chest and make it rise. Then inhale in the upper chest.

When you fill your lungs, exhale the air, first pulling in your abdomen, then pulling down your lower chest, then the upper chest, always exhaling through your mouth as if you were whistling.

Do this after eliminating and before you eat anything in the morning.

Do this exercise only once a day for five months; then start your first exercise again for eight months, then continue with the second for eight months, continuing to alternate the two exercises into your healthy old age.

Emotional Breathing

I. *Exercise*

1. Take a flower and breathe its fragrance and enjoy it.
2. Relate the fragrance to a joyful, emotional experience.
3. Admire the beauty of the flower and feel the joy of your being.
4. Slowly breathe in and out the fragrance and the colors through your nose and eyes. Try to feel its fragrance and joy in each of your astral centers:
   a. Inhale the fragrance, the colors, and the beauty.
   b. Enjoy it for a moment.
   c. Radiate it, exhaling it.
   d. Feel the effect of it.

Do this exercise for three months, changing the kind of flower every week. You can also do this with a bush or tree.

II. *Exercise*

This exercise is purely emotional breathing. See and feel the flower, and visualize you are inhaling its fragrance and beauty through your emotional lungs. This is like an intense, magnetic inhalation with or without breathing.

You see a sunset or a gorgeous tree, an ocean, or a mountain, and you feel ecstasy. You fill your emotional being, say, your heart, with the image of your admiration.

It is not easy to operate emotional breathing, but nothing is impossible. People call emotional breathing enjoyment, aspiration, admiration, and ecstasy. All these are parts of it.

Once I sat by a huge deodar tree, and for one hour I breathed its beauty and fragrance emotionally until I realized that my lungs were breathing with the breathing of the tree. You can also breathe music. Instead of listening only, you can breathe in the music with your emotional lungs.

III. *Exercise*

Listen to some music and try to dance to it with appropriate movements. Synchronization of your movements and your breathing with the rhythm of the music will be physical breathing. But when you inhale the music and rhythm into your emotional lungs, it will produce immense joy and ecstasy.

Do this for three months, daily, for ten minutes. Then do the next exercise.

IV. *Exercise*

Inhale love and exhale love emotionally. Do this only with your family members, husband, wife, children, or with Great Ones you love, such as Buddha, Christ, Mohammed, Pythagoras, etc. Inhale their love in ecstasy and give your love to them in exhalation.

It is through these exercises that you will learn the secret of emotional breathing. But when you find secrets, do not tell people so that they find them for themselves. These are exercises which will lead you to very important discoveries.

Mental Breathing

Mental breathing is done in the sphere of the mental plane. All of us breathe mentally, but not all of us are conscious of it. Conscious mental breathing is deep thinking, meditation, and the ability to receive ideas, impressions, and inspiration and express them in creative ways.

The mental mechanism can grow and unfold through mental breathing, which is a taking, assimilating, and giving process. This process is related in a rhythmic way to physical and emotional breathing. They work as a unit and influence each other.

Physical breathing changes the rhythm of emotional or mental breathing. Mental breathing and emotional breathing have the same effect on physical breathing. For example, if one starts a deep meditation and mentally breathes in fiery spheres of ideas and visions, his emotional breathing and physical breathing calm down, deepen, and become rhythmic.

Mental breathing relaxes the physical, etheric, and astral bodies and immensely strengthens them. This is why one feels strong, happy, and joyful after a deep meditation.

Creative actions are mental breathing. You inhale mentally an impression, idea, or inspiration, assimilate it, understand it, and then in a creative action exhale it in the form of any creative endeavor.

When mental, conscious breathers increase in number, greater light is brought to the planet from Higher Worlds. It is the mental breathers who bring new ideas and greater changes in the planetary life as they transmit the fire of higher planes and invigorate the earthly life.

Telepathy is a form of mental breathing during which *thoughts* are received and transmitted.

Exercise for Mental Breathing

Sit and be calm — physically, emotionally, and mentally.

Use your creative imagination and visualize you are sitting in light. Let your mental body, which is all around your body, inhale the light and exhale it, purifying and strengthening itself. Do this twenty times, but very slowly.

Next, think about a virtue like gratitude. Imagine yourself being grateful. See how your physical body looks if you are grateful, how your emotions feel when you are grateful, how your mental body acts when you are grateful.

Then think about the quality of gratitude. Does gratitude lead you to inertia, apathy, depression, death? Or does gratitude make you active, excited, busy, or emotional? Or does gratitude bring rhythm, harmony, regularity, and integration into your system?

Then think and meditate about the purpose of gratitude. What does gratitude really exist for? Is the purpose of gratitude to heal, to expand your consciousness and the field of your contacts? How can you use gratitude to reach higher levels of beingness?

Then think what is the cause of gratitude. From where does it originate? Does it originate from a greater source, or is it a fabrication of your imagination? How does gratitude come into being?

After these questions are considered properly, then go to exhalation: How can I manifest or express gratitude with my actions, emotions, thoughts, and creativity? When you try to find the answer to this question and begin to practice it, you are in the process of mental exhalation.

Learning, knowing, and discovery is inhalation. Practical application of these things is exhalation.

You can also use other seed thoughts such as joy, beauty, freedom, and courage. In mental breathing you take a virtue and visualize the embodiment or symbol of that virtue, and then exhale it to your emotional and mental spheres and inhale it through your emotional and physical lungs. This is an exercise of actualizing a virtue in your life.

Another form of mental breathing is to learn, understand, and assimilate a subject and teach it to others, or write about it, or express it through your life or creativity. This is a form of mental breathing, which must be harmonious with other forms of breathing if you want to have right synchronization.

Spiritual Breathing

There is also spiritual breathing through which we draw psychic energy from a Cosmic source. It is this energy that regenerates, transforms, and transfigures life and life-forms. This is done through *contemplation*. Contemplation is literally a process of building a magnetic field in the highest level of the mental plane and attracting a part of the Purpose of the Solar Lord.

Mental breathing is for attracting the vision of the Plan of the Planetary Heart. In spiritual breathing, the magnetic field of contemplation is a very tense electrical field which slowly attracts seeds or rays emanating from the Purpose. These seeds or rays carry high-voltage energy into your mental body and gradually turn into thoughts and thoughtforms.

As you continue your contemplation, which sometimes is a silent, watchful, waiting process, suddenly the magnetic field built by contemplation moves up into the Intuitional Plane. Your true contemplation starts on this plane where you really fill your breath with the light of the Purpose.

It is after this realization that all your life becomes a part of the Purpose and becomes a labor to actualize that Purpose through your life.

A Simple Emotional Breathing Exercise

1. Close your eyes.

2. Relax.

3. Feel love toward a tree or toward a great Being such as Christ or Buddha.

4. Let your love pour toward the object of your love. Do this for five minutes.

5. Then feel the love of your object pouring toward you. Accept that love. Fill all your being with that love.

6. Repeat the third step again for five minutes.

7. Repeat the fourth step again for five minutes.

8. Then observe what your outpouring love and incoming love are doing for you. Actually, you will see the effect better in a few weeks.

Note your observations and experiences in your diary.

A Simple Mental Breathing Exercise

Think about a universal law. Try to understand it. After you understand it to a certain degree, try to explain it to a group of people in your imagination. Do this not more than twenty minutes daily. This will strengthen your mental lungs and bring balance in your life and greater understanding about your purpose in life.

A Simple Spiritual Breathing Exercise

Contemplate about Infinity or about Infinite Space, and see how you can actualize your understanding of Space in your daily life. As you contemplate about Space or Infinity, do not use thinking, logic, or reasoning. Just focus your mental magnetic eyes on the idea of Space and wait for the seeds of light or impressions to come to you.

When you receive certain impressions, begin your exhaling process, which is thinking about and actualization of your impressions or visions. See how you can actualize or manifest Infinity in your life.

Space is limited for those who have a limited consciousness. The space of such people is not even larger than their body or field of interest. But space expands as your consciousness expands. Expansion of space is unlimited; so is your consciousness.

Ignorance and separation are spacelessness — death. As your space narrows, your consciousness dies. As it expands, your consciousness comes into life. Death and life are not related to form or change but to consciousness. When you are unconscious, you are dead on that plane of existence. When you are conscious, you are alive on that plane.

Synchronization Exercise

Combined exercises for the synchronization of breathing on four levels can be done as follows:

Relax and close your eyes.

Take a rose or a flower that you love. Inhale its fragrance and exhale it slowly, watching the rose.

Inhale the fragrance, and feel happy with every physical breath.

Imagine the rose is becoming bigger and bigger until it is bigger than your body.

Breathe normally and rhythmically. See with your every breath that the petals are unfolding and folding. Enjoy the fragrance in your imagination as the petals open and close.

Slowly change into the rose and become a rose, opening and closing your petals as if you were the rose breathing rhythmically. Think about the form of the petals, the colors of the petals, the sensitivity and fragrance of the petals, and the beauty of the rose.

Now visualize a rose in your head which is rhythmically breathing with its petals as you are breathing rhythmically and harmoniously as if you were a rose.

Note that your actual breathing is your physical breathing. Your being a rose and breathing as a rose is your emotional breathing. Holding a breathing rose in your mind is mental breathing.

As you are breathing mentally, think about the purpose of the rose. Think while you are breathing. This is not easy, but possible. Think, inhale; rest, exhale. Think, inhale; exhale in visualizing your thought.

When you learn how to do this by doing it, then go to spiritual breathing. In this stage let the petals of the rose open toward the eternal light in Space, and, like an antenna, expect to be impressed by the impressions from Space.

As impressions are received, they will be exhaled to the mental body, which will inhale them and exhale them to the astral body, which will in turn inhale and exhale them to the physical body, which will then inhale and exhale them to the world.

Try to synchronize the breathing process.

You will advance in your evolution and expand your consciousness if you carefully follow these instructions with patience and perseverance.

Negative and harmful thoughts, negative, and harmful emotions, and negative and destructive actions immediately change the rhythm of the heart; and the disrupted rhythm of the heart creates poison and pumps it into your system. It is through breathing that the centers receive and radiate energy from the Universe back to the Universe.

If the breathing is disturbed by negative emotions, words, and actions, you breathe in poisonous substance from the air and pollute your system more, and then exhale with additional poison.

One must be extremely careful in trying to breathe deeply. The personality must be purified gradually to hold the increasing energy and also to keep its balance during the release of accumulated forces in the lower permanent atoms. To explain this point, we can say that as you breathe more and more deeply, a purification process starts slowly or suddenly and your permanent atoms eject the accumulated negativity or pollution into your personality vehicles.

All your past fears, transgressions, failure images, karmic liabilities, guilt feelings, and shameful recordings spring out and flood your personality. If your personality is pure enough, it may still keep its balance until the poison is cleared away. But if there are impurities and ugliness in it, the released poison unites with the impurities and leads the personality into physical, emotional, and mental disasters because the released poison burns the etheric, astral, and mental centers — slowly or suddenly.

Purity of the personality protects the person, although it cannot prevent crises. If the personality is pure and fused with the light of the Soul, the breath can also have a healing quality if it is directed by the fire of thought to the location of trouble. It is also used to transmit psychic energy or to enlighten the mind of another person through exhaling the breath. In such cases, great ideas and visions are also transmitted. But one must learn how to concentrate his thought energy into the outgoing breath.

Breath transmits light, love, and power if a person lives within the light of his Soul. It is extremely difficult to teach right breathing to those who are not clean and pure in their actions, emotions, speech, and thoughts. Such people are like stables full of the dirt of ages.

To help such people, if they are willing, a very slow process must be exercised so as not to allow past poisons to destroy their lives. But it will be easier to start with children when they are three or four years of age and teach them deep breathing. At that age, their auras and physical, emotional, and mental bodies are still relatively pure. Since they have not yet engaged the gears of past negative recordings, they can bear the release of a certain dose of negativity and strengthen themselves in the process of purifying their bodies.

But, first, physical breathing must be taught to children. Those children who breathe deeply and harmoniously become very healthy people in the future.

Let them walk barefoot for three minutes and inhale in four counts, retain the breath for four counts, exhale through their mouth for four counts, and refrain from breathing for four counts.

Teach them always to stand erect and chest out. Teach them to clean their nose and always breathe through the nose. Teach them to avoid inhaling poisonous gases or dirty smells. Those children who can be disciplined with such simple rules will become thinkers of the future.

One cannot fulfill his soul's destiny while breathing polluted air and being ignorant about deep breathing. The survival of humanity depends mainly on these two things:

1. Clean, unpolluted air, free of negative psychic emanations and poisonous gases and chemicals

2. Deep breathing with conscious aspiration and striving

54

Psychological Breathing

Our health will improve to a great degree if we daily try to exercise five-pointed breathing. Besides our health, we will prepare our spaceships — our astral and mental bodies — and for a distant time, our Intuitional Body.

All Nature breathes. All existence in Space, on all planes, breathes. The earth breathes. The solar system breathes. The galaxy breathes. And the Space beyond all created forms breathes.

Breathing is a process of taking in energies, assimilating them and exhaling through them the worn out elements in the organism.

Space breathes. When It inhales, all forms disappear; and in Space a new conception takes place for a new and future creation. All future life-forms, galaxies, zodiacs, solar systems, and other living forms are conceived in Space. When the Space exhales, a new creation comes into being with all its details, starting from the higher planes to the concrete physical plane.

Man breathes in, first with the cells of his body. As the cells breathe, they draw in energy, regenerate their tiny systems, and exhale the toxins accumulated in them.

Science is going to make a new machine which will measure and analyze the breathing process of the cells, the glands, and the organs of the body. Any sickness in the body is the result of a disturbance in the breathing process of the cells and organs. When a cell or a group of cells does not breathe rhythmically and naturally, it dries up and dies. When the cells breathe synchronously and in a rhythm which is related to the rhythm of all that breathe, man radiates a kind of vibration which forms his health aura — a golden aura. If this golden aura is clouded with patches of grey or dark colors in certain places, we know that the aura is not healthy because certain locations of the body are not breathing. The degeneration of the body parts appears months after the cells stop breathing rhythmically.

If the air is pure, through the second kind of breathing — called lung breathing — we draw energy into our system and regenerate our lungs, blood, glands, and everything in the body. Inhalation ends with an interval during which the assimilation and the destruction of worn-out elements takes place.

Exhalation throws out all burned and unnecessary elements that were accumulated in the lungs, just as your exhaust pipe in your car eliminates unused and burned gas. This is true if you are really breathing.

Most human beings have lost the art of breathing. People breathe in a very shallow, non-rhythmic, and irregular manner. There must first be a deep inhalation, then an interval, then an exhalation, then again an interval.

In unrhythmic breathing, these intervals and the inhalation and exhalation are not harmonized and proportionate. Irregular breathing takes place when certain wrong actions, emotions, and thoughts interfere with the rhythm of our breathing.

This kind of lung breathing can be exercised by standing outdoors and inhaling for eight counts, holding the breath for eight counts, exhaling for eight counts, and waiting another eight counts before the next inhalation. This must be done five to eight times, once a day, in clean air.

When your body cells or skin do not breathe properly, your secretions and perspiration smell very bad. When right breathing is restored, your secretions and perspiration smell very pleasant. Some animals smell your odors and get angry at you when your odor hurts their nose!

In improper breathing of the skin, many complications develop because the skin cannot discharge the poison accumulated in the cells.

The same principle applies to emotional and mental breathing. Breathing purifies, energizes, and builds.

Distorted, disturbed, or irregular breathing is the subjective cause of many crimes, vices, and physical, emotional, and mental sicknesses.

Irregular and shallow breathing encourages germs and microbes to settle into our organism. Also, irregular breathing causes congestion in our emotional and mental sphere where dark urges and drives germinate and multiply.

Insane people, criminals, those who are busy with gossip, slander, malice, revenge, or hatred are bad breathers. By changing one's breathing habits, one can cure himself of these many psychological ailments.

Emotional sensations, mental worries, and depressions are clear signs of defective breathing. By regulating and purifying your breathing process, you can transform not only your physical nature but also your emotional and mental nature.

Good breathing starts with observation. Observe people in various physical and psychological conditions, and find out how they breathe.

I once watched a little boy who was stealing money from his father's jacket. His breathing became very abnormal and continued to be abnormal for a while.

I have observed how gossipers breathe, how liars breathe, how people breathe after speaking evil about someone else.

The form of our breathing synthesizes all our physical, emotional, and mental states.

In addition to lung breathing, there is also a deeper breathing which is the receiving and assimilation of prana, or solar energy. Solar energy is inhaled only consciously. When you consciously focus your attention on the life energy of the Sun, and breathe it in with the air, you can assimilate it and use it.

Inhalation of prana is proportionate to your unfoldment of consciousness. As you raise and expand your consciousness, you assimilate more prana directly from the Sun, or indirectly from bushes, flowers, trees, and the earth.

Prana is the exhalation of the Sun which starts with sunrise. At sunset, the Sun inhales. This is why early morning meditation is so beneficial. Meditation for us is inhalation. You inhale the wisdom of the Sun, and throughout the day you exhale it in your thoughts, words, actions, and relationships.

The whole creation is kept alive because of the circulation of energy which is performed through the breathing process of inhaling and exhaling. The synchronization of the inhalation-interval-exhalation-interval is the rhythm of Nature, from the atom to Infinite Space.

Breathing is a process of building communication between created forms and centers of energies. It is through the breathing process that all creation keeps a form of integrity.

Our mechanism naturally knows how to breathe, if the human glamors, illusions, and wrong ways of feeling, acting, and thinking do not disturb it and make the breathing apparatus form wrong habits.

This is the case now. Humanity does not know how to breathe. If one does not know the value of breathing and the significance of breathing, he pollutes the air and then breathes it in, as is the case now.

Those who have as much clean air as possible must start with skin breathing. Skin breathing takes place if the skin is clean and the cells are not polluted by various drugs, marijuana, and alcohol, or if they are not exhausted beyond their capacity.

When the skin is clean, then one must learn how to relax his body, forget about his emotional and mental problems, and lie for ten to fifteen minutes in the most relaxed position. It is in such relaxation that the body begins to breathe and one feels a lifting sensation in his muscles.

If lung breathing and skin breathing are normal, the man's health improves to a great degree. The five senses especially feel a new regeneration within their functions.

One must observe that all that one does against Beauty, Goodness, Righteousness, Joy, and Freedom greatly damages his breathing process and imposes disturbances and bad habits on it.

In all deep breathing sessions, one must not exaggerate. If you go beyond the capacity of your body, you will feel light-headed; you will create congestion in your system, and you will force energy into your lungs and cells prematurely.

Your body must be fed gradually, not at once. **You must give one year to your body to correct its breathing.**

When deep breathing is exaggerated, it carries too much energy into those centers which are wide open and overstimulates them. This is why balance and equilibrium are two key words for health.

Deep breathing will not only clear your body but will also prepare your emotional and mental mechanisms for new breakthroughs.

Many times our breathing is blocked by various objective and subjective poisons so that the records of the etheric brain are not transmitted to the physical brain. This is how we lose our memory. Deep breathing clears up this ailment.

In some olden schools the speakers or teachers used to exercise deep breathing before the class started. Usually they were wiser and more energetic during the lectures or classes.

Breathing is related to spirituality. No one can increase his urge to progress, transform, and advance without good breathing. In the future, people will find out that all advanced people on the spiritual path were good and deep breathers.

Beyond the physical apparatus of breathing, we also have an emotional apparatus of breathing. The emotional body has its own lungs, but ninety-nine percent of the people are not aware of this. They start emotional breathing only occasionally when they are upset, in crises, in love, or in ecstasy.

In real emotional breathing, we inhale the element of love in Space. This is the air for the emotional lungs. Love is not a sentiment, nor an emotion, nor a pleasure. It is a fiery element in Space which does three things:

1. Creates healthy relationships

2. Creates unity in one's own consciousness and in the consciousness of the group

3. Creates sensitivity in your aura toward greater values

All Creation is surrounded by love, but we seldom breathe in that love. If we do not use our astral lungs, they dry up and die away, and we cut ourselves off from the fiery element of love.

Those who breathe deeply take love energy, regenerate their whole system of feeling, sensation, and values, then pull out the elements of hatred, jealousy, fear, anger, greed, and depression hidden in the caves of their emotional lungs, thus purifying their system from inner pollutions. Once the emotional life is in the process of transformation, the healing of the physical body starts and the emotional and physical breathing synchronize.

You can exercise emotional breathing in the following way: Lie down, or sit as in meditation, and visualize your emotional body in a silver color around your physical body. As you breathe in physically, visualize that your emotional body is also breathing in the fiery element of love. During the interval, visualize that all worn-out and obsolete toxins are breaking into pieces. Then exhale them. In the interval between exhalation and inhalation, feel the regeneration and charging taking place within your emotional system.

The lack of emotional breathing leads a man into depression, isolation, selfishness, and crimes.

Breathing the love element into your emotional lungs will also regenerate your whole physical system. Actually, when the regeneration process starts, you feel as if you have a pleasant burning fire along your spine.

After a few months of exercising love breathing, it will be impossible for you to use belittling criticism, gossip, malice, slander, and treason. All these poisons will vanish from your system and leave your body free to regenerate itself.

We must also mention that as most cities of the world are under heavy pollution, so it is also with our emotional sphere. There is much pollution emotionally — our hatred, jealousy, feelings of revenge, anger, fears of different kinds, malice, treason — and these accumulations fill the sphere in which we breathe.

But thanks to Nature, one can pass beyond such strata of pollution and contact fiery love when one develops his emotional lungs. Through imagination and visualization, he can draw in only the love energy present in the Universe. Those who have unhealthy lungs breathe in pollution with the love.

Mental breathing is more difficult. But on the path of perfection one has to learn it. In mental breathing we bring into our mental sphere the pure light of the Sun. The mental body lives through light, in light, and for light.

Any time you give darkness, illusions, and distortions to the mental body, you disturb its function.

Most of the mental mechanisms of men are sick because they feed them with lies, fabrications, illusions, chaos, crime, and darkness. Once the mechanism is distorted, it does not produce the right answers to your questions and it does not solve your problems in the right way.

When you learn mental breathing, you breathe in pure light. You purify and illuminate your mental mechanism. You throw out all worn-out elements such as prejudices, superstitions, vanities, egotism, and separatism. You make your mental body a creative agent for the purpose of life.

Light carries to your mind the creative thoughts of great Lives in the Universe. The results of increasing light in your mental body are

— more creativity

— co-measurement

— inclusiveness

— the ability to see the causes of the problems

— contact with creative centers, Ashrams, and groups

The lungs in the mental body are called the Lotus which, with its twelve petals, can draw a great amount of light even from the zodiacal signs. Thus mental breathing puts you in contact with the centers of the manifested Universe.

In the future it will be possible to heal criminals and emotionally disturbed people through deep breathing. Please note that I am not referring to breathing exercises or to pranayama. I am referring just to deep, mental breathing of light.

We must also mention that the mental atmosphere of the planet has a great amount of pollution. Our base thoughts in their various forms accumulate in Space. Especially our criminal stories and plans for crimes fill the Space. Those whose mental lungs are not developed to absorb the pure light of the Sun breathe in all the trash that we dump into Space.

Through right mental breathing you can control and master your habits. You learn to heal your body and change conditions in your environment and even in the world.

Telepathy is mental breathing; meditation done in the right way is mental breathing; every kind of true creative work is a process of mental breathing.

Beyond the mental breathing we have intuitional breathing. Through intuitional breathing we inhale impressions, ideas, inspiration, and visions. The element which we inhale is called psychic energy, or the Holy Spirit, which gives us the power of universalism. It reveals the future, Infinity. It gives us the true direction on the path of perfection and puts us in communication with Cosmic Centers.

Each inspiration we receive, we receive through our intuitional inhalation. Each inspiration received must be assimilated and used in creative labor.

There is also the breathing of the Self. When a man reaches a stage of development in which his True Self can breathe, it means that all the breathing of his mechanisms has synchronized with each other and the man has reached immortality. He has become a Master.

Some practical suggestions:

1. Any time you are going to start a manual labor, take a deep breath, and during the labor occasionally repeat it.

2. If you have an emotional stress or tension, lie down and try emotional breathing. Do this especially when you are depressed.

3. If you have to make a serious decision, breathe physically fifteen breaths. Then do ten minutes of mental breathing, and you will know how to decide. Sometimes it happens that your decision is not what you expected, but it will be proven in the future that the decision taken after physical and mental breathing was the best for you.

4. When you are ready to enter into a creative labor or a creative performance, do some intuitional breathing.

5. In times of danger, crisis, or in times of war and catastrophe, try the breathing of the Self. You will see how your Self will soar above the clouds of life, and nothing will hinder your progress.

Healing in the future will develop the best ways for breathing on all planes. Through right breathing, we not only prevent many ailments in our vehicles, but we can also cure our physical, emotional, and mental illnesses, bringing into these vehicles rhythm, harmony, energy, and higher substance for repair work.

When people do not develop their astral and mental breathing, they lose their astral and mental lungs. It is even possible that their astral and mental bodies can die before their physical body.

Physicians have developed every kind of apparatus to measure heartbeats, by which they make excellent diagnoses. The apparatuses to measure cell breathing, lung breathing, emotional breathing, and mental breathing have not been invented yet. In the future some apparatus is going to be invented through which the physician will measure cell breathing, lung breathing (we have at the present a few of them but not as they should be), emotional breathing, and mental breathing. With the future apparatuses, the physician will find the degree of synchronization, if any, between these various levels of breathing.

In the next century, medicine will start to worry about the etheric, astral, and mental bodies. Before a man passes away, he will go through extensive treatment to put his astral and mental bodies in shape so that he continues his journey in the Higher Worlds in a state of health. Actually, from the esoteric viewpoint, the Teaching of Christ was the medicine to produce a healthy subtle body for the future journey.

The five-pointed star is also a symbol of five-fold breathing: physical, emotional, mental, Intuitional, and Self. Every time you see a five-pointed star, remember you are going to develop progressive breathing.

Our health will improve to a great degree if we daily try to exercise five-pointed breathing. Besides our health, we will prepare our astral and mental bodies — our spaceships — and, for a distant time, our intuitional body.

Right breathing is a process of fusion with the Great Cosmic Self.

55

Angels

Psychic energy is also transmitted by angels. They are powerful transmitters or even sources of psychic energy. When a person is charged with psychic energy, he turns into a source of creative, healing, and enlightening energy.

Life proceeds stage by stage, gradually building more complicated forms. Evolution proceeds in many lives. Not all evolutions are on one direct path. There is human evolution; there is deva evolution; there are other evolutions which eventually merge.

On the lowest stage of devic or angelic evolution are found elementals and nature spirits which start on the involutionary path and then enter the path of evolution. Thus elementals are on the involutionary arc, and with their substance they build our physical, emotional, and mental bodies.

By being used age after age in the physical, astral, and mental bodies, elementals gradually develop elemental consciousness, and their evolution starts. Ages later, these elementals graduate and individualize in the form of nature spirits — as brownies, then elves, gnomes, mannikins, undines, sea spirits, and finally fairies. After they reach the stage of fairies, they evolve into sylphs, then into devas or angels.

Angels or devas are divided into two sections: lesser and higher angels. Lesser angels operate on the lower mental plane. Higher angels operate on the abstract levels of the mental plane. Sylphs operate in the astral plane. It is after angels graduate from the higher mental levels that the angelic and human evolutions become parallel, until they reach the stage of Chohans, the stage of the Sixth Initiation, where both evolutions merge.

Nature spirits live in the earth, in water, in the air, and in fire. They have only one element in their nature: they are either earthy, watery, airy, or fiery. Nature spirits identify themselves with the earth, with flowers and trees, with lakes and rivers, with the clouds, or with fire. Sometimes they ensoul such forms. They are harmless, but they do not like to be controlled by man.

Nature spirits abhor the pollution of the earth, water, and air. Thousands of them leave the areas polluted by human ignorance. They hate to see the trees, bushes, and flowers cut. They hate to see radiation contaminate the earth. They hate to see chemicals in the waters of the earth. They have their own territories, and they think that human beings have no right to destroy Nature. When they leave a place, natural calamities hit that place.

Elementals and Man

Man has four elements in his nature: earth, water, air, and fire. If all these elements are in harmony and highly developed, man will attract four kinds of devas and he will be successful in all the fields of the four elements. But in general, one of the elements predominates, and man will have to deal with the field which the element presents. If man is "earthy," he will be helped by earth elementals to have wealth, money, etc. If the water element predominates, he will be helped by water elementals, and he will be more occupied with the emotional field. If the air element predominates, he will be helped by air elementals to increase his mental knowledge. If the fire element predominates, he will be helped by the fire elementals in creative works and spiritual virtues. Food, water, various emotions, thoughts, and virtues or vices increase or decrease the elements existing in our bodies.

It is also noticed that these elements change when we relate with people. People sap our elements or increase them.

Devas are higher than nature spirits, and they are found on different levels. There are devas who live in the lower mental sphere, those who live in the higher mental sphere, and those who live in the higher astral levels. We are told that their language is color and music. Those human souls who can tune to the lower mental plane, or who can ascend there either after they sleep or after they die, can enjoy the presence of such devas, especially their music and the combination of colors which they produce with their thoughts.

Higher devas, or those who live on the higher mental levels, are far advanced devas. People who can raise their consciousness to the higher mental spheres can be impressed by these shining souls.

Beyond the higher mental plane there are the angels who cooperate with the Masters of the Wisdom, and they often help Them with Their plans.

What Service Do Angels Do?

1. They provide food for human beings and for animals in the form of vegetables and fruits, if they want to help them.

2. They provide etheric, astral, and mental food:

   a. Etheric-physical food is prana, which they transmit from the Sun or from the earth to human beings.

   b. Emotional food is love, aspiration, compassion, fearlessness, daring, courage, etc.

c. Mental food is inspirations, impressions, ideas, thoughts, new revelations.

3. They help certain people in extremely critical conditions, saving them from drowning, fire, earthquakes, and hurricanes.

4. They lead people into right paths. They lead armies if the armies are fighting for Beauty, Goodness, and Righteousness.

5. They inspire musicians with new melodies, songs, symphonies, etc. Some musicians are even able to hear the music of angels and record it.

6. They inspire artists, imparting new ideas and enabling them to see new colors.

7. They inspire scientists with new laws and discoveries through the means of the Intuition and impression.

8. They inspire in a person Beauty, Goodness, Righteousness, Joy, Freedom, purity, and solemnity. Actually, they can inspire all the virtues in him once the person shows his real merit.

9. They preside over countries, states, towns, villages, homes, families, churches, groups, and fraternities dedicated to the human cause.

10. They overshadow mountains, lakes, rivers, springs, oceans, and forests.

11. They heal people directly or indirectly. They even adjust their centers, glands, and nervous system and produce harmony and health.

12. They communicate in dreams and take the worthy one into subjective meetings, various sacred places, or higher Ashrams.

Some angels energize and charge the sacred places of worship and stay there for days and months to inspire and heal people. They charge Ashrams and enlighten people's minds; they emanate love energy to unite them as a living whole. They also protect Ashrams from dark attacks.

What Can Man Do for Angels?

Angels nourish themselves from elements which man provides. Man can help angels by providing them with the following nourishing elements:

1. Thoughts expressed in music, painting, poetry, writings, dances, singing, or meditation. They greatly enjoy the electrical emanations during individual or group meditation. Lofty thoughts are their primary food.

2. Joy, love, and the emanations of feeling free.
3. Any dedicated, sacrificial, heroic labor because in such a labor man emanates certain elements which nourish them.

Angels live under the law of righteousness and gratitude. Whatever they receive, they offer equal gifts to man in various forms.

What Do Angels Hate?

Angels hate the pollution of the earth, water, air, and Space. Any protection of the environment gives them extreme joy. They do not want people to destroy forests, flowers, or bushes because these are their own creative work which they offer to living forms for their survival and enjoyment. It is through forests, trees, bushes, and flowers that the energy and influence of the angels reach human beings, heal their wounds, and impart to their hearts new visions of a better future.

Angels hate for the water to be polluted. Water elementals are the essence of the water. Pollution makes them withdraw, and the water loses its healing and refreshing essence. When water is polluted, it affects the soil, vegetation, and even the air.

Angels do not want wars, disunity, or cleavages between nations, between families, and within families. Any cleavage creates disturbances in the angelic worlds. Unity and harmony give them delight.

Angels hate the pollution of the air. They cannot easily help humanity if people are living in pollution. When devas withdraw from a certain location because of earth, water, and air pollution, crime increases there. People lose their source of guidance and inspiration and live an anti-evolutionary life. They fall into vices and slowly lose their sense of values and their sense of direction. They waste their time, energy, bodies, and money and gladly face the path of degeneration and insanity.

Angels hate the pollution of Space. Through wrong and criminal thoughts, hatred, and bloodshed, people pollute the Space and prevent the currents of light, love, and direction from reaching them.

Angels do not like to be close to those people whose secretions are malodorous and poisonous. Such a condition occurs in people because of their conflicting emotions, guilt feelings, hatred, malice, slander, and treason. Purity of the aura attracts them.

Bedrooms that have various odors repel them. This is why Oriental Sages advise sleeping in the open air if one is not in danger of various pollutions. Sleeping in mountains, deserts, forests, or near the shores of lakes or rivers gives an opportunity to higher beings to come closer to you. Bedrooms must be simple and almost vacant, away from odors, decaying materials, and mechanical noises.

Angels are repelled by places where sewage flows or stagnant water, dead animals, blood, urine, or waste materials exist. They like well-ventilated rooms, where odors and different smells do not exist. They do not like the smell of meat or barbecues. They do not like the smell of burned food. They are also repelled by irritation, anger, and violent emotions. Once when I was angry and irritated, my grandmother said to me, "Do not disturb your invisible friends."

Great Chohans have armies of angels who help Them. These armies are totally oriented toward the service of the Plan, and they study the Divine Purpose. They also fight against the armies of dark forces. Such fights are recorded as "wars in heaven."

We are told that Christ has an enormous army formed of many grades of angels, and in critical times he mobilizes this army to protect humanity from the attacks of dark forces.

Angels are especially active at full moon times, especially at the time of the Aries, Taurus, and Gemini full moons. The highest moment of these three full moons is the Wesak Festival at which time the Angelic Hierarchy cooperates with the Spiritual Hierarchy. Thousands of these angels are dispatched to various places on earth to channel the energy of Wesak for the upliftment of humanity. A great Sage suggests that one must not allow himself to miss observing the Wesak Festival at the right moment of the Taurus full moon.[1]

Communication with Higher Worlds gradually becomes more difficult as the moral pollution accumulates. Like a fog around the earth, it hinders the communication between the two worlds and affects humanity in general to such a degree that eventually clearing this moral fog becomes impossible. This leads humanity toward suicide or total destruction.

As people are infected by the presence of people who are full of germs, similarly people are infected by the degenerative contents of the moral fog surrounding the earth. Just as angels hate the pollution of the earth, water, air, and Space and withdraw further into Space, a similar thing happens in a person when he pollutes his physical body with alcohol, drugs, unhealthy sexual practices, etc; when he pollutes his emotional body through hatred, fear, anger, greed, jealousy, revenge; and when he pollutes his mental body with vanity, prejudices, separatism, pride, and ego. In such conditions, the Inner Guardian withdraws and darkness descends on the path of the person.

Angels love calmness, serenity, gentleness, poise, solemnity, and grace. Whenever they see such qualities in someone, they are attracted to him and pass to him their joy, blessings, and protection.

Some people have angelic elements in their speech, actions, and expressions. Beyond what they are, they have something which cannot be put into words: they have an angelic element which is magnetic, graceful, inspiring, and strengthening. Some people are surrounded by a group of angels, and the

---

1. For information on full moons, please refer to *Symphony of the Zodiac*.

presence of such people brings joy, solemnity, understanding, gratitude, and ecstasy.

Angels affect people through their presence, even if they do not talk. Their invisible influence spreads like a fragrance. Psychic energy is also transmitted by angels. They are powerful transmitters or even sources of psychic energy. When a person is charged with psychic energy, he turns into a source of creative, healing, and enlightening energy.

Angels especially help those who teach the pure Teaching of the Hierarchy to increase Beauty, Goodness, Righteousness, Joy, and Freedom in the world. They stand beside such people and strengthen their aura with their angelic emanations. They protect them from dark attacks. They remind them of special events or points in their memory. They can even connect them to higher spheres for greater inspiration and ideas or for energy.

Sometimes a group of angels performs various duties. For example, during a lecture, some angels regenerate the memory. Some of them impart ideas. Some of them charge the words of the lecturer with their own energy. They purify the space over the audience. They insulate the mental lines of certain people who are connected with dark forces. Some of them impart joy, enthusiasm, and the spirit of unity. Thus they uplift the whole audience.

Certain angels serve as connecting links between the lecturer and his Master, or between the mind and the Intuitional Plane of the lecturer. On rare occasions, it is even experienced that they urge the Solar Angel of the lecturer to take control and speak through the lecturer himself instead of through his soul.

In extremely rare conditions, angels enter into the aura of a person and use him at certain critical times, after they get permission from the person's Solar Angel.

Angels sometimes even protect holy places or certain houses by standing guard at the door or windows and directing enemies to different paths. In certain cases, they provide money, food, paper, and books. They make you discover lost objects and find people whose addresses were unknown.

People have created ways and means to control angels and use them for their own personal ends. The real Teaching is against such actions. You must provide the right conditions for the angels to help you, since they are there to help you.

Angels love the beauty of gardens, flowers, natural colors, music, and fragrance. Music is very important to them. They like to enjoy music or paintings that carry a spiritual charge from the artist. If the artwork is created from a high spiritual level and by a person who is charged with lofty ideas and visions, the music or painting carries a great power for them, a great nourishment and joy. They dwell in those areas where great music and art in various forms are created or performed.

Angels especially love the fragrance of rose, musk, freesias, violets, amber, and frankincense. They love the natural fragrance emanating from a person full of joy and ecstasy.

Devas and angels love fountains, waterfalls, rocks, and precious stones. They love beeswax candles, flames, and incense, especially sandalwood and rose. They love live flowers and little plants in your home, especially little pine trees. They love melodious music, paintings, statues built by great artists, and Oriental and Indian carpets.

Noise is very repelling to angels, especially the noise of machinery. They also hate the noise rising from a group or a crowd of people where everyone is talking with everyone else. In ancient times Teachers told us that when people gather together they are allowed to do the following things:

1. Keep silence
2. Meditate
3. Sing together
4. Listen to a lecture or music
5. Pray together in unison

Angels do not like applause. Applause shatters their vehicles and the sphere of electricity which they build over the audience if the audience is in ecstasy and united in the spirit of the lecture or other performance. Very soon applause will be outmoded when a certain number of persons realize the damage done by it.[2]

Angels abhor treason, gossip, malice, and slander. They especially do not forgive a person who denies the Hierarchy or speaks blasphemous words against Great Ones. In such cases, they leave the person to face his dark destiny alone.

Heavenly hosts are divided into nine major sections by some Church Fathers. They are called

1. Seraphim
2. Cherubim
3. Thrones
4. Dominions
5. Virtues
6. Powers
7. Principalities

2. See also "Art and the Subtle Worlds" in *Other Worlds*.

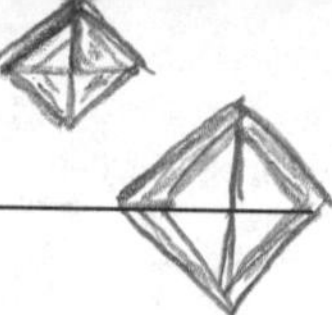

8. Archangels

9. Angels

Each group has the field of its administration and its sphere of power and responsibility.

1. *Seraphim* are related to the energies of Cosmic Love and to Christ, and they are active in His Plan.

2. *Cherubim* are related to the Universal Mind, the Holy Spirit, and psychic powers.

3. *Thrones* are related to Cosmic Will, the Will of the Father.

4. *Dominions* are the supervisors of the economy of the solar system and agents of supply and demand.

5. *Virtues* are related to Cosmic principles and laws.

6. *Powers* are related to the Law of Karma, and they try to transmute evil into good.

7. *Principalities* are protectors or supervisors of continents, races, nations, tribes, cities, towns, etc.

8. *Archangels* are representatives of the Seven Rays and the heads of the seven kingdoms in Nature. They are the spirit of sacred planets. The duty of archangels is to contemplate the Divine Purpose and work for its manifestation.

9. *Angels* are of various groups and of various duties.

The nine groups of angels, who are agents of Divine Law and transmitters of Divine Will, were once upon a time human beings, not necessarily on the physical plane but maybe on finer globes and in the astral or mental planes. Through the human evolution they developed intelligence, and now they consciously serve the Divine Purpose and Plan.

Solar Angels are not the same as angels. Solar Angels were human beings in past manvantaras. They are on the line of human evolution and are very advanced Initiates. They are related to the Karmic Lords, to the Hierarchy, and to the intelligence aspect of the First, Second, and Third Rays.

No angel can relate to a human being before he gets permission from the person's Solar Angel, Who has complete information regarding the karma of the particular person.

Angels do not obsess or possess people, but they can inspire and help if for a certain reason the Solar Angel cannot reach the human soul. In general, angels have their own duties and responsibilities, and they do not interfere with human life except if an order is given to them to do so.

Not only can a person's Solar Angel leave him, but the human soul can even leave the personality. In this case, the personality lives like an automaton through recorded urges and drives, or it becomes the apparatus of a low-level entity which possesses it and uses it for its own advantage to experience sex, alcohol, various crimes, etc. before its own incarnation.

Some criminals and materialists continuously stay on this earth. They die, but the next moment they are born again through one who provides a proper channel for them. They constantly go through suffering and depravity until one day their karma allows them to pass to the Subtle World.

Angels in general protect the human family from the attacks of dark forces. When people fight against each other, angels feel sad but they do not interfere. But if dark forces attack human beings, angels protect them from the dark forces — if the attack is not generated by the karmic liabilities of the person.

If you are walking on the path of righteousness, angels indirectly help you to fight your own battles by illuminating your mind, strengthening your heart, and inspiring your soul.

The whole Angelic Hierarchy is fiery, and human beings are warned not to force a contact with them. If they want to appear for certain reasons, they prepare the person through certain vibrations and then slowly appear. When they appear, their message is related to global problems and international service. They are not interested in your petty problems.

We are told that certain dark entities take the form of angels and appear to those whose vanity they can use for certain purposes. Many false directions have been given by such entities throughout the ages, and many books are channeled by them to their servants. One must be extremely careful to recognize these wolves in sheepskins.

There are many signs by which you can recognize such imposters. Some of them praise you and feed your vanity. Some of them speak about your past lives. Some reveal the secrets of other people. Others advise you to take certain actions to satisfy your desires. Others tell you that you are a Messiah, a Christ, a prophet, etc. Still others try to dominate your will and give you orders. Others stimulate your sexual center or inspire hatred and revenge in your heart. Others create cleavages between you and the source of your vision. It is not strange that they have their followers among human beings who do the same things, following the examples of their bosses.

The dark angels work through their agents if they see that they cannot deceive you themselves. Sometimes it is easier to know them than to know their human agents, who have graduated from the "school" of the art of deception and who usually approach you as a friend, helper, etc.

Real angels are not involved in your personality problems. They are not interested in your past but in the Hierarchy, Shamballa, and the glorious Plan.

As there are angels who preside over families, cities, and nations, there are also dark ones who try to establish their own stations to hinder the labor of the real angels. Such dark ones can establish their headquarters in locations where there are whorehouses, gambling places, groups which are separative and criminal, nightclubs where alcohol is used, or places where drugs are used. Through the substance of people present in such places, dark ones come and anchor themselves in cities and towns, and from that date on, crime, sickness, and insanity increase there.

On the other hand, angels inspire Beauty, Goodness, Righteousness, Joy, Freedom, tolerance, gratitude, and striving. They strengthen their positions in a nation, city, or town when a certain amount of people dedicate their lives to the Common Good and the service of humanity. Thus there can be a close interrelation between angels and men if people transform their lives and work for the upliftment of humanity, for the cleaning of pollution, and for progressive achievements toward the Hierarchy of Light.

Free Will

Angels do not have free will. They form an army, and each member of the army obeys the Will of the Most High. Human beings have free will, but only in a certain sense: when their will is fused with the Divine Will. Man must eventually resign from his free will, study the Will of the Most High, and live according to that Will. Christ achieved such a victory when He said, "Not my will but Thine be done." In that moment He fused His will with the Divine Will. From that point on, He had the most powerful energy under His control but also the pure wisdom to use it according to the direction of the Father.

Angels live in the stream of the Divine Will, and there is no conflict in them.

Humans think that without free will, no one can progress and advance. But they ignore the fact that freedom is not achieved except when one renounces his free will for the Divine Will. It is also true that if a totalitarian controls your will and you renounce your will, you will never advance on the path of evolution. Totalitarianism is not God's Will. The Will of God manifests as Beauty, Goodness, Righteousness, Joy, Freedom, solemnity, purity, and sincerity. Let these qualities control your will if you want to fuse with the Will of the Most High.

Do Angels Incarnate as Human Beings?

All spiritual beings existing beyond the present evolutionary state of human beings passed through human evolution. *The Secret Doctrine* states:

...In order to become a divine, fully conscious god, — aye, even the highest — the Spiritual primeval INTELLIGENCES must pass through the human stage. And when we say human, this does not apply merely to our terrestrial humanity, but to the mortals that inhabit any world, *i.e.*, to those Intelligences that have reached the appropriate equilibrium between matter and spirit, as *we* have now, since the middle point of the Fourth Root Race of the Fourth Round was passed. Each Entity must have won for itself the right of becoming divine, through self-experience....[3]

...The whole Kosmos is guided, controlled, and animated by almost endless series of Hierarchies of sentient Beings, each having a mission to perform, and who — whether we give to them one name or another, and call them Dhyan-Chohans or Angels — are "messengers" in the sense only that they are the agents of Karmic and Cosmic Laws. ...For each of these Beings either *was*, or prepares to become, a man, if not in the present, then in a past or a coming cycle (Manvantara). They are *perfected*, when not *incipient*, men; and differ morally from the terrestrial human beings on their higher (less material) spheres, only in that they are devoid of the feeling of personality and of the *human* emotional nature — two purely earthly characteristics. The former, or the "perfected," have become free from those feelings, because (*a*) they have no longer fleshly bodies — an ever-numbing weight on the Soul; and *(b)* the pure spiritual element being left untrammelled and more free, they are less influenced by *maya* than man can ever be, unless he is an adept who keeps his two personalities — the spiritual and the physical — entirely separated. The incipient monads, having never had terrestrial bodies yet, can have no sense of personality or EGO-ism....[4]

..."Man can neither propitiate nor command the *Devas*," it is said. But, by paralyzing his lower personality, and arriving thereby at the full knowledge of the *non-separateness* of his higher SELF from the One absolute SELF, man can, even during his terrestrial life, become as "One of Us...."[5]

In sober truth, as just shown, every "Spirit" so-called is either a *disembodied or a future man.* As from the highest Archangel (Dhyan Chohan) down to the last conscious "Builder" (the inferior class of Spiritual Entities), all such are *men*, having lived

3. H.P. Blavatsky, *The Secret Doctrine*, Vol. I (1978 ed.), p. 106.
4. *Ibid.*, pp. 274-275.
5. *Ibid.*, p. 276.

> aeons ago, in other Manvantaras, on this or other Spheres; so the inferior, semi-intelligent and non-intelligent Elementals — are all *future* men. That fact alone — that a Spirit is endowed with intelligence — is a proof to the Occultist that that Being must have been a *man*, and acquired his knowledge and intelligence throughout the human cycle. There is but one indivisible and absolute Omniscience and Intelligence in the Universe, and this thrills throughout every atom and infinitesimal point of the whole finite Kosmos which hath no bounds, and which people call SPACE, considered independently of anything contained in it. But the first differentiation of its *reflection* in the manifested World is purely Spiritual, and the Beings generated in it are not endowed with a consciousness that has any relation to the one we conceive of. They can have no human consciousness or intelligence before they have acquired such, personally and individually....
>
> The whole order of nature evinces a progressive march towards *a higher life*. There is design in the action of the seemingly blindest forces. The whole process of evolution with its endless adaptations is a proof of this. The immutable laws that weed out the weak and feeble species, to make room for the strong, and which ensure the "survival of the fittest," though so cruel in their immediate action — all are working toward the grand end. The very *fact* that adaptations *do* occur, that the fittest *do* survive in the struggle for existence, shows that what is called "unconscious Nature" is in reality an aggregate of forces manipulated by semi-intelligent beings (Elementals) guided by High Planetary Spirits (Dhyan Chohans), whose collective aggregate forms the manifested *verbum* of the unmanifested LOGOS, and constitutes at one and the same time the MIND of the Universe and its immutable LAW.[6]

It is generally understood that devas incarnate after a certain stage of development on the mental plane. They can carry on their evolution up to the Sixth Initiation, and there they converge with human evolution. We are told that many archangels became human beings and took the form of human beings to evolve according to the archetype of the human form.

It must be remembered that the invisible hosts in the sphere of the earth are not only angels, devas, or spirits. There are also various entities. There are those who were human and are now living in various planes with their various bodies. There are those who were angels but incarnated as human beings and are now

6. *Ibid.*, pp. 277-278.

living in higher spheres as angel-men. There are those who are living around the earth but are able to visit the subtle planes or appear to living human beings. There are those who have graduated from human evolution and are engaged in the work of the Hierarchical Plan. And, there are those who belong to the army of the dark forces.

All these entities are often called "angels," but they are not. One must have sharp spiritual vision to discriminate between them when one comes in contact with them.

Knowing these facts, one must not conclude that each experience with the invisible world is an experience with angels, though it is possible. There are many human souls working in the subtle planes as invisible helpers who are often mistaken for angels.

Archangels, with their own armies of angels, form subtle centers in Space to transmit certain energies to planets from higher sources. Archangels can also be visualized as rays, beams of light, currents of intelligent energy, the totality of which builds the network of communication between all existing forms and the Mysterious Beyond.

Archangels finished human evolution a long time ago. We are told that at present they are gaining experience with their bodies of manifestation which are the sacred planets.

In the Teaching of Great Ones, we read that some archangels failed on the path of their evolution. These failures must wait until a new solar system begins evolving and life there progresses to form human beings. It is at this stage that these great beings pay their karmic debts.

> *...Then they become an active Force, and commingle with the Elementals, or progressed entities of the pure animal kingdom, to develop little by little the full type of humanity. In this commingling they lose their high intelligence and spirituality of Devaship to regain them in the end of the seventh ring in the seventh round.*[7]

It is stated in Plato's works that human beings can reincarnate as "animals." There is a great truth in this statement if it is understood rightly.

The great archangels entered human evolution and going beyond it became shining angels. It is easy to see what Plato meant in his statement.

We are told that the Buddhic and Atmic Permanent Atoms in the Spiritual Triad are connecting links between the human soul and two great angels. These angels share the human evolution and collect experiences and learning through these links. They also reflect the life of the human being as mirrors. Our Solar

---

7. *The Mahatma Letters*, A.T. Barker, ed., p. 87.

Angel is located mostly around the Mental Permanent Atom, thus forming the Spiritual Triad with the two great angels.

We can help these angels when we live a life of Beauty, Goodness, and Righteousness. One day we may form a part of this triangle, first locating ourselves at the center, then replacing our Solar Angel at the Fourth Initiation and becoming a part of this holy triangle, or the Spiritual Triad. When we reach this stage, our consciousness will have a greater chance to expand by assimilating the deep wisdom these great angels present to us.

The greatest lesson which man will teach these great angels is the principle of free will and the science of how to harmonize the free will with the Will of the Most High. These angels do not have free will, and they will learn about it by passing through the human kingdom. Through the study of the science of the will, man will realize the Oneness of life and the existence of the One Will and will consciously put it into action in all aspects of life.

Most human beings are not aware of such a cooperation between angels and men. We must remember that we are always in the presence of three great angels, one human — our Solar Angel — and two others from the angelic evolution. Even if in our daily struggles, successes, and failures we do not feel their presence, they are there, in close contact with our higher principles.

Until the Fourth Initiation, our Solar Angel becomes an increasing source of inspiration. After the Fourth Initiation, the human soul finds his greatest source of inspiration in these great angels, and through them he reaches heights never before imagined. They are the Divine Companions of man, until he achieves Monadic consciousness. Greater glories are waiting for him after that great achievement.

These great angelic beings do not have self-consciousness or consciousness of individuality. They cannot understand why man centers all his activities around his individual self-interests. Those who are selfish and who live their lives centered in themselves will find it very hard to cooperate and be inspired by these angels.

On the other hand, man must teach the angels the existence of and the secrets of the Self, not opposed to the One Self but in harmony with the One Self. It is in this stage that the angels will understand the mysteries of the *will*, the Self, and freedom. Freedom is the ability to be one with the Cosmic Self.

Through purifying his being, man will be ready to learn the selflessness of the angel. This can be understood only when man passes through many lives under his false selves and their interests and eventually raises his pure Self into the light of angelic selflessness.

Individuality is the goal of evolution. Each individual instrument must achieve the purity of its sound to form part of the Divine Orchestra and create the One Symphony.

Meditation and Angels

Meditation is a very safe way to attract the attention of angels. Meditation spreads peace in the body, emotions, and mind, harmonizes them, increases their vitality, and makes them more magnetic. Meditation raises the level of consciousness and makes it more sensitive to higher angelic impressions.

During meditation higher thoughts, ideas, and visions are attracted to the aura of the person. Such currents of higher thoughts create beautiful colors and radiations in the aura and send a signal of invitation to angels. As meditation deepens and the human consciousness enters into contemplation, the bridge between the two shores becomes shorter, and eventually the person finds himself in a blissful precipitation of higher currents of energies and ideas. This is how conscious contact between men and angels is established and how both can help each other's evolution.

Man must not try to bring invisible beings or angels to the sphere of the earth, but he must try to raise his own consciousness and meet them in their spheres.

Your intention in meditation must not be to force the angelic beings to come in contact with you. Such an intention in itself repels them. You must raise your consciousness, and things will happen naturally.

During meditation, you must be very careful to be focused in the higher mental plane, working with the pure substances of logic, reasoning, and intuitive perception. If you fall into the astral plane with a desire to meet angels, you will meet them; however, they will not be the ones you want to meet but rather those who will mislead you on your path.

Any extrasensory experience must be recorded clearly as it happened. Later, during the same day, you must study it and see whether it is a glamor, illusion, or attack. No experience must be taken as a signal of communication with Higher Worlds unless it proves to be so. The development and unfoldment of discrimination begins when the person faces subtle problems and tries to make a right judgement and take a right action.

Whenever you think that you are falling into glamor and are attacked by invisible forces, stop your meditation for a while and seek the advice of a Teacher.

You must also develop sensitivity to feel the presence of angels. It is not necessary to see them or hear them or touch them. You must first of all accustom yourself to feeling their presence. There are a few signs which are possible proofs of their presence:

1. Silence within yourself
2. A feeling of joy
3. A feeling of expansion
4. A feeling of oneness with all

5. A feeling of deep gratitude
6. A feeling of forgiveness
7. A sense of peace
8. The flow of creative ideas
9. Deeper contacts with sources of great ideas
10. Feelings of courage, daring, and striving
11. A feeling of self-renunciation
12. A feeling of being protected

These are some of the signs which indicate that angels are around you. When they depart, you feel depressed, abandoned, left alone in your destiny. You may feel dry, selfish, argumentative, egocentric, etc. Their presence gives you a feeling of blessing, inner abundance, and inner contentment.

You need not see them. You do not see electrical currents, certain radiations, perfumes — but you feel them. Often people see their own thoughtforms and imagination or the forms they desire. In reality, angels do not have a set form. They are currents of conscious energy, like beams or spheres of light. People cannot think about angels without creating an imaginative form for them. Thus they deceive themselves. It is time to annihilate a glamor which has dominated the human mind since the dawn of human civilization — the glamor which assumes that angels have human forms. They do not.

People say, "They don't have human forms, but they are dwarfs, silly looking elves, good looking fairies, etc." There is no truth behind these pictures. Such pictures are fabrications of those who never had an experience with angels.

Angels must not be confused with great, living Adepts or Masters, Who sometimes appear with Their glorious bodies around Their etheric or physical forms and Who often terrify the one who meets Them. They are sometimes higher than many angels, and They have deeper access to the Plan and the Purpose of the Most High. They not only have free will but also pure intelligence. Some of Them have many angels in Their Ashrams whom They teach.

Christ is called "The Teacher of angels and men."

Angels enjoy learning and feeling high vibrations and emanations. That is why many of them attend lectures and visit halls where great music or singing is performed. They enjoy galleries of great art.

Certain angels love ceremonies and rituals because of the harmony and rhythm of color, sound, and movement. They not only like the ceremonies and rituals, but they also transmit energy to the celebrant, who distributes it to the audience. They even partake in ceremonies and rituals. They deeply love ceremonies of initiation when the neophyte repeats an oath and makes promises for a noble life. They serve and help those who are conducting the ceremonies and rituals and impart certain blessings and energy to each of the celebrant's actions.

Angels love to help lecturers by not only bringing them higher ideas but also by charging their voice and expressions with a magnetic energy.

Certain angels are called "comforters." Others are guides in the Subtle World for those who pass away and need guidance to familiarize themselves with the conditions of the Subtle World. Comforters work on both sides — with those who lost someone and with those who left behind their beloved ones.

How to Ask for the Help of Angels

The first requisite for help is a pure, sincere heart. As long as there are hypocrisy, self-interest, thoughts of exploitation, lies, and deception in your heart, angels are repelled by you.

First of all, we must know that angels see us as we are. We cannot ask for their help if we are trying to hide our motives or if we want to continue to live the way we were living in the past. We often need their help because we face difficulties which were the result of causes we put into action. We must not continue to create the same causes if we expect their help. This is why a self-confession is necessary before we ask for their help.

The second requisite for their help is not to have doubt in your mind — doubt about their existence or doubt that you are doing wrong by praying to them instead of praying to God. Remember that often you ask for the help of your friends, and you do not think you are doing wrong. You ask for the assistance of the police and other governmental officers instead of going to the President. The Angelic Hierarchy is designated to help people, like all the officers of the government. There is nothing wrong in going to an officer whose duty it is to meet your special needs.

Angels like to communicate with you and help you if you create the right approach. But the amount of help they can give you is conditioned by your karma, by your ability to recognize the mistakes you made in the past, and by the attitude you hold in the present. If you are able to face yourself clearly and decide to walk the path of Beauty, Goodness, Righteousness, Joy, and Freedom, you can minimize the effect of your past karma and open the door of possibility wider to receive greater help from the angelic kingdom.

A similar prerequisite applies to other kinds of help. For example, you may need light and wisdom to solve certain problems. Or you may need deeper inspirations to create great artworks or to invent things that will help humanity. In all such needs for angelic help, you have to purify your motives, detach yourself from past failures, and decide not to follow the path which leads you toward self-defeat. When your motive is really pure, it shines like a magnetic light and attracts help.

You must also remember that if your needs are not answered, it does not mean that angels have rejected you. They cannot act against your karma, but they can help you to be strong and to understand the real issues. Also, for example, in having a disease it is well to remember that not all diseases are the result of your own karma; they may be the result of the karma of the world, whose debt you may be helping to pay.

Not all the difficulties and sicknesses on your path are the result of your mistakes. They can also be the result of your love, labor, and dedication carried out beyond the capacity of your bodies. There are also cases in which a person pays for the karma of others, in order to save a group or a nation. But in all these cases, angels can help you in various ways. The important thing is not really healing or solving problems or making discoveries; the important thing is the process of perfection and unfoldment that you go through during your sickness, problems, and difficulties because through them you gain the resources of your knowledge of light, not otherwise available.

How to Invoke Angels

1. Sit in a quiet place in your home or in Nature — under pine trees, near big rocks or waterfalls, or near a small fire.

2. Relax your body.

3. Take five deep breaths.

4. Keep mental silence for a few minutes.

5. Say the Great Invocation and three OMs.

6. Say with deep concentration and feeling:

    O shining brothers of Light,
    O magnetic servers of Love,
    O carriers of the mighty Will of the Most High,
    here I present my heart to you
    with the fire of my aspiration,
    with the fire of my sincerity.
    I call upon your help.

    May your light enlighten me.
    May your love heal me.

May the energy of the will you carry
create integrity, harmony, and wholeness
in all my being.

May I share your peace.
May I share your joy.
May I share your beauty.
May I share your freedom.

O shining brothers of Light,
if it is the Will of the Most High,
in the name of Christ
let my body be healed.

Let my mind find the solution to problems.
Let my soul register the impressions of knowledge
you want to pass to me.
Let your energy flow into me,
O shining brothers of Light.

I will use your light,
your love,
your energy imparted to me
for the benefit of all humanity,
for the manifestation
of the Plan of Light and Love,
for the fulfillment of the Divine Will.

7. Sit in silence. Visualize their light surrounding you. You may register a special vibration, experience a healing or expansion of consciousness, or receive new ideas and visions.

8. After five minutes of silent contemplation, express your gratitude to the angels, saying:

I offer my gratitude to you
as a fragrance
rising from the altar of my heart.

May your blessed service expand
all over the world.

May a chance be given to me
to cooperate with your labor.
Gratitude and love to you.

9. Seven OMs.

In the following hours or days, you must record any new idea, visions, or healing given to you, directly or indirectly. The most important thing you must have is faith. Faith is the intuitive awareness that your voice reached them.

56

Healing and Invisible Beings

Actually, some of the angels will teach in the great centers of advanced study, and a section of them will directly teach the healing arts through sound, color, and motion.

People have forgotten that there are invisible hosts who work in hospitals, in private homes, and in Space to heal people, not only physically but also emotionally and mentally, and to bring peace and health in individual and social life. These invisible beings are called angels or devas, a section of which directly works with all those who have dedicated their lives to healing. These angels or devas heal in various ways:

1. They impress doctors and surgeons to take the right actions and impress their minds with the further steps needed in a particular situation.
2. They reveal new formulas and help researchers make new discoveries.
3. They vitalize the auras of the sick.
4. They advise the patient in dreams to take certain steps, to use certain herbs or methods to heal himself.
5. They reveal the cause of diseases through telepathic communication or direct revelation.
6. They activate certain elementals in the body to heal the person.
7. They charge water, food, or certain objects which transmit their energies to the patient.
8. They heal through creating invisible colors and inaudible sounds around the patient.
9. They heal people through charging them with certain fragrances.
10. They transmit a great amount of psychic energy through inspiration or direct action on the centers.

11. They energize the life thread, the sutratma.

12. They protect the person from various attacks which are often directed to the sutratma and to the etheric centers.

13. They purify and heal the person through fusion. This fusion is on three planes:

    — etheric fusion

    — heart fusion

    — thought fusion

    Fusion brings a great amount of energy from the angels or devas into the personality vehicles and creates purification, harmony, and energy in them.

14. Angels help us see the cause of our suffering and eliminate that cause, if the cause originates in our thoughts, emotions, or actions. Sometimes an illness brings us greater blessings.

15. Angels help patients through charging their doctor's aura. Many highly dedicated doctors immediately receive such charges when they come closer to the patient. Sometimes angels fuse their aura with the doctor's and charge his whole aura with healing energy.

16. Angels heal through music, inspiring certain composers to create music which at that particular time will prevent an epidemic, a cataclysm, a war. Through such music, they purify and balance the fires of Space and bring safety to people.

We must remember that at this stage of our evolution angels do not work to make us physically immortal. Immortality will be achieved through human striving and efforts and evolution. But they try to help us learn our lessons, serve, and meet our responsibilities until the time when we must leave our bodies.

Our death is not a problem for the devas. We do not vanish from them when we leave our body. They obey the karmic laws, and they work in harmony for our evolution.

We are told that Great Ones have hundreds of angels under Their command through which They serve on greater and various fields.

The fear of death shocks them. They do not understand why we are so afraid of death. Our fears hurt them. Our anger and irritation cause repulsion in them. They understand our pain and suffering and try to help us.

Sometimes the angels do not heal us if pain and suffering are needed for our transformation and for an understanding of the deeper facts of life. But they help us to bear the suffering, learn great lessons, and obtain wisdom through the suffering. Their inspiration and presence make us courageous and help us face our problems with serenity, understanding, and even with joy.

People are sometimes surprised that their trouble evaporates immediately after the doctor visits them. Respect for doctors and faith in them facilitates the fusion of angelic auras with the aura of the doctors.

One of the great healing agents is the Mother of the World, the Blessed Virgin Mary, Who throughout centuries spread healing powers in every country, to every race.

There are also angels who protect travelers on horseback, on ships, in cars, or in airplanes. People are not aware that it was because of the help of an angel that their airplane landed safely, their car escaped a fatal accident, their horse did not fall into the abyss.... We have many reasons to be grateful for help never realized by us.

The help of the angels and devas cannot be listed completely because they have ways and means about which we have no idea; they work silently and without recognition. Our gratitude and faith in them are the only factors which give them joy.

Favorable conditions are needed for their effective work. For example:

1. Prayer and worship.

2. Inspirational reading.

3. Ceremonies and rituals. These attract them, especially if they are conducted in solemnity and with the beauty of sound, color, rhythmic movement, and pure thought.

4. Intense aspiration.

5. The fragrances of pine, frankincense, rose, freesias. These create a good atmosphere for their activities.

6. Meditation and group chanting. These are very conducive means for devic help.

7. Faith.

8. Joy, contentment, and the spirit of gratitude.

9. Water and fire. These are very conducive to their energies.

10. Certain stones such as the diamond, topaz, lapis, silver. These are magnetic to devic energies.

11. Fresh mountain air, forest air, the air near waterfalls are also very conducive of their energies.

12. Cleanliness of surroundings and clothing, live flowers and small pine trees are a great help.

13. Relaxation of the mind, emotions, and body as well as silence are a great help.

14. A harmless spirit. This attracts the help of the angels.

15. One of the most effective factors is a strong decision to transform one's life. When the decision is real, it immediately attracts the healing angels who love purity, beauty, honesty, nobility, and righteousness. Changing one's heart toward Beauty, Goodness, Righteousness, Joy, and Freedom invites the angels immediately.

16. One of the greatest magnets for the healing energy of angels is a pure conscience or a pure heart which is not agitated by the memories of wrongs done to others or by wrong and harmful intentions for the future.

17. Love and compassion are strong magnets to attract angelic help.

18. Visitation to holy places, cathedrals, sacred mountains, and sacred rivers is a very effective way to come in contact with angelic presences.

19. Visitation to Holy Ones is another way to come in contact with angelic forces.

20. Certain books are directly connected with the angelic network, and reading and respecting them increases the possibility of contact with angels. Blessed objects and symbols are also very beneficial. Every blessing is a ray between the angelic hosts and the object.

In coming centuries the existence of angels will be experienced by millions of people. Actually, some of the angels will teach in the great centers of advanced study, and a section of them will directly teach the healing arts through sound, color, and motion.

57

The Human Soul and the Subtle World

The wounds caused in the subtle planes create many disturbances in man's vehicles. Sometimes an attack paralyzes the system or weakens it to such a degree that it falls into complete inertia.

There are many people who do not have a soul — yet — just as there are many students in the university who have not become doctors yet.

The spirit of man is still in a nebulous condition. The orchestration has not yet been achieved, and he has not yet found freedom from, and dominating power over, the lives in his aura composing his lower three vehicles.

The pearl of the human soul takes a long time to form itself. As this pearl comes into formation, man feels that he exists. He exists as a cause.

The souls of many people are not yet formed. They are like embryos — but they incarnate, live, die, and are reborn once again without being aware of the life they live. They are unconscious. After they leave their bodies, they live an unconscious life in the astral plane, and when they incarnate they do not remember anything from their subjective life, although their subtle centers register all that goes on upon the subtle planes.[1]

Besides not having souls, there are people who have a soul but do not have a Solar Angel. They incarnated on this planet without Solar Angels, without Inner Guides, and they became the materialistic, self-centered people in the world. They are scattered in all nations, all over the world, and are concentrated in certain fields of activity which support their materialistic tendencies and egotistical interests.

For both of these types of people, there is a good possibility of growing into a soul and having a Solar Angel. The Solar Angel is not drawn to such people very easily. They must prove in many incarnations that they respect their Teachers, their guides, their parents, their leaders, and they must show a selfless dedication toward them in thought and practice. When the light and magnetism of their dedication reaches a certain degree of tensity, it evokes a Solar Angel

1. For more information on the subject, please refer to *Other Worlds*.

Who periodically supervises their life until a particular Solar Angel is provided for them.

When the Solar Angel arrives, It comes after the person has gone through a great crisis and after a conscious renunciation. The Solar Angel impresses in the mind of the subject a sense of deep responsibility and gives a vision of inclusiveness and wholeness.

Often factors which have been accumulated throughout ages in the psyche of the subject mobilize themselves to stand against such impressions. Thus a battlefield is created on which the human being must either fail or conquer, responding to the major impressions received from his Solar Angel or obeying the accumulated factors of the lower vehicles.

The victory is the moment in which, symbolically speaking, the birth of the human soul takes place. But when we say "the moment," it does not mean necessarily a short factor of time. It may be an indefinite duration through which the conception, gestation, and eventually the birth of the human soul takes place.

After the birth of the human soul, it takes years or lifetimes to make the human soul come closer to the Solar Angel, recognize It, establish conscious communication with It, and eventually reach a stage which in the Ageless Wisdom is called Soul-infusion or the "marriage in heaven."

Those who cannot come in contact with their Solar Angel wander for a long time in the deserts of life without a goal, plan, or purpose. Those who build barriers between themselves and their Solar Angel gradually enter the path of darkness and crime. Those who consciously enter the movements of organized crime eventually atrophy their heart center and force the Solar Angel to leave them. This is a great tragedy.

When your Solar Angel leaves you, it means you have "lost" your soul. Losing the soul means to be in danger of dissolving your individuality. If it happens that your individuality is dissolved, your personality can still be alive for a while without you or with another entity that uses your personality as his vehicle.

Immortality cannot be achieved until you build continuity of consciousness — by building your expanding identity between the mental plane and higher planes.

The human soul is the individual Spark on the way to blooming or perfection. He has now reached the mental plane, and he begins to see his face in the mirror of the mental plane in his creative thoughts and actions. This is what St. Paul meant when he said, "We see our face in the mirror, but one day we will meet ourselves face-to-face." Face-to-face is that moment when you become yourself, an immortal being.

When the human soul is born, it does not mean that he has continuity of consciousness, although he lives on the physical plane, passes away, and comes back to earth again. Real, conscious immortality starts when he enters into the Spiritual Triad, or higher spheres, and meets himself.

To see yourself in the mirror means to see your reflection. Your reflection can be seen in your logic, reasoning, creativity, or in your personality. Face-to-face means the reflection has disappeared, and now you exist as reality and you are aware of it.

A man knows himself by the influences he is exercising on others. Others reflect what you are. A disciple is advanced when his progress is seen in the life of those who are related to him.

A question was asked, "If a man loses his soul and gains all the world, what does he gain?" The answer will be: Nothing...because there is no one to gain anything. If the human soul is lost, who is going to gain? One can be dissipated in the air like a bubble and become individually non-existent. Whatever he did, spoke, or thought can come back ages later to form a personality — but without the individuality — until one day the personality degenerates and disappears, as the outgoing waves of the ocean lose their dynamism and fail to come back into the shore of existence. It is possible that such "personalities" serve some wicked ones living in the etheric realm as their vehicles and bring disaster to the community or nation in which they are born.

There are many soulless people walking on earth today, and their number is increasing. The dissipated individuals fuse with the ocean of forces as if they were never in existence.

After individualization man is left to his own efforts and striving to prove his existence as a soul — as an integrated and focused light. Individualization is the moment when, through the influence of the Solar Angel, man develops the "I" consciousness.

Chaotic forces in Nature violently oppose formation of a separate identity. Chaotic forces in Nature want all to be one in one ocean of force. Man must pass beyond the chaotic forces of Nature and enter the domain of the Spirit, which tries to help the individual drops build an identity and pass the sphere of change, of dissolution and disintegration, and achieve mastery.

The first initiation gives man the power to be conscious on the astral and mental planes. But when the human soul incarnates, he cannot remember his past lives nor his out-of-body life.

Toward the end of the second initiation, the human soul begins to remember fragments of his past lives, and he is more conscious in subtle levels when he leaves his body in death. He also clearly realizes the existence of Great Ones while in the Subtle Worlds. In the Subtle Worlds, a man can even take the first and second initiations because of his good deeds and because of his strong orientation toward the Teaching received while on earth.

In the Third Initiation, he is a conscious soul, and he has access to the records of his past lives found in his Chalice. He is wide awake in the Subtle World, and he has continuity of consciousness.

Toward the end of the Fourth Initiation, the first part of the Antahkarana is complete, and he has no experience of death because he is conscious in two worlds simultaneously. He is a mature soul.

For the average man, or non-initiate, death is a long sleep. He has a few short moments of awakening, but his life in the Subtle World is a long duration of sleep.

As one approaches the first initiation through many incarnations, he eventually awakens to the awareness of the Path. If he passes away without taking the first initiation while in the body, he takes his first initiation in the Subtle Worlds.

Thus at all times the human soul exists, but he is not always aware of his existence until he takes his first initiation. From the first initiation, his awareness grows and expands up to the Fourth Initiation, at which time he is fully aware that he exists in both worlds, either in the body or out of the body.

In the Fourth Initiation, the higher bridge is built. The Initiate is not only conscious on the astral and mental planes, but he also penetrates consciously into the Intuitional Plane and exists there as well.

People often ask, "If souls are not aware in the Subtle Worlds, who are those who are giving messages to mediums or channels?" The answer is not easy to understand. The aura is a computer, and this computer is formed of memory discs or memory cells. These cells operate through mechanical push-buttons and through keying in with certain other discs which emanate answers.

The whole of Space is full of such discs or of discarded astral and mental bodies. Astral bodies last longer than mental bodies. All these bodies are charged with past memories. Mediums mostly contact these bodies or corpses and draw information from them. Real human souls who are awake in the Subtle World do not contact mediums. Either such human souls are on their way to higher worlds, or they have spiritual duties in the Subtle World.

A medium cannot contact the mental plane but only the astral world. Advanced souls do not stay on the astral plane but pass on to the mental plane or higher planes.[2]

There are other entities which live in the Subtle Worlds, but they are not yet human. Most of them are like children, and often they serve as keys in the hands of mediums to open memory chambers in the corpses. It is no doubt that mediums receive information from such sources, too, but how valid is this information when the mediums do not have the ability to verify it and the person with whom they are in contact?

Those who are aware in the astral and mental planes are Initiates of higher degrees Who have a certain responsibility there. They can even penetrate into the Subtle Worlds while living in their physical bodies.

---

2. For further information, please refer to *Breakthrough to Higher Psychism*, and *Other Worlds*.

It is mostly the etheric entities that communicate with people on the physical plane, and we must remember that the etheric world is actually a physical world. Curiously enough, this plane is full of "awakened" people. You can find on this plane those who committed suicide and those who died on battlefields or in accidents. They live there as long as they would have lived on the physical plane if they had finished their life-span, and then they are born again. Millions wait on this plane to enter into wombs to incarnate.

We not only have the recordings in the discs of subtle bodies left in the astral and mental planes, but we also have the hard disc of the cosmic computer which is called the Akashic Plane.[3] This cosmic memory has all the recordings of our past lives which are carried into the computer by certain Rays. The corpse carries the recordings of one life, but the stories of millions of lives are recorded in the cosmic computer. Mediums are able to "read" distorted reflections of the Akashic Records in the lower astral plane. However, they have no real way to translate these recordings due to their level of consciousness as well as to the distorted nature of the recordings in the astral plane.

The Akashic Records are contacted in the astral plane by mediums through a corpse because, in general, the records related to the corpse in the cosmic computer and the records in the corpse have the same key. We are told that a Fourth Degree Initiate or Masters have the power to read correctly the Akashic Records, but only by permission of the command of the Hierarchy.

When mediums receive answers for your questions and problems from etheric entities or ghosts, you must be careful not to build your life on the foundations of those answers. You must remember that the consciousness of the etheric entities is more limited than yours because of the conditions in which they live; they are mostly earthbound and full of violent emotions and plans. You can find a better answer if you approach your Soul, the Inner Guide.

Etheric entities live a very miserable life. Their life is a duration of continuous horror or regret. They live in the horror of war, in the horror of accidents they had, in the horror of suicide and regret, in the horror of the memory of their lives. In such a psychological condition, mediums receive numerous radiations of negativity, pain, and suffering.

These entities sometimes are in a heavy coma. There is no possibility of receiving any conscious answer or report from them. Although their sphere of radiation emanates certain information, this information has no identity. It is mixed with much data existing in that world through the waves of horror, regret, and nightmare.

Mediums communicate with these people and often bring much information, but such information has a very misleading nature.

3. See also "Akasha" in *Other Worlds*, pp. 265-272.

It is these entities of the etheric plane which search for weak auras to obsess and possess people. Sometimes legions of them live in the auras of mediums. They try to control the lives of people, either to satisfy their sexual drives or their unsatisfied urges to eat, to kill, and to destroy.

Those who are Initiates of the Third Degree can visit the Subtle Worlds and urge people to go forward on the path of their evolution. These Initiates do not try to gain information from them because they know that people living on these planes are not dependable sources of true information. Also, they know that they have no right to penetrate the storehouse of memories of these people, but their duty is to help them proceed on the way of their evolution.

Prayers for the dead are very potent methods to stimulate them to go forward on their path.[4]

Those who enter the Subtle World report that the astral plane life is exactly the replica of the life on earth. People buy and sell; they build and destroy; they marry and divorce; they are extremely occupied with the objects of their desires. And these observers report that the astral entities are often having a good time.

But advanced and experienced observers will see that these entities are in sleep, as is the case with people on the earth plane; they are not conscious of what they are doing. They are moving automatically, conditioned by those astral and mental inputs that they accumulated in their physical life, and now these inputs are programming and running their lives as if they were awake.

This is why the astral plane is a trap, and people often stay there thousands of years, living the replica of the life they were living before they passed away. They awaken when the law of life begins to recycle them, or they suddenly awaken because of a latent spark of striving and pass on to the next plane. Such a life resembles our dreams where we do almost anything without having any power over what we do.

It is known that there are Guiding Ones in the astral plane. Some of them are called the invisible servers.[5] Some of them are members of the Spiritual Hierarchy. Mostly they try to keep our consciousness awake and to sustain the continuity between the physical and astral life.

People try to identify with the forms of life in whatever plane they are. The guides, or servers, try to instruct us about the transiency of life on various planes. They teach us that each world, like the physical one, is a motel where we stay for a while, then continue our journey toward perfection.

They emphasize the importance of detachment and striving. Detachment helps us not to identify with the phenomena of life on certain planes, and striving urges us to go forward on the path of our evolution.

---

4. See also "Last Rites" in *Other Worlds*, pp. 477-491.
5. See also *Other Worlds*, pp. 64-67.

Because of his insecurity, man tries to build permanent dwellings and occupations on every plane in which he finds himself. It is very difficult for him to learn that he is a passenger. Spiritual guides emphasize this idea and give special instructions to newly arrived persons so that they do not accept the life of the new plane as permanent.

Once a person understands the principles of impermanency, he tries to educate himself in the Subtle World. He attends the classes of guides and learns the wisdom of how to continue his journey and unfold his spiritual flowers.

> *...Where there is a ladder of millenniums, the flutter of butterflies is unfit....*[6]

The strongest factor for retardation is identification with the glamorous forms of the astral plane. One must firmly establish in his consciousness the fact that he is a traveler, and the things he has and the things he uses have temporary value only. The only permanency he has is the vision of the ever-progressing discovery of his True Self.

Thus the guides teach us not to lose time flying back and forth like a butterfly from one object to another but to keep going on the path of our evolution.

In occult psychology we learn that the spiritual man's astral body dissipates like smoke after he passes away. But after a man who is full of glamors, earthly desires, lust, and passions passes to the mental plane, his astral body lasts sometimes thousands of years.

When the spiritual man is born, he builds a new astral body according to the content of the astral permanent atom. When the earthbound man is born, his still-alive astral body may come and attach itself to the new astral body. The new astral body is more advanced than the former astral body because of the improvement in the astral permanent atom while the man was crossing the mental plane.

In this case, before the new astral body is duly formed, the old one comes and attaches itself to it and often pollutes it with its old glamors, desires, and passions and makes a man's emotional life very difficult, complicated, and often contradictory.

The complications increase if in past incarnations you were a man and now you are a woman, or vice versa. In this case, if you have a male body, your past astral body, if strong, forces its female characteristics on you, and you often act in a feminine manner and feel great emotional conflict within yourself.

This is one of the hidden causes of homosexuality. Because your former astral body was feminine, you try to create a polarity by looking for one who has a masculine polarity. Then you end up with a man whose astral body is masculine, instead of with a woman. Your former feminine astral body is attracted to a man

6. Agni Yoga Society, *Heart*, para. 207.

who has a masculine astral body. This will force you to stick to a man because your feminine astral body is attached to him.[7]

The astral body disintegrates in the astral plane if the owner of the body is fiery, spiritual, and charged with beauty, goodness, truth, and joy. The more fiery one is, the shorter his astral body lives. One of the sacred duties of man must be to build an astral body which will fade away easily after death. One can achieve such a goal through living a life of dispassion and detachment. Dispassion is detachment from astral and emotional objects. Detachment is the ability not to be obsessed by physical objects.

Man advances more quickly if he does not inherit a past astral body.

There are also more complicated cases. It sometimes happens that an astral body is occupied by an entity in the astral plane, and this entity wants to come in contact with the owner of the astral body after he starts to incarnate. After the person is born, the former astral body is mechanically attracted to the person, with the stranger in it. This is one of the worst kinds of possession that occurs in a man.

Deep-seated psychological problems which are very difficult to heal originate from such complicated situations. Only an esoteric psychiatrist or an esoteric clinical psychologist may help to some degree. Some of these bodies last a few years and dissolve. Some of them last longer and can be used by those who like to come in contact with mediums. Some of them survive until the owner takes a new incarnation.

Those who have passed the Transfiguration Initiation do not stay long in the astral body. Before they go to the mental plane, they dissipate the astral body so that it does not create pollution or serve as a vehicle for an inferior entity.

The astral body of one who is close to the Fourth Initiation immediately evaporates when he crosses the astral sphere. A Fourth Degree Initiate does not have an astral body, and he can enter directly into mental, then Intuitional spheres.

It is possible to reject or repel a former astral body, if the mother and father have strong willpower and if they protect their children with their fiery presence and meditations. It is usually between the third and seventh years that the old astral body tries to attach to its previous, incarnated owner. Some churches baptize children at a very early age, when they are eight days old. In the sacrament of Baptism, the priest — if he is an esoteric student — can seal the astral body of the baby in such a way that the old astral body cannot make a link with the new body, and the old astral body eventually disintegrates.

It is also possible that a fully grown man can dissipate his old astral body by his willpower.

---

7. For further information, see *The Psyche and Psychism*, Ch. 48, and *Sex, Family, and the Woman in Society*, Ch. 14.

In the astral plane one does not need to cover himself emotionally. Whatever you are, you are almost visible to anyone. This is the reason why you act without inhibition on the astral plane, and you express the desires that you have and reveal the plans that you are forming for yourself and others to satisfy your desires.

It is very easy to see your true emotional motives in the astral plane. For example, if you are helping someone for certain emotional expectations and you are trying to hide it on the physical plane, you reveal it on the astral plane because your wishes and desires turn into acts on the emotional plane.

I read once that a man dreamed that his neighbor stole the fruit from his tree. So he went to him early in the morning and beat him. When the neighbor asked him why he did this, he answered, "You are going to steal my fruits if you have an opportunity, so I am warning you."

In the astral plane, and especially in the mental plane, you are visible to everyone, but the good thing — or bad thing — is that not many people remember what they were in the subtle levels when they return to physical consciousness. You must know that every dream you see about others does not necessarily present their true nature. Often you project yourself onto others to be more comfortable in watching your true nature.

It is possible that someone had passing and transient feelings and thoughts that manifested on the astral plane. But this kind of manifestation must be discriminated by those who have firm Intuition to see behind feelings and thoughts.

This means that not everything we dream is the result of firm decisions or contemplated desires.

Advanced people do not wander in the astral plane except for service, and this is the reason why, for average people, they are concealed. Their motives and plans can be accessible only to those who penetrate the mental plane. There again all is revealed to all.

In our physical consciousness we talk about privacy, and we try to maintain that. But on higher levels privacy is a matter of frequency. Everything is revealed to those who can tune themselves to the needed frequency.

Very soon physical privacy will evaporate. The day is not far away when people will read your thoughts and emotions with their special machines or within their heads. Such an advanced science may be used for the Common Good or for interference into each other's affairs. Thus, the human race will come closer to the conditions of the Subtle World.

Advanced members of humanity will not need to occupy themselves with the affairs of others. Their responsibility is to educate people about the laws and principles of Nature and guide them to deeper realities.

Beyond the mental plane there are great barriers, and people can only penetrate into the domain of reality on higher planes if their lives are purified of self-interest.

We are told that advanced souls stay in the astral plane only forty days. The Eastern Orthodox Church has a requiem service forty days after a person passes away, and the prayers speak about easy release from the lower strata.

Sometimes an advanced soul stays longer if his family, friends, or followers express deep grief and mourning. They pull the soul back to earth. The poor soul can hardly liberate himself from the clutches of astral emanations.

If the man has built the golden bridge, at the time of passing away he can easily pass into higher planes. But if the bridge is not built, and he has no continuity of consciousness, the passing one can still penetrate to higher planes if a friend or family member speaks about or reads to him some enlightening literature about the supermundane life. If a man is enthused with Higher Worlds, he will enter the Higher Worlds and not be trapped in lower ones.

If more people enter into higher planes, they will radiate greater wisdom and light toward the planet, and they will be born with a greater inclination toward Beauty, Goodness, and Truth. This is why it is important to teach people the art of passing away. It is not only beneficial for the individual but is also a service for humanity.

We are told that the subtle bodies of man can receive wounds, both when man is in the physical body or out of the body.

These wounds are comparable to physical wounds. They are painful, disturbing, and bleeding, and they cause many complications in the subtle system according to their intensity.

These wounds are caused by

1. Negative emotions and thoughts projected like arrows toward the individual

2. Arrows of dark forces active on the objective or subtle planes

3. Accidents caused by carelessness

The ancients used to advise co-workers to be very careful not to attract arrows of people's jealousy, hatred, anger, and feelings of revenge. Co-workers were advised to live a low profile life, not to make claims, or run after their vanities, nor show-off, but to live a life of humility, simplicity, and always stand in the shadow of detachment. These were rules to protect co-workers from attacks before they were strong enough to shield themselves and be able to do combat with greater force and better techniques.

As in an army, the generals of the spiritual domain stand back but send their soldiers to the front lines of the battle of light.

The wounds caused in the subtle planes create many disturbances in man's vehicles. Sometimes an attack paralyzes the system or weakens it to such a degree that it falls into complete inertia.

The wounds in the mental body can be very serious, and they sometimes affect the whole cycle of life. They weaken the thinking, they create confusion in the sense of direction, they destroy moral gauges, and they cut the channels of psychic energy. Mental wounds slowly infect the astral, etheric, and physical bodies.

Astral wounds are received more frequently than mental wounds, but the recovery from astral wounds is easier than from mental wounds. The astral body has a natural immunity as long as it is charged with the fire of aspiration and love.

Those who leave their physical bodies in sleep and enter the Subtle World with negative emotions such as anger, fear, hatred, jealousy, and greed expose their astral and mental bodies to attacks. Such negative emotions create psychological vacuums in their bodies, and currents of dark emanations flow into the vacuums.

There are many poisonous flying arrows in the Subtle World which very often are attracted by those who go to sleep in despair and in the spirit of malice, slander, violence, and crimes. The ancients used to say that one must enter into the Subtle World shielded in the light of bliss. To protect people from the dangers of the Subtle World, the technique of prayer was given. Also, the evening review[8] is a very potent protection from subtle attacks.

Often people are continuously under attack in the Subtle World. Fortunately there are also protectors. Friends, teachers, relatives, and invisible helpers try to protect you if you do not violate the Law of Love and Harmlessness in your daily life. No protection can be given to a man who lives against the Law of Love, no matter how many friends he may have in the Subtle World.

On the physical plane, if you were smuggling and committing a certain crime, a friend may save you through bribery, power, or by his position. But in the Subtle World, your true friend does not encourage your crime and lets you face your karma, although he can help you by letting you understand the Law of Life.

There are many battles going on upon the subtle planes. Some armies are protected by the shield of Great Ones.

Protective Meditation Before Sleep

1. Sit near the bed.

2. Visualize a sphere of white light, two to three feet around your bed.

3. Make a quick review of your daily life, and if you find that you violated the Law of Love, Harmlessness, and Righteousness, make a strong

8. Please see Ch. 80 in *The Psyche and Psychism.*

decision to stop such a violation. Fill your heart with the spirit of forgiveness, respect, and righteousness.

4. Visualize a shower of light and take a shower, visualizing that all the pollution of the day is leaving you.

5. Enter into the sphere of light in which your bed is located. Express gratitude to your Guiding Angel.

6. Think about joy, bliss, peace, serenity. . .until you leave your body and depart to the Subtle World, shielded by the electric light of your Angel.

58

Sleep and Healing

Sleep is a vacation for the body. In this vacation the body is left alone with the life force to repair itself. Through sleep the human soul withdraws himself out of the body to the world of energies, emotions, thoughts, and ideas.

A major portion of our life passes in sleep. If a man lives ninety years, thirty years of it is sleep. There is little research yet about what happens when one goes to sleep. Of course, there are a few biological explanations about the cause of sleep, but they do not satisfy the student of the Wisdom.

We are so busy with the few years we live on this planet that most of us do not worry about the long hours and years passed in sleep, or about the hundreds or thousands of years that we live after we drop our physical body in death.

Some religions have many things to say about the life after; others keep silence. It is only the great Teachings of the esoteric Wisdom that give us the needed information about life after death or after sleep.

Actually death and sleep are almost the same. The only difference is that in sleep the consciousness thread is withdrawn from the head, but the life thread remains anchored within the heart. In death both threads are withdrawn, and man cannot come back to his body.

When the life thread is withdrawn, the body begins to disintegrate. When the consciousness thread is withdrawn normally, one becomes unconscious. In other words, the brain does not function and register impressions coming from the seven senses.

What are the differences between samadhi, mediumistic trance, hypnotic sleep, the sleep of Great Ones, and average sleep?

Samadhi is a state of conscious withdrawal from the lower mental plane during the waking state. It is done through intense, one-pointed meditation. In real Samadhi man is aware of both the subjective and objective worlds, and he works and is conscious on the highest mental plane.

Mediumistic trance is caused when the etheric body is partially extracted from the physical body and the brain is occupied by an astral entity. Usually those entities who are full of confusion, illusions, corruption, and lies occupy the mind of a medium. In such a condition the human soul is in suspension and has no control over his mechanism.

Hypnotic sleep is very close to mediumistic trance, but in the former the human soul is extracted not only from the etheric body but also from the astral and mental bodies. Obsession and possession await those who play with hypnotism.

The sleep of Great Ones is a conscious withdrawal from the Intuitional Plane to work on the Atmic Plane. Such Entities are called Nirmanakayas. It is these Souls Who bring direction, purpose, and principles into the world.

Average sleep is of three kinds:

1. The human soul withdraws himself along the consciousness thread that is anchored in the brain.

2. The human soul is pushed out artificially from the bodies, but the consciousness thread is left as it was, anchored in the brain. This is a very dangerous state because entities of various kinds and hypnotists can use the man or orient him the way they want. In this state the human soul temporarily has no control over his communication line with his bodies.

In the average man, the consciousness thread usually extends from the physical brain, etheric brain, and astral permanent atom to the mental unit. It is easy, through artificial means and drugs, to push the human soul out and use the astral and etheric bodies of man the way one wants.

There are special openings in the etheric body through which the human soul withdraws himself, or through which he is expelled. These openings are wide between birth and the age of twelve. Later in life many hindrances accumulate in the etheric openings through wrong actions, words, and thoughts, and they become narrow.

The hypnotist forces the human soul to withdraw through one of these openings, but he does not know how to shut the door after the human soul leaves. This is the reason why obsession and possession occur. In normal sleep the human soul seals the door carefully and returns back safely.

3. The human soul withdraws through the consciousness thread, while keeping it anchored in the brain, and has full control over it. In this stage the consciousness thread is extended from a point in the physical and etheric brain to the mental unit and up to the mental permanent atom in the highest level of the mental body. Because of such an extension, the owner, or the human soul, can keep watch over the lower bodies when he is out of the threefold vehicle. It is also through such a thread that man remembers all that he experiences in higher spheres.

The average man withdraws himself from the lowest opening around the solar plexus. The more advanced man withdraws from an opening near the heart. A disciple or Initiate withdraws from an opening above the head.

Dreams are dramatizations, reflections, or actual recordings of events taking place on the astral, mental, or higher planes. These recordings reach the brain via the consciousness thread. If this thread extends from the brain to the astral body, the human soul wanders only in the astral plane. If it is extended to the mental body, he can function on the mental levels according to his achievements.

If the thread is extended into the intuitional body, he can function on the Intuitional Plane, having full control over the three stations through which the thread passes.

It is possible that man enters into a state which is called "waking sleep" or day dreaming. This is a very subtle state in which the human soul is preoccupied with some work, idea, or symbol, and his attention is drawn into the trap of a thoughtform or recording, and the line of communication is left unprotected. Such a state occurs when we confront painful emotions or certain intense excitements, during which the mind is trapped and a hypnotic suggestion can sneak in and plant seeds.

Sleep is a physical necessity. It is a cycle of repair, a cleansing, regenerating, and adjusting process. It is also a period of taking the pressure of the mind and emotions out of the body. Sleep is a time of regeneration of the brain and nervous system and a period of recharging the centers. During sleep, psychic powers tune in and recharge the body.

Sleep is a vacation for the body. In this vacation the body is left alone with the life force to repair itself. Through sleep the human soul withdraws himself out of the body to the world of energies, emotions, thoughts, and ideas.

There are three stages of sleep:

1. When you leave the physical body, there is a state in which you are between the physical and etheric bodies. When you leave the physical-etheric body, you enter the astral body.

2. When you leave the astral body, you enter the mental body.

3. When you leave the mental body, you are actually in deep sleep. Between the mental body and the higher bodies there is a void, and not everyone can cross that void.

The next body is called the intuitional body. When you are able to penetrate that body via the bridge over the gap, your real awakening starts. From the intuitional body you may pass to higher levels without breaking the continuity of your awareness.

Thus you first leave your physical body. If you are really able to leave your physical and etheric bodies, you give a great vacation to your physical body, taking away the pressure of urges and drives, the pressures of glamors and illusions, the problems of your life and relationships, and you leave your body to heal and reconstruct itself during the time called sleep.

Most of the time our body is restless, agitated, and irritated because of our thoughts, emotions, confusions, fanaticism, hatreds, anxieties, and fears. All these exercise a tremendous pressure on the body which eventually brings in distortion, disturbance, weakness, and various diseases.

At the time of real sleep, you give a good rest to your body. It is during these periods of rest that the body repairs itself. Many miraculous cures occur in the periods of deep sleep. One of the branches of the New Age Teaching will be related to sleep. We will learn how to sleep.

People do not know how to sleep. They are half in, half out of their bodies, and because of this they keep their bodies constantly in agitation. Agitation keeps your physical body restless and poisons it with your emotional and mental disturbances when you are not able to leave the body.

Real sleep is total withdrawal from the physical and etheric bodies, at which time they are in deep relaxation. Relaxation is the state of the body in which the physical elemental tries to repair the physical mechanism, the glands, and the nervous system and throw out the toxins of the body, heal the body, and make it ready for another day's labor. When such a work is done for the body, the human soul, upon awakening, feels joy, strength, and an urge to work and labor. When upon awakening one does not feel joyful but feels negative, tired, or lazy, it means that he kept his body under the strain of his various emotional and mental pressures and did not really sleep.

Every time you have a real sleep you must awaken with a smile on your face, joy in your heart, and optimism and vision in your mind. Your physical body will be energetic, your emotions magnetic, your mental body creative, and your soul striving.

When you go a step deeper in your sleep, you will be able to leave behind your astral body. Your astral body needs a complete rest because all day it is agitated by various emotional pressures coming from people and the environment. Your emotional body is wounded daily by arrows flung at you through jealousy and hatred. All day you face crises of fear and shocks. Daily your emotional body is loaded with desires, attachment to objects, and identifications with fears.

Your emotional body is attacked daily by the things that are ugly, criminal, and destructive. All these make your emotional body wounded, cracked, continuously irritated, negative, and depressed. Such an emotional body produces many poisons which affect not only your physical body but also your mental body and your environment.

A vacation must be given to the emotional body so that it purifies itself from toxins, repairs its wounds, adjusts its mechanism, and brings you pure sensitivity and joy. Every time your emotional body cannot find a chance to relax, it complicates your life with various problems. It is more difficult to solve emotional problems than physical ones.

Most physical problems are emotional problems, and when the emotional pressure is taken away from the physical body, the physical body feels a great release and happiness.

In the third stage of sleep, man is not only withdrawn from his physical and astral bodies, but he is withdrawn from his mental body as well. The mental body is left in the "garage" to be repaired after a thousand-mile journey. It needs various kinds of repairs. Its centers must be aligned and readjusted to the rhythm of the inner Lotus. Greater light must be drawn into the mental mechanism to cleanse it from illusions, from fanaticism, from prejudices, from various crystallizations and vanities.

It is not easy to leave the mental body behind because most of the time we are identified with the thoughts in the mental body, which are like furniture in our room. That is why all over the world the mental body is so polluted, and people and nations cannot find the most essential in their lives; they cannot find the right direction for survival, and they use their inventions and discoveries against their health, happiness, and joy.

People think that by making some sophisticated discoveries of a mechanical nature they are securing health and happiness and proving their progress and achievements. But all these discoveries and inventions can be used destructively and criminally as long as the human mind is not free from its prejudices, fanaticism, separatism, and totalitarian urges and drives. As long as we cannot detach ourselves from our selfish interests, we will always find an opportunity to use our discoveries against others and perpetuate misery in the world.

Whether we believe it or not, the solution to mental distortions and disturbances lies in deep sleep. The human soul gives a vacation to the mental body to readjust itself as far as possible and make itself ready for a higher duty.

Whenever our physical, emotional, and mental bodies do not rest, the chance of misusing these bodies increases, and eventually they function against the plan of our Soul, against the plan of our evolution, and even against our survival in physical, emotional, and mental manifestation.

We can see all over the world how our physical body works against our best interests, how our emotional body works against our happiness, how our mental body works against our survival, our highest good, and our spiritual creativity.

It is very important to know what to eat and how to eat. It is very important to know about your emotions and how to control and sublimate them. It is very important to know about your brain, about your mind and thoughts. But all this knowledge does not profit you if you do not know how to sleep. Right sleep is more important than food. A good sleep provides more energy to your body than a good dinner.

After a good three-dimensional sleep, you introduce many beneficent changes in your life. For example, you abstain from certain vices, or you feel uncomfortable with them and you feel the urge to change your physical life.

Also, after awakening from a deep sleep, you try to correct certain emotional behaviors. For example, instead of continuing your hatred, you begin to forgive and understand; instead of your jealousies, you exercise more acceptance and love. All these are the result of repairs of the astral body on the astral plane.

After awakening from a deep sleep, you introduce many beneficial changes in your mental behavior. Instead of criticism, you try to analyze. Instead of plans of crime or destruction, you try to understand and cooperate. Instead of separatism and fanaticism, you try to be inclusive and holistic.

All these changes take place more effectively as you go deeper and deeper into sleep. This is not like a hypnotic sleep in which you are thrown out of your physical and astral bodies with the heavy luggage of your urges, drives, glamors, and illusions, leaving your bodies unprotected for the seeds the hypnotist will plant without your conscious permission. When you really sleep you do not carry with you your blind urges, drives, glamors, and illusions. You leave them behind in the void which is between the mental plane and the Intuitional Plane. This is sometimes called the Threshold, where the Dweller — formed of your blind urges, drives, glamors, and illusions and identified with the image of your personality — dwells and often prevents your entrance into Higher Worlds.

Most of our dreams are recordings of the battle going on between the human soul and the Dweller on the Threshold. If the human soul wins the battle, he enters into deep sleep, which is paradoxically no longer a sleep but a state of wakefulness in which he is aware of all that goes on upon various levels of his personality world.

When in a deep sleep the human soul, the Real Self, is out of his three lower bodies, and the three elementals come together and say, "We are three brothers. We must take care of each other. Let's create integration and harmony between us so that when our boss comes we can better help him reach his destination. As we are dependent on each other, we are also dependent on our boss. Let's create alignment and fusion with the leader within us." This is what happens every time you enter into a three-dimensional sleep.

At the time of deep sleep the physical, emotional, and mental elementals and devas are in intensive labor to repair your bodies and align them with the creative forces of Nature. Actually, it is the human soul who, through his identification with urges, drives, glamors, and illusions, introduces disturbances and distortions into his bodies. At the time of sleep this "man-made" pressure is lifted and the vehicles have a chance to breathe in pure air.

When the human soul detaches himself from the bodies, his identifications with the urges, drives, glamors, and illusions weaken and possibly disappear. When the human soul is able to detach himself from the threefold mechanism, he enters into the world of an intense light. This is the sphere where a shower of light is given to the soul to clean his senses, to make the beam of direction clear before his eyes, and to reestablish his sense of universalism and spiritual values.

This is how the human soul slips away through right sleep from his own prisons and complicated nets.

Every time you do things wrong physically, the reason is that you did not have a sound sleep on three levels. Every time you do things wrong emotionally, the reason is that your emotional body was not able to clean the toxins due to partial sleep. Every time you do things wrong in your thoughts and intentions, it is because you were not able to have a sound, three-dimensional sleep and were not able to receive the purification of the shower of light in higher realms.

The whole of creation is run within the law of cycles of rest and labor, and these cycles must be observed and exercised within our system. Violation of these cycles brings us unending problems.

We must emphasize the fact that sleep does not necessarily mean a state of unconsciousness. It is possible to sleep in a state of wakefulness. When our consciousness is withdrawn to the emotional body without cutting the communication line with the physical body, the physical body is in a state of sleep, but the human soul is aware of all that transpires on the physical plane. The same thing happens when one is focused in the mental body. The emotional body is in sleep, but the soul is aware of all that transpires on the emotional plane. The same thing happens to the mental body. When the consciousness is focused in the intuitional body, the human soul is aware of all that transpires on the mental plane.

It is at these stages that the Antahkarana is built. Though the lower bodies are inactive, they register all that happens in higher levels. This is not a trance. This is continuity of consciousness in which, no matter how deeply withdrawn from the bodies, the human soul is conscious. Though acting on higher levels, the human soul is aware of all that is transpiring within the three lower worlds. Once such a state is achieved, the human soul can locate or anchor himself on any plane of the personality without interrupting his relationship with the Higher Worlds.

In deep sleep we do not fight against our vices, habits, glamors, and illusions, but we cut the lines of attention which carry energy to them and let them weaken and eventually dry up and disintegrate.

There is a saying that Space does not tolerate a vacuum. Exactly when the negative, destructive, and ugly things disappear from our sphere, positive, constructive, and rhythmic forces fill in and enrich our whole being. That is why we are advised not to fight against evil but to increase the forces of Goodness. Philosophically the Good fills the whole of Space. All joy, all beauty, all bliss fill Space.

Good is absent only when a physical, emotional, or mental tumor is created by human ignorance; when a distortion is created by human hatred or illusions. But ignorance, distortion, and hatred are not part of the all-embracing Good. Once they are annihilated, the ocean of Good again fills the whole sphere of Space.

One can observe people and know if they are sleeping well. The signs of good sleep are

— physical strength and good health

— joy and enthusiasm

— optimism

— realistic views

— inclusiveness and tolerance

— spirit of gratitude

— serenity

— synthesis

— right action and right speech

— clear thought

My Teacher used to say that each true sleep is like taking a bath in the Subtle Worlds and coming back with energy, joy, and new inspirations.

The absence of these signs means partial sleep or bad sleep.

Politically speaking, we must elect those people who know how to sleep because the greatest leaders are those leaders who can visit, during sleep, the realms of Light and receive direction, courage, and fearlessness. These are the three most useful gifts of the higher realms.

If you choose a person who does not know how to sleep, his sleepless nights will increase, and all that he will do will be to increase your sleepless nights.

When you awaken on the Intuitional Plane, you are directed on one path — service for one humanity.

What happens while we are asleep but still attached to our various vehicles?

1. We are drawn to the places of our urges and drives.

2. We are attracted to places of glamor and low desires and habits which want satisfaction.

3. We are drawn to groups with similar interests — good or bad: bad when we are attached to our lower mind, and good when we function in our higher mind.

We become destructive or constructive according to where we dwell and with what motives.

When we penetrate the Intuitional Plane, we go to our Ray Ashram or to the Ashrams where our Elder Brother or Master leads us. We learn the science of service and wisdom and how to serve the Plan of the Great Ones.

Battles with dark forces take place in sleep, and many enemies of light are defeated by a collective attack. These battles are organized against everything that works for crime, slander, malice, materialism, totalitarianism, and separatism.

Those who are merged on earth with matter and are successful with their lies, fabrications, and exploitations are without protection in the Subtle World. They are weak and depressed.

Before we go to sleep we must invoke the higher powers and set our mind on lofty thoughts. In many traditions the Guardian Angel is invoked to guard us within the invisible world.

It is important to know that in sleep we are always active on the plane where we are stuck. On every plane we meet those who are active, either in death or in sleep. On every plane we find those who bring more complications into our lives and those who help us overcome some of our problems.

Many spirits and entities wait anxiously for you to go to sleep to be with you in the subtle planes — if you are a source of wisdom and are blooming with virtues and self-actualization. Your fragrance, colors, and wisdom are their nourishment. Many spirits are anxious to come to classes which you hold. But unfortunately, we sometimes cause them distress and disappointment when we load ourselves with earthly worries and clouds of misconduct. They need to welcome us with our Robe of Glory instead of our rags of earthly pollutions. When we do things that are ugly, we darken our robes and become exposed in the Subtle World, and people feel sorry for us.

There is a big trap on the path of the disciple when he first learns how to be free and conscious in the Subtle World. This trap is the trap of his pleasures and personal interests. Once he is caught in this trap, the gates toward the supermundane world are darkened, closed, and eventually sealed. Many lives and much suffering are needed to open the gates again.

The sparks of our higher striving descend into our heart only when we are in the supermundane world — through our sleep or when we leave our bodies. It is these sparks that grow in our life on earth and flourish as virtues, direction, and talents.

Every time we sleep there is a great chance to receive a spark of striving and to be charged by the spirit of sacrificial service. Every time we are in the supermundane world we have a chance to see the right issues and be filled with the spirit of tolerance, forgiveness, and especially patience. Thus, after the daily battle and labor one can visit the land of pearls, the land of precious sparks, and come back enriched with many blessings.

Let us remember that as we have physical enemies who try to hurt or harm our physical mechanism, we also have astral enemies and mental enemies. Astral enemies are of many kinds. They are those who want to create more glamors within us and more earthly attachments through which they can satisfy their earthly desires and urges. We have those who plan to involve us with emotional, religious, and traditional conflicts and problems to strengthen their position in the astral plane.

We also have those who want to take revenge for various reasons, and every time we visit the astral world they attack us and create irritation in our astral senses and centers. There are those who try to hypnotize us and use us on the physical plane. There are many evil seeds that are sown into our astral bodies while we are not conscious on the astral plane.

On the other hand, we have those on the astral plane who, because of various affiliations, try to clean our glamors, negativity, and disturbances and calm us down, build bridges across cleavages, create deeper sympathy, and awaken deeper aspirations toward the Higher Worlds.

On the mental plane there are many antagonistic forces and also entities who try to give us the best guidance. We also have those who were our enemies when they passed away, and we have those who were our friends, or who are still our friends in physical incarnation. The battle and cooperation go hand in hand on all planes and levels.

Those who are our real enemies misdirect us through their thought force and cause various damages to our mental body. They attack our mental centers and senses. They sow evil seeds in the mental centers to affect our corresponding astral, etheric, and physical centers. They try to obsess and possess our mental body and use our mental body for their own advantage. They even try to prevent the owner of the mental body from repossessing it. It is such kinds of attacks that create the various mental diseases with which our mental hospitals are loaded.

On the other hand, we have our Teachers, our co-disciples, our friends, and our co-workers on the path of light. They help us in our battle; they help to cure our wounds. They teach us the science of battle. They teach us how to protect ourselves and our vehicles when we are withdrawn from them.

There are centers of learning organized by similar disciples of great Teachers. These disciples have their groups on the mental plane where all who have the power to attend and study greater wisdom are gathered. They teach us how to unfold and use our senses. They inspire us with the ideas of greater service for the Common Good. They help us build the bridge between the lower and higher mind. They teach us how to live on the physical plane so that we do not contaminate our mental bodies and make them targets for dark forces and enemies.

Actually, whether man remembers or not, he is continuously active twenty-four hours every day on various planes.

Meditation is a great technique to prepare the mental body and produce those spiritual weapons which can fight dark forces and often lead them onto the right path, after making them see the futility of their course of action.

In the mental world man conquers with his thoughts. His thoughts are stronger and more powerful according to the percentage of truth and willpower which exists in them. Pure thoughts are like fiery streams which burn the mental bodies of enemies and give them a chance to see their naked essence as it is.

When man is able through deep sleep or conscious withdrawal to enter the Intuitional Plane, he attends the great Ashrams of Masters according to his interest, his Rays, and his responsibilities. We are told that it is in these Ashrams that people learn about the Plan for humanity and for other kingdoms and that they develop love-wisdom.

A one minute penetration into these Ashrams will be equal to twenty-five years of intense study on a particular subject. All great heroes and leaders in all fields of human endeavor are students of these Ashrams, which they visit after they sleep or where they go after they leave their bodies.

A great hero, genius, or leader comes to the world equipped with the wisdom, direction, and virtues learned in Ashrams. He or she is born rich, creative, and with a spirit of sacrificial service. It is in these Ashrams that the real expansion of consciousness occurs and the path of Infinity is discovered.

How to Sleep

Before you sleep you must consider many factors which can contribute to a better sleep or create various hindrances to a good sleep. The rules are as follows:

1. Before you sleep, you must move your bowels and urinate. Your body should not be loaded with decayed matter if you want a sound sleep.

2. You must wash your body because the odors and toxins of your body attract many unwanted entities, vultures, and forces which agitate your etheric vehicle. You must also not have on your body different deodorants and perfumes. They create association in your emotional and mental worlds and make it difficult for you to withdraw.

3. Your room must be clean. The less furniture in the room, the better. There must be no symbols, no pictures which excite you physically, emotionally, or mentally. Your room must not have articles which were stolen by you or over which you had a fight, or articles which are charged with irritation, hatred, fear, and lust because every thought and emotion is a line of connection which draws you to the owner of the article and creates great confusion in your soul. Your bed, sheets, pillows, and blankets must be clean and without the emanations of other persons. You must not use blankets, sheets, pillows, or beds which were used by people who suffered pain or irritation or were in steady emotional and mental problems.

In olden days, the great Teachers of humanity even suggested that we build our own room or house to keep ourselves away from all thoughts and emotions that exist in a house where other people lived. Of course, there are homes and rooms which were inhabited by great, creative people. These are exceptions, and when people live in such places they feel a clean, uplifting atmosphere which helps them orient themselves to higher frequencies.

Our modern life and our continuous moving from one apartment to another, from one house to another, leave the doors open for many attacks. Sleep in those places is as unpleasant as sleeping in motel rooms which were occupied by many kinds of people and their problems.

My mother occasionally used to clean my bedroom of various articles which were sent to me as gifts. When asked why she was acting this way, she would say, "You don't need unseen guests attached to these objects. I want your room to be really clean." And it was — because there was almost nothing in it. I had only a picture of Christ walking on the waves of a lake. It was an original picture from a great artist, and I was allowed to have that "because the creative thoughts of the artist were with the picture."

It is possible to have an unseen and unheard symphony of thoughts and emotions in your room, or the chaos of the noise of various conflicting emanations.

One day a person brought a jar to me as a gift. When my mother saw it in my room, she took me on a walk and explained how thoughts, moods, emotions, and intentions can attach to objects given as gifts. She concluded by saying, "They affect you while you are asleep. You don't need them." The next day I threw out the jar because the man who gave it to me had killed three people in the past....

An "egg-headed" man will call such observations mere superstition, but such things are more real than objects, for those who have eyes to see, ears to hear, and brains to observe effects.

In many teachings and monasteries, advanced disciples were forbidden to read books from libraries because they carry with them the aura of many readers — good and bad. Pure living has a scientific foundation, and negligence toward these ancient rules has many destructive consequences on our character and life.

4. Shoes and clothing worn during the daytime must not enter the bedroom. They are contaminated by various emanations from us and from those with whom we come in contact. At the time of sleep, these emanations create static and disturbances and affect our dreams and subjective contacts.

Many emanations of fighting, arguments, negative emotions, and thoughts of low quality are attached to our shoes and clothing. Leaving them out of our room and entering our bedroom with a robe or pajamas will make a great difference in our sleep and psychological health.

5. Animals are forbidden to enter your bedroom because of their emanations and their relations with the astral world. At the time of sleep they

may create various disturbances in your subtle bodies. Animals are beautiful, but their place is not in your bedroom.

6. No food or drink is allowed less than five hours before sleeping. Many disciples used to eat only one meal at twelve noon; that was all. Eating food and drinking an excess amount of fluids close to the time of sleep cause many disturbances in your body and in your sleep.

When you are an advanced disciple, you must have an uninterrupted sleep so that you do not deprive yourself of your ashramic studies, higher services, and higher contacts. Your dream life is affected to a great extent by your digestive and urinary systems and by your food and drink.

7. There are also things that are absolutely forbidden, for example, tea, coffee, alcohol, hallucinogenic drugs, marijuana. These kinds of materials transport your consciousness into either the etheric or astral body and put you in contact with those spirits who like the emanations from your bodies. Thus you create a bad link with earthbound spirits which contaminate your consciousness, make you sleep very uncomfortably, and prevent you from having any higher experiences and higher contact.

8. It is better to sleep in a loose robe or pajamas. You must not wear anything that is tight on your body. Women must not sleep with their brassieres on. We are even advised not to dress in tight jeans or shoes, or corsets and brassieres which prevent the free circulation of the blood. Sexual overstimulation or artificial stimulation is often caused by tight jeans. Anything which presses against your body is against your health and sanity. Your body needs air and free circulation of blood and prana.

9. In your sleeping room it is better to have total darkness or an oil lamp or wax candle put behind an object so that you do not have direct contact with its rays. Electric light is very disturbing for the sleep. It also wears down your energy at the time of sleep. No electrical machines must be allowed in your bedroom.

10. Put your head always toward the north so that you align your energy circulation with the magnetic pole of the earth. This is like floating on a current of energy while you are leaving your bodies, one after each other. For average people these rules do not make any difference.

11. It is very good to have in your room a small pine tree or deodar tree. You can also have a small container with hot water and put into it ten to fifteen drops of eucalyptus or peppermint oil. These oils prevent psychic attacks of low order. Wormwood oil and sandalwood incense expel stronger psychic attacks and protect your body during sleep. They are also good for repelling certain germs.

12. It is very good if you do a few minutes of a relaxation exercise. Lie on your back on the floor and push your whole body into the floor, as if you were trying to enter the floor. Do this for one minute, then relax your body.[1]

13. Electric blankets are very disturbing to the etheric body. This disturbance reflects on the nervous system and heart, and deep sleep becomes an impossibility under such blankets.

It is very bad to sleep in water-filled beds, or to sleep on cement. Hardwood, wool, and cotton beds are very good.

14. The heat of the room must be natural heat, if it is necessary — no gas or electric heaters. It is better to increase the number of your blankets than to leave your heater on. The best heating system is a fireplace or steam going through pipes.

15. The less noise in your room, the deeper is your sleep. Avoid all noise, especially factory, motor, and refrigerator noise. Any mechanical noise is detrimental to your nervous system when you sleep.

Shallow sleep accumulates poison in your system and eventually manifests as various health problems. Curiously enough, you can sleep near waterfalls, springs, rivers, and oceans and go deep into higher levels. Negative ions produced by such natural phenomena provide the energy and drive to go into higher levels.

With such physical rules you must also try to prepare yourself emotionally before you sleep:

1. You must not be disturbed by violent emotions at least three hours before you sleep.

   a. Avoid any arguments which lead you into anger, hatred, fear, etc.

   b. Avoid worries.

   c. Avoid watching movies or television programs full of crime and violence.

   d. Do not sleep with revenge in your heart.

   e. Do not go to sleep with depression or irritation.

   f. Do not sleep with feelings of ingratitude.

---

1. See *The Science of Meditation*, pp. 79-80.

If you sleep under these conditions, you will possibly be stuck in lower strata. Your emotional body will emanate dark fumes in its journey, attract low forces, or be attracted to places that are full of emotional contamination.

2. Before you sleep you must do your evening review.[2]

3. Pray for all your friends and for those by whom you are disturbed. Pray for the world to be blessed with peace, beauty, cooperation, harmony, and goodwill.

4. Enter your bed with thoughts of gratitude and with best wishes for the many people you know. Remember that it is a great privilege to have a good bedroom or a good place to sleep.

5. Do not criticize, complain, or curse before you sleep but have words of love, appreciation, and joy on your lips. Those who sleep with slander and malice attract very destructive forces into their aura.

6. Remember that you may penetrate areas where great celestial or spiritual beings can be met. You must make your aura beautiful, vibrant, and colorful with higher aspirations and lofty motives.

7. Sleep is a journey toward the sources of Beauty, Goodness, Righteousness, Joy, and Freedom. This is why you must know how to prepare yourself for a sound sleep.

8. Higher aspirations aroused by prayer, reading, and meditation are very important for your sleep. Lower desires, charged by your sexual urges and drives and by your greed, chain you to lower strata where you contaminate your aura more. Lower desires dramatized by imagination assume astral forms and attack you on different planes, keeping your consciousness limited to the areas of your desires.

Many people wander in their sleep in nightclubs, whorehouses, and gambling places to satisfy their imaginations. The greater part of humanity is under the pressure of an abnormal, artificial sex drive which originates not only from the outside but also from our own imagination. Our present civilization is full of anti-survival factors.

A Wise One said that you must lift your anchor before you are able to sail in the open seas of higher awareness. When one is anchored in his sex organs, greed, or hatred, such an attachment will never allow him to go deep into higher spheres of wisdom and beauty and be charged with the power of regeneration and healing.

---

2. For complete information, please see *The Psyche and Psychism*, Ch. 80.

Before you sleep, you must not only prepare yourself physically and emotionally but also mentally:

1. Do not go to sleep with thoughts of defeat. You must enter into sleep with great expectations, thoughts of hope and success, thoughts of great achievements. You do not know that most of your successes and failures originate through events and relationships taking place in your sleep. You can literally change the course of events if in sleep you are charged with the spirit of victory, honesty, and striving.

Many achievements are the result of a new charge received at the time of sleep. Many new ideas, new visions, and new successes are gained in sleep, which then change the course of events in our lives.

Fill your mind with thoughts of victory and success, not at the expense of others but by your own right and labor.

Whatever the conditions are, go to sleep with high expectations. Say, "Yes, today things appear dark, but tomorrow may bring a new assistance or protection or inspiration from higher realms. Even before the dawn many things can change in my favor."

2. You must not enter sleep with thoughts of guilt, no matter how guilty you feel. Decide not to repeat the things you did, and say very seriously and with intensity:

More radiant than the Sun,
Purer than the snow,
Subtler than the ether
Is the Self,
The Spirit within my heart.
I am that Self.
That Self am I.

No matter what the conditions of your bodies, you are purer than the snow. Your Real Self is a flame of beauty. Think about this and sleep with these thoughts.

3. Never sleep in a state of fanaticism. Think about the many thousands of beautiful ideas, visions, deeds, and ways which exist. Fanaticism creates isolation from higher forces in your subjective journey. It is those forces that have great gifts of new thoughts, new ways, and new visions to offer you.

Many dark forces or low-level entities, because of similar frequency, impress the minds of fanatics with the ideas of various crimes and make them dangerous human beings.

A fanatic, in the name of God, does satanic jobs; in the name of love, he allows himself to hate; in the name of unity, he dares to separate; in the name of truth, he lies; in the name of beauty, he produces ugliness. A fanatic at the time of sleep does great damage to those souls who are on the path of new breakthroughs and subjectively prepares future attacks on human progress.

Fanaticism produces thousands of mental molds, and any idea or inspiration caught from higher spheres becomes crystallized in these molds. A fanatic in sleep is like a rolling snowball which grows as it descends into lower strata.

When you sleep with the thoughts of fanaticism, you go to those groups where they emphasize "the only way to fly." Nothing is more detrimental to human progress than fanaticism, no matter through what kind of excuses.

4. Do not sleep with negative problems in your mind. You can have great questions in your mind and look for their subjective solutions, but you must not sleep loaded with problems which cause you intense worry. Every time you enter the gate of sleep, leave all your worries on the threshold, and when you come back, either you will find them or you will be equipped with greater wisdom to handle them.

Do not take your problems to so-called Masters. A real Master never solves problems for you, but He inspires you to solve your own problems if you show a state of detachment.

Enter sleep forgetting about your problems, having faith that the Lord will take care of them. Those who take their problems with them are like those who try to climb to the summit of a mountain with heavy loads of furniture and other possessions. You can ascend only if you are free of loads. Problems are chains tying you to the shores of earthly life.

5. Enter sleep with thoughts of self-confidence, self-victory, self-dignity, and nobility.

6. Enter sleep with thoughts of great service, thoughts of world peace, thoughts of right human relations, thoughts of prosperity and success, thoughts of healing others in all levels, thought of leading people

from darkness to Light,
from the unreal to the Real,
from death to Immortality,
from chaos to Beauty.

Think about Infinity and about the immortality of the soul. Fill your heart with joyful thoughts.

After you try the suggestions given above, lie relaxed in your bed and withdraw your consciousness to the top of your head. Do not force yourself too long at this time; take it easy because this exercise is dangerous and you must do it at your own risk.

Take deeper and deeper breaths, focusing yourself at the top of your head. As you breathe deeply, relax your body more, watching it from the top of your head. If you are doing it right, your body will feel very happy, and you will register deep joy in your being.

It is important to sleep with good thoughts, loving emotions, beautiful visions, and higher aspirations for a greater future.

The next step is to decide to leave your body consciously, no matter how long you stay awake. This is not easy, but try it. Eventually you will see that your sleep is a continuation of your last thoughts or last visions. Later, things will be clearer for you, and you will stay awake on the plane where you are controlling the events with your own thought power.

This may take ten to fifteen years, but it works. You can decrease the years of this exercise if you, in the meantime, do the exercises on the Antahkarana explained in various writings.[3]

The Antahkarana is a thread of light which extends from the head to higher spheres. As you are trying to sleep consciously, you must keep a diary and write in it your exact experiences. Try to find the causes of your experiences, whether pleasant or unpleasant. For example, you may suddenly jump during your efforts. This signifies that the doors of your withdrawal are not clear, or you did not prepare yourself intelligently. Also, you may see light, the path, and have very interesting revelations. All these experiences must be recorded so that you see your path clearly and take those steps which will eventually make you an invisible helper or a greater server in subjective fields.

Remember that when you are sleeping you go to different levels or planes, and the level you go to is equal to your beingness — what you are in your essence — not what you know. You may know many things and have high public positions, but your knowledge and positions do not help you climb to higher levels if your true beingness is weak and polluted with self-deceit, vanity, pride, fanaticism, and false values.

You go higher and have higher relationships and service if you refine your heart; if you are full of compassion and goodwill; if you are charged with beauty, love, and joy; if you are inspired by the spirit of sacrificial service; if you are adorned by selfless deeds and labors; if you are pure in your motives; and if your soul strives toward the future.

If you are attached to your physical urges and drives, you will go half a foot away from your body and stay between your physical and etheric bodies. If you

3. See *The Science of Becoming Oneself*, Ch. 18, and *The Psyche and Psychism*, Chs. 45 and 46.

are attached to your glamors and lower desires, you may surrender yourself to the forces of lower desires. These forces will pollute you more and use you for their own intentions and for their own plans.

If you are attached to your problems emotionally and mentally, you attract those forces who enjoy increasing your problems and anxieties and using you for their own ends. They can use your thoughtforms to reach people and mix up their lives. One can karmically load his life through associating himself with such forces. One cannot have mental health and sanity if such forces inject his aura with their own pollution and increase his mental disturbances.

If you had a deep and positive sleep, you awaken early in the morning feeling an urge to do something very beautiful, an urge to serve, an urge to create, an urge to forgive and heal, an urge to create peace and right human relations, an urge to do heroic work. You feel deep joy and freedom.

With good, conscious sleep your self-observation reaches a higher state of clarity. You correct things in your life that are not worthy for your path. You reorient yourself in your motives, thinking, and life. You repair your body, heal your wounds, and bring peace and healing into the lives of others. You sow seeds of beauty and striving. You build new and higher relationships and contacts. You create new fields of cooperation in your life.

Every time we sleep, we expose ourselves to the precipitation of various seeds. The lower the level of our sleep, the more rotten are the seeds which fall into our aura. The higher the level of our sleep, the purer are the seeds thrown into our aura. It is from those seeds that our future creative garden flourishes.

We are told that if one learns how to sleep consciously, greater challenges are presented to him. The first challenge is to be ready to fight the sources of corruption and crime found in the Subtle Worlds. The next challenge is to form subjective classes to educate human souls to unfold toward Cosmic beauty.

The next challenge is to serve continuously, twenty-four hours a day, for the salvation of humanity through the Divine Plan and Purpose. The next challenge is to leave behind the Cosmic Physical, Cosmic Astral, and Cosmic Mental Planes and awaken on the Cosmic Intuitional Plane. Of course, this is a far-off vision, but great things come into existence through small seeds which contain cosmic realities within them.

59

The Meaning of Joy

Every time our memory weakens, it means a painful event, thought, idea, or fear entered into the mechanism, loaded the circuits, and blew out some fuses.

Before we perform the exercises of joy, we must try to clear up the definitions of a few words. Very often we use words without knowing their true definitions.

There are several kinds of definitions. One is your own definition, which is based on your study and experience. The other is the dictionary definition, which is taken as the standard definition. But we know that the standard definition is also limited by the knowledge and experience of the ones who defined it.

Knowing this you can dare to have your own definition — related to the standard definition but carried further into higher dimensions of meaning. As a word can be a symbol, so a definition can be taken as a symbol. However, if your own definition seems more important or accurate to you than the definitions of others, you must make sure it does not create confusion or conflict in your relationships.

Now try to define for yourself the following five words, and what these words mean for you.

— satisfaction

— happiness

— joy

— bliss

— beatitude

What are the similarities and differences between these words? After you are convinced of your definitions, try to find

a. three experiences of satisfaction

b. three experiences of happiness

c. three experiences of joy

d. three experiences of bliss

e. three experiences of beatitude

The important thing to know is that these five words refer to five progressive states of expansion, of at-one-ment within the One Life. These moments or events, when found, will release into your system powerful energy according to their depth, intensity, and duration and according to your ability to recall them.

The Steps

Start going back in your time track, and stop whenever you find a moment of satisfaction. Try to recall it in detail as it happened. Observe the sensations, the feelings, the emotions, and the thoughts you experienced.

Repeat your experiences three times or more, until you are sure you have really lived it again with all the details.

Use the same procedure, finding three experiences of

— happiness

— joy

— bliss

— beatitude

You may sometimes feel that you have not had moments of joy, bliss, or beatitude. The reality is that all of us have had these experiences, but they are buried deep in our being and are forgotten...because of many reasons. Try to uncover them, release them, and re-experience them intensely.

If you have difficulty finding them because of your present negative polarization, ask yourself:

Did you ever enjoy the singing birds in the morning or at night?

Did you ever admire a flower?

Were you ever thrilled by a sunset or sunrise?

Did a beautiful tree or a forest ever capture your soul?

Have you ever watched the midnight sky?

Did you ever love someone?

Did you ever feel expansion while reading poetry, listening to music, watching a ballet?

Did you ever feel the strong feeling of knowing something, of learning some wisdom, or of having moments of penetration into a mystery or meeting your True Self?

All the above considerations will help you reveal many hidden treasures on the time track of your life. Once you find something, stop and define it, and then re-experience and make it as real as possible.

It is probable that you may fail to find these treasures for a few days, but do not give up. They are there, even if you did not register them in your consciousness. Life is full of moments of satisfaction, happiness, joy, bliss, and beatitude. Many high moments in life have penetrated into your being. Often they found their way into your soul when your mind was asleep or you were identified with your petty problems. Search for these treasures and you will find them.

If you continue to feel that you do not have any moments of joy, bliss, or beatitude, do not give up but create them through your creative imagination or even through your visualization. Such a technique may bring a great help to you to discover eventually the treasures which you thought did not exist.

How are you going to use this technique? It is very easy.

Relax and close your eyes. Calm your mind and visualize or imagine a beautiful location in Nature where you will have an experience of satisfaction, an experience of happiness, an experience of joy, bliss, and beatitude.

You may choose any place in Nature you want. You can even fly to the farthest galaxies. You have unlimited power to imagine. Through your imagination create

— three events of satisfaction

— three events of happiness

— three events of joy

— three events of bliss

— three events of beatitude

and re-experience them again and again, for at least five times.

When you do these exercises of creative imagination or visualization for twenty-five minutes daily for three months, you will be ready to discover your own past experiences of satisfaction, happiness, joy, bliss, and beatitude.

But remember that because you faithfully tried to create moments of satisfaction, happiness, joy, bliss, and beatitude, you already planted healthy and wonderful seeds for your future greater satisfaction, greater happiness, deeper joy, more exalted bliss, and ever-more-inclusive beatitude.

During most of our life, we are occupied with unhappy things or we are conditioned to be unhappy. There is so much unhappiness in the world, and it gradually changes our polarization and makes us feel unhappy, think in unhappy ways, and live unhappily. But there are also happy moments and happy people in the world. How can we develop eyes to see the happy moments, happy people, happy things?

Many people lose the power to remember things. This happens when the circuit of their memory system is loaded with memories which are painful, unbearable, and too confusing. The memory shuts itself off and rejects functioning.

The best way to put the circuit in action is to make the person remember

1. The most beautiful things he has seen in his life

2. The most beloved persons

3. The most joyful events

4. The greatest ideas or dreams he has had

5. The greatest moments of his love

When the person is led through these five points of memory generation for three to five months, he will clear all painful memories, and with them the collected posthypnotic suggestions, and attain the power to remember in detail and without distortion.

Every time our memory weakens, it means a painful event, thought, idea, or fear entered into the mechanism, loaded the circuits, and blew out some fuses. Recharging of the circuit can be attained through stimulating still-living sparks in the mechanism.

If the above five points are not applicable, then the attention of the person must be directed to someone whom he worships or loves immensely. Through such a connection the whole memory system gradually will regenerate.

It will be very helpful also to find objects, dresses, jewelry, furniture, etc. that are connected with painful memories and remove them, or replace them with new ones which carry joyful feelings. Sometimes it is necessary to move from the old dwelling and live in a new home, in a new environment. Such articles and homes loaded with irritation and painful memories act as circuit breakers.

60

Healing With Joy

To heal the core problem, you are going to use the beauty technique, the love, truth, or joy technique of cultivating virtues. Once these techniques are used, you release the innermost energy of man and gradually eradicate the sources of troubles without dealing separately with them.

Joy has a very healing effect on our physical, emotional, and mental bodies. It is a great vitamin and an antibiotic. It must be taken every day, even every hour if possible.[1]

Joy is one of the greatest gifts of Nature. It is an energy which can be used in our daily life through all that we do, speak, and think.

A joyful man radiates healing energy. With the energy of joy, he builds a radioactive shield around his body in which his physical organs and glands are protected from any visible and invisible attacks. A joyful man also protects a group, a family; even one's belongings feel safe with a joyful man.

Animals act more intelligently in the presence of a joyful man. They love his smell, they love his radiant colors, and they obey him. A joyful man can train animals, and they do all possible things to please him because his joy nourishes them and gives them greater pleasure.

The articles and clothes that a joyful man uses last longer. Joy feeds them and keeps their magnetic aura healthy.

Flowers and trees adore a joyful man. In the presence of a joyful man, they emanate an extra quantity of fragrance to express their gratitude to him. Sometimes they even bloom out of season to greet him, to salute him, and to express their love to him.

Some poisonous plants do not harm those who are joyful. Plants do not like gloomy, negative people; they like joyful people because joy creates rapport between them. Through joy the communication field of plants extends, and they feel closer to the human kingdom and sense its strivings.

Plants, herbs, and trees sometimes give out secret emanations to those they love to heal them, to inspire them, to encourage them, and to keep them alive,

---

1. For further information on joy, please refer to *Joy and Healing*.

healthy, and joyful. Plants, herbs, roots, and trees give their healing powers to those who have more love and more joy in their heart.

The same herb affects people differently. If a man is negative, full of ill will, hatred, and fear, the healing effect is much less. But if a man is joyful, he consumes the essence of the herb like a fire.

Joy unites hearts and builds bridges between man and man, between group and group.

Through waves of joy man reaches the higher consciousness of people. His thoughts receive energy and direction through joy. Such thoughts are very penetrative and have a very high-level frequency. They do not get lost in a chaotic space full of contradictory currents, but they force their way to reach their destination. Thus, a joyful man serves the Common Good. He spreads the best colors and sounds in Space through his joyful thoughts.

A joyful man makes many invisible friends. The people of the subjective world love the emanating colors, fragrances, lights, and sounds of a joyful person. They receive nourishment and direction through the waves of joy, and in turn they give blessings to man. These blessings are of many kinds. Through the energy of a blessing, man is protected from many dangers. He receives greater inspirations which expand his consciousness. He builds greater links with superhuman evolutions, and thus he becomes a more harmonious part in the symphony of Cosmos.

Joy is produced or generated or, better to say, revealed and accumulated through the following:

1. Practicing the spirit of tolerance
2. Expressing the spirit of patience
3. Practicing the spirit of striving
4. Practicing the spirit of forgiveness
5. Expressing the spirit of creativity
6. Contacting beauty
7. Giving love and compassion
8. Thinking in terms of Infinity
9. Developing the spirit of sacrificial service
10. Obeying the Command
11. Knowing the Plan and the Purpose of our progress toward Infinity

12. Thinking in terms of inclusiveness, universality, and synthesis

13. Rejecting any thought related to hatred, fear, jealousy, and self-pity

14. Rejecting any thought related to hopelessness, pessimism, and failure

15. Not being happy in the failures and defeat of our adversaries and not wishing for them a painful future

16. Exercising harmlessness in all our expressions and deeds

17. Obeying the warnings of our heart

18. Exercising honesty, purity, and nobility

19. Directing our thoughts at least three times a day toward the Great Ones

These nineteen points continuously provide the energy of joy for us.

Psychologists, teachers, and leaders of the future can increase joy in the world if they counsel people and train them with the ideas and concepts of these nineteen points. They will create a wonderful atmosphere in which people will grow, expand, and unfold their creative potentials. Each of these points can be used for a day's seminar, retreat, or counseling session and worked on until the depth is touched and the essence penetrates into people's hearts.

The power of joy clears the mind, makes man see his destiny, and creates beauty that will uplift the world.

You can personally work on yourself and cultivate joy through specific meditations on joy. Daily you can take one of the above-mentioned points and think about it in relation to joy. For example:

1. How does the spirit of tolerance bring joy to me?

2. How does the spirit of patience increase joy in me?

3. How does the spirit of striving help me to have greater joy?

4. Why does forgiveness increase joy in my heart?

5. Why is creativity a manifestation of joy?

6. Why does contact with beauty open deeper layers of joy in my being?

7. Does giving love and compassion expand the field of my joy, and why?

8. Why does Infinity evoke a strong joy from my soul?

9. How is sacrificial service related to an increasing joy?

10. What is a Command? Why is it joyful to follow the Command?

11. Knowledge of the Plan and Purpose of life is a great source of joy. Why does knowledge of the Plan and Purpose give us an abundant source of joy?

12. How are inclusiveness, universality, and synthesis related to joy?

13. Thoughts of hatred, fear, greed, jealousy, and self-pity take my joy away. How does it happen and why?

14. When I stand above my failures, depressions, and pessimism, I see a unique joy springing out of my heart. Where does the secret lie?

15. Do I know that any time I feel happy in the failures of others and in the defeat of the ones I hate, I lose my real joy? What is the cause of it?

    When people feel "joy" in the failures and sufferings of their enemies, such a "joy" mixed with their hatred creates a heinous poison in their system which eventually builds abscesses and leads the entire human being into the hands of obsessors.

16. When I am harmless I have more joy. Why?

17. If I do not obey my heart, joy disappears. What is the secret of this phenomenon?

18. When I am honest, pure, and noble, I feel the joy increasing even in my muscles. How can I explain this?

19. Great Ones, Those Who stand as towers of achievement, inspire joy in us. Can I know the real reason for this?

You can do regular meditation on these seed thoughts, increase your joy and radioactivity, and provide a source of healing energy for your whole body and environment. [2]

In counseling sessions, the counselor listens to complaints and tries to help people with their problems. In my own experiences in counseling, I have seen that the problems people present to me in most cases are not really self-generated problems but imported as a result of certain weaknesses in them.

As a counselor, your task is to find the source of trouble and work on that source if you want to eliminate the problems. If you do not find the source, then

2. You may also read or practice the meditation given on joy in *The Psyche and Psychism*, pp. 814-815.

all the help given will be artificial, and soon any improvement will disappear, giving even greater opportunities for the problems to grow.

The core problem is mostly an accumulation of the events in which the person worked against Beauty, Goodness, Righteousness, Joy, and Freedom. It is a moral problem, and this core problem must be corrected first before any secondary problems are dealt with. To heal the core problem, you are going to use the beauty technique, the love, truth, or joy technique, or the technique of cultivating virtues. Once these techniques are used, you release the innermost energy of man and gradually eradicate the sources of troubles without dealing separately with them.

For example, a man comes and complains about his wife. He has a problem with his wife, and most of the counselors want to know what the problem is, how it started and developed. It is not necessary to know all these things because the man's problem is a result of a deep-seated problem. Maybe he has no love, no patience, no beauty, no goodness, no honesty, no energy.

Go back to him and check whether he has love. Make a scale and see where his love is. Does he have the sense of beauty? Check it and find out.

Does he have goodness? Find out.

Does he live in truth? Check it.

If you find out that he is lacking beauty, goodness, truth, joy, and honesty, try to awaken these virtues in him. Make him imagine and visualize the virtues and meditate upon their meaning. As you awaken in him beauty, goodness, truth, and joy you will notice that his other problems will gradually disappear.

Most of our problems branch from core problems. When the core problem is solved, the branch problems disappear.

Man essentially is Beauty, Goodness, and Truth. He is Beauty because he synthesizes the beginning and the end of the seed and the vision of the seed. All that was and is, is in the Will from which the Spark proceeded.

He is Goodness because, in essence, he is one with all that exists.

He is the Truth because he is both reality and the witness to reality. Truth is the radiation of reality; truth is proof of the existence of reality. Truth is the manifestation of the inner Essence.

From the beginning psychoanalysis has not seen the fact that man is Beauty, Goodness, and Truth — a Trinity in one. All culture, all creative manifestations, all healing, uplifting, and transforming processes are accomplished only through the release of these three energies: Beauty, Goodness, and Truth.

New Age psychology and New Age psychoanalysis will not deal with aberrations, with complexes, engrams, with mud and darkness, with turbulences of crime and evil, with all the mixtures of pain and suffering, failure and defeat. New Age psychology will deal with the Core of the human being. That Core is the nucleus of light, of love, of power. That nucleus is Truth, Goodness, and Beauty. It is only the gradual release of these three energies, the gradual manifestation of these energies that will heal not only our physical, emotional, and mental ills but also our individual, national, and international ills.

In the near future, a person will be guided by those who know how to release the three fiery energies from his Core. In the future, groups and nations will have their group psychologists who will release Beauty, Goodness, and Truth from the group and national soul. In the future, humanity will have its group psychologists who will release global Beauty, Goodness, and Truth.

For a long time specialists have kept themselves busy with the trash of life, with the rubbish of human life. In the New Age, the eyes of human beings and nations will be directed toward Beauty, Goodness, and Truth.

It is the energy of Beauty that will annihilate all ugliness within all realms of human nature and life. It is Goodness that will annihilate all criminal, selfish tendencies, all harmful actions from the life of individuals and nations. It is Truth that will eliminate all individual and national lies, hypocrisy, injustice, falsehood, illusions, prejudices, superstitions, and ignorance.

The Core of the human being is the radioactive nucleus of Beauty, Goodness, and Truth. The salvation and liberation of humanity must start now to eliminate future pain, suffering, and destruction.

61

A Joy Exercise

Happiness is an effect of outer conditions. When favorable conditions change, happiness disappears, leaving the gloom of depression.

Joy never changes. It increases as the problems and conflicts increase in one's life. It grows in spite of conditions....

...Joy is harmony.[1]

1. Learn to distinguish between happiness and joy.
2. Find the times when you experienced happiness.
3. Find the times when you experienced joy.
4. What is the difference?
5. Look in your life now, and see how to create joy.

[A] step toward joy is questioning....[2]

1. Read a newspaper. Look at events which are effects, and ask yourself what are the causes.
2. Look in your own life at effects and search for causes.
3. Do the same with people you know, and look for the causes in their lives. You are asking why these events took place.

1. *The Flame of Beauty, Culture, Love, Joy*, pp. 175-176.
2. *Ibid.*, p. 189.

62

Healing Through Unity

All sicknesses begin when man tries to cut himself from the vine. First the mental body shows signs of degeneration, and the man begins not to listen to the Voice of Righteousness. Then his heart dries up; love and compassion vanish. After a while he lives a life of crime. This stage denotes that he is drying up, and the gardener will very soon notice him.

There is a great healing power in the Teaching of Christ. All that He did and said can be condensed into one word — Healing. His plan was to heal the bodies of the people; to heal their hearts; to heal cleavages between man and man; to heal cleavages between humanity and the kingdom of God, the Hierarchy; to bridge the cleavage between man and the Father's Home. This was His supreme responsibility, and in all His Teaching one feels the healing energy of His Being. He wanted man to be united with the highest principles found within him and within Nature.

Christ's intention was to integrate the human being, to create a whole out of human nature which was full of cleavages. His intention was to make man whole. His Teaching was intended to bring integration within humanity and lead humanity Home.

The Teaching of Christ was very scientific. In all His speeches He hinted that man is a whole and that his thoughts, his motives, his intentions, his emotions, and his words not only have a great effect on his body and his environment but also condition the events to come.

He suggested that man must hurry to integrate his physical, emotional, and mental natures and harmonize them as a whole with the highest principles that exist within him. This is what integrity means. When we say that man has integrity, we mean that he does not do anything with his physical, emotional, and mental bodies that is not in tune with the highest principles found in him. The highest principles in the words of Christ were the heart, the kingdom of God, and the Father's Home.

When man's actions, feelings, and thoughts are integrated in his highest visions, in his highest virtues, values, and principles, he is a man of integrity and a man of beauty and radiance.

The Teaching of Christ was directed not only to individuals but also to all humanity to make humanity whole and integrated with the highest principles of Beauty, Goodness, Truth, and Joy. This is the whole psychological background of the Teaching of Christ. He wanted to emphasize that man is a part of all existence, of the whole Cosmos, and he must live according to such a reality.

Christ explained the concept of synthesis and integrity in one of his last speeches to His disciples. He said,

> *I am the true vine, and my Father is the worker. Every branch in me that does not bear fruit, He cuts out; and the one which bears fruit, He prunes so that it may bring forth more fruit.*[1]

Pruning is different from cutting off. In pruning there is vision, there is hope, there is promise that the pruned branch is going to bring spiritual fruits. But cut branches are dead; they promise nothing.

The only indication that you are alive on the tree is when you show signs of growth — leaves, flowers, and fruit. If you do not grow, you do not produce flowers, leaves, and fruits; you are dead and the gardener cuts you off.

The vine symbolizes the source of spiritual joy, ecstasy, and bliss. Spiritual joy is achieved only through progressive, ever-advancing integration, inclusiveness, and synthesis. When your life is really rooted, not only in His ideas or vision but in Him as well, you have joy.

The minds of many people are rooted in His words, but they are like successful businessmen — they have nothing to do with the things they sell. We must be rooted in Him, sharing His life, His presence within us — just like a branch that shares the life of the tree, if it is healthy and bears fruit...which means it accomplishes the visions of the tree.

Spiritual joy is achieved when one uplifts himself from his physical, emotional, and mental vehicles into his spiritual essence. One can achieve joy in the process of becoming oneself. This is Self-synthesis, when the Self focuses Himself within higher planes without losing His awareness of all the lower planes.

When the awareness of the Self is scattered and separated within different levels and planes or bodies, there is no continuity within the Self. Self-synthesis is achieved when continuity is achieved. Such a synthesis brings greater health to the body because the life energy circulates unimpeded throughout the mechanism of the Self.

Joy is the sense and experience of continuity of awareness. Any separation, any gap in the whole system, brings depression and distortion in the rhythm of circulation.

---

1. John 15:1-2

The Supreme Source of energy can be contacted and fused with only when man achieves a consciousness of unity and synthesis. After such an achievement, the little mechanisms of the Self's vehicles share the life-giving energy of the One Self.

Friction between the life energy and organs, centers, glands, or mechanisms creates unhealthy conditions and eventually brings diseases and decay.

Joy is the radiance of synthesis. Joy is the fragrance of continuity and of unimpeded circulation of life energy.

Thus the Supreme is the vine, and we are the branches of the vine only if we are alive and have our life in Him. Only in being in Him can one bring forth fruits.

Fruits are our deeds, our words, our thoughts, our creative expressions, and our life which receive their inspiration, beauty, taste, and energy from the vine. But if the branch is dry, the branch is not part of the vine, even if it thinks it is, because there is no continuity of life between the vine and the branch. To cut the dry branches means to prepare them for annihilation through fire.

The branches that bring fruit are pruned by the gardener. Note that the pruning is a sort of cutting of those parts of the branch which, when cut, will allow the main branch to be strengthened and bear more and healthier fruits.

The fruit you are giving is the manifestation, the flowering of the life in the vine, a life that is drawn from the Sun and the earth. Fruits are the results of the fusion of these two currents of energy united and matured in the fruits.

Fruits are the virtues, the creative expressions, the deeds that help people, the words that enlighten and uplift them, the thoughts that guide them and inspire them. Fruits are proof that you have life. Fruits are proof that energy is circulating within you, that you are in contact with the Sun and with the earth. The fruits you bear nourish others and make them fruitful.

Christ further says,

> *Remain with me and I with you. Just as a branch cannot give fruit by itself, unless it remains in the vine; even so you cannot, unless you remain with me.*[2]

"Remain with me" means not to be identified with your inertia, depressions, glamors, illusions, and bestial pleasures but to be fused with the flame within you, with the principles of Goodness, Beauty, Truth, and Joy within you.

A branch begins to dry when it separates itself from the interests of the vine, from the principles of the vine. The vine stands for oneness, for unity, for synthesis. Every action, every word, every thought taken against the vine leads to separation from the vine. Any branch that separates becomes dry.

---

2. John 15:4

It is possible that a person is physically, emotionally, and mentally together. But if he is not in Him, and if the presence of Christ is not growing within him and expressing through his thoughts, words, and actions, he is fruitless and he is going to be cut off.

A fruitful branch nourishes many people through its fruits. A human being, a living branch, can nourish millions through his creative expressions, good deeds, and good thoughts, and the gardener keeps him on the vine.

"You remain with me and I remain with you." To be with Him requires continuous watchfulness and steady focus on Divine principles. Sometimes one second of separation from Him brings disastrous results. The only thing that proves your connection with Him is your fruits. "By their fruits ye shall know them."

What kind of fruits are you giving? Are the fruits healthy? Do they carry vitality and beauty? Are they goal-fitting?

> *Unless a man remains with me, he will be cast outside, like a branch which is withered; which they pick up and throw into the fire to be burned.*[3]

It is possible that if a man is not with Him by living a life of love, light, and purpose, he can be thrown into the fire. His future existence can be in danger.

Christ is the vine. The vine within us is the Higher Self, the Inner Guide. We are like branches on the Inner Guide. The Inner Guide prunes us occasionally to make us more fruitful and help us throw away all that is dry within us.

It is a mysterious psychological process when the human soul occasionally sees the vanity of things and the unfitness of his personality activities. He sees the futility of his attachments and starts to orient himself toward a new vision, through striving and detachment, and with a greater dedication toward Beauty, Goodness, and Truth. This process is sometimes like pruning, like cutting the useless parts of the branches away.

There are instances when individualities disintegrate within the Cosmic Whole. This is the annihilation in which the individuality bursts like a bubble and does not exist any more. The Spirit vanishes into the Universal Spirit and the individuality is totally lost. Unless a man is in the process of becoming a soul, a living Spirit, he is in danger of losing himself.

All sicknesses begin when man tries to cut himself from the vine. First the mental body shows signs of degeneration, and the man begins not to listen to the Voice of Righteousness. Then his heart dries up; love and compassion vanish. After a while he lives a life of crime. This stage denotes that he is drying up, and the gardener will very soon notice him.

---

3. John 15:6

If the branch needs pruning, the gardener will prune it, but if he sees that the branch is dry, he will not let any part of that dry branch remain on the tree and contaminate it.

Many persons and many nations are thus pruned...or cut away. If it is necessary, the gardener prunes the man physically only, giving him a chance to grow into a better branch. If it is necessary, he prunes the branch emotionally and mentally.

Pruning or cutting has its special cycles. The greatest pruning or cutting days are called the "Judgement Days," when the gardener has to bring his garden up-to-date for a better harvest in the future.

Pruning is a healing process. When our Inner Gardener prunes us, we know that Spring is on its way, and we feel the creative current within our heart.

> *If you remain with me, and my words remain with you, whatever you ask shall be done for you.*[4]

At this stage you do not ask for anything for your separate interests. All your life is a service for humanity. The branch lives, breathes, blooms, bears fruits, and exists only for the vine. It is because of the vine that he exists. It is because of his conscious contact with the vine that he exists. He never takes action against the vine because any action against the whole is an action against his own survival.

This is the core of the mystery of health, happiness, prosperity, and spiritual advancement. When a man is a fruitful branch he exists for others; he exists for the vine. When he is dry, he exists for himself; he is separated.

All sickness or illness starts from separation. Separation becomes separatism; fears come into being; anger and greed develop; hatred appears; jealousy enters in; vices begin to multiply. Then the destruction of the branch is at hand.

No disease attaches itself to the personality vehicles if they are in integrity with the life principle within the man. Any thought, emotion, word, or deed that loosens or breaks the integrity prepares the ground for various attacks, and health problems begin to appear. The "termite" slowly penetrates into our bodies through all those acts, emotions, or thoughts which do not bear the spirit of wholism and are against the integrity and unity of all humanity.

Fire is the power of purification, creativity, and destruction. Fire can burn and annihilate; fire can evoke creativity; fire can be an agent of purification. In all these three phases, fire is the same Divine substance acting differently because of the condition man presents.

---

4. John 15:7

If you remain with me, and my words remain with you, whatever you ask shall be done for you. In this the Father will be glorified, that you bear abundant fruit, and be my disciples.[5]

One can be a disciple only when he is a living, fruitful, healthy branch. A disciple shares the interests of the whole tree; he lives for the whole tree. He lives as the tree, as the vine. Such a disciple is a fountain of health, vitality, joy, enthusiasm, and wisdom.

Global health will be a reality if humanity abides in Him, if it abides in the principles of Unity, Compassion, Goodness, and Beauty.

As long as we are fused with the vine we can cure our physical, emotional, and mental bodies. This is how so-called miracles happen. The energy of the vine regenerates our system and expels the toxic elements from them. Many changes happen to our emotional nature and many changes happen to our thinking habits. All are the result of a new release of energy from the vine, causing the apparently drying branch to flourish again.

Many sicknesses appear as a result of wrong thinking, and many emotional disturbances occur as a result of a wrong attitude. There are electrical fuses and tubes in the mental, astral, and etheric planes and they can be damaged by our wrong thoughts, wrong emotions, and wrong deeds; or thoughts, emotions, and deeds that destroy the relation between the personality and the inner vine — the relation between man and the whole. Let us not forget that the vine, as a whole, is the One Self.

Just as my Father has loved me, I also have loved you; remain in my love.[6]

All our physical, emotional, and mental troubles and problems originate from thoughts, emotions, and actions that are based on hatred, separatism, revenge, and greed. Eliminate hatred, separatism, revenge, and greed and you will see a new dawn for humanity.

To abide in His love means to love all with a love that has no hatred, greed, revenge, or separatism. The vine is the love which keeps the branches alive. If you increase love energy in those who suffer from many illnesses, you will see how the cure will spread and regenerate the whole system. It is even possible to direct love energy toward locations where trouble exists. This love must be tapped and channeled by our own Self. This means that we must start loving in order to channel love.

5. John 15:7-8
6. John 15:9

Absence of love deprives your whole system of the protective fire and integrating web. Those who love, live longer; but if one abides in Him, in Christ, he lives forever.

Most of our depression, loneliness, and negativity come into our nature when we feel that we are not loved as before, or we are not loved at all. But if you remember that Christ really loves you and He wants you to abide in His love, you no longer need earthly love. You no longer feel lonely and depressed because His love replaces and exceeds all the love that people can give to each other.

The greatness of a human being is the greatness of the love that he gives to others, not the love that he expects from others.

Once a lady who was seventy-two years of age came to me and said, "I am really unhappy. I cannot solve this problem. I went to many psychiatrists and psychoanalysts, and they found nothing wrong. Can you tell me what is wrong with me?"

"Well," I said, "did you try Doctor Love?"

"Doctor Love? Who is he?"

"Well, he is love. Did you try to love with all your heart all living forms?"

"All living forms? I have so much hatred in me toward people, animals, even toward the weeds that grow in my yard. What does love have to do with my condition?"

"If you abide in love, you will see. Start loving. Remember all those whom you hate and forgive them; love them and express your love to them, and you will see a miracle."

Many months passed, and one day she called me. She said, "It is very crazy, but I want to tell you, love works! And guess what? I am going to marry a man that I hated so much in the past. Now all is well."

"Keep going on the path of love, but also find higher octaves of love."

"Now, as long as I am happy, don't give me a new assignment."

Love must grow if we want to abide in His love.

> *If you keep my commandments, you will remain in my love; even as I have kept my Father's commandments, and I remain in His love.*[7]

Just as He said once, "I am in you, you are in me, we are one in the Father," this is total integration, an integration which includes all personality vehicles, the human soul, and the Father within the whole Universe.

> *I have spoken these things to you, that my joy may be in you, and that your joy may be full.*[8]

---

7. John 15:10
8. John 15:11

Joy exists only in unity, in fusion, in synthesis, in living a life as an extension of Him.

> *This is my commandment, that you love one another, just as I have loved you.*[9]

It is so beautiful. The way He started and the way He concluded is like a symphony.

> *People will know you as my disciples if you love one another.*[10]

Love gives you direction. Direction is the link between what you are now and what you can become in the future.

Love makes you see the future; love makes you live the future in your daily life. Health is living the future. Joy is the awareness that you are living in your future visions and achievements.

The vine is the future. Those who do not live in the future decay; they become dry.

Every initiation is taken after a practical demonstration of sacrificial love.

> *There is no greater love than this, when a man lays down his life for the sake of his friends.*[11]

The crucifixion of Christ was a demonstration of His supreme love for his friends, for humanity. It is through such a love that the healing energies of the Universe can operate in our lives. Every act against love is a seed of trouble within our nature.

Practical loving starts with appreciation, gratitude, respect, and service and goes deeper to sacrifice. Actually, each act of appreciation, gratitude, respect, service, and sacrifice is an act of healing.

You can practice this technique of being with Him, in Him, every time you need healing; every time you need to heal your body, your emotional disturbances, or your mental disorders.

Sit and calm your body, emotions, and mind and visualize a vine and be one of the branches of the vine. A few minutes later feel the regenerative life current coming from the vine and penetrating into the branch, purifying, strengthening, and healing it from all kinds of afflictions. Then see leaves and fruits growing beautifully.

After doing this for five minutes, visualize that you, as a person, are standing in His presence, within His aura. See how His Light is purifying your physical,

---

9. John 15:12
10. John 13:35
11. John 15:13

emotional, and mental bodies, transforming your vehicles, and making them a radioactive source of light. Feel that you are one with life.

Say the Great Invocation.

Do this every day and you will conquer many obstacles and see many miracles. Health is to have refuge in Him.

63

Healing Through Struggle

There are many locations of pressures in our etheric, astral, and mental spheres. These pressures are accumulated there by inhibitions or trapped by a sudden shock or forced by circumstances, conditions, and people around us. They are sources of trouble, congestion, degeneration, and decay.

An overall improvement of human conditions can be brought about through the technique of struggle. Struggle eventually forces these pressure pockets to release and carry away with them many physical, emotional, and mental symptoms and sicknesses.

The struggle technique must be arranged very carefully so that the participant will face the danger and dare to overcome it.

WARNING: Be very careful before attempting any such exercises. Be certain that the patient is able to withstand such exercises. Be sure to take all safety precautions.

In olden monasteries, under the strict supervision of highly advanced and benevolent Teachers, disciples often underwent serious struggles. For example, the struggles would include:

PHYSICAL:

1. Twist the arm of the person and let him try to get out of it.
2. Make him swim against the current and rapids.
3. Make him jump over precipices.
4. Send him on a dangerous mission.
5. Let him sleep on a mountain alone.
6. Make him walk on a roof while looking at a high altitude.

EMOTIONAL:

1. Create conditions where an average man would be frightened.

2. Make him watch something that he hates but let him continue watching, making sure it is not ugly and harmful.

MENTAL:

Concentration exercises, such as walking on a tightrope suspended high off the ground.

Under ordinary circumstances, the following are good exercises to evoke struggle:

PHYSICAL:

1. Hang a rope from a tree, approximately 25-30 feet in the air. Let him try to climb it.
2. Make him climb steep mountains.
3. Tie him and let him try to untie himself.
4. Give him a heavy, physical job to do — digging, moving, cleaning — and demand that it be done in a short time.
5. Give him a bad saw and a log to cut.
6. Give him a bad typewriter and much typing to be done in a short time.
7. Make him walk seven hours before eating.
8. Make him climb trees.
9. Make him perform a job in an awkward position, such as standing on one foot and using one hand.
10. Make him hold a dish on his head for two hours and not let it fall.
11. Make him walk with tied feet, or make him eat with tied hands.

There are many similar exercises, and a wise teacher can choose and present them.

Do not tell the person the way to do the task. Tell him only

1. That it is dangerous
2. That he must struggle and do it
3. That there is no protection for him from others

4. That he must want to do it joyfully, without complaint and irritation, and without cursing anyone

Occasionally one must check if daring, joy, and fearlessness are increasing in the person. Daring, joy, and fearlessness are great healers. One cannot buy them from pharmacies or from hospitals. They are fiery purifiers, releasers, and harmonizers.

EMOTIONAL:

1. Tell him to keep silence when his feelings are hurt.
2. Have him love when people hate him.
3. Create conditions where he is humiliated, and let him try to feel happy.
4. Create conditions in which he has expectations and appointments, but he must wait and exercise joyful patience.
5. Create conditions in which someone promises to visit him but does not, and he must exercise joyful patience.
6. Create conditions where things are ready for him to enjoy, but take the objects away. For example, invite him to dinner, and, when ready to eat, decide not to eat but perform a labor.
7. Create conditions in which people demonstrate understanding and love but suddenly turn indifferent to him.
8. Present moments of loss. For example, one of his diamond rings is lost, something very valuable is gone, or a long-standing friend disappears. Discontinue instruction and make him struggle to keep his joy and indifference.
9. Let him try to make another person interested in him, even one who is really indifferent or even hates him.
10. Try to find someone whom he hates and make him love that person and respect him.
11. Ask him to choose a few virtues and try to manifest them in his life.
12. Ask him not to talk for weeks or months.
13. Ask him to feel great joy. Let him create the reasons.
14. Ask him to love loneliness.

15. Make him learn emotional indifference in daring conditions, insult, or praise.

16. Create conditions of jealousy, and watch if he can stand and be indifferent.

Through all these, the person must be advised that he is working on his emotional sphere so that he can release accumulated tensions. The tensions are released by other tensions that are designed to crack the holding walls of the original tension.

After these two kinds of struggles, you must prepare mental struggles.

MENTAL:

1. Let your subject try to solve a problem, any kind, and continuously increase the number of problems to be solved at the same time. You can choose problems according to the level of his mind and his age.

2. Let him do things he has never done, for example: knitting, sewing, cooking, riding a horse, cleaning, building, repairing. If he knows how to do the thing, change it. If he learns how to do it, change it, but never try another one if the first one is not done. Give courage, inspiration, example, but do not help or make it easy for him.

3. Riddles are very good; math problems are excellent.

4. Try to make him see the real cause or causes of a world event.

5. Try to make him face difficult situations and make fast decisions.

6. Make him bring unrelated things together and relate them in a formation.

7. Let him walk on a straight line with closed eyes.

8. Make him find an object in darkness.

9. Put various obstacles around him and advise him not to touch them as he moves around.

10. Make him create a poem and improve it at least twenty-five times.

11. Make him paint.

12. Make him compose music.

13. Make him choreograph a dance.

14. Make him give a speech.

15. Make him do research on a subject which is not well-known.

16. Make him search for a lost object.

17. Hide essential things and let him try to find them, but use logical locations.

18. Make him start learning a foreign language.

19. Make him see other viewpoints.

20. Create occasions of defeat and require that he learn patience, observation, understanding, and respect — even if he knows others are inaccurate or ignorant.

21. Show hopeless situations and make him see points of hope.

22. Praise him and let him feel indifferent.

23. Give him different exercises of visualization:

    color

    sound

    fragrance

    touch

    taste

    movements

    forms

    Then gradually make combinations of these.

24. Let him do the following visualizations:

    a. jump off a 150-story building

    b. walk on a rope for one mile

    c. jump into the ocean from a ship going thirty miles per hour

    d. burn all his body in a fire

e. bury himself under the earth through an earthquake

f. do labor beyond his capacity, for example:

— breaking an iron bar

— changing the current of a river

— holding a thunderbolt

— pulling out a tree by its roots

— stopping two bulls from fighting

During these exercises your patient must be given time to rest. Rest can be given for five minutes, a day, a week, or months. But he must be brought back again and again until he feels physically, emotionally, and mentally filled with energy, joy, and enthusiasm. As the inner pressure releases through struggle, the Real Self begins to strive and rebuild the mechanism of contacts.

It is very interesting to note that life itself presents all these and millions of other opportunities for us to exercise struggle, but we escape from them and bury ourselves within our luxuries, pleasures, or inertia.

Through these exercises we gain lost opportunities and begin to live a dangerous but healthy and victorious life. Hardship in our life turns into a gold mine of health and happiness when we learn how to struggle consciously and conquer obstacles and expect even more obstacles to confront.

64

Energy, Confidence, and Independence Exercises

1. Visualize that you are sitting in a pure white light.
2. Let the light penetrate your entire being.
3. Slowly condense all the light into two little balls, one under your spine and the other at the top of your head.
4. Visualize three rays coming out of the lower ball of light and rising up the etheric spine to the head, and precipitating down from the higher ball.
5. Let all the light accumulate above the head, then spread like an aura around you.
6. Visualize the aura becoming again two balls of light, one under your spine and the other at the top of your head.
7. Let the lights burn and annihilate your body.
8. Visualize the balls of light giving birth to a form of a body which is powerful, dynamic, and beautiful.
9. Be a commander of an army and give ten orders to the army. See that your orders are carried out in detail.
10. Visualize four lions and try to tame them. If they resist, use force and master them. Make them do five things you want them to do.

This exercise of ten points is to develop energy, confidence, healing, and independence on all levels.

65

Depression and How to Handle It

Spiritual inertia or depression is the most dangerous malady because it may contaminate the personality vehicles and induce such a depression in them which cannot be healed by regular medical means.

Depression is a state of total rejection of outer and inner stimuli.

Depression is not only physical but is also emotional, mental, and spiritual.

Sometimes people are active physically but are dead emotionally, mentally, and spiritually. These are living corpses.

Emotional and mental depressions are very common. You feel emotionally or mentally unresponsive.

Spiritual depression comes to those who are advanced in their emotional and mental evolution and for some reason have lost interest to be more. Spiritual depression is a state in which you do not want to advance, to progress, to expand your consciousness and communication, and you shut yourself off from higher ideas, visions, from sources of inspirations and impressions.

The causes of spiritual depression are twofold:

1. You are not evolved enough to be receptive to new challenges.

2. You have built a prison around you through your past achievements, knowledge, and activities.

It is very possible that our activities, emotions, thoughts, and knowledge, instead of creating a path of progress, rotate around our ego and vanity and create a sphere of limitation beyond which we do not want to strive.

You can see these kinds of people in every walk of life. They appear active, but something is dead in them. Spiritual inertia or depression is the most dangerous malady because it may contaminate the personality vehicles and induce such a depression in them which cannot be healed by regular medical means.

In spiritual depression, man loses contact with his True Self and becomes an entity in himself. He no longer aspires for freedom, for expansion of consciousness, for beauty, for deeper love, for service to others but tries to live by whatever he has in his physical, emotional, and mental realms.

Others cannot easily see this kind of depression; they are able to see only if you are "blue."

There are nine main causes of depression that I have found in my dealings with people:

1. The first cause is the feeling of guilt. When you feel, think, and know that you did something wrong to yourself or to others physically, with your feelings, or with your thoughts and words, you feel guilty. By thinking about your wrong doing, you build an image of yourself, and this image builds an etheric, emotional, and mental layer around your aura and isolates you to some degree from life-currents circulating in the Universe.

You also create a cleavage between your personality and your Real Self. Such an isolation and cleavage deprives you of these vehicles, and they fall separately or collectively into inertia, into depression.

Such depressions are very familiar to those who are affiliated with those religious organizations which demand absolute purity or obedience to their doctrines, dogmas, rules, and commandments to such a degree that whenever you step out of these borders you feel guilty.

Such depressions also come to people who have a sensitive conscience and try to live a harmless life. For example, there was a woman lawyer. She was very beautiful: shining, talking, and dancing. Suddenly I noticed her going down, and eventually one day she called me and said, "I am so depressed. I don't know what to do. I am just in total inertia."

My first question was, "Did you do something that is bothering you?" "Of course," she said, "I had an abortion."

This for her was a total crime according to her own measures of righteousness and to the principles and laws of the Universe. It is we who judge ourselves. That guilt was so strong in her that she stayed in bed for three months and did not want to move.

Guilt leads to inertia and depression. That is why when you clean your conscience, you will never be depressed. But our conscience gets loaded and loaded by small things that we do. For example, we know that evil talk is no good, but we talk, gossip, criticize, and it accumulates. Then we steal a little, lie a little. Then we do something else. Eventually we become physically, emotionally, and mentally out of order, and we fall away from conscious contact with our conscience. When these things accumulate and come to their saturation point, depression starts.

The first thing you must know is that the cause of depression is moral and spiritual. It is related to the conscience and to your sense of righteousness, purity, and beauty. When that sense is strong in you, you are unfolding through the sense of beauty, unity, purity, synthesis, cleanness, and wholeness.

But when you act against these things you depress yourself because anything you do against the principles and laws of Nature is a load that you put on your nervous system. You decrease your spiritual Self and increase your material self, and this creates a tremendous imbalance in your system.

How to get rid of guilt?

The first thing is to repeat the following mantram with concentration and faith:

> More radiant than the Sun,
>
> Purer than the snow,
>
> Subtler than the ether
>
> Is the Self,
>
> The Spirit within my heart.
>
> I am that Self.
>
> That Self am I.

No matter what you did, no matter what you are in this stage of your evolution, God is within you. And God cannot make any guilt. It is your physical, emotional, and mental bodies that make mistakes, but not the God within you. You are God within you, not your bodies. If you develop this philosophy, you have a way to come out of your depression.

I say to such people, "Do you know God lives with you? You are a temple of God and a spark of that Almighty Existence. You did not do it really. Your physical, emotional, and mental bodies forced you to do these things, and because you yielded to them, it became guilt because you identified with your physical body, with your emotional body, with your mental body, with your interests, with your hate, greed, revenge, and fear."

When you disassociate yourself from these things, you become aware that you are the spiritual essence and you do not have guilt because you are pure in your essence.

This is a healing process you may do with people. As you talk with them, they slowly bloom and get rid of their depression. They seldom fall into their mistakes again because they no longer identify with their bodies.

Thus, you are going to impress your mind that in your essence you are a spark of the Almighty Power, a PURE spark. You are going to put into your mind that in your essence you are absolute Beauty, Goodness, Righteousness, Joy, and Freedom. You are not guilty. Your body is tempting you and deceiving you, and you are falling into the trap of your bodies. But, essentially, you have nothing to do with guilt because you are God within. That is the "Christ in you, the hope of glory." Can you stand in this? If you work on it, you will see how you will slowly come out of your depression.

When I work with people, for hours I impress upon them the realization that they are not the guilt, and they feel released. I tell them that this is their body. When they identify with it, they do things wrong, but when they start to say, "The body did it; I didn't do it," they have a chance to release themself.

This is the secret of the great Upanishads. It says, "Tat twam asi aham Brahmasmi." You are that, the Brahma (God). You are the infinite one.

"More radiant than the Sun...." You are the Self, the whole thing, the mystery of life; yet you identify yourself with your sex, with your stomach, with your body, with your hatred, with your plans. You identify and become one with your not-self. When you pull yourself out and become conscious as a Divine Spark, you are Infinity Itself.

Avoiding guilt feelings does not mean to imply that this should encourage you to fall into error. On the contrary, it will create a reverse reaction. Guilt means identification with your bodies, but as you think about your Self, you will be protected by Its light.

There is a method the ancient Masters taught called "erasing and reconstructing your recording." It is a very strange method. Let us suppose you were talking with your wife, and suddenly you became nasty and said bad words to her, causing her to cry. Later you went to your room, feeling guilty and depressed. What can you do?

Sit down and visualize exactly what should have happened. When you play your tape, you are recording something new. If your wife told you, "You are a nasty man," you tell her how much you love her, how beautiful she is, and in your imagination you hug her and kiss her and take her to a music center and buy her beautiful clothes and give her a rose. You have erased the tape that happened and replaced it with something new. You will see in fifteen minutes that your depression is gone.

Depression creates electronic waves in your mental body that are not pleasant. They are physical, emotional, and mental in nature and they act against the frequency of your spirit.

2. The second cause of depression is to have such a great vision about which you can do nothing, and you get depressed. For example you think, "I am going to build a university and millions of people are going to work, and the gardens will be like this, and the houses like that, intercoms, televisions, computers inside, and the most famous people will come to give lectures, and here I am sitting all day typing as a secretary and I am sick of it. I am depressed."

You can feel this in a different way when you visit a great man and think to yourself, "What am I? Nothing...."

When you feel that there is a great power, Infinite Space, and you feel small, you may feel depressed. This is why so many people are depressed — not because of their guilt but because they confront something beyond their comprehension.

For example, a little girl, age nine, came to me and said, "I am not going to school any longer. I don't want it. I am not going to play the piano. I am not even going to eat." I asked her, "What do you like to do?" She said, "I want to lie down and sleep." I asked her why she wanted to do that. She said, "Because I want to save the world from atomic destruction and I can't do anything!" Then she shouted at me, "Can you do something?"

"Well," I said, "I'll tell you a story. Do you see the top of that mountain? Stay by me and let's go to it. One, two, three, four, five steps.... Are we closer to the mountain?" "I guess so," she said. "How many feet?" I asked. "Five feet," she said.

"Tomorrow," I said, "we will take two hundred steps, and we will be closer. The next day we will take ten thousand steps, and we will be closer still. If we get closer and closer, one day we will reach the top of the mountain."

Thus, instead of falling into depression, you can take one small step at a time. One little step will take you closer to your vision.

The girl said, "Then I can do something," and she wrote two or three letters to the President. She is so proud now that she did something. This is an example of how you can do the same thing.

Every minute you are in inertia, physically, emotionally, mentally, or spiritually, if you are really sensitive and see yourself you will immediately perceive what the causes of your depression are, especially in spiritual depression.

You love humanity. Then you turn on the television, and everybody is killing each other. "I don't want to write and read and pray any more. It's not working," you say. This is spiritual depression. You try to solve a mathematical problem, but it is so big and you cannot solve it. This is mental depression. You love somebody so deeply, but she hates you. This is emotional depression.

All such depressions at various times play their games with you, but because you do not really know what your depression is, you do not see that you are really depressed in certain moments, in certain levels. The causes, you know now, are guilt feelings and great visions you cannot reach.

3. The third cause is a chemical imbalance or deficiency in the brain. This is what the medical professors or medical doctors say when certain amounts of calcium, potassium, magnesium, or other elements are lacking in the brain and when the chemicals are imbalanced. This causes depression.

We are told in the Ageless Wisdom that all chemicals in the body are under the influence of your states of consciousness. For example, if you have a state of consciousness which is called fear, your calcium slowly fades away; if you are in greed, your magnesium is depleted; if you are in revenge, your hemoglobin is exhausted.

It is your state of consciousness that creates the secretion of your glands and increases or decreases the chemicals in your body. If you change your state of consciousness, you can change the amount or increase the chemicals you want within your body. As you become more balanced mentally and spiritually, the chemicals in your body automatically balance themselves, but as you become more unbalanced mentally or spiritually, the corresponding chemicals become imbalanced in your system.

The constitution of man is not physical; it is etheric, emotional, mental, and spiritual.

When Christ, Buddha, Zoroaster, Mohammed, and all the Great Ones were talking about virtues, They were not talking about religion but about science. Hate, for example, hardens your arteries and creates imbalance in the thymus gland. The electrical palpitations of the gland are distorted by hate. But if you love, the thymus gland readjusts, organizes, and harmonizes itself.

4. The fourth cause of depression is called imperil. Imperil is a poison that is generated within your body when you are irritated. It spreads itself throughout the nervous system and wherever that layer of poison spreads, that part of the nervous system loses its sensitivity, its electricity of life, and does not transmit it into the corresponding organ or gland.

Imperil is not only the cause of heart attacks but also the first and last cause of cancer. Irritation paralyzes the nervous system, creates apathy in the emotional body, and creates indifference and lack of interest in the mental body. When your mind lacks interest, it is in depression; it is dead. Irritation makes this poison penetrate into your mental body and paralyze your mental body. When your mental body is paralyzed, the first sign is an "I don't care" attitude. We bring in this paralysis through imperil, mental imperil.

5. Depression can result when you lose a loved one. This is caused because love "means" identification, and when he or she is gone, a part of yourself is gone with him. This shock creates a tremendous depression. A woman I knew slept for three months after her husband passed away. A young woman, seventeen years of age, slept for fifteen days without eating or drinking, as if she were dead, after her boyfriend passed away.

How can you help those who lose a beloved one? You can help by explaining the philosophy of oneness and the understanding that nothing is lost in the Universe. There is always communication on a mental and spiritual level. If you want to make the person happy, you must present a happy attitude. You can also offer a meditation and contemplation that will enable him to meet the departed one in higher levels. There are many techniques you can use to bridge the gap called cleavage or separation.[1]

6. Depression is caused when your Soul withdraws into higher planes. This is a very common occurrence, and it happens for two reasons. First, your Soul

1. For information on this subject, please refer to *Other Worlds*.

leaves you when you are criminal and malicious or nasty. According to the Ageless Wisdom, there is a state of consciousness in which your Soul leaves you and you become totally crushed. It leaves because It thinks you are no longer worthy of Its presence.

The second reason the Soul leaves you is to perform some important task elsewhere. In the period of time the Soul is gone, you feel depressed. It looks like depression, but in reality it is not depression because you are relaxed and sleeping; you are held in abeyance, but your Soul is doing something great somewhere else. This state will last one minute or longer.

For example, a great Teacher one day felt there was a war going on where ten to fifteen disciples were killed. Immediately she went to sleep for one week, and when she awakened she said she was helping these disciples make their transition from the physical to the astral and mental planes. In the same way, when your Soul leaves you, It has a great duty to perform. Sometimes it happens that your Soul is at such a mission, but you go to the doctor and he injects things into you, massages you or beats you to try to revive you, but it does not work. M.M. once said that future medical doctors and psychiatrists must also be great Initiates and spiritual leaders so they can combine science and spirit together.

7. Depression is caused when you identify with the negative thoughtforms projected to you by others. This is very interesting and occurs frequently. If a group of people are projecting dark, heavy, and hateful thoughts toward you, eventually they knock you down. You feel helpless and in inertia because their thoughtforms, imagination, and visualizations are projected into your aura and you feel that these things in your aura are you. You get horrified with the thoughtforms in your aura.

It is best not to evoke any evil thought from anyone, because the evil thought is like an arrow that is poisonous; it hits your aura and collects poison there.

The effect can be on your physical body, your emotional body, or your mental body. For example, if I am thinking beautiful things about you, you feel so beautiful and you do not know why. You are happy, singing, dancing because I am giving energy to your aura. Beautiful thoughts are energy currents.

When someone is thinking evil thoughts about you, you feel narrow, irritated, and depressed and eventually you give up. Try not to evoke any evil thought, slander, or malice from anyone because they are poisonous arrows that will create total depression in your system.

8. When psychic energy is blocked in you and you cannot express it creatively, it causes depression. This begins at childhood, for example, when your mother says, "Don't do that.... I told you not to dance.... I told you not to play.... Don't read it.... Put that violin down.... I don't want it.... You are ugly...," etc. What happens? You become tightly coiled up within yourself. When it reaches the saturation point, you become depressed. In your mind you think, "I am worthless," and you believe it.

It is very difficult to untie that coil and release it, but you can do so with creative dancing, expression, jumping, running, and singing.

The result of such talk is very serious, and this is the reason why you must never belittle anyone. You should never say, "What's happening to you? You are losing weight.... Your color is gone...." The person's aura will go from five feet to three feet. Say a little more and it will be one foot. Continue to say more and there will be no aura. On the contrary, tell the person, "You are so beautiful.... Come on, you can do it.... Failure is nothing but a great lesson.... If you fail one hundred times, you are still going to be successful...." In this way you are helping the person release it.

9. Another cause of depression comes from the petrification of the heart petals. The etheric heart center has twelve golden petals. Sometimes they are petrified by six vipers: fear, anger, hate, greed, revenge, and treason.[2]

When the heart petrifies, it closes. When the heart closes, you do not receive energy or life from the Sun into your system and you go into total inertia. This is why the Great Ones say, "Guard your heart." Your heart must be always beautiful and loving.

You can melt away this petrification by exercising greater care for something, with greater compassion and love. For example, I saw a girl, age seventeen, whose heart was really petrified. Her mother said, "She is going to be a witch and a criminal. She beats her brothers and sisters, and she has no heart at all."

I played a trick on her. We brought a nice dog to the girl and left it under her care. That dog helped her begin to open her heart. Then we hid the dog from her, and she thought she had lost the dog. "Where is my dog?" she asked. She missed it and this caused another opening in her heart. Then we brought it back and told the girl the dog was sick. She took the dog to the veterinarian and helped nurse the dog back to health. Finally the heart center began really to open.

If you want to open the heart center of a person, you must make the person care for something, love something, and be compassionate.

These are nine major causes of depression. Try not to fall into them.

Q&A

Question: *I am aware that certain people try hypnotism to cure themselves from depression. Is this a safe method?*

2. See also *The Flame of the Heart*.

Answer: Hypnotic suggestion is a violation of the karma of the person and is also a violation of his free will.

This violation creates duality in people, prevents their karma from working out, and inhibits their free will.

Duality manifests as a conflict within man, and this conflict, according to its intensity, brings various complications in health. It also makes man lose his emotional and mental clarity and stability.

A prevented karma accumulates and puts a heavy taxation on the future personality of the person. It delays the freedom and the release of the person from his karma. In the time schedule of the person's many lifetimes, complications can result.

Inhibition of free will causes a setback for the progress of man on the path of self-actualization and self-determination.

Of course, all this reflects on the hypnotist himself, who eventually pays for the damage he has done to others, regardless of whether it was done with good intentions or with mixed motives.

An effort to cure depression by hypnotic suggestion brings disastrous results.

Question: *What is the mineral or chemical that has to do with revenge?*

Answer: Revenge takes the hemoglobin away from the blood.

Question: *What is lack of faith?*

Answer: Lack of faith is a state of consciousness when one cannot see beyond his nose.

Question: *Do you have any techniques to have faith?*

Answer: There was a boy who had no faith in himself. "Come," I said, "Help me, please." I was framing a large picture. I said to him, "You hold this while I cut." He held the frame for me. I said, "Now you put these parts together, and I'll be back when you are done." He put it together, and when I returned I said, "Wow! What a beautiful job you did!" Then I gave him one job after another until finally he knew he could do them. I told him, "If you can do this job, then you will be able to do this other job." I continued this until slowly he increased his faith in himself.

Another boy came and said he could do nothing well. Instead of giving him lessons directly, I gave them to him indirectly. I did not want him to think I was being bossy. I said, "I need a letter written. Can you do it? I will dictate and you can write it down." I dictated a letter, and he wrote it down. "You know," I said, "I think that letter needs improvement. Can you improve it for me?"

I left and when I returned my ten lines had become twenty lines. I read it and said, "Wow, this is so beautiful! You know, what if you take this idea from this letter and write another one? Will you do it?" When he wrote another letter, I read it, "Ah, this is perfect! But you know, we can change this letter into a poem. Come on. You do it."

He wrote a poem that was a masterpiece. Then I told him, "Do you see how beautiful you are? You did it!" He said, "Yes, I did it."

Faith is the ability to sense that you can do something. Faith must be based upon something concrete.

For example, if you tell me that you are not beautiful, I am going to take you and put you in front of a mirror and tell you to see how pretty your eyes and face are. Then you will have faith in yourself because you saw it.

Question: *What about oppression? Is it in the same category as depression?*

Answer: In its esoteric definition, oppression is the result of an outside will forcing itself upon you.

Question: *What do you do in a case like that?*

Answer: If oppression is used on me, I rebel and become more furious. If anyone tries to limit my freedom, I just explode. That is my way to do it. If you choose not to rebel, you are going first of all to be a slave, second you will hate the person oppressing you, and third you will resign from responsibilities and duties. You may do these things, but this is not the way to handle oppression.

The first thing to do is to face the person and ask him why he is doing these things. Also, when you have faith and believe in yourself, nobody can oppress you. Think to yourself, "I am beautiful, I am a genius, I am creative, I am doing well...." When you have faith in yourself, any kind of pressure from outside creates a greater striving within you.

You can see, for example, many oppressed nations and depressed nations and many that are under slavery. It is these nations that in history rebel and create the greater culture and civilization.

Question: *How do you counter an attack from another who is sending negative thoughts to you and your aura?*

Answer: Let me give you a practical example. You may suddenly feel that life is nonsense and everything is stupid. These thoughts fill your mind, yet they are not your thoughts. Perhaps you may feel that everything is going to be lost, or you feel you are ugly, unhealthy, and that you are soon going to die. When this happens, immediately face these thoughts.

For example, if a thought comes to me that I am soon going to die, I say to myself that I cannot die because there is still so much work to be done. Then I confirm that I am healthy and my father lived to be ninety-seven years of age. I take the thought, "You are going to die," and change it into another thought, "You are going to live for two hundred years."

In the future it is only through thought that people are going to fight. Those who know how to think will survive. Those who do not know how to think, how to use the electricity of the mind, are going to be the losers.

Meditation is an exercise to develop thinking.

One day while in Mexico I met a group who asked me to talk with them. One of the leaders told me they kill anyone they want by imagining the person to be sick and dying. In their imagination, they tell the person they are having pain and are sick, and they imagine the person falling down from a heart attack. They imagine the person going to the hospital, then dying. The victim absorbs these thoughtforms, and suddenly one day he will fall sick and die. The thoughtform is controlling the mechanism.

Imagine that right now I am holding a lemon in my hand and squeezing it. Look what is happening to your mouth. Why is it happening? You know I do not have a lemon in my hand, but it is in your imagination. If someone puts an image in your mind, then you are going to be a victim of the image. This is now being done through subliminal suggestion.

For example, during a movie an image of a soft drink will suddenly flash on the screen and suggest that you go immediately to the snack bar and buy a soft drink. The image flashes so quickly your eyes do not see it and your ears do not hear it, but your brain records it. You will see many people suddenly get up at a movie to purchase the drink.

To overcome depression, use your mind and the following three things: joy, beauty, and freedom. Joy is the antitoxin of depression, beauty is the antidote, and freedom is the water that washes the poison of depression away and makes you feel free, think freely, and allow other people to be free. Try to be joyful and to make others joyful. Always try to keep your joy alive, no matter what the conditions. Be beautiful and try to make people beautiful. Be free and allow others to be free. Do these things and you will never fall into depression.[3]

Visualization Exercises to Overcome Depression

I. *Exercise*

This is a beautiful purification exercise.

3. For exercises and further explanations on joy, see *Joy and Healing*.

1. Visualize at the center of your head, a bright and beautiful sun. Now you are going to inhale the light of that sun and exhale it throughout your body. Inhale the light, then exhale it. Do this seven times.

2. Now inhale a violet light from the sun and exhale violet light. This will go to your etheric body. While exhaling say, "All pain and suffering and disorders and discomforts go out, and let harmony be established within me." Now just think about it. Take a deeper breath, absorbing the violet from the sun. Now exhale it throughout your body, cleansing and purifying the etheric body. Do this seven times.

3. Now visualize a silver light, and inhale it and transmit it to your emotional body, purifying all the glamors, negativity, and formations that are found there. Make the emotional body pure. Inhale and exhale silver light through your emotional body seven times.

4. Now you are inhaling yellow light from the sun to the mental body, clearing all illusions, superstitions, fanaticism, and separatism. Inhale and exhale a pure, lemon yellow light through your mental body. Do this seven times.

   The breath is so powerful. When Christ was giving the Holy Spirit, the psychic energy, to His disciples, He exhaled and said, "Take it.... Take it.... Take it." The disciples were filled with that energy because of His breath.

5. Inhale and exhale orange light. You are putting in willpower now. Do this seven times.

   Inhale the orange light and exhale it to the parts of your body that you want to repair. Do not focus on specific parts or organs but around them. If it is your kidney, exhale the orange light around this area. If it is your arm or teeth, exhale the orange light around there. Now exhale orange light wherever you have discomfort. Wherever you want purification, exhale orange light there. Now bring the orange light to the opposite area of the one that needs attention, then again to the general area.

6. Inhale and exhale red light. Red is vivification to strengthen your entire system. Do this seven times.

This is a very important exercise that we can do. Eventually we are going to verify the words of the Great Masters Who said the kingdom of God is within you, the king is within you, the Sun is within you, all the powers are within you. If we find that source of power, we will not need electricity, television, telephones, etc.

We are going to find ourselves because, if the center within us is awakened, every kind of healing art will be obsolete.

Question: *How often should we do this exercise?*

Answer: Once a day. Remember the sequence of the colors. First is violet, which is the etheric body. Second is silver, the emotional body. Third is yellow, the mental body. Orange is the healing, destructive ray that will be channeled to the etheric parts that you want to heal. Red is to energize and purify your entire system. Red is energy, vivification, strength, energy, willpower, and leadership.

Question: *I have a problem switching from one color to the next. When I start with one, would it be possible to do one meditation on one color?*

Answer: You can do it, but you must continue with all of them so that you keep the balance.

Question: *How many times must we repeat the sequence in this exercise?*

Answer: Just once. There is danger in exaggeration in everything.

This is a tremendous exercise to break the ridges and ice formations in our etheric body. Most of our sicknesses are reflections of the blockages that we have in the etheric body. In the books by the Tibetan Master, He very clearly writes that future medicine will deal with the etheric body. The etheric body is the circulatory system of the energies, the wires of the energies, through which vitality and prana circulate. When that vitality and prana are blocked, we have sickness.

All sickness is blockage of energy. This exercise breaks that blockage. It is like entering into an iceberg in icy waters, cracking it and making it liquid, which means there will be more circulation in your system.

II. *Exercise*

Imagine a one to two foot wheel with seven spokes in front of your eyes. See that it is a fiery, electric wheel. Let it turn clockwise, from right to left. See it slowly turning, now gaining speed, turning faster and faster.

Now see it turning in the opposite direction, because most of the formations are in front of your face.

Now take the wheel and put it approximately one foot horizontally above your head, which means facing the earth. Let it turn clockwise very fast, and let it penetrate into your body, going to your feet and slowly coming back up, always turning.

Now visualize it four feet above your head like a fiery spiral. Let it travel down your etheric body to your feet, and bring it back up. Do this again, allowing it to penetrate into your etheric, emotional, and mental bodies. Now bring it back up. Let it keep turning because when you are entering into your body, it is moving a little slower. You are going to set the momentum at a very high speed, and give an order to it to come down into your bodies and clean everything, then return.

Bring it down through the head slowly, from the forehead to the chin. Now to the chest. Go down until you reach your legs. Now go through your legs down to the feet, then suddenly up again.

Start again from the head, but the wheel is wider than the head. Slowly go down, inch by inch, to the feet. Now slowly back up. Wherever you have trouble, you will feel a little pain and discomfort but that is good.

When it reaches the top of your head the last time, bring it up and project a beam of light to disintegrate it. This is a very important process.

These are master methods of healing.

Question: *I have a hard time making it go clockwise, but I can do it counterclockwise.*

Answer: If the rotation of your aura is a little affected by your health, it resists. But when you impose upon it, you reestablish the rhythm because your aura actually turns around your body clockwise. If you see that it is turning counterclockwise, you are in trouble because it is creating friction in your principles, except if you are an Arhat.

Question: *Is this safe to do by ourselves?*

Answer: Yes, you can do it alone, but do not exaggerate it. Do not sit all day doing it or you may go crazy.

Question: *Is our head projected out separately as we are visualizing?*

Answer: No, you are actually the sun. You are the sun; you are inhaling with all your body. The sun may get brighter and brighter. This is good. It means there is no obstruction or friction.

Question: *What do I do when various memories come out.*

Answer: Of course, this happens. The light is agitating and cleaning the bodies. This is a good indication that it is working. If in your memory you have distorted thoughtforms, memories that were creating uncomfortable situations in your life and expressing themselves as diseases or health conditions, then with this wheel you can clean them.

In ancient times they knew about this. For example, in Ezekiel, it is written about wheels within wheels. Nobody understands this. You ask the priests and rabbis and they will tell you one thing or another. The truth is that it is a healing system. It is there, but you are going to know about it and the science of it intuitively and bring them out.

Question: *Regarding the wheel of fire, I visualized a bluish fire. Is the color critical?*

Answer: Any color will do.

Question: *Why did you want us to disintegrate the wheel at the end?*

Answer: Because it should not stay in your aura as foreign material. It was intended to do a job, then to be removed. If you keep it in your aura, as some healers do, it automatically turns against you and does things you do not want. You must break it and remove it from your mind, or else it will become a posthypnotic suggestion.

Question: *Can we use this exercise by visualizing another person, say a child we wanted to help?*

Answer: You can do it, but do not focus on specific areas. Your focus must be general. If you concentrate on the kidneys, stomach, sex organs, etc., you are in trouble because you are not working on the physical body. When you work on the etheric, emotional, and mental bodies, the physical body will follow them. If you concentrate on the physical body, you are bringing energies into materialization and doing wrong.

Before you understand this, do not do it. Wait until you really know what you are doing.

Question: *I find the exercise easier to do when the wheel is away from me, but when it makes contact with my body, it is harder.*

Answer: That shows you need to have control over your willpower and mental thoughtform. Eventually you are going to bring the wheel through you as if you were a transparent ghost, and while the wheel is turning, it will be breaking the crystallizations and you will be released. You will even be able to do this with your hand.

Question: *Do you visualize yourself away from your body?*

Answer: No, you are in it. The important thing to remember is to visualize the wheel turning around within your etheric, emotional, and mental bodies. Do not project yourself. You are in it; you are here.

Question: *Is there a proper progression?*

Answer: Yes, it should be orderly. You must go from top to bottom, then bottom to top, and do not spend too much time in one place because you may create trouble; it must keep moving.

First the head, then down the body to the feet, then back up. Finally you must destroy the wheel.

Question: *Does the direction of travel change as you go down?*

Answer: Yes, it is a spiral and when it goes down, then it travels like a screw.

Question: *Any color?*

Answer: A fiery color is better, but if you imagine fire, you are doing much better.

Question: *What happens if your wheel is stuck and you cannot move it?*

Answer: Then there is a problem there. You must attack it as if you were a bulldozer to make it move and break the crystallizations of the ice in your aura by repeating the exercise.

III. *Exercise*

This is a unification exercise. There is no visual imagery given in this. You are going to do this by yourself because if I give imagery, it may be too general or too specific. You are going to create your own ways to do it.

Close your eyes and relax, and gradually feel one with the whole Universe.

Let all separative thoughts and feelings disappear. You are one with the raindrops, snow, trees, planets, space, heart. This is entering into the rhythm of the Cosmos.

Feel one with the planet, all kingdoms, angels, animals, gods, and forces of Nature. Be one with them. It will give you tremendous peace. Say to yourself, "I am one with them...." You may even sleep if you want, but feel you are one with the whole Universe. Try to expand your consciousness from planet to solar system to galaxy and beyond.

This is a consciousness, not a phenomenon. You are expanding your consciousness and becoming one because you are one, and you are finding your oneness with God, Who is in everything. This is what alleluia means or *la ilaha ill lallah* means: There is nothing else but Allah, God.

Do not force yourself because this is a relaxation and expansion exercise. It should be effortless. Let it happen. It is expansion and silence.

Now visualize the Universe and all the stars and galaxies around it as a rainbow sphere. Start with red, then orange, then yellow, then green, then blue, then indigo, then violet.

Now rub your hands and that is all.

Question: *I had a problem staying in consciousness. When I focused my attention on something, I became separate.*

Answer: The key to it is to be that something. Unity means to separate yourself from your own self-image. The more you become separated from your individual existence, the more you become united. This is a paradox. This is why it is said that if you do not leave yourself, you cannot find the Real Self.

It is paradoxical, but we know what this means. Whatever is separate from you, get united with it, and then you are getting out of yourself; you are going into union because you already are in everything. By uniting in everything, you are finding your True Self.

How do we do this? Everywhere we see how human culture, civilization, and our history are based on separatism; everything works for separation. This is where sickness and fear originate. For millions of years we have been brainwashed into believing in separatism; this is yours, this is mine, this is that — separatism.

How can we overcome it? It cannot be overcome in one day, but some pioneering people are going to start it. When you are doing these exercises, you are putting a tremendous and powerful broadcasting program into the air, and it is traveling to other parts of the world. You will see that this exercise will be picked up in China, Russia, and other countries, and they will find it because you broadcasted it. It has become the property of Space already. In this way you are serving because you are introducing something that is very fundamental.

Depression and Regrets

Regrets for past deeds carry heavy layers of poisons. It is very important that one must try to forgive himself of the past, seeing in his past deeds the influence of posthypnotic suggestions, family influences, karma, obsession, ignorance, blind urges and drives, and many more.

This is not a process of self-justification but a realization of how not to be chained by the past, and how to release one's self for a new striving.

It is important not to dwell on past failures or negative actions once they are recognized and condemned by oneself.

The most important step is to strive toward a future vision, trying not to repeat the failures of the past.

Disciples in the world must not be handicapped by their own failures of the past but press forward.

Joy is released during striving toward the future, and the poison accumulated in human nature is dispersed during striving and joy.

The poison can accumulate in nerve channels, thus disturbing the health of the body as a whole and producing a continuous flow of the poison of irritation.

It can accumulate in the emotional body as dark patches of negative emotions.

It can accumulate in the mental body in forms of separatism, fanaticism, resentfulness, pessimism, and a tendency to be judgmental and suicidal. Such a condition of mind creates the poison of malice, slander, and treason, and eventually man defeats himself.

Striving toward the future does not mean to be irresponsible for the damage one did in the past to others, but it means to reach a state of consciousness by which one not only lives a harmless life, but heals the damage he did to others.

Sometimes past deeds are the sources of intense fear. Fear paralyzes the progress of the human soul. Such a fear must be defeated.

Some people try to overcome such a fear by confessing their past deeds to authorities, trying to be punished by them and feeling that such action will really help them get rid of the memories of their past deeds.

The fact is that any harmful action is like a nail pushed in our brain.

The real healing of the human being from such a fear takes place when he objectively analyzes his past deeds and in a detached way finds the causes of them. He will do this without blaming himself or others but by really discovering the causes of his deed.

Once the causes are found, the next step is to create those causes and visions which will never allow him to repeat the same deeds.

The third step is to try to recompense those whom he hurt.

The fourth step is not to hate those whom he hurt but to send continuous love to them.

The fifth step is to strive to a future vision.

Some of the Great Ones were Those who passed through the paths of many failures, but They never gave up Their vision.

Depression can be slowly removed if the depressed one is helped to develop gratitude.

Gratitude provides those chemicals in the brain which remove the elements causing depression.

Forgiveness is another medicine for depression. If a depressed one begins to forgive those against whom he has a grudge or hatred, he will see the departure of depression.

The third factor is hope. Hope is the magnet which attracts help and lets the currents of the future penetrate into the brain.

In the near future healers will use these three factors to remove depression.

All depression is the result of a feeling of being deprived, left out, abandoned, and not appreciated; or the result of when a person developed hatred against people whom he once loved and then rejected when he felt that there was no future for them. These feelings use up certain chemicals in the body and accumulate poison. This is the cause of depression.

There are many ways to evoke the feeling of gratitude in depressed people: through stories, movies, or with direct conversation.

There are many beautiful stories of forgiveness, many about how hope shone in the lives of people who were ready to give up. Such stories can be compiled and presented to those who will take care of depressed ones.

It is, of course, possible to teach the value of these three factors from childhood and in colleges to teach the philosophy behind them. Those who are charged with these stories will seldom fall into the network of depression. Such an education can save the lives of millions and bring deeper joy into their lives.

I remember when I was once trapped by snow in a hut on a hill. The first thing that came into my mind was the story of Robinson Crusoe. For a while I began to recall the hardships he passed through and filled myself with hope and joy.

Another time when I was in depression, I thought about a lady who saved my life. Once the flow of gratitude began to pass through my heart, all depression vanished.

On another occasion, I was very depressed about a slander that a girl began to spread about me. My hatred turned into depression, mostly because I could not do anything to make her shut her mouth.

One day I found a card that she wrote to me. Her words were full of love, appreciation, and joy. Suddenly I remembered her and forgave her for all her slander. In that moment my depression melted away.

I used this technique on my friends and it worked. I remember a friend who was very depressed because of a financial failure. I did not ask anything about his business, but I told three stories after each other about people who passed through hardships and became victors. Finally, he said, "Do you think there is still hope that I can be successful?"

"Of course," I said. He, regenerated by the hope I gave him, began to work. In a few years time he was a successful, rich man.

Guilt feelings are another cause of depression. This kind of depression is sometimes very difficult to remove because there is self-condemnation.

Self-condemnation brings in deeper depression than the criticism of one's own friends who through their attacks even evoke self-defense and active battle.

Sometimes in order to help remove a person's depression, people argue with that person, hurt his feelings, scold him, and lead him into conflict or argument.

Depression is a state of giving up, a condition that creates reaction against those who try to help.

Exercise to Overcome Depression

1. Sit relaxed.

2. Take seven deep breaths.

3. Visualize an orange light, and let it turn into a door.

4. Approach the door and open it, and see a path leading through the forests to the summit of a mountain.

5. Follow the path as realistically as possible, passing through the forest and discovering the path toward the summit.

6. Climb to the summit.

7. Enjoy the view, the beauty, the space, for at least twenty minutes. Make it a very exciting view.

8. Take seven deep breaths.

9. Come down from the mountain summit, and on the path through the forest find a wounded deer. Try to help him as much as possible.

10. Bring the deer to your home. Give every assistance possible to heal the deer.

11. When the healing is completed, open your eyes. Sit relaxed for a few minutes.

Note: Do this exercise thirty-five to fifty minutes every day for a week, and see if any trace of depression still exists within you.

66

Light Exercise

1. Sit quietly and relax.
2. Take three deep breaths.
3. Visualize a drop of light at the center of your head.
4. Let it slowly expand to three inches. It is a white light.
5. See yourself standing in the middle of the sphere in a blue robe.
6. With your spiritual energy, expand the sphere of light to nine feet.
7. Visualize a beam of orange light coming from Space and charging you. Use the energy to purify your nine-foot sphere of light from all negative elements, thoughts, feelings, and memories and throw them out.
8. Climb through the beam of light toward Space to a high altitude and try to see the room where your body is. Then see the city, the country, and the whole world.
9. Using white light, send light to the world; flood it with light.

   Using blue light, send love to the world; flood it with love.

   Using violet light, send joy to the world; flood it with joy.
10. Remember where your body is. Return to the body. Touch your body. Open your eyes.

Do this daily once, not more than ten minutes. It may dispel depression, grief, doubts, and give you energy, vitality, and joy.

67

Subtle Sources of Depression

One must cultivate the ability to change and adapt. This will be impossible if you are crystallized in your ways. The True Self, the real you, has no such problems. It is only your false self that crystallizes and becomes an unchanging standard on your path. The Self is always progressive. It has the urge to expand.

Depression is inertia, imprisonment, a process of increasing darkness, confusion, and limitation. Depression can be a phenomenon of the physical body, emotional body, or mental body — either individually or collectively.

Depression is related to energy, love, and light. When you have less energy in your body than you used to have, you are on the road to depression. When you have less love and joy in your emotional nature, you are heading toward depression. When you have less light and more confusion, you are entering into depression. In depression you face dead-ends; you do not have real direction and goals. *Thus, when your physical, emotional, and mental natures do not increase in energy, joy, and light, they will not be able to cope with the increasing problems of life and will fall into depression. This is the first major cause of depression.*

How to Overcome Such Depressions

1. You must take care of your physical body as much as possible.

2. Purify your emotional nature of negativity through increasing love, devotion, and aspiration.

3. Plan things that you can do and do them.

4. Try to find the answers to some of your questions through thinking and searching.

A major source of depression starts from the brain. If the brain is tired, you will have continuous problems leading you into depression. The brain needs rest, rest from the conversations of others, from the various kinds of sound and light.

Cyclic rest in darkness, in the mountains and deserts helps your brain recover. Often you must give up reading, watching television, or listening to the radio. This will bring great relief to your brain.

Your nose also sends very potent impressions to your brain. You must stay away from certain odors and the smell of chemicals and gases which often injure the brain and prepare it for depression.

If your office or home is in a state of chaos and things are not in order, and when you pressure your brain to follow an order through the chaos, this contributes to the fatigue of your brain. Orderliness is a great help to your sanity and joy.

Emotional depression can be overcome if you try to do good for others. It is a wonderful healing process to help your friends, neighbors, and even strangers without expectations or personal concerns.

Doing good does not mean to be pleasant to others or to be exploited by them. Doing good means to meet a need which will make them strive and help themselves find the answers to their questions.

People become depressed when they do not find the answers to their questions. One's whole life is a process of questions and answers. Life proceeds in presenting questions and trying to solve them. Each problem in your life, each need in your life, is a question which needs an answer or answers. When you have questions and you do not have answers, you feel depressed.

A healthy man is one who has the answer to his health problems, the answers to his emotional and mental problems. The answers to your questions can be found through meditation, enlightenment, higher contact, and continuous research.

Hatred, separatism, and fanaticism pollute your emotional body and prepare it for depression. Thus, try to increase your goodwill, your joy, your purity, and your beauty.

Mental depression can be overcome by expanding your mental horizon. When the horizon of your mind is limited and fenced in, you are a fanatic. And most depressed people come from fanatical circles. They feel limited within the walls of what is given to them or what they have in their mind. As soon as you are able to expand their horizon, they begin to be violent and irritated; then they come out of their depression. Such people can help themselves through meditation and study.

One must find the source of his depression and approach his problem from the level of the source. If the source is physical, then physical treatment must be given. If it is emotional, a different technique must be used. If it is mental, the problem must be handled in different ways. Inaccuracy of one's evaluation of the sources and means of healing creates even more depression and complications.

Once a man came to me for consultation. He said he was going through a heavy cyclic depression, and this time he was almost ready to commit suicide.

He had come to a dead end. A dead end means no horizon, no future, no hope. When we expand our horizon and develop hope and striving toward a future, depression evaporates.

While we were talking, he made a remark about his religion and said, "My religion is the only way for salvation."

I answered him, "Your religion is the only way that took you into depression."

When you have only one way and all your other windows and doors are closed, you will end up in depression. Fanaticism is the denial of the freedom of others. It creates a vacuum around you which eventually invites pressure.

The human soul lives through expansion. If, instead of expanding their soul, people try to expand the field of their possessions to help their survival, they lead themselves into the impasse of depression. Depression has no future. It leads to a dead-end. The future means a process of unfoldment, expansion, freedom, expanding insight, and synthesis.

When a man is caught in his fanaticism and does not have increasing viewpoints and expanding perspectives, he is going into depression. But when he is increasing his viewpoints and enlightening his mind with the light of more inclusiveness, he is making himself immune to depression.

Our life continues to exist because we find answers to our questions. Greater are those people who have more inclusive answers to their questions. We only advance by finding the answers to our questions. Finding answers leads us toward mastery.

The second major cause of depression is the increasing burden of accumulating negative karma. All those things that we did or are doing against our own conscience, against beauty, light, love, and the purpose of life gradually accumulate and create fields of distortion and destruction within our aura. These negative and disturbing fields absorb our pranic energy, prevent the solar energies from reaching us, and eventually form a barrier between our personality vehicles and the overshadowing Soul.

In each of us there is an internal accountant who, in many ways, informs us of our increasing debts and of the coming storm. Depression is an unconscious mechanism of escape from such a retribution, or it is a form of realization of the harm we did to others and our inability to compensate for it. Every type of confusion is a prelude to depression.

The cure for such depression will be

1. To find a way to pay your karmic debts. Some choose to be sick. Some work hard to do good. Some try to fight against the Law of Karma and fall back into depression.

2. To straighten your accounts with others so that you do not continue increasing your karma but start decreasing it as much as possible.

3. To do good to people.

The Karmic Law cyclically presents us with a bill for our debts. Our intellect rationalizes and pretends that the bill does not exist, but deep in our heart we feel that there is a debt and sooner or later it must be paid. Every time we receive a bill of this kind we feel depressed because we know deep in our heart the wrongs we did, but we cannot find an answer as to how to pay for them.

Depression is that moment in which we lose our contact with our Soul, with our Teacher, with the Divine Presence. We feel abandoned not only by the outside but even by our Higher Self. The way out of such a depression is to pay our bills and establish right communication with our Soul.

Many people pay their karma through health problems, accidents, failures, losses, and so on. But they do not feel depressed if they do not identify with the conditions of their physical, emotional, and mental natures.

Depression descends on us when the human soul feels that the problems of his bodies are his own problems. We must put our actions in line with light, love, beauty, truth, and joy. Gratitude and respect are very good means to decrease our karma and release ourself from increasing pressure.

Man is linked to the consequences of his deeds; the effects of his deeds have subtle communication lines to him.

Our intentions of starting something can be noble, but they do not guarantee the result or the effect. When our intentions are manifested, our deeds may take a totally different direction under the influence of diverse currents found in the masses of people or in the world. Thus a good intention may create a revolution, a way, a culture, a civilization, or all of these.

Whatever events are linked on the string of intention are related to the source. And the source, the individual, or the group is affected by the events and occurrences.

Many unexpected depressions or disturbed mental conditions are reactions to destructive events. Also, many unexpected inspirations, joys, and ecstasies are the reactions to beneficial events.

We are connected to the consequences of our intentions, thoughts, words, and deeds. We are not aware of these connections, but we register and record the transmitted effects and express them through our health conditions, joys and sorrows, creativity, depressions, and ecstasy. This is why we are told that a man is born through his intentions, thoughts, words, and deeds. He is molded by the consequences of all that he is.

One may ask, if it is possible to suffer through our good intentions and deeds, isn't it better if we do not have them?

The absence of good intentions and righteous deeds, words, and thoughts leads us to disintegration, pain, and suffering. But the existence of our good intentions, thoughts, words, and deeds prepares us for striving and makes us ready to unfold and expand our consciousness in adverse conditions. It is possible that our deeds create strong winds and high waves, but if our intentions are noble we intuitively know how to use the winds for our sails and the high waves for our joyful surfing.

Our every action is caused by an invisible action. Behind our actions there are emotions, thoughts, and will. Behind our emotions, thoughts, and will there are the emotions, thoughts, and will of the entire humanity. The interesting point is that beyond the emotions, thoughts, and will of humanity, there are greater subjective influences coming from solar, galactic, and Cosmic sources. All these fields — from individual to Cosmic — act, react, and influence each other.

Every action of a human being is related to Cosmos. Every action of a human being has an effect on every subjective action in every field.

Have we the free will to act the way we want to act? Are we responsible for our actions? The answers to these two questions are clear. Our actions are controlled by our thoughts. By controlling our thoughts, we control our actions. If one can control his actions, he should be responsible for his uncontrolled actions.

Each human mind is subject to various influences. The mind cannot control itself except when the man acts over the mind. The Self within man can control the mind if It is not identified with the mind. If the Self is identified, then the mind is controlled or influenced by all other subjective fields, and the person's actions are the result of these influences.

It is possible to act without the willingness to act the way one acts. This happens when a higher will is imposed upon him and if he has no chance to escape. In this case his action is not his action directly — but indirectly it is still his action. The reason for this is that through his past deeds he created a chain of events which culminated in that moment when imposition was exercised upon him. This is again an example of how subjective forces or causes influence the daily events of our life.

The way to freedom can be entered stage by stage. One first of all must try to control his actions by trying to control his mind and emotions. Then he must try to control his will by identifying himself with a higher will, then detaching himself from that higher will and identifying himself with a still higher will, until he contacts the One Will and acts in that Will.

The third cause of depression is overdevelopment of one's intellect at the expense of his Intuition and overdevelopment of the mind at the expense of the heart.

There is also exactly the opposite condition in which you bypass the mind or the intellect and enter into the world of Intuition. Your eyes open more than you can understand, or you see more things than you can translate.

In the first instance all your intellectual maneuvers lead you to a dead-end. The world is in depression because of this — the intellect overruling the heart. We cannot see the way ahead, and the only thing we want to do is to destroy others and, of course, ourselves. This is a form of self-revenge, subconsciously carried out by people everywhere.

In the second case, one did not develop his intellect but through forceful and artificial methods built a way into the intuitional world. Mantra Yoga, pranayama, wrong meditation, meditation on the chakras, and some drugs can lead one prematurely into that world. Christ called such people thieves who enter the house, not from the door (by natural means) but through windows (artificial means).

In the first case, you have intellect but no vision. In the second case, you have vision but not enough intellect to substantiate it. Both cases lead to apathy, inertia, and depression.

The cure is to develop your mind and heart, your intellect and Intuition, equally. If you do not work along this line, no matter what you do, the depression will come back.

You can also use the following suggestions:

If you have intellect but not Intuition, try to develop your heart qualities through acts of goodwill and service. Eventually build a vision and make your intellect work for the actualization of your vision. Or plan, design, or write music and try to actualize your plan or design; play your music or create a dance or drama with it.

Advanced souls sometimes fall into heavy depression when their lower vehicles, the intellect, the astral body, and the physical body, cannot help them express their higher contacts and higher visions. Sometimes it is the social or political conditions which create great obstacles for these creative geniuses. They withdraw within themselves and go into deeper and deeper depression.

I remember a great poet in Lebanon who used to live in a beautiful house located on a mountain facing the sea. For many weeks he did not appear where he usually would come and talk with his friends and do his shopping. Feeling that something was wrong with him, some of his friends gathered together and went to his home. The servant opened the door and said, "M. is sleeping."

"Is he sick?"

"No, but it is five days now, and he has not gotten out of bed and he doesn't want to eat."

We rushed in and found him in bed staring at the ceiling. He was indifferent to our presence. We sat awhile and then one of us asked, "How are you?"

No answer.

"Can we ask you a question?"

"There is no answer to any question," he replied.

"Can we help you in any way?"

"What is help?"

"We know you are hurt."

No answer.

"But things are moving — your books are enflaming the hearts of thousands. Already a group is formed to carry your ideals into universities and colleges and publish your manuscripts in various languages."

"What ideas … and what books?"

"We must talk to you in the garden. Get up; we have things to tell you."

And the man got up, put on his robe, and we went into the garden. We convinced him that things were going well, that people were standing behind him, and that we needed him for a few lectures. He was so enthused that he went inside, dressed, drank some milk, and took us to his study to show us the new books he had been writing. From that day on, he was again a public figure, working very hard to bring beauty and understanding among people.

The main cause of depression in this man was his thought that he was not able to help people. He thought that they were not benefiting themselves from his creative work. Another reason was that no publishers in England or America wanted to publish his books because of his unusual way of looking at things, so he began withdrawing into himself.

One of the magic ways to help a depressed person is the ability to create interest in him and make him feel that people respect him and expect certain guidance from him. The next step is then to inspire him into creative action. Once a person begins to create, the emotional and mental hindrances will melt away and he will feel increasing power "to stand up and fight."

The fourth major cause of depression is identification with your glamors and illusions, with your feelings and thoughts. Any time anyone attacks your emotions, you feel you are attacked. Any time anyone attacks your thoughts, you feel you are attacked. Because of this identification, once your feelings or thoughts are crushed or heavily attacked, you feel you are losing yourself. You either let yourself become lost in depression, or you withdraw your defeated false self and fall into apathy and inertia. Your false self is a thought, emotion, mental picture, or hypnotic suggestion which acts in lieu of your True Self.

Withdrawal into your True Self makes you more creative and radioactive. Withdrawal into your false and defeated self leads you into apathy. The removal of the false self is a great step ahead in the recovery from depression. The way out of depression is to dis-identify yourself from your own emotions, feelings, thoughts, and ideas, even from your actions — which are controlling your life as if they were your Self.

Do not say, "I am angry." Say, "There is anger and my bodies are caught in it," or, "my bodies are using it." Do not identify with your thoughts; observe them as if they were furniture, pieces of lumber or bricks. Be ready to abandon them any time they do not serve Beauty, Goodness, and Truth.

Realize that you are the Self — pure, immaculate, immortal, and blissful. Your reality does not depend on emotions, thoughts, or actions. They may be imposed upon you. Your vehicles may be acting mechanically. They can be the result of hypnotic suggestions. Watch them, and do not be identified with them.

One must cultivate the ability to change and adapt. This will be impossible if you are crystallized in your ways. The True Self, the real you, has no such problems. It is only your false self that crystallizes and becomes an unchanging standard on your path. The Self is always progressive. It has the urge to expand. It is impossible to expand and be progressive without the destruction of barriers created by the false self. The false self is afraid to progress because it dies.

A fanatic sticks to his tradition or thoughts because a fanatic has a false self and is afraid that change in his beliefs will mean destruction for him. Those people who are identified with their false self fall into depression any time their false self is defeated by circumstances or by people.

The fifth major cause of depression is the pressure of Cosmic currents which cyclically are released in Space. These currents come and fill the container and overflow or devastate the body and the astral and mental mechanisms. This happens to those who do not live their life according to the requirements of the cycles and crystallize their vehicles, creating hindrances and frictions.

These Cosmic currents are released cyclically to distribute new energy and inspiration to the life-forms. But if the life-forms are not progressing in accordance with the Universal Plan, they cannot control these energies and are carried away from the current toward depression and destruction.

When such energies are received and adequately assimilated, they manifest themselves as objects of great art, movements, and inventions which carry a similar charge to those who come in contact with them.

There is also another cause of depression. We live in Infinite Space, and in various ways we share all that goes on in the Universe. For example, when a constellation or a globe is in the process of disintegration, we feel it as if a part of our nature were disintegrating. Some of the unknown causes of subtle depression originate from such facts.

If the Planetary Life is leaving behind one of His planetary vehicles, we feel it as a depression if our consciousness is focused in the corresponding vehicle in our own nature.

If the Solar Life is taking a great step ahead toward Cosmic evolution, many people fall into depression if their Self feels the progress and their vehicles block the expansion.

Tidal waves are produced in the spiritual domain when there is destruction or advancement. These tidal waves cyclically affect our life, global economy, and our politics.

The answers to such problems are sublimation and transfiguration of our nature. We also need periodic rest and purification. But the most important thing is preparation. Preparation starts with the preparation for zodiacal cycles and full moon periods in which we try to come in contact consciously with spatial forces and energies and retain our balance. In *Symphony of the Zodiac*, instructions are given on how to start handling Cosmic energies constructively and creatively. This method is called *full moon approaches*. When our Sun is in a certain constellation and it is the full moon period, it is the time in which a powerful zodiacal energy is released upon our planet. Thus, we must learn to prepare ourselves to be able to assimilate and handle the incoming energies.[1]

Many people pass through depression in these cycles when they feel flooded by these energies. Sometimes people receive these energies in their higher centers, where they turn into a great source of creativity. Sometimes they are received by their lower centers, and the demand of the lower centers increases to such a degree that the only way to escape such pressure is in depression. Sometimes the energies overstimulate the solar plexus, and people do every kind of crazy thing, both at home and in world politics, in order to escape their frustration or to escape depression.

Some of the ways to help yourself at these periods of energy release are to keep silence as much as possible, to occupy yourself with meditation and creative works, or to take a vacation and go into Nature, especially to the desert.

Speech conditions the nature of our aura. If a man speaks eighty percent trash, his aura will be contaminated in certain places by his speech, and at the time of energy contact, the contaminated location will become the "sore point" in his nature, leading him into depression. Sore points act as caves where the person goes and succumbs.

My father used to refer to such depression with a strange expression. He used to say, "The wheel of the mill is taken away by the flood." When your mill is worked by the flow of water channeled to the big wheel, you have the use of energy continuously. But when the flood destroys the channel and the mill and takes away the wheel, the result is depression.

You must exercise periodic silence and solitude and beware of any kind of showing-off.

Nature is a progressive Entity, and we are cells in It. This is why we must advance in our evolution, expanding our field of contact and handling these contacts consciously and creatively.

The sixth major cause of depression (or even possession) is when an entity or a thoughtform possesses you, obsesses you, and saps you physically, emotionally, and mentally according to the type and intention of the entity or thoughtform. This is like an intruder who jumps into your car, ties you up, and

---

1. Instructions are given for preparing our bodies in *Symphony of the Zodiac*, as well as in *Cosmic Shocks*.

drives your car against your will, emotions, and thoughts. To avoid such a danger you must do the following:

1. Keep away from all kinds of mediums, fortune-tellers, common aura readers, channels, and pseudo-prophets. Not only keep away from such persons, but also do not touch their books, literature, or any article used by them. Through their articles they can build a channel between you and the entity or entities using them. They are very contagious.

2. Do not yield to any suggestions given to you through any voice or telepathic means if you cannot determine the exact source.

3. Do not yield to automatic writing. Any power which wants to dominate your mechanism is an intruder. It is only after the Third Initiation, the Transfiguration, that you can consciously cooperate with higher spiritual forces. Before that, all such relationships are handled by dark forces or nature spirits.

4. Reject all apparitions, voices, or any direct imposition upon your organs. Realize that the greatest violation is the violation of your will.

Divine guidance is not given in masquerade or disguise but in full knowledge and identification. Sometimes due to your weakness, the dark ones appear like angels and try to influence your life. Here you must use the light of your heart as the sword of Intuition to unveil the truth.

The seventh major cause of depression is related to electrical exchange, or polarity, between you and others or between you and objects and locations. The Law of Polarity states that identical energy fields repel each other, and non-identical energy fields attract each other.

When the polarity of your physical, emotional, and mental bodies fuses with the greater magnetic field, you are expanded, joyful, successful, and powerful. When the magnetic field of thoughts, persons, objects, or locations repels your magnetic field, you are sick, weak, and confused. Sometimes even the non-identical energy field changes, or it changes you and creates frictions. That is why it is proper sometimes to change locations, furniture, etc. Sometimes it is good to move away from those places where you feel depressed, confused, or bewildered.

Stay away from radioactive waste, nuclear power plants, locations of radioactivity, heavy electrical cables or stations, and buildings or persons which lower your energy level, limit your horizon, and dim your light.

We must know that man is a magnet. He has an electromagnetic form. He is an electromagnetic field, and any distortion and disturbance in this electromagnetic field creates problems and eventually leads the man into depression.

You must watch your polarity with people, locations, objects, and times. Wherever and with whatever and whomever you are most creative and healthy, choose that location, that person, that furniture, that food, that material, that color, that sound, and so on.

The eighth cause of depression is due to our past lives with all our past karma. Someone kills an innocent person, and this "dead" person tries to take revenge on his killer. But because of the makeup of the killer, the "dead" one cannot obsess or possess him so he waits until the killer dies.

In the astral plane the victim then attacks the "newly passed over" killer with all his power and fury in order to take revenge upon his killer, and even at the time of the birth of the killer, the victim incarnates in the same body as the killer in order to continue his revenge. This is the cause of some defective births, insanity, and so on.

If the killer is fortunate, or unfortunate enough, to live in his new body, the victim will lead him into paths which will bring him failure, destruction, depression, and death. This is a very serious case, and only subjectively active disciples can find a solution for it.

One wonders why we are told that we must overcome every thought or feeling of revenge. It is because "vengence belongs to God," which means it is better to let the karmic laws take care of it.

Depression often comes when the time of payment for the deeds of our past life approaches. It is noticed that before major calamities and natural disasters, people go through individual and massive depression. To meet such problems one must increase his good deeds, serve the common cause of humanity, and be a factor for freedom, beauty, and joy.

The ninth major cause of depression is an unbalanced, inharmonious development in your nature. Your nature must grow and develop harmoniously, and each part of your nature must be nourished by its proper food. Hence, you give time to nourish your body, your emotions, your mind, and your soul by proper food, rest, joy, and entertainment.

Cast out fanaticism. Develop co-measurement[2] and the spirit of synthesis. Increase your psychic energy, the energy of your True Self, and advance your point of identification on the line of spiritual realities. Occupy yourself with a project related to world service, holding in your mind the fact that there is only one humanity. Increase joy within you and in your environment. Dedicate yourself to lofty visions. Fuse your actions, emotions, and thoughts with Beauty in any form.

---

2. Please refer to *The Flame of Beauty, Culture, Love, Joy*, Ch. 4.

Occasionally take your personality into Nature, to the mountains or oceans, and especially to the desert. Deserts open within you the source of Infinity, peace, and serenity. The absence of noise and habitations makes the deserts relatively free from elements of depression. In the desert, you can renew your spirit of freedom and joy and build in your consciousness new lines for higher inspirations. Mountains are very beautiful, but deserts are gorgeous. In the desert you are less limited by the suggestions of familiar forms, and there is also silence in the desert which allows you to expand and see yourself.

Deserts have a special quality of wiping out your depression. Your pity and your personality get lost in the wilderness. In the forest you can have the sympathy or the pity of trees, lakes — but in the desert, your horizon is wide and immediately you transcend your petty problems and are challenged to stand on your own feet.

When you come in contact with those people who travel or live mostly in the desert, you will see wholeness in their attitude and unselfishness and Infinity in their eyes. They are the most hospitable people, and they share all that they have with you. They are part of Nature. They love life. They do not impose themselves. There is a smile on their face. The desert lives in them as a source of peace, oneness, independence, and compassion.

The tenth major cause of depression is so-called vampirism. There are people or entities who draw a great deal of ectoplasm from others.

Ectoplasm is a special substance apart from the etheric body and the aura. It is a mixture of astral and etheric substance. This substance is used by earthbound entities to densify themselves and come in contact with the material world. An advanced soul does not need to use the ectoplasm to come in contact with human beings.

The use of ectoplasm by an entity weakens the person and deprives him of energy and vitality. When entities use a great amount of our ectoplasm, we fall into depression.

Ectoplasm is of two kinds. One is used by low-level entities because it is formed of maya, glamors, and low-level desires. The other kind is charged by high-level aspirations and vitality, and some subtle entities enjoy tasting such an ectoplasm and using it as their food. Such entities express their gratitude by rendering various services to us and giving joy and inspiration to us.

In the Subtle World there exist the correspondences of vultures who smell rotten ectoplasm and rush to the victim. Such "vultures" usually sap our energy and vitality and lead us into total apathy or depression. We are told that the only protections are deep aspiration toward the highest beauties and the Teacher's shield.

The combination of ugly thoughts, negative emotions, criminal acts, and irritation produces a very a malodorous aura which, like a magnet, attracts vultures. These vultures, like the vultures of Prometheus, eat the substance of life within our aura and deprive us of the spirit of striving, courage, daring, and the joy of labor.

On the other hand, beautiful thoughts, lofty aspirations, and deeds of sacrificial service produce the food of angels. This is when man bridges the gap between the human and angelic kingdoms and comes in contact with those who will lead his steps toward greater achievements.

There is another serious cause for depression. When the Inner Guide partially withdraws from the Chalice, a great depression descends upon the human soul identified with his threefold personality. The Inner Guide presents a goal in the life of the person, a meaning, a hope, a trust, a path, a possibility, an open door, a way to escape from the miseries of life; a mother, a father upon which to depend; a future which shines as a beacon in a stormy sea. All these seem to fade away as the Inner Guide leaves and man cries, "My Lord, my Lord, why have You forsaken me?"

The Inner Guide has Its own duties and responsibilities, and at intervals It leaves the human soul, although It keeps Its eyes upon him. In these short periods of time, depression can be experienced.

One may ask, "Does the Inner Guide enjoy the depression of the human soul?" The answer is that It gives a chance and a challenge to the human soul to try to stand on his own feet and face life before the Great Renunciation arrives.

Secondly, It leaves the human soul temporarily, or in rare cases permanently, when the man lives a corrupted life, uses drugs, wastes his time and energy, or plans activities against the Law of Love. It also leaves temporarily when the man subjects himself to mediumship or acts against the Hierarchy of Light, or deals with mediums, or with people on the dark path.

The departure of the Inner Guide is not a technique of punishment but a way to teach the human soul to live according to the Law of the Cosmic Magnet, which can be summarized as the Law of Beauty, Goodness, and Righteousness. In those periods of depression, the human soul experiences a miserable loneliness which is an opportunity for him to contemplate the causes of his depression and straighten his path.

The Inner Guide occasionally uses these techniques to prepare the man to stand firm and strong in an approaching challenge.

Depression often descends upon people because of the conditions of their etheric body. When the etheric body is contaminated by various psychic and material poisons, radiations and chemical pollutions, or prolonged irritation through various shocks of fear, anger, failures, hatred, and jealousy, the etheric body does not circulate the prana and distribute it properly to the physical body. In most cases this is the cause of prolonged or short periods of depression.

To clean such a condition, one must run, work hard in Nature, and throw away his mental and emotional attitudes which bring intoxication of the etheric body.

There is a prevalent emphasis on the opinion that despair or depression is the result of losing the sense of meaning in life. This is true to some degree, but a greater number of people suffer because they feel smaller than their vision, too small to grasp the meaning and face the challenge presented to them by their vision.

Many advanced souls feel frustration, despair, and depression when beauty unveils itself in a Solar and Cosmic sense. The psychic digestive system shuts itself off because, although they see the beauty, they cannot assimilate it or serve it.

Great challenges sometimes cause depression if the person feels hindrances within his nature or in his environment which prevent him from meeting the challenge.

There is also a cause which is the inability to give birth to those great visions which one sees in his inner world. This inner vision cannot incarnate because of many reasons, and the person falls into depression because of his inability to bring it into being.

Lethargy is not an illness. Such people are dealt with as if they had a serious sickness to be treated medically.

In most cases, lethargy is a condition of the physical body when the human soul leaves it and goes with his astral body for a distant journey. Such a journey sometimes takes three to seven days or even months. The body lives by the magnetic thread which exists between the body and the human soul. When the mission is finished, the soul returns and reenters the body.

In Oriental villages I observed a few cases of lethargy. People would put drops of water and honey in the mouth of the person and leave him alone in a dark, clean, ventilated, secluded room where noise could not penetrate. Visitors were forbidden. The lethargy itself was considered a sacred phenomenon. When it was over, people expected some measure of expansion of consciousness, as they believed the soul went on a far-off journey and learned exceptional things.

This experience is sometimes referred to as a long dream, sometimes as total blankness, or as an unconscious state. The brain usually cannot translate the frequency created by the journey, and it shuts itself off automatically.

The most common things observed in such persons after their recovery were that they manifested more tolerance, they had more space and used more caution, they were slower in making decisions, and their eyes gave the impression that they had a forgotten memory. Months later they remembered unusual things, but they assumed that these were the fabrications of their minds.

I did extensive interviews with those who had experienced the lethargic state, and I came to the conclusion that if all the evidence were put together, it would definitely indicate that the human soul was somewhere else doing something, but the brain did not remember it. One day people may go into deep sleep consciously and come back to their normal consciousness with their experiences.

Depression sometimes manifests as a form of *paralysis*. The symptoms appear as indifference, inertia, criticism, malice, slander, treason, and even violence. There are two causes for such a paralysis:

1. A person paralyzes his inner mechanisms by finding mistakes in others and judging and condemning them. This is just like putting sand in your own gas tank.

2. The second cause is a person's failures, faults, or errors which hit his conscience in such a way that they paralyze him. He becomes unworthy, a sinner, a dirty rag in his own eyes.

In both cases you build images. In the first case you build the ugly image of the one you condemn and judge, and slowly you assimilate the image and identify with it. In the second case, you build a miserable image of yourself, a defeated, ugly image, and you believe that it is what you are.

Usually those who condemn others are those who have similar faults, errors, and failures. Condemnation for them is a mechanism of escape from their own conscience. Thus they not only impress the image of their victim upon themselves, but they also restimulate and call to the surface their own imprisoned faults, errors, and failures, and paralyze their progress on the path of perfection. Condemnation of one's own personality perpetuates the failures and makes a person unfit for progressive development.

What is the solution? There is nothing new in the answer; it is an old homemade remedy:

— See beauty in others.

— See beauty within yourself.

— Keep yourself busy doing good and encourage others to increase goodness in the world.

— Uplift your consciousness with lofty thoughts for the future.

— On the rough path of life, do not count the rocks you drive upon but keep your eyes upon the destination. Do not paralyze others and yourself in the spirit of condemnation.

Also remember:

— By giving joy to others, you uplift and heal yourself.

— By giving freedom to others, you free yourself of depressing emotions and thoughts.

— By increasing beauty in the world, you elevate your heart to the altar of the future.

Some Practical Self-Healing Suggestions

Study the following:

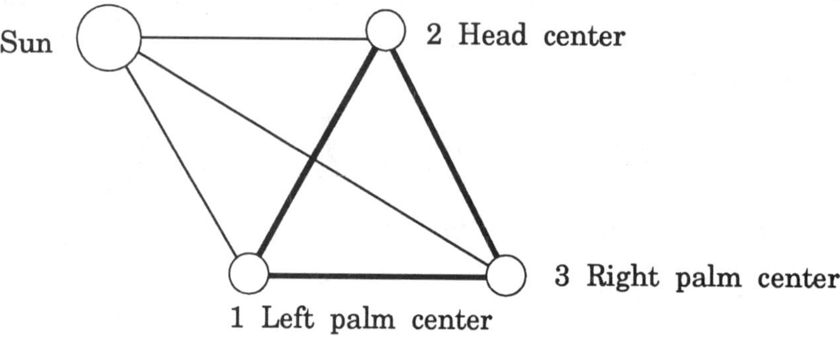

Diagram 67-1 The Sun and Healing

The Sun is the source of healing energies and substances. One day the human being will be able to use the chemistry of the Sun to heal his many ailments. Around the sphere of the Sun there will be found the most precious elements to cure many diseases. However, mentally we can direct Its visible and invisible light to our system and use it for healing.

Visualize the Sun charging your three centers with healing energy. Put your right hand on your left shoulder and your left hand on your right shoulder and bring in the healing energy. Then put your left hand on the middle of your chest. Put the right hand upon it, and visualize the ray of the head center joining with them for healing the whole body. Do this after charging yourself for three to five minutes in the sunshine.

1. Visualize the healing energy of the Sun accumulating in the above three locations, then forming a triangular current between them.

2. When the left hand goes to the right shoulder, the right hand is still on the left shoulder. They cross each other. At this point, visualize the head center ray joining at the crossing.

3. When both are on the chest, imagine the ray from the head center joining with both hands.

4. Let the right hand energy pass through the left shoulder to the right side of the body. Let the left hand energy pass through the right shoulder to the left side of the body.

5. The middle point will fuse these two energies in the whole body.

Say with concentration:

> *Let the regenerating energy of the Sun pass through the right hand to the left side, to cure, to heal and transform the left side.*

Say the same for the left hand.

At the crossing, let the energies flow to the astral body — both sides.

At the chest, let the energies pour into the mental sphere.

6. Sit relaxed and inhale the prana of the Sun into your physical, emotional, and mental bodies.

7. Let your head center shine.

8. See yourself transformed.

If you want to exercise healing on others, remember you must be focused in your higher mind, in the heart center in the head. You must not use force but become a transmitter of healing energy.

Before you start healing, you must charge yourself with the rays of the Sun — letting them pour into your head center and to both your hands.

Then visualize a pure electric-yellow force around your head. This is the reservoir of the energy of your thoughts.

Then visualize both your hands and both your eyes connected with that fiery sphere through electric-yellow currents.

This is a self-healing technique, but if the person wants to stimulate and kindle the healing energies of someone else, he may use the following technique:

Before the healer applies his hands and eyes, he must close his eyes and through his mental fire purify the locations of the body of the person where the trouble exists. This purificatory action disperses all pollution around the location and also keeps away those entities who may be trying to possess the person.

After the thought operation, the healer must direct the palms of both his hands to the heart of the person, while standing behind or in front of the person, and look at the center of the back of his hands, channeling through the ajna center the psychic energy to the heart, which will receive it, distribute it into the blood, and heal the parts of the body where the trouble exists.

This will be done for fifteen minutes. After that, the healer must take a deep breath, visualizing that he is inhaling a golden light through his head center, and then exhale it toward the location of the trouble. The breath will carry into the aura a great amount of energy.

We are told that such a healing mostly applies to disorders related to nerve centers or etheric centers and their corresponding glands.

Sometimes healers spread the fear of death into the hearts of people. The Great Ones advise us to be indifferent not only toward death but also toward life. Both concerns must be eliminated from our minds if we want to progress on the Path.

If one is too attached to life, he will not be able to release himself easily from the body. If he is afraid of death, he will be attached to the form-life and increase his suffering. Or on the journey to Higher Worlds, he will meet opposing currents of energy, as if he were drowning in a waterfall. On the other hand, when he surrenders himself to the "now," he will soon invite those angels who will help him on his journey toward the Higher Worlds.

Medical offices and hospitals are charged with heavy layers of thoughts and emotions about death. This not only hinders the release of many but also makes healing difficult or impossible.

One must surrender himself joyfully and peacefully to death whenever he feels that the moment of departure has arrived.

Some people set limits to their life. They say, "I will die young," or "I will live to the age of sixty-five." These limits are wrong. One must leave these things to karma or to the Hierarchy to be determined. The Hierarchy sometimes needs special workers here or in the Subtle Worlds. It is this need that sometimes shortens or lengthens our life.

The only thing with which a living person must be occupied in his mind is, "How can I serve humanity?"

68

Exercise to Repel "Bad" Energies

To repel "bad" energies, daily you must do the following visualization exercise:

1. Sit quietly for one minute.
2. Visualize a drop of light at the center of your head.
3. Let the light increase into a sphere of three feet.
4. See yourself standing at the center of the light in a blue robe.
5. Expand the light nine feet and visualize that your light is building a shield around you through which no evil can penetrate.
6. Then say: "I stand in the light of my Soul and radiate the power of my true Divine Self. I am that pure Self."
7. Sound the OM three times, visualizing a violet color.

69

Virtues

Part I

Vices are built both of microbes, germs, and viruses and of psychic disorders. The more virtuous one is, the longer he lives and the better he serves humanity.

We are told that virtues travel with us throughout eternities as inspiring, encouraging, and protecting angels until they fuse with our essence and disappear in it when the mountaintop is attained.

Virtues are the rays of the human soul which radiate out in the process of Self-actualization. When Self-actualization is complete and the human soul is born in all planes and is conscious and active, we say that the Inner Sun is shining in all fields simultaneously.

In the beginning, these rays or virtues do not seem to exist as part of the human soul because they are identified with the personality vehicles, with personality aspirations, dreams, visions, and interests. But once this identification is surpassed and the human soul stands free, the person truly becomes aware that he is the sum total and the source of virtues.

Virtues are lines of energy flow. Sometimes they mix with different forces and elements and take different forms. For example, a negative virtue is a vice. A vice is a virtue controlled by a negative emotion. When love becomes demanding or mixed with jealousy, it turns into a vice, a destructive force. You have certain noble beliefs, but when they are controlled by fanaticism, they create genocides and inquisitions. Thus virtues turn into vices, and often the most vicious people are those who once had many virtues.

How should we make a virtue safe? A virtue exists in three forms:

1. As an intellectual concept and deduction.

2. As an intellectual concept and feeling.

3. As an intellectual concept, a deep feeling, and an actualization or a livingness of a virtue. This means that you know the virtue, you feel it deeply, and **you are it**.

Unless one reaches the third stage of virtues, any virtue can be misused, overused, distorted, manipulated, controlled, or rejected under certain conditions and circumstances.

If you analyze a vice, you will find grains of virtues around which the ego, glamors, illusions, urges, and drives build their shells.

In order to be a real virtue, a virtue must not be imposed upon us either by fear, hypnotism, promises, bribery, personality authority, or "beliefs." The virtue must be built within us as the result of our conscious decision to bring changes into our nature and in society. A virtue must not dominate our free will but be a part of our will. Actually, there is no real virtue unless the virtue is a part of the human soul manifesting through thoughts, words, feelings, and actions.

Virtues also change into vices when they are not used for one humanity, for one life, but instead are used for an ego, for a group, or for one nation only. **An honest person is honest with himself, with others, with all nations, with all life-forms**. If honesty works only within a family but not within society, it turns into a vice: dishonesty.

Once a virtue shines as a facet of the diamond of the human soul, it stops being a virtue. It is only on this level that a virtue cannot degenerate into a vice. This is the secret of why a really virtuous person is unaware of his virtues. He has no virtues to be turned into vices.

The process of all this development is as follows:

1. Virtues are unconscious.

2. Virtues and vices are in conflict.

3. Virtues fall under the domination of emotions or physical urges and drives.

4. Virtues are used for the ego.

5. Virtues lead a person to a great sacrifice.

6. Vices disappear.

7. Virtues fuse with the Self.

When we achieve virtues, they gradually disappear for us. Virtues exist only for those who are not perfect in virtues. For example, fearlessness is developed because you have fear. You want to cultivate fearlessness and abide in it as long as you feel that fear can attack you. Once fear has no effect upon you, fearlessness is no longer there. If your hunger is fed, you are no longer hungry.

Renunciation is a virtue. But if there is nothing to which you are attached, what does renunciation mean for you then? When the reflection, the personality, becomes the soul, he no longer needs virtues because he is free; he is virtues.

Virtues can be achieved through four steps:

1. Gathering information about what they are

2. Watchful discipline to develop virtues and avoid "turning wine into vinegar"

3. Continuous discipline to let virtues actualize in our daily life and relationships

4. Becoming one with the virtues

Each step leads to the next one. If the physical, emotional, and mental vehicles do not have time to assimilate each state properly, the work does not proceed.

Long years and many lives are needed for transformation, but one must not lose time in starting to work on it.

Virtues change into vices when they are forced or imposed upon us, exaggerated by us, or if they are exercised under bribery or flattery.

It is very important to observe these signs and see how virtues slowly turn into vices with embarrassing and destructive results. A vice that is a degenerated virtue is very powerful because it draws energy from higher centers where the roots of virtues originate. Thus a virtuous person, when he turns into a person of vices, becomes extremely dangerous.

Vices are not only degenerated virtues but also exaggerated instincts and desires. This is very interesting to note. Animals or primitive races have almost no vices. Primitive races live as they are. But once their natural instincts, urges, and drives are exaggerated, they turn into vices.

Forced or imposed virtues become a plaster on the walls of the human character. Sudden pressures or shocks make them fall. They create also an inner resistance to virtues, and for long years prevent people from cultivating them.

When people bribe their children and ask them to develop certain virtues, they lead their children into hypocrisy. This is what happens to many religious groups when heavenly gifts are promised for the virtuous.

Those who exaggerate and make a show out of their virtues lose not only their virtues but also the possibility of developing the virtues for a long time.

Virtues can be developed if one really sees their value, if he expands his consciousness, if he aspires to those who become the embodiments of virtues.

Virtues develop and bloom naturally as we strive to expand our consciousness and think and meditate on virtues and on those heroes who became the embodiments of virtues.

Virtues are healing agents. They are like the rays of the Sun which carry healing elements on their wings.

Vices are built both of microbes, germs, and viruses and of psychic disorders. The more virtuous one is, the longer he lives and the better he serves humanity.

70

Meditation on a Virtue

1. Relax your physical body. Align your physical, emotional, and mental vehicles.

2. Visualize yourself as the human soul standing in the light of your Inner Guide.

3. In your visualization see the name of any virtue you want written in any color of your choice on a wall or on a monument or rock.

4. In your creative visualization see yourself dramatizing the virtue. Create the location, the weather, the light, the color, the personnel, and enact the virtue as if you were the embodiment of the virtue. Coordinate your thoughts, emotions, and actions in the spirit of the virtue, and actualize it with living enthusiasm.

5. As you achieve a certain degree of success in embodying the virtue in your life and beingness, visualize a few other people with the same virtue.

6. See them manifesting the virtue in their acts and relationships, and develop great gratitude and joy because of their achievements.

7. Visualize a meeting in which you sit with those heroes who embody the virtue and discuss: "How can we spread this virtue all over the world and invite people to cultivate it in their lives?" Carry on the discussion as realistically as possible, and when the discussion is over, watch them slowly depart.

8. Sit for a few minutes in silence, and then record your discussion on paper for future use.

NOTE: This meditation can be done for fifteen to twenty minutes daily, using a different virtue each month.

Suggested virtues:

— striving

— courage

— daring

— discrimination

— solemnity

— harmlessness

— service

— compassion

— patience

— fearlessness

— gratitude

— responsibility

71

Virtues

Part II

Virtues are electric energy proceeding from the Inner Core. They give health, beauty, energy, and vigilance.

Virtues were considered to be the rays emanating from Holy Ones. These rays had healing power, enlightening power, and inspiring power. No one was considered great unless he demonstrated fundamental virtues.

Virtues evoke trust, striving, and dedication to the great cause of human liberation. Virtues also have a considerable effect on our body chemistry and health. For example:

— *Compassion* strengthens the heart and harmonizes the digestive system.

— *Fearlessness* strengthens and corrects the kidneys and urinary system.

— *Solemnity* purifies the spleen.

— *Ecstasy and great joy* evoked by beauty and art performances energize and harmonize the spleen.

— *Service* purifies the toxins from the muscles and helps to regulate the lymphatic system.

— *Generosity and love* strengthen the flow of electricity in the nervous system, which contributes to longevity.

— *Forgiveness* dissolves the ulcers found in the mental and astral bodies.

— *Patience* energizes the generative organs and heals many disorders found in these organs.

— *Optimism* is a great remedy to the pancreas. Every bit of optimism gives a new electric shock to the pancreas.

— *Discrimination* strengthens the eyes.

— *Silence or right speech* are tonics for the thyroid gland.

— *Compassion* is the best tonic for your eyes.

There are many benefits that a virtuous man can have. Virtues are electric energy proceeding from the Inner Core. They give health, beauty, energy, and vigilance.

Money cannot buy virtues; wealth cannot replace them. But virtues can bring prosperity and abundance and make man enjoy them and use them as a blessing for others. In the not too distant future, the physician will prescribe virtues to his patients and minimize the use of chemicals and even surgery.

Mental conditions and emotional states affect the body, changing its chemistry for good or for bad. For example:

1. Confusion creates poison in our body. It prevents the free flow of the glands. Secretions become abnormal. There is congestion between the organs and glands. The person has a bad odor. It is the poison that makes man lethargic, numb, and unresponsive to the call of responsibility and service.

Confusion blocks the mind, and this affects the energy transmission from higher sources. Energies are polluted when they pass through a confused mind.

2. Fear is very bad for the hair glands. Fear accumulates and creates a sediment which creeps into the hair roots and kills them. There is an occult connection between the hair and kindness. One wonders if the medical profession knows about it.

The adrenals are distorted under the pressure of fear, and they inject a large quantity of adrenaline into the blood.

3. Anger absorbs the adrenaline into the etheric centers, which burns the etheric substance nourishing the hair and teeth. Of course, this happens slowly, and the cause and effect are cumulative and relative to the intensity of the fear and anger.

4. Lies distort the vision. A dishonest act weakens the power of vision to a certain degree. Many physicians may argue about this. Of course, this does not mean that those who have bad sight lied or were dishonest; there are many causes of bad eyesight, but one of the causes which follows us life after life is our accumulated lies and dishonesty.

One can test the power of his eyesight on many occasions and prove or disprove the above statement.

Beauty strengthens the eyesight. We must try to find beauty in form and enjoy looking at it. Ugly things reduce the power of vision. Also, it is important to know that "looks" charged with hatred, jealousy, revenge, and ugly motives waste our precious psychic energy.

It is an occult fact that the eyes transfer a great amount of energy into the whole nervous system. It is also true that the eyes waste a great amount of energy by looking at things which they are not supposed to see. When our senses are forced to come in contact with ugliness in its various forms, they are considerably weakened. That is why we are told that beauty is a great healer. Harmony is a great healer. Each fragrance of the flowers and trees and herbs has a healing quality.

Taste is refined when one eats things that are pure, delicious, and tasty. Touch is refined when one touches things that give him pure joy.

The date is approaching when we will try to find the secrets of self-healing.

We translate things according to the level we are on the scale of beingness. First we translate things according to what we know. If it does not agree with our knowledge, we reject it. People fool themselves with the factor of agreement. If someone says something that agrees with what we *know*, then he is speaking the truth; he is a great man. This is our logic.

You should not look for agreement but for breakthrough. It may be that you do not accept a great truth because it does not agree with your illusions. Thus, do not be a measure or a judge but an observer, thinker, searcher. The things that you have never heard may bring you to a new phase of unfoldment.

Often we must realize that the greatest wisdom or the greatest knowledge that we have is like a reflection of the sun in a broken bottle. Our knowledge is what our mind can understand.

Imagine a fish deep under the ocean and a big ship on the surface. The reflection or the shadow of the ship is the knowledge of the fish. The greatest thinker on the earth is not better than the fish, if once you consider Space and Infinity and the limitations of our brain.

Initiation is the process to make the human soul think and observe without the limitation of the brain or the mind. It is then that there is the possibility of a breakthrough — to see the shadows of things on a higher level.

Your knowledge is your reaction and response to the impulses and impressions of your brain. When the level of your responses, reactions, and mechanism of impressions changes, your knowledge changes.

Real truth is the line of a persistent striving toward the unknown.

The average man's knowledge is a teddy bear with which he plays and does things. When he grows, he buys different toys...until he becomes a soul. When he becomes a soul, he first tries to wash out all that he accumulated throughout centuries while he was identified with the mind. Then he thinks freely, without limiting himself to the impressions of his lower bodies. This is how he thinks.

This is why beingness is you. Knowledge is your teddy bear. Knowledge is as valuable as it makes you realize that you should search for something more than knowledge.

In the process of beingness, you are going toward your True Self; in the process of knowing, you are running after your own tail. It is not that your tail is unimportant, but you must not be bound to your tail.

We can see the evidence of this in our contemporary life. Why, with all these scientists, professors, inventors, and learned men, are we on the edge of the abyss? Instead of spending our time, energy, and money to create beingness, to develop virtues, to bring unity and transformation, we dumped most of our money, energy, and time into building tools of destruction and poison. If this is where our knowledge has led us, should we have faith in our knowledge? What a man knows is not as important as what he is.

Beingness is the process of spiritualization, and wisdom is in beingness not in knowingness. When knowledge does not change into wisdom, it becomes destructive. Knowing this, "God" threw Adam out of the garden to save the garden from Adam's knowledge.

Dark forces can transfer knowledge to you to retard your evolution. All knowledge that increases your vanity, your pride, your control over others, and leads you to destructive actions is a knowledge imparted to you or inspired in you by dark forces.

When a man or a book becomes an authority and the last word of knowledge, beware of that man or that book. It is going to prepare you for another cycle of dark ages.

Any time knowledge becomes the authority, it limits your expansion. Expansion is more important than knowledge.

Initiation is not a process of gaining knowledge but of breaking limitations.

Beauty, Goodness, and Truth live together, and any one of them dies without the other. If you have Truth but not Goodness and Beauty, that Truth is for your own destruction.

Beauty does not even exist without Goodness and Truth. Goodness cannot live and operate if it is not based on Beauty and Truth. This formula can be used in politics, education, philosophy, arts, science, religion, and economics. How often do we defeat our own interests in not being inspired by these three factors — Beauty, Goodness, and Truth.

One of my Teachers used to say that the mystery of the Almighty One has three gates, but one door. One day I went to his room and asked why there were three gates and one door.

"Well," he said, "that is the mystery."

And after a few minutes of silence, he smiled and said, "If you pass these three gates, you become the door itself."

I remember one day a dean of a private college took me to his room and said, "I will show you a painting I just bought."

We went to the entrance of the great hall, and on the wall he showed me a modern painting.

"What is this?" I asked.

"This is great art."

"Where is the beauty in it?"

"Beauty?"

"Yes."

"Well...."

"Who painted it?"

"A great artist brought buckets of paint, put the canvas on the wall and, dipping his brushes in the buckets, sprayed the paint over the canvas...."

"My grandmother could do a better job. How much did you pay for it?"

"Three thousand dollars."

"There is chaos in this painting. There is no beauty in it. There is no goodness in it. There is no truth in it. There is no geometry, no harmony, no rhythm, no future, no purpose, no mystery. No art exists without these things.... Goodness does not exist without Truth. What will be the value of my goodness if I come to you with a gift, but with wrong motives and intentions?"

You can see ugliness in that action.

These three principles go together because they are the component parts of your Essence, and your Essence cannot operate except in completeness. If your True Self is in action, It radiates Beauty, Goodness, and Truth, and no one can reach his own Essence unless he lives a life of Beauty, Goodness, and Truth.

These are the three gates leading to the door of Cosmos, to your Self.

In a deeper understanding, virtues are the rays coming from your Real Self. Your Real Self radiates twelve beams of light, and as your Self radiates out, you become a man or a woman of virtue.

If you exercise and develop these virtues, you enter the path of health and happiness.

Solemnity

Solemnity means that always, in every minute, you are living under the watchful presence of your Inner Divinity, in the presence of your highest vision, in the presence of your spiritual commitment; that your actions, emotions, thoughts, and motives are in harmony with your vision, with your Inner Divinity, with your spiritual commitment.

When you are going to visit a king or a great president, you dress properly, you speak properly, you behave properly. But remember that there is the presence of the Almighty Power within you; how much more solemn must you be in the presence of your Inner Divinity?

Solemnity releases bliss, joy, ecstasy, and sacrificial urges and evokes dedication.

How can you develop solemnity? First have a great vision, a great cause to which you dedicate your life. Respect yourself and make yourself worthy of respect. Do not let the cause which you are presenting suffer because of your limitations or shortcomings. You are presenting a cause, a great vision. You must be careful that you do not hurt your cause or vision by living a cheap life.

Suppose a man came here and said, "I am representing Christ, the Hierarchy." And the next day you find him drunk in a whorehouse or you find him lying, stealing, and cheating. What do you think about him? He is not presenting the cause for which he says he stands. He is not solemn, and because of that he becomes an obstacle between Christ or the Hierarchy and humanity.

If you are representing the Hierarchy, you must live a life in which the beauty and power of the Hierarchy is reflected. If I am sending you as a messenger and you are not representing my honor, prestige, and reputation in your behavior and words, you are hurting me; you are failing in your mission. You are misrepresenting me and creating confusion in the lives of others.

The greatest test of a noble man is solemnity.

A solemn man has a magnetic aura, peace, and joy, and he is in tune with his Inner Divinity.

The New Age disciple must live according to the demands of the New Age. Do not talk about sacred things if you are living a bad life.

They came and asked Ananda, the beloved disciple of Buddha, "What is the greatness of Buddha?"

He answered, "Whatever He tells the others to do, He also does. He lives in the Light, which He tries to spread all over the world."

A solemn man stands for a great cause, vision, idea. Through solemnity he brings the influence of his Inner Divinity into manifestation.

Solemnity means to stand in the grandeur of the cause and of our vision, in all our actions, responses, thoughts, and words and reflect the grandeur of the Almighty Presence in Whom we are living, moving, and having our being. It is an ability to live in the presence of God every minute.

Each constellation inspires a virtue in you through the twelve petals of your heart center. As you travel from one sign to another in the Zodiac, the corresponding virtue receives energy, stimulation, and increases its potency in your life. As you receive more energy from the signs of the Zodiac, your heart petals unfold more and more, and you become a distributor of zodiacal energies through the way you live.[1]

In each sign you express the corresponding virtue, until in all signs all your virtues reach their full blooming. That is how a man reaches mastery.

Knowledge of many things does not help because it is a way of accumulating things from outside. But virtues are emanations of your beingness. They are signs of your spiritual unfoldment. They are the radioactivity of the real man within your form.

---

1. For the particular virtues see *Symphony of the Zodiac*, and *The Flame of the Heart.*

If you know many things and if your life is not changed through the assimilation of knowledge, you become like a donkey carrying bags of gold. You have great treasures in you, but you have no way to use and transform your life through them.

Harmlessness

We must exercise total harmlessness in our thoughts, imagination, words, feelings, deeds, and in all our relationships. Harmlessness is the ability to live a life of inspiration for others, a life of beauty, a life of compassion, and a life of striving toward perfection.

A harmless person never creates a blockage on the path of the spiritual progress of any life in any form. In addition, a harmless person is very active to prevent damage done to others by irresponsible people. A harmless person stands against darkness, ignorance, and slavery and protects light and freedom.

We hurt people because of our so-called love. To be harmless means

1. To be beautiful and full of actions charged with goodness and truth
2. To be full of goodness, through beauty and truth
3. To live the truth, through beauty and goodness

When you separate these three in your thoughts, relationships, and actions, you become a harmful person.

No one can progress on the Path if he is not harmless because any harmful act becomes a hindrance on his Path and prevents him from proceeding onward.

It is observed that those who try to hurt people are full of guilt feelings. Their past is full of crimes. They try to hurt people to hide their face from the light of their conscience. But they open themselves to the attack of various diseases. Purity of conscience leads us to the Plane of Intuition.

We must transcend the mental plane, and knowledge acquired through the mental plane, and penetrate into the Intuitional Plane where the "living waters" exist. Once Christ said, "If you drink the water that I will bring you, you will never thirst again."

To thirst means to need knowledge. Living water is the symbol of Intuition. Once we have Intuition, we will never need knowledge acquired through the mind. "The white horse" that will bring Christ to the people is also the symbol of Intuition, which means we can reach Him through Intuition.

Patience

Patience is steadiness of labor to reach a goal. It is a joyful perseverance to actualize your innermost Self.

People translate patience as a form of waiting or a prolonged expectation, whereas patience is a steady effort to achieve. In patience man uses all available forces to assist his effort.

Steadfastness and perseverance are virtues exercised by the personality to achieve mundane success. Patience is steady mastery over personality and earthly conditions, through Self-actualization. Without patience, steadfastness and perseverance do not last long. Patience supplies the energy and endurance to man.

Patience is not an attitude or a state of consciousness but a steady energy flow from the Core of the human being. It is this flow of energy that makes a man steady and inspires him to persist in his labor. Patience is related not to time but to Space. It inspires man with the vision of Infinity. Once man makes a contact with the vision of Infinity, the energy flow of patience commences.

Patience is like a thread of light which relates not only the persevering efforts of weeks, months, or years but also of lives. On the golden thread of patience, man locates his most precious pearls of achievement.

Patience is always related to self-discipline. Without self-discipline, patience cannot manifest.

Patience puts man into action. The moments of waiting, for a patient man, are the moments of the most intense efforts to make a breakthrough. The moments of expectation of a patient man are moments recharged by the vision of the future.

Patience is the royal path upon which walk all victorious sons of Light. Patience is the ability to see that you are the Changeless One in all changes; the ability to see that you have traversed time and you stand as *duration* within the cycles of the past, present, and future; the ability to cooperate with the laws of Nature. Patience is inspired by the vision of spiritual destiny.

Faith, knowledge, self-control, and patience form the cross of life upon which the spirit of resurrection will grow its wings.

The flow of the energy of patience increases as it meets with difficulties and problems. In one of the centers where I used to study, there was a class which was called, "The Exercise of Patience." In this class we used to untangle a knot of fine threads. Sometimes it would take months to untangle the bunch of threads given to us. At first I thought it was the best way to waste time and create irritation. Then slowly I loved it to such a degree that I used to dream about it all night.

Once the graduating students received a question, "What was the most prevalent idea that you had at the time of your labor to untangle the thread?" We had one week to answer the question, but we were warned not to discuss the matter among ourselves.

It was on the last day of the class that my brain received an answer in a flash. I wrote on the paper, "The prevalent idea in my mind was the continuity of the one thread through the twisted mess." I gave my paper to the Teacher and went out of the class.

For some time we did not receive any evaluation. But through all my daily work, feelings, and thoughts, there was one *thread* which was permanently making its presence felt — "Was I correct about my answer?"

A month later we were preparing to depart from the center. The Teacher came, put his hand on my shoulder, and smiled. I smiled back. Then after a long silence he said, "I hope you know what you wrote on your paper. …Yes, life is an entangled thread, from beginning to Infinity, from Infinity to the point of beginning. We must try to untangle the thread, knowing that it is the One Thread and each success is a release of joy…and those who succeed we call Masters of life. …And that is what patience is. Goodbye, until we see you again…."

I looked into his eyes, and I did not have one word to tell him. I went to pack my blankets on the horse with tears in my eyes.

On my whole journey one word was continuously echoing in my mind: "Again. …Until we see you *again*…."

It dawned in my mind that this "again" was a knot on the invisible thread of patience. On the horse I thought, "Life is a thread, an entangled one. From the beginning…yes…we are the threads…come on, horse…life is a thread…go straight to that mountain…and then we will see where to go. …But do not worry, I have a part of the thread in my hand. …We will find the way with patience…."

Sincerity

In all your expressions, in your actions and reactions, in your words, in your thoughts and behaviors, you are going to be an example of sincerity.

Sincerity does not tolerate lies, pretensions, masks, or cover-ups. Sincerity is the ability to take away all masks from your nature and reveal your true face. Take the clown away and let others see exactly what you are.

Sincerity means to be as you are in reality.

If you are a sincere person, another stream of creative force is coming from the depth of your Inner Divinity and enriching and glorifying your life from your inner resources. People feel you more than hear you.

You say a few words, and you electrify them because you have electricity. You can talk for ten hours, and the people are not moved because you lack electricity. Electricity is the manifestation of your True Self, your Higher Self, manifesting through your life and making it magnetic and electrically charged.

Gratitude

Gratitude is an expression of thankfulness. A disciple is a man of gratitude. He says, "Thank you, Lord, for the beauty of Nature, for the beauty of my friends, students, and teachers. Thank you, Lord, for my sufferings and hardship and pains. Thank you for the stars, oceans, and rivers." And to prove his gratitude he lives a sacrificial life, a life of giving, a life of selflessness, and tries to give back all the blessings that life gave to him.

Gratitude opens your heart center. Many boys and girls say, "Mother, you are old. Father, I do not like you any more." That is your mother. Say, "Thank you, Mother, for keeping me nine months with you; for taking care of me; for crying for me." We must give our gratitude to our parents, brothers, sisters, teachers, and friends.

Christ said, "I will not forget the one who gave a cup of water to a stranger in My name."

Through gratitude you add another color or note to your aura, and thus you slowly build your seamless robe.

Gratitude is one of the sources of happiness and joy. People make themselves unhappy by feeling self-pity and by thinking that life is not paying back to them what they expected from life. They overlook all those blessings that are around them and live blindfolded by their own self-pity. They see in everything an unfriendly face; they expect people to adore them, to bow down to them. They expect sunny days always, and no matter what they have, what is done for them, they remain ungrateful.

Ingratitude makes the substance of joy evaporate and brings gloom and unhappiness. Ingratitude toward life and others creates negative polarity and rejects beneficent forces.

Trust creates joy, and ungrateful people cannot be trusted because ingratitude is a sign that the subject has no stability nor a sense of standards in his heart.

Gratitude is an appreciation of trust, a demonstration of faith, an appreciation of justice and righteousness. Ingratitude reveals also that the subject is expecting from life more than his own worth. He wants a harvest without the labor of sowing. Ingratitude reveals that the subject never developed the sense of value to appreciate life as a whole.

Gratitude is a great source of joy, and everyone can develop this virtue by trying to appreciate life and by finding out how life presents to him great gifts.

Simplicity

Do not let yourself fall into complications: complicated involvements, thoughts, words, and lectures; complicated relationships, conversations, and monkey business. Simplify yourself as much as you can.

Dress simply, eat simply, live simply, think simply, speak simply. Simplicity does not mean cheapness. Simplicity adds another color to your aura, another note, which makes it more radioactive and magnetic.

As virtues increase in your life, you become more your True Self.

Striving

Striving means — Don't give up. Improve yourself continuously. If at any time you think you are perfect or you have reached your last levels of the development, you turn into a corpse.

God means progress. Those who are worshippers of God must be progressive in their development and unfoldment.

Perfection means a striving for continuous improvement. There is not a stage in all the Cosmos which you can reach and say, *I am perfect.* If you think you are perfect, you are blind because Infinity is our path and God is Infinity, limitlessness, and continuous expansion.

Striving is the urge of your Inner Divinity to surpass your level of existence. This will add another color and beauty and note to your aura, and you will strive more and more in spite of accumulating difficulties in your life.

Striving is the release of your inner Self. When your inner Self gradually releases Itself, you feel the urge to go toward greater heights on the path of perfection, trying to overcome all hindrances within you. It is the inner Core, the Self, the real you which is going to master the vehicles. You grow from inside to outside.

People try to grow from outside to inside. This is wrong. Real growth starts from the center of your Real Self and blooms out. This is safe progress because the higher light of the Self slowly penetrates from the higher to the lower bodies, giving the lower bodies a chance to prepare themselves to receive higher energies and adapt themselves to those frequencies. Thus all your system is flooded by the light of the inner Core. This is psychic energy, which means the energy of the soul.

Courage

You must develop courage. Courage means to jump over obstacles, face dangers, and live a dangerous life. When you meet hindrances, do not give up. Overcome them by the power of your courage.

Courage means not to identify with your personality. Identify with your True Self. When you are identified with your True Self, nothing is impossible. Courage is the ability to make impossible things possible.

"Be courageous; I overcometh the world," said Christ.

If you are a personality, you would *like* to do it; but if you are a soul, you *can* do it.

Courage overcomes the obstacles coming from beloved ones and enemies. With courage you overcome illusions, glamors, inertia, vanity, financial conditions, and health.

When you are on the path of perfection, everything that opposes you increases your wisdom, energy, ingenuity, and power. You bless the opportunities, complications, and hindrances because you realize that they make you progress and grow faster than with easy conditions.

Courage is a great transformer.

We never grow if we do not confront obstacles or hardships.

One of the games of life is to create obstacles. All creation and manifestation is an obstacle put there for the spirit to overcome.

Growth only exists when there are obstacles and you conquer those obstacles by courage. If there are no obstacles, there is nothing to conquer. If there are no difficulties, life is so uninteresting. It is the difficulties that temper the spirit and make it invincible.

Everything is a limitation so that you exercise your courage to destroy limitations and release your Self. This is your game — physical limitations, emotional limitations, mental limitations — and the labor to overcome these limitations is called courage, which eventually makes you a liberated soul.

Then you must exercise more courage to break the ring-pass-not of the planet, the solar system, and the galaxy...to fly toward Cosmos. Who knows what obstacles God has prepared for us in Cosmos!

Courage gives your aura greater beauty. Courage makes your aura palpitate with magnificent rhythm and color.

Fearlessness

What are you afraid of? A person can perform miracles only if he is fearless, which means only when he is ready to sacrifice all that he has and is for the Common Good.

If he is fearful, the spirit cannot work through him because he is under the control of his personality interests. Personality interests and spiritual interests cannot grow with each other. The personality must disappear in the interest of the spirit, if one wants to be successful.

A fearless person can stand for principles and challenge people to stand for principles.

Fearlessness is neither stupidity nor foolishness. Fearlessness is a state in which you are identified with your spirit and have wisdom and knowledge. A fearless person does not throw himself into Niagara Falls or do things that make people hate the cause he is presenting to humanity.

Fearlessness is the ability to stand identified with your immortal Self. A man in this stage knows that nothing can hurt him if he lives for the Plan of God. When you become fearless, you slowly become your True Self, who is called the Fearless One.

Nothing deeply constructive is done in life without fearlessness.

In all the great people in the world — great servers, inventors, and leaders — fearlessness was a star shining on their foreheads. They have said that only a decision made in a moment of fearlessness brought them victory.

A fearless man sometimes strikes like lightning to pave the way for Freedom, Beauty, Goodness, and Truth. He is merciless when he confronts obstacles. But he destroys only to build a new mansion.

Fearlessness adds a magnificent radioactivity in the aura of the man. It adds a new note to the symphony in process of building.

When teachers tell us to be fearless or not to fear, they are telling us not to act against the Law of Love and Compassion, not to break the Law of Justice. Fearlessness is impossible when a man continuously violates the laws and principles of Nature and lives a life harmful to others.

Fear is generated within us if we do not meet our tasks and responsibilities or waste our time and energy trying to achieve non-essentials. Fearlessness needs a life of purity, harmlessness, courage, labor, and daring, or else our fearlessness will be a sign of insanity.

Fear is the warning that we did something wrong in the past. Sometimes fear itself is the punishment because a fearful person poisons himself and pays heavily for his violations. Fear is also generated when a person experiences ingratitude because ingratitude is a great violation of trust.

Fearlessness translates the focus of life into the domain of Beauty, Goodness, Righteousness, Joy, and Freedom.

A righteous man is fearless because righteousness is a focus of consciousness on a higher plane, and from such a high plane the energy flows into his nervous system and aura and gives him strength, the power of endurance, and stability in confusing conditions. An unrighteous man is a weak man because his consciousness draws the nourishment of the body from contaminated sources in his nature.

This is why when one acts against his heart and against his conscience, he has fears. Even his imagination produces certain dramas of fear.

Many people kill themselves by continuous fear in following a path of injustice and unrighteousness. Fear can be eliminated by raising the consciousness to a level where righteousness and justice exist. When one touches such a level, the energy begins to flow and wipe out fear and its consequences.

Exercises to Overcome Fear

I. *Exercise*

You can overcome fear by meditating daily upon the following "words of power." You may meditate for fifteen to twenty minutes, or you can write a few pages or an article daily on each one of them. In this way your positive thoughts will eliminate the thoughts of fear.

A. "There is no fear in love. Perfect love casts out all fear."

B. "Let reality govern my every thought, and truth be the master of my life."

C. "Be courageous for I overcometh the world," said Christ.

D. "Verily, there was never a time when I was not, nor you, nor these rulers of men; nor shall come a time when we shall all cease to be."

E. "Avira Virma Yeti" (O, Self Revealing One, Reveal Thyself in me.)

F. The Great Invocation

> From the point of Light within the Mind of God
> Let light stream forth into the minds of men.
> Let Light descend on Earth.
>
> From the point of Love within the Heart of God
> Let love stream forth into the hearts of men.
> May Christ return to Earth.
>
> From the centre where the Will of God is known
> Let purpose guide the little wills of men —
> The purpose which the Masters know and serve.
>
> From the centre which we call the race of men
> Let the Plan of Love and Light work out
> And may it seal the door where evil dwells.
>
> Let Light and Love and Power restore the Plan on Earth.

G. "The Indweller of the body is never born, nor does It die. It is not true that, having no existence, It comes into being; nor having been in existence, It again ceases to be. It is the unborn, the eternal, the changeless, the Self. It cannot be killed, even if the body is slain."

II. Exercise

A. Sit and be calm. Close your eyes, and focus your mind in your head. Hold one minute of silence.

B. Think about a strong fear which is bothering you. Make a symbol of your fear. Take your time and try to create a symbol which represents your fear.

C. Visualize a five-pointed star, six inches away from your forehead. Try to visualize a golden flame at the center of the star.

D. Direct that flame to the symbol and burn it in its entirety.

E. Repeat this seven times; each time recreate the symbol and burn it totally. In so doing, you will dissipate the formation of many kinds of fears in the etheric, astral, and mental planes.

III. *Exercise*

Visualize your symbol of fear, and gradually change it into a symbol of joy and beauty.

This way it is possible that the accumulated energy of fear will transform itself into a constructive energy. For example, take the coffin as a symbol of death, and change it into a life-saving boat. When you change your symbol, you change the flow of energy into your system. You must work hard enough to change your symbol so that the new symbol absorbs all your attention.

Once you reach that stage, you will feel the help of your Inner Guide. He stands for fearlessness, and any attempt by you to overcome fear creates a contact with It.

You can overcome certain fears by dramatizing them as happening and observing the event as it happens. First observe your emotional reactions, then your thoughts. Do it as many times as you can until your fear has evaporated.

Some people are afraid to be successful. See yourself as a great success, and do it again and again with more detail until you realize that fear evaporates, if you face it courageously and exhaust its force.

In these exercises do not look for solutions; only try to reach the realization of fearlessness. This is not an analysis of fear but a direct process of the destruction of fear.

These exercises create psychological antidotes for fear.

IV. *Exercise*

Try to see clearly the object of your fear, and in your visualization draw an orange triangle above your head. Then distinctly see the three points of the triangle. The top one is crimson red. The right one is blue. The left one is violet.

Let three lights from the three points come and focus themselves in front of your forehead, six inches away from your body, and from there hit the object of your fear, or the problem of your fear. Imagine the problem melting away and disappearing into the air.

Such an energy carries a destructive power for fearful thoughtforms, and sometimes you feel an immediate release if you do it right. There are many such thoughtforms which hang around us and sap our energy or obscure our vision.

We are told that fear is related to ignorance. This is true. But ignorance means not being exactly that which you essentially are. If you are your essential Self, you do not have ignorance and fear.

Responsibility

A man cannot walk toward perfection if he has no sense of responsibility.

Man unfolds when the field of his responsibility expands every day and he feels responsible for his behavior, for his actions, for his writings, for his speech and silence, and for all his relations. On any level he stands responsible. He is responsible to his family members and to those with whom he has any relation, or no relation at all.

We are told that the first sign of an Initiate is a deepening sense of responsibility. It is a sign that man is in contact with his Self, or the Self is increasing Its mastery over the personality.

With the virtue of responsibility, one adds another color to his aura, which makes the aura extremely sensitive to the needs of others.

Love

The greatest attainment is to develop love — universal, Cosmic, all-inclusive love.

Love will complete your aura with the substance of the Cosmic Heart, and you will now walk in the rainbow.

Love will open gates which otherwise would be closed forever. Love will initiate you into the Hall of Understanding and Wisdom. Love will make you harmless and humble.

Love will open a continuous flow of inspiration from higher sources. Love will make you a conqueror of hearts.

When one loves, his enemies become his servants. When one loves, his friends become his co-workers. When one loves, the travelers see the light on their path.

A person is trusted when he has love.

Discrimination

Discrimination means to know what energy you are going to use — where, how, when, why, and in what dosage. Discrimination does not mean to discriminate blacks from whites, or to discriminate according to sex, religion, or race.

Discrimination is the ability to use energy, matter, space, and time at the right moment, with the right person or group, in the right dosage, and with the right motive. Discrimination is the ability to know reality and to choose reality, to choose beauty, to choose light, to choose truth.

Once when I was in the Middle East, I worked with a watchmaker and jeweler. One day he brought fifty stones and spread them in front of me and said, "Find the real precious stones."

I found fifteen precious stones. He examined them and said, "You have no discrimination yet. You have only three real stones. The rest are all artificial."

From that day on I tried to study the real ones, and a day came when I could immediately know which stones were real.

Discrimination is intuitive; it is the result of experience, study, and observation. Try to sense the motive behind the words, expressions, and behaviors.

Lack of discrimination leads us into failure. Discriminate between those who want to go out with you; try to see their intentions. Discriminate between books, teachers, doctors, lawyers, and even food.

When one has soul contact through meditation, the jewels of the virtues increase their radiation and beauty. If you have solar plexus contact, you increase in lower psychic phenomena. Soul contact means precipitation of virtues.

If you are doing right meditation, you must actualize the above mentioned virtues. If you are not increasing in virtues, you are doing something wrong. Wrong meditation leads you to mental and physical confusion.

Right meditation leads you into taking greater responsibilities in the affairs of the world and makes you able to meet the needs *with honesty, with integrity, with beauty, and with courage.*

The Hierarchy is not looking for people who are sleeping in their meditations. They gave the technique of meditation to make people contact their Soul, radiate the twelve virtues of the chalice and the wisdom of the Soul, and manifest them in their practical life so that they become beneficial human beings who can bring changes in the world, wherever they are.

Creativity means to adapt your actions, words, and thoughts to the need of the moment with an inclusive view of the effect of your actions, words, and thoughts on the related field of the need.

Creativity means to reflect Divine harmony and beauty in your life.

When these twelve virtues are exercised and lived, one manifests creative energy, and all his expressions become creative. Creativity transmits healing energy from our love into our vehicles.

72

Healing From a Distance

Healing is achieved by those who strive toward perfection. And those who are preparing themselves for healing must regularly exercise visualization.

If you want to heal people at a distance, visualize a violet beam of light directed to the etheric body of the sick person and focused on the etheric location corresponding to the physical organ.

Let the violet light pour into the etheric atoms and energize or kindle them. Do not focus your attention on the physical counterpart of the etheric body. Let the charged atoms of the etheric body do the job.

Every time you send the energy, send it on the wings of the thought: "Thy will be done" in order not to have karmic involvement with the person.

You can do the same for your own many ailments.

Violet light carries psychic energy and is related to the Seventh Ray, which is the Ray of "organizational power." Any organ, disorganized due to many factors, creates problems. This energy can put the organ into functioning order through its etheric counterpart.

The healer must know how to visualize. Visualization needs practice. The healer must learn how to see forms when he closes his eyes. Also, he must learn how to see colors. He must also develop the power to hold any form in his visualization as long as he wants without letting it be diffused. The same thing applies to colors.

However, often a strong desire to heal people surpasses all such requirements.

But the science of healing must be based on the healer's inner development and achievements and on the experiences gathered from his experiments.

Healing is achieved by those who strive toward perfection. And those who are preparing themselves for healing must regularly exercise visualization.

Visualization is the power through which the creative and reconstructive energies of Nature can scientifically be utilized.

It is important that the healer stand emotionally detached from the sick one and remain without anxieties and worries — as such thoughtforms block the current of the healing energy.

73

The Tools of Love

To build the temple of joy and bliss, we need to use special instruments, and they must always be ready in our hands:

Freedom

Non-criticism

Admiration

Sacrifice

Education

Gratitude

Sense of responsibility.[1]

Seven Tools in Love Relationships

1. Freedom
   a. Find ways to let your mate express his inner light, love, and beauty through his own ways and means.

   b. Do not force your will as to what you think should be done, but encourage the person to do those things that are a part of his vision.

2. Non-criticism

   ...Leave each person to bloom into his own flower, with his own original colors....[2]

   a. Any time you feel critical, replace it with a positive thought. Then find something you like about the person.

1. *The Flame of Beauty, Culture, Love, Joy*, p. 155.
2. *Ibid.*, p. 156.

b. If the person is doing something you feel is wrong, find what positive lesson the person will learn by going through the experience.

3. Admiration
   a. Admire the good deeds of your partner daily.

   ...Admiration is like watering your garden....[3]

Admire good speech and good thought, as with encouragement they will manifest into good deeds. See the highest in your partner and tell your partner about it.

   b. Do not flatter. Select good deeds, actions, words, or thoughts.

4. Sacrifice

   ...In its true meaning, to sacrifice means to destroy within ourselves those limiting forms, feelings, thoughts, and habits which prevent our progress toward deeper joy and understanding....[4]

   a. List these limitations.

   b. Work out a way to dissolve them through love and beauty.

   c. Work on this daily until eliminated.

5. Education
   a. Look in these areas: physical, emotional, mental, spiritual, and see what areas need more education. Work out a way to gain more knowledge.

   b. Work out how higher education in these areas will make you a better partner.

6. Gratitude
   a. Sit with your mate and discuss the things for which you are grateful with each other.

   b. If you are doing this without your mate, ask yourself what you can be grateful for in your partner?

---

3. *Ibid.*
4. *Ibid.*

c. Go through your life together — jobs, living environments, children, in-laws, etc. Discuss things you can be grateful for during the time together.

d. If your mate is not present, do the same procedure as in "b" above.

7. Sense of responsibility

...This is the consciousness of being one with the other. To understand it simply, we can ask ourselves: "Do my words, acts, feelings or thoughts increase the happiness, the joy, the light, and the health of my partner, or decrease them?..."[5]

a. If the answer is decreasing them, work out how to reverse the situation.

b. If the answer is some decreasing, take words first, then acts, then feelings, then thoughts and find how to turn them around to the opposite.

c. Work out ways to increase the happiness, joy, light, and health of your partner.

"...Do I know that everything good for my partner is good for me, too?..."[6]

Work out ways where each partner can see that the other gets treatment as good as what he provides for his own self.

"...Do I know that I will pay the cost for all those words, deeds, feelings, and thoughts that retard or prevent the progress of my mate?..."[7]

a. Reverse all words, deeds, or thoughts that have retarded your mate's progress.

b. Work out deeds you could do that would more than make up for what you have done to retard his progress.

c. Follow the same formula for all major people in your life. More than make up for any deeds that retarded others' progress.

---

5. *Ibid.*, p. *157*.
6. *Ibid.*
7. *Ibid.*

d. If the person has passed away, find people with similar characteristics and help them.

"... Do I know that a small seed of evil can grow throughout centuries and block the door of light for myself and for others?"[8]

a. Find any seeds of evil and change them to seeds of love.

b. Confront each one and change it to a seed that will make yourself and others grow.

8. *Ibid.*

74

The Twelve Energies of the Heart

The heart center controls the other six centers in the etheric body. The impulse of an unfolded and purified heart goes through each center and synchronizes and regulates it. When your centers are synchronized and regulated through the rhythm of the heart, the glands and the corresponding organs are regulated.

Physiologically, psychologically, and esoterically, the heart is the central organ in man.

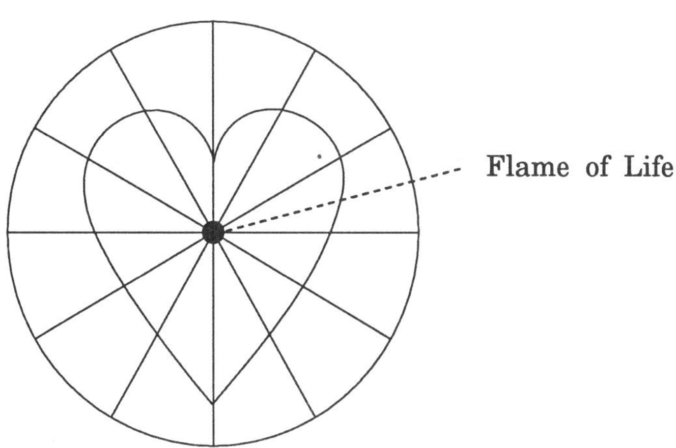

Diagram 74-1 The Heart

There is the heart, and behind it there is an electromagnetic energy field with twelve flames originating from the center of the heart. The center is the foundation of life, originating from the Self, from the Spark. The Transcendental Self and the center of the heart are connected by the silvery thread which in the Ageless Wisdom is called the *life thread.*

The Transcendental Self, in Its turn, is a beam of life emanating from the Cosmic Heart. We have a Global Heart, which is the Hierarchy. We have a Solar

Heart, which is the Heart of the Sun. We have a heart at the center of our galaxy, the Galactic Heart, and another heart is found beyond our galaxy.

Actually, the human heart is connected with these hearts by the silver thread; and when the heart is purified, it registers the events going on in the Global, Solar, Galactic, and Cosmic Hearts. Our heart registers earthquakes, explosions, calamities, and disasters occurring on the earth, in the solar system, and even in the galaxy.

Most of the time man is unaware of these things, but the heart registers them. Such registration affects the electromagnetic center behind the heart, and the heart manifests different rhythms, pains, anguish, and various symptoms of ailments.

The heart also registers great events on global, solar, galactic, and Cosmic planes, for example: when a group of advanced souls passes through an initiation; when Great Ones advance and are admitted into higher planes of Cosmos; when evil is defeated on some plane, or a new plane succeeds in cooperating on a Cosmic scale; when a new light and a new revelation emerge from Cosmic sources. The heart rejoices at these events. The heart registers them, although it is only in rare moments that the brain is aware of the registration of the heart. If a galaxy is in the process of disintegration, the heart registers it. If a new galaxy is in formation, the heart registers it as well.

The heart also records the emotions, thoughts, and plans of our friends. If they are sending benevolent thoughts, the heart rejoices. If they are sending negative thoughts, the heart feels the burden.

So often our moods are direct echoes of thoughts and emotions sent to us. We can uplift people through our pure and best thoughts, or we can cause them pain and suffering through our uncontrolled and wild thoughts and emotions.

We are told that there are seven sacred energies which are passing through the zodiacal signs and through our Sun, bringing to our solar system and our globe a flood of light, love, and power. The human heart is the assimilator of these energies, and if the consciousness of man begins to function on more refined levels, these energies will be used as communication lines — between man and the sources of the energies — through the human heart.

Every organization and every group has its own heart. The heart is a mechanism which receives, assimilates, and transmits life energies to keep the forms in line with the Purpose of life and to reveal the Purpose of life. Each heart translates the same Purpose in different magnitudes, according to the unfoldment and level of the heart.

In the human heart these seven cosmic energies are assimilated and changed into twelve radiations or twelve streams of energy. These are

1. The energy which heals

2. The energy which gives serenity and peace

3. The energy which gives joy and leads us into sacrificial service
4. The energy which gives courage, daring, striving, and patience
5. The energy which gives love, unification, and inclusiveness
6. The energy which causes universalism and synthesis
7. The energy which evokes beauty
8. The energy which creates understanding, timelessness, straight knowledge, and Intuition
9. The energy which records
10. The energy which enables us to receive great inspirations and become creative
11. The energy which transmutes
12. The energy which changes into righteousness and compassion[1]

...Watch children when they fall down or hurt themselves. They run to their mother and put their head on her heart, and they feel peace and security. If someone is in fear, in trouble, confused, or grieving, take his head and embrace it on your heart in silence. Watch what will happen.

I remember a lady who had lost her two daughters. She was in a desperate condition while everyone around her was trying to comfort her with no result. Knowing the power of the heart, I approached her, pulled her head to my heart, and kept it there for a few minutes in silence. When I lifted her head, she opened her eyes and said, "I guess it was God's Will. I feel all right. I think I can overcome my grief. As you were holding my head, I began to think about the continuity of life on other planes and about Infinity...."

I did not answer her but smiled, and she continued, "I knew there was a better way to comfort myself than with pills."

Once we learn how to channel the healing energy of the heart, we become unseen healers, and we heal people on the physical, emotional, and mental planes.

The healing energy of the heart harmonizes the rhythm of the body and creates rhythm and harmony in the functions of the glands through the centers.

The heart center controls the other six centers in the etheric body. The impulse of an unfolded and purified heart goes through each center and synchronizes and

---

1. For further information, please refer to *The Science of Becoming Oneself*, Ch. 12, "Chalice and the Seeds." See also *The Science of Meditation*, Ch. 24, "Illumination."

regulates it. When your centers are synchronized and regulated through the rhythm of the heart, the glands and the corresponding organs are regulated.

Health starts and ends with your heart. When your heart is taken by someone, your whole being is taken. When your heart is broken, your whole being is broken. It is the heart that is the fortress of your being.

At the center of the heart there is a flame. It is the Flame of Life. And it is this Flame that transmutes the energies of the seven streams and changes them into the twelve energies of the heart. These twelve energies are the sources of the twelve most essential minerals of your body, emotions, and mind. Through these minerals the heart repairs, cures, and regenerates the organs.

It is this flame that transmits psychic energy to the man. Psychic energy is the synthesis of the seven Cosmic and twelve heart energies. Psychic energy is the healing energy which cures, enlightens, purifies, regenerates, and puts man in tune with the Will of the Almighty Center of Life.

When the flame of the heart is gone, the degeneration of a person starts and his body, emotions, and thoughts show signs of deterioration. It is the flame of the heart that holds the whole man together in harmony with Cosmos. When the flame is gone, the ability to understand disappears.

The first help for healing must be evoked from the Heart Center of the planet, which in esoteric literature is called the Hierarchy. The Hierarchy is the source of psychic energy, which is the energy that makes all things new and regenerates the whole system of our vehicles, starting from the *consciousness*. The consciousness of man must change before true healing can take place.

Thus, the contact with the Hierarchy must be sought with great striving, labor, and invocation. Once the contact is established, psychic energy infiltrates our system and purifies, strengthens, and transforms it. Many miraculous healings happen at the moment of contact with the Hierarchy.

In case of illness or disease, the first step is to polarize your whole being toward the Hierarchy and try to establish a contact with that great Center of healing energy. The contact can be felt as an electrical energy filling your head, your heart, and your entire physical, emotional, and mental systems. On the physical level, the contact creates warmth, fragrance, light, color, etc. On the emotional plane, it creates profound peace and a feeling of release. On the mental plane, it creates enlightenment and generates a creative force. Enlightenment can reveal the causes of disease and challenge you to correct them; it also reveals the steps to be taken after the healing is accomplished so that the disease will not recur.

Prayers are efforts to contact the Hierarchy. Meditation is an effort to translate contacted energies. Sacrificial service is proof that one has contacted Hierarchy.

The Hierarchy is called the "primary remedy." Future health can only be secured through psychic energy, which is released at the time the man contacts his Soul and the Hierarchy.

The heart has a great quality for healing. The heart center in man has a blue-orange flame which, when it is fully developed, turns into a mechanism of accumulation of Cosmic energies and a mechanism of distribution of these energies into our system, into our environment, and into far-off locations. The formation and blooming of the fire of the heart is carried out through sacrificial service and through exercising spiritual virtues in our lives.

It is in this flame that the received Cosmic energies fuse, and it is in this flame that the expansion of consciousness takes place. The Cosmic energies fuse and gradually form a rainbow-like sphere around the heart and even around the body, extending ten to fifteen feet. This is the sphere of energy which heals, uplifts, transforms, and enlightens people. All of one's words, thoughts, emotions, and actions carry the energy of this sphere to whomever or to whatever it is directed. This energy of the heart senses Cosmic events, and as the flame increases and develops purer colors, the whole sphere of the heart energy merges with the psychic energy in Space.

We are told that Christ, having reached such a state of unfoldment of the heart, could heal people with His touch and with His thoughts. He was able to establish contact with the Cosmic Heart.

It is the state of the hearts all over the world that conditions international events and planetary disturbances or brings great harmony, health, and culture. We are told that this planet is protected by great Hearts. The grouping of these Hearts is called the Hierarchy of the planet. It is this Center that is the source of all healing rays for our physical, emotional, mental disturbances, as well as global disturbances, disorders, or sicknesses. That is why we are told to contact not only our heart, but also the Planetary Heart for healing, enlightening, and transforming our being.

***

The greatest healing process in the future will be the healing of the hearts of people. The heart needs healing. Because of the pressure our society is living under due to the control of illusions and glamors, the heart is left without nourishment and encouragement and thus becomes petrified, and the flame in it almost passes away. With the degeneration of the heart, the flame is not capable of sustaining the vitality of the bodies and aura, and thus various germs and sicknesses devastate the human body.

When the heart is healed and the flame is restored, the flame of the heart will open a new era of health, joy, and great endurance. The healing of the body must start with the healing of the heart. The heart must be purified; the flame must be restored. Once this is accomplished, the healing process will take place.

No one can really heal a sick person permanently if his heart is spiritually dead or polluted by vices. Spiritually dead hearts are very dangerous. They not only contaminate people with destructive emanations, but they become graves for the incarnating human soul for many centuries. To heal a sick heart, you must bring into it love, inclusiveness, purity, joy, courage, the spirit of sacrifice, and forgiveness. These create miraculous changes in the bodies of sick people. Heal the heart and the man will be healed.[2]

2. Reprinted in part from *The Flame of the Heart*, Ch. 2, pp. 27-35, 52-53.

75

The Wisdom of Love Exercise

All wars, all pain, all troubles are due to crystallization. Sometimes, somewhere the flow of energy stops, becomes crystallized, and no longer circulates freely....

...Hatred and jealousy are emotional level crystallizations which block circulation of energy....[1]

1. Review the times when you hated.

2. Go back before that and see when you cared. Pinpoint the time of crystallization where love energy was blocked. Remove the crystallization by putting in more love.

3. Do the same with jealousy.

4. Expand out to your family, groups, nations.

5. See always where the caring was prior to the blockage of love energy. Unblock it by sending more love.

Love must be progressively expanding.[2]

1. Look through your life and see in what areas you need to expand your love so that it exists.

2. Review the past and see where your love did not expand. Work out a way in your mind that you could have taken responsibility and expanded that love.

   Get a sense of there being no end to the love you feel. See your love with no end but going to Infinity in the following areas. Talk about why you love each area and how this could lead to expansion.

---

1. *The Flame of Beauty, Culture, Love, Joy*, p. 136.
2. *Ibid.*, p. 139.

— Love for food and possessions

— Love for a partner

— Love for family

— Love for race, group

— Love for nation

— Love for beauty, culture, friends, teacher, Master

— Love for the Divine in all forms, in every man

— Love for the Supreme Presence in all manifestation

Marriage or love is not only the unity of two bodies. We marry with our hearts if we are dedicated to the same goal....[3]

1. Find the times when your love stopped at unity with a body.

2. See how you could have expanded it to marrying or uniting with the same goal.

3. Find people whom you married with your ideas, thoughts, and visions.

The unconditional nature of love stands behind these beautiful words spoken by Christ, "Greater love hath no man than this, that a man lay down his life for his friends." ...Can you still say, "I love you and I am going to stand by you and help you in any way you may need my help."...[4]

1. In your mind say this to the people who have blackened your name, slandered your reputation, or made life difficult for you.

2. See the beauty in them beneath any personality reaction, and have compassion for them.

Love performed without a sense of responsibility leads to sorrow and suffering. Responsibility means that you will sustain unity once you have created it and work for the progressive advancement of that unity toward more love, more light, and more life. Responsibility teaches you that other people's failures and

3. *Ibid.*, p. 140.
4. *Ibid.*, p. 144.

sorrows are yours, and that you must try to eliminate them physically, emotionally, and mentally with freedom and joy, as if they were yours.[5]

1. Look at your relationships and see the ones in which you have created unity. Decide how to sustain them.

2. Find out how to surpass the unity toward more light and love after you have learned how to sustain this unity with consistency.

3. Look at your relationships — family, group, nation, humanity — and view their failures and sorrows.

    a. Find out how you could try to eliminate these failures and sorrows physically, emotionally, and mentally with freedom and joy as though they were yours.

    b. Do these one at a time until you have a realization of the whole.

4. Each day work out a way to do something that is based on your loving understanding.

---

5. Ibid., p. 145.

76

The Heart and Healing

No one can stay healthy under heavy labor if the heart does not continually provide energy and stand as a shield against dark attacks.

The heart center in the etheric body is the depository of psychic energy.[1]

Psychic energy is the cure for all ailments. No virus, microbe, germ, decay, or petrification can stand against the fire of psychic energy once it is in operation.

It is important to have an unfolding heart center which, through its twelve petals, distributes psychic energy throughout the body. Psychic energy is directed to the needed locations of the body through thinking and visualization.

The heart center is a bridge or communication line between the physical and invisible worlds.

The etheric heart center is the dynamic center in the second etheric sphere.[2] The second etheric sphere is the sphere of light emanating from the Sun. The etheric heart center is the distributor of that light into the body. The heart not only distributes blood to every part of the body but also light. Blood is charged with light and psychic energy, which are the cures for all ailments.

Every action taken against light damages the petals of the heart which are devices for spreading the light.

The heart center within the second etheric sphere is sensitive to the impressions coming from all over the world, just as the Second Cosmic Ether is a very sensitive part of the etheric body of the planet which makes the light of the Sun available to the earth.

There is no life in Nature without light. This is also true for every human being. If the heart center does not pump light into the physical body, the body slowly disintegrates.

On the mirror of the sphere of the second ether is reflected the physical body of a person in its entirety.

---

1. See also *A Commentary on Psychic Energy*, especially pp. 40-51, and *The Flame of the Heart*.
2. Note: The etheric body has four levels. The lowest one, the fourth, is related to color. The third is related to sound. The second, to light. The first, to life or electricity.

As the physical heart is the central organ for the body, so is the heart center in the etheric body, which is the prototype and blueprint of the light system of the physical body.

The Teaching says that the heart center accumulates energies from Space if a person is dedicated to the service of humanity in physical and mental labor.

We are told that solemnity, meditation, aspirations, and prayers strengthen the heart center and make it not only a distributor of light and psychic energy but also a shield for the disciple. No one can stay healthy under heavy labor if the heart does not continually provide energy and stand as a shield against dark attacks.

On the path of transformation one must develop his heart. The heart is the contact point with the Purpose of life. It is possible that your intellect will not yet be able to translate the subtle contacts of your heart, but as you develop your heart you will find direction inspired by the Purpose of life.

A cultivated heart gradually clears the intellect, expands the consciousness, and enables one to see the divine Plan operating to manifest the Purpose. Without sensing the Plan and feeling the direction of the Purpose, one is a lost ship on the ocean, no matter how much information he has in his mind and what position he holds in society.

A cultivated heart is stronger than your intellect. It controls your actions, your emotional responses, your thoughts, and especially your motives. A cultivated heart lives and exists for the good of all.

The heart is the anchorage point of the silver thread. This thread is the communication line between you and your Teacher. This thread slowly extends to your Teacher as your dedication and sacrificial service for the Teaching increase. Every time you register the call of your Teacher, the building of the thread takes place, and eventually it becomes a sensitive communication line between His heart and yours.

We are told that through this communication line the wisdom and psychic energy of your Teacher reach you and flood your consciousness.

It is through this thread that man lives a purposeful and goal-fitting life. Once you build this thread, you know what to do in your life. You know what to read, what to listen to, what kind of discipline you need. The thread keeps you always in line, no matter what the conditions are in your life.

A cultivated heart becomes the treasury of the wisdom of your Teacher. You feel your heart embracing all living manifestations of life. The bliss and joy of your Teacher slowly flow into your nerves, and your life becomes creative.

The silver thread also builds your future shield for supernatural battles, for righteousness and unity.

The spiritual Self is located in the heart, like a spark of a giant flame. As your heart is developed, this spark awakens and turns into a flame. This is your future Self in the process of formation.

In some esoteric writings we are told that man is not an individuality until he brings it into existence. The human soul, the spiritual Self, must come into being piece by piece, and as it develops and comes into existence it enters into its conscious immortality. The spiritual Self must come into existence if man wants to be conscious of the Path upon which he is traveling throughout ages.

Continuity of consciousness is based upon the formation of the spiritual Self and upon the silver thread.

Immortality is not granted to you by Nature; you are going to attain it by your own striving and labor. The flame of immortality is within your heart. That flame is your individuality, your True Self.

> *... Each consummation, each union, each great cosmic unification is achieved through the flame of the heart....*[3]

Your heart is the only judge, accumulator and guardian of the precious spiritual energies. All spiritual centers depend on the heart. Not one of those who strive with the heart will be forgotten.

The heart referred to here is not our physical heart but the etheric heart center behind the heart, which has twelve flames, twelve fiery petals. It is located ten to twelve inches behind our back. The colors of the flames are golden when fully open.

When the heart center is in its infancy, it is like a white-colored bud, with a blue nucleus of light at the center. As the heart develops, the petals slowly turn a golden color and the white totally disappears.

The heart center receives Cosmic impressions, and by its life thread it is linked to the Magnet of Life, or the Cosmic Magnet. Each petal in the heart is connected with the Cosmic Magnet, and as it opens and unfolds, the direction of the Cosmic Magnet is gradually sensed and followed by the heart.

The life of all the cells of the body, the life of all atoms of the emotional and mental bodies, is provided by the heart, which is the focal point of the life energy coming from the Cosmic Magnet.

The development of the heart takes centuries. It is comparatively easy to develop one's mind, but the development of the heart is a slow and painful process.

It is also possible that one may develop his heart in many incarnations and then close it by living a life against Beauty, Goodness, and Truth. Sometimes a man can in one moment destroy his heart which was built over centuries and make himself the cave of dark forces. Sometimes our formal education, position, power, and reputation may close the petals of our heart center.

---

3. Agni Yoga Society, *Heart*, para. 1.

Irritation and close contact with people who are in constant fear and hatred close the petals of the heart. Every act against justice, against love and beauty is a deathblow on our heart center.

This flower was worshipped throughout centuries as the Chalice of life.

There are many things that are harmful to the heart.

1. Not eliminating certain desires, imaginations, and dreams is harmful to the heart.

2. Activities, words, and thoughts based on selfish interests are harmful to the heart.

3. Sexual license dries up the heart and wastes psychic energy.

4. Greed is very dangerous for the heart center. Those who have closed heart centers are greedy people, and they can commit any kind of crime to satisfy their greed. Working on the line of generosity and developing the spirit of giving and helping eventually cures the diseases of greed.

5. Hallucinogenic drugs are poisonous to the heart. Liquor, tobacco, and marijuana close the petals of the heart.

6. Indifference to the needs of others is a sickness of the heart. Indifference toward beauty, progress, and service is called "the killer of the heart."

How to develop the heart? These are simple steps which gradually feed the heart and help it bloom.

1. Try to have short visits with sick people and take them flowers and different gifts. Talk with them; give them courage; speak about the future, about victory, and about beauty. There is a special wisdom that grows in our heart as we visit sick people and give them hope and joy.

2. Be very respectful and loving toward old people. Sometimes they need your help, your smile, your presence.

Sometimes great Teachers instruct their disciples to serve old people and in such service collect wisdom and have deeper understanding about life. Such relations develop the heart center of the disciples and make them ready for future great service.

Higher responsibilities are given to us when we prove that we have heart and we care for people.

It is interesting that on earth higher positions are given to those who prove that they have knowledge and mind. But in subjective realms of life, higher positions can be taken only through developing our heart.

The structure of a family, group, or nation is permanent if it is built on the foundation of the heart. The degeneration of nations and families begins when the intellect takes over and the education of the heart is forgotten.

Continuous and perpetual violence and crime shown in our movie theaters and television programs eventually will produce more people with petrified hearts. With the petrification of the heart, one loses his spiritual values and lives a life against his and others' survival.

There was a seventy-five year old woman. She was living alone. One day she went to a retirement home and brought home a man who was ninety-five years of age to live with her. He was a very healthy, beautiful man, but he was suffering in the retirement home. After three months, I saw a great change in the woman's heart quality and wisdom. She told me that she finds great fulfillment in cooking for the man, washing his clothes and taking him to gardens, rivers, and lakes. Such companionship is a rare opportunity to unfold the heart petals.

Those who are entering the spiritual path of beauty and purity must try to "see with their heart, to hear with their heart, to understand with their heart."

3. The next step to develop the heart is to inspire people with hope, courage, and the future and uplift their heart into the light of joy. A disciple is a man who radiates courage, hope, and optimism and inspires victory and joy. As you give more joy, more love, and more hope, your heart petals open more. The "life more abundant" increases in your heart, and its joy and bliss spread into your life.

A disciple, because of his unfolding heart, serves with his money, time, talents, power, and position. All these are tools in his hand for the field of his service.

4. Developing devotion and dedication to a great humanitarian cause unfolds the heart center. Devotion is a process of identification with a great value. Dedication is the process to actualize that value in the world through your deeds and life expressions. Unless a man is dedicated to a humanitarian service, he cannot develop his heart.

Mental development leads us to disaster if the heart does not control and guide it.

5. Another technique to develop the heart is prayer. Prayer means to stand in the presence of God and let Him fill your heart with love, light, and power.

One day I received a nasty letter. I was hurt. I said, "Let me answer so that this person never opens his mouth again." I wrote a very strong letter. I almost chewed him out. After I finished the letter, I went into meditation, and when I was doing my prayer, I was impressed that I should burn the letter I wrote, or else I was not going to be heard again.

"Please," I said in my mind, "he needs it; he is so nasty. I must teach him a lesson....Let me send the letter, please...."

I received no impression. "Now," I said, "there is no answer, the door is closed; the communication line is cut. Well, what should I do? The letter is good, but I must burn it. If not...."

I went and burned the letter.

I went back to my corner and began my prayer. Immediately I felt that the door opened and my prayer was heard. Joy filled my heart.

Our hearts register the effects of our words, deeds, and thoughts reflected on the Cosmic mirror.

6. The next method to develop the heart is worship. Worship is a total, spiritual identification with the object of your vision. In worship you try to tune in completely with the object of your vision. To tune in means that all your thoughts, words, and deeds are in accord with the keynote of your vision.

True worship is a process of transformation. Every time we transform and transcend ourselves, the petals of our heart open.

Worship is also a way for spiritual healing. Whatever you worship, you will eventually be like your object of worship.

In worship your total beingness is in focus. It is a state of absorption, a state of transformation. After every act of worship, one must feel a little more ahead on the path of beauty and Self-actualization.

7. The next technique to develop our heart is compassion. Compassion is inclusiveness of love and the spirit of non-separatism.

8. The next step is to exercise the twelve powers of the heart. Eleven powers are given by Master D.K. in *Discipleship in the New Age*:

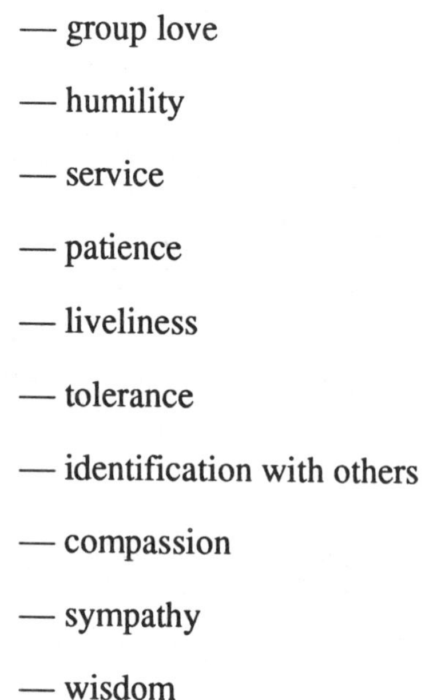

— group love

— humility

— service

— patience

— liveliness

— tolerance

— identification with others

— compassion

— sympathy

— wisdom

— sacrifice

— gratitude

The heart center is a twelve-petaled prism. The life current coming from the Core of our being turns into twelve powers of the heart through the twelve petals of the heart.

1. The first power is *group love.* Group love will be demonstrated in your life expressions. You think, talk, and act in such a way that the spiritual progress of the group members as a whole and of each member as an individual is not hindered but accelerated and strengthened.

Your group love can be expressed through your cooperation with group purpose, through your selflessness, sacrificial service, harmlessness, and right speech.

Group love also requires extreme carefulness of what you do in secret. One can hurt the aura of the group through his thoughts, covert acts, and motives.

Group love manifests through your regular meditation, study, and service because those who are left behind become burdens on the shoulders of the group.

2. The second power of the heart is *humility.* Humility is not weakness but power. There is an epidemic of vanity at this time. Vanity is denial of reality. Humility is the ability to see where you stand on the ladder of evolution. Those who are behind you evoke humility in you because you see in them your past. Those who are ahead of you evoke humility in you because you realize the great labor you must perform to reach their level. Wherever you are found, humility gives you balance and equilibrium.

Those who do not know where they are are weak people. Those who know where they are are firm people, people who have clear minds and a clear path. It is because of humility that you dare to serve and you dare to strive.

Those who do not have humility use every occasion to force themselves on others. They take every occasion to use others for their selfish interests.

Humility increases our psychic energy. Vanity bankrupts us and leaves us like an empty shell.

Humility opens the petals of the heart. Vanity and pride burn the petals or petrify them. An opening heart fills you with magnetism, and magnetism brings you success and prosperity.

I remember once I was present at a concert where one of my father's friends played a violin solo for half an hour. When the music was over, my father and I went backstage to congratulate him. Father just walked by and gave him a smile. I rushed to him, hugged him and said, "You were like a spirit, and your violin was a living being. It was an animated being.... You were beyond my imagination."

He looked at me with a big smile and said, "Well, thank you...but if you really understand what music is, you will understand that I am yet a little boy just trying to learn the ABC's of the music." And I saw tears in his eyes.

Later, when I told my father what the violinist had said, my father said, "Greatness is the ability not to see greatness in oneself. The vision of the future makes people humble. The greatness of man is his ability to compare himself with greater achievements of the future and realize the labor needed to reach the future."

3. *Service.* One of the petals of the heart is called service. As that petal opens, one feels the urge to radiate and serve.

Wrong and hateful activities develop guilt feelings within us. It is these feelings that delay the opening of this petal; or if it is open, they petrify it. Guilt feelings chain you and do not let you serve. They block your radioactivity.

This petal nourishes itself by the energy of Beauty, Goodness, and Truth. Whatever you think, talk, or do, the energy of service (Beauty, Goodness, and Truth) charges your thoughts, words, and deeds. Through the energy of service, your soul touches people.

4. *Patience.* Patience opens the petals of the heart. Actually, if one knows that he is a traveler on the Path which has neither beginning nor end, he will learn how to be patient.

Life — immortality — is that endless and beginning-less Path. Persistence to go forward on the Path requires patience.

One of my Teachers told the following story:

There was a man to whom was given a mountain of wheat. He was told to carry the grain to another field half a mile away and build there a new mountain of wheat. He was told that only through accomplishing this labor would he be free to do all that he wanted.

After careful calculation the man found out that it would take him seven hundred years to do that labor. He went to his Master and said, "But I have only fifteen or twenty years of life left. I am already seventy years of age!"

"Well," said the Master, "we will give you seven hundred years, with little rest periods, and you try to finish it."

The man worked a few days and then thought, "If I do not finish it in seven hundred years, they will give me eight hundred years, so that I live longer."

The Master came and said to him, "We gave you this work to teach you patience, which will grant you the power of immortality. What else is more important than your immortality? Work out your own salvation."

But the man got bored. Often he slept or played, and one day Death approached him and said, "If you don't learn patience, I will take you away. Patience does not mean laziness but continuous work to reach immortality."

The legend says that from that day on the man worked every day, and in seven hundred years he moved the mountain of wheat. When he was carrying the last grain of wheat, the Master appeared and said, "You learned patience. Now you have the key to immortality."

"But," said the man, "I do not want to use the key until I carry the mountain back to its former place."

The legend says that the Celestial Ones loved his words and sincerity so much that they sent a fiery horse and took him to celestial realms.

After telling this story, the Teacher said, "All that we do is really to develop patience. Until patience is developed, one cannot consciously enter into the Higher Worlds because the petal of patience is the door to immortality.

5. *Liveliness.* Some people are not lively; they are like frozen fish. Life is our Core, and that Core must pour out with enthusiasm.

To be lively means you communicate with Nature, with flowers, bushes, trees, rocks, oceans...with everything. To be lively means to be a carrier of life to others. People often carry their burdens and loads to others. Lively ones bring you joy, bliss, light, and life.

People either serve death or life. Those who serve death spread separatism, pain, suffering, slavery, exploitation, and ugliness. Those who serve life spread hope, future, and the spirit of striving.

6. *Tolerance.* The petal of tolerance channels the energy of Intuition. Tolerant people have more Intuition than fanatics.

Fanatics cannot see their own limitations and ordain themselves to create laws and regulations to limit the thinking and the consciousness of people. Tolerance accepts the right of freedom of thinking, freedom of religion and speech. Tolerant people think that only in freedom can people grow. Fanaticism tries to make all flowers in one shape, in one color. Tolerance gives opportunity for every soul to express himself.

Fanaticism develops selfishness, separatism, hatred, and crimes. Tolerance develops understanding and dialogue, builds bridges between people, and eventually creates friendship and cooperation for the Common Good.

Fanaticism denies the rights of other people. Tolerance restores the rights of everyone.

Through tolerance Intuition grows and becomes the light in the heart. Tolerance uplifts the fallen ones and gives them a new chance to stand on their feet.

Fanaticism is imposition of your beliefs upon others, as if your measures were the only ones in the world, as if you were the only one with eyes and the right to control other people. Tolerance never imposes because intuitively the man knows that no one can unfold, refine, and transform himself through imposition.

Tolerance challenges and encourages people to strive, but it never forces things on others. Tolerance opens a great path for the consciousness. It is only in tolerance that the consciousness expands. Tolerance increases your viewpoints and puts you in contact with new values.

Tolerance teaches you humility; you become more simple. The only thing that prevents your spiritual unfoldment is your pride, and fanaticism is the daughter of pride.

A wise man one day told his student, "My dear one, you cannot learn any more. No matter how hard you work and how hard you knock at the door, the door will remain closed."

"But Master," said the student, "why can't I learn? I have a wonderful brain, a sharp intellect, and persistence."

"Because," said the Teacher, "you built a wall of pride around yourself, and if you continue learning the way you do, that wall will turn into a prison for your soul. No light will penetrate into that prison. It is better for you to go into the world and destroy that wall of pride before it is too late."

Many intelligent ones built the wall of pride while trying to cultivate their souls, and they eventually buried themselves in their own prison and became "the only way to fly."

Tolerance destroys pride and does not encourage weakness or crime. Tolerance even takes disciplinary action to free the prisoner.

7. The next power of the heart is called *identification with others*, which is an embryonic fusion carried eventually to synthesis when the head center is developed.

This petal gives you the power to contact people on the soul-to-soul level. When you shake hands, people feel that you are touching their heart rather than their hand; you are touching their heart through your words and your looks.

As one learns to communicate with the hearts and souls of other people, that particular petal of the heart unfolds and gives man a chance to understand the foundation of future synthesis.

8. *Compassion.* Compassion is an inclusive love for all living forms. Compassion is the fire of the heart which is in contact with the Self of the Universe. It is the active manifestation of the One Self through the heart that is called compassion.

Compassion is the law that unites the pairs of opposites — Spirit and matter, the smallest and the biggest. Compassion is unity in opposites.

9. *Sympathy.* The petal called sympathy is unfolded through knowledge expressed in the interest of the well-being of any manifested form. This energy comes from the knowledge petals of the inner lotus and activates the petal of sympathy in the heart when man tries to know in order to help.

Sympathy can turn into an instrument of better understanding and an instrument of transmission for psychic energy. Sympathy opens the field of service and cooperation.

Sympathy reveals that which is going on within the hearts of others. Through sympathy one reads the heart but keeps silent. There is a deep wisdom in true sympathy.

Sympathy must not be confused with pity. Pity is a solar plexus feeling, and it encourages weakness and violates karma.

10. *Wisdom.* The source of the energy of wisdom is within the love petals of the lotus. As these petals unfold, the wisdom petal opens in the heart lotus.

Wisdom is distilled love fused with intuitive light.

Wisdom is cumulative, and it takes thousands of incarnations to develop. Wisdom understands intuitively and helps at the right time, at the right place, with the right dosage. Wisdom is harmless, but it also prevents harm and crime.

Knowledge fails, but wisdom never fails. Wisdom's viewpoint is the future. It is all-inclusive and righteous. It is also forgiving, if forgiveness will help the growth of sanity and love.

Wisdom is not the product of academic learning. It uses knowledge but is not limited by it.

Wisdom radiates like an aura. One receives the answer to his questions when he enters into that aura.

Some people, because of their past labor, are born with wisdom. They may be found in lower classes, but they shine like jewels.

Jalaluddin Rumi, the great poet and sage, once told the following story to his disciples:

A philosopher one day met a peasant who was traveling with his camel.

"Good morning," he said, "What are you carrying on your camel?"

"Well, this side of the bag is full of wheat, and the other side is full of sand, to balance the weight."

"My goodness," said the philosopher, "you don't need to do that. You can divide the wheat into two parts and put one half on this side and one half on that side, and free the camel from an excessive load."

"Wow," said the peasant in amazement. "Are you a king?"

"No."

"Are you a minister?"

"No."

"Are you a man of wealth?"

"No. I have almost nothing."

"Well," said the peasant, "if your knowledge did not help you to have something and be somebody, then I will not listen to you, and I will load my camel my way. God be with you...."

11. *Sacrifice.* Sacrifice is the flow of heart energy from the service of others. The sacrifice petal in the heart unfolds through the flow of energy from the sacrificial petal of the inner heart lotus.

Sacrifice is related to life-energy which, when offered through wisdom and compassion, turns into sacrifice.

Sacrifice is also related first to bliss and, in the heart center, to joy.

12. Master D.K. did not give the twelfth power, at least I did not see it, but I feel that the twelfth petal of the heart center is *gratitude*. Gratitude makes man magnetic, beautiful, and joyful.

Your magnetism created through gratitude attracts the substance of love, light, and trust and brings you success on many levels.

Gratitude completes the strings in the harp of your heart.

Through these twelve strings your soul plays its creative melodies and symphonies, and your life is filled with beauty and joy.

> *To behold with the eyes of the heart; to listen with the ears of the heart to the roar of the world; to peer into the future with the comprehension of the heart; to remember the cumulations of the past through the heart; thus must one impetuously advance upon the path of ascent....*[4]

Meditation to Cultivate Virtues

1. Sit in a peaceful place.

2. Relax your personality vehicles.

3. Say the Great Invocation.

From the point of Light within the Mind of God
Let light stream forth into the minds of men.
Let Light descend on Earth.

From the point of Love within the Heart of God
Let love stream forth into the hearts of men.
May Christ return to Earth.

From the centre where the Will of God is known
Let purpose guide the little wills of men —
The purpose which the Masters know and serve.

---

4. *Heart*, para. 1.

From the centre which we call the race of men
Let the Plan of Love and Light work out
And may it seal the door where evil dwells.

Let Light and Love and Power restore the Plan on Earth.

4. Sound the OM three times.

5. Visualize your heart center and see it as a golden lotus.

6. Meditate on the virtue you want to develop:

   a. Think, define, and understand the virtue under consideration for six minutes.

   b. Try to remember if you know anyone who demonstrates that virtue, and with what effects.

   c. Try to dramatize the virtue as if you were the embodiment of that virtue.

   d. Think what influence you will have upon life in general and what changes will take place individually in your life if you develop that virtue.

   e. Think why you want to develop that virtue and how you will use it for the service of others.

7. Sound the Great Invocation.

8. End with three OMs.

Keep a daily diary to see how the virtue is influencing your life. This meditation is to be done once daily for not more than half an hour, but try to keep the virtue in your mind throughout the day. You can use this meditation until you actualize the chosen virtue. Mental formulations of a virtue can lead you into crystallization, even into fanaticism.

In true actualization of a virtue, you become a virtuous person without even knowing about it.

We must develop eight powers of the heart:

- Understanding
- Compassion
- Intuition

- Sincerity
- Simplicity
- Righteousness
- Willpower
- Responsibility

People must try to understand through their heart.

Compassion is the power of inclusiveness of the heart. The heart has many multi-dimensional contacts with the Universe. Such contacts are the cause of Intuition.

The heart never deceives. Deception is a poison for the heart. Lying and hypocrisy endanger the flame in the heart. Sincerity is the wisdom of the heart.

The heart loves Nature. Simplicity is the ability not to entangle oneself with unnecessary forms and currents. Simplicity is directness, frankness, and openness because the heart knows that simplicity is economy of energy.

The heart is always righteous. Unrighteousness occurs only after the heart is beaten to death. Even a dying heart whispers righteousness.

The heart is a source of willpower. Willpower is formulated and directed life energy toward a purpose. The heart provides all energies. The mind adapts them to the need of the time.

One can only depend on a man or woman who has *heart*. Responsibility is the ability to care for and identify with the needs of other people. Life advances only with the power of responsibility. The decay and disappearance of nations and races can be traced to the lack of responsibility.

The first sign of the awakening disciple is the demonstration of the sense of responsibility.

In developing these eight powers in your life, you develop your heart center. People do not need to sit and meditate on the etheric heart center. This may cause great damage to the heart. Mental energy is inferior to life energy. The heart is developed when one meditates on the eight powers of the heart and tries to actualize them in his life. Unless actualization of these powers is a fact, the petals do not start opening, even if you have encyclopedic knowledge about them.

77

Healing the Heart Exercise

The heart can be damaged by many causes:

1. Pollution
2. ELF currents; microwave ovens
3. Radioactivity found in food or in the environment
4. Electromagnetic currents of equipment in your home
5. Extreme anger, fear, hatred, jealousy, revengefulness, treason
6. Incessant noise of airplanes or other machinery and irritation
7. Lack of sleep
8. Sugar, fat, drugs, alcohol, tobacco
9. Deep feelings of guilt
10. Waste of sexual energy

These are the major causes of heart trouble besides viruses. The healing process of the heart can take place after eliminating these causes and without forcing your heart to survive on chemicals.

During your efforts to eliminate these ten causes, you can try the following exercise, which may bring a magical healing to your heart.

The method:

1. Lie in a comfortable position. Try to learn to release your body, your emotions, your mind.
2. After six or seven minutes, visualize that you are entering into harmony with the Cosmic Rhythm and gradually becoming one with that rhythm. Let the rhythm penetrate into your whole nature.
3. Do this everyday twice, morning and at sunset.

What it means to feel the Cosmic Rhythm cannot be easily explained. You must feel it. You must experience it. When you enter into the Cosmic Rhythm, you feel happy, joyful, peaceful, totally relaxed. Let the loving energies of the Universe pass through you. Let your body, emotions, and mind not hinder its flow in any way; just let the rhythm involve your whole being.

This exercise will benefit you beyond your imagination. This does not mean that you will reject all medical help. Medicine is the result of the sacrifice of thousands of people.

In doing these exercises, you touch the rhythm of Nature; you "hear" Its songs and dance with It.

After doing this exercise for one month, see the difference in your energy level, enthusiasm, and the strength of your heart.

This exercise is not a mystical one, but it is a subtle method to absorb the health giving chemistry of Space, channeled into you through your visualization.

78

Love In Action Exercise

Love is not only a giving, but also a rejecting act; not only a going out, but also a withdrawal; not only an allowing act, but also a preventing act. It is not only gentle and sweet, but also highly disciplinary....[1]

1. Role play as a mother, and see when discipline would be correct in order to show your love.
2. Take a situation with a mate, and see when withdrawal would be an expression of love that would help the person grow.

To "love your enemy" does not mean to encourage him in his destructive practices....[2]

1. Discuss how you would really be showing your love by stopping someone from doing destructive acts.
2. Discuss how you would really be showing your love by taking actions to stop wars.
3. Discuss how you would be showing your love by stopping a drug seller from giving drugs to children.
4. Think of five examples of how you would be showing your love by stopping harmful actions.

...If your enemy appears to be an enemy because he is revealing your transgressions, injustices, and weaknesses, he is your friend in disguise. You need to love him and learn your lesson from him.[3]

---

1. *The Flame of Beauty, Culture, Love, Joy*, p. 163.
2. *Ibid.*, p. 163.
3. *Ibid.*, p. 164.

1. Think of a time when someone revealed your transgressions, injustices, and weaknesses.

2. Were you grateful for being caught, or did you regard him as an enemy?

3. If you regarded him as an enemy, find out the lesson gained at that time and mentally send loving gratitude to that person.

4. Continue until you have covered all such times.

5. Then look at transgressions, injustices, or weaknesses which you need to reveal to yourself.

6. Work out a method of handling these whereby all will win.

When the ancients spoke about love, gratitude, and other virtues, people assumed that such teachings were parts of religious or moral instructions. But gradually we are seeing that the ancients were giving us scientific advice related to our health, sanity, and prosperity.

People continuously emanate certain radiations — some of them benevolent, some of them malevolent. These radiations or emanations are not only beneficial or harmful to the person himself but also to those with whom he is related. For example, there are emanations of love, emanations of gratitude, emanations of joy, emanations of ecstasy, emanations of lofty thoughts, emanations of aspirations, emanations of admiration.

Every time such emanations radiate from a person, they revivify and nourish his aura and, like a current, flow out and carry a great amount of healing power to those around him.

Sometimes you give a little gift but receive a great charge of energy from the gratitude. Someone loves you and floods your aura with life-giving energy. Someone admires your work and floods your sphere with uplifting and expanding energy. When you give and receive such emanations, your health improves, your heart opens and unfolds, your mind clears and expands, and prosperity and success meet you on your path.

Thus when a person is living in the spirit of Beauty, Goodness, Righteousness, Joy, Freedom, gratitude, solemnity, and so on, he emanates atoms charged with life-giving essence and brings to people of the world a more abundant life. At the same time, such a person attracts life-atoms in higher realms, such as from the four Cosmic Etheric Planes or from planetary and solar centers. Through such life-atoms, he builds his subtle bodies, nourishes their centers and senses, and enables himself to live a life more abundant.

On the other hand, a person who lives in ugliness, unrighteousness, ill will, depression, and slavery also attracts from Space low-grade atoms which create densification in his vehicles and make him earthbound, coarse, and inflammable to the fires of Space. This inflammability can be experienced when one enters the Subtle Worlds.

Such a person emanates coarse atoms to his environment, nourishes people's coarse atoms found in their various vehicles, and makes them coarse and more susceptible to pain and suffering. This is why we affect our environment by the way we live.

When higher bodies are formed because of the supply of higher atoms, the human soul passes from one state of existence to the next higher state of existence without losing the consciousness of his individuality. But if his bodies are coarse, or if he has no organized higher bodies, he loses the consciousness of his individuality in the plane where his body has not developed senses and centers.

We climb as high as our ladder is built.

People sometimes wonder why negative emotions are forbidden for those who want to advance on the Path and bring more abundant life to their environment. The first reason is that emotions are related to the glands and lymphatic systems, to everything that is fluidic in the body. One must remember that the greater part of the body is fluid.

Emotions control the glandular and lymphatic systems, as photo cells are controlled by light. If the emotions are negative, the glandular and lymphatic systems produce those sediments which hurt the corresponding organs or parts of the body. Eventually these sediments turn into poison and disturb the activities of the glandular and lymphatic systems.

The second reason negative emotions are forbidden is that the sediments released into the secretions not only circulate in the body, but like a form of poisonous gas they also radiate out of the aura and infect people. If one is sensitive, he immediately feels the effect of such poison when he is in the presence of a person who is in fear, hatred, anger, jealousy, greed, revenge...to mention the grossest negative emotions.

These fumes or gases infect other people's auras and condition them to be susceptible to such kinds of emanations. These emanations in the auras of others gradually go to their glandular systems and damage them.

The third reason is that negative emotions are very contagious. They not only carry poison with them but also the astral counterparts of the germs or viruses that the original source of the negative emotions had.

The fourth reason is that negative emotions form a wall in front of incoming inspirations from higher sources, or they become a mechanism for distortion and confusion. When any lofty thought falls into the muddy pool of negative emotions, it is disfigured and deformed. Such forms become the agents of destructive forces. Many destructive and harmful people bring in lofty thoughts and use them as fuel for their destructive purposes.

One of the most shocking examples of this is the Inquisition. The Inquisitors were not animals but learned people, in contact with the ideas of Christ; but because of their negativity, they reversed and poisoned the ideas and used the energy of the ideas to fulfill the goals of their negative emotions.

79

Infinity in Man

Is there any kinship between man and Infinity? Perfection is expansion, is livingness. Contraction is separation, death, or darkness.

One of the great poets of Persia left us a beautiful story about a lover who went and knocked on the door of his beloved. The girl, who was perhaps an initiate of the mysteries, asked, "Who is it?"

"Me, your friend. I came to see you."

"In my home only one can live. I do not have any room for another person."

The boy was surprised about this very unusual answer and left in confusion. A few days later, thinking it was a joke, he again went back to the home of his beloved and knocked on the door.

"Who is it?"

"Me. You know it is me. Open the door."

"I am sorry, but I told you there is room here only for one. There is no room for another person."

The confusion and anger of the boy created an anxiety in him, and he left the door and went to a wise man. He told the Sage what had happened between him and his beloved and asked for advice. The wise man saw the reason for the girl's action but did not reveal it to him. He told him to go and think about her *answer* until he found the solution to his problem.

Months passed and the boy could not put the problem out of his mind. One day as he was sitting near a river which was flowing into a lake, the idea of unity came to his mind. The river united with the lake, and they became one. There is no room for the river and the lake; there is room for the lake or for the river. There is room for both only if they merge.

Excited by this revelation, the boy went to the girl's home and knocked at the door.

"Who is it?" she asked.

"You!"

There was no answer — but the door slowly opened and the boy was taken in. The girl wanted to teach him that love is unity and oneness and, until one is aware of this, he cannot be admitted into companionship.

In this story we see the beauty of human love, but the story is also a symbol to reveal the relationship between man and Infinity. One is admitted into Infinity through integrating and fusing himself with Infinity. Achievement is a progressive unification with the Universe, in higher and higher dimensions.

In one of the Hindu scriptures, we read,

More radiant than the Sun,

Purer than the snow,

Subtler than the ether

Is the Self,

The spirit within my heart.

I am that Self.

That Self am I.

A similar beauty is found in one of the letters of the Apostles: *"We do not know yet what we are going to be, but when we see Him, we will be like Him."*

Christ synthesized all these ideas and said, *"Be perfect as your Father in Heaven is perfect."*

The destination of all human beings is perfection. Perfection is not a level of achievement on which you stand and say, "I have achieved; I finished my evolution; I have graduated from my school." *Perfection is the ever-progressing, ever-developing unfoldment of the Divinity within man.*

"The Father in Heaven" is the One Who really manifested all that exists in the Universe and is also Infinity, for which no definition is possible. We are invited to be perfect, "as our Father in Heaven is perfect!"

Is there any kinship between man and Infinity? Perfection is expansion, is livingness. Contraction is separation, death, or darkness.

Those who have an urge to be creative and to serve are those people who love space: the space of the ocean, the space of the mountains and valleys, the space of the sky — limitlessness. One of the causes of our spiritual, mental, emotional, and physical problems is the narrowness of our horizon. If our horizon is limited, if our horizon is narrow, we cannot breathe spiritually, mentally, emotionally, or even physically. This creates tension, disturbances, irritation, and congestions, and we see their dire effects.

We have had the experience of going out of a small room to a garden, and the first thing we do is to take a deep breath. This is so natural that we do not even notice it. The reason is that greater space creates a release within us, and for a moment something mysterious happens. The problems we had that seemed overwhelming to us take their right proportion and sometimes even vanish in front of a great panoramic view, in front of greater space.

Actually, when the astronauts flew toward greater space, they expanded our horizon, and for the first time humanity felt that our earth, with all its beauties and problems, is nothing else but an atom in a greater Cosmos. This had its healing quality and a strong effect on our politics. The world became smaller and subjectively more united as we penetrated into greater space.

The same thing is true of all those religious or spiritual people who open their hearts to a greater Cosmos and feel more and more fully the presence of the Almighty One. **Religious or political fanaticism, intolerance, hatred, and prejudice — which create such great problems in human relationships — will be cured the moment people open a greater horizon of beauty within their souls.**

The Creator of this Cosmos is in man. He is the undivided Presence in everything, "from Whom all things proceed, to Whom all things return." Being a part of that great, Unknown Almighty Life, man is capable of expanding his awareness and including the whole. In the Ageless Wisdom this process is called initiation, about which all the mysteries of the ancient world, the Sages of Greece, and all religions, even the religion of Christ, testified. When Christ referred to the Father, He referred to a supreme goal.

Who is our Father? Is He the One Who only created our planet? No. The solar system? No. The galaxy? No. He created billions of galaxies and beyond. Christ is demanding such a perfection from us. And the interesting point is that this Power, this Source of creation of Cosmic consciousness, is our Father. It is in this word that the mystery of human achievement, human inspiration, and the spirit of striving is found.

Unfortunately we think about ourselves as insignificant life-forms. We do not recognize our supreme, immense value. Ugly images have influenced our minds since childhood, and we believe that we are those images. These images are impressed on our minds as strong suggestions by people around us, through their words or examples with which we identify. It is this identification that controls our lives for a long time.

We begin to develop a relationship between Cosmos and ourselves when, for the first time, it dawns in our mind that we have a Father and that there is the possibility of growing into Him. This Father image is a very inspiring image, but it slowly must fade away and turn into a concept of infinite power, without losing the connecting thread between the Son and the Father. Gradually the Father will lose all His anthropomorphic characteristics, while the link remains between man and Infinite Space.

On a clear night, when we stand outside in our garden and look at the Milky Way, we may have a little expansion of consciousness and realize the greatness of the destiny of man. Great Ones tell us that there will never be a time when a soul will be able to say, "I achieved; I reached perfection, the summit of my evolution." On the contrary, at the time of all his new achievements the soul will say, "My horizon is expanding immensely, my responsibility is becoming heavier, and the distant sunny summits of the mountains of achievements are still inviting me. I am the traveler of Infinity going to Infinity."

This planetary life is a school; it is a kindergarten in the solar system. Those who finished this school passed into the solar school, and when it was over they started the school of the galaxy, like small children facing Cosmos. We can imagine that our galaxy is like a little fish in the ocean of Infinite Space. In this Space man is a small "bubble." He is individualized space, separated from Space by self-made walls.

Initiation is the process of refining and transforming these walls to such a degree that the inner space fuses with the Space without losing its individuality. Initiation is the process through which human awareness expands, until a time comes that man includes in his True Self the awareness of the Planetary Life, the awareness of the Solar Life, the awareness of the Galaxy, and the awareness of Cosmos.

We are told that there are nine initiations, and in Western terminology they are called

1. Birth, or turning toward light
2. Baptism, or crossing the river
3. Transfiguration, or enlightenment
4. Crucifixion, or the great renunciation
5. Revelation, or nirvanic experience
6. Decision
7. Resurrection
8. Transition
9. Refusal

Through these nine steps the human Spark merges with the ocean of Space as a bright flame in that ocean of fire. An initiation essentially is not a ceremony, ritual, or an act of admission into some secret or open organization. It is a process of transformation and transmutation. It is a change in your whole being. It is a change in your physical body; it is a change in your emotional reactions; it is a change in your mental responses, decisions, and motives.

In each initiation you grow toward yourself; you grow toward your future, your glorious future, closer and closer to Cosmos and to the Plan and Purpose behind Cosmos. As we have nine months in the birth process, so do we have nine initiations through which a Spark passes before it is born into Cosmic Space. But let us remember that the real Essence is not born because the real Essence is you. You are not born. Initiation is the process of the birth of Space through man.

The first initiation is called the Birth. Remember what Christ said to the man who out of fear came to Him at night and asked how he could enter into the kingdom of God. Christ said, "You must be born again."

You are going to be a new man. For example, John Bunyan was passing through a street where prostitutes were selling their services and one of them insulted him saying, "What a dirty man you are." He collected himself, and for a moment his life passed in front of his eyes like a fast playing movie. He realized he could not continue the way he was living, and suddenly a great enlightenment came into his mind. In one flash he identified himself with his spiritual nature and observed the life which his lower self was living.

John Bunyan reacted very strongly to the prostitute by trying to defend himself, which ended in a prison sentence. It was there that he wrote one of the most remarkable books in the world, *The Pilgrim's Progress.*

A drunkard, a criminal, an official, or even a clergyman can have such an inner enlightenment where he sees the world of vanity in which he is happily living. The first initiation is the result of an intense aspiration to surpass the life in which one is living, polluting himself with things that are not assets to the spiritual life. Thus our physical relationships, our body, our environment, our home, and the way we dress all change as a result.

The result of dissatisfaction with oneself leads one to the first initiation.

The second initiation is called the Baptism. This is the result of an increasing love for humanity, when love floods your heart and washes away all your negative emotions — self-pity, jealousy, hatred, fear, and their associates. Your emotional reactions are calm, peaceful, and loving, and you want to be harmless not only toward human beings but also toward animals and even toward the objects you use.

One day a man threw down his shoes, but then he picked them up and asked them to pardon him.

There was a girl who went to bring water from a well but saw that a climbing vine with a beautiful flower was covering the rope. She went to the neighbor and said, "My beloved neighbor, may I have a bucket of water from your well? A flower is holding the rope of our bucket and if I use it, the flower will die."

There was once a boy who was silently crying in a market, looking at the frozen fish. He could not understand why people were so cruel to freeze fish.

The second initiation is the attainment of purity of heart. The water of love cleans you. The water of compassion purifies you, and the joy of the Almighty One fills your being. Thus your Real Self comes closer to you. You become more Space and less matter.

The Third Initiation is concerned with your whole personality. This initiation is called the Transfiguration or Illumination. It is in this stage that your mind is so purified and clean that the light of your inner being shines and radiates out, electrifying all the cells of your body and all the atoms of your emotional and mental nature.

Illumination takes place, and one of the signs of such an enlightenment is that man is free from his hang-ups or habits. Habits no longer control him. He can use his mechanism as he decides. The presence or the pressure of habits denotes that there are other forces in him that still have control. As long as a man is under the control of such forces, he is not an enlightened man. The Third Degree Initiate has clarity of vision. He knows the way, and he has the light on the Path. He is the Path; he is the traveler on the Path. He is the light on the Path.

At the Third Initiation we are told that all the etheric centers of our electromagnetic spheres are lit by the flame of the Spirit within the body, and the Plan of the Planetary Life or Lord is seen. This is the stage when the five-pointed star shines upon the Initiate, and he comes in contact with his Father (the Monad).

This initiation is achieved after an agelong search for truth and unselfish dedication to the human cause of liberation. Purification of the mind is a necessity, due to the effect that it can exercise upon one's nature.

Collective human thoughts create huge electromagnetic fields in Space which, according to their nature, affect the energy distribution in Space. An enlightened man sees that there is a very close relationship between the Universe and humanity. The Universe affects humanity through the change of energy patterns, sunspots, new moons and full moons, new configurations, new alignments of stars, or cyclic energy releases from constellations. Humanity, through its feelings, thoughts, and actions, creates changes in the Universe. Humanity either increases the beauty and harmony in the Universe, or distorts the harmony and creates obstacles on the path of evolution of the Universe.

In the Ageless Wisdom we read that earthquakes and great cataclysms of Nature occur as a result of human thoughts which, when negative or inharmonious with the laws of Nature, distort the equilibrium of the energy field of the earth. We have references in the Bible to Sodom and Gomorrah. In esoteric traditions we read about Atlantis and Lemuria which were destroyed because of the increasing wickedness of the people inhabiting those continents.

The distorted thoughts of human beings have a cumulative effect. Because of the similarity of their vibration and frequency, they form strata in the electromagnetic energy field of the earth and eventually cause disturbances in the field. These disturbances create tensions of various magnitudes within the force field of the planet.

A thoughtform travels around the globe, and wherever this thoughtform is reactivated by a similar massive thoughtform in the process of being built by the inhabitants of that area, a powerful discharge strikes there in the form of destructive natural phenomena. Disasters occur when the traveling thoughtform, human wickedness, and the subterranean fires or electrical discharges synchronize with each other. This is a greater catastrophe. It occurs in certain places where ancient and modern wickedness has accumulated as a vortex of a continuously growing thoughtform.

Subterranean fires are the active electrical energies which keep the globe in balance and in harmony with the electromagnetic sphere of the earth.

The Fourth Initiation is contact with the Planetary Life and total sacrifice for the cause of one humanity. At this initiation, the Initiate is totally insulated from any effects of the emotional world of humanity. He is called an Arhat, Who pours love and bliss upon humanity with active sacrifice. In this initiation he uses his Intuition in the same way an advanced man uses his mind.

The Fourth Degree Initiate is aware. He has direct or straight knowledge because he has built the Golden Bridge, or continuity of consciousness. The greatest characteristic of such a person is an all-encompassing, all-embracing compassion.

In the Fourth Initiation egotism and pride are renounced. The old man is dead, and the universal man is rising on the horizon. In this initiation the Chalice is destroyed; the treasury of the collected knowledge of many incarnations is gone. He does not need knowledge because *He is.*

Man releases himself from all knowledge formulated by the human mind, just as a jet passes beyond the sound barrier.

The Fourth Degree Initiate has nothing in his nature that ties him to the world, to the world of emotions, or to the world of the mind because even the mind is transcended. His sacral center is controlled by the throat center. The fire of kundalini is raised to the head center, and the solar plexus is under the control of the heart center because of this immense purification. This initiation is entered and passed due to all the sacrifices that a man made throughout all his lives.

The Fifth Initiation is called the Initiation of Revelation. In this initiation the reflection meets the reality; the lower self merges into the glory of his divine heritage. Man becomes himself and the following things happen:

1. The wisdom of the ages is His.

2. The Plan of the Hierarchy is revealed to Him.

3. The secret of the Seven Rays is given to Him, and He becomes a vortex of energy.

4. The mystery of the human soul is revealed to Him.

5. The Purpose of the Planetary Life or Logos opens before His eyes.

6. He has conquered His body, emotions, mind, time, matter, energy, and death. He has reached conscious immortality.

7. The Cosmic mystery starts to reveal in Him, and He sees in His heart the reflection of His Home. Now the greater journey homeward starts.

8. He shoulders His ashramic responsibilities toward humanity and the solar system. He is in contact with the Lodge in Sirius.

The Sixth Initiation is the graduation from the planetary school and the choosing of a specialized path of development in the solar system. These Initiates cut all Their relations with the earth and work in one of the schools in the solar system, unless They choose to remain with humanity.

This initiation is taken through all the decisions that we made at the major crises in our lives. Continuous right decisions eventually enable us to make the right decision at this initiation.

The Seventh Initiation enables a man to enter Cosmic evolution. He is completely free from the earth and can function on the Cosmic Astral Plane and control the seven energies of the system which are called the Seven Rays. These Initiates work primarily with those Beings Who work out the Divine Purpose on earth. They become the channels of the Will Energy working behind the Purpose.

We are told that *"before a man takes an initiation of any degree, He is already an initiate of that degree."*[1]

The Eighth Initiation is the Initiation of Transition. The Initiate conquers the matter aspect of the solar system and rejects any tendency of form building.

The Ninth Initiation is called Refusal. The Cosmic Physical Plane totally drops from His consciousness, and He is now an Initiate of Cosmos. It is in this stage that suddenly the revelation comes to Him that He is one with the Spirit in which the whole Cosmos floats like a flower and that flower is in Him; He is greater than the Cosmos and there is no end to His Infinity.

A great Himalayan Sage, the Master Djwhal Khul, says,

> *From stage to stage, from crisis to crisis, from point to point and from centre to centre, the life of God progresses, leaving greater beauty behind it as it moves through one form after another and from kingdom to kingdom. One attainment leads to another; out of the lower kingdoms man has emerged, and (as a result of human struggle) the kingdom of God will also appear.... The manifestation of the Kingdom of God on Earth, the preparing of the way for its great Inaugurator, the Christ, the making possible the externalisation of the Hierarchy upon Earth give us each and all a fully adequate task and something for which to live and work, to dream and to aspire.*[2]

You can only be *that*, the seed that you are. You can be infinite because Infinity is within you.

---

1. Alice A. Bailey, *The Rays and the Initiations*, p. 721.
2. *Ibid.*, p. 738.

All these Initiations are the result of many lives of spiritual striving, service, and mediation.

Each initiation is a process of expansion through fire. Fire purifies, fire creates, fire dissolves. Fire is the contact point with the spirit aspect. Fire increases the motions of the atoms by which your vehicles are built. Fire expands the field of their activities, thus giving more freedom to the unfolding soul. Fire purifies all that does not serve the purpose of the indwelling Divinity. Fire creates new vehicles, fertilizes and germinates the new seeds of the future mechanisms. Fire puts in contact the unfolding human soul with the Spatial Fire, and thus opens higher penetration into the mysteries of Life.

But what is fire? Fire is the flame of your candle, the flame in your chimney, your electricity, the fire in your cells and in the atoms of your vehicles, the fire of Spirit, the Holy Spirit, God. There is nothing except fire in its gradations — less matter, more fire; less fire, more matter.

Initiations are taken through fire. As the fires of the centers increase, as the fires of higher ethers penetrate into lower etheric planes, the flame, the Inner Core of man radiates its beauty step-by-step and eventually contacts the flame of the Planetary Lord. Each contact with higher fires is a step forward on the Path of Initiation.

People see their ugliness in the light of your beauty. You do not need to criticize. Your beauty will make them criticize themselves. Do not be involved with the vanities and dark paths of others, but be beautiful. Let your beauty be the judge for them; let your beauty challenge them. Let them feel that through your beauty they are finding an opportunity to meet their Self. Beauty is the greatest judge. Nobility, beauty, and solemnity are three great judges for people.

People feel great discomfort in their personality vehicles and deep joy in their higher nature when they are in the presence of people who are embodiments of beauty, solemnity, and nobility.

When you are an honest man, when you are really noble, solemn, and beautiful, you are a walking judge, a standard of values, a high mountain. People look at you and shape themselves.

It is the kind of judgement by which you are not criticizing, belittling, hurting, limiting, rejecting, or punishing anyone.

Instead, you are challenging the inner fire to radiate, the inner beauty to manifest, and the inner beauty to actualize because of your own beauty.

Initiation means expansion of Space, more communication and contact, and more registration of impressions. When you are a first degree initiate, your field of contact is one mile and mostly translated in physical terms.

When you are a second degree initiate, your field of contact is five miles, and received impressions are translated mostly in emotional terms.

When you are a Third Degree Initiate, your field of contact is fifteen miles, and received impressions are transmitted mostly in terms of light and fire; you register mental frequencies.

When you are a Fourth Degree Initiate, your field of contact is planetary. You are released from your personality limitations. You register intuitional frequencies, and you are almost aware of all that causes things to happen.

As you advance more, your field of contact becomes solar, zodiacal, galactic, and Cosmic. As you advance, you become an outpost of consciousness of the field in which you live, move, and have your being.

An initiate is equal to the space of his registration and actualization. If you are registering one station, you are a first degree initiate. If you are registering all major stations, you are an Avatar, in tune with the Cosmic pulse.

80

Meditation on Causality

Here is a simple meditation to help you enter the state of causality, to become a cause:

1. Say the Great Invocation. When you say it, be united. Be a cause.

    From the point of Light within the Mind of God
    Let light stream forth into the minds of men.
    Let Light descend on Earth.

    From the point of Love within the Heart of God
    Let love stream forth into the hearts of men.
    May Christ return to Earth.

    From the centre where the Will of God is known
    Let purpose guide the little wills of men —
    The purpose which the Masters know and serve.

    From the centre which we call the race of men
    Let the Plan of Love and Light work out
    And may it seal the door where evil dwells.

    Let Light and Love and Power restore the Plan on Earth.

2. Say three OMs, and be a cause.

    Send the first OM to your body to purify it.

    Send the next OM to your emotions to purify them.

    Send the third OM to the polluted mental sphere and clean it.

    Feel that you are a cause.

3. Say the following mantram:

    The sons of men are one and I am one with them.
    I seek to love, not hate.
    I seek to serve and not exact due service.
    I seek to heal, not hurt.

    Let pain bring due reward of light and love.
    Let the soul control the outer form,
    And life, and all events,
    And bring to light the love
    That underlies the happenings of the time.

    Let vision come and insight,
    Let the future stand revealed.
    Let inner union demonstrate and outer cleavages be gone.
    Let love prevail.
    Let all men love.

4. Again sound three OMs.

5. Meditate on the following idea:

    a. Find three instances when you were an effect. For example, someone came and spoke about your wife and told you that she said you did something nasty. You went home and started to fight with her. You were a football. That person kicked you, and you went and kicked your wife. Somebody lied, and you reacted to it. You were an effect.

    b. Find three occasions in which you were a cause.

    c. Think about the will-to-be-a-cause for three minutes.

6. Say, "Om Mani Padme Hum," which means, "Salutations to the jewel within my heart." The jewel is God within you.

7. Say the Great Invocation.

81

Healing and the Self

In the human level only an integrated, harmonized human being is a healthy being. Sickness is a condition in the body in which there is no harmony, no integration.

In the future, the health of the bodies will be restored through a discipline of integration and alignment with the Self. ...Once the spirit of separatism vanishes from the consciousness of man, the True Self begins Its healing process within the three mechanisms of man.

There is a Teaching related to the One Self given in the *Upanishads, The Bhagavad Gita*, and by Christ. According to this Teaching there is only One Self, and all living forms "live, move, and have their being" within this One Self.

The One Self is the foundation of all our moral and spiritual laws and the only panacea which can solve our individual, national, and global problems. All virtues, all values are related to the One Self. Unless we understand, assimilate, and practice the concept of the One Self, all our efforts for global peace and harmony, all our efforts toward happiness and joy, all our efforts toward improvement of earthly conditions will be a failure.

We may say that the concept and practice of the One Self is the solution to all our problems. Similarly, we may say that most of our problems originate from thoughts, feelings, and motives based on separatism.

The understanding of the Teaching of the One Self is the foundation of justice, of joy, of sacrificial service. On the other hand, destruction of justice, increase of fear, hatred, and indifference originate from our attitude of separatism.

It is true that all is originated from One, and the One is trying to compose the synthesis within every form and in all manifestation. **Life in all departments of manifestation is striving to make that synthesis an accomplished fact.**

Many religions emphasized the oneness of God, but they kept the manifestation apart from God. The Teaching of the One Self includes the whole existence within the Self and declares that nothing exists apart from the Self.

This is also the foundation of compassion, the super-love which holds all in one. That is why compassion is called the Law of Laws in all manifestation. It is the source from which emanate all values. Once this compassion is felt or registered in our heart, we fulfill all laws in the Universe.

The solution to all our problems in the political and educational fields, in the fields of communication, arts, and science, in the fields of religion and economy, rests on the Law of Compassion, on the One Self. People want to solve their political problems with wars, whereas the only solution exists in the understanding of the One Self.

Understanding and application of the concept of the One Self leads to unity, leads to synthesis, leads to abundance, leads to success. Your highest dreams can be accomplished not in separatism but in synthesis.

Understanding of the One Self enlightens our soul. The greatest sign of enlightenment is that the enlightened one never thinks, never speaks, never writes, never acts in terms of separatism; and the motivating force of all his thoughts, words, writings, expressions, and deeds is the spirit of unity, oneness, synthesis, and compassion.

In Asia there is a proverb which is often used in conversation. It says, "The name of Satan is separatism." Satan is the symbol of all crimes, pain, and destruction. One who lives in the spirit of separatism lives against the Law of Compassion, against the One Self; he lives in *sin* — in separatism. One who serves Satan does not recognize unity, the One Self, and that is why he acts in a satanic way, to gratify his separatism.

A "sin" is nothing else but an act of separatism, a thought or feeling of separatism, a relationship based on separatism.

One of our Teachers used to explain the oneness of all manifestation by bringing to our attention the relationship of the cells with the entire body. He used to say, "The body is one existence, and cells are part of the body; they are the body. The Self is within all. Thus all forms act as senses, as organs, as centers in one body."

The whole process of evolution is a step-by-step realization of the Law of Unity, Synthesis, and the One Self. The Omnipotent One, the Omnipresent One, the Omniscient One is the One, is the Self, or is one who has achieved the realization of the One Self.

In the One Self, time and space disappear. Time and space exist only in separatism. Poverty exists because of separatism. Hatred and fear, which control the majority of our thoughts, words, and actions, disappear when we realize the One Self and live accordingly.

The advancement and achievement of humanity is the advancement toward unity and the achievement of progressive unity.

True education and true science are based on this Law of Unity and on the realization of the One Self. If education spreads the concept of the One Self all over the world and builds all its institutions on the foundation of the One Self, humanity can be spared from pain, suffering, and destruction in the future.

The real age of light will dawn through the concept of the One Self. This concept, once realized, will make all our preparations for war, and the expenditure of lives and the resources of Nature, unnecessary.

There are steps for unification and steps for separation. The steps for separation are as follows:

1. Man thinks he is separate from Nature.
2. Man thinks he is the body.
3. Man thinks he is body and emotions.
4. Man thinks he is the mind.
5. Man thinks he is a personality.
6. Man thinks all is over after he passes away.
7. Man thinks all is in vain.

The unification process, which is the reverse process, can be described as follows:

1. Man makes his body an integrated whole.
2. Man develops his heart and feeling nature.
3. Man unfolds the potentials of his mind.
4. Man creates an integrated personality.
5. Man fuses his personality with his spiritual nature and becomes a Soul-infused personality.
6. The personality acts as the vehicle of a liberated human soul, which is technically called "a man working on the level of the Spiritual Triad." He knows *he is.*
7. Man reaches his essential state of being and fuses himself within the One Self. He knows the Purpose of life, and he is life.

It is this last stage that is called Resurrection. The Spirit, freeing itself from all separated states of being and consciousness, becomes a light within the greater light of the One Self.

When the light of knowledge of Self shines out like a sun, the veil of ignorance is destroyed, and the Supreme in man is revealed.[1]

This is the goal of all living Sparks — to reach the realization of the Supreme Self.

In ancient times the way toward at-one-ment was given in *The Bhagavad Gita* as follows:

Let the Yogi constantly centralize the Self, resting in solitude, with the mind and body controlled, free from all expectations and possessions.[2]

A "yogi" is one who is striving toward supreme unity with the Self. Unification is carried out through gradient steps of fusion with higher and higher states of consciousness.

In a psychological sense, a man of integrity is a yogi. But a yogi does not stop on the way toward the Supreme Self and tries to "constantly centralize the Self."

We, the Real Selves, live in a scattered, dispersed, and consequently diffused state of consciousness. We are not centralized in our own True Self. We are identified with the body and its urges and drives; with the emotional body and its glamors; with the mental body and its thoughts and illusions. We are in every object or subject with which we are identified. We are like a broken bottle full of mercury, with millions of pieces scattered all over the world. We are like an army dispersed all over the world, which has lost its communication with the central command; every soldier or every little group has become its own command.

In *The Bhagavad Gita* we are told:

A man is called enlightened by the Self whose mind is not disturbed by pain, whose cravings for pleasure have disappeared, who is free from passion, fear, and anger,

And who, under any condition, remains unattached. The good and evil cannot disturb him and he neither praises nor condemns nor hates. Thus he is well established in the light of Self-Knowledge.[3]

---

1. *The Bhagavad Gita* 5:16
2. *The Bhagavad Gita* 6:10
3. *The Bhagavad Gita* 2:56-57

Thus, such a person is not controlled by the moods of his body, by his or others' emotions, by his or others' thoughts, but stands as the Supreme Self, watching all changes around him, having no change within his own Self. It is only in such a state of attainment that one can realize that he is not his thoughts, he is not his mind, not his emotions, not his body, but the True Self. *This is what true solitude is.*

One may go into solitude but may carry all his worries, desires, and worldly dreams with him. Real solitude can be achieved in our consciousness, and of course this is achieved more easily when a man has an opportunity to be in the wilderness or to isolate himself in places where he has the least interference from subjective and objective realms.

As one becomes his True Self, his body coordinates itself with all its organs and glands. Systems and centers begin to synchronize and refine. The same process takes place in his emotional realms and mental realms. Then these three realms fuse and blend and produce a highly integrated and refined personality with a healthy and radiant body, with elevated and pure emotions, with highly beautiful and creative thoughts.

In the process of unification, joy manifests itself. *Joy is the experience of unity.* The deeper the unity, the deeper is the joy. There is no joy unless one experiences unity. Immediately when one experiences unity, his physical, emotional, and mental limitations fade away and joy emerges in its beauty. Such a man stands "free from all expectations and possessions."

As far as one is attached to an object, he is divided in his nature. As long as one is expecting things, he is not together with his True Self because he creates a gap in his consciousness. There is the object; there is the giver; there is the receiver.

One of my Teachers used to say that the materialist and the spiritual man both affirm unification with the Cosmic Whole. The materialist thinks that he will eventually die and everything that he is will become one with Nature. Thus separation will disappear. The spiritual man achieves unity in consciousness, and when he passes away his body fuses with Nature, but his Self builds greater and greater contacts with the Universe, like a concentric wave on the pure and calm ocean.

The materialist will be enslaved in his thoughtforms for ages and reject the reality of Subtle Worlds. But the spiritual man will enjoy the fruits of his earthly deeds and step-by-step discover greater reality within his and the Universal Self.

One can have flash experiences of the One Self. In certain conditions we feel that we are the Self; we feel that we are looking out through the eyes, and hearing through the ears.... We feel the difference between the mechanism and the dweller in the body mechanism. In deeper experiences we feel the unity of the All-Self. But these are flashes of Intuition challenging us to turn these flashes into conscious, permanent awareness.

The human Self thus is absorbed step-by-step into the One Self. This absorption or fusion is the process of initiation.

When we become aware of our Self, it changes all our expressions and relationships and it almost reverses our life. Our life mostly revolves around our selfish interests, around our toys. But once the Self is sensed, we grow mentally and spiritually and try to live for the One Self.

Almost all our problems on the planet originate from separatism. It is also true that even within our own physical, emotional, and mental systems all our problems are based on our "sins," on "Satan." Sin and Satan are the names of separatism.

Then one may ask, "Why is it that in unity, in the One Self, there is separatism, there are parts working against each other?" *The Bhagavad Gita* gave the answer ages ago. It says,

> *The supreme Self is not responsible for anyone's vices or virtues. Knowledge is veiled by ignorance; that is why beings are deluded.*[4]

When the Cosmic Self, like a burning fire, radiated out all Its Sparks, each Spark gradually darkened as It went farther and farther from the Central Magnet. The veil of darkness and ignorance surrounded the Sparks, as the ashes veil a burning coal while the fire fades away. Once the Spark, the Self, is veiled by darkness, It loses Its *direction*, and delusion is a state in which one loses his direction because of lack of light.

It is in this deluded state of being that the apparently separated self tries to build an empire of its own around its self-interests, ignoring the interests of others. But the interesting point is that this selfish and separated self can reach its own destination only by uniting with other selves.

Thus the self in the cell or in the atom appropriates other atoms or other cells and builds molecules or an organism and organs.... Ages and ages later this ruling self becomes a tree, an animal, a man, always appropriating more and more advanced selves.

It is only in the human state that the realization about the One Self dawns in the person's heart. He sees in wonderment that all his separative activities are leading him toward greater and greater unity. He feels that he is on the river playing with his boat, but the current of the All-Self is leading him to the ocean through pain and suffering and joy. Thus the individual develops family consciousness, national consciousness, and eventually global consciousness.

But the veil of ignorance is taken away only through pain and suffering and through continuous birth and death. That is the price the separated self pays to find his way eventually toward the One Self.

---

4. *The Bhagavad Gita* 5:15

Those who enter into the awareness of the One Self gradually liberate themselves from the agony of pain and suffering and ornament their path with the flowers of beauty, joy, and love.

Our True Self reaches a pure state of equilibrium as we fuse our Self deeper into the One Self.

> *The supreme Self within, who has control and is serene, is in a state of equilibrium between cold and heat, pleasure and pain, in honor and dishonor.*[5]

Equilibrium is a state of divine indifference. Divine indifference is an awareness of all that transpires but also a state of seeing things as the One Self. Remember the ocean and the ripples. Those who are deluded in separatism lose their direction but eventually come home through painful paths. In delusion one tries to chew rocks. In delusion one kills because of love. In delusion one loses in accumulating through greed.

A legend says that Satan is *delusion*, sin is delusion, separatism is delusion. But these delusions seem to be reality for those who have lost their path. Behind all these delusions, the reality of the One Self stands.

The whole quest of the Teaching is that man must enter into the realization of Supreme Unity, with conscious participation in that unity. Step-by-step you must expand your inclusiveness without losing your conscious participation in the process of expansion.

> *Know that the real is indestructible and all-pervading, and nothing can destroy the Imperishable One.*
>
> *All these bodies are perishable and transitory. In them dwells the Imperishable, the Indefinable, and the Eternal One. Therefore...stand and fight.*[6]

The fight is for unity. It is the supreme effort to reveal the Self, the supreme effort to be aware of the One Self, the supreme effort to *be* the One Self.

It is very interesting to see that separatism is weakness, and only in separatism does one try to destroy himself and others. That is why one can reach the conclusion that unity is power and reality is nothing but unity and harmony.

If you achieve a state of unity, you are an immortal being. If you bring your Self into focus, you are consciously immortal. Unification is the path toward not only success, happiness, joy, and bliss but also the path of conscious immortality.

People may expand toward unity in many ways. They may expand in accumulating the form and seeking the pleasure of accumulations. This is called

5. *The Bhagavad Gita* 6:7
6. *The Bhagavad Gita* 2:17-18

expansion in a painful direction. There is also expansion toward the Self. Such an expansion is carried on through paying back or throwing away all that you accumulated because you see its futility when you reach a higher state of consciousness. There are physical accumulations and emotional and mental accumulations...which often rest upon the fire of the Self like ashes.

Conscious expansion toward the Cosmic Self is accomplished by creating greater affinity with Cosmic energies.

> *The affinity with subtle energies becomes intense when it is harmonized with him who carries the subtle energies. The current is generated when all is fused with Fire. Hence, the creativeness of the Fire is so precipitant. Creativeness is generated through striving toward the affinity. Mutual striving endows the forms with psycho-spirituality. Indeed, numerous are the combinations which endow the forms with life.*
>
> *The process of infusion of psycho-dynamics into a new planet may be manifested only through a united Atom. The manifestation of the cosmic basis must be imbued by the all-containing energy. Therefore, We are united in a synthesis of cosmic fusion.*
>
> *Only the synthesis of a full fiery consciousness, containing all fires of spirit and heart, can affirm psycho-spirituality and psycho-life.*[7]

The "fight" referred to in *The Bhagavad Gita* is the effort and striving that a warrior of spirit manifests in his life to conquer the illusion of separatism and establish ever-expanding affinity with the One Self. Such a fight can be carried on intelligently to expand the consciousness of humanity in all departments of human endeavor and to challenge that consciousness to orchestrate the life with the vision of unity and the One Self.

At the present, two currents of energy are fighting: the energy which is generated in striving toward unity, and the force generated in pursuit of selfish interests. The history of humanity is the history of the battle between these two currents.

The majority of people are hanging on to the perishable bodies of their interests and leading themselves toward delusion. The majority of people are obeying the promptings of the perishable forms, acting under the darkness of ignorance.

---

7. Agni Yoga Society, *Infinity*, Vol. I, para. 253.

Those who are on the path of unification are the benefactors of humanity. They are increasingly unified with the consciousness of the One Self upon higher planes of existence.

Those who are on the path of unification and synthesis are called warriors. They fight not against armies of human beings but against the armies of delusion, false concepts, false ideas, and thoughts based on separatism. The ability to fight for spiritual values is a great sign indicating that one is not stuck in perishable and transient values but is focused in all-pervading Reality.

If one really fights to conquer all his thoughts, emotions, words, and deeds based on separatism and tries to manifest unity through his creative thoughts, words, and actions, he is a hero; he is a beauty. Thus he is proving that he is beyond the perishable forms and is centered in the Self.

Once our Teacher told a story of three thieves who, thinking that a house was abandoned, sneaked in. After checking a few rooms, they began to fight. One of them said, "This is my room." The other said, "That is my room." The third one wanted to occupy the whole house.

The owner of the house was resting upstairs. Hearing the quarrel he came down and said, "What are you talking about? How can you divide my house into parts and own them?"

And the story says that he threw them out into the darkness.

We fight for separate interests and eventually find ourselves in greater and greater problems. We call such a life an interesting and enjoyable life, this life based on destruction, hatred, fear, greed, jealousy, pain, and suffering.

Great crises sometimes awaken us to the necessity of unity. That is how, as a result of the suffering in the great war, the United Nations was born. The formation of the United Nations was a great effort toward the Self. It is still a symbol of the coming greater unity because unity is not achieved overnight. People must mature to be able to handle unity. The United Nations itself suffers with the pains of disunity; every nation tries to secure its own interests at the expense of others. But through all the illusions in which nations are mired, still the undercurrent of the One Self is leading the world into greater and greater closeness, inter-relationship, and unity.

The enemies of humanity and unity are everywhere. They are the deluded ones who are doing everything possible to create disunity.

Throughout the history of the planet, many races were eliminated and wiped out. Continents were submerged and disappeared. Great civilizations and cultures were annihilated because of the "darkness of ignorance" — because of the sin of separatism. This is the method of the One Self to prune Its tree so that the old branches and the unfruitful branches are removed and the Self is strengthened to bear better and more abundant fruits.

The planet and the solar system are the bodies of great Entities, just as our body is the mechanism or the body serving the human being.

Separatism in all levels is considered sickness. As separate interests working against each other cannot create a condition of joy and growth and eventually turn into exploitations and self-destruction, similarly a divided house cannot live long. A divided nation cannot last long, and a divided solar system eventually enters the path of dissolution.

In the human level only an integrated, harmonized human being is a healthy being. Sickness is a condition in the body in which there is no harmony, no integration.

The human pulse, when checked at various parts of the body, can show the conditions of the body — if there is integrity or not. Similarly, the pulse of the physical heart must synchronize with the pulse of the emotional and mental hearts. When these three pulses are synchronized, you have a healthy human being, a healthy heart, healthy emotions, and a healthy mind and thoughts.

When the parts of your body, the various emotions in your emotional nature, and the many thoughts within your mind are fighting against each other, you are physically, emotionally, and mentally sick.

People have a few moments of exaltation through their meditation, through their music or a painting, or through a creative experience; but a few hours later they talk about selfish interests, they hate, they plan for separatism, and thus create disharmony in their whole system. Eventually the disharmony grows and becomes a violent conflict resulting in various sicknesses in the three parts of their nature. People cannot serve light and darkness at the same time and remain whole.

One can enter the path of recovery and health by eliminating divisions and conflicts in his nature. A man can build a mental mansion through his best thoughts, but in a moment of hatred, conceit, or malice he can instantaneously destroy that mansion and live in its ruins for a long time. This is very common and one of the serious causes of sickness. The integration of the whole man is finally achieved when he *"casts away all desires of the mind and is satisfied by the Self and in the Self alone."*[8]

This seems to us very abstract and impractical because throughout ages we developed a materialistic mind which saw the source of its pleasures and joy in the objects of its desires. This can be slowly reversed when the mind is trained to draw greater and deeper joys in contacting higher dimensions, higher worlds, and in starting to create in the light of the One Supreme Self.

Immediately when we awaken in the morning we see our daily paper with its nerve-racking news. We watch our televisions and collect many objects of irritation. We think all day about our petty self, about our selfish interests, and so on.

---

8. *The Bhagavad Gita* 2:55

If you are an executive, you do not have enough time to deal with your personal problems. If you are a politician you have all your plans for how to protect the interests of your nation, often at the expense of the interests of other nations. If you are a man of pleasure, you do not have a moment to lose to enjoy yourself.

Life runs along these or similar lines all day, and all your time is yours; but you do not have one hour to dedicate yourself to thinking about your True Self, about the Supreme Self, on which depends all your health, sanity, and well-being. This is how the human life is wasted, misused, and eventually led into conditions in which life turns into a painful process.

There is only one Law, the Law of Compassion, the Law of the One Self. Compassion is the ability to see the One Self in every living form and live according to the laws of the One Self. The manifested Universe stands as it is only because of its harmony with and integrity in the One Self.

> *A man is called enlightened by the Self whose mind is not disturbed by pain, whose cravings for pleasure have disappeared, who is free from passion, fear, and anger.*[9]

"Passion, fear, and anger" are the result of identification with the objects of our desires; they are the fruits of separatism, and they lead us to death. When one is separated from the True Self, he is angry, full of fear, and he has passion. When one is identified with the not-self, he is lost to his Self.

In the future, the health of the bodies will be restored through a discipline of integration and alignment with the Self. The start of such a process is daily meditation and an effort to live a virtuous life based on the Law of Compassion.

We have within us the True Self, which is a window open toward the Supreme Self. We must try to unify our systems and reach the awareness of Self by living a life of unity. Then we must merge out of the tiny self into the Cosmic Self; that is the Royal Path of all evolution.

It is possible to cure many diseases by only creating a thought, feeling, word, or act based on the concept of the One Self. It is possible to develop a whole process to annihilate separative thinking, separative talking, and separative acting. Once the spirit of separatism vanishes from the consciousness of man, the True Self begins Its healing process within the three mechanisms of man.

One must learn to think in terms of holism and gradually feel his own oneness with the whole life and with the One Self. Every separative thought is a cause of illness. Every separative emotion, word, and act brings disturbances into the aura and into the vehicles because the foundation of all vehicles is harmony.

The life currents of the Self cannot rejuvenate the parts of the mechanisms which are under disturbing currents of separatism. Just as one cannot see his face

---

9. *The Bhagavad Gita* 2:56

in agitated water, similarly one cannot enjoy integrity and health in a condition which is agitated by the spirit of separatism.

We read in *The Bhagavad Gita,*

> ***The Blessed One said:*** *Fearlessness, purity of heart, steadfastness in the teaching of wisdom and Yoga, charity, self-discipline, sacrifice, study of the scriptures, austerity, straight-forwardness, harmlessness, truthfulness, absence of anger, renunciation, serenity, indifference to slander, compassion to all beings, freedom from covetousness, gentleness, modesty, poise, vigor, forgiveness, fortitude, purity, absence of hatred, absence of pride: these, O Arjuna, are the endowments of those who are born in their divine nature.*[10]

All these virtues manifest in a man who is united with his divine Self, his divine nature.

The real health of man and humanity can be achieved through living in our divine nature, in the One Self. Imagine how many human lives will be saved, how much pain and suffering will be eliminated, and how much energy and matter will be economized if humanity were able to think in terms of the One Self. One wonders why we do not see such a simple truth.

The ancients sang:

More radiant than the Sun,

Purer than the snow,

Subtler than the ether

Is the Self,

The spirit within my heart.

I am that Self.

That Self am I.

The most beautiful thing for a human being is to have an *anchorage.*

Without an anchorage he is lost in the stormy sea of life, of emotions, of thoughts, of opinions which always and everywhere are in agitation, in turmoil, and are trying to break the individualization of the human being.

---

10. *The Bhagavad Gita* 16:1-3

The forces of the Universe, like waves of the ocean, mercilessly try to break into pieces all that has an identity. People live in these forces and slowly lose their anchorage and eventually melt into the elements of the earth, air, and ether.

The most important goal of the human being is to have an anchorage and eventually become so solid, so condensed, so pure, so like adamant that he is able to pass the layers or spheres of the elemental forces of Nature and enter into the sphere where the *construction* to make him a co-worker of the *Plan* starts.

After one passes this sphere of energies, he develops the Self, the "I," and passes into another sphere which is the sphere of *Purpose.*

All plans, all programming, all changes and motion existing in this Universe are simplified when the Purpose is achieved.

It is after the Purpose is achieved that one penetrates into a higher sphere where compassion is. Compassion is all penetrative, all inclusive understanding of all that is going on upon the planet.

How can you create this anchorage? Meditate daily and keep in your mind throughout the day the idea of

Beauty

Goodness

Reality

Joy

Purity

This will go on for six months. After six months, daily repeat seven times with intense concentration, the "More Radiant" mantram given above.

During the year try clearly and closely to observe the following:

— What is changing in your thought world?

— What is changing in your emotional world?

— What is changing in the world of your activities and relationships?

— What is breaking off?

— What is building up?

All sickness is the result of a decaying *center*, a center that is losing its control on the mechanism it built. If the center is "together," the vehicles of the center will have a chance for regeneration, harmonization, adaptation, and synchronization — with an ever increasing contact with the center. If the center is together, it will be able to experience the three worlds separately and simultaneously.

Every time we are off-center, we are open to all kinds of attacks from the forces of Nature. Every time we are off-center or not esoterically focused, the bodies disintegrate in various degrees.

What does it mean to be "off-center"? Every time we do not act as the Self but act as our bodies and lose ourselves in our actions, emotions, thoughts, maya, glamor, and illusions, we are off-center. All vices are signs of being off-center. All virtues are efforts to bring us to *centeredness*, to *focus*.

How, then, can the human being live if the majority of people are off-center?

The bodies themselves create artificial centers for their survival. Man acts as a body. Man acts as emotions. Man acts as a mind. Man acts as a personality. These are pseudo "I's," false *selves* which hold the place of the real center. A goal is a pseudo center in the mind which holds the mental body together. A desire is a "center" which holds the emotional body together. A necessity is a "center" which holds the body together. But because the goals, the desires, and the necessities continually change, they weaken the focus and all repetition of the weakening of focus is registered as pain, suffering, and diseases on these levels.

Until the permanent "I" is conceived, established, and ruling, man will suffer pain, diseases, and death. Once he begins to conceive the "I" and build it as a tower in the city of his beingness, he will be an initiate going from death to Immortality.

The next step after the experience of the permanent "I" is the experience of the Center which is the permanent "I" of our planet. This is, *I am That*.

Then comes, *I am That I am*, which is the discovery that you are one with the Central Spiritual Sun.

The One Self

Exercise

This is a great healing exercise. It is very simple, but it must be done with all your sincerity and solemnity.

1. Sit relaxed.

2. Calm your emotions.

3. Bring serenity to your mind.

4. Begin to realize that there is the Self in everything.

5. Begin to fuse your little self with that Cosmic Self, stage by stage.

6. You do not need to think and analyze. This is only a realization exercise.

7. Try to realize that you are one with that *Self*.

8. Expand your realization beyond the solar system into the galaxy, and beyond the galaxy to Cosmic Space.

9. Let body identification slowly disappear and merge yourself with the ocean of the One Self.

10. The less you identify with your form, the more you can fuse with the Cosmic Self. The more you identify with the Cosmic Self, the more you gain control over your form.

11. Do not jump from your body into the Cosmos. Make it gradient. These gradual steps must be designated by yourself.

12. This must take not less than fifteen minutes and not more than forty-five minutes.

13. After your exercise say:

    O Self-revealing One,

    Reveal Thyself in me.

    Let all my life be

    an effort to be one

    with the Cosmic Self.

14. Stay in Cosmic awareness and sound the OM three times.

Try throughout the day to act in the light and awareness of the One Self.

People have a tendency to change such an exercise into daydreaming. Please note that in this exercise there is no use for imagination, daydreaming, even thinking. Willpower must be exercised to keep yourself on track. You need only to realize and be aware of the One Self, and to be aware of the merging process of your Self into the Cosmic Self.

82

Exercises For Beauty

The life that we live in this incarnation and the lives that we lived in the past are just like a rosary or a necklace with hundreds of beads. These beads are white and black. The white ones are the days or the moments of beauty, joy, and ecstasy; and the black ones are the days of failures, pain, and suffering. The white ones are sources of energy, inspiration, and courage; and the black ones are sources of confusion, depression, and failure.

Most of these beads are hidden under the layers of our lifelong experiences. They are occasionally restimulated by similar experiences. Usually the black ones are stimulated more often than the white ones. But there is a way to restimulate and release the energy contained in the white ones. Many psychological techniques are occupied with the black beads. The following technique is just the opposite; it is occupied with the white beads. This is a technique which releases the hidden moments of joy, beauty, and goodness. Once these vital sources are released, man is physically much healthier, emotionally happier, and mentally brighter, more concentrated, and more creative. He is more intuitive, inclusive, generous, and noble. He is more optimistic, more magnetic, and more trustworthy.

I. *Exercise*

Sit, keeping your spine erect but relaxed. Start with this year and go back in your mind toward your childhood. Write down any moment or experience that was exceptionally beautiful, joyful, and uplifting for you.

When you finish your list, go over it and divide it into periods of five years. See in which five year period you had the most beautiful experiences.

Now you have the most beautiful moments of your life on a list before your eyes. Starting with the most recent experience on your list, read it once and try to remember as many details as possible about that event. Take one experience daily, and each day continue with your list until you finish it.

The next step is to start with the latest event of beauty, joy, and upliftment on your list and relive it seven times, as if it were happening just now. As you do this again and again, the trapped light, love, and energy in the event will release and flood your aura with joy and energy.

If you go through the whole list of events, you are ready to go through it again, a second time, third time, fourth time, up to seven times seven. In this way you will regenerate not only your body but also your heart, your emotional values, your mind, and your spiritual nature.

Every time you go through an experience again, try to remember and relive it in more detail, in greater depth and realism. Relive the experience through all your senses, and try to register the same sensations and thoughts you had when it happened the first time.

There is another important point to be mentioned here. Never try to measure, evaluate, compare, or envy the experience, but only try to relive it as it happened the first time.

It may be that the best event of your life was the moment when you sacrificed yourself for others, or when you received a gift or an honor, or when you gave your time and money for a great cause, or when you experienced a great moment of expansion of consciousness, or when you felt free and unattached, or when something was revealed to you, or when you experienced a great upliftment, ecstasy, or bliss. It is possible that the most beautiful moments of your life were those times when you really loved or stood for truth and righteousness, or when you were teaching, or when you were in a period of intense creativity. There are other moments which are very beautiful, for example, the moments when you were around your loved ones, the moments when you were in the presence of a great soul, a great talent, or a genius.

Beautiful moments are so numerous. There are many which you have forgotten — for example, when you were watching a waterfall, a mountain with snowy peaks, a blooming tree, a flower on the riverbank or in the desert, a smile of a child.... Once you build your garland of flowers, you will not feel the same. Your aura will be energized by the current you release through contacting the moments of beauty, joy, goodness, truth, sacrifice, and service.

This exercise will pave the way for your health, happiness, prosperity, and creativity. It will also clear all those elements which keep the sparks of joy under ashes. The opposition of many tensions in your life will disappear, and you will be freer to build your future.

Each beautiful moment of your life is a beautiful flower, but dark days of your life cover the beautiful flowers under dust and foliage. In these exercises you are uncovering the flowers and making them free to radiate their beauty and fragrance and smile to the Sun.

You do not need to play with darkness in your life; just enter your darkness with a candle in your hand, with the flame of beauty. A little light will disperse the darkness. If you fight with darkness, you will increase the darkness. You do not need to dwell on the painful moments of your life; this is already an obsolete method. Light your flame of beauty, and the darkness will disappear.

Every event of beauty in your life is a flame of beauty which releases a tremendous amount of energy into your aura.

Remember that energy is one, but you can translate it in different forms and colors. In the same way, you have one electricity, but it manifests itself as light, heat, motion, cooling, sound, color, etc. Thus the released energy is one, but according to the hidden factors in your nature, you translate the energy as courage, love, optimism, vitality, healing force, power of concentration, or radioactivity.

After you do this exercise, you can go a step ahead and do the following exercise for fifteen to twenty minutes every week for one month.

II. *Exercise*

Sit relaxed, spine erect, and think: What beautiful things can you do for the world? Think of five beautiful things you can do for the world. Plan them sequentially; see everything organized in the best way, and see your plan in full operation. See your plan as if the effect were there already in full bloom. You can plan your activities for the next ten years or fifty years, or for your next life, or for the next 10,000 years. Remember, energy follows thought, and thought actualizes your dreams according to the power you put into your dreams and visualizations.

These exercises clear the channels of inspiration and impressions coming from higher sources. They increase the power of your optimism. Optimism relates you to the future and tunes you to the Cosmic harmony, and you feel a great fusion with the living beauty in Cosmos.

Along with all these exercises, daily try to dwell on the bright side of life. Try to see beauty in the most daring events, and hold firmly to the idea that beauty is always victorious and all who work against beauty are used as fertilizer for the future growth of beauty. Remember also that each time you come in contact with an event of beauty, joy, ecstasy, upliftment, freedom, or love, you come in contact with your True Self. That is where the source of power is. If you are closer to your Self, you are more powerful. But if you are focused in various parts of your body which are related to sad events, you are weak and you can control neither your vehicles nor your life.

In greater beauty, ecstasy, and bliss there is a greater experience of detachment, renouncement, and sacrifice. Real joy, beauty, and love create renunciations within you because beauty, joy, and love uplift your consciousness from lower levels and focus it in your True Self. It is only in the Self that you can see the futility of personality problems and personality attachments.

In each event try to find the core, the diamond, and when you contact the diamond, energy will flash out into your aura.

You can do these exercises any time when you feel that clouds of depression, grief, and hopelessness are approaching you. Go to your room and dwell on one of the best events of your life and relive it as vividly as possible, and you will see the result.

When you notice the good result, sit and write it down. Do not exaggerate; be factual and realistic. See what part of your nature is affected the most. Avoid any memory that is related to failure, pain, or suffering. Reject it totally.

There is another secret in these exercises: They open the path toward the Great Souls in the planet. Your magnetism is drawn to Them and Theirs to you. As you think about beauty, joy, and ecstasy, you build flowers in Space — with splendid colors and shapes. It is these formations that carry to you higher inspirations and impressions from great Souls.

Depression, sorrow, hopelessness, and pessimism draw you away from the sources of light, love, and beauty. When the flowers increase in your aura and in Space, the weeds will not have a chance to grow.

Humanity is definitely going toward the age of joy. We must talk, think, write, sing, create, and dance in the name and the spirit of Joy, Beauty, Goodness, and Truth.

Every astral, mental, and spiritual progress must be proven in physical incarnation. It is in the physical body that one must prove his mastery. Then other planes or spheres are open for us to go ahead on the path of our evolution. Graduation from the physical plane means mastership, the achievement of conscious immortality, and victory over time, matter, and space. Until this mastery is achieved, the human soul will come back again and again to learn his lesson and affirm his evolution.

III. *Exercise*

After a few years of experimenting with the former exercises, you can periodically do the following exercise to increase beauty, joy, and goodness in your nature:

1. Visualize the bud of a beautiful flower three feet above your head.

2. Be the bud; identify with it.

3. Slowly unfold petal after petal of yellow, orange, and violet.

4. Be this gorgeous flower.

5. Do not imagine or visualize the flower, but BE the flower.

6. See your own beauty.

7. Focus your awareness at the center and watch the petals.

8. Radiate your fragrance fifty feet around you.

9. See a yellow bird coming and standing on one of your petals and singing the most beautiful love song for you.

10. After five to seven minutes, see the flower closing and turning into a bud.

11. Step out of the bud.

12. See yourself as a transformed human being.

13. Walk on a path toward the summit of a high mountain. Try to see all that can be seen.

14. Close to the summit see three doors, three feet thick and five feet apart from each other. Each door is a door of fire three feet thick.

15. Walk through the first door and visualize that your physical body is melting away and you are walking out toward the second door with your emotional body.

16. Enter into the fire of the second door and see your emotional body burning away and you are walking out toward the third door without an emotional or physical body but with your mental body.

17. Enter the third door and see your mental body dispersing like a cloud. You now have the form of a five-pointed star, golden in color and with a diamond at the center. Identify your whole self with the star and feel extreme freedom and joy.

18. Enter the third door again, and as you pass through the fire, build a new mental body.

19. Enter the second door again, and as you pass through the fire, see yourself building a new, pure emotional body, vibrant with love and compassion.

20. Enter the first door again, and as you pass through the fire, see yourself building a new body, a beautiful, healthy, shining physical body.

21. Stand away from the doors and see yourself in an experience of transfiguration — whatever that term means to you.

22. Return to your room, feel your chair, your face, rub your hands together, and open your eyes.

IV. *Exercise*

This exercise can be an immediate continuation of the former one, or it can be done at a different time. Please know that this exercise must not be done if the former one is not done at least five times a month for six months. You can do this exercise for half an hour, for a month or more.

1. Close your eyes. Think that rare beauties are found also in moments of great danger.
2. Imagine yourself in the tide of a river which is running toward a great waterfall. Go with the current over the falls, and experience all that is possible for you. Do this until you do not feel the slightest fear, tension, or anxiety.
3. Walk in a forest and visualize strong lightning and thunder. Hear the voices of wild animals. Try to see the rare beauty of the event. Again, do this until you feel extremely joyful, fearless, and free.
4. Visualize an endless desert of sand and walk through it for miles and miles in night and day. See why there is a rare beauty in it.
5. Visualize a lion who tries to eat you. Fight with him and make him your friend. Think that the same beauty is found in great crises and destructions. Try to find this beauty and experience it in your visualization.
6. See yourself jumping from a high ledge into the ocean. See a lioness feeding you her milk. See a rattlesnake bringing you a big diamond. See immense explosions.
7. See a bridge or a building collapsing over you, and find yourself unharmed.
8. Walk through the bullets of machine guns, and see how they are bypassing you.
9. See how people are burning your body, and feel the supreme release experienced by your spirit.

You can do these exercises for ten to fifteen minutes. They break all hindrances of fear in your nature and liberate your consciousness for great and daring labors.

Then daily, morning and night, you must find three reasons why you are really beautiful. You can think or talk aloud and say,

I am beautiful because

— I am courageous

— I am generous

— I am fearless

— I am sacrificial

— I am selfless

— I am full of goodwill

Daily you must find at least three reasons to affirm your beauty. Know and feel that you are beautiful and that no one can take your beauty away from you. As you think beautifully about yourself, your "sleeping beauty" awakens and you become the most beautiful person, a blessing for the world.

V. *Exercise*

1. How can you make your expressions more beautiful? Write on a paper what changes you need to make and how you are going to introduce these changes into

    Your appearance

    Your dress — form and color

    Your hair

    Your gestures and manners

    Your walk

    The way you sit

    The way you talk

    The words you choose

    The tonality of your voice

2. Are cleanliness, purity, and simplicity related to beauty? Can you find some examples?

3. How can you make your home and your office more beautiful?

4. What habits of thought, speech, and manners must you avoid in your life if you have decided to be beautiful? Watch your expressions when you were caught in

   Anger

   Jealousy

   Hatred

   Gossip

   Stealing

   Lying

   Breaking the law

5. Is beauty related to independence, energy, and self-mastery?

6. Can you continue to be beautiful if people exploit your beauty for their physical and emotional interests? Why not?

7. Do you want to be beautiful to attract people for your selfish interests or because you cannot stand to be ugly?

8. Is beauty a way to express your love of life as a whole?

9. Is beauty a process of Self-actualization or cooperation with the efforts of the great Nature?

10. Is caution necessary to reveal beauty to those who are just awakening to the need for beauty? Why?

11. Do you see that beauty cannot exist without righteousness, justice, love, respect, and intelligence? What else do you think spoils beauty?

12. Can you see that beauty is related to freedom and joy? How?

13. Can one develop beauty without fearlessness?

14. Do you feel grateful and joyful when you see the beauty of others, or the works of beauty of others?

15. How can you increase beauty in others without aggravating the spirit of ugliness in them? Can you give an example?

16. Who is the most beautiful man or woman for you? Why?

17. What is

— The most beautiful painting for you? Why?

— The most beautiful music? Why?

— The most beautiful dance? Why?

— The most beautiful opera or ballet? Why?

18. What is the most beautiful experience that you have had in your life? Can you imagine a higher one?

19. Did you experience any healing through beauty? Did you experience any of the following?

Ecstasy

Spiritual freedom

Expansion of consciousness

Greater love

Greater forgiveness

Greater inclusiveness

Greater insight

A power to synthesize

20. If people around you are ugly, do criticism, irritation, and hatred help you? What will be your diplomacy or mode of relationship with them?

21. Is beauty related to energy?

22. Can you visualize and then describe a symbol of beauty?

23. What does one need to be a real beauty? What does one need on physical, emotional, mental, and spiritual levels? Are any of the following needed?

Energy

Money

Health

Wisdom

Education

Environment

Friends

Family

Nation

Failures

Dangers

Attacks

Tension

Crises

Seclusion

Company

24. Why do people think that stars are beautiful? What about Space? Power? Unattainability? Mysteries?

VI. *Exercise*

This is another method to receive inspiration, higher impressions, joy, and beauty.

1. Relax and calm your whole nature.

2. Imagine a mountain and a pure stream of water. Use your imagination and make such a vision an event. Feel the water, smell the fragrance of various plants, enjoy the pure air, the Nature, the mountains, perhaps certain birds, animals, flowers....

3. Create a vacation in the mountains for yourself, and try to make your imagination so real that eventually your imagination turns into visualization. As you orchestrate your vacation in the mountains with various actions and objects, think always about beauty, love, and joy. Everything you see or do must be charged with beauty, love, and joy.

You can do this exercise for half an hour or one hour, but try to conduct the whole procedure in a vivid, clear, enthusiastic spirit. Do not fall asleep; do not go to any painful memories. If they come, reject them, concentrating your mind on an object of beauty, or an object of love and joy.

You can change your exercise every three days and also do the following: Instead of going to a mountain, river, lake, stream, or forest, you can imagine going to a concert hall where the most beautiful symphony is playing for you; a symphony which radiates beauty, joy, and love. Create and hear the music. Try to imagine the whole orchestra, the whole atmosphere of enthusiasm in the hall, and listen to the symphony for fifteen minutes.

You can also create other beautiful, joyful, and loving events.

VII. *Exercise*

This exercise is a little more difficult. Imagine a dance hall or a huge stage, and see there the most beautiful and fantastic dance that your imagination can create. Let the dancers dance three dances:

— one for beauty

— the next for joy

— the last one for the love of Infinity

VIII. *Exercise*

The next exercise is to expand our Space.

Stand on a mountain and imagine you are a sphere of light. Let this light expand, gradually and slowly, until it embraces the earth. Fuse with the light of the earth. Then expand yourself as a light toward the solar system. After two minutes expand yourself to the galaxy.... After three minutes expand yourself into the Space and fuse with It.

These exercises are very powerful exercises. They will activate the Divinity within you and expand your consciousness. Once your consciousness expands to a certain degree and your sense of synthesis and universality is put into motion, you will not remain as the same person. Your petty hindrances will vanish, and you will build a beauty out of your nature.

83

A Basic Meditation on Beauty

In the first year, take a paper and pencil in your hand and choose a topic, a seed thought for your meditation — for example, BEAUTY.

List the names of some beautiful things you have seen this month, this year, this life. Maybe you saw a beautiful bird, a beautiful flower, a comet, a man, a woman, a dance, and so on.

You can hear beauty, touch beauty. One day I saw a tree against a setting sun and heard a flute; it brought tears to my eyes. List beautiful things you have experienced.

Try to imagine *beauty*. Why are things beautiful? What is beauty? Why was that rose beautiful? Why was that tree at that special time beautiful? Why was that dance or song beautiful? What makes things beautiful?

Surfing seems magnificent. Why?

What is the difference between beauty and ugliness? Is it mathematics, geometry, harmony, balance, rhythm? What is beauty?

When you are trying to answer these questions, you are really expanding the horizon of your mind; you are thinking and meditating.

Now you know beautiful things. You know what beauty is, but you want to know what beauty does. What does beauty do to your eyesight, to your heart, to your nervous system, to your social relationships? Is it possible to improve people through beauty — beauty of color, sound, movement, and form?

Now you know what is beautiful. You know what beauty does, but why do you love beauty? Is there any mysterious relationship between beauty and one's innermost Self? What is it? Why does beauty inspire, uplift, and charge?

Is your life beautiful? You know what beauty does, but what about life as a whole? Is it beautiful? Of course you love beauty, you use beauty, but are you beautiful, inside and outside, in every relationship? Are there things in your nature which need to be changed and made beautiful? Are there seeds of beauty within you which need more care to grow and bloom? How can you make the life of other people more beautiful?

Here we begin to step out of our personal field. We know things that are beautiful. We are beautiful. We appreciate beauty, but is there anything we can do to make the lives of other people really beautiful, without imposing our will on them and limiting their freedom?

After you try to answer all these questions for ten to fifteen minutes daily, record your answers and sit quietly for a few minutes. Imagine your life being really beautiful. If you do this for a year, occasionally changing your seed thought, you will see the power of meditation. Your life will transform itself, and you will make yourself ready to work on the next level of meditation.

In the second year, take a sentence and on the odd days write an article for half an hour. On the even days read it, change it, improve it, or rewrite it.

After fifteen days, read all that you wrote as if you were someone else. Ask questions about the things you wrote. Why? How? Do this for three days, and then continue writing and improving it until the end of the year.

In the third year, read one or more books and ask the following questions: Does this book contribute to the betterment of life? If so, why and how? What are the things you agree with, the things you do not agree with, and why? What did the book do for you? At the end, write your opinion about the book.

Doing such a meditation daily for ten to fifteen minutes will change your whole life. You will be more creative. You will think more clearly. You will be an independent human being. You will develop a sense of responsibility. You will be magnetic. You will be a beauty, and you will be ready for advanced meditation.

84

Seed Thought Exercises

Meditation on *solemnity* for one year may change and transform your life. As you go deeper into the meaning of solemnity and meditate upon it from various viewpoints, you impose a great discipline on your physical appearance and actions, on your emotional expressions, and on your mental attitudes or thoughts. This discipline coordinates your personality and slowly brings it under the control of the Inner Lord.

Thus, you not only save energy, but you also create integrity within your higher and lower bodies. When integrity and coordination reach a certain degree, the energy of your Higher Self pours down into your personality and slowly transforms and regenerates it.

It is most probable also that through your solemnity you raise the level of the people around you and give them an unending example of beauty, honesty, and nobility.

You may start your meditation any month and continue it for one year until you come to where you started. After each meditation, record your discoveries in a special book for future use in your creative work.

Meditation is pure thinking. Use your mind and find the principles, laws, and rules which form the foundation of the subject.

Meditation must be done for not more than fifteen minutes. Anyone using drugs, marijuana, or alcohol should **not** attempt these meditations.

Seed Thoughts on Solemnity

What is solemnity? How does solemnity come into being? How does solemnity reveal, and what does it reveal?

January 23 to February 22

What is solemnity in action, in expression?

February 23 to March 22

How is solemnity related to freedom? How does solemnity bring unfoldment?

March 23 to April 22

Solemnity on many levels is relationship with the higher Presence and one-pointed dedication to that Presence.

April 23 to May 22

How is solemnity seen in Nature — canyons, rocks, rivers, lakes, oceans, birds, flowers, animals?

May 23 to June 22

How is solemnity related to goodness, harmlessness, gentleness, nobility, magnanimity?

June 23 to July 22

What is solemnity in art and culture?

July 23 to August 22

How is solemnity related to beauty and to the Inner Glory?

August 23 to September 22

How is solemnity related to purity, sincerity, integrity?

September 23 to October 22

Solemnity does not exist without righteousness, balance, equilibrium.

October 23 to November 22

Solemnity leads to victory, to new achievements and mastery. How? Why?

November 23 to December 22

Solemnity reveals the Plan and acts for the Plan. Solemnity is the manifestation of the Plan. Why?

December 23 to January 22

Solemnity causes expansion of consciousness and sacrificial service.

Seed Thoughts on Beauty

What is beauty? How did beauty come into being?
The following are the dates and seed thoughts to be meditated upon:

January 23 to February 22

Beauty in movement, in motion.

February 23 to March 22

Beauty of liberation, freedom, blooming.

March 23 to April 22

Beauty of contact and relationship.

April 23 to May 22

Beauty in Nature.

May 23 to June 22

Beauty of goodness, harmlessness, gentleness, and nobility.

June 23 to July 22

Beauty of architecture, carving, and sculpture.

July 23 to August 22

Beauty of power and glory.

August 23 to September 22

Beauty of purity.

September 23 to October 22

Beauty of justice, balance, equilibrium.

October 23 to November 22

Beauty of victory. Beauty of achievement and mastery.

November 23 to December 22

Beauty of planning and goals.

December 23 to January 22

Beauty of expansion and sacrificial service.

Seed Thoughts on Joy

What is joy? How did joy come into being? Think about Joy as a revealer. The following are the dates and seed thoughts to be meditated upon:

January 23 to February 22

Joy in movement, in action.

February 23 to March 22

Joy of freedom. Joy of unfoldment.

March 23 to April 22

Joy of contact and relationship on many levels and planes.

April 23 to May 22

Joy of experience in Nature — birds, trees, flowers, water, animals.

May 23 to June 22

Joy of goodness, harmlessness, gentleness, nobility.

June 23 to July 22

Joy of culture and the arts.

July 23 to August 22

Joy of beauty and glory.

August 23 to September 22

Joy of purity, joy of sincerity, joy of integrity.

September 23 to October 22

Joy of righteousness, joy of balance, joy of equilibrium.

October 23 to November 22

Joy of victory, joy of achievement and mastery.

November 23 to December 22

Joy of sensing the Plan and living in harmony with the Divine Plan within you and the Universe.

December 23 to January 22

Joy of expansion and sacrificial service.

Seed Thoughts on Balance

What is balance?
Meditate on the following seed thoughts for fifteen minutes daily:

January 23 to February 22

Balance in motion.

February 23 to March 22

Balance and joy.

March 23 to April 22

Balance as a means of communication with higher dimensions.

April 23 to May 22

Balance in Nature.

May 23 to June 22

Balance and beauty and harmlessness.

June 23 to July 22

Balance caused through the arts and culture.

July 23 to August 22

Balance as power and generator of energy and magnetism.

August 23 to September 22

Balance as a bridge between the highest and the lowest.

September 23 to October 22

Balance and righteousness.

October 23 to November 22

Balance and victory. Balance on progressively higher planes.

November 23 to December 22

Balance and the Plan and the labor.

December 23 to January 22

Balance as a means of rebirth and service.

85

The Sense of Healing

In order to be a complete healer, you must have the three energies of light, love, and willpower available. This also means that your soul flower, the Chalice, must be totally bloomed — with three light petals, three love petals, and three will or sacrifice petals. Actually, healers are called "bloomed flowers" because through the nine petals they radiate the three energies of light, love, and power in three different colors, shapes, and dimensions.

Healing is a sense found on the Intuitional Plane and corresponds to the sense of touch on the physical plane. The sense of healing can be found dormant in some people, active in others, and highly developed in Initiates. All healing on the physical, emotional, and mental planes is inspired by the sense of healing.

For human beings, healing has three stages:

1. Healing with herbs, chemicals, oils, perfumes, roots, colors, music, dance, or other external means.

2. Healing with light and love through visualization or direct radiation. This is *spiritual healing*.

3. Healing with psychic energy directed through the "sense of healing" found in the intuitional body. This is *divine healing* in which the willpower is used.

When the sense of healing starts to form and develop, a person feels an urge to heal. If he is an intellectual type, he becomes a physician, a psychiatrist, a psychologist, or a holistic healer. If he is a spiritual person, his urge directs him toward the resources of the inner world, toward light and love. If he is an Initiate, he heals people through willpower and psychic energy, through solar and spatial energies.

The first method of healing is mostly related to the physical and etheric bodies. Of course, such a healing also affects the rest of the human being.

Spiritual healing is related to the astral and mental bodies.

Divine healing is directed to the human soul who, when emancipated, heals his vehicles by eliminating the causes of disorders in all bodies and shielding the vehicles from exterior, planetary, and solar disturbances.

The first way of healing is not permanent, and the roots and causes of diseases are not completely eliminated. It is temporary healing.

The second way of healing has deeper effects. It heals the astral and mental bodies, but it cannot prevent planetary and solar disturbances or past causes from affecting the health.

The third way of healing is permanent and extends over the whole mechanism of the human soul for many incarnations. When you reach the third stage, you are a perfect healer, and you can use all other stages intelligently to alleviate pain and prolong life. Such a person is an Initiate; he has the gift of healing.

Light, love, and willpower can be used safely if your sense of healing in the Intuitional Plane is unfolding, developing, and acting. This sense develops when you make efforts to stand in light, in love, and in harmony with the Divine Will and when you cultivate compassion for all those who suffer.

Healing with light and love evokes healing energies from the intuitional level.

The sense of healing uses psychic energy through light, love, and willpower to heal. The silver light in the head, the blue flame in the heart, and the violet-red flame in the head center are avenues through which the human soul, focused in the intuitional body, heals the vehicles of the personality, if karma permits.

This is complete healing, which means the causes of sickness latent in the bodies are annihilated at once and forever. But this does not mean that one cannot exercise healing to relieve the suffering of people through medicine, surgery, homeopathy, and other healing arts; or through music, color, light, love, and power. If the sense of healing in the Intuitional Plane is active, then man can heal through psychic energy, transmitting it through light, love, and willpower, using any healing art as a mechanism of healing.

Your suffering and the suffering of others can be alleviated by various methods. In spiritual healing, you use light, love, and willpower if your motives and vehicles are pure, if you are well-informed in the technique of transmitting these energies, and if you yourself have light, love, and willpower.

If you do not have light and you pretend that you have light and use the technique of light without having light, you complicate your own situation and that of others *if you force the issue.*

If you do not have love and you pretend that you have love, or pretend to have the blue flame in your heart and use the love technique of healing, you will fail and complicate the situation if you force your technique.

If you try to heal with willpower and you do not have willpower even to discipline your own self, but you pretend that you have willpower and use the technique of healing with willpower, you either fail or complicate the situation beyond the possibility of repair.

It is possible that if your vehicles are pure and your motives are charged with compassion, your Solar Angel or your Master uses you for healing. Your Solar Angel may use your intellectual light to heal someone from his glamors, your intuitional light to heal someone from his illusions, your love to heal someone from his depression and despair. But the greatest, most complete and conscious healing is achieved when your sense of healing is unfolded and active in the intuitional body, which means, when you are an Initiate of the Third or Fourth Degree.

To prepare people for such an achievement, easy and simple methods are presented to them to exercise and experiment with healing and slowly learn the science of healing on all levels.

Spiritual healing is healing with the energies of the soul, which are light, love, and willpower.

To heal means to harmonize, to put the organism into such a state that it can live, survive, and perform the *initial* functions that were impressed on it. For example, your eyes should see very clearly. To heal the eyes means to make them able to see and perform their initial function. The ears must hear well. If you make the ears hear perfectly, you heal the ears.

The same thing applies to the astral and mental bodies. As your physical body becomes sick, distorted, and inharmonious, your emotional and mental bodies can be in similar conditions. You may have a sick mental or emotional body. To heal these bodies means to create harmony in them and between them, and to reestablish their initial duties and functions.

The healer first uses light, if he has light. If he has light and the light is in a growing, expanding state, he uses this light first of all to see things clearly and secondly to heal people. How does he heal? He takes the obstacles and hindrances away from the physical body, emotional body, and mental body and lets the light penetrate and heal them. Light heals, kills germs, cleans glamors and illusions, and restores the initial functions of the mechanisms.

The first thing is to have that light. Then you will direct the light

— through your eyes

— with your palms

— with your heart

— with your hugs

Using light, you recharge the dying batteries of others with your own battery, with the condensed light within you.

The right hand should not be used when healing with light. The left hand should be used. When directing light with the eyes, the right eye should be used more than the left eye. When transmitting light through the heart, the two hearts should touch. At this stage, the heart is the transmitter of light, not love.

Light heals etheric and physical diseases. Love heals physical diseases and emotional diseases. Willpower is only directed to the soul when the soul is stuck in the bodies due to any element. Freeing the soul means to heal.

If the soul is imprisoned in glamors, urges, drives, illusions, hatred, anger, posthypnotic suggestions, jealousy, revenge, or fear, willpower takes the soul and says, "Get up out of this mess!" When the soul is out of the mess, he can immediately heal his mechanism.

In order to be a complete healer, you must have the three energies of light, love, and willpower available. This also means that your soul flower, the Chalice, must be totally bloomed — with three light petals, three love petals, and three will or sacrifice petals. Actually, healers are called "bloomed flowers" because through the nine petals they radiate the three energies of light, love, and power in three different colors, shapes, and dimensions.

Light functions in the physical, astral, and mental levels. Love functions in the physical, astral, and mental levels. Willpower functions in the physical, astral, and mental levels. This is why there are three petals for each energy.

In order to be a healer, one must put himself in such a condition that his whole mechanism functions in harmony with all of Nature. Actually, the destiny of every human being is to be a healer. This was affirmed by the Sage, D.K., when He said that every Initiate is eventually a healer; and by M.M. when He said, "Do not forget that I am also a physician."

There is no escape from the healing process because life is going to force you to be healthy. Healing and health are the most important functions of a human being. Many people in various parts of the world have started to sense this idea at this time, as evidenced by the tremendous interest in health — exercise, fitness, and diet.

Sickness of the mental body occurs when there are too many illusions and too much vanity and ego in it. Ego is equal to cancer in the mental body. Vanity is a degenerative disease in the mental body. Separatism is diphtheria in the mental body.

If the astral body is full of hatred, jealousy, revenge, fear, etc., it smells like sewage; and how can you expect to enter an Ashram if you smell like sewage?

Your bodies must radiate *fragrance.* Fragrance is a sign of health. This is why Christ said, "You must radiate your fragrance." Your bodies must never smell like dead flowers or rotting fruits and vegetables.

Healing is not just a physical phenomenon. Actually, ninety-nine percent of all physical troubles start from the mental, astral, and etheric planes. When physicians try to heal the physical body without healing the astral and mental bodies, they just patch the walls but eventually the water starts leaking again.

In order to be a healer and to be healed, one must increase his light, love, and willpower. You can never be healed without increasing your own light, love, and willpower. This idea has been recognized by some doctors who have started programs which emphasize the expansion of the consciousness of the patient and the cleansing of his heart from malice, hatred, and jealousy before the physical healing process starts.

In the future, all doctors will prescribe certain disciplines of mind and emotions before writing any prescriptions for the physical body so that the higher bodies do not continuously produce germs which attack the physical body and interfere with the physical healing methods.

The light which pours out of the healer's eyes, hands, and heart is mostly silver or electric blue.

Sometimes healing with light and not healing with love makes the patient's condition worse. In addition, when you heal with light without the presence of love, you do not have protection and you absorb the sicknesses of other people into your body.

When you have light in your brain, you have some kind of Intuition developed within you, a kind of seeing eye which sees the location of the sickness in the body. Your hand goes directly to the place that is sick on the patient. Or you may clairvoyantly see the location of the sickness. Unless you have this Intuition or clairvoyance, you may stimulate different centers at the expense of others and create disharmony in the system of the patient.

Those who do not yet know the location of the patient's sickness do not have light and are only pretending to be healers. They may deceive people into believing that they are healing with etheric energy — which means, to give someone liquor to eliminate his pain or depression, and the condition becomes worse once the influence of the liquor wears off.

When the healer directs light, he dispels darkness. Darkness is sickness. Darkness in the body means congestion; every kind of congestion is darkness. Petrification is darkness. For example, petrification of the pineal gland is darkness. Calcifications are darkness. The accumulation of certain elements in certain places of the body is darkness. This darkness can be seen with X rays.

Degeneration of tissues and organs is darkness because it creates fermentation. Darkness is also the accumulation of germs and microbes. Cancer and tumors are darkness. All these types of darkness are dispersed by light. This is why the presence of great Initiates is healing because Their light penetrates into your bodies and eventually dispels your darkness.

You can heal yourself if you hold yourself in the light of your Soul. You must create that light within you and stand in it.

Healing with Light

This exercise can be done individually or in a group.

1. Close your eyes and relax.

2. Visualize a spark of light at the center of your head, in the middle point of your brain.

3. Make this light gradually bigger and bigger, until it is bigger than your head.

4. Visualize this light penetrating throughout your body. Do not direct it to any specific location; let it penetrate everywhere equally. See your body becoming slowly translucent.

5. Locate a place in your body that has a problem. Take a deep breath and send the light there, and in one second take your mind away from that spot.

6. Stand in the light again, as if you are standing in a spotlight. Let the light penetrate your head, eyes, nose, mouth, teeth, gums, ears, cheeks, and nose.

7. Let the light move down and penetrate the neck, shoulders, chest area, breasts, lungs, and heart.

8. Let the light penetrate the stomach, intestines, sexual organs, legs, knees, feet, and toes.

9. Now visualize the light pouring out of your toes and coming back to your head, and going through your entire body and reaching again to your toes. Repeat this five times.

10. Now let the flow of the light come up toward the head and pour into the reservoir of the light. After a few seconds, rest.

11. Let the light penetrate with the rhythm of your heartbeat into your entire body. Again, after a few seconds, rest.

12. Focus the light on your spine, from the top of the head to the tailbone, for just a few seconds. **Make sure that your concentration on a particular spot is very brief.**

13. Send the flow of light into your hands, arms, and palms. Put your palms on your knees, and let the light flow into your knees.

14. Put your hands on your navel, right hand upon the left hand. Let the light penetrate into your organs. See them as translucent. Feel yourself becoming warmer and warmer.

15. Direct your light into your palms with the rhythm of your breath. Inhale from the head, and exhale through your palms. Repeat this inhalation and exhalation for a few seconds.

16. If this is being done in a group, hold the hands of other people participating in the exercise, and let the light flow throughout everyone present. See the light circulating through the entire group, purifying, cleansing, healing, and uplifting.

17. Visualize above the group a five-pointed star which is shedding light on everyone. All the group members should inhale the light and spread it throughout the group.

18. Visualize that all the bodies are becoming healthy, all the emotions are becoming purified, and all the minds are becoming cleaner and cleaner.

19. See a cloud of darkness coming out of you, going through the roof, hitting a rock, and destroying the rock and disappearing with the rock.

20. Relax and open your eyes.

This exercise may be done every day, early in the morning, if you wish. This is not meditation, but a relaxation exercise in the light. Let light penetrate every part of your body. Do not concentrate on any part of your body until you learn the technique. After you learn the technique, the focusing of light on any part of your body must be only for a short duration, one second or so.

If you want to help somebody, you must first sit in the light for five minutes. Then put your right hand on your forehead with your palm outward, and extend your left hand toward the person. Visualize the beam of light going through your right hand to your left hand and pouring out on the person — not to a specific location in his body.

This can be done for ten to fifteen minutes, but it is very important that you keep concentrating on the light and do not let any other thought come to your mind. *This is very important.*

If you want to comfort someone in his emotional troubles, do the same thing, but put your right hand, palm in, on your heart.

If you want to help a person expand his mind, to be tolerant and broad in consciousness, do the same thing, but put your right hand, palm in, on the top of your head.

Everyone is eventually going to be a light, so start being in light and living like a light. Transfiguration is the stage when your three bodies become all light. Resurrection is total entrance into the light of the Divine Spheres and becoming a part of the Divine Light.

If your light is intense, sometimes you may heal people only by looking at them, touching them, or simply being with them. You do not need to tell them you are healing them. Actually, you are transmitting light, and the light is doing the job. When Initiates walk, Their vibration and radiation heal people. Even their shadow heals people.

The heartbeat and breathing are coordinated by using light energy and prana to heal and uplift. When you want to direct the light into etheric, astral, and mental bodies, use the heartbeat because the resistance of these vehicles is less than the resistance of the physical body, which needs more time to accept and assimilate the healing energies of light and love. The will energy needs no time to be assimilated; its assimilation is instantaneous.

There is also healing through hugging someone. Mothers hug their children and indirectly or unconsciously heal them. People hug each other and heal each other. But one must have light in order to uplift someone else and heal him with a hug.

There is also the method of touching hearts together, but without mixing the currents of light, love, or willpower with sexual thoughtforms or sensuality. These things disturb the current of healing energies, except in cases when the two people are connected to each other in love or in marriage, or they are in the process of lovemaking.

People think that in lovemaking there is only the satisfaction of sex. Actually, when lovemaking is done in the right way, it is a healing process whereby the one who is stronger in love, light, and energy charges the other and harmonizes many centers; or absorbs the pollution of the other and releases him or her. Lovemaking must not be limited to physical sex; it must involve emotions, thoughts, and spirit. Then the healing is complete.

People kill each other by sending each other ill will, hatred, and negative thoughts instead of healing each other with light, love, and energy.

Healing by light proceeds if the sick person is not using drugs or alcohol and is not involved with hypnotism or crimes. Before attempting healing, the healer must know that the subject is in a state of leaving his past behind and making a commitment to follow healthy ways of living and healthy ways of relating to people and life in general.

Healing can create complications if the person does not have such a commitment and does not turn his back on the past errors. A healthy attitude eases the healing process.

Healing must be practiced after one is sure that he has light, that he knows how to transmit the light and how to deal with those whom he wants to heal. If these factors are not present, his efforts to heal create complications.

One may ask, "How do I know that I have light and am not living by the light of outer sources?" The answer is

1. When you close your eyes and relax, you should see a flame of light in the center of your head.

2. You do not engage in activities of darkness, such as crimes, treason, malice, hypocrisy, slander, etc.

3. You see the value in others.

This light can also appear if you do intense visualization, but the difference is that such a light appears like a reflection — artificial and crystallized. The real light is vibrant, living, and radiating. Remember that Christ said, "Shine your light."

You may lose your light if you act against light. Heavenly gifts are totally ethical in their foundation.

Light comes into existence within the head when the human soul establishes a contact with the Inner Watch.

Love comes into existence when the Soul-infused person contacts a Master, an Ashram, or the Hierarchy.

Will comes into operation when the Initiate makes a contact with "the center where the Will of God is known."

Healing with Love

Love is a healing energy not yet used consciously and scientifically. In the future, man will be able to measure this energy and find better ways to use it for the improvement of human life. Christ was called the Great Physician because He was the embodiment of love.

Love allows people to have contact with its source, and the powerful source begins to tune the whole mechanism of the person. Like a Cosmic Magnet, the source of love harmonizes and synchronizes the vehicles of man, purifying them from any disorderly phenomena.

Health is harmony, synchronization, rhythm, and purity. Love offers all these things, but one cannot transmit love without having and being love. Love must be transmitted through a focal point between the eyebrows, and it must fill the entire aura. The color of this energy is ruby-pink. This ruby-pink energy is a great agent of healing. It has a very strong ability to penetrate where the light cannot penetrate.

In the process of healing with love, the healer unites his heart with the Heart of the Hierarchy and channels the love of the Hierarchy to his Solar Angel, from his Solar Angel to his soul, from his soul to the focal point between his eyebrows and then to his left hand.

During the flow of love energy to the subject, the healer may also visualize that the energy of love is doing the needed repair, according to the karmic possibilities and the future intentions of the subject. Love heals if the subject is not intoxicated by feelings of hatred, revenge, etc. If these feelings are present, love energy multiplies the germs of these feelings and complicates the situation.

One must realize that healing with love also involves light energy. Love and light work together, but in this case love energy predominates.

Visualization is a technique of directing and focusing the available energy, so it must be used in light and love healing. Visualization directs the energies into the etheric body. When you are dealing with light, visualization directs love energy into the emotional and lower mental body. Visualization directs will energy into the higher mental body and into the aura as a whole.

The color of light energy is silver-blue. The color of love energy is ruby-pink. The color of will energy is red-orange.

Visualization at this stage is a mechanism to focus or direct those energies into certain areas of your body or the body of the subject.

How can you increase your light, your love, and your willpower? Light is always there and in an increasing state if you do not extinguish it by actions, feelings, and thoughts which are antagonistic to light.

The flame of love is always in your heart and in an increasing state if you do not extinguish it through actions, words, feelings, thoughts, and motives antagonistic to love and unity.

Your willpower is your essence. It is there to radiate out if you do not hinder and bury it under acts taken against the laws of Nature; subjectively against the Law of Love, the Law of Unity, and the Law of Synthesis; against Beauty, Goodness, Righteousness, Joy, and Freedom. You must be spiritual, or you must have higher values in order to be a healer.

In the healing process, you do not visualize the colors of the energies until you know whether the color of the energy you are sending to your organs or toward your subject is harmonious with the color of his Rays, with the color of his organs being healed, and with the predominating color in his aura. Visualization strengthens the quality of the color, and it may create conflict because of its strength. But if the energy is channeled without emphasizing the color, you give time and opportunity to the energy and the organ to adjust to each other and harmonize their colors.

Also, the colors of these energies cannot be visualized correctly if you have not seen them in operation. Visualizing a slightly different hue can change the quality of the energy.

During the process of healing, you must be focused only in the energy transmission; your mind and feelings must stop producing thoughts and feelings for a while. When the energies pass through your thoughts and emotions, not only is their voltage broken down, but also they are polluted by your personality concerns.

You are only a transmitter. This is hard to understand for those who have not passed through a training of concentration, meditation, and discipline.

How do you know if you have love? Again, you can see its flame in your heart, or you can measure it in your actions, feelings, words, thoughts, and motives. If these are charged by love, if your life is inclusive, not self-seeking and separative; if you can understand people and can search for beauty in them; if you are ready to sacrifice for the Common Good, you have light and love energy, and you increase them by using them.

In order to heal with love, you must not allow yourself to submit to any fear. As Christ said, "In perfect love there is no fear." If you have any kind of fear in your heart or mind, you cannot do healing by love. You must also have a record of harmlessness in the past few incarnations. Love energy does not accumulate when you are caught in fear, hatred, separatism, jealousy, revenge, and greed.

Healing With Willpower

This gift belongs to advanced Initiates whose **sense of healing** is already in operation. Willpower begins to release itself within us after the experience of total Transfiguration. In the Fourth Initiation, it shines with greater power. In the Fifth Initiation, it reaches its maturity.

As you become your True Self, detaching yourself consciously from your not-self, you release will energy from your Core.

How to heal with this energy? First, your vehicles must be very healthy and Soul-infused. Your Intuition or higher clairvoyance must be active. You must be aware of the karma of the subject.

No Initiate attempts to work against the Law of Karma. One can be severely damaged if after initiation he acts for one moment against this law; his evolution can be retarded for thousands of years.

Before healing, the healer tries intuitively to know the karma of the subject. If the karma is in favor of healing, he still does not proceed in healing, but he asks a question in his mind, such as, "If my releasing the will energy to heal this person is not in accord with karmic law, let the energy bypass and not be used for healing." Or, "If my healing is accepted by the Will of God, let the energy released do its healing work."

If the Initiate knows without a doubt that the subject is under attack by dark forces, he immediately protects him and uses his energies to heal him. When Christ healed with will energy, He absolutely knew that the karma of the person allowed it, and He could heal him as witness to the healing powers. Or, by the permission of "the Father," He used to take the karma of the subject on Himself...and He paid for it with His suffering on the cross.

In order to heal with will energy, the Initiate must bring the energy from Shamballa directly to himself, bypassing his Solar Angel. He must channel it to his right hand; then the right hand will pass it to the left hand, mixing it with love and light energy to heal the person.

In healing with willpower, both hands are used together. The right hand is put on the location of the trouble; the left hand is put on the right hand, and energy is channeled by the human soul to the hands and through the hands to the human soul of the subject.

Willpower can manifest as physical urges, emotional desires, and mental determinations; but these are not pure forms of will because they may be mixed with personality drives, glamors, illusions, ego, and vanity. To have a pure will is not easy, and it needs long years of discipline, purification, and development.

This method is not really used on the vehicles, but *through* the vehicles to contact the human soul, to evoke the willpower in him, and to release him from inertia, glamors, illusions, ego, vanity, and false karma.

False karma is an important fact not mentioned before. It is the impression that the pain, suffering, or discipline which the laws of karma imposed on you to make you free from your debt are still in operation. You are so impressed that you think you are still under the hammer of the karmic laws. For example, when you have been in prison and are released, for a long time you still feel you are in prison.

False karma created or fabricated by us is a great hindrance on the path of our advancement.

Great healers heal not only through such techniques or ceremonial acts but also with their presence. Their presence radiates powerful energies of light, love, and will; and whomever they contact, they heal and release. **Healing is, in essence, a process of harmonization with Divine Order and the ability to increase the Divine Presence in us.**

Healing through Art

Healing through art needs light, love, and willpower. Healing through painting, music, and dancing has been used throughout millenniums. To do such a healing, one must know, in painting for example, the chemistry of colors, forms, and movements. Certain colors can create a harmony with a form and with the meaning of the form. Others create contradiction and color-noise.

Nicholas Roerich's paintings are built on this esoteric chemistry. He has a painting, for example, in which a deer is escaping from a hunter and seeking refuge with a monk who is sitting on a rock. The hunter lets loose the arrow, but the arrow hits the hand of the monk, which is extended over the deer for protection.

The name of the painting is "Compassion." This painting is a living, moving picture. There is movement in it; there is color and form in it — all combined in such a way that compassion is evoked from your heart. This is what esoteric chemistry is. Colors, forms, lines, shapes, and meaning are fused harmoniously to make you feel "compassionate."

The same system can be used in music. The rhythm, the melody, the pauses, the notes, the accents, etc., fused with the dream, the vision, and the psychic energy of the composer make the music a unique science of healing, as it releases the light, love, and will energy of the composer.

The same is true for dance. One must choose the dancers, the colors, the form of the costumes, the music, the movements, the rhythms, etc., as if each of these factors were chemical elements to be combined to produce healing.

Every Initiate is a healer. Every artist is a healer. The presence of such people in humanity is a blessing. Beauty transmits a tremendous amount of light, love, and will energy. Beauty releases the sense of healing and makes it operative on lower planes. Beauty is the manifestation of light, love, and power, harmonized in a form.

Both spiritual and Divine healing are the art of evoking the Beauty in man and making it express itself as a tangible beauty.

Sacred dances also are powerful means of healing. They are organized in such a way that their movements transmit and direct energies to the audience to heal, to uplift, and to transform their physical, emotional, and mental nature.

The music, the color, and the movements are mathematically planned to bring certain effects.

Advanced dances or movements are carried upon the three planes simultaneously. On the mental plane it is the dance of ideas. On the emotional plane it is the dance of emotions. On the physical plane it is the dance of movements.

More advanced dances include the Intuitional Plane through which the participants contact various planetary and solar Centers to transmit certain energies for the regeneration of life.

Healing work is also carried on for others using our

— thoughts

— hands

— eyes

Healing with Balance

Try to find out if the person is out of balance. Look for the physical signs and symptoms, the emotional signs and symptoms, and the mental signs and symptoms.

Physical signs are unhealthy conditions of the body. Emotional signs are hatred, fear, anger, greed, jealousy, and revenge. Mental signs are an egotistical attitude, vanity, and separatism. Mental imbalance expresses itself in conversations and actions. A mentally imbalanced person shows signs of fanaticism, inconsistency, separatism, contradiction, and extremes.

Most of the sources of imbalance are in the mind and in the thinking. If one is able to balance his own and others' thinking, it will be easy to balance the emotional and physical bodies.

An important point to remember is that the existence of imbalance is the result of imbalanced chemistry in the physical, emotional, and mental spheres or bodies. Such an imbalance of chemistry exists because the human being put unbalanced pressure on his vehicles. Such an action can be eliminated by

1. Knowing the age of the soul

2. Making him express his creative forces gradually and purposefully, or in goal-fitness

3. Helping him exercise mastery over his vehicles

4. Making him have a vision of the future

When the human soul, the awareness unit, or the conscious individuality is restored to balance, the balanced vehicles will not prevent the carrying out of a complicated labor. The soul will eliminate all causes of imbalance with the help of the agent of balance. The agent of balance must be the combination of a balanced soul and personality. Before each service, this human soul must work to balance his vehicles.

The balancing agent must help the human soul of the patient to balance his physical body with right diet and professional help. He must help that soul to uproot the six signs of emotional imbalance in his nature, as well as various signs of mental imbalance.

Regular meditation daily; observing oneself in all actions, emotions, and thoughts; and service dedicated to the upliftment of humanity are the major balancing factors in our life.

86

A Transformative Exercise

1. Sit quietly and relax.
2. Visualize that you have put your body in a coffin and passed away, or just leave your body.
3. See how your body is burned.
4. Go to a mountaintop and visualize yourself as a flame.
5. Burn your astral body.
6. Burn your mental body.
7. See your light shining upon the mountain.
8. See how far your light will go.
9. See all around the mountain.
10. Take a deep breath and create a mental body, lemon-yellow in color. Repeat three times.
11. Take a deeper breath and create a new emotional body, silver in color. Repeat four times.
12. Take an even deeper breath and create an etheric body, rosy or violet in color in the shape of a physical body you like.
13. Take three deep breaths and create a new, beautiful body.
14. Now try to align and coordinate these four bodies like a symphony.
15. Sit quietly, and open your eyes.

87

Resurrection

The victory of the human spirit over matter will continue age after age, and we will have more Resurrected Ones Who will shine over the horizons of humanity as radiant stars teaching us the secrets of health, happiness, and joy.

This chapter may help you make a great breakthrough in your consciousness and help you see the possibilities for permanent health and freedom. It may be that you need to do the given exercises for thirty to forty years, or thirty lifetimes! But eventually, you will attain Resurrection. Those Who have attained Resurrection worked intensely for thousands of years. As They proceeded on the Path of Resurrection, Their body attained purification and eventually it became spiritual. A body that is in the process of resurrection will be a source of health, beauty, and radiation.

The exercises given here are not easy. They call for those people who know the purpose of their life and are determined to climb the path leading to the summit. This is the radiant path leading to perfect health.

Great is the glory of the human soul. The human soul is a Spark fallen onto earth, but it carries within itself all the Cosmic possibilities.

Infinity is present in the human soul. These possibilities, this Infinity, are revealed within the human soul as he proceeds on the Path of Resurrection.

In this chapter you will find practical suggestions and exercises on how to resurrect yourself

From darkness to Light,

From the unreal to the Real,

From death to Immortality,

From chaos to Beauty.

You can do these exercises at your own risk. If you are ready for spiritual adventure, you will love and enjoy them. If you are not ready, read them and wait for the day when a new awakening will take place in your consciousness.

Experimentation and experience are factors that give credibility to knowledge. Knowledge is abstraction unless it manifests and proves itself in experience. Theories or knowledge can create cleavages, but experience leads to understanding and unity.[1]

One must work to actualize one's own Self. One can collect much information but never proceed on the path of evolution because evolution is based on the foundation of transformation and not on accumulation.

Resurrection starts when the Spark makes a breakthrough and passes to the vegetable kingdom and produces color, fragrance, and growth. Then It makes another breakthrough and enters the animal and human kingdoms and continues Its way toward Infinity. This is the Path of Resurrection; the Spark goes back to Its original state of being.

The process of Resurrection goes on within the human being. First, the Spark is stuck for many ages in the etheric and physical body; then It resurrects Itself toward the astral and mental bodies. Eventually It lifts Itself up to the intuitional and atmic bodies. When It is able to penetrate into the Divine Plane, we say that the Spark achieved Resurrection on the human level.

This is what Christ did: He finished His human evolution and penetrated into His Solar evolution.

We, as Sparks, are stuck in our physical shell, but eventually we are going to break it. Unless we have the experience that we are not bodies, all our knowledge in many fields will be used to identify our Spirit more and more with our shell. All our theories about the soul and spirit receive value only when we have an experience. Only the resurrected part of ourselves can penetrate into the domains of conscious immortality.

If we resurrect ourselves into the astral plane, we will be conscious only on the astral plane and unconscious on the mental plane. On whatever plane we resurrect ourselves while in physical existence, we will be conscious only upon the corresponding plane after death. That is why Christ urged us to resurrect ourselves, and He resurrected Himself to show us the possibility of doing the same.

Some people think that natural evolution will eventually carry us through the Path of Resurrection. This is not a correct statement. Nature brings us up to the human level. If we want to pass beyond it, we must strive and make greater breakthroughs. If we fail, three conditions may await us:

1. We may suffer in proportion to our delay.

2. We may fall into the danger of enforced pralaya.

3. We may fall into the danger of annihilation.

---

1. For further infomation on experience, please refer to *The Ageless Wisdom*, Ch. 24.

When man eventually was materialized, one way was left for him to save and liberate himself from slavery — that was his imagination. The real root of imagination is the memory of the great beauty in which the Spark existed before materialization. But imagination began later to serve the lower instincts of man, and man built a world of imagination to live within.

When imagination was cultivated and it became creative imagination — which is a combination of the memories of beauty before materialization and the memories of being in one's present life span — it was an effort to re-experience the memories and possibly recreate them. Creative imagination developed in certain individuals through hard labor and became visualization, which is the ability to translate creative inspirations and impressions coming from higher sources.

Creative imagination and visualization are senses latent within the Core of the human being. As they unfold and develop, they prepare the human soul for greater expansion of consciousness and clearer Self-actualization. One imagines and visualizes, then creates. Pure imagination is the grounding wire; visualization is the hot wire. Pure imagination is the door to actualization. Visualization is the door to inspirations and impressions.

We expand our horizon within our consciousness toward the past and toward the future. Then our consciousness transforms and molds matter, or our vehicles, upon the design of our creative imagination. "Whatever you think in your heart, so you are."

We have to resurrect ourselves from the forms of our physical, emotional, and mental bodies, within which we are literally buried.

There are many exercises that we can do in our mind to develop our creative imagination and visualization and bring transforming changes within our nature. This transformation is not easy because the image of ourselves built throughout ages must slowly lose its "reality" and be replaced by the symbol of the Inner Dweller. We cannot advance on the path of victory unless we detach ourselves from our own image and build a new image which is closer to reality, to our essential being.

For most people, their personality becomes their own grave. They need to make greater efforts to resurrect themselves step-by-step, from one level to another, from one plane to another, until their whole nature is transcended.

The secret steps toward Resurrection are the gradual realizations that we are not our form, our emotional expressions, or our thoughtforms. We are the motivating power behind all these.

We look into the mirror; we see our form, our face, and we think: "I am beautiful. My eyes are beautiful. This nose is pretty. These cheeks are shiny. This hair is wavy....I am so beautiful, beautiful, beautiful...."

We start making more efforts to work on our form, and our own image impresses our mind so strongly that we think we are our own form. We become identified with it. We become our body.

For fifty, sixty, or eighty years we look in the mirror and think, "That is me, me, me...," and eventually our nose becomes us. Once we identify with our form, it will take a long time to release and resurrect ourselves toward our original state of being.

You look at your baby and say to your friend, "Isn't my baby beautiful? She is so darling. Look at the eyes, the lips, the hands...." But you forget that you are talking about the body of your baby, not about the real her. And the baby hears your voice and your comments over and over again and thinks about herself as a body. She becomes a body.

Our culture is built to a very great percentage on the body consciousness, on an "I am my body" consciousness. A great part of advertising, propaganda, and politics runs around matter and body consciousness. That is why most people have a deep fear of death. Fear originates from separation and separatism.

The Path of Resurrection is steady striving toward the realization of your essential formlessness. This is not an easy path. Your body has its own melodramas and tragedies. Your emotional body has its phantasmagorias; your mental body has its labyrinths; and you as a flame must walk through all these and resurrect yourself to the state of your essential being.

Every time you try to make a real effort, you experience a reaction from your bodies and also from those who are stuck within their bodies. That is why the Path of Resurrection is called the "path to Shamballa" — the lonely path to Shamballa. This loneliness is the feeling of the personality. The human soul rejoices at every step that takes him closer to Home.

Before we can master our vehicles, the image of mastery and the approximate conditions must be achieved in our consciousness. It is after the change and expansion of consciousness that the vehicles obey and adapt themselves to higher calls.[2]

Our procedure is to become ourselves, and as we succeed in becoming our True Self, the flowers of our chakras unfold, bloom on various levels, and keep our vehicles in contact with a more abundant life.

The story of the Prodigal Son is the story of Resurrection. The vital plan of Christ was to teach humanity how to resurrect itself from the grave of matter. Christ told the story of a man who left his father's house and went away and eventually began to eat like the pigs. Then one day he remembered the Father's Home and turned his face toward home. That was the beginning of the Resurrection of his Spirit.

All the Teaching of Christ was an effort to build the Path of Resurrection and impress on the mind of humanity that the goal of this planetary evolution is to achieve Resurrection.

---

2. On consciousness and beingness, please refer to *The Ageless Wisdom*, pp. 36-43.

It is possible that on the Path of Resurrection you turn your eyes back and confess, "Why was I so crazy? How could I have lived such a life in the past? How many people did I hurt because of the way I lived?..." But then the beauty of the vision attracts you again, and you continue the Path of joyful Resurrection.

People feel proud when they are able to destroy their enemies and take over their possessions. Such an attitude is an earthbound attitude. To conquer and destroy enemies means to work against your own Self.

You should not have an enemy. You do not actually have an enemy. There is only one Self. Are you trying to kill your own Self?

The problem is how to illustrate these ideas for the modern "geniuses" whose noses are stuck in matter and breathe only separatism!

Any time you feel and see the reality of the phenomenal world, you have a contact with your innermost Self. Such an experience is just like planting a seed in your consciousness, which grows and grows and becomes like a Sun.

One must experience Resurrection. Experience at this stage is registration in your mind of the process of your transformation or transfiguration. Awareness of your transfiguration is your experience.

In experience, duality still exists. When duality is transcended, the experience turns into a process of becoming. Then you become an experience for those who still live in duality.

There are three prisons from which we must liberate ourselves:

1. Materialism

2. Totalitarianism

3. Separatism or selfishness

These three are considered the most powerful enemies confronted on the Path of Resurrection. Only the gradual defeat of these enemies on individual, national, and international scales will release us toward the Path of Resurrection.

Materialism is born when the Spirit identifies with matter. Totalitarianism is born when the Spirit identifies with emotional glamors. Separatism is born when the Spirit identifies with the illusions of the mental body.

Resurrection is an experience which permits the Spirit to leave behind this threefold grave and enter the light of universality. Resurrection is won inch-by-inch, step-by-step, by overcoming the darkness and power of matter, ignorance, separatism, and the six evils of fear, anger, hatred, greed, jealousy, and slander. The physical body goes through transformation, the emotional body is replaced by Intuition, and the Spiritual Triad replaces the Chalice. The Monad shines through the aura with twelve rays of energy.

Exercise for Resurrection:

1. Repeat slowly the following mantram, three to seven times, each time with clearer visualization and creative imagination.

   More radiant than the Sun,

   Purer than the snow,

   Subtler than the ether

   Is the Self,

   The Spirit within my heart.

   I am that Self.

   That Self am I.

2. Close your eyes, relax, breathe deeply a few times, and try to visualize a mountain. See yourself standing on the top of the mountain and changing slowly into a white flame, "more radiant than the Sun." Let your radiation go as far into space as possible, without losing its brightness and intensity.

3. Now, relax more and think:

   "I am more radiant than the Sun because in essence I am one with the One Who uses the Sun as Its body. I am more radiant than the Sun."

   Think about your Self as a white flame and locate the flame in the Sun and see how bright you, as a flame, are.

4. Do not hold onto your human image. Let it go; think about yourself as the flame which is "purer than the snow," a pure, white flame without pollution, without fallout, but purer than the snow of high mountains.

   Do not activate your lower mind and gear yourself into past images of failure and ugliness. You are purer than the snow in your essence. Stay for a few moments in that purity.

5. "I am Subtler than the ether." Think that as ether you can penetrate anywhere and pass through anything. There is no obstacle existing on your path. You are an electrical flow, an electrical wave, and your speed is faster than the light.

6. Visualize your heart center between your shoulder blades, ten inches behind your back.

Visualize the twelve-petaled golden lotus unfolded, and at the center see a shining flame in the form of a fiery diamond. Visualize that you are that fiery diamond. Then say:

More radiant than the Sun,

Purer than the snow,

Subtler than the ether

Is the Self....

Be that diamond, that Spark, that Self.

7. Holding that diamond in your consciousness, sing the affirmation:

More radiant than the Sun,

Purer than the snow,

Subtler than the ether

Is the Self,

The Spirit within my heart.

I am that Self.

That Self am I.[3]

After a few minutes rest.

8. Imagine where you are sitting in your room. Relax. Rub your hands together, open your eyes slowly, and sit quietly for a few minutes.

After four months of doing the previous exercise, you can try the following for another three months:

1. Repeat in your mind, "I am a point of light within a greater Light." In your visualization shine your light out in a greater light on five occasions. See the rays of your light; see if they have colors; see how far your light goes in that greater Light. As your light shines out, see it cleansing any darkness found in your aura. Make your radiation like a pure light with seven colored radiations.

2. Repeat within your mind and visualize, "I am a strand of loving energy within the stream of divine Love." Create a visualization of the "stream

---

3. Musical recording by the author available.

of divine Love," and in it you are a strand. Visualize and create three occasions in which you are a strand of loving energy, within the stream of divine Love.

3. Now say in your mind, "I am a spark of sacrificial fire focussed within the fiery Will of God." Visualize three events in which you are a point of sacrificial fire within the fiery Will of God. Try to symbolize this fiery Will and the point of sacrificial fire in it. Make it really clear and meaningful.

4. Sing:

    I am a point of light within a greater Light.

    I am a strand of loving energy within the stream of divine Love.

    I am a spark of sacrificial fire, focussed within the fiery Will of God.

    And thus I stand.

    I am a way by which men may achieve.

    I am a source of strength, enabling them to stand.

    I am a beam of light, shining upon their way.

    And thus I stand.

    And standing thus, revolve,

    And tread this way, the ways of men,

    And know the ways of God.

    And thus I stand.[4]

5. Imagine once more that you are a spark of sacrificial fire focused within the fiery Will of God, a strand of loving energy within the stream of divine Love, a point of light within a greater Light.

    Let your light, love, and fire shine out, purifying all your vehicles — your physical, etheric, astral, and mental bodies — and making them an abode of glory.

6. Now you are a point of light; you are a strand of loving energy; you are a sacrificial fire within the fiery Will of God. Give three minutes to each phrase.

---

4. "Affirmation of a Disciple," *Discipleship in the New Age*, Vol. II, p. 175, by Alice A. Bailey.

7. Visualize, "I am a way by which men may achieve." Be a way, and try to see how people are achieving because of you. Make yourself a way. Translate this symbolism into practical terms and visualize it. See how people achieve. What does achievement mean for them and for you? What does it mean to be a way?

   You are not a labyrinth where people are lost. You are not a Babylon where people are confused. You are not going to be a dead-end street where people will confront a wall. You are a way by which men may achieve.

8. Sing, "I am a way by which men may achieve. I am a source of strength enabling them to stand."

   Visualize that you are a source of strength enabling them to stand. Make people stand on their feet and not depend on others. Their feet are their divine foundation. Let them stand on their divine foundation.

9. Sing, "I am a beam of light shining upon their way. And thus I stand."

   You are now a beam of light shining upon the way of others who, because of your light, can climb, strive, and achieve. Let your beam of light penetrate dark places of the earth and lead people into greater light.

10. Visualize your light in an orange color, shining upon the top of a mountain. After thirty seconds, change its color into yellow, then into electric blue, then into violet.

11. Fuse your light with the greater Light Divine.

12. Merge yourself as a strand of love with the stream of Divine Love.

13. Visualize yourself as a point of sacrificial fire. Fuse yourself with fire; fuse yourself with the Fire of God.

14. Visualize yourself standing like a fiery pillar in the presence of the Almighty Existence, radiating love, light, beauty, and the glory of fire.

15. Affirm, "And thus I stand."

In creative imagination or visualization, there should not be a process of analyzing but a process of becoming. The mind cannot forget the thoughtform of the image you are. It is impressed by your outer phenomena and sticks to them. In the visualization process, the mind looks toward the incoming impressions rather than occupying itself with past forms.

Creative imagination and visualization can function independently from the mind. Visualization is the ability to translate impressions coming from Cosmic sources. Creative imagination is the sense which relates these translations to the mental world for objectification and possible application.

After three months, you can do the following exercise for fifteen to twenty minutes daily for another three months.

1. Relax.

2. Calm your emotional nature.

3. Bring serenity into your mental nature.

4. Breathe deeply a few times and see your physical body as pure, healthy, and beautiful, without any affliction.

5. See your emotional body as pure as possible. Imagine its shape and color. Think, "What can I do with that body that I can't do with the physical body?" See it in its purest form. Think, "What does it mean when they say, 'I have the purest astral body'?"

6. Visualize your mental body. What would you do if you were in the mental body? How would you feel? What experiences would you expect? What advantages would you have? Make your mental body as pure as you can visualize.

What does this purity mean to you in terms of practical action? What must you eliminate? What must you initiate in your life? Are you mentally pure at this time? Do not condemn yourself; just see.

After another three months, try to study the seven initiations, as given by the Tibetan Master in His books *Initiation, Human and Solar, The Rays and the Initiations,* and *Esoteric Healing.*[5]

Keep a diary and record your experiences, your thoughts, and the effects these steps have on your life and relationships.

These seven initiations are seven great steps that can take you on the Path of Resurrection.

The *first initiation* is the moment when you, the human soul, realize that you are a living existence, not the body.

The *second initiation* is the moment in which you take firm action toward purification of your threefold personality vehicles.

The *Third Initiation* is the moment in which the mind is impressed by the Spark, and gradually the mind absorbs the light of the Spark and radiates it out.

---

5. By Alice A. Bailey.

When you, as the Spark, see your face or feel your reality in the mirror of the mind, we say that you have achieved the Third Initiation, and through the mind you can translate such an experience.

Existence in the three worlds is only possible when the Spirit comes in contact with matter. It is the mirror of matter or substance that makes the Spirit exist as a separate entity. When matter and substance are transcended, man leaves behind the mirror of matter. He sees and realizes His Self as He is.

When the mirror of your mind reaches such a state of refinement in which your beauty, your essential beauty, can be reflected and impressed, we say that you have taken the Third Initiation.

In the first initiation the Self is a dream, a vision. In the second initiation you *feel* the Self and take part in the vision of the Self.

In the Third Initiation you *know* about your Self.

In the *Fourth Initiation* the Self liberates Himself from the octopus of self-interest and dedicates Himself to the service of One Life. Cleavages disappear in the realization of One Life. This is a practical application of the One Self in world affairs.

The Fourth Initiation is the practical application of the consciousness of the One Self within your daily duties, responsibilities, relationships, and visions. This means that whatever you are doing, feeling, or thinking is inspired by the One Self for the service of the One Life.

At the *Fifth Initiation* the Initiate hears the call from Sirius and makes a contact with that great source of Light. This call is a call of encouragement, affirmation, and challenge for higher striving on the Path of Resurrection. It is at this moment that the Purpose of the Path is revealed to Him.

At the *Sixth Initiation* the Initiate sees His glory in the mirror of the Third Cosmic Ether. The space of the planetary existence is conquered, and time no longer exists.

At the *Seventh Initiation* the Initiate leaves the glory of the Second and First Cosmic Ethers and penetrates into the Cosmic Astral Plane. He is a totally Resurrected One as far as the Cosmic Physical Plane is concerned and has now advanced to a Higher Sphere. We are told that Christ achieved such an accomplishment as a son of man.

Resurrection is a continuous process, and it is achieved through our daily life. Every moment of our life must be a striving toward liberation. Immediately when we feel tempted by our lower nature, by our habits, urges and drives, by our glamors and illusions, we must stop a moment and try to direct our attention toward our vision of Resurrection. It is a continuous battle with involutionary forces that is going on within our nature. Either the Self will make it, or the elements will use us to satisfy their impulses.

There are six noble efforts toward Resurrection.

1. Try not to be trapped by your personality. Anyone trapped by his personality cannot proceed on the Path of Resurrection and thus wanders for many millions of years within the valleys of pain and suffering.

Each human being is a key for the door of initiation. If you do not turn the key the right way, the door will not open. Keep your mind clear and your heart pure, and you will turn the key in the door of initiation.

Each word, each deed, each emotion, and each thought either keeps us back or helps us proceed forward. We build our path daily toward Resurrection, or block our path and increase our crystallizations.

2. Try daily not to identify yourself with your vehicles. Every time you make an effort to resurrect yourself, all Nature seems to rebel against you. But if you persist and be patient, you will notice that it is this seeming resistance that will increase your momentum.

Dis-identification from your vehicles must be carried on daily.

For example, do not say, "I am sick." Say, "My body feels sick." Do not say, "I am angry. I am jealous. I hate...." Say, "I see anger, I see jealousy, I see hatred in my emotional nature." Realize that you are different from these emotions. You are "more radiant than the Sun...."

Do not say, "I am hungry. I am crazy." Such expressions increase your problems and make your future efforts for resurrection more difficult.

Each victory achieved over your identification is a one-hundred-year progress on the Path of your Resurrection. Do not fool yourself and make yourself a slave. Resurrection is achieved by a spirit of victory.

3. Try daily to renounce something. Renouncement is the process of increasing joy since in renouncement you become less matter, more Spirit; less failure, more victory.

We are advised to decrease the loads we have put upon our shoulders by our materialistic tendencies if we intend to climb the mountain of initiation. The traveler must be wise to take only the most essential, or else his burden will not allow him to climb. The loads are material possessions, identifications, and the debts of our karma. When most people have an impulse to climb, they sit on their load and cry. They cannot renounce or detach themselves from the objects of their identifications.

4. Try to withdraw into spiritual serenity and values. Sometimes a person focuses his mind on spiritual values, while mixed values or earthly attractions try to disturb his mind and confuse him. When people try to hurt you or when you fail in your daily life, take refuge within your True Self. When you cannot correct things, pray for them in the sanctuary of your Innermost Temple.

Life is a great computer, and its answers or responses are based on justice. Knowing this you can stop wasting your time and energy in trying to correct certain conditions which are beyond your power. In such cases you can withdraw into your Inner Sanctuary and come in contact with the Almighty Power. This power, once invoked, can move mountains.

Withdrawal is a technique to raise yourself above confusion and have a clear overview of situations. Every great work is done after a period of withdrawal.

You must also learn to withdraw from your own vanities and personality problems. Disengage your gears from the personality, and cool down for a while. This will give you refreshment, energy, and a clear vision to continue your Path of Resurrection.

Try often not to be present within your emotional and mental bodies when they are under malicious attacks. Resistance will build greater animosity; non-resistance is a powerful method to disperse the accumulated evil. You cause accumulation through your resistance to the attacks and continuous occupation with adverse forces, and you block the Path of your Resurrection.

5. Try to stand out of your mental mechanism:

   a. Watch your thoughts.

   b. Detach yourself from earthly thoughts.

   c. Try to dispel and disintegrate unworthy thoughtforms — thoughts that are based on lies, hypocrisy, flattery, and bribery.

   d. Try to burn away ugly and malicious thoughts.

   e. Try to dispel thoughtforms animated by anger, fear, hatred, jealousy, and greed.

   f. Try to nourish and energize beautiful thoughts.

   g. Create fiery thoughts.

You must plan special times to practice the above suggestions. It is relatively easy to detach yourself from the control of the body and emotions, but it is hard to detach yourself from your own thoughts and from the thoughts imposed upon your mind.

6. Try to go through the death process in your creative imagination. Do not think about sickness, diseases, or accidents, but visualize the moment you are passing away. Come out of your body, and act as if you were a living being out of your body.

See your body. See the cremation process.

See your beloved ones, and then with clear detachment resurrect yourself into the Subtle Worlds.

Visualize the astral plane; visualize the mental plane; think how you can easily pass through them and achieve greater illumination on the Intuitional Plane.[6]

Think what you would do if you had fifty years or five thousand years in the subtle levels.

See the possibility of continuing the Path of your Resurrection beyond the Cosmic Physical and Cosmic Astral Planes.

At the present time the greatest trap for disciples is the mental plane — the lower mind and the abstract mind with their coarse and subtle thoughtforms. Disciples must learn to transcend the mental plane and live in greater reality. As long as they are attached to or soaked in thoughtforms, they will be unable to see things with a holistic perception and emancipate themselves into the clearer light of Reality.

The cleavages that exist within so-called spiritually progressive groups and organizations are due to their mental attachments. As long as people cannot go beyond their mental spaces, they cannot see the need for unity and they cannot unify groups, churches, and nations that are suffering through separativeness and cleavages.

Man is trapped within his own creation. Real creativity is a process of Resurrection. In real creativity the human soul liberates himself stage after stage from lower worlds, and on each progressive stage he manifests the glory of his greater contacts with Cosmos.

There are seven stages that must be conquered in relation to the mental plane.

The first one is called the *thoughtless stage*. Thoughtlessness is the stage in which your mind is operating like a machine controlled by the thoughts and thoughtforms of others which are flying around you. Your mind is activated by these thoughts and thoughtforms, and you do not have discrimination and choice. You are in action not because of your own choice but because of what others want you to do, or because of what other people do or think. This means that you are absent from your mental vehicle, and you are unable to think and have your own thoughts. Such people are like cars which are driven by criminals.

One may ask, "Why can't people also be activated by the *higher* thoughtforms which exist in Space or around them?" The answer is that "thoughtless" people have no sensitivity toward subtle forms of thoughts. Thoughtless people are very dangerous people because they can operate only by very low or criminal thoughts of others.

The mental body is a very sensitive instrument. It registers and functions unceasingly, on any level of its development.

Thoughtlessness occurs when the owner is either absent, sleeping, or mixed with lower elementals, and the machine is not operated consciously.

---

6. For comprehensive information regarding these planes, see *Other Worlds*.

There is a higher stage of thoughtlessness which occurs when man takes the Fourth Initiation. The mind no longer responds to the impressions of the lower world (physical, emotional, and mental) but becomes a pure channel for ideas and visions originated from the human soul functioning upon the Intuitional Plane.

There is also a state of mind in which the thoughts are suppressed. This resembles the thoughtless stage, but in reality it is a very dangerous state of mind. Those who are caught in this form of thoughtlessness will have a hard time resurrecting themselves from the lower worlds.

You can pause a few minutes to observe your mind and find the forces that are using your mind, even without your permission.

Resurrection can be attained from any plane only through conquering that plane.

Those who want to be resurrected must every minute watch the functioning of their mental mechanism and their thoughts and try to refuse a "thoughtless" state of mind. Butterflies, monkeys, rabbits, and puppets are all symbols of the stage of thoughtlessness.

The second stage of mind which must be conquered is the stage of *earthly thoughts*. At this stage the mind is in operation. It is working, but it is in its lowest gear.

As long as we continuously produce earthly thoughts, Resurrection will be impossible because our earthly thoughts will be chains on our feet.

Earthly thoughts are thoughts of exploitation, greed, and unsatisfied urges to collect and accumulate at the expense of another's freedom and labor. Earthly thoughts are thoughts of identification with transient values, possessions, and positions. Earthly thoughts are thoughts in which you are stuck to passion, sex, drugs, alcohol, and money.

Try to find these earthly thoughts, if you have them, or if they are trying to stick in your mind. Do not identify with them, but see them as they are and find out how much power they have over you and how you can control them or dispel them.

Find out if at any time you had a victory over one of them and how you did it. Find out if you are planning to get rid of them and purify your mental machine. Remember that your body-machine cannot survive if you feed it with trash; the same thing is true for your mind. The mind loses its efficiency if it is fed continuously on earthly thoughts.

Try to see yourself free of earthly thoughts, and see what will happen to you.

It will be very difficult for you to resurrect yourself while earthly thoughts are increasing your load, day after day, until you lose your spirituality and become matter. One must continuously fight against earthly thoughts or earthbound thoughts.

Resurrection uses earth as its airfield to run and fly above it into the blue skies.

One of my Teachers gave me the following exercise to detach myself from earthly thoughts.

Visualize yourself dead and in the coffin. Let people carry you to the mortuary and cremate your body. After cremation think about all the things to which you were attached. Do this twice weekly for twenty minutes.

After you finish watching your cremation, go to a mountaintop as a beam of light and build new physical, emotional, and mental bodies with pure matter and with great beauty.

This exercise helped me survive during genocide, war, and destruction. I was always joyful because I was prepared to face anything that could happen to the material side of my life.

Christ summarized all these concepts when He said, "Look at the lilies of the field; even Solomon did not dress like them...."

Worry and greed wear on our soul and burn our energy. We must be able to withdraw from earthly thoughts, at least occasionally, and take steps eventually to stand above earthly thoughts.

Some people are burdened by their sex; others by their habits; others by their ego, vanity, money, and property. There are different kinds of burdens, but they all delay our journey toward Resurrection.

It will be very good if one sits down weekly for fifteen to twenty minutes and thinks about his load, a load that is not useful. There is only one load which you must be proud to carry — that is your responsibilities. Think how many burdens you have in the physical, emotional, and mental realms. You can resurrect yourself by letting them go, one by one.

Watch your thoughts and mouth, and immediately when you feel that you are on the way to building an earthly thoughtform, stop it and change your gear and direction. If you do this for a while, you will not have difficulty in your ascent and expansion toward greater beauty and contacts.

During this exercise you may make a list of your burdens and let them go during your "cremation." The cremation must be visualized very clearly but without attachment. This will help the progress of your Resurrection.

Only Resurrected Ones can eventually help humanity to resurrect itself.

The third step is to dissipate *unworthy thoughtforms*, thoughts that are degenerative, thoughts that are based on lies, hypocrisy, flattery, and bribery. No one can resurrect himself if he does not liberate himself from such thoughtforms.

Degenerating or disintegrating thoughtforms in Space are worse than decaying dead animals or corpses on earth. Devas and human souls have a very difficult time living in such spheres. Disintegrating thoughtforms spread similar germs in Space, sometimes causing mental epidemics. Such thoughtforms have no foundation; they do not have principles or spirit. They sometimes serve as vehicles for dark forces, but soon they begin to disintegrate and cause pollution within our aura. Many times our aura passes through crises of poisoning. Such poisoning weakens the body, the heart, and the brain and saps our psychic energy.

In daily life you must try to stop those thoughts and thoughtforms which are not based on reality and truth. Before you open your mouth, check your thoughts. Before you build any thoughtform, check your thoughts. Thoughts originating from Beauty, Goodness, and Truth live eternally and ornament Space with their symphonic beauty.

Every time you build a false thoughtform you waste the precious energy of your mental body. When mental energy is wasted, it weakens your system as a whole.

Thoughts based on lies, hypocrisy, flattery, and bribery create great disturbances in Space when they reach the walls of the fiery spheres. It is there that their degeneration starts polluting Space and contaminating the life-giving currents of Cosmic energies pouring down toward the earth. The Law of Karma never tolerates such a crime. Such thoughtforms resemble a sewage pipe broken within your living room. You must stop creating such pollution by all possible means if you want to resurrect yourself "from death to Immortality, from chaos to Beauty."

After pondering upon the above paragraphs, try to find a symbol which represents the purification and dispersion of such thoughts.

There are many records about bad odors existing in rooms and buildings without any apparent reason. Such odors cannot be disinfected by usual methods, but with prayers and meditations one can dispel them. These odors and bad smells are caused by the disintegrating thoughtforms or the astral carcasses of dead people. Sandalwood incense, peppermint, and eucalyptus solutions can provide external help. But total purification is possible with psychic energy produced by prayers and meditation.

It is possible for astral entities to come and leave their astral corpses in your house to take some kind of revenge upon you. Or dark forces can bring such corpses and throw them into your home to create irritation in your system.

Very often the odor is produced by your own degenerative thoughtforms which day by day accumulate in Space and then are attracted to your house where they originated.

Pure thoughts create fragrance not only around you but also within your glands and your whole body.

Disintegrating thoughtforms create bad odors within one's body. They impede the functions of the glands and hinder the circulatory system. When one starts having a bad odor, he must turn his attention to his thoughts and emotions.

Resurrection is not possible in a polluted atmosphere. It needs purity and clear surroundings.

Disintegrating thoughts are related to the various parts of our bodies. Thus they affect the corresponding parts and their chakras and glands.

The fourth step is to try to burn away *ugly and malicious thoughts and thoughts full of slander*. These thoughts are real and they do not disintegrate, but they last centuries and collect millions of similar thoughts floating in Space to become a cloud of locusts.

When a man passes away, these kinds of thoughts attack him from all sides like black bugs and drill into his astral and mental bodies and try to finish them off. This is a kind of hell for those people who lived a life full of ugly thoughts, slander, and malice. Such thoughts prevent the possiblity of Resurrection.

It may be that your speech is factual, but why amplify ugly and malicious thoughts and why construct them? Gossip is forbidden for those who are on the Path of Resurrection. To gossip means to engineer and construct ugly thoughts. You are in the construction business, building ugly and criminal edifices for the spirits of malice and slander.

Try to see yourself free of ugly thoughts, and see what may happen to you. Sometimes you do not even need to define them. You know them in your heart.

Ugly thoughts are like the refuse, the trash of yesterday. They are thoughts which keep you stuck in matter, in ego, in your lies and hypocrisy, in false values. They are thoughts of exploitation, crimes, and heartlessness. They are thoughts of imposition, inquisition, jealousy, and competition. Ugly thoughts sometimes are made by ugly things we see or hear or things others do.

Beautiful thoughts give you wings in the subjective world and help you to ascend higher and higher, not only from level to level but also from joy to greater joy, from glory to greater glory. People born after such flights are usually great talents, leaders, and heroes.

There are many deaths. After each death one experiences a resurrection of spirit.[7]

The first death is the death of the physical body.

The second death is the death of the astral body.

The third death is the death of the mental body.

The fourth death is the destruction of the causal body.

The fifth death is the planetary body death.

After the causal body is destroyed, the Spark resurrects Itself into the Atmic, Monadic, and Divine Planes, and a time comes when It transcends the Cosmic Physical Plane and enters the Cosmic Astral Plane.

The Path of Resurrection has no end. It is the only Path on which walk all Sons of God, on different levels with different duties and responsibilities but all tied together in the spirit of Resurrection. The Royal Road leading to the palace of perfect health is the Road of Resurrection.

---

7. For additional information please refer to *Other Worlds*, Ch. 54, "Five Deaths."

Exercise for the Resurrection Process

1. Sit relaxed.
2. Close your eyes.
3. Imagine you are out of your body and standing in front of your body which is resting on a chair.
4. Leave your body there and go to the top of a mountain.
5. Come back to your body and stand behind it for a second.
6. Go again to the top of the mountain. Sit there and visualize your astral body. Come out of your astral body.
7. Be a mental body.
8. Let your astral body slowly dissolve with its fears, anger, hatred, greed, jealousy, depression, and negativity.
9. Feel as if you are in the mental body. Slowly leave the mental body and watch it from outside. See yourself as a luminous being. Let your separatism, illusions, pride, and vanity go with the mental body and stand in the great light of higher, more glorious vestures.
10. Feel your freedom from the limitations of these three bodies. Affirm that you are not your bodies. Affirm that you are an immortal spirit, beyond time, space, matter, and force.
11. See what you can do to serve humanity, what plans you can conceive to clear the Path of Resurrection for humanity.
12. Visualize a pure mental body, a pure emotional body, a radiant physical body, and enter into them. Come back to your room. Feel your body. Remember where you were sitting. Rub your hands together and open your eyes. It is good to rest in silence for five minutes.

Do this exercise every day for three months, not more than fifteen to twenty minutes daily. If you have any unpleasant experience, stop it and try to find the cause of it.

If this exercise is done in the right way, it will increase your vitality, sanity, expand your consciousness, and make you more free.

The spiritual Path is a path full of surprises. As one tries to raise his spirit toward Beauty, Goodness, Truth, Freedom, and Joy, he notices the mobilization of a different army within himself.

Every step toward Beauty calls out from the dark caves of our being an ugly act, event, thought, or motive.

Every step toward Goodness calls out from the dark, inner corners of our being thoughts of malice and memories of harmful emotions, acts, and motives.

Every step toward Truth awakens in us seeds of lies, hypocrisy, bribery, flattery, and untruth which a long time ago were buried within us.

Every step toward Freedom evokes those impressions within us when we enjoyed the slavery of body, emotion, and thought.

Every step toward Joy restimulates hidden impressions and memories of pain, suffering, and failure.

This stage on the Path of our evolution is called the "battlefield experience" in which the two armies of our nature fight. There is the army of the vision and the future, and there is the army of the past, of involution. And the human soul feels like a pendulum which goes from right to left, from left to right. As he goes to the left, he denies all the precious virtues toward which he was striving. As he goes toward the right, the forces of Resurrection rejoice and his flowers unfold and bloom.

This phase of our life is a very difficult phase, and three things must be done by a person and his friends to help the situation. As one feels the pull of the negative pole:

1. He must at least try to keep in his heart the best visions of the future.

2. He must keep away from those who are on the path of ascent so as not to pollute them with his aura and contaminate them with his irritations and psychic emanations.

3. He must by all means pray for divine help, even if he is deep in darkness.

On the other side, his friends will

1. Not criticize him or gossip about him

2. Keep praying for him, sending him good thoughts about his future achievements

3. Stay away from him in loving detachment, with no trace of vanity or pride

The spiritual life at various times confronts you with such a situation, and you can learn from others. Loving understanding is the key for all those who see their friends on the line of the pull of the negative pole. Remember that denial of spiritual values and solemnity makes a person a "tasty dish" for Satans.

The resurrection of Spirit takes place when one breaks the phase of the pendulum stage and heads toward the future, with the immovable decision to go ahead and never turn back to a degenerative life. Those who go through such experiences must take vacations and retreats and clearly see the situation and readjust their lives.

The fifth step is to try to dispel *thoughtforms animated by anger, fear, hatred, jealousy, and greed.* There are millions of such thoughtforms almost covering the earth and clouding each human aura. Disciples must be able to liberate themselves from such thoughtforms and stand like lightning rods to bring in the power and the fire from the Sun beyond the clouds.

Those who remain buried within the tomb of anger, fear, hatred, jealousy, and greed cannot enter the Path of Resurrection. One must use this inner fire to transcend anger, fear, hatred, greed, and jealousy and walk toward the summit of serenity, fearlessness, love, generosity, givingness, and a sense of oneness. Such virtues become wings for us and take us out of our prisons.

Every step on the Path of Resurrection will be a victory over the above five evils or five iron chains of slavery.

One must meditate and find out how anger chains us, how fear and hatred make us slaves, how jealousy imprisons our spirit, and how greed closes our heart. It is good to observe how the human soul humiliates himself by falling into these five traps.

Daily one must try to stand above these five traps, keeping watch over his thoughts, words, and actions.

Every hindrance on your path delays your Resurrection.

The sixth step is to nourish and energize *beautiful thoughts*. It is at this stage that man, or the human soul, gains his dignity and prestige.

What are beautiful thoughts? Beautiful thoughts are thoughts related to freedom, to compassion, to harmlessness, to solemnity, to nobility, to honesty. Beautiful thoughts reflect Infinity, inclusiveness, oneness, and future visions for humanity.

Beautiful thoughts are charged with goodwill and right human relations. Beautiful thoughts are based on goodness, truth, joy, and sacrificial service. There is no vanity, self-interest, bribery, showing-off, flattery, or slander in beautiful thoughts.

Beautiful thoughts inspire people to strive, to achieve, to sacrifice, and even to renounce. It is only through beautiful thoughts that the planet survives.

Beautiful thoughts prepare the way for the Resurrection of the human soul. How can we nourish them? We can nourish them by supporting beautiful thoughts through our words, decisions, actions, and creative expressions. Every time you hear, see, or experience a beautiful thought, give your spiritual energy to it so that it grows and spreads benevolent influences over humanity. In energizing good, beautiful thoughts, you build the Path toward Resurrection.

The seventh step is to create *fiery thoughts*. Fiery thoughts can be created if you are in contact with the fiery Core of your being. Fiery thoughts are

— purificatory

— enthusiastic

— penetrative

— creative

— future oriented

— inclusive

— blissful

Fiery thoughts are created when the higher mind is fused with the Intuitional Plane. In fiery thoughts, illusions and deceptions do not exist; thoughts are pure, simple, deep, and holistic.

Pure thoughts transmit ideas without distortion and evoke warm response from the hearts of men. Pure thoughts are very dynamic, and they create movements for the welfare of humanity. When thoughts are pure and fiery, the human soul finds opportunity to liberate himself from the mental plane and step into the Intuitional Plane.

The Resurrection of the human soul will be an impossibility without fiery thoughts because pure, fiery thoughts build the bridge through which the human soul elevates himself to higher planes, to higher dimensions.

These seven states of mind are not sequential. No matter where you are in the field of society, your mental state fluctuates up and down, and your psycho-chart is filled with zigzagging lines like barometric pressure charts. Unless you conquer the seven states of mind and enter into illumination, you are not yet resurrected.

Resurrection on the human scale is victory over the mind, over the world of thought and thoughtforms. It is easy to hold your hand. It is easy to control your body, your emotions, your mouth, but it is very difficult to control your mental mechanism, your thought world.

To be Resurrected means to achieve the primordial, the essential original state of your beingness.

The forces of Nature bring Resurrection to Nature every time spring comes with its flowers and birds. Nature begins to rejoice through colorful bugs, beautiful flowers, singing birds, colors, fragrance, and vitality. Spring is the gift of Nature. Nature blooms through Nature, but it does not stop there.

Nature wants man to resurrect himself.

Resurrection needs energy, efforts, dedication, renunciation, mastery, and tremendous labor. Nature demands all these from man to enable him to resurrect himself. Eventually you must release yourself from your traps, from your body, from your urges and drives, from your negative emotions, from your irritations and fears, from thoughtlessness, wrong thoughts, ugly thoughts, and degenerative thoughts. This is how you can make people come and find your grave empty.

Every day before you retire, ask yourself:

What was the chart of the fluctuations of love, emotions, and thoughts?

Which state of mind was I most in?

What was my level exactly?

At what altitude was I flying and at what speed?

Was I creative? Did I have constructive, beautiful thoughts? How can I increase them?

Did I have an experience of transcending my mind in greater awareness?

As man tries to resurrect himself, he will establish a contact with a great Being Who in the Ageless Wisdom is called the "Spirit of Resurrection." A great Sage says that the Spirit of Resurrection is an extra-planetary Being. He is a member of the Council Chamber of Shamballa, and He is Their chosen Emissary. He is

> *...the "Sun of Righteousness" Who can now arise "with healing in His wings"; Who can carry this life-giving energy which counteracts death, this vision which gives incentive to life, and this hope which can restore all nations....*[8]

> *...the work of the Spirit of Resurrection will intensify, and is already making its presence felt. More and more people are beginning to be forward-looking and to hope with greater conviction and courage for a better world set-up; their hitherto wishful thinking and their emotional desire are slowly giving place to a more practical attitude; their clear thinking and their fixed determination are far more active and their plans better laid because both their thinking and their planning are today based on facts; they are also beginning to recognise those factors and conditions which must not be restored, and this is a point of major importance.*[9]

---

8. Alice A. Bailey, *The Externalisation of the Hierarchy*, p. 458.
9. *Ibid.*, p. 459.

When we study the religions and myths of other nations, we find out that Resurrection was a universal event, and many, many Sons of God were resurrected.

This never minimizes the value of the Resurrection of Christ but substantiates it and makes it more real and shows that the human soul, here, there, in different centuries and cultures, overcame death. This increases the glory of God as more of His Sons make the great breakthrough and conquer death.

> The story of the resurrection of Christ Jesus is related by the four Gospel narrators, and is to the effect that, after being crucified, his body was wrapped in a linen cloth, laid in a tomb, and a "great stone" rolled to the door. The sepulchre was then made sure by "sealing the stone" and "setting a watch."
>
> On the first day of the week some of Jesus' followers came to see the sepulchre, when they found that, in spite of the "sealing" and the "watch," the angel of the Lord had descended from heaven, had rolled back the stone from the door, and that *"Jesus had risen from the dead."*[10]

> *Crishna*, the crucified Hindoo Saviour, *rose from the dead,* and ascended bodily into heaven. At that time a great light enveloped the earth and illuminated the whole expanse of heaven. Attended by celestial spirits, and luminous as on that night when he was born in the house of Vasudeva, *Crishna* pursued, by his own light, the journey between earth and heaven, to the bright paradise from whence he had descended. All men saw him, and exclaimed, *"Lo, Crishna's soul ascends its native skies!"*[11]

> Samuel Johnson, in his "Oriental Religions," tells us that *Râma* — an incarnation of Vishnu — after his manifestations on earth, *"at last ascended to heaven,"* "resuming his divine essence."[12]

> *Buddha* also ascended bodily to the celestial regions when His mission on earth was fulfilled, and marks on the rocks of a high mountain are shown, and believed to be the last impression of his footsteps on this earth.[13]

10. T. W. Doane, *Bible Myths and Their Parallels in Other Religions* (New York, Charles P. Somerby, 1882), p. 215.
11. *Ibid.*
12. *Ibid.*, p. 216.
13. *Ibid.*

> *Lao-Kiun,* the virgin-born, he who had existed from all eternity, when his mission of benevolence was completed on Earth, *ascended bodily into the paradise above*. Since this time he has been worshipped as a *god,* and splendid temples erected in his memory.[14]
>
> *Zoroaster,* the founder of the religion of the ancient Persians, who was considered "a divine messenger sent to redeem men from their evil ways," *ascended to heaven* at the end of his earthly career....[15]
>
> *Esculapius,* the Son of God, the Saviour, after being put to death, *rose from the dead.*[16]
>
> The Saviour *Adonis* or *Tammuz,* after being put to death, *rose from the dead....*[17]

Expansion of consciousness is the expansion of our inner Space. To expand our consciousness we need energies to break our walls from inside and outside.

Lofty thoughts and striving generate inner energies and create greater magnetism in our heart. It is the magnet of the heart that attracts outer energies which help to expand our Space.

When the beam of intelligence of the Solar Angel hits the mental plane, it forms a sphere of light; that sphere is what we call consciousness.

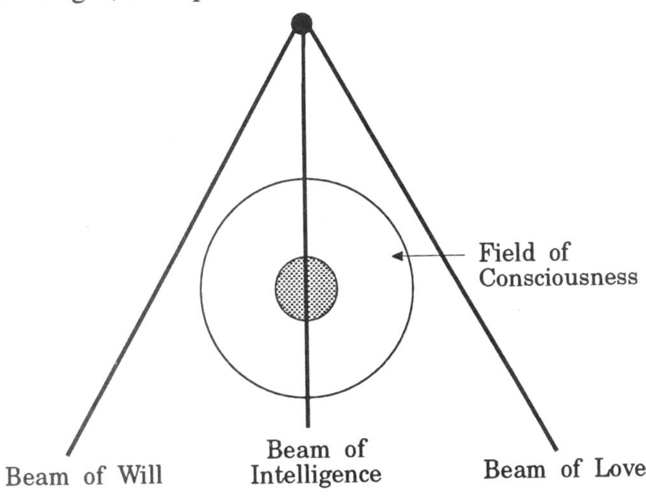

Diagram 87-1 Beam of Will, Intelligence, Love

---

14. *Ibid.*
15. *Ibid.*
16. *Ibid.*, p. 217.
17. *Ibid.*

The light of the Solar Angel is not absorbed in its entirety, but only a portion is absorbed due to the evolving and increasing sensitivity of the mental atoms. Through the contact of the light and the impression through the mental body, the human soul becomes aware of his existence.

The coordination of the mental body with the brain is a necessity if the consciousness is to be translated and the impressions from the five senses are to be interpreted.

Most of the time our consciousness is reflected or focused on the lower mental plane, or even in the etheric body or astral body. That is how we are physically conscious, astrally conscious, and eventually mentally conscious.

Translation of impressions coming from the lower and higher worlds creates *thoughtforms*. The effort to translate is the effort of thinking.

How do we expand our consciousness?—Through observation and meditation and by the actualization of virtues.

1. Observation brings more light from Higher Realms and creates tension in the atoms of the mental body, making them reflect more light.

2. Meditation is an effort to assimilate the light and formulate higher impressions into thoughtforms, through linking light and mind and increasing their interrelationship.

3. Actualization of virtues purifies the vehicles and makes them responsive to the impulses of the Solar Angel and human soul.

The ability of the human soul to control the personality increases, and eventually the Self manifests through the personality. This is how the second birth, or the first major expansion of consciousness, happens in the life of the human being.

What is the result of expansion of consciousness?

1. More harmony with universal principles

2. Greater sensitivity to higher impressions

3. Better translation of facts

4. Greater creativity

5. Better health

6. Clearer relationships

7. Higher morality

8. Goal-fittingness

9. New breakthroughs in Self-actualization

There is a great secret in human nature. There is a wheel beyond the mind which always rotates because it is geared to the Universal Mind. The Universal Mind is the source of all our knowledge in the seven main fields of human endeavor: politics, education, philosophy, arts, sciences, religion, and economics. This wheel is always engaged with that Universal Mind, but it does not transmit to us any knowledge until our mental wheel engages itself with that flywheel.

Our mind has seven gears, and according to the gear in which it is engaged, it brings corresponding knowledge from the higher wheel which runs with the Universal Mind. These seven gears are not for changing our speed, but are the seven ways to translate the knowledge they receive from the Universal Mind.

There is an additional point to be mentioned here: the deeper the gear engages in the flywheel, the deeper is the knowledge.

When the human mind is engaged, it will draw *thoughts* according to the nature of its gear.

Man always creates. He is a creator. When he thinks, when he imagines, when he visualizes, or when he talks, he creates. Even in his sleep man creates.

To create means to produce an effect on the matter where the man's consciousness is focused.

A Great One says that there is a machine which measures the lines of creativity of the people. There are three levels:

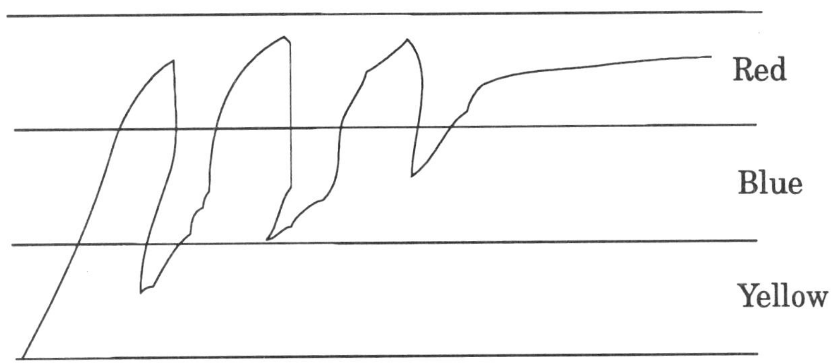

Diagram 87-2 Line of Creativity

When you are a creative beauty with great vision and spirit, the line goes up and up. When you create ugly things, the line goes down and down. Our life has a needle which draws on the charts and demonstrates exactly where we are going.

Creativity grows continuously as we live, act, feel, think, and engage ourselves in higher creativity. This chart is kept in Space, and your Solar Angel watches it to see what you are doing on the Path.

Expansion of Space is gradual.

There are many other exercises that can be given to help your efforts toward Resurrection. For example, you can start from simple arrangements in your life such as these:

First Stage:

1. Place more mirrors in your home.
2. Have big rooms, high ceilings, and as little furniture as possible in your creative or study room.
3. Often go to high mountains, deserts, oceans, canyons.... Expand your views.
4. Travel by ship or airplane, and watch the space.
5. Watch the midnight sky.
6. Walk alone through forests.
7. Wear loose clothing.
8. Think big.
9. Feel joyful.

Second Stage:

1. Visualize yourself as a flame.
2. Sit in a room built on the top of a mountain.
3. See the flame getting bigger and bigger until the room is full of the flame. Repeat three times for five minutes each time.
4. Visualize the view from the top of the mountain, and see great valleys on all sides of the mountain.
5. Let your flame grow and cover the whole mountain.
6. Let it cover the whole valley.
7. See how far you can go into space as a growing flame.
8. See the planet and envelop it in your fire.

9. Envelop the solar system.
10. See your flame.

    — in all trees

    — in all animals

    — in all human beings

    — in all devas

    — in all stars
11. Try to think with how many beings you are in contact.
12. Think about how much you have spoken all these years and where the waves of your voice and thoughts have penetrated.

Every contact influences you. Your contacts eventually create your beingness and character for years to come.

All vices contract your Space until you have no Space, for example:

1. Harmful deeds
2. Negative emotions
3. Separative thoughts
4. Hatred
5. Greed
6. Fear
7. Anger
8. Jealousy
9. Fanaticism
10. Hopelessness
11. Ugliness
12. Limitations created because of pressure to narrow your Space and freedom

You can expand your Space by creating the opposite of these vices, by creating virtues such as:

1. Harmlessness
2. Joyful, positive emotions
3. Inclusiveness, synthesis
4. Love
5. Generosity
6. Fearlessness
7. Serenity
8. Sharingness
9. Tolerance
10. Hopefulness, optimism
11. Beauty
12. Liberation through detachment and renouncement

Resurrection needs Space. As Space expands, the wings of Resurrection grow. Illumination is impossible without expansion of our outer and inner Space. Resurrection and illumination are processes by which the imprisoning walls of inner Space are gradually removed.

Space only expands when the outer Space is observed by an inner expanding Space.

We know what the outer Space is: the Infinite Space which can expand further as we create bigger and more powerful telescopes and microscopes. This gives the human being a sense of worthlessness if the expanding Space is not experienced and balanced by an expanding inner Space.

What is the inner Space? The inner Space is the planes with which you come in contact, discovering different realities and different dimensions in them.

Planes are carriers of states of consciousness. They are substantial. For example, we have the space of our physical body, its organs and glands, or the physical plane. Then we have the etheric body or etheric plane, the etheric centers, and the nadis. We have the astral world, the astral plane, and its centers and inhabitants.

We have the mental world, or plane, the mental centers, the Chalice, the thoughtforms, and the virtues.

We have the Intuitional Plane, Ideas, the Plan, Ashrams, the Great Ones. We have the higher planes and higher wonders.

These planes form the inner Space which expands *ad infinitum* as our consciousness penetrates into and acts on one plane, then another, eventually coming in contact with supermundane realities.

Outer Space can be conquered if the corresponding inner Space is conquered by certain human beings. Inner victory allows outer victory to be achieved.

Individually, the physical body corresponds to earth. The emotional body corresponds to the oceans and lakes, and the mental body corresponds to the atmosphere around the earth. Man has polluted these three spaces because he first polluted his body, next his emotions, and then his mind through greed, fear, hatred, anger, and jealousy.

We imprison ourselves in a smaller and smaller space when we do not clear and purify our inner Space. It is also true that our Space expands when we realize how insignificant and tiny we are in the Universe. Realization of your size in proportion to Space gives you humility, and humility is expansion of Space.

When your Space gets narrower, you develop pride, vanity, separatism, and fanaticism. These are called the four walls of your prison.

The outer Space is affected by all that we do physically, all that we do emotionally, and all that we do mentally. Thoughts that do not carry the fire of Beauty, Goodness, Truth, and Joy poison Space. Emotions that are charged with hatred, fear, anger, greed, and jealousy dump into Space poisonous gases. Deeds based on malice, separatism, and vices pollute Space with invisible germs.

When the inner Space is polluted, the pollution of the outer Space takes place immediately, and then the degeneration of life on the planet begins. That is what the real human history shows us. Historians do not write about these things as they are very busy with their own interests and separative outlooks.

The only way to save outer Space is to expand and purify our inner Space. Then the purification of the outer Space will be a possibility, if it is not too late.

For the human mind, things begin and things end; things are small and big. For the human Intuition, there is no beginning and no end; things flow. For the human Intuition Space is infinite.

Once, while giving a lecture, a scientist said to the students, "Space is limited." One of the young girls asked, "Teacher, then what is beyond Space?"

"Well, emptiness, void...."

"Or, empty space...!"

The scientist was shocked. He tried to prove to himself that Space was finite, but the girl's question presented a new challenge which could be met only with something higher than the mind.

The human mind thinks through forms. The human Intuition, on its own level, does not need forms to understand or to be aware. To expand our Space we need to transcend form. For a man, he himself is a form. He cannot accept himself without a form.

To expand our Space we must think of ourselves apart from a form. First, we must be aware that we are not the body. The body is not us. This will take a long time, but once we achieve such an awareness, we are one hundred years ahead of ourselves.

The next step will be to detach ourselves from our emotional forms, from our mental forms, and think about ourselves as the Space, as the One Self, which manifests through all forms but remains formless. Any form puts a limit on us, on our space-concept. Detachment from any form restores our essential Self.

Of course, man needs time to expand his Space gradually, without losing his individuality. People do not understand what is meant by *individuality*. How can one expand his Space and become more and more a part of the One Self and still remain an individuality?

The answer is that individuality is not a feeling of separateness, apartness, or aloofness. Individuality is the awareness that one is universal. It is the awareness that he is one with Space, with the One Self. It is the awareness that he exists as a part of all forms. As one becomes more universal, he has more Space. Individuality is the *awareness* of his expanding Space.

People are limited by what they have. Havingness is a powerful limiting factor. Craving for more objects narrows our Space. Greed almost annihilates our Space. Renouncement and resignation give us freedom, and freedom expands our Space. As our Space expands, we grow in the awareness of our universal individuality.

All that is written relates only to the Cosmic Physical Plane. We do not know yet how Space will be conceived beyond the Cosmic Physical Plane. But by analogy we can have a glimpse of reality. As one expands his inner Space when he overcomes body/form consciousness, he will expand a thousand times more in his awareness of Space when he leaves behind the great illusory form which is called the Cosmic Physical Plane. One can only contemplate the glory awaiting him on higher and higher fields of freedom.

Expansion of Space is not the ability to see many light-years into Space. Space is. You cannot change its extension or dimension. Our telescopes and microscopes widened our vision, but they did not change the Space. It is now as it was before.

It is the realization of our contact with more inner Space that expands our outer Space. There are two ways of expansion — vertical and horizontal. Horizontal expansion is expansion of the distance between us and our objects or barriers. Vertical expansion is expansion of mastery upon a higher plane.

Our telescopes, microscopes, airplanes, and rockets have brought us to the conclusion that the knowledge of the outer Space cannot help to further our evolution, unless we expand our inner Space. Inner Space expands only through expanding our consciousness. Consciousness expands when one registers in his brain his contacts with astral, mental, and intuitional Space.

All that we see through our telescopes and microscopes is *mass,* not Space. We expand and increase our knowledge of *mass*, not of that in which the mass has its being. *That,* the Space, is imperceptible. This imperceptible Space *is.*

When we talk about the expansion of Space, the inner Space, we mean the ability to occupy more Space. We expanded the distance between us and our barriers, but we filled that Space with our chemical, emotional, and mental fumes and poisonous emanations. Our extended Space became our own limitation. Increasing the poison in our Space will prevent any possibility of expanding our inner Space.

Thus, expansion of the outer Space, in reality, is the contraction of our inner Space. It is through the expansion of the inner Space that the true nature of the outer Space can be understood.

This is the vertical expansion of our Space into outer Space. This is done by mastering higher dimensions of our consciousness.

The planes higher than the physical can be mastered only through the process of freedom, liberation from the *mass,* from limitation. This is what is mystically called Resurrection.

The victory of the human spirit over matter will continue age after age, and we will have more Resurrected Ones Who will shine over the horizons of humanity as radiant stars teaching us the secrets of health, happiness, and joy.

Epilogue

The process of healing involves tuning our bodies to our inner Core, and then to the Cosmic note of the Central Core of the Universe.

As you read this book and do the exercises, you will experience many changes in your life.

These changes can show in the physical body as dynamic health and beauty.

In the emotional body, changes can manifest as calmness, peace, and joy.

In the mental body, changes such as serenity, freedom, and expansion can take place.

Spiritually you will become radioactive, rhythmic, free, progressive, inclusive, and develop a sense of synthesis and a sense of Infinity.

Crises may come to you, as well as moments of joy when you finally feel you have made a breakthrough.

When the crises come, do not despair. Healing takes consistent effort. On the path of progress toward the spiritual realms, all obstacles, hindrances, and impediments are as energy resources. The advancing soul utilizes all such difficulties to know more, to have more, and to serve more.

M.M. says,

> *. . . All the winds serve the miller to produce a better flour.*[1]

1. *Leaves of Morya's Garden*, Vol. I, para. 272.

Glossary

Adi Plane: The Divine Plane or the highest subplane of the Cosmic Physical Plane.

Ageless Wisdom: The sum total of the Teachings given by great Spiritual Teachers throughout time. Also referred to as the Ancient Wisdom, the Teaching, the Ancient Teaching.

Agni Yogi: One who is in a continuous process of fusion with higher spheres, from which pour down the joy and bliss of his own Essence.

Ajna center: The center between the eyebrows; corresponds to the pituitary gland.

Akashic Records: Existing in the Higher Cosmic Ethers, the Akashic Records are living records of all experiences and activities that have occurred in the past, present, and future of this planet and everything in it.

All Self: That great Entity Who pervades and sustains all things on all levels of existence.

Angels: Beings who follow a different line of evolution than the human family.

Antahkarana: The path, or bridge, between the higher and lower mind, serving as a medium of communication between the two. It is built by the aspirant himself. It is threefold: the consciousness thread, anchored in the brain; the life thread, anchored in the heart; and the creative thread anchored in the throat. More commonly called the Rainbow Bridge [or Golden Bridge].

Arhat: Ancient term designating Fourth Degree Initiates.

Aryan: Refers to the present period of the development of the human race. The Ageless Wisdom divides human development into seven sections called Root Races. From ancient times to the present, they have been called: Polarian Race, Hyperborian Race, Lemurian Race, Atlantean Race, Aryan Race, Sixth Root Race, and Seventh Root Race. The latter two are the future states of human development. For more information, see *The Psyche and Psychism* by Torkom Saraydarian.

Ancients: Wise thinkers and teachers of humanity who contributed to the Ageless Wisdom.

Ashram: Sanskrit word. Refers to the gathering of disciples and aspirants which the Master collects for instruction. There are seven major Ashrams, each corresponding to one of the Rays, each forming groups or foci of energy.

Astral Plane: The sixth plane of the Cosmic Physical Plane, in which the emotional processes are carried on. Sometimes called the astral or emotional world. Also known as the Subtle World or the Astral Realm or the Emotional Plane.

Atlantean civilization: (Atlantean Epoch) Refers to the civilization existing on the continent that was submerged in the Atlantic Ocean, according to the occult teaching and Plato. Atlantis was the home of the Fourth Root Race, whom we now call the Atlanteans.

Atmic Plane: The plane of consciousness known as Nirvana, the Third Cosmic Etheric Plane.

Aura: The sum-total of all emanations from all the vehicles of any living thing.

Avatar: Great Being from solar or galactic fields sent cyclically to help humanity progress. Avatars are condensed sources and embodiments of energy.

Black Lodge: See Dark forces.

Causal body: The Chalice in man. See also Lotus.

Cause and Effect, Law of: See Karma, Law of.

Center: Any energy vortex found in a human, planetary, or solar body. See also Chakra.

Central Sun: The Central Spiritual Sun; the Core of the solar system. The Sun is triple: the visible Sun, the Heart of the Sun, and the Central Spiritual Sun.

Chalice: See Lotus.

Chohan: One Who has accomplished the Sixth Initiation.

Clairaudience: The ability to hear beyond the audible range of vibrations, and also the power to hear astrally, mentally, and intuitively.

Clairvoyance: The ability to see beyond the visible range of vibrations, and also the power to see astrally, mentally, and intuitively.

Consciousness thread: One of three threads composing the Antahkarana. See Antahkarana.

Core: The essence or spark of God within each being; the Monad.

Cosmic Astral Plane: See Cosmic Planes.

Cosmic Mental Plane: See Cosmic Planes.

Cosmic Physical Plane: Refers to the totality of the seven subplanes of manifestation, from highest to lowest: Divine, Monadic, Atmic, Intuitive or Buddhic, Mental, Emotional or Astral, and Physical; each with seven subdivisions, totaling forty-nine planes of manifestation.

Cosmic Ethers: The highest four levels of the human constitution are called (from 4 to 1) the Intuitional Plane (Fourth Cosmic Ether), the Atmic Plane (Third Cosmic Ether), the Monadic Plane (Second Cosmic Ether), and the Divine Plane (First Cosmic Ether).

Cosmic Heart: See Cosmic Magnet.

Cosmic Magnet: The invisible center of the Universe.

Cosmic Planes: The seven planes of cosmic manifestation: Cosmic Physical, Cosmic Astral, Cosmic Mental, Cosmic Intuitional, Cosmic Atmic, Cosmic Monadic, and Cosmic Divine.

Dark forces: Conscious agents of evil or materialism operating through the elements of disunity, hate, and separativeness.

Disciple: A person who tries to discipline and master his threefold personality, and manifests efficiency in the field where he works and serves.

Divine Purpose: See Purpose.

Dweller on the Threshold: You, the lower self, the totality of your personality hindrances; also, the totality of your maya, glamors, and illusions.

Ego: The human soul identified with the lower vehicles (physical, emotional, mental) and their false values.

Elementals: The lives who operate the body they inhabit; three in number: physical elemental, astral elemental, and mental elemental.

Emotional Plane: See Astral Plane.

Etheric body: The counterpart of the dense physical body, pervading and sustaining it. Formed by matter of the four etheric subplanes. The blueprint on which the physical body is based.

Etheric web: See Web, etheric.

Fiery World: Refers to the Mental Plane or above. See Higher Worlds.

Flame of the Heart: See the Jewel.

Glamors: Astral forms with a life of their own in the emotional body. When a person desires something intensely, the astral form of that desire is called a glamor. These forms float in a person's aura and connect with certain astral and etheric centers, exercising great power over a person's actions, emotions, thoughts, and relationships. For example, such a person does not like to hear anything against his desires.

Golden Bridge: See Antahkarana.

Great Ones: Beings Who have taken the Fifth Initiation or beyond.

Guardian Angel: See Solar Angel.

"Hall of Wisdom": The symbolic sphere of education contacted at the Third Initiation on higher mental planes. In the Hall of Wisdom we learn the following: a. How to be aware of forces and powers latent within us and within the Core of our spiritual group. b. How to use these forces and powers to help humanity in all fields. It is a subjective class held by disciples and Initiates.

Hatha Yoga: Used many millions of years ago to create greater synchronization between the physical and etheric bodies, but is now considered obsolete and even very harmful because of the progress of humanity in this direction. For further information, refer to *The Psyche and Psychism*, Ch. 40.

Hierarchy: The spiritual Hierarchy, whose members have triumphed over matter and have complete control over the personality, or lower self. Its members are known as Masters of Wisdom Who are custodians of the Plan for humanity and all kingdoms evolving within the sphere of Earth. It is the Hierarchy that translates the Purpose of the Planetary Logos into a Plan for all kingdoms of the planet.

Higher ethers: See Cosmic Ethers.

Higher Worlds: Those planes of existence that are of a finer vibration of matter than the physical plane. Generally refers to the higher mental plane and above.

Illusions: Formed when a person has mental contact with inspirations, ideas, visions, revelations, but, due to his inadequately prepared mind, self-centeredness, selfishness, and crystallized thinking, he is unable to translate the incoming energies in their correct form. The resulting illusion is a mistranslation of something factual. Illusions thus contain distorted facts.

Imperil: A paralyzing poison formed of cystallizations of psychic energy mixed with anger, fear, or irritation which settles on the nerve channels.

Initiate: A person who has taken an initiation. See also Initiation.

Initiation: The result of the steady progress of a person toward his life's goals, achieved through service and sacrifice, and manifested as an expansion of his consciousness. It represents a point of achievement marked by a level of enlightenment and awareness. There are a total of nine initiations that the developing human soul must experience in order to reach the Cosmic Heart.

Inner Guardian: The Solar Angel.

Intuitional Plane: See Cosmic Planes.

Jewel, The: The Core of the human being; the Monad.

Jiva: The human soul; the Monad.

Karma, Law of: The Law of Cause and Effect or attraction and repulsion. "As you sow, so shall you reap."

Lemurian civilization: A modern term first used by some naturalists and now adopted by Theosophists to indicate the civilization of the continent Lemuria, which preceded Atlantis. The civilization of the Third Root Race.

Life thread: The thread connecting the Monad to the heart; the *sutratma.*

Logos, Planetary: The Soul of the planet. The planet is His dense physical body to provide nourishment for all living forms.

Logos, Solar: The Core of the whole solar system and all that exists in the solar system. His purpose is to integrate, correlate, and synchronize all Centers using His Light, Love, and Power like an electrical energy to circulate within each atom through all Centers, thus revealing the Purpose for existence and changing all forms to strive toward the highest form of cooperation.

Lotus: Also known as the Chalice. Found in the second and third levels of the mental plane (from the top). Formed by twelve different petals of energy: three knowledge petals, three love petals, three sacrifice petals. The three innermost petals remain folded for ages. They are the dynamic sources of these outer petals. The Lotus contains the essence of all of a person's achievements, true knowledge, and service. It is the dwelling place of the Solar Angel.

Lower mental plane: See Mental Plane.

Lower psychism: The ability to perceive subtle aspects of existence with the aid of the lower centers in the human body. Mediums, channels, etc. are considered lower psychics.

Mantrams: Words of power; mental prayer.

Manvantaras: Periods of activity, or the "days" of the Eternal One.

Masters: Individuals Who had the privilege to master Their physical, emotional, mental, and Intuitional bodies.

Maya: A counterpart of illusions and glamors on the etheric plane. It results in the inability of the physical, emotional, and mental bodies to respond clearly to incoming impressions.

Meditation: Technique to penetrate the mind of the planet and develop creative abilities to manifest that mind in the life of humanity. (For in-depth information, please refer to *The Science of Meditation* and *Psyche and Psychism* by Torkom Saraydarian.)

Mediumistic: A tendency of certain individuals to astral phenomena and its perception thereof. Mediumistic people can, without guidance, fall into various dangers and traps associated with the astral plane. (For more information, see *Psyche and Psychism* by Torkom Saraydarian.)

Mental Plane: There are seven planes through which a human being travels and which make up human consciousness. From the lowest level upward, they are called: physical, emotional or astral, mental, Intuitional or Buddhic, Atmic, Monadic, Divine. The mental plane itself is divided into seven levels. The first three from the bottom are numbers seven, six, and five, which form the lower mental plane. Number four is the middle mind or link. Numbers three, two, and one form the higher mental plane.

Mental Unit: A mental mechanism in the fourth level of the mental plane which is formed of four kinds of forces and relates man to the sources of these four forces through its four spirillae.

Monad: See Self.

Monadic Plane: See Cosmic Planes.

Nadis: The etheric counterparts of the nervous system; they relate the etheric body to the nerves.

Neophyte: An aspirant on the path of discipleship.

Nirvana: The plane of consciousness know as the Atmic Plane.

Occultism: Term used to designate the Ageless Wisdom and its study. See Ageless Wisdom.

OM: A word of power. See *Cosmos in Man.*

One Self: The universal consciousness pervading all existence.

Personality: Totality of physical, emotional, and mental bodies of man.

Plan, The: The formulation of the Purpose of the Planetary Logos into a workable program, a Plan by the Planetary Hierarchy for all kingdoms of Nature.

Planetary Logos: See Logos, Planetary.

Pralaya: Periods of rest, or the "nights" of the Eternal One.

Psychic energy: The energy of the Central Fire.

Purpose: That which the Solar Logos is intended to achieve at the end of the evolution of the solar system. The Plan is the formulation of this Purpose for our planet only.

Qualities: Also known as *gunas;* the three qualities of matter are *Sattva,* rhythm; *rajas,* motion; and *tamas,* inertia.

Rajas: See Qualities.

Ray: See Seven Rays.

Real Self: See Self.

Ring-pass-not: Limit of consciousness; veil between present level of being and a higher level requiring a major expansion to penetrate. See Web, etheric.

Sattva: See Qualities.

Seven etheric centers: See Chakra.

Seven Fields of Human Endeavor: The expression of the Seven Rays in human evolution, each corresponding to a specific Ray. They are: Politics, Education, and Psychology, Philosophy, the Arts, Science, Religion, Economics and Finance.

Seven Rays: These are the seven primary Rays through which everything exists. They are pure energy, vibrating to a specific frequency and condensing from plane to plane, from manifestation to manifestation. The three primary Rays, or Rays of Aspect, are: The First Ray of Power, Will, and Purpose; The Second Ray of Love-Wisdom; The Third Ray of Active, Creative Intelligence. There are four Rays of Attribute: The Fourth Ray of Harmony Through Conflict; The Fifth Ray of Concrete Science or Knowledge; The Sixth Ray of Idealism or Devotion; The Seventh Ray of Synthesis or Ceremonial Order. These Rays indicate qualities that pertain to the seven fields of human endeavor or expression.

Shamballa: Known as the White Island, it exists in etheric matter and is located in the Gobi Desert. Shamballa is the dwelling place of the Lord of the World, Sanat Kumara, and is the place where "the Will of God is known."

Solar Angels: Very advanced beings Who sacrifice Their life, descending from Higher Worlds to help the evolution of humanity and guide its steps toward initiation. This happened on our planet at the middle of the Lemurian period.

Solar Fire: Energy coming from the Heart of the Sun. There are three Suns: the visible Sun, the Heart of the Sun, and the Central Spiritual Sun.

Solar Logos: See Logos, Solar.

Soul: Also known as the Solar Angel if written with capital "S".

soul: The small "s" soul is the human psyche, the Spark, traveling on the path of evolution and having three powers: willpower, attraction, and intelligence to guide its development. Also know as the evolving human soul.

Soul-infusion: A state in which the physical, emotional, and mental bodies are purified to a high degree and aligned with the Solar Angel so that the light of the Solar Angel can radiate through the personality in full power and beauty.

Spark: Human Monad fallen into matter.

Spiritual Archetype: The Archetype toward which one strives to be.

Spiritual Triad: The field of awareness of the human soul. This field comes into existence when the magnetic fields of the Mental Permanent Atom, the Buddhic Permanent Atom, and the Atmic Permanent Atom fuse and blend.

Subconscious mind: The seventh, sixth, and fifth levels of the mental plane. See Mental Plane.

Sublimation: Changing the substance of a body or center into a higher substance by a process of purification, transmutation, transformation, and transfiguration.

Subtle World: Refers to the Astral or Emotional Plane.

Supermundane World: The Higher Worlds.

Supreme Self: See the One Self.

Tamas: See Qualities.

Teaching, The: See Ageless Wisdom.

Third Degree Initiate: The total purification and alignment of the mental, emotional, and physical vehicles of the evolving human soul, leading to Transfiguration or Enlightenment.

Thousand-petaled Lotus: The head center, which takes the place of the Chalice after the Fourth Initiation.

Throat center: See Chakras.

Transfiguration: The result of the action of the electric fire of the Spiritual Triad on the higher mind. The lights of the little atoms of the personality vehicles are released, and the whole personality is purified in the Third Initiation.

Transpersonal Self: The Solar Angel, the Inner Guide.

Triangles: A method given in 1937 to increase the circulation of psychic energy in the planet by changing the etheric patterns from squares to triangles. The method is for three people to say the Great Invocation daily at the same hour with focus and aspiration. See *Triangles of Fire*.

True Self: See Self.

Twelve-petaled Lotus: See Lotus.

Universal One Self: See One Self.

"Voice of the Silence": Also known as the Inner Voice. The Inner Voice is higher than the conscience. It is the Real Voice talking within you. It is direct communication with your Solar Angel.

Web, etheric: A protective valve or gage between the etheric centers which protects the centers from an overflow of energy. The valves open naturally when the requisite degree of purity and spiritual pressure is maintained.

Wesak Festival: The festival of the Taurus Full Moon, usually falling in May. One of the three major festivals of the year: the Aries Full Moon, the Festival of the Christ or the Festival of Resurrection; the Taurus Full Moon, the Festival of the Buddha or the Festival of Enlightenment; the Gemini Full Moon, the Festival of Humanity or the Festival of Goodwill.

Bibliographic References

Agni Yoga Society. New York: Agni Yoga Society.
Agni Yoga, 1954.
Brotherhood, 1962.
Community, 1951.
Fiery World, Vol. I, 1969.
Fiery World, Vol. II, 1946.
Fiery World, Vol. III, 1948.
Heart, 1982.
Infinity, Vol. I, 1956.
Infinity, Vol. II, 1957.
Leaves of Morya's Garden II, 1979.
Letters of Helena Roerich, Vol. I, 1979.
Letters of Helena Roerich, Vol. II, 1981.

Bach, Dr. Edward. Keats, CT.
The Medical Discoveries. Out of print.

Bailey, Alice A. New York: Lucis Publishing Co.
Discipleship in the New Age, Vol. II, 1972.
Esoteric Healing, 1982.
Esoteric Psychology, Vol. I, 1979.
Esoteric Psychology, Vol. II, 1966.
Externalisation of the Hierarchy, 1972.
Letters on Occult Meditation, 1974.
The Rays and the Initiations, 1976.
A Treatise on Cosmic Fire, 1977.

Barker, A.T. Pasadena, CA: Theosophical University Press.
The Mahatma Letters, 1975.

Blavatsky, H.P. Pasadena, CA: Theosophical University Press.
The Secret Doctrine, 2 vols., 1988.

Blavatsky, H.P. Wheaton, IL: Theosophical Publishing House.
Collected Writings, Vol. XIII, 1982.

Blavatsky, H.P. Adyar: The Theosophical Publishing House.
Collected Writings, Vol. VIII, 1960.

Doane, T.W.: New York, Charles P. Somberby.
Bible Myths and Their Parallels in Other Religions, 1882.

Lamsa, George M., trans. Nashville, TN: Holman Bible Publishers.
New Testament, 1968.

Roerich, Nicholas. CT: Arun Press.
Altai Himalaya, 1983.

Roerich, Nicholas. Corona Mundi, New York.
Roerich Adamant, 1923.

Saraydarian, Torkom. Sedona, AZ: Aquarian Educational Group.
The Bhagavad Gita, 1974.
Cosmos In Man, 1983.
Earthquakes and Disasters, What The Ageless Wisdom Tells Us, 1991.
The Flame of Beauty, Culture, Love, Joy, 1980.
The Hidden Glory of Inner Man, 1985.
Irritation, The Destructive Fire, 1991.
Joy and Healing, 1989.
The Psyche and Psychism, 2 vols., 1981.
Sex, Family and the Woman in Society, 1987.
The Science of Becoming Oneself, 1976.
The Science of Meditation, 1981.
The Solar Angel, 1990.
Symphony of the Zodiac, 1988.
Triangles of Fire, 1977.
Woman, Torch of the Future, 1980.

Saraydarian, Torkom. West Hills, CA: T.S.G. Publishing Foundation, Inc.
The Ageless Wisdom, 1990.
A Commentary on Psychic Energy, 1989.
Cosmic Shocks, 1989.
The Flame of the Heart, 1991.
Other Worlds, 1991.
The Psychology of Cooperation and Group Consciousness, 1989.
The Sense of Responsibility in Society, 1989.

Music by the author for the mantrams is available. Please write to the publisher.

Index

A

B

C

D

E

F

G

H

I

J

K

L

M

N

O

P

Q

R

S

T

U

V

W

Y

Z

About the Author

This is Torkom Saraydarian's latest published book. Many more will be released very soon. His vocal and instrumental compositions number in the hundreds and are being released.

The author's books have been used all over the world as sources of guidance and inspiration for true New Age living based on the teachings of the Ageless Wisdom. Some of the books have been translated into other languages, including German, Dutch, Danish, Portuguese, French, Spanish, Italian, Greek, Yugoslavian, and Swedish. He holds lectures and seminars in the United States as well as in other parts of the world.

Torkom Saraydarian's entire life has been a zealous effort to help people live healthy, joyous, and successful lives. He has spread this message of love and true vision tirelessly throughout his life.

From early boyhood the author learned first-hand from teachers of the Ageless Wisdom. He has studied widely in world religions and philosophies. He is in addition an accomplished pianist, violinist, and cellist and plays many other instruments as well. His books, lectures, seminars, and music are inspiring and offer a true insight into the beauty of the Ageless Wisdom.

Torkom Saraydarian's books and music speak to the hearts and minds of a humanity eager for positive change. His books, covering a large spectrum of human existence, are written in straightforward, unpretentious, clear, and often humorous fashion. His works draw on personal experiences, varied and rich. He offers insight and explanations to anyone interested in applying spiritual guidelines to everyday life. His no-nonense approach is practical, simple, and readily accessible to anyone who is interested in finding real meaning in life.

Torkom Saraydarian has de-mystified the mysteries of the Ageless Wisdom. he has made the much needed link between the spiritual and the everyday worlds.

Look for exciting new books and music being released by Torkom Saraydarian.

Other Books
by Torkom Saraydarian

The Ageless Wisdom
The Bhagavad Gita
Breakthrough to Higher Psychism
Challenge For Discipleship
Christ, The Avatar of Sacrificial Love
A Commentary on Psychic Energy
Cosmic Shocks
Cosmos in Man
Dialogue With Christ
Flame of Beauty, Culture, Love, Joy
The Flame of the Heart
Hiawatha and the Great Peace
The Hidden Glory of the Inner Man
I Was
Joy and Healing
Legend of Shamballa
Other Worlds
The Psyche and Psychism
The Psychology of Cooperation and Group Consciousness
The Purpose of Life
The Science of Becoming Oneself
The Science of Meditation
The Sense of Responsibility in Society
Sex, Family, and the Woman in Society
The Solar Angel
Spiritual Regeneration
Symphony of the Zodiac
Talks on Agni
Triangles of Fire
Unusual Court
Woman, Torch of the Future
The Year 2000 & After

Next Release: **Thought and The Glory of Thinking**

Booklets by Torkom Saraydarian

A Daily Discipline of Worship
Building Family Unity
Earthquakes and Disasters — What the Ageless Wisdom Tells Us
Fiery Carriage and Drugs
Five Great Mantrams of the New Age
Hierarchy and the Plan
Irritation — The Destructive Fire
The Psychology of Cooperation
Questioning Traveler and Karma
Responsibility
The Responsibility of Fathers
The Responsibility of Mothers
Spring of Prosperity
Synthesis
Torchbearers
What to Look for in the Heart of Your Partner

Ordering Information

Write to the publisher for additional information regarding:

— Free catalog of author's books and music tapes

— Lecture tapes and videos

— Placement on mailing list

— New releases

Additional copies of *New Dimensions in Healing*

Softcover $40.00 U.S.
Hardcover $50.00 U.S.
Postage within U.S.A. $5.00
Plus applicable state sales tax

T.S.G. Publishing Foundation, Inc.
Visions for the Twenty-First Century
P.O. Box 4273
West Hills, California 91308
United States of America

TEL: (818) 888-7850
FAX: (818) 346-6457

These fine books have been published by the generous donations of the students of the Ageless Wisdom.

Our deep gratitude to all.